READINGS AND CASES IN
MACRO-
ECONOMICS

T117 $15.95

READINGS AND CASES IN MACRO-ECONOMICS

Ben Bernanke
Woodrow Wilson School
Princeton University

McGraw-Hill
Book
Company

New York • St. Louis
San Francisco • Auckland
Bogotá • Hamburg
Johannesburg • London
Madrid • Mexico
Milan • Montreal
New Delhi • Panama
Paris • São Paulo
Singapore • Sydney
Tokyo • Toronto

1 2 3 4 5 6 7 8 9 0   DOC   DOC   8 9 2 1 0 9 8 7

ISBN 0-07-017779-1

This book was set in Times Roman by J. M. Post Graphics, Corp.

The editor was Paul Short; the designer was Jo Jones;
the production supervisor was Diane Renda.

The drawings were done by Accurate Art, Inc.

R. R. Donnelley & Sons Company was printer and binder.

Library of Congress Cataloging-in-Publication Data

Readings and cases in macroeconomics.

  Supplement to: Macroeconomics/Rudiger Dornbusch,
Stanley Fischer. 4th ed.
  1. Macroeconomics.   I. Bernanke, Ben.   II. Dornbusch,
Rudiger. Macroeconomics (4th ed.)
HB172.5D67 Suppl.   339   86-27423
ISBN 0-07-017779-1

CONTENTS

PART FIVE   INTERNATIONAL MACROECONOMICS, TRADE, AND DEVELOPMENT

PREFACE

Each of the thirty-nine readings in this book was chosen for its potential value as an aid to the teaching of undergraduate macroeconomics, at the level of *Macroeconomics, fourth edition,* by Rudiger Dornbusch and Stanley Fischer. The readings cover a variety of areas in modern macroeconomics. These areas include:

Theoretical concepts (time inconsistency, real business cycles, sources of wage rigidity, and so on)

Policy debates (rules versus discretion in monetary policy; supply-side economics versus industrial policy as the key to growth)

Recent developments in the macroeconomy (disinflation of the 1980s; the budget deficit and the trade deficit)

As is appropriate for an intermediate-level course, the readings are more challenging than the products of the popular media (most were written by professional economists). At the same time, care was taken to be sure that all the articles would be accessible to students without advanced mathematical preparation.

There are a variety of ways in which the articles reprinted here can be usefully incorporated into a macroeconomics course. Some possibilities are:

1 As *supplementary reading materials.* Texts operate under severe space constraints, which prevent them from including extensive applications of the theory or going deeply into some important concepts. The readings in this book can act as a "supplementary text," from which the instructor (or the motivated student) can choose topics for further exploration. A guide which matches up the readings with related chapters of the Dornbusch-Fischer text is given below.

2 As a *basis for classroom discussion.* Each article comes with a set of questions about its contents, written by the editor. These questions emphasize concepts, not minor details. Working through these questions in class can provide a springboard for a general discussion about issues raised in the text or in the reading.

3 As an *alternative to mechanical problem sets.* Instead of assigning problems from the text each week, a possibility is occasionally to require written answers to the discussion questions from one or two of the readings. This will help the students learn to apply the concepts of the text in context that is more "realistic" than the manipulation of algebraic or graphical models.

4 As a *source of term paper ideas.* In many cases, extending or varying the analysis of one of the readings is a challenging yet doable research project for an undergraduate. For example, Tatom's decomposition of the federal deficit into its sources for the 1980–1984 period (Reading 10) is straightforward to update, to expand to include state and local governments, or to modify in other ways. Most of the readings also have useful bibliographies, to aid further research.

MATCHING UP THE READINGS WITH TEXT CHAPTERS

There are two ways to fit these readings into the course schedule. The first way is to place emphasis alternately on the text and on the readings. For example, after using the text to develop the basic *IS-LM* model, the course could then turn to the readings in order to focus intensively on, say, monetary policy for two or three sessions. To facilitate this approach, the readings are grouped under major subject headings; under each heading, an attempt has been made to choose articles that are complementary in coverage and viewpoint.

The second way to integrate the readings is in a parallel fashion, by adding a few readings each week to the regular text assignment. The accompanying table matches the chapters of *Macroeconomics,* fourth edition, by Rudiger Dornbusch and Stanley Fischer (McGraw-Hill, 1987) with the appropriate readings in this book. It will be noted that some text chapters have several suggested readings, while others have relatively few or none. Also, some readings are listed as appropriate for more than one chapter in the text. It is important that the table be treated as a menu listing the range of possibilities. The actual assignments made should depend on the interests of the instructor and the students and on the specific goals of the course. In the Appendix are two additional tables matching the chapters of other texts with the appropriate readings.

Text chapter	Suggested readings	Text chapter	Suggested readings
1	—	11	14–16, 18
2	1, 2	12	3, 4, 17, 19, 20
3	4–6, 9	13	25, 26, 29
4	—	14	16, 17, 22–24, 27
5	8, 10, 15, 16	15	28
6	32–35	16	9–13, 32
7	—	17	—
8	4–6, 13	18	5, 14, 15, 20, 21, 30
9	5, 7, 8	19	5, 30, 31, 36
10	—	20	34, 35, 37–39

ACKNOWLEDGMENTS

Thanks are due to Stanley Fischer, for suggesting this project, and to the McGraw-Hill staff, especially Joseph Marcelle and Paul Short, for seeing it through. Andy Atkeson, Cindy Long, Dan Sichel, and Richard Stuebi did an excellent job of searching the libraries for readings. Gwendolyn Hatcher provided efficient secretarial support.

Ben Bernanke

PART **ONE**

MEASUREMENT

NATIONAL INCOME ACCOUNTING AND ECONOMIC WELFARE: THE CONCEPTS OF GNP AND MEW

Kenneth Stewart

The gross national product (GNP) is the best-known indicator of the state of the economy; it is widely used by both economists and policy makers as a general measure of economic performance. Some years ago, however, Yale economists William Nordhaus and James Tobin raised an objection to heavy reliance on GNP figures; namely, that while GNP may be a reasonable measure of *production,* it is perhaps not so good a measure of the ultimate goal of an economy, which is (or should be) the general well-being of the population. Nordhaus and Tobin proposed an alternative statistic, MEW (measure of economic welfare), which was supposed to be an improved measure of economic well-being. The concepts of MEW and GNP are compared and evaluated in the following article.

MEW, it should be said, has not caught on as an alternative to GNP. However, the point made by Nordhaus and Tobin—that a higher GNP does not *necessarily* mean than an economy is better off—remains a very important one.

The most comprehensive indicator of economic performance in the nation in a given year is gross national product (GNP). Changes in GNP reflect both changes in prices and changes in the physical volume of output. GNP adjusted for price level changes is generally accepted as a reliable indicator of growth in the nation's total production and is used by economic analysts to indicate whether the economy is expanding or contracting. Policymakers use GNP data, along with other measures of economic activity, in the formulation and subsequent evaluation of stabilization policy.

Kenneth Stewart, "National Income Accounting and Economic Welfare: The Concepts of GNP and MEW," *Review,* St. Louis Federal Reserve Bank, April 1974, pp. 18–24.

A growing GNP is generally associated with expanding opportunities for employ-ment and an increasing amount of material welfare. Economic policy facilitating GNP growth is formulated, in part, as a means of reducing both unemployment and poverty. But a growing GNP has also been accompanied by urban decay and pollution, which are not accounted for in national income data. Critics of economic growth, as measured by national income data, argue that such data tend to emphasize the growth of material welfare while ignoring what is happening to the "quality of life" or "social welfare." GNP has been growing, but what has been happening to total welfare?

William Nordhaus and James Tobin recently proposed an indicator to obtain a measure of "economic welfare" or "standard of living" to complement GNP.[1] This indicator, referred to as "Measure of Economic Welfare" (MEW), would modify the present GNP measure primarily in three ways: 1) by subtracting estimates of certain costs or "bads," such as pollution, from the national income total; 2) by excluding some services, such as police services, since it is possible that increased police budgets to combat rising crime do not indicate an increase in welfare; and 3) by adding to GNP some activities, such as household activities (housework, home repairs, etc.) and leisure, which are not included in the GNP total.

This article discusses the Nordhaus-Tobin measure of economic welfare. Since they use GNP as a point of departure, the concept of GNP is reviewed in the first part of this paper and then compared with the proposed MEW concept.

DEFINITION AND CONCEPT OF GNP

Gross national product can be defined as the market value of domestic current final output. It provides a measure of the nation's aggregate economic activity—income or output—measured in terms of current market prices over a given period of time, usually a year.

Two methods can be used in measuring the nation's income or output—the income approach and the expenditure approach. The income approach determines gross national income by totaling the various income shares of the factors of production, such as compensation of employees, rental income, proprietors' income, net interest, and corporate profits (and adding in an allowance for depreciation, indirect business taxes, and other smaller items). The expenditure approach determines the current value of production basically by totaling all expenditures for final goods and services based on type of purchase and expenditure (plus the net change in business inventory). Expen-ditures in the national income accounts are classified as personal consumption expen-ditures, gross private domestic investment, government purchases of goods and ser-vices, and net exports. The two approaches provide approximately the same total, for expenditures on final goods and services provide income to the factors of production which produced these items.

In general, nonmarketed goods, such as goods and services produced and consumed by the household (which would include meals prepared in the home and home repairs) are not included as part of the nation's measured income. The exclusion of such

[1]William Nordhaus and James Tobin, "Is Growth Obsolete?" *Economic Growth,* Fiftieth Anniversary Colloquium, Vol. 5 (New York: National Bureau of Economic Research, 1972).

productive work performed by household members limits the validity of the GNP concept as a measure of the nation's *total* product.

It also should be stressed that not all market transactions are included in determining GNP, for this would involve double-counting. Final products are not normally resold; intermediate products are resold in some form. For example, flour sold by a miller to a baker is resold in the form of bread. To count the flour sold by the miller and the bread sold by the baker as part of GNP would involve double-counting the value of the flour.

Market transactions involving the exchange of wealth or claims to wealth are also excluded in the determination of GNP. Exchange of stocks on the stock market and exchange of bonds in the securities markets only shift ownership of claims to existing assets from one person to another. For the most part, the sale of a used car has a similar effect. In both cases, no increase in production or productive capacity is directly related to the exchange of these assets. Included in GNP, however, are some of the dealer costs associated with these transactions. These costs include, among other things, the salaries and the commissions of the stock and security brokers and used car salesmen, since they provide a current service in the exchange of existing assets. In determining what is included in GNP, the emphasis is on current economic activities which are "productive" in the sense of creating income. A sale of a new car would be included in GNP for this is an end item of current productive activity.

The concept of GNP then necessarily implies selection of what one considers "productive activity." In determining GNP, one must use some criteria of production which are based on an implicit or explicit value judgment. To quote Simon Kuznets, a pioneer in developing national income accounting concepts:

> . . . if no criteria of social productivity are used, national income becomes a mechanical total of all net receipts of individuals and business agencies, regardless for what activity or even whether there is any activity. It would include the compensation of robbers, murderers, drug peddlers, and smugglers, differential gains from the transfer of claims, and pure transfers such as gifts and contributions, which, in the absence of a productivity criterion, cannot be distinguished from payments for services. Such a judgmentless estimate would be of little use, since, to measure all market transactions, some gross rather than net total is requisite. It would measure neither the positive contribution of the country's economic system to the needs of its members for purposes of consumption or capital formation nor the sum total of what the inhabitants of the country *think* their income is.[2]

Kuznets favored a policy of making any underlying "scheme of values or social philosophy" explicit and allow it to guide the selection of the data.

HISTORICAL DEVELOPMENT OF GNP

The concept of "production" or "productive activity" in the measurement of national income has been given different meanings by various writers and governments. In *The Wealth of Nations,* which was first published in 1776, Adam Smith distinguished

---

[2]Simon Kuznets, *National Income and Its Composition, 1919–1938,* Vol. 1 (New York: National Bureau of Economic Research, 1941), p. 4. In 1971, Kuznets received the Nobel Prize in Economics, which was awarded, in part, for his work on developing measurements of national income.

productive activities as the making of material goods only; all services, such as those provided by churchmen, lawyers, doctors, musicians, etc., were considered unproductive since "the work of all of them perishes in the very instant of its production."[3]

Smith's concept of productivity was perpetuated in the writings of David Ricardo and John Stuart Mill and formed the basis of the primary national income estimates in England and France for nearly a century. It was not until Alfred Marshall identified the production of goods and services with the creation of utility in the latter part of the nineteenth century that estimators in these two countries returned to a broader concept of production.[4] This broader concept included services as well as material commodities in the measurement of output. Karl Marx accepted Smith's distinction, and consequently, the Soviet Union and other communist countries of Eastern Europe adopted a concept of national product that basically excludes all those services which do not contribute to material production.[5]

In the United States, studies on the measurement of national income appeared in the mid-nineteenth century, and the National Bureau of Economic Research published several studies in the 1920s. Spurred by the economic depression and increasing government involvement in economic affairs, the Department of Commerce established a National Income Division in the late 1930s which prepared estimates of national income data on an official basis. Official figures of U.S. national income and product first appeared in the *Survey of Current Business* in 1942 and were published in accounting form for the first time in 1947. Various revisions and refinements have been made since, but the basic structure of national income accounting has not been altered greatly.

PROPOSED MEASURE OF ECONOMIC WELFARE

National income or GNP in the United States today is basically a measure of the market value of goods and services produced during a given period of time.[6] As two proponents of an indicator to measure economic welfare, William Nordhaus and James Tobin do not question the usefulness of the GNP data as a measure of production. They consider GNP data indispensable for short-run stabilization policy and for assessing the economy's long-run growth in productive capacity. They do question, however, the usefulness of GNP data in evaluating the growth of economic welfare.

Nordhaus and Tobin would like to see the development of a new concept to measure the growth of economic welfare, and their argument for the development of such a concept is as follows:

---

[3]Adam Smith, *The Wealth of Nations* (New York: The Modern Library, 1937), p. 315.

[4]Earlier estimators of national income had used a more comprehensive production concept. See International Encyclopedia of the Social Sciences, s.v. "National Income and Product Accounts: Developments up to World War I."

[5]See Moshe Yanovsky, *Social Accounting Systems* (Chicago: Aldine Publishing Company, 1965), pp. 112–115. Other aspects of national income accounting in the Soviet Union are also influenced by the writings of Marx. For example, following Marx's theory of value, income is related to only one factor of production—social labor.

[6]The major exceptions concerning production of goods and services which are not marketed but included in the measurement of GNP are estimates of food produced and consumed on farms, financial services of commercial banks and other financial intermediaries, and the rental value of owner-occupied houses.

An obvious shortcoming of GNP is that it is an index of production, not consumption. The goal of economic activity, after all, is consumption. Although this is the central premise of economics, the profession has been slow to develop, either conceptually or statistically, a measure of economic performance oriented to consumption, broadly defined and carefully calculated. We have constructed a primitive and experimental 'measure of economic welfare' (MEW), in which we attempt to allow for the more obvious discrepancies between GNP and economic welfare.[7]

To construct their measure of welfare or consumption, Nordhaus and Tobin make several modifications to the existing national income accounts. These modifications fall into three general categories: 1) reclassification of GNP expenditures as consumption, investment, and intermediate; 2) imputation for the services of consumer capital, leisure, and household activities; and 3) correction for some of the disamenities of urbanization and industrialization.[8]

Sustainable MEW

These modifications are shown in Table 1. In essence, this table provides various additions and subtractions to gross national product, or net national product, to arrive at what is labeled sustainable MEW.[9]

[7]Nordhaus and Tobin, "Is Growth Obsolete?", p. 4.
[8]Ibid., p. 5.
[9]Another concept, labeled actual MEW, consists only of total consumption for a given period and does not take into account any investment expenditures.

TABLE 1
GROSS NATIONAL PRODUCT AND MEASURE OF ECONOMIC WELFARE (MEW):
1929 AND 1965
(Billions of Dollars, 1958 Prices)

	1929	1965
Gross national product	$203.6	$ 617.8
Less: capital consumption, NIPA[1]	−20.6	−54.7
Net national product, NIPA	183.6	563.1
Less: NIPA final output reclassified as regrettables and intermediates		
a) Government	−6.7	−63.2
b) Private	−10.3	−30.9
Imputations for items not included in NIPA		
Plus: a) Leisure	339.5	626.9
b) Nonmarket activity	87.5	295.4
c) Services of public and private capital	29.7	78.9
Less: d) Disamenities	−12.5	−34.6
Less: Additional capital consumption	−19.3	−92.7
Less: Growth requirement	−46.1	−101.8
Sustainable MEW[2]	$43.6	1241.1

[1]NIPA refers to National Income and Product Accounts.
[2]MEW figures are based on using variant B as a deflator.
Source: William Nordhaus and James Tobin, "Is Growth Obsolete?", *Economic Growth*, Fiftieth Anniversary Colloquium, Vol. 5 (New York: National Bureau of Economic Research, 1972), p. 66.

Capital Consumption Sustainable MEW as a measure of consumption is somewhat similar to the concept of net national product (NNP) as a measure of production. Part of the output included in GNP will be used to repair and replace the existing stock of capital goods. This portion of output is classified as the capital consumption allowance. The subtraction of the capital consumption allowance from GNP gives NNP. NNP tells us how much current income or production can be consumed consistent with the maintenance of productive capacity or income potential.

In a similar manner, the Nordhaus-Tobin concept of sustainable MEW provides a measure of "the amount of consumption in any year that is consistent with sustained steady growth in per capita consumption at the trend rate of technological progress." The sustainable MEW concept then considers not only the amount of capital which must be replaced in a period to maintain consumption at the existing level, but also how much additional investment or abstention from consumption in the current period must be made in order to keep consumption per capita growing at some rate which is based on technological progress. After estimates for both the capital consumption allowance and the growth requirement are made, these estimates are subtracted from GNP.

Intermediates and Regrettables Some output, classified as final output for GNP purposes, is reclassified as regrettables and intermediates by Nordhaus and Tobin and is excluded from MEW.

By intermediate product, Nordhaus and Tobin mean "goods and services whose contributions to present or future consumer welfare are completely counted in the values of other goods and services"; they are "not directly sources of utility themselves but are regrettably necessary inputs to activities that may yield utility." Regrettables represent expenditures for national security, prestige, or diplomacy, which in the judgement of Nordhaus and Tobin, do not directly increase the economic welfare of households. No sharp dividing line exists between what is classified as intermediates or regrettables.

Some private expenditures and some Government expenditures are reclassified as intermediate products or regrettables. Private expenditures, such as personal business expenses and a part of transportation expenditures in the GNP accounts, would be reclassified as intermediate products. A major portion of Government purchases, such as national defense, space research and technology, international affairs and finance, veterans benefits, general government, and civilian safety (police, fire, and correction) are reclassified as regrettables or intermediate products and subtracted from GNP.

Imputations The authors impute an estimate for many activities which they feel have a positive or negative effect on social welfare but are not considered in the determination of GNP. Specifically, imputations are made for leisure, nonmarket activity, disamenities, and services of public and private capital.

The most substantial modifications to GNP in obtaining a measure for sustainable MEW are the result of the imputations for leisure and nonmarket activity. Leisure is important to a welfare index, for welfare could rise (consumption of leisure) while GNP falls if employees voluntarily decide to work less. An estimate for nonmarket activity or household production and consumption, such as meals, cleaning, and home repairs, is also added to GNP to obtain MEW.

An estimate for the disamenities of urbanization is subtracted from the GNP data in determining MEW. This estimate considers social costs which are not included in the costs of producing consumption goods and services. These costs would include pollution, litter, congestion, noise, and insecurity. The estimate of these costs is based on the income differentials between large cities and smaller towns and rural areas. Assuming that people can choose residential locations, a portion of the observed income differential can be considered a "disamenity premium" which compensates individuals for unpleasantness associated with living in urban areas.[10]

Services of public and private capital is the last category of imputations for items not included in GNP. The only imputation made for the services of capital in determining GNP is the addition of an estimate for the services received from owner-occupied housing. The MEW concept would extend imputations from capital to include services from Government structures (excluding military) and services from consumer durable goods (under the MEW concept, consumer durables are reclassified as investment goods rather than consumption).

Assessment of MEW

Nordhaus and Tobin state that they are after a measure of consumption, "broadly defined and carefully calculated," but then label this measure a "measure of economic welfare." However, consumption and welfare are two different (although related) concepts. Welfare would depend on the amount of total satisfaction one receives from total consumption, and, among other things, would depend also on the distribution of income. Nordhaus and Tobin realize the problems involved in trying to measure welfare and state that they "cannot . . . estimate how well individual and collective happiness are correlated with consumption."[11] In a comment on the Nordhaus-Tobin MEW concept, Robin C. O. Matthews points out that debates in the 1940s recognized such distinctions between consumption and welfare, and argues that the MEW concept is a measure of consumption not a measure of welfare.[12]

Obtaining reliable estimates of various economic activities which are not included in the national income accounts poses a serious problem in computing MEW. The problems involved in obtaining an accurate measure of household activities is one of the reasons why such activities are not included in measured GNP. The authors of MEW recognize this problem and attempt to estimate the reliability of various components of MEW.

Nordhaus and Tobin rank the reliability of the components of MEW as having a low error, medium error, high error, or very high error. Data in the national income

---

[10]According to the authors, the disamenity premium was about 8 percent of average family disposable income in 1965. Since income differentials have tended to induce migration to urban areas, only a portion of the estimated income differential is subtracted from the GNP accounts as a disamenity premium.

[11]Nordhaus and Tobin, "Is Growth Obsolete?", p. 25.

[12]Robin C. O. Matthews, "Discussion," *Economic Growth,* Fiftieth Anniversary Colloquium, Vol. 5 (New York: National Bureau of Economic Research, 1972), p. 91.

accounts, such as GNP, are used as a benchmark in determining reliability and are put in the low error category. Components in the very high error category are judged to have about ten times the percentage error of GNP. The imputations for leisure, nonmarket activities, and disamenity fall into this very high error category. The imputations for these activities, however, account for much of the difference between GNP and MEW.

The imputations for leisure and household activities, in terms of constant prices, vary greatly depending on how current price estimates are deflated. The authors obtained constant price estimates of both activities by deflating current prices by a consumption deflator and by deflating by wage rates. The accompanying chart presents three different growth paths of sustainable MEW which depend on how leisure and

Per Capita Net National Product and Per Capita Sustainable Measure of Economic Welfare (MEW), 1929–1965. *Note:* Data on MEW are available only for the years 1928, 1935, 1945, 1947, 1954, 1958 and 1965. For comparability, the NNP series is plotted only for those years, even though this series is available on a continuous basis over this period. (Source: *William Nordhaus and James Tobin, "Is Growth Obsolete?,"* Economic Growth, *Fiftieth Anniversary Colloquium, vol. 5, New York: National Bureau of Economic Research, 1972, pp. 53, 57.*)

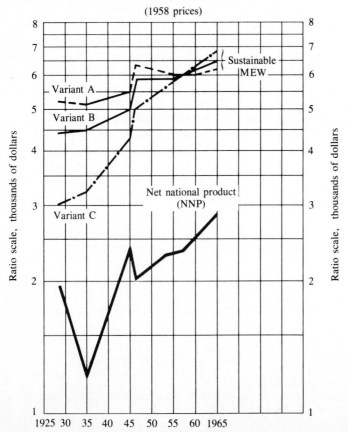

(1958 prices)

nonmarket activities are deflated. The authors indicate a preference for variant B which deflates leisure by a wage index and which deflates nonmarket activity by a consumption deflator.[13]

All three variants of MEW show a positive rate of growth over time, which indicates that real consumption per capita has been increasing. According to variant C, per capita sustainable MEW grew at a 3.6 percent average compound annual rate from 1929 to 1965, which is slightly faster than the 3.1 percent rate for NNP. In the same time period, variant B grew at a 2.3 percent rate and variant A at a 1.8 percent rate.

Nordhaus and Tobin have provided an estimate of sustainable consumption over time. After allowing for some of the disamenities of modern production techniques and urban congestion, their estimates show that net consumption has been growing, but probably at a slower rate than total measured output. They recognize that many unsolved problems are posed by their MEW concept, but view the measure as an attempt to obtain an indicator of the growth in economic welfare. Perhaps the intent and conclusions of their study can best be summed up by the authors themselves:

> We recognize that our proposal is controversial on conceptual and theoretical grounds and that many of the numerical expedients in its execution are dubious. Nevertheless, the challenge to economists to produce relevant welfare-oriented measures seems compelling enough to justify some risk-taking. We hope that others will be challenged, or provoked, to tackle the problem with different assumptions, more refined procedures, and better data. We hope also that further investigations will be concerned with the distribution, as well as the mean value, of a measure of economic welfare, an aspect we have not been able to consider.[14]

SUMMARY

GNP, in general, provides a measure of current production in the United States for which a money income has been received. As a production or income measure, it has been used in forming policy goals for output, employment, and price level changes.

Criticism has been directed against the GNP concept as emphasizing the quantity of goods and services produced while ignoring what is happening to the "quality" of life. Proponents of a new measure to obtain such a quality indicator, or an economic welfare measure, would modify the present national income accounts in several ways. They would subtract from GNP any costs incurred in maintaining clean air and water in the production of goods and services, subtract an estimated cost of urban congestion, subtract expenditures for police and national defense, and include an estimate for the value of nonmarket activities such as household activities and leisure time.

In obtaining their measurement, however, Nordhaus and Tobin have had to resort to a number of crude estimates and rely considerably on their own value judgments concerning the classification of goods and services as consumption or intermediate product. In particular, Nordhaus and Tobin make estimates of many activities, such as household activities, that official national income estimators have avoided because of lack of data. Their judgments concerning what is or is not an intermediate product

---

[13]Variant A deflates both leisure and nonmarket activity by a wage index, and variant C deflates both activities by a consumption deflator.

[14]Nordhaus and Tobin, "Is Growth Obsolete?", p. 26.

also play a significant part in this measure. The problem of defining intermediate products is not unique to this measure of consumption, however, as the problem of defining intermediate goods remains an unsettled issue among various national income estimators. For example, Simon Kuznets supports the notion that many governmental services should be treated as intermediate products rather than final products in the national income accounts.

Although the proponents of this new concept refer to it as a measure of welfare, it more accurately provides a broad measure of consumption. A welfare measure would quantify the amount of satisfaction or utility received from consumption and would depend, in part, on the distribution of income. As a measure of consumption, however, the MEW concept attempts to provide an indicator more closely associated with the concept of welfare than that provided by a production measure such as GNP. Unfortunately, in view of the high error content associated with this measure, the proposed MEW concept does little more than break the ice in an attempt to provide an accurate estimate of economic welfare.

QUESTIONS FOR DISCUSSION

1 The article states that the income and expenditure approaches to measuring GNP give essentially the same results.
   a Explain why this is the case.
   b Suppose that a firm produces some final goods but does not sell them before the end of the year. How would this unsold production get "picked up" by the income approach? The expenditure approach?
2 Why are the following excluded from GNP?
   a Intermediate products (flour sold to a baker)
   b Exchanges of assets (sale of stock or of an old house)
   c Meals prepared at home and home repairs
3 MEW excludes most government spending as "regrettables." Why? Do you agree with this?
4 People work far fewer hours per week today than they did in 1900. On this dimension, does the growth of GNP between 1900 and today understate or overstate the growth in economic welfare?
5 Here are some other differences between 1900 and today:
   a Life expectancy is higher and general health is much better today. We also spend a great deal more on hospitals and doctors.
   b Spending on pollution control equipment is much higher today than in 1900.
   c The country is much more urbanized today than in 1900.
   How are each of these changes reflected in GNP? In economic welfare?
6 Critics of MEW have argued that it measures total consumption, not well-being. Explain how two countries of equal population could have the same total consumption but different levels of well-being. (Some factors you should consider include income distribution, political freedoms, social mobility, and family structure.)
7 Why do you think MEW has not replaced GNP as the leading measure of economic performance?

THE UNMEASURABLE ECONOMY
Susan Lee

A LITTLE BIT OF SPILLAGE
Jane Sasseen

The government and private sources release hundreds of economic statistics each month. Should economists, business people, and policy makers watch each of these and respond to every slight fluctuation in the data? The first of the following two companion articles, by Susan Lee, takes a skeptical view of the value of economic statistics for analyzing the economy in the short run. In the second piece, Jane Sasseen discusses a particular data problem—the failure to adjust measured computer prices for changes over time in computational efficiency.

The Unmeasurable Economy

Susan Lee

The headlines could not be clearer. Just released government figures show that the economy is turning sluggish. What should you, as a business person, do? Drop your newspaper and race to the phone to halt production before inventories pile up? Or yawn and turn to the sports page? You would be better off doing the latter, because that headline is probably meaningless. Chances are that the sluggish GNP figure will be revised, and chances are even-up that the new figures will suggest stepping up your production rather than cutting it back.

Are we saying the government's economic figures are useless? We're certainly saying that they are unreliable and that smart business people rarely pay them much attention.

Consider economist David Munro of General Motors. In the fourth quarter of last year Munro had a feeling that the economy was growing at about 4% and things were looking good. Then the flash GNP figure came out showing 2.8% growth. Munro was nonplussed: "We stopped to see what we'd missed. We looked at our sales, talked to our dealers and marketing staff. I phoned Eastman Kodak and asked about camera sales, GE about refrigerators, J.C. Penney about soft goods. Their orders, and ours, were heavy."

In the end Munro decided to ignore the official flash figure. Wisely. A short time later the Commerce Department revised the figure to 4.9%.

Like Munro, most economists feel that the economy is basically stable. It changes only once in a while, not every week, not even from month to month. These economists disdain looking at every last wiggle in a number. And they are suspicious of drastic changes. Murray Foss of the American Enterprise Institute says that if the numbers zoom down all at once, it doesn't mean the economy is heading into a recession but that there is "something funny going on, like bad weather." In short, suspect the figures before suspecting the economy.

The government puts out these statistics to help policymakers and business people plan for the future. It feeds them figures on money supply, unemployment rates, housing starts, labor productivity, business inventories, retail sales, car sales and so on and so forth.

Ideally, people are supposed to take these figures as a call to action. A strong GNP number—say putting growth over 4%—is supposed to cue managers to speed up production to avoid getting caught with too little inventory. And a big unemployment figure is supposed to alert Congress to the possible need for jobs legislation, or the Federal Reserve to the necessity for zipping up the economy with a little extra money.

Increasingly, however, sophisticated business people and economists regard the figures with amusement. They are still taken seriously only by newspaper editors, TV commentators, politicians with an ax to grind and market players with a phone in their hands.

Consider something as routine as the Commerce Department's tracking of expenditures on plant and equipment. For 1983 the initial numbers showed that expenditures dropped 4.8%, exciting cries of alarm that America was disinvesting itself. The revised numbers, however, now show the average annual rate of change was down only a modest 1.9%.

Are the government number-collectors stupid, inefficient or dishonest? No. Sheer common sense would indicate that an economy as big and as complicated as ours is tough to call. Especially at a time like this, when an increasing part of the economy is underground. This underground economy includes criminal activity, off-the-books cash transactions and barter arrangements. That can add up to a rather large chunk. Baruch College Professor Peter Gutmann estimates that 15% of the GNP is missed. Or about $550 billion worth.

Even with the aboveground economy, the numbers can be unreal for other reasons: Some samples or databases are out of date, the seasonal adjustments are inappropriate or the method of measurement is utterly amateurish. Take the government's measure of plant capacity, called capacity utilization. Some factories are obsolete, yet are counted. Others, which are not on line but could be brought on easily, aren't counted.

So what is a poor economist to do when his or her livelihood depends on measuring the course of business?

When data seem off, most economists let experience and wisdom be their guide. Edward Denison of the Brookings Institution, whose career covers some 45 years in the business, says: "If you just plain don't believe it, you change the numbers. It's almost an instinct about what a particular number can or can't be."

Politicians constitute another group dependent on a feel for the economy to perform their jobs. If the economic news is gloomy, their traditional response is to make pious statements but do nothing. Say, for example, unemployment figures for April rocket. Rather than motoring out a jobs bill in May, Congress will content itself with words of dismay and then wait for a few more months of figures. Not that they are shirking their responsibilities: The chances are that the figures for May—or June—will reverse the bad news.

Or reverse the good news: The Reagan Administration's initial forecast of the budget deficit for 1982 was $45 billion. It was revised later in the year to more than double that. A small error. Who calls $45 billion small? According to Lawrence Kudlow, then chief economist at the Office of Management & Budget, "If that figure had been public ten months earlier, Reagan's fiscal program wouldn't have gotten through."

When waiting around fails, politicians do their own form of punting by putting what's called political spin on the numbers. Says William Niskanen, formerly a member of the Council of Economic Advisers, "The Reagan White House press office puts a big political spin on the numbers. Take the growth of government spending. It's way down in nominal terms, but it's almost as high as the Carter years in real terms." How can this be? Simple. With inflation down, the increase looks smaller. Of course, it's the nominal figure that the Administration punches in on.

Of course, politicians make fiscal policy and fiscal policy is a long time in the making. But what about the Fed, which—as maker of monetary policy—is in a position to react, and react quickly, to the numbers?

Here, again, the watchword is caution. In July 1984 the Fed was confronted with the following bad news: Consumer credit had shown a big jump in May, both first- and second-quarter GNP had been significantly revised upward, capacity utilization was very high, and the money supply figures had leapt by 12.8% in May and 11.3% in June. Since the Fed had tightened money in March and interest rates had risen in spring, it looked as though the economy was really coming on strong.

Did Paul Volcker and company step hard on the brakes? They did not. To do so would have thrown a lot of people through the windshield. The Fed had to worry about Third World debts, the thrift industry and agriculture. All of these were suffering from high interest rates and might have been killed by yet higher rates. But wasn't the Fed, in ignoring those strong growth numbers, risking an inflationary outburst? Answers Preston Martin, vice chairman of the Federal Reserve: "We knew that there was idle capacity in the world and that wage settlements were still low."

The Fed's instinct proved correct: Revised money supply figures showed that May's increase had been only 7.3%, and 10.6% in June. Second-quarter GNP was revised downward. "The numbers just don't give us a good handle on how the economy is performing," says Federal Reserve Governor Martha Seger. "We shouldn't react to the monthly numbers, let alone the weekly ones."

So much for official Washington. What about the rest of the country? Many smart business people almost instinctively adjust the official figures on the side of optimism. They suspect a pessimistic bias to the numbers. Like Dave Munro at GM, they tend to jump on the phone and call around until they hear some good news. (This is not self-serving, either. The fact that official statistics miss up to 15% of the economy's total activity means that figures like GNP are understated, while other indicators, like unemployment, are overstated.)

Indeed, reliance on anecdotal evidence is strong. It's what business people call putting a finger in the wind. On any Saturday night, for instance, business people at cocktail parties across the country are listening to their peers say things like "Gee, houses are really turning over, and the prices we are getting are fantastic. The recession? I guess it is hitting somewhere else."

By far the most popular finger in the wind is the shopping center indicator. Francis Schott of Equitable Life Assurance, who lives in northern New Jersey near four major shopping centers, always watches to see if the parking lots are full the day after Thanksgiving. So does Rosanne Cole of IBM, who also wants to know "if the cash registers are jingling or if people are just looking."

Rick Preiss of IC Industries has a personally tailored coincident indicator—how long it takes him to get to work. At the height of the 1982 recession, Preiss could drive from suburban Lake Forest to Chicago in an hour. Now, with more people on the road also driving to work, it takes him an hour and a quarter.

Except for journalists, then, does anybody take government's data seriously? The financial markets do. And they take it very seriously in the very short term, like minute to minute.

Consider the impact of GNP figures on the markets. The players assume that a weak number means interest rates are going down and a strong number means rates are going up. As Schott describes it: "When the flash figure comes out—especially if it's not what's expected—traders start screaming for a reaction from the economist. So the economist grabs his or her bag of tricks and says something, and that goes out over the wire and the reaction begins."

What if—as usually happens—the numbers turn out to be wrong? More turmoil. If bond traders have bought heavily on down news that begins to look as if it might have been a fluke, they simply unload the position they accumulated.

If nothing else, it's an interesting spectacle. In one corner, we have the government, which generates all these numbers. In the other corner, we have the users. The government comes out slugging, its numbers flying. The users feint and jab. It looks like fun, but does anybody get hurt?

The only real harm is done to those who react to the numbers as they come out. As all the constant revisions demonstrate, it's silly to take the numbers seriously over the short term. Smart people, who hunt trends in the economy, look for them over the long term. As Rosanne Cole says, "If short-term evidence plays any role at all, it is almost a posturing one in that it convinces people to do what they were going to do anyway."

Not that this continual bombardment of government data doesn't have defenders. Most players argue that some information is better than none. Nonetheless, each has his own bête noire, which he or she would cheerfully see vanish from the newspaper. As Bill Niskanen says, "I occasionally yearn for a world in which bilateral trade statistics do not exist. The great concern Congress has about the trade deficit with Japan is wholly inappropriate. It's a number that has a political content several orders of magnitude more important than its economic content."

Is the country better off for all the information we now get that we didn't get 20 years ago? Well, consider Francis Schott's answer: "I have my serious doubts. I mean, I *really* have serious doubts."

The age of information is not necessarily the age of wisdom.

A Little Bit of Spillage

Jane Sasseen

To help drive home our point that economic statistics ought to be looked at skeptically, when at all, FORBES has devised a quick little test. Guess which of the following is true: Over the last decade computer prices have . . .

A) Dropped dramatically.

B) Held steady, without changing at all.

Chances are, you answered A. You would be correct in the real world but wrong in a statistical sense. If you answered B, congratulations. You would be wrong in the real world, but there might be a job for you at the Commerce Department's Bureau of Economic Analysis.

That's because the BEA, in calculating the inflation-adjusted "real" Gross National Product figures, makes a simple little assumption that reduces GNP by more than a full percentage point. In adding up real investment in computers each year, the BEA assumes that computer prices haven't changed at all since 1972.

You don't have to be Steven Jobs to know how ridiculous that is. An IBM PC that today brings about $2,500 would have been about $1,200 more than that just four years ago. On average, computers now cost less than a third what they cost in 1972.

But ridiculous or not, the BEA's assumption makes for some of the worst statistics flowing out of Washington. Real spending on computers by U.S. business last year was around $35 billion. But by simply factoring in a 10% yearly drop in computer prices since 1972—a conservative figure—the Council of Economic Advisers estimates

Reprinted by permission of *Forbes* Magazine, June 3, 1985, p. 102. © Forbes, Inc., 1985.

that real computer spending last year was actually closer to $120 billion. A little spillage there. Some $85 billion worth of error.

That increase ripples through the GNP statistics. Real GNP would have jumped more than a point in each of the last three years if computer spending had been measured more accurately; inflation, on the other hand, would have dropped by a point. Spending on plant and equipment would have doubled, from its anemic 3%-a-year average growth rate to a far healthier 6%.

Put another way, the BEA is saying that $10,000 spent on computers in 1984 bought the same amount of "computer power" as $10,000 spent on computers in 1972. In fact, a $5 million processor today is about eight times more powerful than a $5 million 1972 model. With most goods, that kind of quality increase would lead to a big jump in the real GNP figure. But not with computers. Because of the outdated price assumption, none of that productivity gain gets reflected in real GNP.

Originally, the BEA made that assumption decades ago, when computers were still a tiny speck of GNP. But in the last year, with the "real" figures moving grossly out of line with reality, the BEA decided to correct the miscalculation. The problem now is coming up with a decent index to measure changes in computer prices.

Normally the BEA gets that kind of information from the Bureau of Labor Statistics, but it, too, has lousy computer price information. So the BEA is busy concocting a new way to tally real computer spending. The most likely outcome is that the BEA will start logging a 10% annual decline in prices when it publishes the 1985 GNP figures.

But don't expect that change to be obvious. At the same time, the BEA plans to change the way it figures real GNP. By late this year, real GNP will be based on 1982 dollars instead of 1972 dollars, as is currently done. That rebasing means that the new 1982 "real" figures will be incomparable with current 1972 real figures. Warns one BEA statistician, "It will be a couple of years before people figure out what these new numbers really mean." Would you buy a used car from this man?

QUESTIONS FOR DISCUSSION

1 Until recently, the U.S. Department of Commerce reported a very early "flash estimate" of quarterly GNP, based on preliminary information available even before the end of the quarter. The flash estimate was often heavily revised but probably did, on average, contain some information about the direction of the economy. The department stopped reporting the flash estimate largely because of criticism about the estimate's relative inaccuracy.

  Was the department right to stop reporting the flash estimate? How could reporting this estimate be helpful to the economy? How could it be counterproductive?

2 What is the "underground economy"? Why is its size poorly measured? Can you think of some ways in which the government might try to get an estimate of how big the underground economy is? (*Hint:* People in the underground economy are more likely to use cash than checks.)

3 While it is probably true that the underground economy (see question 2) is a large portion of the total economy, it is also probably true that its share of the total economy changes slowly over time. What are the implications of this for using measured GNP (*a*) as an indicator of short-run booms and busts; (*b*) as a measure of long-run economic growth?

4 Susan Lee states that traders in financial markets do pay close attention to economic statistics. Is this consistent with her view that the numbers are "usually wrong"? Why or why not?

5 *Seasonal adjustment* is a procedure that removes *regularly recurring* seasonal patterns from the data. What would be the effect on the seasonally adjusted and seasonally unadjusted unemployment rates of:

a The surge in department stores hires that takes place each year during the Christmas season?

b Less severe than normal winter weather? (*Note:* Construction and other major industries lay off workers when the weather is bad.)

c A general economic recovery?

6 The types of computer products offered to the public have varied dramatically over the years; many on the market today were not even available a few years ago. In what sense, then, does Jane Sasseen claim that "the" price of computers has dropped radically over the last ten years? How would replacing the BEA's official assumption about computer prices with Sasseen's view affect (*a*) measured inflation, (*b*) measured real GNP growth, and (*c*) the share of computers in current real GNP?

Note: The U.S. Department of Commerce *News* of December 20, 1985, describes a "comprehensive revision of the National Income and Product Account." Included in the revisions are (*a*) a change in the base year from 1972 to 1982, (*b*) adjustments, based on IRS studies of unreported income, to include more of the underground economy in GNP, and (*c*) a significantly revised price index for computers.

A DESCRIPTIVE ANALYSIS OF ECONOMIC INDICATORS

Ronald A. Ratti*

The *index of leading indicators* is a measure of economic performance often reported in the media. The following article discusses the construction and uses of this index and of the less well known coincident and lagging indexes.

Each month the U.S. Department of Commerce publishes a series of economic indicators, the most widely followed of which are the composite indexes of leading, coincident and lagging indicators.[1] The significance attached to these series is attested to by the promptness with which their month-to-month movements are reported and analyzed by the news media.[2] Economic agents monitor the behavior of these indexes

---

Ronald A. Ratti, "A Descriptive Analysis of Economic Indicators," *Review,* St. Louis Federal Reserve Bank, January 1985, pp. 14–24.

*Ronald A. Ratti, associate professor of economics, University of Missouri-Columbia, is a visiting scholar at the Federal Reserve Bank of St. Louis. Laura Prives and John G. Schulte provided research assistance.

[1]Published monthly in *Business Conditions Digest* by the U.S. Department of Commerce.

[2]For example, an estimate of the behavior of the Index of Leading Indicators for August 1984 was released by the Department of Commerce on September 28. That same day, the *New York Times* carried a lengthy article with the headline "Economic Index Up by 0.5%" (Hershey [1984]). *United Press International* (1984) carried a story headed "Indicators Rise Slightly in August." On October 1, the *Christian Science Monitor* carried stories focusing on the behavior of the leading index for August 1984 (Cook [1984] and Nenneman [1984]), and *The Wall Street Journal* ran a story headed "Economic Index Eases Worries Over Slowdown" (Murray [1984]).

because, historically, they have been thought to provide useful information on current and future changes in the economy.[3]

The objective of this paper is to describe how these indexes are constructed and revised, to provide a descriptive explanation for why they might provide information on future economic conditions, and to examine critically their usefulness.[4] In the final section of the paper, the difficulties inherent in using the index of leading indicators as a forecaster of future economic conditions are discussed. Emphasis is placed on the leading indicator index since it is the most widely reported and well known of the indexes considered.

A DESCRIPTION OF COMPOSITE INDEXES

Individual and composite indicators are used to predict downturns and upturns in the economy and to monitor the degree of strength or weakness in a recession or recovery. Analysts generally acknowledge that in order for individual indicators to provide useful information they should have the following characteristics: (1) they should represent and accurately measure important economic variables or processes; (2) they should bear a consistent relationship over time with business cycle movements and turns; (3) they should not be dominated by irregular and non-cyclical movements; and (4) they should be promptly and frequently reported.[5] These requirements ensure that the best indicators regularly provide timely economic information on the stages of the business cycle.

On the basis of these criteria, the Bureau of Economic Analysis has evaluated, and continues to evaluate, hundreds of economic time series. Only those series with a good overall performance that are available monthly with a short time lag and are not subject to large revisions are candidates for inclusion in the three major composite indexes.

The composite indexes of leading, coincident and lagging cyclical indicators each measure the average behavior of series showing similar leading, coincident and lagging timing at business cycle turns. Components of the indexes are also chosen so as to represent as broad an array of diverse activities and sectors as possible. This requirement is meant to ensure that the composite indicators continue to monitor and closely shadow economic activity, even if the causes and nature of cyclical change vary over time

---

[3]For an authoritative discussion of the use of composite indicators for forecasting, see Zarnowitz and Moore (1982). On the use of the leading series for forecasting, see Hymans (1973), Stekler and Schepsman (1973) and Neftci (1979). For a summary of work on the use of the index of leading indicators for forecasting, see Gorton (1982).

[4]This work draws on the following basic sources: Zarnowitz and Boschan (1975a, 1975b), Moore (1984) and Zarnowitz and Moore (1982).

[5]If a series did not bear a consistent relationship over time with the business cycle, it would not be useful as an indicator of business cycle conditions. If a series was dominated by non-cyclical factors, it would not be possible to "read" cyclical developments from the behavior of the series. A series should be promptly and regularly reported in order to provide a steady stream of timely information. For a demonstration of the formal application of the criteria used for evaluating the usefulness of economic series as indicators, see Zarnowitz and Boschan (1975a).

and the performances of some individual indicators deteriorate. Since each business cycle has unique characteristics, individual series can be expected to perform better during some cycles than others. Without prior information on the causes of current economic change, it seems best to rely for information on groupings of series rather than individual series.

The Index of Leading Indicators

Table 1 lists the components of the three composite indexes. The leading index consists of individual components that might lead measures of economic activity.[6] For example, housing starts, new incorporations, contracts for construction and new orders for machinery and equipment are leading indicators, since they represent early commitments to future economic activity.

The inclusion of some other components in the leading index is less obvious and more involved. This is partly because there is no single well-developed theory linking each of the indicators to the business cycle. The economic series that make up the composite indicators are included primarily because they perform well statistically in relation to the cycle, not because they are the operational counterparts of variables in an economic theory of business cycles.

There is usually some economic rationale, however, for including each series in the index. An increase in average weekly hours worked, for instance, presumably leads the business cycle since it is easier for employers to move to higher output levels in the initial stages of an expansion by increasing the utilization of labor than by increasing the number of employees.

The remaining components of the index of leading indicators and the rationale for including them in the index are the following: Initial claims for unemployment insurance represent first claims filed by workers newly unemployed or claims for subsequent periods of unemployment. Slower deliveries, which inversely reflect the volume of business of firms supplying purchasing agents in the Greater Chicago area, has been found to precede changes in the actual volume of business.[7] The sum of changes in inventories on hand and on order are assumed to reflect changes in the desired stock of inventories. The desired stock of inventories is assumed to rise if the anticipated level of sales increases.

"Change in sensitive materials prices, smoothed" is based on indexes of crude and intermediate materials prices and spot market prices of raw industrial materials. Movements in these prices are assumed to reflect variations in demand relative to supply in the process of building up or drawing down raw material inventories. A rise in prices is taken to indicate increased demand for the output of the manufacturing and construction sectors. Stock price movements affect and measure the general state of

---

[6]A discussion of why the components of the Index of Leading Indicators lead the economy is provided in Moore (1984), chapter 21. A detailed discussion of the relative strengths of the components of the Index of Leading Indicators is given in Zarnowitz and Boschan (1975a).

[7]This is an ad hoc statistical criterion that seems in contrast to the "economic" reasoning behind other components. The use of this indicator is being questioned on the grounds that faster deliveries reflect better management rather than slack demand, especially in light of increasing computerization.

TABLE 1
STANDARDIZATION FACTORS AND WEIGHTS
FOR COMPOSITE INDEX COMPONENTS

BEA series number and title	Standardization factor[1]	Weight[2]
Leading index components		
1. Average weekly hours of production of nonsupervisory workers, manufacturing	0.467	1.014
5. Average weekly initial claims for unemployment insurance, State program[3]	5.374	1.041
8. Manufacturers' new orders in 1972 dollars, consumer goods and materials industries	2.818	.973
32. *Vendor performance, percent of companies receiving slower deliveries	3.840	1.081
12. Index of net business formation	.996	.973
20. Contracts and orders for plant and equipment in 1972 dollars	6.194	.946
29. Index of new private housing units authorized by local building permits	5.064	1.054
36. *Change in manufacturing and trade inventories on hand and on order in 1972 dollars, smoothed[4]	2.530	.986
99. *Change in sensitive materials prices, smoothed[4]	.324	.892
19. Index of stock prices, 500 common stocks	2.633	1.149
106. Money supply M2 in 1972 dollars	.417	.932
111. *Change in business and consumer credit outstanding	2.627	.959
Coincident index components		
41. Employees on nonagricultural payrolls	.321	1.064
51. Personal income less transfer payments in 1972 dollars	.502	1.003
47. Index of industrial production	.924	1.028
57. Manufacturing and trade sales in 1972 dollars	1.021	.905
Lagging index components		
91. Average duration of unemployment in weeks[3]	3.587	1.098
77. *Ratio, manufacturing and trade inventories to sales in 1972 dollars	0.016	.894
62. *Index of labor cost per unit of output, manufacturing— actual data as a percent of trend	.557	.868
109. *Average prime rate charged by banks	.376[5]	1.123
101. Commercial and industrial loans outstanding in 1972 dollars	.901	1.009
95. *Ratio, consumer installment credit outstanding to personal income	.062	1.009

*First differences rather than symmetrical percent changes are computed for this series.
[1]Standardization factors are computed over the period 1948–81.
[2]The weight for a given series is the ratio of its performance score to the average score of all series in that index.
[3]Changes for this series are inverted; i.e., they are multipled by −1.
[4]This series is a four-term moving average (weighted 1,2,2,1) placed on the terminal month of the span.
[5]This standardization factor is computed over the period 1966–81.
Source: U.S. Department of Commerce, *Handbook of Cyclical Indicators* (1984).

business expectations about future profits. When prospects for profits deteriorate, investment plans are shelved and expansionary business operations are contracted.

The inclusion of money and credit indicators capture the impact of changes in real balances and the availability of credit on future activity. During the late stages of a boom, bank deposit creation is limited by the availability of reserves, and the rate of increase in consumer prices begins to accelerate. The opposite is true during a downturn. These effects cause the turning points in the business cycle. The change in business and consumer credit also is a leading indicator, since many economic actions require financial arrangements before their inception.

The Index of Coincident Indicators

The components of the Index of Coincident Indicators are measures of aggregate economic activity in the areas of employment, real income, production and real sales. The Index of Coincident Indicators, together with other coincident indicators, show how well the economy is faring and is used to identify and date the peaks and troughs in the business cycle. This identification and dating, however, can only be done after the turning points have occurred.

The Index of Lagging Indicators

The Index of Lagging Indicators is designed to confirm both downturns and upturns in business activity. Lagging indicators can also be useful for forecasting purposes, because their turns sometimes lead the opposite turns of the leading indicators. Lagging indicators, such as bank interest rates, unit labor costs, inventory holdings and outstanding debt are associated with the costs of doing business. Reductions in these items during a recession lay the basis for the subsequent upturn, as well as having an enhancing effect on such leading indicators as commitments to invest, inventory accumulation and new credit outstanding.

CONSTRUCTION OF COMPOSITE INDEXES

Construction of the composite indexes involves several statistical operations on both the individual data series that make up the indexes and on the indexes themselves. These steps are described in this section. The accompanying insert provides an illustration of how the indexes are constructed.

The first step in constructing the composite indexes involves standardizing the individual series. Standardization prevents the relatively volatile series from dominating movements in the composite index. If, for example, a series typically exhibits large percentage changes, a failure to standardize would cause this series to swamp the effects of series that typically change by more modest amounts.

For each individual series, the month-to-month percentage change is calculated. (For series already in percentage form or in ratio form the month-to-month difference is taken.) The percentage changes in a component series are then standardized by dividing them by the long-run average percentage change in that series without regard to sign (the standardization factor).[8] These standardization factors are shown in table 1.

A composite index is constructed by weighting the standardized changes of its components. The weight assigned each component is determined by the overall score each series receives on the basis of a number of economic and statistical criteria. The application of these criteria involves both objective and subjective evaluations of such factors as economic significance, timely recognition of business cycle turning points, degree of conformity to the stages of the business cycle, quality and availability of current data, and the importance of non-cyclical movements in the series.[9] The largest weights are attached to those components with the best overall performance on the basis of these criteria. The weights attached to the components of the composite indexes are shown in table 1. As can be seen, these weights do not vary between components by as much as the standardization factors do.[10]

The raw percentage changes in the leading and lagging indexes, given by the sum of the weighted standardized percentage changes of their components, are then adjusted so as to facilitate comparison with the coincident index. This is done by equating the cumulative sum over time of the absolute values of changes in the leading and lagging index with the sum of the absolute values of changes in the coincident index. The index standardization factors based on data over 1948–81 appear in table 2.

In addition, a trend adjustment procedure is used to make the trends in the three major composite indexes equal to the average of the trends in the components of the

---

[8]The sum of the percentage changes of even a highly volatile series might be zero if large negative values are just as likely to be followed by large positive values as more negative values. For this reason, the sum of the absolute values of the percentage changes is used as a measure of volatility. This means that the standardization factor of a series that alternates in value between $+1$ and -1 is the same as the standardization factor of a series that has values of only $+1$.

[9]For a detailed explanation of the principles upon which the scoring system is based, see Zarnowitz and Boschan (1975a) and U.S. Department of Commerce (1984).

[10]Auerbach (1982) has argued that a simple average weighting scheme yields a leading composite index that is very similar to the official leading index and that elaborate procedures for determining weights are therefore unnecessary.

TABLE 2
INDEX STANDARDIZATION AND TREND ADJUSTMENT FACTORS: 1948–81

Composite index	Average absolute change[1]	Index standardization factor[2]	Trend in raw index	Trend adjustment factor[3]
Leading index	0.496	0.582	0.132%	+0.139%
Coincident index	.852	1.000	.466	−.175
Lagging index	.602	.707	.253	+.018

[1]The average absolute change for each index is obtained as follows: (a) for each month, a weighted average of the standardized changes of all components in that index is computed; (b) a long-term (1948–81) average without regard to sign is calculated from these monthly averages.

[2]This measure is the ratio of the average absolute change in each index to the average absolute change in the coincident index.

[3]The trend adjustment factor is 0.271 minus the trend in the raw index.

Source: U.S. Department of Commerce, *Handbook of Cyclical Indicators* (1984).

coincident index. This is done by subtracting the trends in the leading, coincident and lagging indexes (0.132, 0.446 and 0.253, respectively) and adding in the average of the monthly trends in the components of the coincident indexes (0.271).[11] The trend adjustment facilitates the use of the three indexes as indicators of levels of activity. The trend adjustment factors are listed in table 2.

THE IMPORTANCE OF REVISIONS

A preliminary estimate of the performance of the composite indexes for a given month appears toward the end of the following month. The July issue of *Business Conditions Digest*, for example, carries a preliminary estimate of the composite indexes in June. The August issue of *Business Conditions Digest* will then carry a revised estimate of the June indexes. The second estimate typically differs from the first because data on some series were not originally available and because data that were originally available have been updated.

The net effect of these revisions is often a significant change in the estimate of the performance of the composite indicators. Table 3 illustrates that the absolute size of the first revision in the indexes of leading, coincident and lagging indicators averaged about 0.5, 0.3 and 0.3 percentage points, respectively, for the first nine months of 1984. These revisions appear to be substantial, given that the preliminary estimates of the monthly changes in these indexes have average absolute values of only about 0.7, 0.7 and 1.0 percentage points.

[11]Details on trend adjustment can be obtained from U.S. Department of Commerce (1984).

TABLE 3
FIRST AND SECOND ESTIMATES OF COMPOSITE INDEXES: 1984
(Percent Changes)

	Leading		Coincident		Lagging	
	First[1]	Second[2]	First	Second	First	Second
January	1.1%	1.0%	1.0%	1.4%	−0.9%	−0.9%
February	0.7	1.3	0.9	0.8	0.9	1.6
March	−1.1	−0.1	0.3	0.0	1.1	1.3
April	0.5	0.5	0.8	0.9	1.7	1.8
May	−0.1	0.4	0.5	0.9	1.0	1.7
June	−0.9	−1.3	0.7	0.9	0.6	0.9
July	−0.8	−1.8	0.8	0.1	0.9	1.2
August	0.5	−0.1	0.2	0.0	1.1	1.0
September	0.4	0.6	0.1	0.0	0.6	0.8
Average absolute revision	0.5		0.3		0.3	

[1]First estimate for a month is obtained from the issue of *Business Conditions Digest* for the following month.
[2]Second estimate for a month is obtained from the issue of *Business Conditions Digest* dated two months later.
Source: U.S. Department of Commerce, *Business Conditions Digest*, various issues.

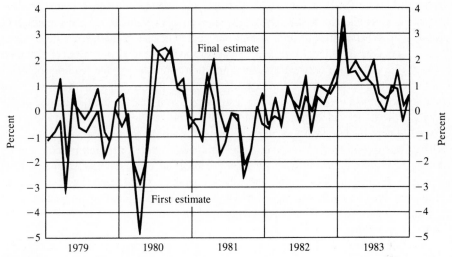

CHART 1
First and Final Estimates of Leading Index.

The sources of revisions in the three indexes vary from one month to the next. It appears, however, that for the monthly estimates during 1984 the subsequent availability of data on series *not available initially* accounts, on the average, for over two-thirds of the first revision in leading and lagging indexes and about one-half of the revision in the coincident index. The balance of the revisions are due to updated estimates of data *that were available* for the initial estimates.

Estimates of the composite indexes are subject to revision for a period of 12 months. The first and last available estimates of the leading indicator from 1979 to 1983 appear in chart 1. As we can see, these estimates sometimes diverge by substantial amounts. In table 4, the average absolute values of successive revisions in estimates of changes in each composite indicator from 1979 to 1983 are presented. For purposes of comparison, the table also includes the average absolute value of selected estimates of the percentage change in each index. The average absolute value of the

TABLE 4
AVERAGE ABSOLUTE VALUES OF ESTIMATES AND REVISIONS OF
COMPOSITE INDICATORS: 1979–83

	Leading	Coincident	Lagging
First estimate	1.1	0.7	2.5
Second estimate	1.1	0.7	1.8
Final estimate	1.0	0.7	0.9
First revision	0.4	0.4	0.8
Revisions subsequent to first revision	0.5	0.2	1.2
Revision from first to final estimates	0.6	0.4	1.9

Source: U.S. Department of Commerce, *Business Conditions Digest,* various issues.

first revision (the difference between the first and second estimates) in the leading indicator is calculated to be 0.4, and the average absolute value of revision subsequent to the first revision (the difference between the final and second estimates) in the leading indicator is found to be 0.5. Since the average absolute value of the total revision (the difference between the final and first estimates) in the leading indicator (0.6) is less than the sum of the individual revisions (0.9), it is apparent that successive revisions sometimes overshoot the final estimate. Given that the final estimates of the leading, coincident and lagging indicators have average absolute values of only 1.0, 0.7 and 0.9, respectively, errors in early estimates would seem to be substantial.

The difficulty created by error in early estimates can be illustrated by considering recent months during 1984. From table 3, it can be seen that the first estimate of the percentage change in the leading indicator in May was negative. The second and subsequent (not shown) estimates for May are positive. The first and subsequent estimates for June and July (as of the middle of December) are negative. This makes the behavior of the index during August of some interest. For August, the first estimate was positive ($+0.5$), the second negative (-0.1), and the third (available in November) positive ($+0.1$). A further illustration of the difficulties created for forecasting is taken up in the next section.

THE USEFULNESS OF THE INDEX OF LEADING INDICATORS IN FORECASTING

One way of evaluating the index of leading indicators is to examine its ability to predict the onset of a recovery or a recession. This is usually done by observing the number of consecutive monthly declines or increases in the index.[12] If the index has been rising steadily and the economy has been expanding, a fall in the index for several months heralds a recession. Likewise, if the index has been falling for several months and the economy has been depressed, a rise in the index over several months heralds a recovery.

This approach to forecasting the business cycle begins by specifying the number of successive months of reversal in the index's behavior necessary to predict a turning point in the cycle. In general, the method is more reliable the greater the number of consecutive months of decline or increase required to forecast a turning point. When the lead time in the forecast is increased, however, it reduces the number of consecutive months of reversal required to make a forecast.

Using both two and three months of consecutive movement in the index as a criteria for prediction, Wood (1984) has reported the reliability and lead time of using the leading index to forecast turning points in the economy's rate of growth. His observations are reported in table 5.

These data reveal that the index of leading indicators has forecasted every recession

---

[12]For a discussion of an alternative criteria for forecasting turning points, see Zarnowitz and Moore (1982). Work by Zarnowitz and Boschan (1975b) suggests that the ratio of the coincident indicator to the lagging indicator would be a useful predictor of turning points. Moore (1969) first suggested the use of the ratio of the coincident to lagging indicators for forecasting purposes. For a history of the basic idea that lagging indicators might lead, see Moore (1984), chapter 23.

TABLE 5

EX ANTE TIMING OF THE LEADING INDICATORS
DURING GROWTH CYCLE TURNING POINTS: 1948–82

Growth cycle peaks	Two consecutive monthly decreases	Three consecutive monthly decreases	Growth cycle trough	Two consecutive monthly increases	Three consecutive monthly increases
Nov. 1948	− 1	0	Oct. 1949	− 3	− 2
Mar. 1951*	− 4	− 3	July 1952	− 5	− 4
July 1953	− 1	0	May 1954	− 5	− 4
Aug. 1957	− 19	− 18	Apr. 1958	+ 1	+ 2
Apr. 1960	− 9	− 8	Feb. 1961	− 8	− 7
May 1962*	+ 1	+ 2	Oct. 1964	missed	missed
June 1966*	0	+ 1	Oct. 1967	− 6	− 5
Dec. 1969	− 9	− 5	Nov. 1970	+ 1	+ 2
Nov. 1973	− 4	− 3	Mar. 1975	+ 1	+ 2
Jan. 1980	− 13	− 5	July 1980	0	+ 1
July 1981	− 6	− 5	Dec. 1982	− 7	− 1
Average	− 6	− 4	Average	− 3	− 2

Note: *indicates that a growth recession followed. Negative numbers indicate a positive lead time.

and growth recession (which occurs when the rate of growth in the economy slows down) since 1948.[13] A negative number indicates the number of months by which either a two- or three-month rule leads a peak or trough in the rate of growth. A positive number indicates the number of months by which the use of the rule lagged behind a turning point. For example, since the leading indicator declined for several months starting in August 1948, two- and three-month declines in the indicator lead the growth cycle peak in November 1948 by one and zero months, respectively.

Use of a two-month rule for forecasting a growth cycle peak gives a longer lead time than the three-month rule by more than one month for the recessions starting in both December 1969 and January 1980. This means that there were isolated consecutive monthly declines in the index in February and March 1969 and in November and December 1978, that is, declines that were not immediately followed by recession.

The lead times in table 5 refer to the forecasting performance of the final estimates of the leading indicator. In general, the final estimates are not the same as the initial estimates. These differences between early and final estimates of the indexes can sometimes create serious problems in forecasting turning points in the growth cycle. For example, table 5 indicates that three consecutive monthly declines in the leading

[13]A growth cycle is a fluctuation around the long-run trend in economic growth. Most business cycles contain, and coincide with, one growth cycle. The business cycle starting at the end of 1948 contained two growth cycles. The dates in table 5 indicate that economic growth slowed down from March 1951 to July 1952, then picked up again to peak in July 1953, at which time a recession began. The very long business cycle starting during 1960 contained three growth cycles, with slowdowns in growth starting immediately after May 1962 and June 1966, and upturns in growth starting in October 1964 and October 1967. A recession did not begin until December 1969. For a discussion of the concept of growth cycles, see Moore (1984), chapter 5.

TABLE 6
ESTIMATES OF THE LEADING INDICATOR: 1979
(Percent Changes)

	Final estimate	First estimate	Second estimate
May	0.8%	0.4%	0.3%
June	− 0.7	− 0.1	− 0.3
July	− 0.9	− 0.4	− 0.2
August	− 0.5	0.0	0.1
September	0.0	0.8	0.2
October	− 1.9	− 0.9	− 1.4
November	− 1.1	.− 1.3	− 1.2
December	0.3	0.0	− 0.2

Source: U.S. Department of Commerce, *Business Conditions Digest,* various issues.

indicator forecasted the onset of the 1980 recession by five months. These declines in the final estimate of the leading indicator, which occurred during June, July and August 1979, are shown in table 6. The problem with this analysis from a forecasting viewpoint is that the first and second estimates of the leading indicator did not register declines for August. The second estimate for August 1979, which became available at the end of October 1979, showed a positive rise in the leading indicator of 0.1 percent. As this example illustrates, the likely magnitude of revisions in preliminary estimates of change in the composite indexes complicates the interpretation of signals in the short run.

Additional qualifications also need to be made concerning the forecasting ability of the index of leading indicators:

1 The leading index has falsely forecasted the onset of recession on at least three occasions. The index declined for three consecutive months in late 1960 and a recession didn't start until 17 months later. The index fell for two consecutive months in mid-1963 and mid-1971 and recessions did not begin until two or three years later.

2 The is no clear a priori criteria as to whether declines in the index forecast a full-blown recession or merely a significant slowing in the economy. Consecutive monthly declines in the index preceded slowdowns, but not recessions, in economic growth in 1951, 1962 and 1966.

3 The lead times by which the leading indicator predicts a turning point are highly variable. Indeed, the three monthly declines in the index in December 1955, January and February 1956 were so far ahead of the business cycle peak that occurred in August 1957 that they can almost be regarded as a false signal. Given the historical tendency of the U.S. economy to exhibit cyclical fluctuations, a recession eventually will follow a decline (or any other movement for that matter) in the indicator. In order for the indicator to be a really useful forecaster, it also would need to forecast the timing of a recession within narrower bounds than it has since 1948.

4 By using the most up-to-date version of the index, a favorable bias is introduced into this evaluation of the predictive performance of the leading indicator. The components of the index and the standardization, weighting and trend factors have been altered continually through the years. Currently, they are based on data from 1948–81. The current index has been designed so as to obtain as favorable an ex post record as possible. While this is the appropriate means for constructing an index that will lead future economic activity as reliably as possible, the application of the current index to historical business cycle data does not measure the forecasting performance of the leading indicator actually in use when the forecasts were made.

In summary, the usefulness of the index of leading economic indicators for forecasting would seem to be seriously circumscribed by the problem of the highly variable lags by which economic activity follows the index, and by the large revisions by which initial estimates of the index are adjusted.

REFERENCES

Auerbach, Alan J. "The Index of Leading Indicators: 'Measurement without Theory,' Thirty-five Years Later," *The Review of Economics and Statistics* (November 1982), pp. 589–95.

Cook, David T. "Fed Meets This Week Amid Fresh Signs of Slower Economy," *Christian Science Monitor,* October 1, 1984.

Gorton, Gary. "Forecasting with the Index of Leading Indicators," Federal Reserve Bank of Philadelphia *Business Review* (November/December 1982), pp. 15–27.

Hershey, Robert D. Jr. "Economic Index Up by 0.5%," *New York Times,* September 29, 1984.

Hymans, Saul H. "On the Use of Leading Indicators to Predict Cyclical Turning Points," *Brookings Papers on Economic Activity* (February 1973), pp. 339–84.

Moore, Geoffrey H. "Generating Leading Indicators From Lagging Indicators," *Western Economic Journal* (June 1969), pp. 135–44.

———. *Business Cycles, Inflation and Forecasting,* National Bureau of Economic Research Studies in Business Cycles No. 24, 2nd ed. (Ballinger Publishing Company, 1984).

Murray, Alan. "Economic Index Eases Worries Over Slowdown," *The Wall Street Journal,* October 1, 1984.

Neftci, Salih N. "Lead-Lag Relations, Exogeneity and Prediction of Economic Time Series," *Econometrica* (January 1979), pp. 101–13.

Nenneman, Richard A. "Latest Economic Data, Dip in the Prime Rate Look Good for the Economy," *Christian Science Monitor,* October 1, 1984.

Stekler, H. O., and Martin Schepsman. "Forecasting With An Index of Leading Series," *Journal of the American Statistical Association* (June 1973), pp. 291–96.

United Press International. "Indicators Rise Slightly in August," *N.Y. Journal of Commerce,* October 1, 1984.

U.S. Department of Commerce. *Business Conditions Digest,* various issues.

———. *Handbook of Cyclical Indicators,* 1984.

Wood, Steven A. "The Index of Leading Indicators: What is it Telling Us?" *Chase Econometrics* (September 1984), pp. A.24–A.33.

Zarnowitz, Victor, and Charlotte Boschan. "Cyclical Indicators: An Evaluation and New Indices," *Business Conditions Digest* (U.S. Department of Commerce, May 1975), pp. V–XIX.

———. "New Composite Indexes of Coincident and Lagging Indicators," *Business Conditions Digest* (U.S. Department of Commerce, November 1984), pp. V–XXI.

Zarnowitz, Victor, and Geoffrey H. Moore. "Sequential Signals of Recession and Recovery," *Journal of Business* (January 1982).

APPENDIX: Construction of Composite Indexes: An Example

The procedures for constructing composite indexes from the basic monthly data series are illustrated in the example below. In the example, the preliminary estimates of the leading coincident and lagging indicators are calculated for June 1984. The data, taken from the July 1984 issue of *Business Conditions Digest,* are presented in the table that follows.

Note that data on several components—change in inventories, business and consumer credit, manufacturing and trade sales, the ratio of manufacturing and trade inventories to sales, and the ratio of consumer installment credit outstanding to personal income—were not available. These omissions and subsequent revisions in the original data will be sources of change in successive estimates of the three indexes.

The column headed "weighted and standardized percentage change" is obtained by dividing the percentage change in each component by its standardization factor, then multiplying by its weight, both of which are presented in table 1 and explained in the text.[1] The sum of the numbers in this column provide estimates of the movements during June in each of the indexes that have not yet been standardized for compatibility across the three indexes or detrended. For the leading coincident and lagging indicators, these figures are $-0.577, 0.888$ and 0.398 percent, respectively. Dividing each of those numbers by the index standardization factors and then adding the trend factors, both of which are given in table 2, yields the following preliminary estimates of the changes in the three indexes for June:

Percentage change in
Leading Index $= -(0.577/0.582) + .139 = -0.9$;
Coincident Index $= (0.888/1.000) - .175 = 0.7$;
Lagging Index $= (0.398/0.707) + .018 = 0.16$.

[1] The numbers are also divided by the sum of the weights on the components included in an index. These sums are 10.005, 3.095 and 4.098 for the available components of the leading, coincident and lagging indexes, respectively.

QUESTIONS FOR DISCUSSION

1 What are the three types of indicators? What is the difference among them?

2 What are the four criteria for useful indicators? What role does economic theory play in selecting indicators?

3 Why are individual indicators combined into "indexes," instead of being used separately? Discuss the importance of "standardization" and "weighting" in the construction of useful indexes.

4 How important are revisions to the indexes? (Compare with the discussion in the Susan Lee article of Reading 2.) What are the principal sources of index revisions? How do these revisions affect the way indicators are used for forecasting?

5 Nobel Prize–winning economist Paul Samuelson once wryly "praised" the stock market, an important leading indicator, for having "predicted nine of the last five recessions." To what general problem with leading indicators was he alluding?

CONSTRUCTION OF COMPOSITE INDEXES: AN ILLUSTRATION

Index and BEA series number	Basic data		Percentage change	Weighted and standardized percentage change[1]
	May 1984	June 1984	May to June 1984	May to June 1984
Leading index components				
1.	40.6	40.6	0	0.000
5.	348	350	−0.6	−0.012
8.	34.46	36.18	−0.9	−0.203
32.	70	66	−4	−0.112
12.	116.2	115.8	−0.3	−0.029
20.	17.11	15.59	−8.9	−0.135
29.	141	142.8	1.3	0.027
36.	34.26	NA	NA	NA
99.	0.27	−0.12	−0.39	−0.107
19.	156.55	153.12	−2.2	−0.095
106.	914	917.8	0.4	0.089
111.	26.2	NA	NA	NA
				−0.577
				−0.577/0.582 +0.139
			Leading index =	−0.9
Coincident index components				
41.	93.72	94.02	0.3	0.321
51.	1170.5	1177.3	0.6	0.387
47.	162.8	163.6	0.5	0.180
57.	177.35	NA	NA	NA
				0.888
				0.888 −0.175
			Coincident index =	0.7
Lagging index components				
91.	18.4	18.6	−1.1	−0.068
77.	1.52	NA	NA	NA
62.	86.6	86.2	−0.4	−0.152
109.	12.39	12.60	0.21	0.153
101.	114.20	116.19	1.7	0.465
95.	14.17	NA	NA	NA
				0.398
				0.398/0.707 +0.018
			Lagging index =	0.6

[1]Percentage change in component series is divided by the relevant standardization factors and multiplied by the relevant weight given in tables 1 and 2.

NA = not available

Source: U.S. Department of Commerce, *Business Conditions Digest* (July 1984).

PART TWO

FISCAL POLICY, SAVING, AND INVESTMENT

CHANGING RATIONALES FOR TAX CUTS

The 1964 Kennedy-Johnson tax cut and the 1981 Kemp-Roth-Reagan cut were objectively quite similar. Both were substantial, permanent cuts in the level of income tax rates, including the top rates. Both offered significant incentives to capital formation. Both tried to eliminate a number of inefficiencies and inequities from the tax code. Yet, because of different political orientations and changing views on economic policy, the arguments offered in favor of the two tax cuts, and their proponents' expectations about the tax cuts' ultimate effects, seem (at least superficially) rather different.

The next two readings offer an interesting comparison of rationales for tax cuts. The first reading, from the Kennedy administration's 1963 *Economic Report of the President*, provides arguments for the proposed 1964 tax bill. The second reading, from the Reagan administration's 1982 *Report,* explains why the administration supported the 1981 tax cut.

Reading 4 U.S. Council of Economic Advisers, *Economic Report of the President: 1963*, Chap. 2 (excerpt), "A Tax Program for the Mid-1960's," pp. 43–52.

Reading 5 U.S. Council of Economic Advisers, *Economic Report of the President: 1982*, chap. 5 (excerpt), "The Economic Effects of Tax Policy," pp. 117–133.

A TAX PROGRAM
FOR THE MID-1960'S

The Administration's 1963 tax program will be presented in a forthcoming Presidential message. Its major outlines are sketched here to serve as the basis for a review of its impact on total demand and thus on production, income, and employment.

In the first stage, beginning on July 1, 1963, the rate reductions will cut individual liabilities by a total of $6 billion at annual rate. For wage-earners, most of this cut will be translated immediately into greater take-home pay, through a reduction in the withholding rate; other taxpayers will realize the benefit of this reduction in rates by adjusting their quarterly tax payments; some will receive refunds during the first half of 1964 for overpayment of 1963 tax liabilities. Further reductions will occur in the rates applicable to 1964 and 1965 incomes, and these will be offset only partially by enlargements of the tax base.

The proposed gross annual reduction in individual and corporate income tax liabilities, occurring in three stages, is estimated at $13^1/$_2$ billion, based on current levels of income. Most of this gross reduction—$11 billion—is in individual income tax liabilities. The proposed final rate structure will range from 14 to 65 percent, contrasted with the present range of 20 to 91 percent. The largest part of the total reduction will be received by the lower and middle income groups of taxpayers.*

The corporate profits tax rate will be reduced in stages from the current 52 percent to 47 percent. This represents a reduction in corporate tax liabilities of about $2^1/$_2$ billion annually at current levels of profits. Payment of corporate income taxes will,

U.S. Council of Economic Advisers, *Economic Report of the President: 1963*, chap. 2 (excerpt), "A Tax Program for the Mid-1960's," pp. 43–52.

Editor's note: The actual rate structure passed by Congress ranged from 14 to 70 percent. The corporate tax rate was reduced to 48 percent, not 47 percent as stated.

however, be placed on a more nearly current basis, adding about $1 $^1/_2$ billion annually to administrative budget revenues for the next several years.

In addition to the tax rate reductions described above, the program incorporates structural changes—offsetting about 3^1/_2$ billion of the rate reduction—designed to improve the equity of the tax system and to encourage greater efficiency in the use of resources. The present income tax system contains numerous provisions that allow special treatment for income derived from particular sources, for expenses incurred in certain ways, for capital gains that are sometimes thinly disguised transformations of current income. Such exceptions have a number of consequences: (1) they provide a strong element of "horizontal" inequity, taxing differently persons in essentially similar income positions; (2) they complicate enormously the task—for the taxpayer and the Government—of ascertaining any individual's liability, and they divert energies from productive activities to tax avoidance and enforcement; (3) because some forms of production receive preferential tax treatment, resources are allocated to the production of certain goods at the expense of others whose value to the economy is greater; and (4) because they reduce the tax base, the exceptions compel higher rates on incomes that remain subject to tax, compounding the inequity and resulting in rates that may interfere with incentives to work, to assume risks, and to invest.

To eliminate in a single step all forms of unjustifiable special treatment is not feasible. But the President's program will make decisive progress in this direction.

Much, though not by any means all, of the income that currently escapes full taxation is received by persons who are, or would be, in the higher income tax brackets, paying rates on marginal income ranging up to 91 percent. The very height of these rates is, of course, partly the reason for the exceptions: taxpayers looking for ways to escape rates which seem oppressive have sought special treatment, and have often obtained sympathetic response. Those high rates, where paid, undoubtedly have a dampening effect on incentives to invest and take risks, and they impair the ability to accumulate investment funds. Since a higher rate of investment of risk capital is essential to a higher rate of growth, it is appropriate to reduce significantly the highest income tax rates at the same time that a more comprehensive tax base is provided. For these reasons, the President is recommending a top marginal rate of 65 percent on taxable income, together with measures to deal with tax preferences that pull resources away from their most efficient uses.

TAX REVISION: IMPACT ON OUTPUT AND EMPLOYMENT

Tax reduction will directly increase the disposable income and purchasing power of consumers and business, strengthen incentives and expectations, and raise the net returns on new capital investment. This will lead to initial increases in private consumption and investment expenditures. These increases in spending will set off a cumulative expansion, generating further increases in consumption and investment spending and a general rise in production, income, and employment. This process is discussed in some detail in this section. Tax reduction may also have financial effects associated with the increased budget deficit that it will initially produce. Since these effects—in the first instance, at least—depend on the methods used to finance the deficit, they are left for discussion in a later section dealing with monetary and debt management policy.

Initial Effects: Consumption

Effects on Disposable Income   The proposed reduction in personal income tax rates will directly add to the disposable income of households. In addition, the reduction in corporate tax rates will increase the after-tax profits of corporations as a result of which corporations may be expected to increase their dividend payments. The initial direct effect on the disposable income of households resulting from the entire program of tax reductions should be approximately 8^1/_2$ billion, at current levels of income.

Consumer Response to Increase in Disposable Income   The ratio of total consumption expenditures to total personal disposable income has in each recent calendar year fallen within the range of 92 to 94 percent. Although there are lags and irregularities from quarter to quarter or even year to year, the change in personal consumption expenditures has in the past, after a few quarters, averaged roughly 93 percent of any change in personal disposable income. On this basis, the initial addition to consumer expenditures associated with tax reductions would be on the order of $8 billion, although all would not be spent at once.

Additions to after-tax incomes resulting from tax reduction are likely to be spent in the same way as other additions to income. The largest part of the proposed tax reduction will be reflected in reduced withholding of taxes from wages and salaries, and therefore in larger wage and salary checks; thus, it will be indistinguishable from additional income arising from wage or salary increases, greater employment, or longer hours of work. Similarly, part of the reduced corporate taxes will be passed along to stockholders in increased dividend checks. Stockholders will not be able to identify the source of their additional dividends. Tax reduction dollars carry no identifying label, and there is no reason to expect recipients to treat them differently from other dollars.

Recent experience with tax reduction demonstrates clearly that additions to disposable income from this source are spent as completely as any other additions. Taxes were reduced by about $4.7 billion on May 1, 1948, retroactive to January 1, with resulting large refunds in mid-1949. Again taxes were cut, net, by about $6 billion, effective January 1, 1954, with further cuts later that year. Table 1 shows that the percentage of disposable income spent by consumers remained within the normal range of quarterly fluctuation during the periods following the enactment of each of these tax reductions.

It is sometimes suggested that tax reductions which add only a few dollars to the weekly pay check of the typical worker would do little good even if the money was spent, since the amounts involved would not be large enough to permit major expenditures—say on washing machines or automobiles. Instead, the money would be "frittered away" on minor expenditures and would do little good for the economy. But all purchases lead to production which generates income and provides employment.

TABLE 1
PERSONAL CONSUMPTION EXPENDITURES AS PERCENT OF DISPOSABLE
PERSONAL INCOME DURING TWO POSTWAR PERIODS OF TAX REDUCTION

1948–49		1953–55	
Quarter	**Percent**	**Quarter**	**Percent**
1948: I	97.3	1953: IV	91.5
II	94.0	1954: I	91.8
III	92.6	II	92.8
IV	93.2	III	98.0
1949: I	93.9	IV	93.2
II	95.2	1955: I	94.5
III	95.7	II	93.5

Note: Based on seasonally adjusted data.
Source: Department of Commerce.

Therefore, the purpose of tax reduction is achieved when the proceeds are spent on any kind of goods or services.

Actually, of course, tax reduction which expands take-home pay even by a relatively small amount each week or month may induce recipients to purchase durable goods or houses of higher quality, since the increased income would permit them to handle larger monthly installment payments. It may even induce a rearrangement of expenditure patterns and thus bring about purchases of durable goods that would not otherwise be made.

Initial Effects: Investment

Investment is a more volatile element than consumption in national expenditure. The timing and magnitude of its response to tax changes is less predictable. But a cut in tax rates on business income will stimulate spending on new plants and new machinery in two ways. First, it will strengthen investment incentives by increasing the after-tax profits that businessmen can expect to earn on new productive facilities. Second, it will add to the supply of internal funds, a large part of which is normally reinvested in the business (though part of this effect may initially be offset by the proposed acceleration of corporate tax payments).

Since the largest part of business investment is made by corporations, the proposed cuts in the corporate income tax are especially significant. But investments of unincorporated businesses will also be encouraged by cuts in personal income tax rates, especially in the upper brackets.

Two important reforms affecting the taxation of business income designed to stimulate investment in plant and equipment were put into effect during 1962: the new depreciation guidelines and the investment tax credit.

Evidence to date clearly indicates that these measures are already stimulating some capital spending that would not otherwise have taken place. The impact of the 1962 actions and the 1963 proposals to reduce taxes on business will, of course, differ from company to company and industry to industry, depending in part on the adequacy of their internal funds and their levels of capacity utilization. Though the speed of response may vary, industry after industry will begin to feel pressure on its capital facilities and funds as markets for its products are expanded by the 1963 tax program.

Furthermore, there are many individual companies for which the supply of internal funds is a constraint on investment, and many others that do not have excess capacity. Moreover, it is estimated that some 70 percent of the investment in plant and equipment is for modernization and replacement rather than expansion, that is, it is designed to produce new or better products, or to reduce production costs rather than primarily to expand productive capacity. For this large segment of capital spending, the stronger inducement to invest provided by the business tax changes already adopted and those now proposed will translate much more readily into actual purchases of plant and equipment.

As production expands and existing capacity is more fully utilized, the depreciation guidelines and the investment tax credit and the new business tax reductions will provide an even stronger stimulus to investment.

Cumulative Expansion: The Consumption Multiplier

Tax reduction will start a process of cumulative expansion throughout the economy. If the economy is already undergoing slow expansion, this cumulative process will be superimposed upon it. The initial increases in spending will stimulate production and employment, generating additional incomes. The details and timing of this process will vary from industry to industry. The first impact may be to draw down inventories rather than to expand production. But as inventories are depleted, retailers will quickly expand orders. As manufacturers' sales rise in response and their own inventories of finished goods decline, they will activate idle production lines, hire additional workers, place orders for materials and components. Thus the expansion will spread to other industries, leading to further expansion of production, employment, and orders.

Expanded sales mean increased profits. Increased employment means greater wage and salary income. Each additional dollar's worth of gross production necessarily generates a dollar of additional gross income.

But expansion does not proceed without limit. A considerable fraction of the value of gross production is shared with governments or becomes part of corporate retained earnings and does not become part of consumers' after-tax income. Some of the increase goes to pay additional excise and other indirect business taxes. Typically, when GNP is rising toward potential, corporate profits increase by about one-fourth of the rise in GNP. But a substantial part of this increase in profits is absorbed by Federal and State corporate income taxes, and another part is ordinarily retained by the corporations. Only the remainder is passed on to the households in dividend payments. Part of the additional wage and salary incomes associated with added production is absorbed by higher social security contributions. At the same time, increased employment means a drop in payments for unemployment insurance benefits.

When all of these "leakages" are taken into account, a little less than two-thirds of an additional dollar of GNP finds its way into the before-tax incomes of consumers in the form of wages, dividends, and other incomes. Part is absorbed by personal taxes, Federal, State, and local. The increase in personal disposable income is 50 to 55 percent. Of this amount a small fraction—about 7 percent— is set aside in personal saving, and the remainder—about 93 percent—is spent on consumption, as indicated earlier. Thus, out of each additional dollar of GNP, initially generated by the tax cut, roughly half ends up as added consumption expenditure. But the process does not stop here.

The additional expenditure on consumption that is brought about by the rise in GNP generates, in its turn, further production, which generates additional incomes and consumption, and so on, in a continuous sequence of expansion which economists call the "multiplier process." The "multiplier" applicable to the initial increase in spending resulting from tax reduction, with account taken of the various leakages discussed above, works out to roughly 2. If we apply this multiplier only to the initial increase in consumption (about $8 billion), the total ultimate effect will be an increase in annual consumption—and in production (and GNP)—of roughly $16 billion. Lags in the process of expansion will spread this increase in GNP over time, but studies of the relationships between changes in disposable income, consumption, and production of consumer goods suggest that at least half of the total stimulus of an initial increase in disposable income is realized within 6 months of that increase.

Cumulative Expansion: The Investment Response

Tax reduction will also have important cumulative indirect effects on investment in inventories and in fixed productive facilities. These effects are much more difficult to predict than the induced effects on consumption.

Inventory Investment   The stocks of goods that businessmen which to hold depend upon current and expected rates of sales and production and the volume of new and unfilled orders, as well as on price expectations and other factors. An expansion of aggregate demand can be expected to raise business inventory targets. Production for inventory will generate further increases in demand and income over and above the multiplier effects discussed above, and will in turn induce further increases in consumption spending.

Inventory investment is volatile, and induced inventory accumulation can add significantly to the expansionary effects of tax reduction within a few months. At the same time, it should be recognized that inventory investment is exceedingly difficult to forecast. As the increase in production and sales tapers off, stocks and the rate of inventory investment will be correspondingly adjusted.

Business Investment in Plant and Equipment   A tax reduction large enough to move the economy toward full employment will also stimulate business investment in plant and equipment. General economic expansion will reinforce the initial stimulus to investment of cuts in business taxes. In the first place, narrowing the gap between actual and potential output—now estimated at $30–40 billion—will increase the utilization of existing plant and equipment. As excess capacity declines, more and more businesses will feel increasing pressure to expand capacity. At the same time, increases in the volume of sales and in productivity will raise corporate profits—in absolute terms, relative to GNP, and as a rate of return on investment. Internal funds available for investment will rise, while at the same time higher rates of return on existing capital will cause businessmen to raise their estimates of returns on new investment. When investment incentives are strengthened by rising demand, internal funds are more consistently translated into increased investment than when markets are slack.

Residential Construction The demand for housing depends on growth in the number of families, on the existing stock of houses, and on the cost and availability of mortgage credit. But housing demand also responds, to some extent, to changes in disposable income. Thus, tax reduction will have some direct effect on residential construction. And as production, employment, and income generally expand, the demand for new homes can be expected to increase further. This increase will, in turn, reinforce the other expansionary effects of tax reduction.

State and Local Government Expenditures

State and local government units have found it difficult to finance the needed expansion of their activities. Given the present importance of income and sales taxes in State and local tax systems, government revenues at the State and local level expand automatically as GNP rises. The additional State-local revenues generated by economic expansion will assist these governments to meet their pressing needs. Moreover, since Federal tax liabilities are deductible under many State income tax laws, reduction in Federal tax rates will automatically generate some further addition to State-local tax revenues. Finally, a reduction in Federal taxes will enlarge the tax base available to State and local government units and may make it easier for them to raise rates or impose new taxes.

Undoubtedly, some of the added State-local tax revenues will be used either to retire existing debt or to reduce current borrowing rather than to increase expenditures. Whether the net result will be expansionary will depend upon whether the proportion of additional tax revenues spent on goods and services by State and local government units is greater or smaller than the proportion which would have been spent by the taxpayers from whom they collect the additional taxes. But whether or not the response of State and local government units is such as to strengthen the aggregate impact of Federal tax reduction on income and employment, the Federal tax program will ease, to some extent, the problems of these units in obtaining revenues needed to finance urgent public activities, such as education, transportation facilities, and urban development.

Summary of Effects on GNP

Tax reductions for consumers will have initial direct effects on the demand for goods and services, as consumers raise their spending level to reflect their higher after-tax incomes. Corporate tax reductions and the lower tax rates applicable to the highest personal income brackets will stimulate investment directly, through raising the rate of return on new investments and providing additional funds for their financing. Some of the tax reforms will also have a directly stimulating effect on productive investment.

These direct or initial effects on spending would occur even if total output, employment, and incomes remained unchanged. But the increased spending cannot fail to increase total output, employment, and incomes. And as activity responds to the initially increased level of spending, cumulative impacts begin to develop in which the several elements interact to carry the expansion far beyond its initial point.

The higher incomes which consumers receive from the added production of both consumer and capital goods will lead to a further step-up in the rate of spending, creating further increases in incomes and spending. The same expansion process raises rates of capacity utilization, thereby interacting with the initial impact of tax reduction on business incomes to make investment both for modernization and expansion more profitable. This in turn generates higher consumer incomes and more spending, helping to provide the added demand which justifies the higher investment.

If there were no investment stimulus—either initially, or as a result of the cumulative process of expansion—we could expect that GNP would ultimately expand by about $16 billion. If the result were no more than this, the tax reduction would still be abundantly rewarding in terms of greater production, employment, purchasing power, and profits. What will really be given up to produce added output will be only unwanted idleness of workers (whose families have reduced neither their needs nor aspirations) and incomplete utilization of plant and machinery (which have continued to depreciate).

But the pay-off is much more than this purely consumption impact. There is also an investment impact, and each extra dollar of investment that is stimulated should bring roughly another dollar of added consumption and encourage still further investment.

A strong expansion can alter profoundly the whole climate within which investment decisions are made. If not at once, then somewhat later, subtle but significant changes in business attitudes occur in response to the trend in the economic outcome. We have referred earlier to the cautious investment attitudes that more than 5 years of slack markets have generated. This caution did not arise at once in mid-1957, when output first began to fall away from the track of potential expansion. It developed gradually, fed on itself, and in part helped to justify itself. The reverse can and will happen.

No one can pretend to estimate with precision the ultimate impact of a program so far-reaching as that which the President will propose: it would come into operation in stages extending from July 1, 1963 to January 1, 1965, and its effects would cumulate and spread into 1966 and beyond.

Our study of the program, and our tentative projections based upon it do, however, convince us that the program measures up to the challenge that the 1960's present to our economy: that it will surely set us on a path toward our interim employment target; and that it will lay the foundation for more rapid long-run growth.

TAX REVISION: IMPACT ON THE BUDGET

When the Congress legislates changes in income taxes, it defines or redefines the income subject to taxation—by setting the exclusions, exemptions, and deductions allowable for various reasons—and sets the new tax rates that are applicable to various fractions of that income. Given the levels and structure of current incomes, these new definitions and rates can be translated into fairly precise estimates of the new tax yield in billions of dollars. This can be compared with the actual yield at the old rates and definitions. The difference is the gross cost of (or gain from) tax revision, and it also measures the initial change in deficit or surplus.

This would be the whole story if the tax revision had no effect on incomes. But a prime purpose of tax revision is precisely to affect production, employment, and incomes. The President's tax program for 1963 is designed to end 5 years of under-capacity production, excessive unemployment, and unnecessarily depressed incomes.

Tax revenues do not depend on tax rates alone, but on the tax base as well. The tax base is determined by the level of income. Because tax revision will raise incomes, it will also raise tax revenues, through a "feedback" out of the expanding tax base. Greater prosperity will also reduce some important types of Federal expenditures, such as unemployment insurance, area redevelopment assistance, and public works accel-eration. For these reasons, the net cost of tax revision will be less—substantially less— than the gross cost.

QUESTIONS FOR DISCUSSION

1 The Kennedy administration economists who wrote the 1963 *Report* considered the potential effects of the proposed tax cuts on aggregate demand to be quite important. Why did they feel it was important to stimulate aggregate demand? Through what channels did they believe the tax cut would affect aggregate demand?

2 Does the 1963 *Report* ignore the aggregate supply implications of tax changes? List any references you can find to aggregate supply effects. If you have also read the excerpt from the 1982 *Report* in Reading 5, compare the discussions of the impact of tax cuts on aggregate supply in the two readings. Are there substantive differences in economic reasoning? In emphasis?

3 How strong an effect of tax cuts on consumption was predicted by the 1963 *Report*? Do you think their argument was reasonable? What if the 1964 tax cut had been a one-year, one-time cut instead of a permanent reduction in rates?

4 The article suggests a number of different ways in which the tax cut might stimulate investment. Find as many of these as you can. Explain in each case how the tax law changes were supposed to affect (*a*) the returns earned by capital and (*b*) the cost of making a capital investment.

5 The tax cut multiplier is calculated in this article to be roughly 2.0. Work through the details of the calculation. Does it appear reasonable? What is being assumed about (*a*) the MPC, (*b*) the effect of GNP growth on investment, (*c*) the behavior of monetary policy, and (*d*) the response of the national price level to increases in aggregate demand?

6 The last sentence of the article predicts that "the net cost of tax revision [in terms of government revenue loss] will be less—substantially less—than the gross cost." Explain this statement. You many find it helpful to use a simple algebraic Keynesian model.

READING 5

THE ECONOMIC EFFECTS OF TAX POLICY

In making the decisions that determine national output and capital formation households consider their options. Each household makes decisions on consumption, savings, and work based on the household's current and future resources. These include the household's net worth (the current market value of all financial and real assets minus liabilities), the household's expected inheritances, the household's expected receipt of government transfer payments, and the household's human capital endowment. The endowment of human capital is the present value of after-tax income the household would earn if it was solely interested in maximizing its labor earnings.

Household choices between consumption and saving and between work and leisure are influenced by after-tax wage rates and after-tax rates of return on capital. When the government changes either the level or the structure of taxes, it ultimately alters household decisions about consumption, saving, and work effort. All aspects of the tax system, including both personal and business taxes, influence these decisions. For example, higher after-tax returns on capital income make present consumption more expensive than future consumption; forgoing a dollar of consumption today and investing that dollar provides more than a dollar of consumption tomorrow, with the additional amount determined by the after-tax return on the investment.

It is customary to associate taxes on wage income with changes in incentives to work and to associate taxes on capital income with changes in incentives to consume or to save. Wage taxes also influence consumption and saving decisions, however, and taxes on capital income influence labor and leisure decisions. Lowering taxes on capital income raises the after-tax return on that income. The larger after-tax return effectively lowers the cost of enjoying leisure as well as consuming in the future

U.S. Council of Economic Advisers, *Economic Report of the President: 1982*, chap. 5 (excerpt), "The Economic Effects of Tax Policy," pp. 117–133.

relative to the present. Hence, a reduction in taxes on capital income increases the incentive to work now and can thus stimulate the supply of labor.

U.S. households and businesses face, at best, a highly uncertain economic environment resulting from continuing changes in preferences, prices, and productivity. Uncertainty with respect to government fiscal and monetary policy increases the uncertainty under which households make current and future consumption and labor supply decisions. In such an environment, households may choose to postpone supplying labor and businesses may decide to postpone new investment until the economic environment is more settled.

The Administration and the Congress have greatly reduced uncertainty with respect to the tax policy. The Economic Recovery Tax Act of 1981 clearly spells out the major features of the U.S. tax system for the next several years; the indexation of the Federal income tax slated to begin in 1985 will reduce the uncertainty associated with inflation pushing households into higher marginal tax brackets.

THE STRUCTURE OF THE TAX SYSTEM

The United States has a complex tax system that influences the choices households make between current and future consumption and current and future work effort. The tax system also influences the types of investments businesses undertake and the set of commodities households choose to purchase. The Federal personal and corporate income taxes, the social security program, the welfare system, and the money creation process all affect the economic behavior of firms and households. This section describes the changes introduced by the Economic Recovery Tax Act of 1981 to the personal and corporate income tax systems, and discusses the likely effects of these changes on labor supply and saving rates. Tax aspects of the social security system, the welfare system, and monetary policy are also addressed.

THE PERSONAL INCOME TAX

Last year's tax legislation made three important changes in the Federal personal income tax. First, marginal tax rates on given levels of nominal income will be reduced, in three stages, by 23 percent by 1984. Beginning in 1985 the personal income tax structure will be indexed to inflation. In addition, the top rate on income from capital was reduced from 70 percent to 50 percent. Table 1 presents marginal tax rates (excluding the social security tax on earnings) at various levels of real income for the next 5 years, based on Administration projections of future inflation. This table also presents the marginal tax rates that would have occurred in the absence of the Economic Recovery Tax Act of 1981.

Two points are clear from this table. First, without the tax cut, marginal tax rates for low- and middle-income households would have been 30 percent to 50 percent higher. Second, although the tax cut will significantly lower marginal tax rates at all levels of income, tax rates at given levels of real income will decline by much less. Bracket creep will offset much of the effect of the tax cut between 1981 and 1985. Under the Administration's inflation projections, most households will still face mar-

TABLE 1

COMPARISON OF MARGINAL PERSONAL INCOME TAX RATES BY REAL INCOME LEVEL UNDER THE ECONOMIC RECOVERY TAX ACT OF 1981 AND OLD LAW, 1979–86[1]
(Percent)

Real income (1979 dollars)	1979	1980	1981[2]	1982	1983	1984	1985	1986
Single:								
$10,000:								
Old law	21	21	21	24	24	24	24	26
New law			21	22	19	18	18	18
$20,000:								
Old law	30	30	34	34	34	34	39	39
New law			34	31	28	26	26	26
$30,000:								
Old law	39	39	39	44	44	49	49	49
New law			39	40	36	38	38	34
$50,000:								
Old law	49	50	50	50	50	50	50	50
New law			49	50	45	48	48	48
Married, two workers:								
$10,000:								
Old law	16	16	18	18	18	18	18	18
New law			18	16	15	14	14	14
$20,000:								
Old law	21	24	24	24	28	28	28	28
New law			24	22	19	22	18	18
$30,000:								
Old law	28	32	32	32	37	37	37	43
New law			32	29	26	28	28	28
$50,000:								
Old law	43	43	43	49	49	49	49	49
New law			42	44	40	38	38	38

[1]Excludes social security taxes and State and local income taxes.
[2]Tax rates for 1981 under new law rounded to nearest whole percent.
Source: Department of the Treasury, Office of Tax Analysis.

ginal tax rates that are high by historical standards. Table 2 presents past and projected marginal tax rates for households at 3 points in the income distribution from 1965 to 1984. For the projected inflation path, marginal tax rates for median income households in 1984 will decline to roughly their 1977–80 levels, but will remain considerably above earlier rates. Thus, despite the substantial reductions introduced by the 1981 tax cut, most rates in 1984 will remain near the historical high rates on real income.

To discuss the effects of the tax cuts on labor supply and saving decisions, it is necessary to understand the various incentives on household behavior created by reductions in marginal tax rates. Cutting tax rates increases an individual's after-tax wage rate. With the Federal Government taking a smaller share of the last dollar of earnings, the return to an individual from an extra hour of work or a more demanding

TABLE 2

MARGINAL PERSONAL INCOME TAX RATES FOR FOUR-PERSON FAMILIES,
SELECTED YEARS, 1965–81[1]

(Percent)

| | Family income | | |
| | One-half | | Twice median |
Year	median income	Median income	income
1965	14	17	22
1970	15	20	26
1975	17	22	32
1980	18	24	43
	Under Economic Recovery Tax Act of 1981		
1981	17.8	27.7	42.5
1982	16	25	39
1983	15	23	40
1984	16	25	38
	Under old law		
1981	18	28	43
1982	18	28	43
1983	18	28	49
1984	21	32	49

[1]Excludes social security taxes and State and local income taxes.
Source: Department of the Treasury, Office of Tax Analysis.

job will increase, strengthening the incentive to work more hours, or accept a more demanding job.

Similarly, cutting tax rates increases after-tax interest rates. The higher the after-tax interest rate, the higher the level of future consumption possible for a given reduction of current consumption. The increase in after-tax interest rates resulting from the tax cuts will thus tend to decrease present consumption, including consumption of leisure as well as goods. In other words, households will tend both to work more and to save more.

Operating in the other direction is the effect of the tax cut on household income. As marginal tax rates fall, the total tax bill paid by a household will fall and its after-tax income will rise. As disposable incomes rise, both in the present and in the future, consumption of both goods and leisure will rise. Thus the effect of increased income will tend to decrease saving and decrease work effort. The net effect of the tax cut on saving and labor supply will vary according to household circumstances. The preponderance of empirical studies suggests that the labor supply effects of a tax cut are small for married men, somewhat larger for unmarried people, and substantial for married women. The most important effect of these changes in personal marginal income tax rates may thus be to increase labor force participation rates and hours of work by married women.

The second important change in the personal income tax introduced by last year's tax legislation was the extension of the opportunity to use Individual Retirement Accounts (IRAs) to all working households. Under the new law, each worker may contribute up to $2,000 to these accounts regardless of whether the worker is already covered under an employer-sponsored pension plan. One-earner couples can contribute up to $2,250. IRAs provide two tax advantages to contributors. First, contributions are deductible from taxable income. Second, returns on IRA investments accumulate tax-free as long as the funds are not withdrawn from the account. Given the sizable tax savings available from IRAs, the total amount of money invested in them can be expected to rise sharply. Some of this money will simply be transferred from other types of savings, including stocks, bonds, and savings accounts. However, for many households without sufficient liquid assets to transfer to IRAs, the last dollar contributed to an IRA will correspond to their marginal saving. That is, the last dollar of current consumption forgone will correspond to the last dollar invested in an IRA. Since the marginal tax rate on capital income obtained from these accounts is quite low, this provision is expected to increase the national saving rate as well as contribute to an increase in the labor supply.

The prospect of moving into higher marginal income tax brackets biases households away from activities that would generate higher future incomes. Hence, income tax progressivity encourages current consumption and leisure and discourages saving for the future. In the presence of inflation and an unindexed tax system, "bracket creep" strengthens this disincentive for generating future income. Indexation of the tax system in 1985 will, therefore, provide further stimulus for saving and economic growth.

Other changes in the tax code will also provide taxpayers with greater incentives to join the work force. The new law provides married couples filing a joint 1982 return with a 5 percent deduction in 1982 and a 10 percent deduction starting in 1983 on the earnings up to $30,000 of the lower earning spouse. If the couple's marginal tax rate would otherwise be 30 percent, the 10 percent deduction after 1982 will reduce the marginal tax rate on earnings of the second spouse to 27 percent. The spousal deduction will also place certain households in lower marginal tax brackets, thus further lowering marginal tax rates. This change should help sustain the growth of female labor force participation.

TAXATION OF INCOME FROM BUSINESS INVESTMENT

The Economic Recovery Tax Act of 1981 also made major changes in the taxation of business income. The most important change is the more generous treatment of the way in which capital can be depreciated for tax purposes, known as the accelerated cost recovery system (ACRS). A second change was the introduction of leasing rules that provide businesses with temporarily low taxable income the same investment incentives as other businesses. A third provision of the act is an increase in the investment tax credit for some types of equipment. Finally, a fourth provision allows small businesses to expense up to $5,000 of new investment in 1982 and 1983. The $5,000 limit will rise to $7,500 in 1984 and 1985, and $10,000 thereafter. These changes should substantially increase business investment by increasing the after-tax return available on new business projects.

TAX TREATMENT OF DEPRECIABLE PROPERTY

The ACRS will encourage business investment by shortening the period over which assets can be fully depreciated and by allowing firms to claim more of the depreciation early in the tax life of the asset. Before the adoption of ACRS, businesses were permitted to write off industrial equipment over an average period of 8.6 years. The ACRS asset life for this equipment is 5 years. For industrial plant, asset lives have been reduced by 37 percent, from an average of 23.8 years to 15 years. The ACRS depreciation schedules represent a combination of the declining balance and straightline method of depreciation through 1984. For 1985 and beyond, declining balance switching to sum of years digits is used. The depreciation schedules for the years after 1984 provide increasingly more acceleration of depreciation. The combined result of the ACRS and the investment tax credit will be a decline in effective tax rates on new investment over the period 1982 to 1987.

Table 3 shows historic and projected before-tax real rates of return in new capital investment required to provide a 4 percent after-tax real return. This real return is a commonly used analytical assumption. These numbers reflect the combined effect of the depreciation provisions and the investment tax credit. Historical numbers are based on historical rates of inflation. Rates of return in future years are based on the Administration's inflation projections. A before tax rate of return of 8 percent, for example, implies an effective tax rate of 50 percent on new investments. The calculations assume

TABLE 3
REAL BEFORE-TAX RATE OF RETURN REQUIRED TO PROVIDE
A 4 PERCENT REAL AFTER-TAX RETURN, 1955–86
(Percent)

Period	Construction machinery	General industrial equipment	Trucks, buses, and trailers	Industrial buildings	Commercial buildings
1955–59	8.9	9.5	10.8	8.0	8.0
1960–64	7.4	7.8	8.7	7.9	7.9
1965–69	6.5	6.9	7.5	7.6	7.6
1970–74	6.6	6.7	7.6	8.6	8.4
1975–79	6.1	6.4	7.6	9.0	8.7
1981	3.4	3.5	3.5	6.6	6.2
1982	3.1	3.3	3.1	6.4	6.1
1983	2.9	3.2	3.0	6.4	6.0
1984	2.9	3.1	2.9	6.4	6.0
1985	2.3	2.7	2.6	6.3	6.0
1986	2.2	2.6	2.5	6.3	6.0

Note: Data for 1955–79 are based on Auerbach and Jorgenson calculations of expected inflation in each year. Data for 1981–86 are based on the Administration's projections of inflation (year-over-year percent change in the GNP implicit price deflator): 1982, 7.9; 1983, 6.0; 1984, 5.0; 1985, 4.7; 1986, 4.6; and 1987 and beyond 4.5.
Sources: Auerbach, Alan and Jorgenson, Dale, "Inflation Proof Depreciation of Assets," *Harvard Business Review,* Sept.-Oct. 1980 (1955–79), and Council of Economic Advisers (1981–86, based on Economic Recovery Tax Act of 1981).

TABLE 4
REAL BEFORE-TAX RATE OF RETURN REQUIRED TO PROVIDE A 4 PERCENT
AFTER-TAX RETURN IN 1986 AT SELECTED RATES OF INFLATION
(Percent)

Type of capital	Inflation rate (percent)		
	5	8	12
Construction machinery	2.3	2.9	3.7
General industrial equipment	2.7	3.2	3.7
Trucks, buses, and trailers	2.5	3.1	3.7
Industrial buildings	6.4	6.9	7.4
Commercial buildings	6.1	6.5	6.9

Source: Council of Economic Advisers.

the new investment is equity financed. Hence, the tax advantages from the deduction of interest expense associated with debt financing are not included.

Under the assumptions made here, in comparison with the years 1975 to 1979, the 1982 real before-tax rate of return required to justify a new investment in general industrial equipment has been reduced from 6.4 to 3.3 percent. For investment in plant the required rate of return estimated here declines from 9.0 to 6.2 percent. The effective tax rates associated with these numbers decline between 1982 and 1986. This reflects both the more favorable depreciation schedules after 1984 and projections of continued declines in inflation.

Since depreciation allowances are not indexed, higher rates of inflation will raise effective tax rates. Table 4 presents the before-tax rates of return required in 1986 to provide a 4 percent after-tax return under different assumptions about the rate of inflation prevailing in 1986 and beyond. The table shows that a reduction in inflation from 8 percent to 5 percent will lower the required before-tax rate of return from 3.2 percent to 2.7 percent in general industrial equipment and from 6.9 percent to 6.4 percent on plant. Conversely, a 1986 level of inflation of 12 percent would raise required before-tax rates of return to 3.7 percent for equipment and 7.4 percent for plant.

Tables 3 and 4 also indicate that the ACRS does not treat all types of business investment equally. Although favorable to all new investment, ACRS is relatively more favorable to investment in equipment. As a consequence, industries for which short-lived equipment represents a large fraction of their total capital will face lower effective tax rates than industries with a low equipment-intensive capital structure. Table 5 presents calculations of industry specific tax rates on new investment for 1982. There are two sets of numbers; the first indicates the tax rates that would have prevailed under the old law, while the second column indicates tax rates in 1982 under the Accelerated Cost Recovery System.

The table shows substantial reductions in tax rates for all industries, but differences among industries in the rate of tax reduction. The effect on each industry is different because each industry uses a different mix of capital. Tax rates vary across industries,

TABLE 5
EFFECTIVE TAX RATES ON NEW DEPRECIABLE ASSETS, SELECTED INDUSTRIES, 1982[1]

Industry	Old law	New law
Agriculture	32.7	16.6
Mining	28.4	−3.4
Primary metals	34.0	7.5
Machinery and instruments	38.2	18.6
Motor vehicles	25.8	−11.3
Food	44.1	20.8
Pulp and paper	28.5	.9
Chemicals	28.8	8.6
Petroleum refining	35.0	1.1
Transportation services	31.0	−2.9
Utilities	43.2	30.6
Communications	39.8	14.1
Services and trade	53.2	37.1

[1]Industries chosen had at least $5 billion in new investment in 1981.
Note: Assumes a 4 percent real after-tax rate of return and 8 percent inflation.
Source: Department of the Treasury, Office of Tax Analysis.

from a high of 37 percent in the services and trade sector to a low of − 11 percent in the motor vehicle industry. Effective tax rates on new investment are negative for some industries. The result will be lower total corporate tax liabilities rather than direct payments by the Treasury. These differential rates of taxation at the industry level will probably lead to relatively more investment in industries with lower tax rates.

LEASING PROVISIONS

The ACRS provides the same investment incentives to firms with taxable income and those with nontaxable income. The leasing provision of the Economic Recovery Tax Act of 1981 should enhance efficient allocation of capital across industries and across firms within the same industry. The fundamental principle underlying the leasing provisions is that investment incentives should be equal for all businesses in a given industry and across industries; that is, investment incentives should not favor investment in one firm over another. Prior to the establishment of these leasing provisions, firms with temporary tax losses (a condition especially characteristic of new enterprises) were often unable to take advantage of investment tax incentives. The reason was that temporarily unprofitable companies had no taxable income against which to apply the investment tax deductions. As a result, these companies were placed at a relative disadvantage, although the new investment undertaken by these companies was potentially as profitable as investment undertaken by firms with temporarily positive profits.

The leasing provisions will permit companies with no current taxable income to take advantage of investment incentives by transferring their tax credits and additional deductions associated with investment to firms with taxable income. For example, American automobile manufacturers who are currently reporting losses will now be able to take the same advantage of the incentives as more profitable firms. In the absence of the leasing provisions, investment would probably be too low in the automobile industry relative to the most productive mix of investment.

The leasing provisions will also have the advantage of reducing incentives for mergers. Under the old law, companies with positive taxable income had an incentive to merge with companies with tax losses because these tax losses could be used to offset the parent company's taxable income. The leasing provisions, by permitting companies with positive taxable income to effectively purchase the negative taxable income of other companies, will eliminate this motivation for mergers.

EFFECTS OF TAX ACT ON HOUSING AND CONSUMER DURABLES

The 1981 act will alter the allocation of existing capital and labor among industries. It will also affect the allocation of new business investment, the fraction of investment allocated to business as opposed to residential investment, and the division of consumption between durable commodities—such as residential real estate, automobiles, and furniture—and nondurable commodities.

The Tax Act improves the attractiveness of business investment relative to other forms of investment. As relative returns rise for business investment, financial institutions will tend to increase their business lending and decrease their consumer and mortgage lending. Households themselves will tend to lower their investments in these goods in order to put more of their savings directly into business capital by purchasing corporate stocks and bonds, or indirectly by placing their savings with financial institutions who will make these investments for them. In either case, more money will be channeled to business investment and less to housing and consumer durables than would have occurred without the ACRS.

To understand the effects of the new depreciation system on the consumption of durables versus nondurables, one must first realize that the implicit price of consuming durable goods is the after-tax return the owners of these durables would otherwise receive if they sold these assets and invested the proceeds.

The sizable reductions in tax rates on capital income mean that real after-tax returns on household saving will be substantially higher than they have been in the recent past. As a result, the implicit price of consumer durables has risen, and a long-run shift in demand away from housing, automobiles, and other consumer durables may result. While housing and durables provide important service flows, the tax treatment of service flows from durables may have led to over investment in them in the 1970s. Much of the spectacular rise in housing prices during the last decade was associated with the increasingly pro-durables bias imbedded in a very inflation-sensitive system of capital income taxation. As inflation rose, so did effective taxes on capital income. This rise lowered the relative price of consuming durables because it lowered the opportunity costs of holding these durables. As a result, the demand for consumer durables in general, and housing in particular, was greatly stimulated. In the short run, housing prices were bid up dramatically, reflecting the tax-induced increased demand for housing services. The higher housing prices, in turn, stimulated construction of new housing, since it increased the price at which newly constructed houses could be sold.

An offsetting consideration with respect to the durables industries is the relatively more favorable treatment of the motor vehicle industry under the 1981 Tax Act (Table 5). The effective tax rate on the return to new investment in the motor vehicle industry has been cut from 26 to − 11 percent.

Another pertinent point is that the tax structure is simply one of numerous determinants of the demand for different commodities. The surge in new family formation resulting from the baby-boom of the 1950s will lead to a strong demand for housing that could well swamp the effects of the tax change on residential investment. The same is likely to be true of other durables that are in relatively greater demand by young families setting up a household.

IMPLICIT TAXATION OF LABOR SUPPLY
BY THE SOCIAL SECURITY AND WELFARE SYSTEMS

It is ironic that the social security and welfare programs may, themselves, contribute to the relatively low income levels of the elderly and the poor. Social security and welfare recipients may well face the highest marginal tax rates of any members of our society. These systems provide very small incentives to work. Not surprisingly, therefore, relatively few beneficiaries of these two programs work, especially at full-time jobs.

There is mounting evidence that the social security earnings test has contributed significantly to the dramatic increase in early retirement. In 1950 the labor force participation rate of males 65 and over was 46 percent; today it is only 20 percent. Not only are there fewer older men working on any given day during the year, but there are fewer older men who work at any time during the year. The fraction of men 65 to 69 who are completely retired has risen from 40 percent to 60 percent since 1960. For males 60 to 64 the retirement rate is now 30 percent, double the 1960 figure of 15 percent. Those older males who do choose to work are working fewer hours. Since 1967 the fraction of working males 65 and over who work part-time has increased form one-third to almost one-half. This reduction in work has occurred despite a substantial increase in the general health of people in this age group.

The social security earnings test currently reduces benefits by 50 cents for every dollar of earnings above $6,000 and represents a 50 percent implicit tax for workers aged 65 to 72. In combination with the Federal and State income taxes and the social security payroll tax, this 50 percent tax on earnings penalized the work effort of the elderly at rates that can easily exceed 80 percent. These exceedingly large tax rates extend over a wide range of the typical older worker's potential supply of labor hours.

Eliminating the earnings test, as has been proposed by the Administration, would unquestionably increase the income of older workers as well as generate tax revenues that would offset a portion of the costs of doing so. Because of impending changes in the demographic structure of the population, it is important to reverse the trend toward early retirement. By the year 2025 the proportion of the population age 62 and over will rise to 24.5 percent, compared to 13.6 percent in 1981. The ratio of workers paying social security taxes to retired beneficiaries will fall from a current level of 3.7 to 2.4. If the work disincentives for older citizens were reduced, U.S. per capita income would rise more rapidly and social security's long-run financial position would be improved.

Current provisions of the social security system also generate work disincentives for a significant fraction of married women. While married women are joining the labor force in increasing numbers, the typical wife's earnings are still one-third to one-half that of husbands. Hence, the marginal tax contributions to social security of many wives will yield them no marginal social security benefits because they will collect benefits based on their husband's earnings record. (This applies only to retirement and medicare benefits. A wife who becomes disabled cannot currently collect disability benefits based on her husband's account.) The combined employer-employee retirement and medicare tax rates total 11.75 percent and represent a pure marginal tax on the work effort of married women. The response to females to the level of net compensation is estimated to be quite high. Hence, the bias in the current structure regarding dependent and survivor benefits may represent a significant disincentive to the participation of married females in the labor force.

Similar work disincentives potentially reduce the labor supply of welfare recipients. Welfare recipients do not face a single and easily understood tax schedule relating their gross earnings to their net disposable income. Instead, they are confronted with eight different and highly complicated implicit and explicit tax schedules. These include the work and income tests of Aid to Families with Dependent Children (AFDC), food stamps, housing assistance, social security insurance and medicaid, the earned income tax credit, the Federal income tax, and State income taxes. Each of the welfare programs has its own eligibility requirements, its own definition of income, its own set of deductions and exclusions, and its own tax rates. These explicit and implicit tax systems differ across States as well. Even within a State, implicit tax schedules vary, depending on both the characteristics of the recipient and the discretion of the social service worker. The result of all this is a complex set of uncoordinated rules and regulations that surely leave welfare recipients confused and dismayed. Past reforms of the system simply added more and more programs, with little emphasis on how the work disincentives of new programs would interact with those of old programs.

The efficacy of any particular income transfer program cannot be determined in isolation from the rest of the system. Analyses of marginal tax rates arising from the combined earnings tests of the various welfare programs and the explicit Federal and State tax systems suggest that typical welfare recipients, namely single mothers with children, face marginal tax rates in excess of 75 percent. Reductions in these very high implicit and explicit tax rates might generate a sufficiently large addition to their labor supply to pay for themselves. As State and local governments assume fuller responsibility for the welfare system, they could effectively offset these high, marginal tax rates by providing additional work incentives.

As this section has shown, many households still face considerable work disincentives, despite the substantial changes enacted in the Economic Recovery Tax Act of

1981. Future reforms of social security and welfare policy should take account of these concerns.

STRUCTURAL TAX POLICY AND ECONOMIC GROWTH

Structural tax policy probably constitutes the Federal Government's most powerful tool for influencing economic growth. If households anticipate their own and their descendants' future tax liabilities, changes in the tax structure generating the same revenue have only "substitution" effects on their decisions; "income" effects are zero or negligible. If households consider only their own future tax liabilities and not those of their descendants, income effects do arise for different age groups, but they are largely offsetting. Such changes in the tax structure do not change household budgets, in the aggregate, but they do change household incentives to work and save. The rate of savings and capital formation can be increased significantly by switching away from taxes on capital income to some other tax base, such as wages or consumption. As described earlier, reductions in the tax rates on capital income reduce the relative cost of future consumption and leisure and encourage the substitution of future consumption and leisure for current consumption and leisure. Such substitution leads to increases in the current supplies of both capital and labor.

The 1981 Tax Act's reduction in marginal tax rates on capital income under both personal and corporate income taxes, the provision for substantial increases in Individual Retirement Accounts and Keogh accounts, and the recent expansion of pension fund savings all constitute major reductions in taxation of capital income. These historic changes in the structure of taxation, assuming they are maintained for the indefinite future, are expected to lead to a significant long-term rise in the private business capital stock and increases in labor supply over what would otherwise be the case.

While capital formation and economic growth are predicted to be enhanced, it should be emphasized that the choice of a tax base should be determined on grounds of economic welfare and efficiency, rather than simply the effect of structural tax change on factor supplies. Economic research suggests that rather sizable efficiency and welfare gains are available from switching from the taxation of wage and capital income to the taxation of consumption. In contrast, there is evidence that switching from wage and capital income taxation to wage taxation alone can reduce economic welfare and efficiency, even though this structural tax change would lead to more capital formation. In recent years, Federal tax policy has increasingly moved away from marginal taxation of capital income toward an alternative structure that can best be described as a hybrid mixture of wage and consumption taxation.

The change in the structure of taxation will increase labor supply and capital formation over time, provided there is no significant deterioration in the government's real net debt position. While the move away from marginal capital income taxation is necessary to stimulate saving, the Nation still retains a tax system that is overly complex, that is still sensitive to inflation (especially with respect to effective business taxation), that is administratively expensive, and that absorbs too much talent in the fundamentally nonproductive endeavor of what is gently termed "tax planning." In short, there is a need for further simplification and rationalization of the U.S. tax code.

QUESTIONS FOR DISCUSSION

1 What are the primary channels by which the 1982 *Report* argues that a tax cut will increase GNP? If you have read the excerpt from the 1963 *Report* in Reading 4, compare the channels emphasized here with those emphasized in the earlier article.

2 An individual's *average* tax rate is the total tax paid divided by total income. The *marginal* tax rate is the percentage of *additional* income paid in taxes, when income is increased from the current level. Do the authors of the 1982 *Report* consider the effect of the 1981 tax cut on average rates or on marginal rates to be relatively more important? Explain. How do the authors of the 1963 *Report* (Reading 4) feel about the relative importance of marginal and average tax rate cuts?

3 The article describes one channel by which lower taxes increase work effort and another by which they reduce it. What are these channels? Why do the authors still feel that the effect of tax cuts on work effort (labor supply) will be positive on net?

4 What is an IRA? Give one channel by which the existence of IRAs stimulates household saving and one by which it reduces saving. How would you expect the introduction of IRAs to affect the behavior of families who already have substantial savings in checking and savings accounts? (*Hint:* Given the limits on annual IRA contributions, would you expect these families to do any substantial *new* saving?)

5 What is *tax indexation*? (Refer to your text.) Why do the authors of the 1982 *Report* consider indexation to be an important tax reform? Why do you think the introduction of indexation was delayed to 1985?

6 Refer to your text for discussion of the tax deduction for depreciation received by owners of capital goods. How did the ACRS provision, which shortened the period over which a piece of capital can be depreciated for tax purposes, affect the after-tax return to investment? Did the sharp drop in inflation in the early 1980s offset or reinforce the impact of ACRS?

7 The article argues that the Social Security earnings test is effectively a tax. In what way is this true? Why does the article argue for the elimination of the earnings test? How does this logic extend to the work and income tests associated with welfare and food stamp programs? Why is it more feasible to eliminate or reduce the income test for Social Security than for the welfare program?

8 The last sentence of the reading foreshadows the additional tax reform that took place in 1986. Make a list of the major changes introduced in 1986 (you might look in the 1987 *Economic Report*). What major provisions of the 1981 act were extended or enhanced? What provisions were eliminated or cut back? Is the 1986 tax program consistent with the goals of supply-side economics? With the goal of tax simplification?

THE 1981 PERSONAL INCOME TAX CUTS: A RETROSPECTIVE LOOK AT THEIR EFFECTS ON THE FEDERAL TAX BURDEN

John A. Tatom*

The 1981 Kemp-Roth tax cuts significantly reduced federal personal income tax rates. In this article, John Tatom of the St. Louis Fed compares the federal tax burdens faced by families of different incomes in 1980 and 1984. He argues that, despite the statutory rate cuts, the federal tax burden fell very little during the early 1980s; and that, as of 1984, this burden remained much larger than it was in 1965.

The tax structure in 1984 is an excellent watershed from which to assess the effects of the 1981 personal income tax changes on the federal tax burden. This is the first year in which the phased reduction of marginal tax rates became fully effective; it is the last year in which the personal tax structure was not indexed. Under the 1981 tax act, the brackets used to compute personal income tax liability will be indexed to inflation beginning in 1985.

Since 1981, analysts have examined the effects of these tax changes using various assumptions about economic performance. Some analysts focused only on the 23 percent rate reductions, suggesting that taxes were being reduced. Casual observers questioned the relevance of such a view, since it was difficult, especially at the individual or family level, to observe any actual reduction in tax burden. Other analysts compared the rate reductions to indexing, suggesting that inflation would raise nominal incomes and add to the tax burden, roughly offsetting the effect of rate reductions.

John A. Tatom, "The 1981 Personal Income Tax Cuts: A Retrospective Look at Their Effects on the Federal Tax Burden," *Review,* St. Louis Federal Reserve Bank, December 1984, pp. 5–17.

*John A. Tatom is an assistant vice president at the Federal Reserve Bank of St. Louis. Thomas A. Pollmann provided research assistance.

More recently, some analysts have attempted to use post-1981 data from income tax returns to analyze the impact of the tax rate changes on actual reported tax burdens. Ironically, while early analyses required assumptions about 1981–84 economic developments, recent analyses often have neglected the effect of changing economic conditions on their conclusions.

This article examines the effects of the personal income tax rate reductions on the burden of federal taxes.[1] The impact of assumptions about the 1981–84 economic conditions, particularly inflation, is minimal since these conditions are now largely known. Alternative assumptions are employed, however, to highlight the importance of changes in real income. The effects of the tax law are standardized by examining the change in the tax burden facing three representative households: families with the 1980 median family income, and families that earned one-half or twice the median level.

The federal personal income tax has become increasingly complex. Differences in the economic circumstances and choices made by households led to different taxes in 1980 or 1984 and to different tax changes even for households with the same income levels. Interested readers may wish to pull out their own 1980 federal income tax return and preliminary data for 1984 to determine the outcome for their household. Are you better off, taxwise, in 1984 than in 1980? Do the changes in your tax burden since 1980 suggest that your tax changes are a source of recent and prospective deficits?

THE 1980 TAX BURDEN

The median family income in 1980 was about $21,000.[2] Table 1 shows the 1980 federal personal income tax and Social Security tax liabilities for this level of income and for one-half and twice this median income. In computing personal taxes, it is assumed that there are four people (exemptions) in each household, that a joint return is filed, that all income is adjusted gross income and that there are no other deductions, credits or income adjustments.

In 1980, the employee-paid Social Security tax equaled 6.13 percent of wages up to a maximum of $25,900, with an equal amount being collected from the employer. Since the cost of employment includes both payments, the tax burden borne by the recipients of the respective income levels are given both ways: including and excluding the employer-paid Social Security tax. It is the former that represents the total federal tax burden. The analysis here concerns wage income; the overall tax burden, at the

---

[1]Only personal income and social security taxes are analyzed here; federal excise and corporate income taxes and state and local government receipts are not. These other taxes have risen substantially since 1980. From 1980 to the first half of 1984, federal excise tax liabilities rose 41 percent to $55 billion, and corporate income taxes rose 5.7 percent to $74.3 billion. State and local government tax receipts rose from $297.4 to $515.1 billion, a 73.2 percent increase over the same period.

[2]In 1980, the median family money income was $21,023. The median measure indicates the level at which one-half of all families receive more income and one-half receive less. The average size family in 1980 contained 3.27 members and the average number of wage earners per family was 1.63. The range of income in 1980 considered here encompasses most families. In 1980, 18.9 percent of families had incomes below $10,000 and 13.5 percent of families had incomes in excess of $40,000. See *Statistical Abstract of the United States* (1982–83), pp. 432–34.

TABLE 1
THE 1980 FEDERAL TAX BURDEN AT THREE LEVELS OF INCOME

	One-half median income	Median income	Twice median income	
			One wage earner	Two wage earners
1980 income	$10,500	$21,000	$42,000	$42,000
Personal income tax	$454	$2,505	$9,366	$9,366
Average tax rate	4.3%	11.9%	22.3%	22.3%
Marginal tax rate	16.0%	24.0%	43.0%	43.0%
Employee-paid Social Security tax	$644	$1,287	$1,588	$2,575
Personal tax plus employee-paid Social Security tax				
Average tax rate	10.5%	18.1%	26.1%	28.4%
Marginal tax rate	22.1%	30.1%	43.0%	49.1%
Total tax burden[1]				
Average tax rate	16.6%	24.2%	29.9%	34.6%
Marginal tax rate	28.3%	36.3%	43.0%	55.3%

[1]Includes personal income tax and employee- and employer-paid Social Security tax.

personal level, on such capital income as dividends, or interest is limited to the personal income tax rates. The additional taxation of income from capital at the corporate level, however, is generally greater than the additional burden of Social Security taxes shown here.

The tax burden is measured in two ways: by the average tax rate and the marginal tax rate. The average tax rate is simply the amount of taxes paid per dollar of total income. The marginal tax rate is the increase in federal tax liability per dollar of additional income; it is the relevant measure of the impact of the federal taxes on incentives to work, save and invest. Both measures are shown in table 1.

The tax calculations apply to a one- or two-wage-earner family at the $10,500 and $21,000 levels. At $42,000, however, the taxes are calculated for both one-wage-earner and two-wage-earner families. For the latter, it is assumed that each wage earner earns less than the Social Security maximum tax base of $25,900 in that year.

If one worker's earnings exceed this base in 1980, then the relevant marginal tax rate applicable for the high wage-earner is that indicated in the one-worker calculation, while the rate applicable for the low wage-earner is that indicated for the two-worker calculation. The average tax rates for such a family are in the range bounded by the average tax rates for the one- or two-wage-earner families. For example, if one worker earns $26,000 and the other earns $16,000, the former faces an overall marginal tax rate of 43 percent, while the latter faces a marginal tax rate of 55.3 percent. Such a household had an average tax rate of 34.5 percent, based on the $9,366 paid in personal income taxes, the maximum Social Security payment of $3,175 by the high wage-earner, and the $1,962 paid in Social Security for the low wage-earner for a total of $14,503 on $42,000 of income.

Some General Properties of the Federal Tax Structure

The data in table 1 provide not only a benchmark from which to assess 1981–84 tax rate changes, but also an illustration of some important properties of the tax system. Moving from left to right in the table, one observes how marginal and average tax rates rise as income rises, because the marginal tax rate exceeds the average tax rate. In addition, one can observe the relative importance of social security taxation on both average and marginal tax rates.

At the low income, the employee-paid Social Security tax (one-half the total) exceeds the personal income tax liability. Even at the 1980 median income, the total Social Security tax liability [(.1226)($21,000) = $2,575] exceeds the personal income tax liability ($2,505). Moreover, the Social Security tax is regressive since, at wage-income levels above $25,900 in 1980, the marginal Social Security tax rate is zero. Thus, the gap between the average or marginal personal income tax rates and the average or marginal tax rate measures of the total burden narrows as income moves above $25,900. For example, at $42,000 (one worker), the difference between the overall tax burden and personal income tax average rates is only 7.6 percentage points (29.9 − 22.3); for the marginal tax rates, the difference is zero. At the lower two income levels, this difference is 12.3 percentage points.

THE CASE FOR THE PERSONAL INCOME TAX RATE REDUCTIONS

Although one argument favoring the marginal tax rate cuts under the 1981 tax act is essentially a normative case, it can be illustrated using the data in table 1. The marginal tax rates shown appear to be "high," even at relatively low levels of income. In the case of a two-worker couple earning $42,000 with each earning less than $25,900, each worker faced a marginal tax rate of over 50 percent (55.3 percent).

A stronger case for the 1981 rate-reduction legislation can be made based on what would have happened to tax burdens if the tax changes had not been made. Had no income tax rate changes been approved, inflation would have pushed all families into higher tax brackets. Coupled with existing provisions for Social Security taxation in 1980, these increases would have raised the average and marginal tax burden substantially, even if the purchasing power of family income (real income) had been unchanged. These effects are shown in table 2.[3]

Income in table 2 equals the 1980 levels adjusted for the 26 percent increase in the general level of prices (consumer price index for all urban consumers) from 1980 to 1984; since income rises at the same rate as prices, no real income gain occurs. The 1980 tax tables are used to compute the personal tax liabilities. The Social Security tax calculations include both the rate increase to 13.7 percent (6.7 percent for employee-

---

[3]In 1981, the strongest case for a tax cut was based on the mounting tax burden since 1965. A comparison of the 1980 families tax burden using 1965 and 1980 rates is given in the appendix.

TABLE 2
WHAT THE 1984 FEDERAL TAX BURDEN WOULD HAVE BEEN
UNDER THE 1980 PERSONAL INCOME TAX LAW: NO CHANGE IN REAL INCOME

	One-half 1980 median income	1980 Median income	Twice 1980 median income	
			One wage earner	Two wage earners
1984 income	$13,230	$26,460	$52,920	$52,920
Personal income tax	$923	$3,906	$14,249	$14,249
Average tax rate	7.0%	14.8%	26.9%	26.9%
Marginal tax rate	18.0%	28.0%	49.0%	49.0%
Employee-paid Social Security tax	$886	$1,773	$2,533	$3,546
Personal tax plus employee-paid Social Security tax				
Average tax rate	13.7%	21.5%	31.7%	33.6%
Marginal tax rate	24.7%	34.7%	49.0%	55.7%
Total tax burden[1]				
Average tax rate	20.7%	28.5%	36.7%	40.6%
Marginal tax rate	31.7%	41.7%	49.0%	62.7%

[1]Includes personal income tax and employee- and employer-paid Social Security tax.

paid and 7.0 percent for employer-paid components) and the 46 percent rise in the tax base of $37,800, provided under the 1977 and 1983 Social Security Act amendments.

Despite unchanged real incomes, the families in table 2 would have been subject to substantial jumps in their tax burdens form 1980 to 1984 under the 1980 tax law. Compared with 1980, the total tax burden, measured by taxes per dollar of income, shown at the bottom of tables 1 and 2, would have risen by 17.8 percent for the median-income family (28.5 percent divided by 24.2 percent = 1.178), 17.3 percent for a two-worker, high-income family and over 22 percent for the low-income and one-worker, high-income families.

Bracket creep, the taxation of purely inflation-induced changes in wages, would have raised the average tax rate for the personal income tax by over 20 percent in most cases (see insert on pages 66 and 67). The rise for the lowest income level, from a 4.3 to a 7.0 percent average tax rate, would have been a staggering 63 percent increase. Even marginal tax rates would have risen sharply despite the unchanged real income. The change from table 1 to table 2 indicates that total marginal tax rates would have risen by 12 to 15 percent under 1980 tax laws. These relatively large percentage increases are associated with much smaller changes in the marginal tax rate for the personal income tax of 2 to 6 percentage points and a 1.44 percentage-point increase in the marginal tax rate for Social Security (12.26 percent to 13.7 percent).

Higher Real Income Raises the Federal Tax Burden

Of course, average and marginal tax rates actually would have increased more than the comparison of tables 1 and 2 indicates, because of typical real income increases and the progressive personal income tax system. From 1980 to 1984, real GNP per capita rose about 8 percent, or slightly less than 2 percent per year.

If each of the families in table 2 had experienced similar growth in their real incomes, their incomes would have been 8 percent higher than those shown in table 2 and their tax burdens would have been higher as well, given the progressive personal income tax. The overall average tax rates in table 2 would have risen by 2.5 percent to 4.2 percent above those shown in table 2.

For the 1980 median-income family shown in table 2, the personal income tax average rate, the component of the tax system most sensitive to real growth, would have risen from 14.8 percent to 15.7 percent, a 6.1 percent rise due to 8 percent real growth. At relatively low incomes, the average tax rate is most sensitive to income changes because marginal tax rates exceed average tax rates by the greatest amount; 8 percent real income growth for the low-income families in table 2 would raise their personal income taxes much more, so that the average tax rate would rise from 4.3 cents per dollar of income to 7 cents per dollar, an 11.4 percent rise in the average tax rate. Such real income growth would have raised the average tax rate for the high-income family in table 2 by about the same percent as that for the median-income family. None of the families shown in table 2 would have moved into higher marginal tax brackets due to typical real income growth from 1980 to 1984 under the old tax law.

THE 1981 PERSONAL INCOME TAX RATE REDUCTIONS

To offset the escalating tax burden due to inflation and the rise in marginal tax rates, which reduced incentives to earn additional income through work, saving or investment, Congress approved a 23 percent cut in all personal income marginal tax rates to be phased in fully by 1984. For our purposes here, the major components of the 1981 tax act were a 23 percent cut in all marginal tax rates, phased in as a 5 percent cut in October 1981, 10 percent in 1983 and 10 percent in 1984, and the "indexing" of bracket incomes and personal exemptions beginning in 1985.

Other Provisions of the Economic Recovery Tax Act of 1981

There were other important changes in the 1981 tax act, especially the adoption of the accelerated cost recovery system, extended investment tax credits and reductions in tax rates on business income. These changes have been highly successful in stimulating business investment and productivity growth, as intended, and are not examined here.[4] Two other non-rate provisions had important effects on personal income taxes: the extension of tax-deferred income treatment through IRAs and the all-savers cer-

---

[4]See Ott (1984), Meyer (1983) and Tatom (1981). Also, see the *Economic Recovery Tax Act of 1981* for details of other none-rate provisions affecting the personal income tax.

tificates (July 1981 to November 1982), and an earned income credit for two-wage-earner families.[5] These are not formally analyzed here. Another important change was to end the differential tax treatment of capital income for relatively high-income families. In 1980, marginal personal income tax rates on income from capital rose from 54 percent to 70 percent as taxable income rose from $60,000 to $215,400. This distinction was dropped in 1982, so that all taxable income was subject to the same marginal tax rate.

[5]In 1984, personal income taxes can be reduced by contributions of up to $2,000 to IRA or deferred income plans that were not allowed for many taxpayers in 1980. As a percent of income, these benefits are, in the limit, equal to the marginal tax rate times $2,000 divided by income.

The new deduction for married couples when both work is limited to 10 percent of the lower income up to $30,000. The benefit subtracts the marginal tax rate times a maximum of one-half of income for a two-wage-earner family. The maximum reduction in the average personal income tax rates in table 3 are thus (0.05 × 14 percent) 0.7 percent at the lowest income, (0.05 × 22 percent) 1.1 percent at the median-income level, and (0.05 × 38 percent) 1.9 percent for the high-income family.

HOW TYPICAL IS BRACKET CREEP?

The accompanying table shows the brackets for taxable income for married persons filing joint returns under 1980 and 1984 income tax schedules. The income brackets were unchanged from 1980 to 1984, except that the top two were phased out because of reductions in the income level at which the maximum 50 percent marginal tax rate is achieved. For a family of four, the size of the brackets spans increases in income ranging from 15.6 to 46.7 percent. Focusing on those brackets up to $109,400 of taxable income, the average bracket size is 25.7 percent of the income at the bottom of the bracket. This is the maximum extent of income gain necessary to move from one bracket to the next.

Such percentage changes in money income are quite easily obtained over four-year periods, when inflation proceeds at 6 percent per year or so. When real income rises at 2 to 3 percent per year, bracket changes due to real growth alone occur for the average bracket size only within 8 to 12 years. At the smallest bracket differences taxable incomes of $16,000 and $35,200, bracket movements proceed much more rapidly and the marginal tax rate rises quite sharply. Under the 1980 tax law, the marginal rate at $16,000 of taxable income was 24 percent, and, at $35,200, it was 43 percent. Without indexation, inflation created a manifest problem of bracket creep over relatively short periods of time.

Bracket creep, however, does not simply refer to periodic inflation-induced shifts into higher marginal income tax brackets. It also includes the effects of inflation on average tax burdens within a bracket due to inflation-induced wage gains. For example, consider the low-income family in 1980 shown in table 1 in the text. In 1980, this family earned $10,500, had a taxable income of $6,500 after four personal exemptions and was in the bracket for taxable income that ranged from $5,500 to $7,600. The tax in this bracket was $294 plus 16 percent of the excess of taxable income over $5,500. At the low end of the bracket, the average tax rate was 3.1 percent, while at the high end of the bracket, the average tax rate was 5.4 percent. The low-income family at $10,500 paid 4.3 percent.

Inflation initially pushes up nominal income within the bracket—income rises from $10,500 to the top of the bracket, $11,600, a 10.5 percent income increase. Within the bracket, bracket creep pushes the average tax rate for the family with an unchanged real income from the 4.3

1980 AND 1984 PERSONAL INCOME TAX BRACKETS
FOR PERSONS MARRIED AND FILING JOINT RETURNS

Taxable income	Income	Percent change in income in bracket
$ 3,400 to $ 5,500	$ 7,400 to $ 9,500	28.3%
$ 5,500 to $ 7,600	$ 9,500 to $ 11,600	22.1
$ 7,600 to $ 11,900	$ 11,600 to $ 15,900	37.1
$ 11,900 to $ 16,000	$ 15,900 to $ 20,000	25.8
$ 16,000 to $ 20,200	$ 20,000 to $ 24,200	21.0
$ 20,200 to $ 24,600	$ 24,200 to $ 28,600	18.2
$ 24,600 to $ 29,900	$ 28,600 to $ 33,900	18.5
$ 29,900 to $ 35,200	$ 33,900 to $ 39,200	15.6
$ 35,200 to $ 45,800	$ 39,200 to $ 49,800	27.0
$ 45,800 to $ 60,000	$ 49,800 to $ 64,000	28.5
$ 60,000 to $ 85,000	$ 64,000 to $ 89,000	39.1
$ 85,000 to $109,400	$ 89,000 to $113,400	27.4
$109,400 to $162,400	$113,400 to $166,400	46.7
$162,400 to $215,400[2]	$166,400 to $219,400	31.9
$215,400 and over[2]	$219,400 and over	—

[1]Includes a $4,000 exemption for four dependents.
[2]These brackets were phased out under the 1981 tax act.

percent average tax rate, up to the 5.4 percent rate before a bracket rate change is triggered, further accelerating the climb in the average tax rate.

The rise in the average tax rate within the bracket arises because of the fixed nominal value of the exemptions, which decline in real value because of inflation and because the marginal tax rates applied to the inflation-induced income changes exceed the average tax rate. For example, for the 1980 low-income family, the marginal rate of 16 percent exceeded the 4.3 percent average tax rate shown in table 1 in the text. Thus, a $1,000 rise in income resulting solely from about a 10 percent increase in all prices would be taxed at the marginal rate of 16 percent, adding $160 to the $454 paid on the lower income instead of at the average rate of 4.3 percent, or $43. As a result, taxes of ($160 + $454) $614 on the higher income of $11,500 would yield an average tax rate, or tax per dollar of income, of 5.3 percent.

If the $1,000 gain income had resulted from real income growth, not from inflation, the rise in the tax burden would be consistent with the "vertical equity" principle built into the progressive income tax; this principle is that higher real income families should pay higher average tax rates. When the $1,000 gain reflects inflation-induced bracket creep, however, families with the same real income will pay higher average tax rates after prices rise than they did before. The intertemporal change in the tax burden on a family with the same real income violates the horizontal equity principle that "equals should be taxed equally."

The sensitivity of the average tax rate to changes in income, whether due to price increases or real income gains, is indicated by the ratio of the marginal tax rate to the average tax rate at any level of income. This ratio is largest at relatively low income levels. Thus, a given percentage rise in income raises the average tax rate the most at low income levels; similarly, a given reduction in real income reduces the average tax rate more at low income levels than at high ones.

The Effects of the 1981–85 Rate Reductions

With the rate reductions included in the 1981 tax act, the three families shown in table 2 faced the tax burden shown in table 3.[6] Compared with what they would have been (table 2), taxes were reduced substantially. For the personal income taxes considered alone, the cuts in average and marginal tax rates were close to the target. Average tax rates fell by 22.9 to 23.6 percent for the three family incomes. Similarly, marginal tax rates fell by 21.4 to 22.4 percent.

But the results shown in table 2 never actually occurred. A comparison of table 3 with the table 1 tax burdens, the actual taxes paid in 1980, indicates the effect of the

[6]The marginal personal income tax rate for the low-income family here masks the marginal tax burden at lower incomes. For incomes between $6,000 and $10,000, the earned income credit declines at a 12.5 percent rate on additional income. Thus, for a family of four, the marginal personal income tax rate is 12.5 percent for incomes from $6,000 to $7,400, to 23.5 percent from $7,400 to $9,600, and 24.5 percent from $9,600 to $10,000. At $10,000 the marginal personal income tax on additional income drops to 12 percent and remains there until income reaches $11,600, where it rises to the 14 percent indicated in table 3. Thus, at the margin, the tax burden on families with incomes from $7,400 to $10,000 exceeded that of 1980 median-income families. The situation is even worse for a head of household with one dependent, where the marginal personal income tax rate of 23.5 percent begins at an income of $6,000 and rises to 26.5 percent as income approaches $10,000. Bracket creep falls most heavily on persons in these brackets because of both the large difference between marginal and average tax rates at low incomes and the complicated and non-indexed earned income credit.

TABLE 3
THE 1984 FEDERAL TAX BURDEN FOR SELECTED 1980 REAL INCOMES

	One-half 1980 median income	1980 median income	Twice 1980 median income	
			One wage earner	Two wage earners
1984 income	$13,230	$26,460	$52,920	$52,920
Personal income tax	$711	$2,994	$10,958	$10,958
Average tax rate	5.4%	11.3%	20.7%	20.7%
Marginal tax rate	14.0%	22.0%	38.0%	38.0%
Employee-paid Social Security tax	$886	$1,773	$2,533	$3,546
Personal tax plus one-half Social Security tax				
Average tax rate	12.1%	18.0%	25.5%	27.4%
Marginal tax rate	20.7%	28.7%	38.0%	44.7%
Total tax burden[1]				
Average tax rate	19.1%	25.0%	30.5%	34.4%
Marginal tax rate	27.7%	35.7%	38.0%	51.7%

[1]Includes personal income tax and employee- and employer-paid Social Security tax.

TABLE 4
CHANGES IN TAX BURDENS FROM 1980 TO 1984 FOR SELECTED INCOMES:
NO REAL INCOME GROWTH

	One-half 1980 median income	1980 median income	Twice 1980 median income	
			One wage earner	Two wage earners
Personal income tax rates				
Average	25.6%	−5.0%	−7.2%	−7.2%
Marginal	−12.5	−8.3	−11.6	−11.6
Personal income tax plus employee-paid Social Security rate				
Average	15.2	−0.6	−2.3	−3.5
Marginal	−6.3	−4.7	−11.6	−9.0
Total tax rate				
Average	15.1	3.3	2.0	−0.6
Marginal	−2.1	−1.7	−11.6	−6.5

[1]Percent change; excludes "deduction for a married couple when both work."

1981 rate changes on actual tax burdens, with no real income changes. Again, focusing only on the personal income tax liability, it appears that tax burdens were reduced. For the median-income family, the average personal income tax rate fell from 11.9 percent in 1980 to 11.3 percent in 1984, a 5 percent reduction; the marginal tax rate fell from 24.0 percent in 1980 to 22.0 percent in 1984, an 8.3 percent cut. These changes are shown in table 4. For all three groups, the marginal tax rates fell, but by far less than the 22 percent observed when comparing tables 2 and 3. For 1980 median-income taxpayers and higher-income families, average personal income taxes declined, but, again, by much less than 22 percent. At the relatively low income level, however, the average tax rate actually *rose* from 4.3 to 5.4 percent, a 25.6 percent increase.

It should be emphasized that the modest declines in the personal income tax rates from 1980 to 1984 shown in table 5 were fortuitous. They occurred primarily because inflation was not high enough to entirely erode away the gains from the personal income tax cuts for some families. The 6 percent average inflation rate over the four years was well below the 7.8 percent average rate projected by the administration in 1981. Even that forecast was viewed as a rosy scenario at the time; for example, the Congressional Budget Office projected a 9.8 percent average annual inflation rate for the four years. Instead of the 26 percent rise in prices and income that occurred due to inflation since 1980, these forecasts envisioned 35 and 45.3 percent increases, respectively. Either outcome would have led to higher average and marginal personal income tax rates for most families in 1984 than they faced in 1980, despite the 1981 tax cuts and unchanged real incomes.

TABLE 5
1980-TO-1984 CHANGES IN TAX BURDENS FOR SELECTED INCOMES:
REAL INCOME GAIN OF 8 PERCENT

| | One-half median income | | | 1980 median income | | | Twice 1980 median income | | | | | | |
| | | | | | | | One wage earner | | | Two wage earners | | |
	1980	1984[1]	Percent change	1980	1984[1]	Percent change	1980	1984[1]	Percent change	1980	1984[1]	Percent change
Personal income tax rates												
Average	4.3%	6.0%	39.5%	11.9%	12.1%	1.7%	22.3%	22.0%	−1.3%	22.3%	22.0%	−1.3%
Marginal	16.0	14.0	−12.5	24.0	22.0[2]	−8.3	43.0	38.0	−11.6	43.0	38.0	−11.6
Personal income tax plus employee-paid Social Security rate												
Average	10.5	12.7	21.0	18.1	18.8	3.9	26.1	26.4	1.1	28.4	28.7	1.1
Marginal	22.1	20.7	−6.3	30.1	28.7[2]	−4.7	43.0	38.0	−11.6	49.1	44.7	−9.0
Total tax rate												
Average	16.6	19.7	18.7	24.2	25.8	6.6	29.9	31.0	3.7	34.6	35.7	3.2
Marginal	28.3	27.7	−2.1	36.3	35.7[2]	−1.7	43.0	38.0	−11.6	55.3	51.7	−6.5

[1] Excludes "deduction for a married couple when both work."
[2] Income is $23 below next personal income tax bracket, where the marginal tax rate rises 3 percentage points.

When the social security tax boosts since 1980 are taken into account, however, even the modest gains cited above generally disappear. At the bottom of table 4, the measures of the total tax burden indicate that average tax rates generally increased and that marginal tax rates fell only slightly for 1980 median- and low-income families. Only two-wage-earner, high-income families appear to have received a slight reduction in their average tax rate. One-wage-earner families at the same income level fared worse, on average, because the rise in the average tax burden due to social security tax hikes was larger for families that earned more than the maximum social security tax base in 1980.

Changes in the Actual Tax Burden

The assumption of no real income growth used to derive the tax rates in table 3 is appropriate for assessing the tax cut effects alone. Actual tax changes from 1980 to 1984, however, include not only the effects of inflation on income and the tax law changes, but also the effects of real income changes on income. Families typically earned higher real income in 1984 than in 1980 and paid higher tax burdens because of the progressive income tax.

Representative actual tax burden changes for the 1980 median-income families are shown in table 5. There, nominal income (from table 2) has been raised 8 percent to reflect the rise in per capita real GNP over the 1980–84 period. The table provides a comparison of 1980 and 1984 tax burdens assuming this typical growth.

Table 5 shows that the average personal income tax rate *rose* from 1980 to 1984 for 1980 median- and low-income families. When the higher 1984 Social Security taxes are included, the overall average tax rate *rose for every group shown*. Marginal tax rates generally declined slightly over the period.

It is clear that the rise in the tax burden from 1980 to 1984, despite the enacted tax rate reductions, fell disproportionately on low-income groups. In table 5, the rise in the overall average tax rate is smaller at higher incomes, raising the possibility that some high-income families actually paid lower average tax rates in 1984 than in 1980. Indeed, there is a "break-even" 1980 income level of $55,537 at which the 1984 average tax rate under the assumptions above equals that paid in 1980. Only about 6 percent of tax returns had an income in excess of $50,000 in 1980. More important, these returns totaled about 15.9 percent of all taxable income. Moreover, the tax reductions from 1980 to 1984 for these taxpayers were generally quite small either as a percent of 1980 average tax rates or in absolute percentage-point reductions. The largest tax reductions were about 2 percentage points for 1980 incomes from about $80,000 to $100,000, where, under the assumptions above, the average tax was about 40 to 42 percent in 1980.

Two Myths About the 1981–84 Tax Rate Changes

Public discussion of the 1981 personal income tax cuts has been dominated by two pervasive myths. The first is that the tax rate reductions led to lower personal income taxes for high-income families but little reduction in taxes for low-income families.

The second myth is that personal federal taxes fell from 1980 to 1984 (either absolutely or relative to income), thus contributing to higher federal deficits.

Table 4 clarifies the source of the conflicting claims that 1981 tax changes either resulted in greater benefits for those with higher incomes or reduced marginal and average tax rates equally. Both the personal income and overall average tax rate changes in table 4 indicate that the tax increases shown there fell disproportionately on lower-income families. The differential impact of the tax cuts shown in table 4, however, does not arise from the tax rate changes since 1980; indeed, the comparison of tables 2 and 3 shows that average and marginal tax rates were lowered by about the same percentage across income levels by the tax cuts enacted. The discriminatory tax changes shown in table 4 arose from bracket creep and Social Security tax hikes, increases that fall disproportionately on lower-income families. Fortunately, the greatest culprit, bracket creep, was largely eliminated by the 1981 tax act, though not until 1985.

The second myth is that the tax changes contributed to the surge in the deficit in late 1981 and 1982, and to the magnitude of recent and prospective deficits. Table 5 clearly indicates that, for representative families, the average tax burden rose from 1980 to 1984. Thus, personal tax rate cuts alone are not a likely candidate as a source of the increased federal deficit. While personal taxes as a percent of income did decline slightly at very high incomes, these reductions did not fully offset the generally larger increases in tax liabilities of lower-income groups that earn the larger share of income.

Of course, federal revenues would have been larger and the deficit correspondingly smaller in 1984, had the 1981–84 personal income tax rate changes not occurred. A comparison of tables 1 and 2 shows that 1984 revenues would have been about 22 percent larger under the old tax schedule. For fiscal year 1984, actual personal income taxes amounted to about $300 billion; this would have been about $85 billion larger under the 1980 tax rates. This "loss," however, was more than offset by the effect of inflation alone on federal tax receipts. The apparent decline in the size of taxes relative to GNP was largely due to the cyclical decline in the economy and to cuts in business taxes.

SUMMARY AND IMPLICATIONS

Personal income tax rate reductions were offset by bracket creep and increased Social Security taxes for most families between 1980 and 1984. Typical households, whose income merely kept pace with inflation and economy-wide real income gains during the past four years, faced higher average tax rates in 1984 than they did in 1980. Although this may seem implausible given the large declines (about 22 percent) in marginal and average tax rates provided by the 1981 tax act, it is easily explained. The failure of tax rates, on average, to decline is the result of both the massive extent of bracket creep produced by inflation over the 1980–84 period and the sharp rise in Social Security taxes since 1980.

The most important undercurrent of the analysis here is the role of indexation in eliminating bracket creep. Such indexation, as provided in the 1981 tax act, will begin in 1985. Contrary to most discussion, indexation will not lower average tax rates or taxes per dollar of income, unless real incomes decline. Instead, indexation allows inflation-induced income changes to be taxed at average tax rates, not at higher marginal tax rates that would push up taxes faster than incomes, even if real incomes are unchanged.

The analysis indicates that, at relatively low incomes, the effects of bracket creep are the strongest. Thus, not surprisingly, the 1980–84 rise in tax burdens has been largest at the lowest income levels. These increases were reinforced by Social Security tax hikes, which also add disproportionately to the tax burden of relatively low-income households and families.

Tax reform is high on the political agenda, but some of the implications of the analysis here have not been central to the discussion. Supply-side analysts could conclude from the analysis here that little effective cutting of marginal tax rates has resulted from the 1981–84 changes. To the extent such changes are desirable, a new initiative would be in order. At least three recent reform proposals include sharp reductions in marginal tax rates. Against a backdrop of an indexed tax system, another round of such cuts would be more likely to be effective.

REFERENCES

Bureau of the Census. *Statistical Abstract of the United States: 1982–83* (103d edition), Washington, D.C., 1982.

Economic Recovery Tax Act of 1981: Law and Explanation (Commerce Clearing House, August 1981).

Meyer, Stephen A., "Tax Cuts: Reality or Illusion?" Federal Reserve Bank of Philadelphia *Business Review* (November/December 1981), pp. 3–12.

Ott, Mack. "Depreciation, Inflation, and Investment Incentives: the Effects of the Tax Acts of 1981 and 1982," this *Review* (November 1984), pp. 17–30.

Tatom, John A. "We Are All Supply-Siders Now!" this *Review* (May 1981), pp. 18–30.

APPENDIX: The 1965 Tax Structure

Before 1981, marginal tax rates under the personal income tax had not been altered since 1965.[1] The increasingly onerous burden of the level of average and marginal tax rates in 1980 shown in table 1 in the text can be seen by comparison to the 1965 income tax structure.

Table A-1 shows the three representative 1980 families' tax positions, from table 1 in the text, based on 1965 taxes and prices for one-wage-earner families. In 1965, the social security tax was only 3.625 percent on wages up to $4,800 for both the employee- and the employer-paid amount. In 1965 prices, the 1980 income levels are considerably smaller, but purchasing power has been held constant. At the smaller 1965 nominal earnings, the 1980 median real income exceeded the maximum social security tax.

It should be noted that at the income levels given for 1965, the 1980 families had considerably more real income than similarly placed families in 1965; the 1965 median-family income was only $6,957. The examples in table A-1 are for families that were comparatively better off than

---

[1]From 1965 to 1981, many changes did occur in the personal income tax. These changes included alterations in standard deductions and personal exemptions, and changes in the incomes associated with brackets. The number of brackets and bracket rates, however, did not change.

TABLE A-1
THE FEDERAL TAX BURDEN ON SELECTED 1980 REAL INCOMES IN 1965[1]

	One-half 1980 median income	1980 median income	Twice 1980 median income
1980 income	$10,500	$21,000	$42,000
1965 equivalent	$4,021	$8,041	$16,082
1965 personal income tax	$143	$779	$2,431
Average tax rate	3.6%	9.7%	15.1%
Marginal tax rate	15.0%	19.0%	25.0%
1965 employee-paid Social Security tax	$146	$174	$174
Personal tax plus one-half Social Security tax			
Average tax rate	7.2%	11.9%	16.2%
Marginal tax rate	18.6%	19.0%	25.0%
Total tax burden			
Average tax rate	10.8%	14.0%	17.3%
Marginal tax rate	22.3%	19.0%	25.0%

[1]Assume one-wage-earner family for Social Security tax calculations.

their 1965 counterparts; their real incomes were about 15.6 percent above the respective multiples of median income in 1965. Thus, their tax treatment represents higher tax rates for income than their 1965 counterparts.

The average personal income tax at each income rose substantially from 1965 to 1980. For the 1980 median income, the increase is 22.7 percent of the 1965 tax burden of 9.7 percent. Even at the low income, the average tax burden rose sharply (19.4 percent). At twice the 1980 median income, the average personal income tax rate rose from 15.1 percent in 1965 to 22.3 percent in 1980, a 48 percent increase in taxes per dollar of income, despite no change in real income. The marginal personal income tax rates rose sharply as well, increasing $6^2/_3$ percent at the low income, 26.3 percent at the 1980 median and 72 percent at the high income.

The overall tax burden on these unchanged real incomes ballooned much more. The overall marginal tax rate on the 1980 median income almost doubled, rising from 19 percent to 36.3 percent. The total marginal tax rate at the low income rose from 22.3 percent to 28.3 percent, a 27 percent increase, while that for the high-income family rose 72 percent. The overall average tax rates on these real incomes rose 53.7 percent for the low-income family, 72.9 percent for the median-income family and 72.8 percent for the high-income family. Except at the high income, the biggest shares of the increase in the tax burden, on average or at the margin, was due to increases in both the Social Security tax rate and its tax base. At the relatively high-income level, almost two-thirds of the overall average and marginal tax burden increase occurred due to inflation-induced bracket creep. Even at the 1980 median real income, the jump in the tax burden due to bracket creep was substantial.

In summary, by 1980, marginal and average tax rates at all levels of income had risen dramatically from 1965 levels due to rising Social Security tax rates and its tax base, and to the effects of inflation pushing families into higher average and marginal personal income tax brackets. These forces continued from 1980 to 1984 and, in the absence of the 1981 tax cuts, would have further boosted the tax burden.

QUESTIONS FOR DISCUSSION

1 This article disputes the conventional wisdom that the 1981 tax bill was effective in sharply reducing the federal tax burden. What factors does the author point out as having offset the sharp reductions in tax rates instituted by the 1981 bill?

2 What is the difference between marginal and average tax rates? Give a simple numerical example. If you have read the article from the 1982 *Report* on the 1981 tax bill (Reading 5), explain why supply-siders emphasize the distribution between average and marginal tax rates.

3 What two alternative measures of the burden of Social Security taxes does the author cite? Why does he argue that it is the broader measure that is the appropriate one to include when measuring the total tax burden?

4 For a family with one-half the 1980 median income, what was the overall average tax rate in 1980 and in 1984? Break this down into personal income taxes and Social Security taxes (including both employer- and employee-paid). Now do the same thing for a family at twice the median income with one wage earner. Why are Social Security taxes called "regressive"?

5 How much did Social Security taxes contribute to *marginal* tax rates, in 1980 and in 1984, for each of the two representative families of question 4 above?

6 If the 1981 tax bill had not been passed, the author argues that the average tax burden would have risen substantially by 1984. For what two reasons would this have happened?

7 According to this article, how did the tax burden borne by different income groups shift between 1980 and 1984? What were the reasons for this shift?

8 Why did "bracket creep" end in 1985?

9 How did total average tax burdens in 1984 compare with those in 1965, according to this author?

10 The tax burden studied here is actually not the total tax burden faced by U.S. citizens. What are some important taxes omitted in this analysis? Would inclusion of these omitted taxes likely make the estimated tax burden more progressive or more regressive than that given here?

THE EFFECTS OF 1981–1982 FISCAL POLICY CHANGES ON BUSINESS INVESTMENT

A principal goal of the 1981 tax bill was to stimulate investment spending by giving a more favorable treatment to firms that purchased capital goods. In the first of two articles on this subject, Stephen A. Meyer documents that the net effect of tax legislation in 1981 and 1982 was to lower the "cost of capital" at any given real interest rate. However, in the second article, Adrian W. Throop argues that the overall impact of fiscal policy in the early eighties was to weaken investment; and that to explain the 1983–1984 investment boom, we must look to other factors.

Reading 7 Stephen A. Meyer, "Tax Policy Effects on Investment: The 1981 and 1982 Tax Acts," *Business Review,* Philadelphia Federal Reserve Bank, November-December 1984, pp. 3–14.

Reading 8 Adrian W. Throop, "A Supply-Side Miracle?" *Weekly Letter,* San Francisco Federal Reserve Bank, November 2, 1984.

TAX POLICY EFFECTS ON INVESTMENT: THE 1981 AND 1982 TAX ACTS

Stephen A. Meyer*

Investment spending by businesses has grown with unusual vigor during the current economic expansion. During the first year-and-one-half of the current expansion, business fixed investment grew at a 17 percent annual rate, almost twice as fast as its average growth during the equivalent period in the six previous recoveries. Yet market interest rates have been high during the past three years compared to historical experience; high interest rates tend to reduce investment, other factors being equal, by making it more costly for firms to finance investment. Why has investment spending been so strong?

Part of the answer is that changes in business tax laws enacted in 1981 and 1982 increase businesses' incentives to invest, on balance. The net effect of these changes is to lower, on average, the tax-adjusted real financing costs that firms face at any given interest rate. Thus the changes in tax law modify the historical relationship between investment behavior and interest rates by making it more attractive to invest at any given interest rate.

One of the objectives of the 1981 tax act was to spur investment spending. The 1981 tax act did substantially increase incentives to invest in virtually all kinds of buildings and equipment. The 1982 tax act, however, took back much of the increase. The net effect of the two tax acts is to reduce incentives to invest in certain kinds of

Stephen A. Meyer, "Tax Policy Effects on Investment: The 1981 and 1982 Tax Acts," *Business Review,* Philadelphia Federal Reserve Bank, November-December 1984, pp. 3–14.

*Stephen A. Meyer is a Senior Economist and Research Advisor in the Research Department of the Federal Reserve Bank of Philadelphia. He also teaches macroeconomics and international finance at the Wharton School, University of Pennsylvania.

projects, while making other projects somewhat more attractive by reducing tax-adjusted real financing costs.

Of course, financing costs—even tax-adjusted real financing costs—are not the only factors affecting firms' investment decisions. Expected future profits from a new investment and the actual cost of the investment also will affect firms' decisions. But the cost of financing investment projects is one important element helping to determine how much investment firms will undertake.

In addition to increasing businesses' incentives to invest, on average, the 1981 and 1982 tax acts also change the relative attractiveness of various kinds of real investment. Even though such changes may be unintentional effects of the new tax laws, the 1981 and 1982 tax acts do help to explain changes in the composition of business investment, as well as its strength, during the current economic recovery.[1]

THE COST-OF-CAPITAL APPROACH

Businesses have undertaken more investment during the past three years than we would have expected on the basis of historical experience, given how high not only market interest rates have been, but also how high real interest rates have been. To get real interest rates, subtract expected inflation from market interest rates.[2] The inflation premium included in market interest rates should not be counted as part of firms' real financing costs, because firms can expect that inflation premium to be offset by rising prices for the goods they produce, on average.

The real interest rate alone does not give us the actual cost of financing an investment project. To get firms' actual financing costs we must also adjust for the effects of tax laws. Adjusting for inflation and also for the effects of tax laws gets us to the *net cost-of-capital*, which we can think of as the tax-adjusted real interest rate faced by a firm which borrows to finance an investment project.

An investment project is worthwhile only if the expected rate of return (net of actual depreciation) from the investment is at least as large as the cost (expressed as a rate) of financing the project. Because interest payments are a deductible expense in calculating taxable profits, and because the firm can benefit from investment tax credits, depreciation allowances, and other provisions of the tax code, the net cost-of-capital for financing the investment project differs from both market and real interest rates. One way of evaluating investment projects is to compare the expected rate of return (net of actual depreciation) on each project, before taxes, with the net cost-of-capital for borrowed funds. If the expected rate of return from an investment project is sufficiently larger than the *net cost of capital* for financing the project to compensate for the risk inherent in undertaking the project, then a firm will want to undertake that investment. A reduction in the net cost-of-capital increases the number of investment projects for which expected return is greater than financing cost, so a cut in the net cost-of-capital provides firms with an incentive to invest more.

---

[1] The 1981 and 1982 tax acts also changed personal income taxes. For a discussion of the economic effects of the *personal* tax changes, see S. A. Meyer, "Tax Cuts: Reality or Illusion?" *Business Review* (July-August 1983).

[2] For a discussion of the meaning of real (inflation-adjusted) interest rates, see H. Taylor, "Interest Rates: How Much Does Expected Inflation Matter?" *Business Review* (July-August 1982).

The Tax Code and the Cost-of-Capital

The net cost-of-capital is affected by three major parts of the tax code. The *ability to deduct interest payments* as a business expense in calculating taxable income is one. Consider as an example a corporation that borrows money to finance some investment project. Each time the corporation pays out a dollar of interest on that loan, it also reduces its taxable income by one dollar. Because the statutory federal corporate income tax rate is 46 percent, our corporation saves 46 cents in federal corporate income tax when it reduces its taxable income by paying out one dollar of interest. In terms of cash flow, our corporation must pay out 54 cents, net, rather than one dollar, to meet its interest obligation. So the ability to deduct interest payments reduces the net cost-of-capital relative to market interest rates.

The *ability to deduct allowable depreciation* (as defined in the tax code) as a business expense is a second part of the tax code that affects the net cost-of-capital. When a firm undertakes some new investment, such as buying and installing a new machine, it also incurs some real costs of depreciation—the new machine must be maintained and eventually it will wear out and need to be replaced. The tax code recognizes that depreciation is a real cost of doing business; the tax code allows firms to subtract a depreciation allowance from gross profits to calculate their taxable income. But the depreciation allowances specified by the tax code rarely equal the *actual* depreciation costs incurred by a firm on its new machines. If the depreciation allowances written into the tax code are larger than actual depreciation incurred by the firm, then the tax code permits the firm to report taxable profits smaller than its actual profits (net of true depreciation) and thereby increases the net cash flows from investment in new machines by reducing cash outlays for tax payments.

To see exactly how much the depreciation allowances specified by the tax code differ from actual depreciation costs over the lifetime of a new investment project, the firm can look at the *net-present-value* (NPV) of depreciation allowances and costs. (NPV is the value today of future receipts or payments. One way to think of NPV is to ask: How much must I deposit in a bank today, earning today's interest rate, in order to be able to make a specified series of future payments?) If the NPV of depreciation allowances specified by the tax code is larger than the NPV of actual depreciation costs over the lifetime of the investment project, then the tax code will reduce the net cost-of-capital. This is so because the extra depreciation allowances reduce the firm's tax liability, which increases the net cash flows from the investment project by the amount that otherwise would have gone to pay taxes. The tax savings effectively reduce the real cost of borrowing to finance the project. On the other hand, if the NPV of depreciation allowances is smaller than the NPV of actual depreciation costs, then the tax code increases the net cost-of-capital for borrowing to invest in such a machine.[3]

The *opportunity to claim an investment tax credit* is the third major part of the tax code that affects the net cost-of-capital. When a firm undertakes some kinds of new

---

[3]The tax code bases depreciation allowances on the initial, or historical, cost of investment projects. Actual depreciation costs depend on the replacement, or current, cost of comparable machines. So in an economy which is experiencing inflation, it is likely that the NPV of depreciation allowances will be smaller than the NPV of actual depreciation costs, which raises the net cost-of-capital. And the higher the inflation rate, the larger will be the amount by which depreciation allowances understate actual depreciation costs.

investment, the tax code allows it to claim an investment tax credit which immediately reduces the firm's tax liability. So the firm can pay out less cash to the taxman. The reduction in cash outflows generated by the investment tax credit reduces the net cost-of-capital to the firm.

These three major aspects of the tax code—deductions for interest payments, depreciation allowances, and investment tax credits—combine with market interest rates and expected inflation to determine firms' net cost-of-capital for new investment projects. The interplay among all these factors typically makes the net cost-of-capital lower than the market interest rate at which a firm can borrow, but the net cost-of-capital may be higher or lower than the real interest rate (the market rate less the expected inflation rate).

Changes in the tax code can raise or lower the net cost-of-capital, even though market interest rates and expected inflation remain unchanged. Because the net cost-of-capital measures firms' cost of borrowing to finance an investment project, changes in the tax code can make investment less or more attractive even with no change in interest rates. In other words, changes in the tax code, especially in the three major aspects of the tax code that we identified earlier, can change the relationship between observed, market interest rates and investment spending.

HOW DID THE 1981 AND 1982 TAX ACTS CHANGE THE COST-OF-CAPITAL?

The 1981 tax act, formally called the Economic Recovery Tax Act of 1981, liberalized two of the three major aspects of the tax code that affect the cost-of-capital—allowable depreciation and investment tax credits. The 1981 tax act shortened the period over which assets can be depreciated, which substantially increased depreciation allowances for the early years of useful life of most types of investment, and thus raised the NPV of tax depreciation allowances. The new depreciation rules let firms which undertake new investment pay less tax than they would have before 1981, at least in the first few years after undertaking the investment. Even though firms may eventually have to pay those taxes, postponing the tax payments is equivalent to obtaining an interest-free loan and thus improves firms' cash flow. Because the new depreciation rules reduce the cash outlays associated with new investment, they reduce the net cost-of-capital.

The 1981 tax act also liberalized the investment tax credit for purchasing new short-lived capital equipment, that with a useful life of less than seven years (under 1980 tax law). Increasing the investment tax credit reduces the net cost-of-capital because it provides new tax savings that reduce the cash outlays required to undertake investments which qualify for the tax credit.

The 1982 tax act, officially named the Tax Equity and Fiscal Responsibility Act of 1982, continued the accelerated depreciation methods enacted in 1981; however, it introduced a new requirement that firms subtract one-half of the investment tax credit available on new investment projects from the cost of such projects, and then

calculate allowable depreciation deductions on the remainder. (So a firm would calculate depreciation allowances using 95 percent of the cost of a project which qualifies
for a 10 percent investment tax credit, for example.) This new requirement reduces
the NPV of depreciation allowances, compared to 1981.[4] So this new requirement
raises the net cost-of-capital, compared to 1981 tax law. Neither the 1981 nor 1982
tax acts changed the provisions of the tax code which specify that interest payments
are a tax-deductible business expense.

HOW MUCH WAS THE NET COST-OF-CAPITAL CHANGED?

Exactly how much the 1981 and 1982 tax acts changed the cost-of-capital for a
particular investment project depends upon the kind of investment being undertaken,
and also upon the level of interest rates and expected inflation. But the changes in net
cost-of-capital for most kinds of investment *within* a few broad categories that encompass all kinds of investment are quite similar, even though the effects of tax changes
differ *across* those categories.

Let us take a coupon interest rate of 13.5 percent and an expected inflation rate of
5 percent as representative of the situation that a firm faces today if it wants to borrow
to finance an investment project.[5] Using those rates, one can calculate the net cost-
of-capital under 1980 tax law, and under current tax law.

Taking a weighted average of the change in net cost-of-capital for *all* the different
kinds of investment undertaken in the U.S. economy shows that the net effect of the
1981 and 1982 tax acts was to reduce the *average* net cost-of-capital by slightly more
than one-eighth, from 2.64 percent to 2.29 percent.[6] For other combinations of market
interest rates and expected inflation, the reductions in net cost-of-capital may be larger
or smaller. But for all combinations of market interest rates between 10 and 16 percent
and expected inflation between 4 and 8 percent, the net effect of the 1981 and 1982
tax acts was to reduce the average net cost-of-capital by at least one-tenth.[7]

Breaking down investment into the broad categories used by the U.S. Department
of Commerce for the National Income and Product Accounts reveals the degree to

[4]For a more detailed treatment of depreciation allowances on various types of investments, and a
description of how the new tax laws change depreciation allowances for each specific kind of investment,
see C. R. Hulten and J. W. Robertson, "Corporate Tax Policy and Economic Growth: An Analysis of the
1981 and 1982 Tax Acts," Urban Institute Discussion Paper (December 1982).

[5]In principle, one should choose for each investment an interest rate that measures the cost of borrowing
over the lifetime of the project. Thus one normally would use a higher interest rate to calculate the net
cost-of-capital for a long-lived project than for a short-lived project. Because market interest rates are now
essentially equal for all maturities of three years or more, I have simplified the argument by using one
interest rate for all types of investment.

[6]The weights used in calculating this average net cost-of-capital are the shares of each kind of investment
(as a fraction of total fixed investment) in the U.S. in 1982. Weights are calculated from data in the July
1983 issue of the *Survey of Current Business* (U.S. Department of Commerce).

[7]For combinations of market interest rates and expected inflation rates which imply a before-tax real
interest rate less than 5 percent, the net cost-of-capital becomes negative, on average, under current tax
law. The net effect of the 1981 and 1982 tax acts is still to reduce the net cost-of-capital, on average.

TABLE 1
NET COST-OF-CAPITAL

Category	Net cost-of-capital (%) (rounded to nearest hundredth)		
	1980	**1981**	**1982**
Buildings	4.58	3.36	3.36
Residential structures	3.59	2.97	2.97
Utilities and structures	2.92	2.77	2.83
Equipment	1.55	0.84	1.49

Note: (1) The figures in this table were calculated using a coupon interest rate of 13.5 percent and an expected inflation rate of 5 percent, roughly corresponding to market conditions in mid-1984.

(2) The disaggregation shown here corresponds to that given by the U.S. Department of Commerce when it presents detailed National Income and Product Accounts data for the United States in the July issue of *Survey of Current Business* each year.

which "the 1981 tax law giveth and the 1982 tax law taketh away" (see Table 1). For the two categories covering most construction, the 1981 tax act cut the net cost-of-capital and the 1982 tax act left those cuts virtually untouched. The 1981 tax act cut the net cost-of-capital for *building new plant* (such as factories and commercial buildings) by about one quarter. The cut in the net cost-of-capital results from the larger NPV of depreciation allowances generated by the new accelerated depreciation methods introduced in the 1981 tax act.[8] The 1982 tax act did not change the tax treatment of buildings further. The 1981 tax act also cut the net cost-of-capital associated with borrowing to finance *residential construction,* such as construction of new apartment buildings. The change in depreciation rules for rental housing cut the net cost-of-capital for this kind of investment by roughly one-sixth.

While most kinds of construction activity benefited from large cuts in net cost-of-capital, the tax-adjusted real cost of borrowing to finance investment in the kinds of structures built by utilities did not benefit much from the 1981 and 1982 tax acts, on balance. The net cost-of-capital for this type of investment was barely cut.

Investment in *equipment* benefited from the largest cut in net cost-of-capital under the 1981 tax act, but that cut was largely reversed by the 1982 tax act, on average. The effect of the accelerated depreciation rules and liberalized investment tax credits introduced by the 1981 tax act was to reduce the net cost of capital for investment in equipment by nearly one-half, on average. But the 1982 tax act raised the net cost-of-capital by allowing firms to depreciate less than the full cost of a project that

---

[8]The 1981 tax act also cut the cost-of-capital for *rehabilitating* existing factories and commercial buildings by substantially increasing an investment tax credit (from 10 percent to as much as 25 percent) for rehabilitation expenditures on buildings more than 30 years old. The provisions of the tax code which apply to such projects are so complicated, however, that it is not possible to calculate the change in net cost-of-capital for rehabilitation of existing buildings except on a project-by-project basis. But the net cost-of-capital for financing the rehabilitation portion of such a project (but not the purchase of the old building and its site) was cut by roughly 35 percent, given the rates used in our example.

qualifies for an investment tax credit. The net effect of the 1981 and 1982 tax acts was to reduce the net cost-of-capital associated with borrowing to finance investment in equipment by one-twentieth from its 1980 level.

A tax-induced reduction in the net cost-of-capital makes it less costly for firms to undertake new investment, at any given interest rate. It follows that the business tax changes enacted in the 1981 and 1982 tax acts are part of the reason why investment spending has been strong even though interest rates seem high by historical standards. Firms have discovered that the real, after-tax, cost of borrowing to finance new investment is much lower than market interest rates, and lower than would have been the case if the tax laws had not been changed since 1980.

DIFFERENTIAL EFFECTS OF THE 1981 AND '82 TAX CHANGES

Looking at the average change in net cost-of-capital due to the 1981 and 1982 tax acts does not tell us all that we would like to know, however. We have already seen that the reduction in net cost-of-capital was larger on average for investment in plant than for investment in equipment. The differences in the tax laws' effect upon the net cost-of-capital for some *specific* kinds of investments is even larger. (For complete details see the table on page 84.) The two tax acts reduced the net cost-of-capital for some kinds of investment by much more than the average, not at all for some other kinds of investment, and raised the net cost-of-capital for some types. These differences are important because they can affect the composition of new investment in the U.S. economy.

Some Investments Benefited Greatly

The net cost-of-capital associated with borrowing to finance the purchase of *automobiles* for business use was cut by the largest amount. Suppose we continue with our example of a firm which borrows at a coupon interest rate equal to 13.5 percent, and which expects 5 percent inflation each year over the useful life of its investments. Such a firm would find that the 1981 and 1982 tax acts reduced the net cost-of-capital for investing in new automobiles by almost one-third on balance. This reduction is more than twice as large as the average cut in the net cost-of-capital; recall that the average net cost-of-capital, averaging over all kinds of investment, was cut by slightly more than one-eighth. The large reduction in net cost-of-capital for *automobiles* stems from changes in the investment tax credit (ITC). For automobiles used in business, the ITC is now 6 percent of the value of the investment, almost twice the 3.3 percent credit allowed under 1980 tax law.

For *ships and boats* used in business, the reduction in net cost-of-capital was almost as large, and still substantially larger than the average cut for all investment. The net cost-of-capital associated with borrowing to finance purchases of ships and boats for business use was cut by more than one-quarter. The net cost-of-capital for financing purchases of *engines and turbines* was also cut substantially more than the average. For this kind of machinery the net cost-of-capital was cut by one-quarter, on balance,

NET COST-OF-CAPITAL FOR 35 TYPES OF INVESTMENT PROJECTS (*continued*)

	Net cost-of-capital (%) (rounded to nearest hundredth)		
	1980	1981	1982
Largest to smallest cuts in net cost-of-capital			
Automobiles	2.04	0.62	1.44
Commercial buildings	4.58	3.24	3.24
Hospital buildings	4.47	3.19	3.19
Ships and boats	2.41	1.39	1.74
Religious buildings	4.24	3.08	3.08
Educational buildings	4.24	3.08	3.08
Engines and turbines	2.30	1.36	1.72
Other nonfarm buildings	5.05	3.79	3.79
Industrial buildings	4.54	3.54	3.54
Other nonbuilding facilities	4.18	3.35	3.35
Railroad equipment	2.16	1.45	1.76
Residential buildings	3.59	2.97	2.97
Metalworking machinery	1.87	1.07	1.59
General industrial equipment	1.87	1.07	1.59
Electrical and communications equipment	1.87	1.10	1.61
Special industry machinery	1.89	1.20	1.65
Fabricated metal products	1.90	1.27	1.69
Trucks, buses, and trailers	1.34	0.20	1.20
Farm structures	3.52	3.22	3.22
Gas storage and distribution structures	2.51	2.14	2.30
Petroleum pipelines	2.58	2.18	2.39
Tractors	1.56	0.80	1.47
Instruments	1.61	0.91	1.52
Little or no change in net cost-of-capital			
Railroads	2.57	2.41	2.52
Telephone and telegraph structures	2.69	2.56	2.72
Electric light and power structures	2.66	2.53	2.68
Mining, shafts and wells	3.01	2.92	2.92
Smallest to largest increases in net cost-of-capital			
Agricultural machinery	1.56	1.24	1.67
Furniture and fixtures	1.51	1.15	1.63
Other equipment	1.36	0.91	1.52
Mining and oil field machinery	1.29	0.79	1.47
Service industry machinery	1.29	0.79	1.47
Construction machinery	1.27	0.74	1.45
Aircraft	0.91	0.67	1.41
Office, computing, and calculating machinery	0.43	0.07	1.15

Note: (1) The figures in this table were calculated using a coupon interest rate of 13.5 percent and expected inflation rate of 5 percent, roughly corresponding to market conditions in mid-1984.

(2) The disaggregation shown here corresponds to that given by the U.S. Department of Commerce when it presents detailed National Income and Product Accounts data for the United States in the July issue of *Survey of Current Business* each year.

by the 1981 and 1982 tax acts (still assuming that the firm borrows at a 13.5 percent market rate and expects continuing 5 percent inflation).

The large reductions in net cost-of-capital for financing purchases of *ships and boats,* and of *engines and turbines,* stem from the new accelerated depreciation rules enacted in 1981. The time period over which these investments can be depreciated was shortened so substantially that the NPV of depreciation allowances is higher under current tax law than under 1980 tax law, even though the firm cannot now depreciate the full cost of such investments.

Finally, investments in new buildings, especially *commercial buildings,* benefited from large reductions in the net cost-of-capital. The new depreciation rules included in the 1981 tax act reduced the net cost-of-capital for this type of building by three-tenths. *Industrial buildings* benefited almost as much; the net cost-of-capital for financing construction of such buildings was cut by one-fifth. The 1982 tax act did not change the net cost-of-capital for buildings further.

Utilities' Structures Benefited Much Less

While some kinds of investments benefited from larger than average reductions in net cost-of-capital, the tax-adjusted real cost of borrowing to finance investment in the kinds of structures built by utilities did not benefit much, if at all, from the 1981 and 1982 tax acts. The net cost-of-capital for financing investment in *telephone and telegraph structures* and in *electric light and power systems* was left unchanged. The net cost-of-capital for financing investment in *railroad structures, gas storage and distribution structures,* and *petroleum pipelines* was cut by the new tax laws, but not appreciably. Compared to 1980 tax law, the 1981 and '82 tax acts cut the net cost-of-capital for such investments less than one-tenth, on balance.

The 1981 tax act shortened the number of years over which utilities are allowed to depreciate most of these investments. Doing so modestly reduced the net cost-of-capital for these investments. The investment tax credit offset enacted in 1982 reduced the size of depreciation allowances for many kinds of investment projects undertaken by utilities, and thus raised the net cost-of-capital. On balance, the net cost-of-capital for most investments undertaken by utilities was not changed appreciably by the new tax laws.

Some Investments Were Adversely Affected

While the new accelerated depreciation schedules introduced in the 1981 tax act substantially reduced the net cost-of-capital for financing investment in all kinds of equipment, the 1982 tax act took back much of the cut. Indeed, the tax adjusted real cost of financing purchases of some kinds of equipment was raised substantially, after 1982.

For *office, computing and calculating machinery* (the category covering electronic computers, including personal computers), the net cost-of-capital was almost tripled by the new tax laws. The net cost-of-capital for such investments remains lower than for any other type, however.

The large increase in net cost-of-capital for office, computing, and calculating equipment results from the investment tax credit offset built into the 1982 tax act. The 1981 tax act shortens the period over which firms calculate depreciation allowances from 7 years to $4^1/_2$ years for office, computing, and calculating equipment. But the 1982 tax act, which prevents firms from depreciating the full cost of such equipment, more than reverses those gains.

A similar, although smaller, increase occurred in the net cost-of-capital for financing purchase of aircraft. The net effect of the 1981 and 1982 tax acts was to raise the net cost-of-capital by one-half. (Again, these results are based upon a market interest rate of 13.5 percent and 5 percent expected inflation.) The net cost-of-capital for financing investments in construction machinery, mining and oil field machinery, and service industry machinery also rose as a result of the combined tax changes, by roughly one-seventh. In all of these cases the new investment tax credit offset introduced in 1982 outweighs the depreciation rules introduced in 1981.

Did Tax Changes Affect the Composition of Investment?

The fact that the 1981 and 1982 tax acts changed the net cost-of-capital for various kinds of investment by different amounts has implications for the composition of investment during the current economic recovery and expansion. Large cuts in the net cost-of-capital for financing investment in ships and boats, in engines and turbines, in automobiles, and in new commercial buildings, suggest that business firms would have an incentive to undertake larger purchases of those items. In fact, the net cost-of-capital for almost all kinds of buildings was cut substantially by the 1981 and 1982 tax acts. We might expect firms to respond to the reductions in net cost-of-capital by investing more in new buildings, in general. On the other hand, utilities might be reluctant to undertake new construction, because the kinds of structures that they use received almost no cut in the net cost-of-capital.

And the increases in net cost-of-capital for financing purchases of office, computing and calculating machinery, of aircraft, and of some other kinds of machinery suggest that firms will be less likely to undertake investment projects which require purchases of those types of equipment. The net effect of the 1981 and '82 tax acts was to make such investment projects relatively less attractive.

Did the composition of new investment undertaken by firms in the U.S. actually change in the way suggested by changes in the net cost-of-capital? In general, the answer is that changes in the composition of investment do seem to be related to the changes in net cost-of-capital that was generated by the 1981 and 1982 tax acts, but not very closely. Construction of new factories and commercial buildings has grown more rapidly than in previous expansion periods, as suggested by large cuts in the net cost-of-capital for financing such investments. Construction of new buildings and structures grew at a 7 percent annual rate during the first six quarters of this expansion. That rate is about one quarter higher than the average growth rate during comparable periods in six previous recoveries. Utilities have undertaken very little investment during the current economic expansion, consistent with unchanged cost-of-capital for their investment.[9] On the other hand, new investment in equipment, including office equipment and computers, has grown especially strongly during the current economic expansion even though the net cost-of-capital for equipment was cut only slightly, on average. Business investment in equipment in general grew at nearly a 22 percent annual rate during the first year-and-a-half of the current economic expansion. That rate is twice as fast as the average growth rate of equipment investment during the same period in six previous expansions, and faster than during any other expansion since World War II.[10]

The observation that tax-induced changes in the net cost-of-capital for financing investments do not fully explain the changing composition of business investment should not be surprising. Changes in expected future profits from investment projects, and in the actual cost of projects, as well as in tax-adjusted real financing costs, all influence firms' investment decisions. Investment in high-technology equipment, such as computers, illustrates the point. Prices of computers have fallen so dramatically as the number of potential applications has risen, that computers are more attractive investments than they were in 1980. Even though the real, tax-adjusted cost of financing investment in computers was increased by changes in tax law, the expected rate of return from investing in computers has risen even more. While the changes in net cost-of-capital which resulted from the 1981 and 1982 tax acts are not the only reason for the pattern of investment that has occurred in the current economic expansion, they have played a role in determining the composition as well as the strength of new investment.

SUMMARY AND CONCLUSIONS

The net effect of the 1981 and 1982 tax acts was to make new investment more attractive by reducing the net cost-of-capital compared to what it would be under 1980 tax law. The *net cost-of-capital* is a measure of the tax-adjusted real financing cost faced by a firm that borrows to finance an investment project. Furthermore, the 1981 and 1982 changes in business taxes cut the net cost-of-capital for some investment projects more than for others. So these tax acts also changed the relative attractiveness of various kinds of investment projects.

The 1981 tax act made two major changes in business taxes: it increased the net present value of depreciation allowances, as specified by the tax code, for most kinds of new investment; and it increased investment tax credits for some kinds of investment. Both of these changes generate tax savings which reduce the net cost-of-capital. The 1982 tax act introduced a new investment tax credit offset which reduced the net present value of depreciation allowances for many kinds of investment, especially for

---

[9]Sluggish investment by utilities reflects both slower growth of demand for energy, and increased construction costs for utilities' structures. Construction of nuclear power generating stations has been particularly hard hit by these two factors. These factors reduce the expected return on new investment by utilities, and thus make investment less attractive even at a constant net cost-of-capital.

[10]These observations about investment behavior are based on data published by the U.S. Department of Commerce in *Survey of Current Business,* July 1984 and earlier issues.

equipment. The net effect of the changes in business taxes that were enacted in 1981 and 1982 is to reduce the net cost-of-capital for firms which borrow to finance new investment by one-eighth, on average, from what it would be under prior tax law (using an example in which market interest rates are 13.5 percent and inflation is expected to be 5 percent per year over the useful life of the investment project).

Because the net cost-of-capital measures the financing cost (in real terms) faced by firms which borrow to finance an investment project, firms will undertake more investment if the net cost-of-capital is reduced than they would otherwise. By reducing the net cost-of-capital, the 1981 and 1982 tax acts made firms more willing to undertake new investment. And investment projects which benefit from the largest cuts in net cost-of-capital will appear especially attractive. The net cost-of-capital for financing construction of new buildings was cut substantially more than was the net cost-of-capital for investing in new equipment. But within the equipment category, some types of equipment benefited from large cuts in net cost-of-capital, while other types faced large increases.

Investment has grown exceptionally strongly during the current economic recovery and expansion, considering how high interest rates have been. The strength of investment is explained, in part, by reductions in the net cost-of-capital which resulted from the 1981 and 1982 tax acts. The changes in the composition of investment spending that occurred during the first year-and-a-half of the current economic expansion do not appear to be closely tied to the changes in relative cost-of-capital that were generated by the two tax acts, however. These results indicate that while the business tax changes contained in the 1981 and 1982 tax acts did provide some stimulus to investment, they can explain only part of the unusually strong growth of investment spending during the current economic expansion.

QUESTIONS FOR DISCUSSION

1 Broadly speaking, what is the *cost of capital?* Why is it an important influence on the volume of investment spending? What other factors affect the willingness of businesspeople to invest?

2 What is the difference between real and market (or nominal) interest rates? Which belongs in the cost of capital? Why? (It may help to construct a two-period numerical example. Assume the firm borrows $1 to buy a machine in period 1. In period 2, the machine produces a fixed amount of output, which is sold. At the end of period 2, the machine wears out and the loan is repaid. Keep in mind that the price at which the output is sold should grow at the rate of inflation between period 1 and period 2.)

3 What are the three parts of the tax code that affect the cost of capital? Explain how each affects the tax bill of a firm that makes an investment. What happens to the cost of capital of a firm which has no taxable income (say, due to losses)?

4 Suppose that a $1,000 investment may be depreciated (for tax purposes) at $250 a year for four years (straight-line depreciation). The market interest rate is 10 percent and the corporate profits tax rate is 50 percent.

a What is the *net present value* of the depreciation deductions associated with this investment? (Use a calculator.)

b The tax law is changed to allow the investment to be fully depreciated in two years. Now what is the NPV of the depreciation deductions?

   c On top of the tax law change in (*b*), the market interest rate drops to 6 percent (due to lower inflation). Now what is the NPV? Does lower inflation reinforce or offset the effects of accelerated cost recovery?

5 Investment in computers grew strongly during the 1983–1984 economic recovery, despite the fact that the cost of capital for "equipment" was cut only slightly. What explanation does the author give for this?

6 What conclusion about the effectiveness of the 1981 tax bill at affecting investment does the author draw from the pattern of growth among different *types* of investments after the tax cut?

7 Find out what were the major provisions affecting business investment in the 1986 tax reform act. Do you think the 1986 changes will increase or reduce the cost of capital?

A "SUPPLY-SIDE MIRACLE"?

Adrian W. Throop

The U.S. economy is experiencing an investment boom in plant and equipment of major proportions. Nonresidential fixed investment set a postwar record by growing at a 16.8 percent annual rate during the first six quarters of the current expansion. More importantly, investment spending also reached a record high in relation to current levels of GNP. Nonresidential fixed investment has averaged 11.5 percent of GNP in the current expansion, compared to an average of 9.5 percent of GNP in earlier business cycle upswings.

Have the tax incentives for business investment provided in the Economic Recovery and Tax Act of 1981 caused the current investment boom? This *Weekly Letter* presents evidence showing that any reduction in the cost of investment created by these new tax incentives has been offset by recent increases in real interest rates.

POSSIBLE EXPLANATIONS

Various explanations have been advanced for the current investment boom in plant and equipment. One is based on the momentum of the recovery from the 1981-82 recession which was quicker than normal and thus may have created a greater need to expand capacity. However, real GNP grew by a 7.2 percent annual rate in the first 6 quarters of this expansion, compared to an average rate of 6.8 percent in previous postwar expansions; and the speed of the decline in real GNP during the prior recession was no more than average. These differences are not great enough to explain the large disparity in investment behavior. Nor can the strength of investment spending simply

Adrian W. Throop, "A Supply-Side Miracle?" *Weekly Letter,* San Francisco Federal Reserve Bank, November 2, 1984.

be explained by a relatively low level in the prior recession. The ratio of investment spending to GNP was not any lower than usual for a recession.

Two other explanations have more validity. Since the cyclical expansion of the mid-1970s, many new forms of "high-technology" investment have become available in the areas of electronic equipment, communications gear, and office machines. Since these investments allow firms to cut costs by using new technologies, they can be highly profitable even if the financial cost of investment is greater than normal. According to unpublished data compiled by the Commerce Department, such "high tech" investment has recently taken a quantum leap, jumping from 25 percent to nearly 50 percent of total investment since 1978. Since most "high tech" investment takes the form of equipment, this explanation is consistent with the below-average ratio of investment in structures to GNP at the same time that the ratio of investment in equipment to GNP has been at a postwar high.

A second explanation for the current investment boom in plant and equipment is the obsolescence of the capital stock. Higher energy prices in the 1970s, as well as regulations to reduce pollution and enhance occupational safety, made production facilities that had been regarded as fully competitive in an earlier environment relatively inefficient. If, as demand increases during an expansion and older facilities are brought into use, the cost of running them exceeds the cost of investing in new capital, then investment is stimulated.

The most widely discussed possible explanation of the current investment boom is the potential effect of the tax cuts for business provided in the Economic Recovery Tax Act of 1981. This Act substantially reduced effective tax rates on the capital cost of business fixed investment without changing the corporate income tax rate. First, an Accelerated Cost Recovery System (ACRS) replaced the previous system of basing tax lives on expected useful lives. For most assets the new tax lives are considerably shorter than their economic lives. Second, the 1981 Act increased the value of investment tax credits for investment in equipment. The Tax Equity and Fiscal Responsibility Act of 1982 took back a portion of these cuts as part of a package to reduce the size of the federal budget deficit, but its net effect on tax incentives for business was relatively minor.

Whether the tax cuts for business are actually generating the investment boom in plant and equipment depends upon whether the incentives they provide have been offset by higher real interest rates. If the amount of available saving were fixed and other kinds of investment had received equal tax breaks, interest rates would have to rise to an exactly offsetting extent in order to ration the given amount of saving. But interest rates need *not* have increased to this extent since several other kinds of investment (such as consumer durables, owner occupied housing and foreign investment) did not get equal tax breaks. With a given amount of saving, business fixed investment would then gain at the expense of other types of investment.

The pressure on interest rates would be further reduced to the extent that the supply of private domestic saving was augmented by tax incentives or inflows of foreign saving. But the pressure would be increased if other factors were simultaneously contributing to larger federal budget deficits, which represent a reduction in governmental contributions to total saving. Although the 1981 Act reduced the average marginal tax rate for individuals by several percentage points (after taking into account the effect of "bracket creep"), there has actually been no perceptible increase in the private saving rate. Instead, the main effect of cutting personal income taxes has been to create large losses in revenue and therefore further reductions in government saving. The result has been a substantial upward pressure on real interest rates.

TAX INCENTIVES VS. REAL INTEREST RATES

The real cost of capital investment, including the effects of taxes, can be measured with an approach developed by Professors Robert Hall and Dale Jorgenson. In their method, the real cost of capital has three main determinants besides debt and equity costs: (1) the tax rate on corporate profits, which is applied to returns on equity capital, (2) deductions allowed for depreciation, and (3) an investment tax credit of up to 10 percent of the original cost for expenditures on equipment, but not for structures. The present economic value of depreciation allowances varies inversely with the life of the investment for tax purposes and also inversely with nominal interest rates. The economic value of depreciation allowances and that of the investment tax credit have varied substantially over the post-war period due to changes in the tax law and variations in nominal interest rates.

The real cost of capital investment in the Hall and Jorgenson formula is equal to a weighted average of real debt and equity costs plus the physical rate of depreciation, all multiplied by one plus the effective tax rate. The effective tax rate is influenced by the economic value of depreciation allowances and the investment tax credit, as well as the corporate income tax rate itself. The accompanying chart shows the behavior of the Hall and Jorgenson measure of the real cost of capital and its two major components (real debt and equity costs plus depreciation and the effective tax rate) for nonresidential fixed investment in recent years.

Nonresidential Fixed Investment: The Real Cost of Capital and Its Two Main Components. (Sources: *Federal Reserve Bank of San Francisco, Board of Governors of the Federal Reserve System, and Data Resources, Inc.*)

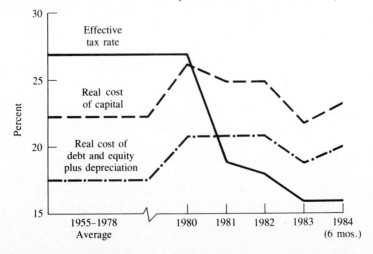

Effective tax rates on the cost of capital investment in equipment and structures have been marked by strong, but divergent, trends between 1955 and 1980. As inflation and nominal interest rates rose, the economic value of depreciation fell, raising the effective tax rate on investment in structures from 36 to 58 percent. For equipment, however, the introduction of the investment tax credit in 1962 and subsequent changes in the tax law were enough to offset the effect of higher inflation, resulting in an actual decline in the effective tax rate from 24 to 13 percent. Although the disparity in the treatment of equipment and structures became quite large, by 1980 nonresidential fixed investment as a whole was not taxed any more heavily than in earlier years. The 27 percent average effective tax rate then was actually a little lower than in 1955.

Effective tax rates on both types of investment were reduced substantially by the 1981 Tax Act, with the average effective tax rate on all nonresidential fixed investment falling from 27 to 16 percent by 1984. Other things being equal, lower tax rates reduce the effective real cost of capital and raise the optimum capital/output ratio. Such an increase in the desired capital/output ratio would then raise the level of investment spending. During the current expansion, however, other things have not been equal. In particular, the real cost of debt and equity has been pulled up by the federal government's increased demand for credit (or, equivalently, the decrease in government saving) stemming from large and growing structural budget deficits.

Real debt and equity costs were abnormally high in 1980-82, as a temporary consequence of the process of disinflation brought about by a slowing in monetary growth. Ordinarily, real debt and equity costs would have fallen back to normal levels during the 1983-84 expansion. However, due to the growing pressure on interest rates created by federal budget deficits, by the first half of 1984, real debt and equity costs were still 2.5 percentage points above the average of earlier postwar years. This kept the real cost of capital investment in structures and equipment as measured by the Hall and Jorgenson formula at 23.2 percent, compared to an average of 22.2 percent in earlier years. This measure of the cost of capital was also higher over the first six quarters of the current expansion than in previous comparable periods—at 22.3 percent versus 20.8 percent.

Thus, the effect of the tax cuts in stimulating nonresidential fixed investment has been more than offset by the upward pressure on real debt and equity costs. Because of this, the current investment boom in plant and equipment cannot be explained by incentives provided in the 1981 Tax Act.

IMPORTANCE OF OVERALL FISCAL PACKAGE

A major objective of the supply-side program was to provide tax incentives to stimulate business investment and economic growth. For such a program to work, real interest rates must not rise to such an extent that they nullify the effects of the tax incentives. Monetary policy cannot permanently alter real interest rates, so the problem lies with the overall fiscal package itself. The difficulty with current fiscal policy is that the effects of tax cuts for households have overwhelmed the incentives provided to business. Personal income tax cuts have not produced the hoped-for increase in the private saving rate, but, instead, have only increased the federal government's demand for credit (or reduced government saving) as a result of the loss in government revenues.

As a consequence, real debt and equity costs have risen by enough to offset the reduction in the cost of capital for investment in structures and equipment that would otherwise have occurred.

The evidence provides no support for the view that the current investment boom is a "supply-side miracle" produced by recent cuts in business taxes. The thrust of the overall fiscal package since 1980 has actually been counter-productive for that purpose, being "pro-consumption" rather than "pro-investment." The investment boom is better explained by other factors—particularly the availability of "high tech" investment and the obsolescence of a portion of the capital stock. Once the strength of these factors fades, as is likely, so too will the investment boom, unless the pro-consumption thrust of current fiscal policy is changed.

QUESTIONS FOR DISCUSSION

1 In this article, Throop argues that the 1981 and 1982 tax bills were not responsible for the investment boom that began in 1983. Yet, in the previous reading, Meyer showed that the tax changes lowered the cost of capital at any real interest rate. Explain why the findings of the two authors are not necessarily inconsistent.

2 In an *IS-LM* model, analyze the effects of a change in the investment tax laws which makes investment relatively more attractive, but (because of offsetting increases elsewhere) does not change the overall tax burden of the economy. Explain why, even though real interest rates rise, the overall cost of capital must fall. Where does the saving to finance the increase in investment come from?

3 Suppose that, in addition to the tax change described in question 2, there is a large cut in personal income taxes. In an *IS-LM* context, explain why the cost of capital is likely to rise overall despite the favorable changes in the taxation of investment. If investment falls (due to a higher cost of capital) and savings rise (due to higher disposable income), where do the "extra" savings generated go? Why does Throop call the overall fiscal package "pro-consumption" rather than "pro-investment"?

4 Tatom (Readings 6 and 10) views the 1981 tax cuts as largely illusory, arguing that they were offset by Social Security tax increases and "bracket creep." He believes the federal deficit is largely due to increased spending, especially on transfers. If this is the case, how does it affect Throop's argument that the overall fiscal package was pro-consumption?

5 To what factors does Throop attribute the boom in investment? Why is it important to his overall argument to be able to invoke these "autonomous" sources of increased investment?

WILL THE REAL FEDERAL DEFICIT STAND UP?

Robert Eisner*

Everybody worries about the "huge" federal deficits. But how big are the deficits, really? Northwestern University economist Robert Eisner explains how fundamental measurement issues obscure the true size of the deficit and cloud the debate.

In some circles, the federal budget deficit has become the hottest political issue since Vietnam. Democrats and Republicans echo each others' proclamations of disaster and largely restrict their differences to proposed remedies and the casting of blame. Scoring political points has replaced almost all efforts at sober economic analysis.

Deficits do matter, but to know how and how much, you have to measure them right. And deficits can be good as well as bad.

By official measure, the federal budget has been in deficit in all but eight of the fifty-five years from 1931 through 1985. In fact, in the twenty-five years since 1960 only one, 1969, had no deficit. The last sixteen years have presented an unbroken picture of deficits.

World War II saw what were then huge deficits, totaling $170 billion for the years 1942 through 1945. The total gross federal debt over that period rose by $203 billion.

From 1946 through 1984, budget deficits, net of surpluses, totaled $988 billion; including off-budget outlays, they totaled $1,112 billion. Over that period, the gross

Robert Eisner, "Will the Real Federal Deficit Stand Up?" *Challenge,* May-June 1986, pp. 13–21. Reprinted by permission of the author.

*Robert Eisner is William R. Kenan Professor of Economics, Northwestern University. This article is adapted for *Challenge* from a much longer paper presented at the Symposium and is drawn from the author's new book. *How Real Is the Federal Deficit?* (New York: The Free Press. A Division of Macmillan. Inc., May 1986).

federal public debt increased by $1,317 billion. This is a history that, at least in general terms, is well etched into the public consciousness. It has been the stuff of many sober pronouncements and warnings and has frequently agitated political debate. A number of additional items of information, however, complicate the picture and also put it in better perspective.

First, when numbers are changing rapidly over time, particularly with economic growth and inflation, it is important to put the figures in some kind of relative terms. The gross federal debt held by the public, for example, grew from $235 billion at the end of the 1945 fiscal year to $1,313 billion by the end of the 1984 fiscal year. But our national income and gross national product grew relatively more over these years. The gross federal debt held by the public was 108.4 percent of GNP at the end of fiscal 1945. Despite the very large dollar growth in that debt over the following years, it had fallen, as a percentage of GNP, to 27.8 percent by the end of the 1980 fiscal year. And with all the subsequent red ink and increase in the debt, at the end of the 1984 fiscal year the debt as a ratio of GNP had risen to only 36.7 percent, still well below the 108.4 percent figure of 1945 (and the 119.8 percent figure of 1946).

There are some analogous observations to make with regard to our annual budget deficits. They surged during the years of World War II, but then were generally modest until they rose toward the end of the Vietnam War and surged again after 1981. Over all these years federal outlays and receipts have been fluctuating—albeit growing—and GNP has increased enormously. How can we get an appropriate view of the *relative* size of the deficit?

One way to get a broader perspective is to note what has happened to the deficit as a percentage of budget outlays. We see in Table 1 that, while the proportion of federal outlays that are deficit-financed stood at a substantial 21.8 percent in fiscal 1984, this was far from a record. During the Depression fiscal year of 1932 (from July 1, 1931, through June 30, 1932), although the deficit was "only" $2.7 billion, 58.7 percent of federal outlays were deficit-financed. And during the war years that proportion soared, rising to 70 percent in 1943. In the presumably fiscally responsible administration of Dwight Eisenhower, in fiscal 1959, the ratio rose to 13.96 percent. During the peak-deficit, Vietnam fiscal year of 1968, the ratio was slightly higher, some 14.13 percent.

The size of the deficit relative to the economy as a whole may be reasonably captured by the ratio of the deficit to GNP. That ratio was also relatively high in Depression and war years, but fairly small over the rest of the period until 1982.

DEFICITS AND THE ECONOMY

But how can we measure the effects of deficits on the economy? Do they cause inflation or recession? Do they reduce unemployment or crowd out investment? Do they stifle economic growth or stimulate it? Do they increase our foreign debt and wreck our balance of trade, or do they contribute to world prosperity?

A simple, naive approach would be to relate the federal deficit to some of the broad aggregates in which we are interested. We might check the correlations among deficits

TABLE 1
FEDERAL RECEIPTS AND OUTLAYS, AND SURPLUS OR DEFICIT
AS PERCENTAGE OF OUTLAYS AND GNP, FISCAL YEARS 1929–84

Fiscal year	Receipts	Outlays†		Surplus or deficit (−)		
(1)	(2) Billions of dollars	(3) Billions of dollars	(4) Percentage of GNP	(5) Billions of dollars	(6) Percentage of outlays	(7) Percentage of GNP
1929	3.9	3.1	3.03	0.7	23.47	0.71
1932	1.9	4.7	6.96	−2.7	−58.70	−4.09
1943	23.6	78.5	44.37	−5.9	−69.89	−31.01
1945	45.2	92.7	42.71	−47.5	−51.22	−21.88
1946	39.3	55.2	27.32	−15.9	−28.73	−7.85
1959	79.2	92.1	19.41	−12.9	−13.96	−2.71
1960	92.5	92.2	18.52	0.3	0.29	0.05
1965	116.8	118.2	17.92	−1.6	−1.35	−0.24
1966	130.8	134.5	18.57	−3.8	−2.82	−0.52
1967	148.8	157.5	20.26	−8.7	−5.53	−1.12
1968	153.0	178.1	21.42	−25.2	−14.13	−3.03
1969	186.9	183.6	20.16	3.2	1.76	0.36
1970	192.8	195.6	20.19	−2.8	1.45	−0.29
1971	187.1	210.2	20.38	−23.0	−10.96	−2.23
1972	207.3	230.7	20.44	−23.4	−10.13	−2.07
1973	230.8	245.7	19.62	−14.9	−6.06	−1.19
1974	263.2	269.4	19.53	−6.1	−2.26	−0.44
1975	279.1	332.3	22.45	−53.2	−16.01	−3.59
1976	298.1	371.8	22.67	−73.7	−19.82	−4.49
1976*	81.2	96.0	22.21	−14.7	−15.31	−3.40
1977	355.6	409.2	21.97	−53.6	−13.10	−2.88
1978	399.7	458.7	21.93	−59.0	−12.86	−2.82
1979	463.3	503.5	21.36	−40.2	−7.98	−1.71
1980	517.1	590.9	22.94	−73.8	−12.49	−2.87
1981	599.3	678.2	23.50	−78.9	−11.63	−2.73
1982	617.8	745.7	24.48	−127.9	−17.15	−4.20
1983	600.6	808.3	25.09	−207.8	−25.71	−6.45
1984	666.5	851.8	23.79	−185.3	−21.75	−5.17

Note: Fiscal years until 1976 ran from July 1 of the preceding calendar year to June 30. From 1977 on, the fiscal years began on October 1.

*Transition quarter, July 1 to September 30, 1976.

†Including off-budget outlays.

Source: Economic Report of the President, February 1985, Table B-72, p. 318. U.S. Department of the Treasury, Office of Management and Budget, Bureau of Economic Analysis, and author's own calculations.

and GNP, business investment, or the rates of unemployment or inflation. The difficulty, a common one in economics, is especially serious here: we cannot distinguish between cause and effect.

The problem is that the economy affects the deficit, perhaps as much as or more than the deficit can be expected to affect the economy. When economic conditions are good, incomes, profits, and employment are high. Treasury receipts, tied as they are to individual and business income taxes and payroll taxes on employment, are hence high. Further, government expenditures for unemployment benefits and welfare payments will be less when the economy is prosperous.

The combination of higher tax receipts and lower expenditures means a lower deficit. But it is clearly the high GNP, income, profits, and employment that have caused the low deficit, and not the reverse. Since high rates of saving and investment generally accompany high GNP, incomes, and profits, they too would be associated with smaller deficits. The inference that the smaller deficits brought on the higher saving and investment would be similarly unwarranted.

The inverse relation between deficits and inflation is somewhat more complex. At first blush it might appear that inflation would have a neutral effect on the deficit. While higher prices would mean larger nominal incomes and hence greater tax payments to the Treasury, the government would also have to pay more for what it buys. If federal salaries and Social Security benefits are indexed to the cost of living, we might conclude that expenditures and receipts would both be increased by inflation and the deficit therefore not changed.

There are, however, a number of complications. First, income taxes historically have risen more, proportionately, than increases in income brought on by inflation. This has happened because of the notorious "bracket creep"—inflation has pushed more of the income into taxable brackets and into higher brackets with higher tax rates.

While indexing of exemptions and tax brackets to the price level has not essentially ended that contribution of inflation to a more-than-proportional enhancing of individual income-tax payments, the effect of inflation in bringing more-than-proportional increases in business tax payments remains. This stems from the failure of original-cost depreciation deductions to rise with inflation, as well as from swollen inventory profits of firms that use FIFO ("first-in, first-out") accounting. This occurs because revenues reflect current higher prices, while accounting costs of materials and fixed capital are based on the lower prices of bygone days.

Inflation also brings about more-than-proportionate increases on the expenditure side. These stem from the higher interest rates and hence greater Treasury interest payments as inflation expectations take hold.

In the past, bracket-creep effects of higher prices were such that inflation tended on balance to reduce deficits. But such an association of higher inflation and lower deficits does *not* imply the inverse relation—that deficits reduce inflation.

Actual budget deficits are therefore not a good measure of fiscal policy. The administration and the Congress might be following a tight fiscal policy, keeping discretionary expenditures down and tax rates up, and yet a recession would create a substantial deficit. Indeed the tight fiscal policy, by depressing aggregate demand, might bring on such a recession.

THE HIGH-EMPLOYMENT BUDGET

To ascertain what deficits do to the economy, we need a measure that is uncontaminated by what the economy does to deficits. Economists have been able to develop one that removes some of the contamination—brought on by cyclical fluctuations in income and employment. It has been variously called the full-employment, high-employment, standardized-employment, cyclically adjusted, and structural budget.

Whatever its name, the important thing about this budget is that it presents estimates of what expenditures and receipts, and hence the deficit, *would be* if the economy were at a level of activity independent of cyclical variations in employment, output, and income. Since the cyclical variations in output and income are closely associated with those of employment and unemployment, the budget has usually been defined for a constant rate of unemployment.

Beginning in 1955, the Bureau of Economic Analysis of the Department of Commerce constructed a series of high-employment budget surpluses and deficits. "High" employment was initially taken to mean 4 percent unemployment, but that figure was subsequently raised, apparently on the assumption that structural or demographic change in the economy was increasing the amount of unemployment—unfortunately often called the "natural" rate of employment—which should be accepted as consistent with high employment. It was argued, particularly, that the population contained increasing proportions of youths and urban blacks, with high rates of even noncyclical unemployment, and these increasing proportions were forcing up the national average of unemployment which was attainable.

The comparison of actual and high-employment budgets is intriguing. From 1955 to 1965, as shown in Table 2, the actual budget was in deficit five times and in surplus six. The high-employment budget was never in deficit. When the actual budget was in surplus, the high-employment budget was more so. All this reflected the fact that actual unemployment was more than the high-employment rate over this period. Hence, actual tax revenues were less while government expenditures were more.

From 1966 to 1969, with the boom aggregate demand produced by the Vietnam War, actual unemployment was less than the 4 percent rate associated with high employment. (That is an interesting commentary on our view of "high employment" even then. Quite ignoring the Humphrey-Hawkins Full Employment and Balanced Growth Act, we now cheerfully project unemployment in the 6 and 7 percent range.) The low unemployment of those years caused the three actual deficits to be *less* than the deficit associated with high employment and the 1969 surplus to be greater.

The 1970s ushered in the era of unrelenting federal deficits. For none of the last sixteen years has the budget been balanced, let alone in surplus. Those who saw deficits as evidence of unbridled government spending contributing to inflation seemed to have some support for their views. Inflation rose through most of the decade of the seventies, peaking in 1981. But then, as deficits soared to unprecedented heights in 1982, inflation rates dropped precipitously.

TABLE 2
ACTUAL AND HIGH EMPLOYMENT FEDERAL BUDGET SURPLUSES AND DEFICITS ON
NATIONAL INCOME ACCOUNT, 1955–84

Year	Actual	High-employment	Actual	High-employment
	Billions of dollars		Percentage of GNP	
(1)	(2)	(3)	(4)	(5)
1955	4.4	5.2	1.10	1.30
1956	6.1	7.9	1.44	1.87
1957	2.3	6.1	0.51	1.37
1958	− 10.3	0.0	− 2.28	0.00
1959	− 1.1	5.4	− 0.23	1.11
1960	3.0	12.1	0.60	2.39
1961	− 3.9	7.1	− 0.74	1.35
1962	− 4.2	3.0	− 0.75	0.53
1963	0.3	7.4	0.04	1.24
1964	− 3.3	1.1	− 0.51	0.17
1965	0.5	0.9	0.08	0.13
1966	− 1.8	− 5.6	− 0.24	− 0.74
1967	− 13.2	− 15.1	− 1.65	− 1.89
1968	− 6.0	− 11.0	− 0.69	− 1.26
1969	8.4	4.9	0.89	0.52
1970	− 12.4	− 4.6	− 1.25	− 0.46
1971	− 22.0	− 11.3	− 2.04	− 1.05
1972	− 16.8	− 12.1	− 1.42	− 1.02
1973	− 5.5	− 9.5	− 0.42	− 0.72
1974	− 11.5	− 0.3	− 0.80	− 0.02
1975	− 69.3	− 29.1	− 4.47	− 1.88
1976	− 53.1	− 17.4	− 3.09	− 1.01
1977	− 45.9	− 20.4	− 2.39	− 1.06
1978	− 29.5	− 15.9	− 1.36	− 0.73
1979	− 16.1	− 2.0	− 0.67	− 0.08
1980	− 61.2	− 17.1	− 2.33	− 0.65
1981	− 64.3	− 3.2	− 2.17	− 0.11
1982	− 148.2	− 32.6	− 4.83	− 1.06
1983	− 178.6	− 57.0	− 5.40	− 1.72
1984	− 175.8	− 91.8	− 4.80	− 2.51

Sources: Frank de Leeuw and Thomas M. Holloway, "The High Employment Budget: Revised Estimates and Automatic Inflation Effects," *Survey of Current Business,* 62 (April 1982), pp. 21–33, subsequent issues of the *Survey of Current Business,* and author's adjustments to maintain a 5.1 percent base for "high employment" in 1983 and 1984. These last estimates have been revised downward somewhat from those published in *How Real Is the Federal Deficit?*

The deficits were widely interpreted, nevertheless, as evidence of expansionist fiscal policy. Richard Nixon had said in 1972, "We are all Keynesians now." If the Keynesian analysis, which had presumably come to dominate policymaking, were correct, should not unemployment have been low and the economy sizzling? In fact, unemployment was inching up and the economy was sluggish. What was wrong?

One try at an answer was that it was the actual budget that was showing the repeated and generally growing deficits. As we have observed, these deficits may have been essentially the product of poor economic conditions, rather than their cause. We may point, for example, to the then-record deficit of $69 billion in 1975. Clearly that was largely the result of the sharp 1974–75 recession. Unemployment, after all, averaged 8.5 percent in 1975. If we had looked at the high-employment budget might we have had a different picture?

But now comes the shocker. The high-employment budget deficit was less than the actual deficit throughout the 1970s and into the 1980s, but it too was never quite balanced, coming close only in 1974. Indeed, in 1975 the high-employment deficits seemed generally to be getting larger, not smaller.

It might be said that with growth in the economy and inflation everything was getting larger. The deficit figures would be more comparable over time if they were adjusted for this growth. A simple way to do this is to present the deficit figures as percentages of GNP. As we can also see in Table 2, however, this does not change the basic picture. Actual deficits as a percentage of GNP set post-World War II records. Even high-employment budgets showed an unmistakable trend to deficit.

At least until the Vietnam War, the high-employment budget was never in deficit and was usually substantially in surplus. By 1966, however, the high-employment budget moved to deficit, and stayed in deficit, with the solitary exception of the tax-surcharge year of 1969. It would thus appear that the original charge that fiscal policy had been overly expansive is supported—or at least not contradicted—by the history of the high-employment budget deficit.

DEFICITS ADJUSTED FOR INFLATION

We come now to our critical departure. We must adjust deficits for inflation. The real surplus or deficit may be viewed as essentially the sum of three components: (1) the nominal surplus or deficit as currently measured; (2) an adjustment for changes in the market value of government financial assets and liabilities due to changes in interest rates; and (3) an adjustment for changes in real value due to changing general price levels incident to inflation. An identical or analogous set of adjustments is appropriate for the high-employment budget surplus or deficit.

We can then calculate the adjusted high-employment budgets, which, by correcting for these inflation effects, come closer to measuring real surpluses or deficits and the consequent thrust of fiscal policy on aggregate demand. Applying our calculations of net revaluations on actual net federal debt, we originally adjusted the official high-employment budget surplus series for the years 1955 through 1981. Maintaining the 5.1 percent unemployment benchmark for high employment in effect in the official series since 1975, we have now extended our calculations to 1984.

TABLE 3
HIGH-EMPLOYMENT SURPLUS AS PERCENTAGE OF GNP, 1955–84

Year	Official	Adjusted for price effects	Adjusted for interest effects	Adjusted for price and interest effects	Percent change in GNP
		Percentage of GNP			
(1)	(2)	(3)	(4)	(5)	(6)
1955	1.30	2.81	2.26	3.77	6.72
1956	1.87	3.83	2.79	4.74	2.14
1957	1.37	2.46	0.11	1.20	1.82
1958	0.00	0.93	1.32	2.24	−0.42
1959	1.11	2.09	1.96	2.94	5.99
1960	2.39	2.83	0.45	0.89	2.15
1961	1.35	1.99	1.81	2.45	2.63
1962	0.53	1.28	0.12	0.87	5.78
1963	1.24	1.79	1.70	2.25	4.02
1964	0.17	0.78	0.12	0.72	5.27
1965	0.13	0.98	0.58	1.43	6.04
1966	−0.74	0.33	−0.97	0.11	5.97
1967	−1.89	−0.89	−1.33	−0.34	2.70
1968	−1.26	0.06	−1.14	0.18	4.62
1969	0.52	1.94	1.32	2.74	2.79
1970	−0.46	0.77	−1.87	−0.64	−0.18
1971	−1.05	0.11	−1.41	−0.25	3.39
1972	−1.02	0.02	−0.66	0.39	5.66
1973	−0.72	0.89	−0.46	1.14	5.77
1974	−0.02	2.15	−0.16	2.01	−0.64
1975	−1.88	−0.38	−2.04	−0.54	−1.18
1976	−1.01	0.22	−1.75	−0.52	5.41
1977	−1.06	0.46	−0.23	1.30	5.51
1978	−0.73	1.26	0.15	2.15	5.03
1979	−0.08	1.72	0.11	1.91	2.84
1980	−0.65	1.45	−0.13	1.97	−0.30
1981	−0.11	1.57	−0.23	1.45	2.52
1982	−1.06	0.02	−3.10	−2.01	−2.13
1983	−1.72	−1.66	−0.44	−0.62	3.70
1984	−2.51	−1.36	−3.07	−1.92	6.78

Note: Surplus or deficit (−) on national-income-accounts basis.
Source: Frank de Leeuw and Thomas M. Holloway, "The High Employment Budget: Revised Estimates and Automatic Inflation Effects," *Survey of Current Business,* 62 (April 1982), pp. 21–33, subsequent issues of the *Survey of Current Business, Economic Report of the President, February 1985,* author's adjustments to maintain a 5.1 percent base for "high employment" in 1983 and 1984, and author's calculations explained in *How Real Is the Federal Deficit?* with deficit figures for 1983 and 1984 revised downward from those published there.

The results, shown in Table 3, are dramatic. Inflation and rates of interest were low and relatively steady in the early 1960s prior to escalation of our military involvement in Vietnam. Corrections to the official high-employment budget surplus are hence generally small in those early years.

But in later, more inflationary years, when the official high-employment budget as well as the actual budget moved substantially into deficit, the corrections are striking. In the 1970s, the entire perceived trend in the direction of fiscal ease or expansion is eliminated or reversed. The high-employment budget surplus, fully adjusted for price and interest effects, was higher as a percent of GNP for every year from 1977 through 1981 than the surplus of all but two of the years from 1966 through 1976. The only exceptions were the tax-surcharge year of 1969 and the oil-price-shock year of 1974.

With similar exceptions, the surplus adjusted only for price (and not interest) effects was higher in every year from 1978 to 1981 than in any other year back to 1963. And since we have accepted Bureau of Economic Analysis increases in the "high-employment" bench mark from 4.0 percent to 5.1 percent unemployment over the period of its "official" series, we may well understate the move to fiscal tightness. The high-employment surpluses would have been even greater in later years if calculated at 4.0 percent unemployment.

NEW LIGHT ON ECONOMIC HISTORY

So some significant rewriting of recent economic history is in order. Inflation could hardly be ascribed to excess demand associated with increasing fiscal ease and stimulus if, at least by the appropriately corrected high-employment budget measure, there was no such movement to fiscal ease. Some explanation of sluggishness in the economy, climaxed by the severe 1981–82 recession, might then be found in a relatively tight fiscal policy, as measured by the adjusted high-employment budget surplus, as well as in the widely blamed (or credited) role of monetary policy.

The record of deficits beginning in 1982 is another matter. We shall come to that later. For now we want to show the relation of budget deficits to the economy. And we will find that prevailing views reflect the distortions of improper measures, the most important of which, again, are those tricks played by the effects of inflation.

A few charts can begin to set the record straight and tell a dramatic new story. First, Figure 1 shows the widening gap between official and price-adjusted high-employment budget surpluses or deficits as inflation began to heat up in the late 1960s. The two measures moved up and down in broadly similar fashion. But by the mid-1970s the inflation-adjusted budget were some 1.5 to 2 percentage points more in surplus or less in deficit than the unadjusted, official high-employment budgets.

What about the relation between budget deficits and the economy? A single picture may be worth a thousand words, or as many statistics. Figure 2 juxtaposes the percentage change in real GNP and the previous year's price-adjusted high-employment deficit as a percentage of real GNP.

The two curves, it must be conceded, show a remarkable fit. The greater the deficit, the greater the next year's increase in GNP. The less the deficit, the less the increase or the greater the decline in the next year's GNP.

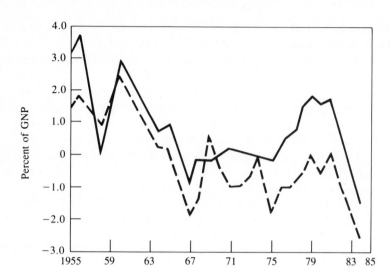

- - Official high-employment budget surplus

—— Price-adjusted high-employment budget surplus

FIGURE 1
Official and Price-Adjusted High-Employment Budget Surplus.

FIGURE 2
Lagged Price-Adjusted High-Employment Deficit and Change in GNP.

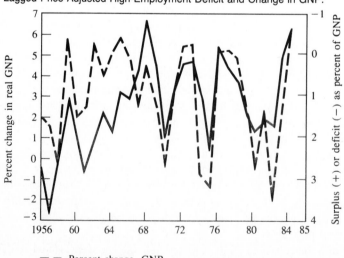

- - Percent change, GNP

—— Price-adjusted high-employment deficit

Changes in real GNP, as is well known, are closely but inversely related to changes in unemployment. Production requires labor, and the more people working the greater the output. When unemployment goes up, real GNP growth slackens or actually becomes negative. When unemployment goes down, GNP goes up. And the faster unemployment goes down, the faster GNP rises.

In view of the relation between the deficit and GNP, we should thus expect a similar close, but inverse, relation between the deficit and changes in unemployment. Figure 3 confirms this. Converting the inverse relation with the deficit into a direct one, it plots the percentage-point change in unemployment and the *previous* year's ratio of the price-adjusted high-employment *surplus* (the negative of the deficit).

The close fit of the two curves is again outstanding. Higher surpluses—or lower deficits—are associated with greater increases or smaller decreases in unemployment.

This relation indicating the stimulative effect of budget deficits has held up under a substantial amount of more vigorous statistical analysis, reported in my new book, *How Real Is the Federal Deficit?* That analysis indicates that monetary policy, as measured by changes in the monetary base, also affects rates of growth of gross national product and unemployment. The independent effect of budget deficits remains substantial, however, probably greater (when the deficit is adjusted for inflation) than effects of changes in the monetary base.

Budget deficits are found to be positively associated not only with increases in consumption but also with increases in investment. Deficits in the past have generally "crowded in" investment, not crowded it out. There is evidence as well, however, that budget deficits have contributed to the increase in our trade deficit, particularly

FIGURE 3
Lagged Price-Adjusted High-Employment Surplus and
Change in Unemployment.

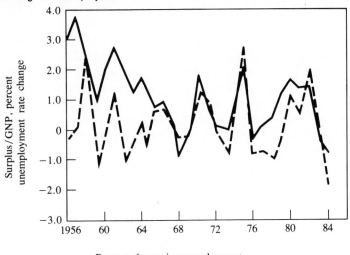

- - Percent change in unemployment

—— Price-adjusted high-employment surplus

in their association with substantial increases in imports. It should be added that these increases in our imports have in turn stimulated growth in output in our OECD partners. And it may be added, finally, that, after adjustment for inflation, it turns out that Japan had the greatest deficits in recent years along with the fastest growth. And the very slow-growing United Kingdom had substantial budget surpluses after inflation adjustment.

THE IMPACT OF THE DEFICIT

Where does all this leave us? The officially reported federal debt has been growing at astronomical rates. Since President Reagan took office in 1981 the gross public debt has more than doubled, from $930 billion to $1.9 trillion. The increase has reflected huge and repeated annual deficits, reaching $212 billion in fiscal 1985.

But this has not been all bad! Indeed, given the economic collapse of 1981-82, smaller deficits would have made the deep recession worse. Unemployment would have risen above the official 10.7 percent figure, which was already the highest since the Great Depression of the 1930s. Total production and business profits would have been less. Without the huge deficits, we would not have had the brisk recovery of 1983 and 1984. And the 1984 election results—for good or for ill—might well have been quite different.

Up to about 1966, when inflation was relatively minor, budget deficits were really budget deficits. In the period from 1966 on, however, when inflation became substantial, the officially balanced budget turned into one of surplus after inflation corrections were made. A balanced, inflation-adjusted, high-employment budget would have been substantially expansionary, producing high rates of growth of GNP and declines in unemployment. As late as 1981, however, we had a roughly balanced *official* high-employment budget, while the budget adjusted for inflation was substantially in surplus.

The Carter administration, which, along with most outside critics, ignored indications of sluggishness in the economy, interpreted the combination of apparent deficits and inflation as indicating excess demand. It initiated moves to combat inflation by encouraging a tight-money policy and, in its final years, striving to reduce budget deficits. This policy continued through the first year of the Reagan administration, as domestic spending was further restrained and more taxes rose than declined.

But in fact, fiscal policy was not stimulative. The high inflation and rising interest rates meant that budgets seemingly in deficit were actually in substantial surplus. Our statistical relations indicate strongly that these inflation-adjusted surpluses contributed significantly to the 1981-83 recession.

This suggests two important correctives to widespread views of fiscal and monetary policy. First, the 1981-83 recession cannot properly be interpreted as a triumph of all-powerful monetary constraints over relatively ineffective fiscal ease. Tight monetary policy *and* tight fiscal policy were its proximate causes.

Thus, those who acquiesced in tight money as the only way to slow a presumedly overheated, inflationary economy were wrong on two counts. First, the inflation had come from supply shocks—with critical energy prices up some 500 percent in a decade—rather than excess demand, an inference reinforced by the absence of real increases in fiscal thrust. And second, strong-willed rejection of accommodative monetary policy, rather than balancing budget excesses, offered a near-lethal combination of monetary and fiscal contraction.

But fiscal policy moved in a sharply different direction in 1982. A combination of major tax cuts and increases in military expenditures with a fall in inflation and interest rates converted the adjusted high-employment budget from a very high surplus to a very high deficit. Indeed, the change of 3.46 percentage points, from a surplus of 1.45 percent of GNP in 1981 to a deficit of 2.01 percent in 1982, was one of the greatest such swings to expansion on record. Our estimate of relations between budget deficits and changes in GNP and unemployment predicted a major swing to economic recovery and lower unemployment in 1983 and on into 1984, and that is of course precisely what occurred.

Prior to both the fiscal 1986 Congressional Budget Resolution and the Gramm-Rudman program to "balance the budget" by 1991, Congressional Budget Office estimates indicated very large and increasing deficits in the years ahead. August 1985 projections of the official high-employment ("standardized-employment") budget, reduced to a 5.1 percent unemployment rate, showed a deficit of $185 billion by 1990. This corresponds to an actual projected deficit in the national income accounts of $258 billion for that year.

Adjustment for price effects, however, brings the high-employment deficit down substantially, to $29 billion in 1986, but shows it rising to $79 billion by 1990. The price- and interest-adjusted deficit in 1990 is projected at $76 billion. We thus had projections of substantial high-employment deficits over the rest of this decade. The adjustments for anticipated inflation reduced those projected deficits, but still left them high. The projected adjusted deficits, therefore, while initially less than their 1982–84 peaks, were substantial, and turning higher.

Indeed, make no mistake about it. From a historical perspective, these deficits are enormous. From 1986 to 1990 they would average 2.15 percent of GNP, while up to 1982 the largest inflation-adjusted deficit we had ever had, in any year since the high-employment series began in 1955, was 0.64 percent. From 1955 to 1981, the adjusted high-employment budget was, on average, in *surplus* by 1.35 percent of GNP.

Deficits this large, according to my analysis—and probably those of any major econometric model—imply considerable excess demand. Unchecked, they would be pushing the economy toward rates of growth of GNP and declines of unemployment— the latter to negative figures!—that are clearly unattainable.

Initially, however, it should be recognized that the large deficits would be expected to contribute to a reduction of our 7 percent overall unemployment rate. Once unemployment is driven as low as possible with aggregative measures, further fiscal stimulus would generate inflation. The Federal Reserve would then be expected to tighten the money supply, and interest rates, both nominal and real, would rise.

The curious consequence is that associated declining real market values of the public holdings of government debt would mean that the *real* federal deficit would be reduced. It would have been reduced, however, by an inflation tax rather than explicit tax increases or reductions in government expenditures.

The deficit reductions envisaged in the Congressional Budget Resolution for fiscal 1986 were in fact substantial. With adjustment for inflation, the high-employment budget, calculated at an unemployment rate of 5.1 percent, would be brought into balance in 1986 and would be in some surplus in subsequent years. While none of this can be predicted with great accuracy or confidence, it would appear that such a path for the high-employment budget, and the associated relatively moderate actual budget deficits that it implies, would be consistent with relatively low unemployment and reasonably noninflationary economic growth.

The Gramm-Rudman program, on the other hand, envisages very drastic deficit reduction from 1987 on. By bringing the actual budget to balance by 1991, it would create a surplus in the official high-employment budget and, most important, very substantial surpluses in the high-employment budget adjusted to include the inflation tax. Gramm-Rudman would, in a real sense, give us high-employment budget surpluses, when adjusted for inflation, comparable to those that have usually been associated in the past with a sluggish economy or sharp recessions.

A NEW LOOK AT DEFICITS

Once we get over the notion that deficits are automatically sinful, and once we learn to measure them right, a lot of the easy answers have to be rejected. It is not true that deficits must always be reduced. The current mix of fiscal and monetary policy, with high real interest rates and a huge trade imbalance accountable to an expensive dollar, is far from ideal. Our budget priorities may be all wrong. But it is hard to sustain the knee-jerk reaction that wiping out all the overall official deficit will solve our problems.

The public has feared that budget deficits add to their own debt burden and that of future generations. What we really bequeath to the future, however, is our physical and human capital. A "deficit" that finances the construction and maintenance of our roads, bridges, harbors, and airports is an investment in the future. So are expenditures to preserve and enhance our natural resources or to educate our people and keep them healthy. Federal budgets that are balanced by running down our country's capital or mindlessly selling public assets to private exploiters are real national deficits.

As for that bottom line on what to do about the current federal deficit—it depends. If we were to carry out the projections of the fiscal 1986 Joint Congressional Budget Resolution, and we are seriously committed to a high-employment economy, we would probably have gone far enough in overall budget cutting. The increase in debt for the last five years has been such that even our slower rate of inflation generates a substantial inflation tax. The inflation tax rate is less, but the public debt on which it is paid is more.

Inflation-adjusted budget deficits, on the basis of the budget resolution projections, did not promise to be unduly large. For those who prize economic growth and low unemployment, the risk of insufficient fiscal stimulus must be weighted heavily. One cannot properly counsel budget-balancing in an economy with unemployment still at 7 percent and real economic growth well below its potential. A budget balanced by current federal rules of accounting is an invitation to the worst economic downturn in half a century.

The budget mix is another matter. We may wish to spend more on investment in our public infrastructure and human capital and less on subsidies and support to those with the most political clout. We may also wish to devote more to our nation's welfare and less to warfare. And we may wish to finance our expenditures with a more equitable tax system.

With a sound and balanced fiscal policy, we should look all the more to a monetary policy that permits the economy to move at full speed. No artificial shortage of money should be allowed to drag down private investment or so distort the value of the dollar as to cripple the significant sectors of the American economy that do and should compete in world markets.

A competitive, market-oriented economy is capable of stunning successes. But there remains a major role for government policy to ensure the aggregate demand necessary for full employment and maximum growth. With correct measures, the macroeconomic theory of the past half century can continue to show the way.

QUESTIONS FOR DISCUSSION

1 The gross federal debt has risen sharply in dollar terms since World War II; yet today it is a much smaller percentage of GNP than it was in 1945. Explain how this can occur, being sure to include in your analysis (*a*) economic growth and (*b*) the effects of inflation on the value of outstanding government debt.

2 In order to measure the effects of deficits, we might simply check the correlation of the official deficit with some key economic variables. Why does the author argue that this is not a good approach? Specifically, why would the correlations of official deficits with (*a*) GNP and (*b*) interest rates not provide good measures of the effects of fiscal policy on those variables? How does the use of the "full-employment deficit" help solve this problem?

3 Eisner's main departure from the standard practice is to adjust the budget deficit for inflation. One of his principal adjustments is illustrated by the following example:

	Economy A	Economy B
Government spending less interest	100	100
Initial debt	1,000	1,000
Inflation rate	0	0.10
Interest rate	0.02	0.12
Taxes	120	120

Economy A and economy B are identical, except that economy B has 10 percent more inflation and therefore (assuming real interest rates are 2 percent in both economies) a 10 percent higher nominal interest rate than economy A. It is assumed that the initial price levels of A and B are identical.

a What are government interest payments in the two economies? What is the official government deficit in each of the two economies?

b Show that the real value of outstanding government debt at the end of the fiscal year is the same in both economies, so that the difference in official deficits does not reflect any real difference in the governments' net debt positions.

    c Show that, if one counts only *real* interest payments (not total interest payments) in the deficit, then A's and B's deficits are the same. (This is essentially the correction used by Eisner.)

    d In periods of high inflation, do official deficit measures tend to understate or overstate the "true" value of the deficit?

4 How does the author's adjusted deficit measure lead him to reinterpret the macroeconomic effects of fiscal policy during Reagan's first term? How do they lead him to view the probable effects of the Gramm-Rudman attempt to balance the budget (in *official* deficit terms) by 1991?

A PERSPECTIVE
ON THE FEDERAL
DEFICIT PROBLEM

John A. Tatom*

None of us really understands what's going on with all these numbers.

David Stockman,
Atlantic Monthly,
December 1981

Large federal budget deficits are, or at least are perceived to be, a major problem for macroeconomic policy makers. Below, John Tatom of the St. Louis Fed offers a breakdown of why the deficit grew. He concludes that a number of factors have contributed to the increase in deficits; and that the "cyclical" deficits of the early 1980s are being transformed into "structural" deficits as the decade progresses.

Federal budget deficits of $200 billion or more have created considerable controversy and confusion among analysts, policymakers and voters. The important problem, of course, concerns the consequences of current and projected spending, receipts and deficits. Public concern about these problems began, however, with the ballooning of deficits in 1982 and 1983.

Many analysts conjecture that recent and projected large deficits have deleterious effects on the economy—raising interest rates, exchange rates, the inflation rate, crowding out private sector investment and economic growth and threatening the

John A. Tatom, "A Perspective on the Federal Deficit Problem," *Review,* St. Louis Federal Reserve Bank, June-July 1984, pp. 5–16.
*John A. Tatom is a research officer at the Federal Reserve Bank of St. Louis. Thomas H. Gregory provided research assistance.

economic recovery. Others are more sanguine, arguing instead that recent deficits have not significantly affected interest rates, exchange rates or price behavior.[1]

The purpose of this article is to assess these contrasting views on the causes and consequences of recent and prospective deficits. Most of the controversy arises from differences in theoretical and empirical judgments about the effects of deficits on the demand for goods and services. After examining these relevant conceptual issues, recent trends in the federal budget are taken up. Then these conceptual distinctions are used to clarify the source and potential economic effects of recent and projected deficits.

In the view of many analysts, both current deficits and future projections indicate a major break with the U.S. postwar experience. It is suggested below that this view is unwarranted when applied to recent deficits. While recent deficits have been large compared with earlier ones, they have arisen largely from the unusual cyclical experience in the U.S. economy, not from unprecedented fiscal policy actions that raised spending and/or reduced tax receipts. Future deficits, however, may represent a major break from the current and past experience. If so, past relationships between deficits and economic performance may prove to be of little use in judging their likely effects.

THE THEORY OF ACTIVE AND PASSIVE DEFICITS

The federal budget deficit is the excess of federal government expenditures over receipts. In analyzing the sources of the deficit and its effect on the economy, it is necessary to distinguish between "active" and "passive" components of the deficit. Spending, taxes, and, therefore, the actual deficit are affected by both direct policy actions and changes in the level of economic activity, prices and interest rates. The latter changes occur passively, that is, without fiscal policy actions. Active deficits, in contrast, are those that arise from legislated changes in spending or taxes, *given* the other economic conditions that influence the deficit.

One attempt to deal with this difference is the measurement of the so-called high-employment budget. It involves measuring expenditures and tax receipts at a high-employment level of real GNP, given actual prices and interest rates. This measure is useful because it removes that part of the actual deficit that arises from passive adjustment to cyclical fluctuations in real GNP.

For example, as real income expands, tax receipts rise and spending (primarily transfer payments) declines, so that the actual deficit shrinks. This decrease (or increase when real incomes fall) reflects *automatic* movements that are built-in to existing tax and spending legislation. This automatic response of the deficit to economic conditions is referred to as a change in the passive deficit. In contrast, legislated increases in spending or tax reductions raise the actual deficit at any level of GNP and produce a change in the active deficit. At each point in time, the observed deficit reflects both an active component—the size of the deficit at, for example, a high-employment level of real output—and a passive component—the part due to the business cycle.

---

[1]An example of the latter argument is the study by the U.S. Department of the Treasury (1984). There does appear to be general agreement about the possibility that deficits can be "monetized," that is, financed by money creation. To the extent this occurs, inflation would accelerate.

Conventional economic analysis, which forms the basis for much of the current popular discussion, focuses on the effects of a higher active deficit that arises from either a discretionary increase in federal expenditures or a cut in taxes. The conventional wisdom indicates that an increase in the active deficit causes spending on goods and services to rise. A federal purchase of goods or services directly raises total aggregate spending; increased transfer payments or tax reductions allow greater spending in the private sector. Thus, a change in the active deficit is important because it affects the level of real GNP.

At its simplest level, the conventional analysis indicates that, if the money stock is unaltered, interest rates will rise along with real GNP. At higher levels of spending and income, the demand for money will be higher. Thus, in this view, interest rates must go up to ration the available money stock. Of course, a rise in rates tends to choke off some of the expansion in spending and income that results from an increase in the active deficit. This latter effect is called "crowding-out" because the rise in interest rates discourages (crowds out) private investment and consumer purchases.

If income and spending rise as a result of an increase in the active deficit, prices are likely to rise as well. At unchanged prices, the higher level of demand for real output is unlikely to be produced. To induce suppliers to produce more output, the general level of prices will have to be bid up. A higher level of prices induces more crowding out, since it causes a reduction in the supply of purchasing power available from a given nominal money stock relative to the demand for it. Thus, interest rates rise further and more private spending is crowded out.

In summary, a simple version of conventional theory states that a rise in the active deficit raises not only the level of output and employment, but prices and interest rates as well. Crowding-out of private investment occurs, slowing the growth rate of economic capacity.

A rise in the passive deficit, in contrast, reflects a cyclical decline in real GNP and employment. Passive deficit increases do not exert an independent effect on economic activity.[2] Moreover, such deficit increases in the simple conventional analysis, are typically associated with a decline in interest rates and/or prices, since cyclical declines in real GNP reflect declining demand for goods and services and credit.

There are many linkages in the results above that are open to question. Mainstream macroeconomic conclusions depend heavily on alternative hypotheses about the sensitivity of investment, consumer spending, money demand and aggregate supply to interest rate and price level fluctuations. Depending on these assumptions, considerably different conclusions about the effects of an increase in the active deficit can emerge.

Central to the conventional analysis is the conclusion that an increase in the active deficit raises the demand for goods and services at unchanged prices and interest rates. Even this result is, in principle, problematic. Some analysts emphasize that the demand for goods and services is *not* raised by an increase in the active deficit. Federal spending, they point out, must be financed—if not in the present, then in the future. Thus, households will tend to discount the increased *future* tax liability that arises from an

[2]Movements in the passive deficit are endogenous with respect to movements in real GNP, while active deficits are not. A rise in the passive deficit, when real GNP falls, may reduce the extent of the real GNP decline itself and the interest rate decline as well. Those adjustments, however, are endogenous because they are built-in to the structure of the economy.

Seasonally adjusted

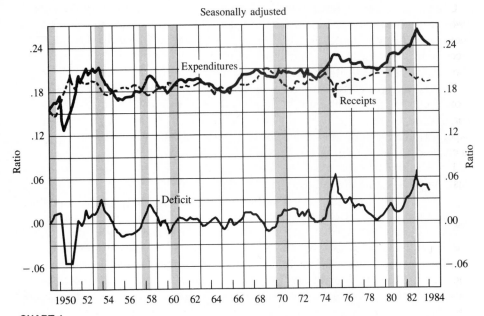

CHART 1
Federal Government Budget as a Share of GNP. Shaded areas represent periods of business recessions. Latest data plotted: 1st quarter. (Source: *National Income and Product Accounts.*)

increase in the active deficit. In effect, households match the increased deficit by an equivalent increase in personal saving (or cut in consumption). Thus, total spending, given interest rates and prices, does not rise.[3]

If such discounting of future taxes occurs, the conventional conclusions about the effects of active deficits fail to hold, except for those concerning crowding-out, capital formation and economic growth. Others have noted the theoretical ambiguity of mainstream theory in this regard.[4] Thus, while the channels of influence of a change in the deficit are clear, especially the importance of the active-passive distinction, the assessment of the effects of a rise in the active deficit remains essentially an empirical question.

RECENT BUDGET TRENDS

The federal budget deficit soared to $147 billion (National Income Account, NIA, basis) in calendar year 1982, then rose to about $183 billion in 1983. Projections for the next several years range from a slight decline to a near doubling by the end of the decade. It is useful to compare the budget developments of the past two years with past trends to gain some understanding of how the deficit became so large.

---

[3]This result is referred to as the Ricardian Equivalence Theorem. See Barro (1974, 1978), as well as Buchanan and Wagner (1977).
[4]See, especially, the recent analysis by the U.S. Department of the Treasury.

Chart 1 shows the growth of federal spending and receipts as shares of GNP from 1948 to 1983. The deficit, the difference between expenditures and receipts, also is shown as a share of GNP. In the fourth quarter of 1982, the deficit reached a peacetime record 6.7 percent of GNP. While this proportion subsequently declined, it remained above 5 percent through 1983.

The surge in the deficit is associated with an acceleration in federal expenditure growth and a decline in receipts growth, when both are measured relative to GNP. For example, from 1980 to 1983, when GNP grew at a 7.9 percent annual rate, expenditures grew at an 11.1 percent rate and federal receipts rose at only a 6.0 percent rate. As a result, expenditures rose from 22.9 percent of GNP in 1980 to 25.0 percent in 1983, and the share of receipts fell from 20.6 percent to 19.5 percent. Thus, over this time interval, the deficit widened from 2.3 percent to 5.5 percent of GNP.

The Growth of Federal Expenditures

The sharp surge upward in federal expenditures as a share of GNP is shown again in chart 2, where expenditures are broken into two major categories: the purchase of goods and services and transfer payments (including transfers to persons, state and local governments, net interest on the federal debt and subsidies to government enterprises). From 1967 to 1979, the share of expenditures in GNP rose little (except

CHART 2
Federal Government Expenditures as a Share of GNP. Shaded areas represent periods of business recessions. Latest data plotted: 1st quarter. (Source: *National Income and Product Accounts.*)

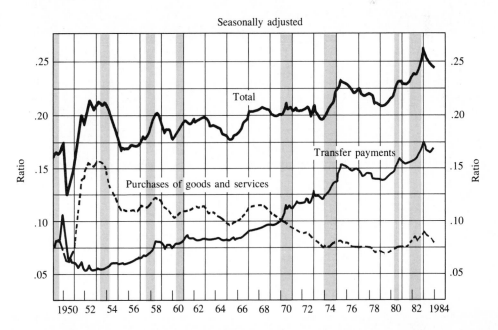

for a temporary spurt in 1975), with the surge in transfer payments almost offset by the decline in purchases of goods and services. Since 1979, however, both components of federal expenditures have risen relative to GNP. Purchases of goods and services rose from 7.0 percent to 8.3 percent of GNP from 1979 to 1983, while transfer payments continued their previous trend of rising faster than GNP, increasing from 14.1 percent to 16.6 percent of GNP.

The pattern of federal purchases of goods and services closely mirrors that of national defense expenditures (not shown), since the remainder, non-defense purchases, has remained about 2 percent to 3 percent of GNP since the early 1960s. National defense purchases, after declining from 1968 to 1979, rose from 4.6 percent of GNP in 1979 to 6.0 percent in 1983. This rise accounts for all of the rise in the share of purchases in GNP, but only 36 percent of the increase in the share of expenditures in GNP and an even smaller percentage of the increase in the deficit measured relative to GNP.

Federal Receipts as a Share of GNP

The share of federal receipts in GNP is shown in chart 3 along with its major components: personal tax and non-tax receipts, social security contributions and corporate income taxes. From 1979 to 1983, the share of social security taxes in GNP continued

CHART 3
Federal Government Receipts as a Share of GNP. Latest data plotted: 1st quarter. (Source: *National Income and Product Accounts.*)

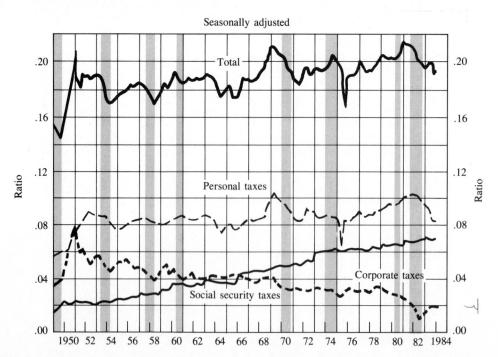

its upward climb, rising from 6.6 percent to 7.1 percent. This increase largely offset the decline in the share of personal taxes from 9.5 percent to 8.9 percent over the same period. Corporate taxes declined from 3.1 percent to 1.8 percent of GNP from 1979 to 1983, a decline that reflected an actual decline in such receipts from $74.2 billion to $59.3 billion. In large part, this was due to a similar percentage decline in corporate profits from $252.7 billion in 1979 to about $207.6 billion in 1983.

The Sources of Recent Deficits

It appears that the recent ballooning of federal deficits has been associated with a combination of adverse budgetary developments rather than a single cause. Expenditures have surged upward relative to the nation's GNP, primarily because of the continued rapid growth of transfer programs such as social security payments, Medicare, unemployment benefits and interest on the national debt. At the same time, receipts have grown more slowly than GNP, largely because of a decline in corporate income and corporate income tax receipts.

Simple explanations that attribute recent deficits to the defense buildup that began in 1979 or to tax cuts are inadequate for understanding recent deficits.[5] From 1979 to 1983, growth in the share of defense spending in GNP accounts for only 1.4 percentage points of a 4.8 percentage-point rise in the deficit as a percent of GNP (from 0.7 percent to 5.5 percent). Other expenditures, in particular transfer payments, account for a considerably larger part of the rise.

The tax cut argument is simply wrong. Personal tax rates generally have risen since the passage of the 1981 tax cut, a "cut" that evidently was a poor substitute for indexing (which begins in 1985). Confusion arises because, while tax rates and taxes obviously were cut from levels that they would otherwise have attained, actual tax rates tended to rise from 1980 to 1984. The cut in personal marginal tax rates was largely offset by inflation-induced "bracket creep" and social security tax hikes.[6]

Business tax cuts, provided primarily through accelerated depreciation (the Accelerated Cost Recovery System) substantially reduced effective tax rates on income from new investments, but had only a minor impact on average tax rates or on the real tax burden on business income from 1980 to 1983. The lion's share of the observed decline in corporate income taxes as a share of GNP has been related to the business cycle. Lower tax rates on corporate income and accelerated depreciation have been largely offset by new indirect business taxes. Moreover, the taxation of capital, which arises from the use of historical costs in calculating depreciation in the face of inflation-induced boosts in replacement costs, has continued to increase.

Charts 1–3 show clearly that recent budget developments are largely related to the business cycle. During the shaded recession periods, expenditures (especially transfer programs) typically rise and receipts generally fall relative to GNP. Indeed, with the exception of the 1953–54 recession, when expenditures fell relative to GNP as a result

[5]See "How to Cut the Deficit" (1984), p. 50, for example.
[6]See Tatom (1981), McKenzie (1982) and Meyer (1983), for example.

of a sharp decline in national defense expenditures, this pattern has been observed in each postwar recession. The greater extent of the recent recession has amplified the cyclical swing in the deficit.

A further example of the effect of the cycle on the federal budget is given in chart 4, where a measure of the average tax rate on "earned" personal income is given. Transfer payments are excluded from personal income in the chart, because they are not subject to federal taxes; social security contributions are added to federal personal income taxes, because they are considered to be as direct and personal as income taxes. A cyclically adjusted average tax rate measure also is shown.

The rates in chart 4 provide little indication of the so-called tax cut. The actual rate rose from 22.9 percent in 1979 to 23.1 percent in 1980, then fell slightly to 22.7 percent in 1983. There is some indication of a decline after mid-1982, but the average level for 1983 was virtually unchanged from its 1979 and 1980 levels.

On a cyclically adjusted basis, the evidence that taxes were cut is even weaker. On this basis, the average tax rate rose from 23.1 percent in 1979 to 23.5 percent in 1980 and reached 24.0 percent in 1983. While the tax rate declined somewhat in 1983 from its 1982 level, it was still above its 1980 level, the year before the "tax cut" began.

The 1.3 percentage-point difference between the actual and the cyclically adjusted average tax rates represents a $30.4 billion shortfall in federal receipts based on the level of income in 1983. Moreover, such income would have been substantially higher if the unemployment rate had averaged 5 percent in 1983, instead of the actual 9.6 percent rate. Each percentage point of unemployment is associated with about a 2 to

CHART 4
Personal Taxes as a Share of Earned Personal Income. Personal taxes include social security taxes. Earned personal income is personal income less transfer payments. Shaded areas represent periods of business recessions. Latest data plotted: 1st quarter. (Source: *National Income and Product Accounts.*)

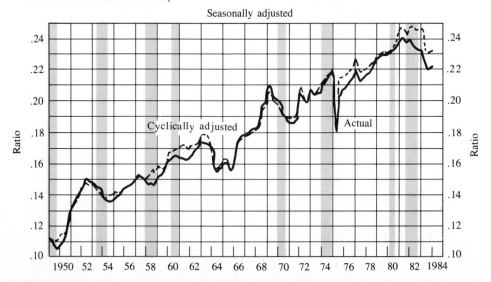

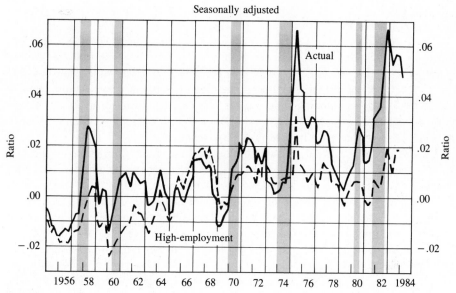

CHART 5
Deficits as a Share of GNP. Shaded areas represent periods of business recessions. Latest data plotted: High-employment—4th quarter; Actual—1st quarter. (Source: *National Income and Product Accounts.*)

$2^1/_2$ percentage-point loss in real and nominal GNP and a $2^1/_4$ to $2^3/_4$ percentage-point decline in personal income less transfer payments. Thus, the loss in personal tax receipts alone in 1983 was about $72 billion, a substantial share of the observed budget deficit.

Chart 5 shows the deficit as a percent of GNP and the high-employment deficit as a percent of high-employment of GNP.[7] Typically, the high-employment deficit as a share of high-employment GNP has ranged between plus or minus 2 percent. While actual deficits have risen substantially as a share of GNP since mid-1981, deficits measured on a high-employment basis have remained within that range. For example, using fiscal year periods (ending in the third quarter of each year), the 1.6 percent high-employment deficit registered in 1983 was equaled or exceeded in 1967 and 1968 (1.8 percent and 1.6 percent, respectively).

THE DEFICIT OUTLOOK: FROM PASSIVE TO ACTIVE DEFICITS?

While recent budget deficits appear to have been largely the result of the 1980 and 1981–82 recessions, projections of future expenditures, receipts and deficits show a

---

[7]The high-employment budget data are prepared by the Bureau of Economic Analysis, U.S. Department of Commerce, following methods described in deLeeuw and others (1980). Their analysis uses a more disaggregated form of the cyclical adjustment procedure. The high-employment budget data indicate the point above concerning "tax cuts." In fiscal 1980, the share of high-employment budget receipts in potential GNP was 20.7 percent. This ratio fell only slightly to 20.4 percent in fiscal 1983.

different picture. Such projections are shown in table 1, with earlier actual data for comparison purposes.

The first column in table 1 shows the estimated deficit for fiscal years 1983 to 1989, based on the assumptions used in the preparation of the fiscal 1985 budget for the economy on a "current services" basis. The current services budget measures assume that all federal programs and activities in the future remain the same as those adopted for the 1984 fiscal year (ending in September 1984) and that there are no policy changes in such programs. They also incorporate assumptions about future spending, real GNP growth, inflation, interest rates and unemployment.

The projected total deficits remain substantial through 1989, providing support for recent concerns about "large" deficits. Note, however, that relative to the size of the economy or GNP, the actual deficit declines after 1983.

The table also provides a breakdown of the deficit into "cyclical" and "structural" components. This distinction is similar to the high-employment vs. actual deficit categories used previously. In this instance, however, the cyclical deficit arises from the departure of real GNP from its 1969-to-1981 trend, rather than from a high-employment level. The structural deficit is the level that would exist if real GNP were at its trend level; the smaller high-employment deficit measures the deficit that would exist were real GNP at a high-employment level.

While the total deficit declines relative to GNP in the table, the structural deficit

TABLE 1
THE CYCLICAL AND STRUCTURAL COMPONENTS OF THE DEFICIT: 1980–89
(Dollar Amounts in Billions)

Fiscal year	Total deficit	Deficit as percent of GNP	Cyclical com- ponent	Structural com- ponent	Structural component as percent of trend GNP	High- employ- ment deficit	High- employment deficit as percent of potential GNP
			Actual				
1980	$ 60	2.3%	$ 4	$ 55	2.1%	$16.7	0.6%
1981	58	2.0	19	39	1.3	1.0	0.0
1982	111	3.6	62	48	1.5	20.2	0.6
1983	195	6.1	95	101	2.9	56.8	1.6
			Projected				
1984	$187	5.3%	$49	$138	3.7%		
1985	208	5.3	44	163	4.2		
1986	216	5.1	45	171	4.1		
1987	220	4.8	34	187	3.9		
1988	203	4.1	16	187	3.8		
1989	193	3.6	−4	197	3.8		

[1]Deficit estimates for 1984–89 are from the current services budget, January 1984.

balloons up relative to GNP until 1985, then remains quite high as real GNP approaches trend. These estimates show an unprecedented rise in the structural deficit and record levels persisting through the decade.

There are a number of reasons for viewing such conclusions with extreme caution. First, estimates of the structural deficit tend to be raised by the use of trend GNP, since it is somewhat below the path of high-employment GNP. The table also includes high-employment measures of the deficit for 1980 to 1983, for comparison purposes. The trend-based estimates of the structural deficit in 1980–83 average about 1.3 percentage points higher than structural deficits that are measured on a high-employment basis. The size of projected structural deficits in the current budget estimates are likely to be similarly overstated; thus, the projections for 1984 to 1989 do not represent a major break from the record shown in chart 5. Adjusted for this difference, the projected 1988–89 deficits are slightly more than twice the standard deviation of the high-employment deficit ratio from 1955 to 1983, instead of over three times as large.

Also, the deficits in table 1 are current services estimates. Currently proposed Administration policies would reduce the structural deficit shown for 1989 to about 2.3 percent of actual or, roughly, trend GNP, instead of the 3.8 percent shown in the table.

Third, if actual economic conditions differ from the economic assumptions used for the projections, future deficits could be higher or lower than indicated. Some analysts have been critical of a decline in interest rates assumed in making the projection. If interest rates are higher than projected from 1984 to 1989, the actual and structural deficits would be larger. Others have criticized the projected rate of economic growth as too low; a higher growth rate would lower the actual and projected deficit.

Economic assumptions are extremely important to deficit projections. Carlson (1983) demonstrates, for example, that changes in assumptions about economic conditions for fiscal 1986, between projections made in March 1981 and projections made in January 1983, accounted for most of a nearly tenfold rise in the projected deficit from $21.0 billion to $203.1 billion. Policy changes between the two projections *reduced* the projected deficit by about $39 billion, but downward revisions in the projected levels of prices and real GNP for 1986 raised it by $221 billion.

Even departures from near-term assumptions can have relatively large effects on projected deficits. For example, at the end of July 1983, the Office of Management and Budget (1983) estimated that the unified budget deficit for fiscal 1983, which ended two months later, would show a deficit of $209.8 billion. Two months later, the actual deficit ended up at $195.4 billion, primarily because outlays were about $13 billion lower than estimated two months earlier, when most of the fiscal year had been completed.

THE CONSEQUENCES OF LARGE DEFICITS

Conventional economic theory suggests that rising deficits may tend to raise prices, output and interest rates, while depressing capital formation. Obtaining empirical support for all but the last of these hypotheses has proved quite difficult, however.

In 1981, concern over rising deficits associated with the Economic Recovery Tax

Act of 1981 focused on the anticipation that increasing deficits would overheat the economy and raise inflation, just as inflation measures began to plummet and the economy entered the worst recession since the 1930s. Since then, increased attention has been focused on the effect of deficits on interest rates and capital formation during a period in which, until recently, interest rates were declining and capital spending was unusually high relative to GNP. In part, finding evidence on the consequences of deficit increases becomes difficult because of a failure to account for the active/passive deficit distinction. This problem is most apparent when one looks at the investigation of the deficit-interest rate link.

The actual pattern of deficits and interest rates over the past four years runs counter to the higher-deficit, higher-interest rate hypothesis. Interest rates skyrocketed from III/1979 to III/1981; long-term Treasury security yields, for example, rose from about 9 percent to 14 percent. During the same period, the high-employment deficit for the most recent four quarters fell from about $2 billion to $1 billion, and the actual deficit rose from about $14 billion to $56 billion. Over the next two years (III/1981 to III/1983), long-term Treasury security yields fell from 14 percent to 11.6 percent. Yet, in the latter period, the actual deficit ballooned up to $186 billion and the high-employment deficit rose from near zero to about $57 billion.

A principal difficulty in interpreting these movements in interest rates and deficits is the failure to account for the active/passive deficit distinction. In the past, deficits have been in large part passive, as chart 5 indicates. Thus, it is not surprising that, during and following periods of recession, deficits were rising or "high," and interest rates were falling or remained "low." The dominance of this negative cyclical relationship between passive deficits and interest rates interferes substantially with empirical investigations of the impact of deficits on interest rates.

The second problem with testing the interest rate-deficit hypothesis is that the U.S economy has had only limited peacetime experience with either large or variable active deficits, measured relative to GNP. As chart 5 indicates, deficits or surpluses rarely have exceeded 2 percent of GNP on a high-employment basis.

Thus, should future federal structural deficits be larger than they were in the earlier postwar experience, past empirical evidence would provide little guidance concerning the potential adverse effects on inflation and interest rate levels. Although past evidence suggests there are none, the economy has had no peacetime experience with large, persistent structural deficits, as some analysts have suggested will occur from 1983 to 1989. Thus, the past may offer little relevant evidence for assessing the future effects of deficits. Of course, financial market participants have been warned of the potential magnitude of future deficits and, to the extent such deficits could be expected to raise interest rates, such effects already should have been incorporated into the structure of rates. Interestingly enough, however, interest rates have generally fallen since late 1981, even though it has been only since then that the adverse deficit information began to be discerned and disseminated.

SUMMARY

In 1982–1983, federal deficits surged to triple-digit levels. Moreover, administration and CBO projections indicate they will remain so, at least through 1989. These deficits have arisen from the unsatisfactory cyclical performance of the U.S. economy. Typically, federal expenditures are raised when unemployment is higher and tax receipts are lower. Recessions in 1980 and 1981–82 have left the unemployment rate at unusually high levels since 1980. Suggestions that either a rise in defense spending or cuts in tax rates have played major roles in the creation of recent deficits are misleading.

Projections tend to show deficits declining as a share of GNP, but structural deficit projections show a worsening trend in 1984–85 and little improvement in 1986–89. Should the current cyclical deficit be transformed into a structural deficit, it is not clear what consequences such a development would have. There is little evidence supporting the adverse consequences of a sharp increase in the structural deficit. The lack of such evidence, however, may arise from the fact that the United States has had no experience with "large" peacetime structural deficits.

REFERENCES

Barro, Robert J. "Comment From An Unreconstructed Ricardian," *Journal of Monetary Economics* (August 1978), pp. 569–81.
————"Are Goverment Bonds Net Wealth?" *Journal of Political Economy* (November/December 1974), pp. 1095–117.
Buchanan, J. M., and R. Wagner. *Democracy in Deficit* (Academic Press, 1977).
Greider, William. "The Education of David Stockman," *The Atlantic Monthly* (December 1981), pp. 27–54.
"How to Cut the Deficit." *Business Week,* Special Report (March 26, 184), pp. 49–106.
deLeeuw, Frank, and others. "The High-Employment Budget: New Estimates, 1955–80," *Survey of Current Business* (November 1980), pp. 13–43.
McKenzie, Richard B. "Supply-Side Economics and the Vanishing Tax Cut," Federal Reserve Bank of Atlanta *Economic Review* (May 1982), pp. 20–24.
Meyer, Stephen A. "Tax Cuts: Reality or Illusion." Federal Reserve Bank of Philadelphia *Business Review* (July/August 1983), pp. 3–16.
Tatom, John A. "We Are All Supply-Siders Now!" *Review* (May 1981), pp. 18–30, reprinted in Bruce Bartlett and Timothy P. Roth. *The Supply-Side Solution* (Chatham House Publishers, Inc., 1983), pp. 6–25.
U.S. Department of the Treasury. *The Effects of Deficits on Prices of Financial Assets: Theory and Evidence* (GPO, March 1984).

QUESTIONS FOR DISCUSSION

1 Tatom uses the term "active deficit" to mean "full-employment deficit," and "passive deficit" to mean "the actual deficit less the full-employment deficit." Use the *IS-LM* framework to explain his argument that active deficits expand GNP and employment, but passive deficits do not. According to Tatom, were federal deficits primarily active or passive during 1980–82? How about after 1982?

2 A striking feature of Chart 2 in this article is the large recent increase in "transfer payments." Use the *Economic Report of the President,* the *Survey of Current Business,* or some other recent data source to break down this growth of transfer payments into its major component parts. Has this growth continued since 1984, when this article was written? How much of the growth is due to increasing interest payments? Social Security? Medicare? Aid to families

with dependent children (AFDC)? It is useful to measure everything relative to GNP. How much has the change in transfer payments since 1981 contributed to the change in the current federal deficit?

3 Using the same sources as in question 2, find recent data on national defense spending and nondefense government spending. How much of the increase in the federal deficit since 1981 is due to changes in these categories? Again, measure relative to GNP.

4 Finally, again using the most recent available data, calculate how much of the change in the deficit since 1981 (as a percentage of GNP) is due to the change in federal receipts. Look at personal income taxes, Social Security taxes, and corporate taxes separately. Based on your results for questions 2 to 4, do you agree or disagree with the author's overall assessment of the sources of the deficits?

POLITICS OF DEFICIT REDUCTION REMAINS DEADLOCKED DESPITE BALANCED BUDGET ACT

Jonathan Rauch

Unable to reduce federal deficits through the conventional budgetary process, Congress in 1985 passed the Gramm-Rudman-Hollings (GRH) bill. GRH sets a series of deficit-reduction targets, with the ultimate goal of a zero deficit by 1991; more significantly, it sets up a procedure by which the budget is to be automatically cut if Congress misses those targets.

The following article, written shortly after GRH was passed, describes how the bill is supposed to work and discusses the question of its ultimate effects on the federal budget.

The name of the budget game is still chicken.

Congress, by enacting radical legislation that will cut spending automatically if deficits are not reduced each year, hoped to raise the game's stakes dramatically—to make the consequences of failure so severe as to force Congress and the White House to break free of the deadlocked politics of deficit reduction.

But many people think that raising the stakes does not change the underlying dynamic that has perpetuated 12-digit budget deficits: Whichever player—President Reagan, Senate Republicans or House Democrats—takes the first step toward compromise risks being clobbered politically by the others.

Under rules of the game until now, Reagan protects the defense budget and refuses to agree to a tax increase, House Democrats protect social security and other domestic programs and Senate Republicans come out somewhere in between. So far, no one has given way, no one has blinked. The result has been uncontrolled federal deficits.

"We've been playing budget chicken for the last few years, wondering if the deficits would reach crisis proportions and in that sense force action," Rep. Leon E. Panetta, D-Calif., said. Until now, however, no crisis has developed sufficient to break the deadlock.

The 1985 Balanced Budget and Emergency Deficit Control Act, better known as the Gramm-Rudman-Hollings bill after three of its leading Senate sponsors, Phil Gramm, R-Texas, Warren Rudman, R-N.H., and Ernest F. Hollings, D-S.C., attempts to generate crisis artificially: If no one blinks and deficits are not reduced by $36 billion a year, programs cherished by all the players could be savaged by automatic spending cuts. Half of the automatic cuts (or sequestration, as the new law calls it) would come out of defense, half out of a limited proportion of domestic spending. (For details on how the law will work, see appendix 1; for how automatic cuts would be calculated, see appendix 2; for where the ax would fall, see appendix 4.)

It may work. But many fear that the measure could just as easily do the opposite of what its sponsors intended: intensify the budget paralysis.

"It plays both ways," said House Budget Committee chairman William H. Gray III, D-Pa., who opposed the measure. "I see Gramm-Rudman as a disincentive for making the hard choices. What happens if your favorite programs are slated for elimination or you see the consensus moving to cut them 50-75 per cent? It is not in your interest to have a budget."

Sen. J. Bennett Johnston Jr., D-La., another opponent of the measure, said: "Gridlock is entirely possible, because you can blame this inanimate Gramm-Rudman machine and say, 'I didn't vote for the cuts.' You may well be setting the scene for the automatic spending cuts."

The consensus is broad on Capitol Hill that it is politically impossible to reduce the deficit as quickly as the Balanced Budget Act requires without a tax increase. "I don't see any way to avoid a sequester without some revenue increases," Rep. Willis D. Gradison, Jr., R-Ohio, said. As was true late last summer, many lawmakers see taxes as the key to the puzzle.

But who will propose a tax increase? Reagan? It seems unlikely: If he accedes to tax increases, he risks losing the spending cuts he wants. House Democrats? They remember being clobbered on taxes in the 1984 presidential election and are adamant that Reagan must go first. Senate Republicans? It's tough in an election year when Republicans are fighting to maintain their hold on the Senate. Gray said, "The only person who can put revenues on the table is the President."

Large automatic spending cuts have the potential to ravage defense programs; many people think that ultimately the measure will trap Reagan into agreeing to a tax increase so as to save defense. But he has yet to show signs of willingness to reduce deficits Congress's way rather than his own. His budget for fiscal 1987 is expected to cleave to the well-established Reagan priorities: It will call for a defense spending increase, no new taxes and probably the most radical domestic spending cuts that Reagan has yet proposed.

To avoid automatic cuts, someone or everyone will have to give way, unless the law is overturned or repealed. The uncertainty created by the Balanced Budget Act makes it harder than ever to foresee who, if anyone, will do so. The act, like a ball balanced on a rooftop, could easily go in either of two very different directions, breaking the deadlock or worsening it. So as the fiscal 1987 debate begins, the game of budgetary chicken goes on.

PARALYSIS OR PROGRESS

One useful place to look for clues to the way the game might be played out is the fiscal 1986 budget debate. In many key respects, the political equation a year ago looked just the way it does now.

"We're in essentially the same position, except we have fewer options," said John H. Makin, an economist with the American Enterprise Institute for Public Policy Research (AEI). "Half of spending has been taken off the table by Reagan and Congress, and the rhetoric on taxes is the same."

A year ago, Reagan and the Democrats emerged from the election swearing that they would not allow social security, which accounts for 20 per cent of federal spending, to be touched. Their position hasn't changed.

Everyone agreed as the last budget debate began that programs for the poor, which account for about 7 per cent of spending, should not take deep cuts. That consensus still holds. Interest on the national debt, about 14 per cent of spending, remains off limits.

Defense, which accounts for 28 per cent of spending, is Reagan's top spending priority; for fiscal 1986, he asked for an increase, and he will do so again for fiscal 1987. Although Congress will reduce his request, the deep reductions in Pentagon budget growth in fiscal 1986 make defense reductions far harder to find next year.

As for taxes, both parties took the 1984 election results to be a firm rejection of new taxes by the voters. Democrats were not about to offer a tax increase and let Reagan chop them up politically. Reagan was not about to let Congress slip out of cutting spending by proferring new tax revenue.

In July, any chance of a grand compromise on all the big issues got shot down when Reagan and House Democrats agreed that there would be no new taxes and no cuts in social security. The result was a business-as-usual budget that helped somewhat in reducing the deficit—largely by sharply slowing growth in defense spending—but it failed to break the political gridlock. In the coming debate for fiscal 1987, social security, taxes and, to a lesser degree, defense and domestic spending are all still being held off the bargaining table by one or more of the players.

Frustrated, desperate and seeing no way out under the old rules, the Republican Senate proposed writing new ones. The proposal grew into the Balanced Budget Act, which was signed into law on Dec. 12.

In theory, the threat of automatic spending cuts will tie all the players' fates together, because if all do not cooperate, all will hit the automatic spending cut "wall," as many people on Capitol Hill called it. In effect, the measure's supporters hope to rearrange the political incentives by making it more painful for everyone to do nothing about deficits than to reduce them. Whether that strategy works turns largely on the problem of so-called double hits—the fact that if a program is cut during the budget cycle and automatic spending cuts kick in anyway, the program will be cut again.

Two responses are possible. One is foreseen by Senate Budget Committee chairman Pete V. Domenici, R-N.M., and other Senate sponsors of the act: The Senate and House will make sufficient deficit cuts through the regular budget cycle to ensure that there are no automatic spending cuts and thus that double hits are prevented. "Everybody in the government, except the excluded programs, will be hit the second time if we do not meet the targets," Domenici said in floor debate. "If that's not an incentive, what is?"

But there is a much different way the game could be played. If Members believe that automatic cuts are coming, they may try to protect their favorite programs from initial cuts to avoid taking the second hit later on. Few cuts would be made—if a budget could be approved at all—and the expectation of automatic spending cuts would become a self-fulfilling prophecy.

"It will be very difficult," Panetta said, "to pass a budget resolution or reconciliation"—that is, to set guidelines to reduce the deficit and enact legislation implementing them—"because Members will be afraid of double hits on their programs." Guy L. Clough, a budget aide to Sen. Nancy Landon Kassebaum, R-Kan., said, "If you see a sequester [automatic cut] coming down the line, the last thing you want to do is take a 20 per cent cut up front."

Moreover, for some of the players, automatic spending cuts might not be such a bad deal. For some Members, as Gray put it, automatic spending cuts may be more like a safe harbor than a wall.

Many of the programs Democrats and liberals most cherish—social security, medicare and programs for the poor—are exempt or largely exempt from automatic cuts; in fiscal 1986, probably less than $100 billion of domestic spending could be cut deeply by automatic reductions, although the cuts in that portion would be deep. Members most interested in the exempt programs, Clough said, know that if no budget resolution is passed and automatic cuts kick in, "they're going totally free. And the people who want to cut defense know that all they have to do is stand pat and they'll get 50 per cent [of automatic cuts] out of defense."

Clough estimates that a core of about 20 conservatives in the Senate would rather cut spending, even if defense is hurt, than raise taxes. They also might prefer automatic cuts to any congressionally adopted budget with new revenues.

"You have a brand new dynamic in the budget process," he said. "Under the old process, there was no alternative scenario that would kick in without a budget resolution. You were flying blind. Now, if we don't get a resolution with $50 billion in cuts, you can sit down with a pencil and see what a sequester is going to do to you."

It is therefore possible that the presence of an alternative to adoption of a congressional budget will create "paralysis" during the regular budget cycle, said Rep. James R. Jones, D-Okla., who was chairman of the Budget Committee from 1981-84. Panetta speculated that Congress will be unable to reach agreement on a budget resolution; instead, it may wait until soon before automatic spending cuts are scheduled to kick in and then, at the last minute, draft deficit reduction measures aimed at meeting the new law's deficit targets and attach them to such "must-pass" legislation as an increase in the federal debt ceiling. "That could be a huge vehicle for budget negotiations with the President," he said.

Allen Schick, a visiting scholar at AEI, said there was "a very high probability [that Members of Congress will] lie in wait for a debt limit bill or some other vehicle they can use."

Gradison said, "What you're doing is creating new categories of winners and losers." But no one knows who they are or whether the result will be paralysis or progress.

GAMBLING ON TAXES

People will just be beginning to find out who the winners and losers are on Feb. 1, when the President is required to issue an order for automatic spending cuts for the last seven months of fiscal 1986, March through September. It is thus into a climate of vast budgetary uncertainty that Reagan will inject his fiscal 1987 budget proposal on Feb. 3.

The broad outlines of Reagan's budget are already clear: no tax increase, no social security cuts, a 3 per cent real increase in defense and draconian cuts in domestic spending. Gradison said, "It sounds like in many respects a repeat of last year's budget."

Office of Management and Budget (OMB) director James C. Miller III, however, has a harder job than his predecessor, Dave Stockman, did last February. For fiscal 1987, OMB estimates that it needs to cut spending by $50 billion to reduce the 1987 deficit to the Balanced Budget Act's target level of $144 billion.

Last year, too, the Administration sought about $50 billion in cuts, but $9 billion of those cuts came out of a reduction in the size of the defense increase Reagan wanted. This year, the Administration must find all of the $50 billion in cuts from a pot of about $400 billion in domestic spending. To do that, Congressional Budget Office (CBO) director Rudolph G. Penner said, "they have to take all the cuts of last year and add some." To find such deep cuts, the Administration has been considering proposing such severe measures as shutting down the Interstate Commerce Commission.

Last year, Congress rejected most of Reagan's proposed spending cuts, and there is little reason to suppose that it will do differently this year, although Reagan's budgets always have an important effect in shaping the debate. "The one thing that's clear," Sen. Johnston said, "is that this budget, like last year's, will be dead on arrival. I think it'll be laughed out of town."

If so, the question will once again become where to find a substitute for Reagan's approach that Reagan, House Democrats and Senate Republicans can all agree to. "We're no closer to an agreement or a consensus on what to do or how to do it," Johnston said.

Rep. Dick Cheney, R-Wyo., one of the leading sponsors of the original Gramm-Rudman-Hollings bill in the House, said the Balanced Budget Act may force earlier and more serious consideration of all the available options. "I would think that Democrats would have to look at social security," he said. "To some extent, their choice will be between putting social security on the table or standing by and watching some of their favorite programs go down in flames."

But Mark Johnson, a spokesman for the Democratic Congressional Campaign Committee, said: "I think chances are slim that Democrats will touch social security. And it's not going to come from the Democratic side. I think any proposal before the 1986 election to cut social security will only come from the Republican side—and I really doubt even that."

Defense is almost certain to get less than Reagan wants, but Congress imposed a real-dollar freeze on the Pentagon budget this year, and any proposal to cut defense below this year's level is sure to be in for a fight with Reagan and many Republicans. As for the kind of radical domestic cuts that Reagan will propose, the fiscal 1986 budget cycle clearly demonstrated Congress's reluctance to accept them. "Congress doesn't have the will to make those cuts," Makin said. "They'll have to raise taxes."

But who will call for higher taxes in an election year? Domenici and the Senate Budget Committee might; Johnston, a committee member, said the panel is likely to adopt a package that includes both tax increases and spending cuts. He said that the package is likely to look much like the one that a bipartisan coalition of Senate budget negotiators, without the public support of Domenici or Majority Leader Robert Dole, R-Kan., proposed to the House last June in an attempt to break a House-Senate deadlock. Because the package included new taxes, Reagan shot it down.

Still, even if the Budget Committee does propose such a package and, what's less likely, the Senate goes along, the Democratic leadership in the House has been adamant that Reagan must publicly support a tax increase before Democrats will vote for it. "We are not going to bring [a tax increase] up," Speaker Thomas P. O'Neill Jr., D-Mass., said in November.

For many of its congressional supporters, the Balanced Budget Act represented a gamble that they could force Reagan to support new taxes. Sen. Slade Gorton, R-Wash., said on the Senate floor, "I think sooner or later we will force the President to choose between what he honestly believes necessary for the appropriate defense of the United States and his refusal to consider any revenue increase whatsoever."

It's a big gamble. Reagan has often shown his ability to slip out of reach of schemes to force him to accept congressional priorities. And he has also shown the depth of his feeling on taxes.

"The Reagan you see in the tax issue is the real Reagan," Schick said. "He's had God knows how many times to choose taxes, and he hasn't. He is convinced that if you raise taxes, you increase spending—and he's not entirely wrong. So why should he support a tax increase?" On the other hand, he added "if the President doesn't agree to a tax increase and Congress succeeds [only] in nickel-and-diming [domestic] programs, you've got a real problem." The game of chicken might once again create a long budget standoff, ending in automatic spending cuts, a last-minute effort to avoid them, or who knows what else.

Schick, like Domenici, Gorton, Panetta, Jones and many others, believes that ultimately the Balanced Budget Act is likely to force Reagan to choose between higher taxes and less defense. But no one knows how or when he will choose, or, for that matter, how Congress and the President will behave in the new budgetary dynamic. The feeling on Capitol Hill is that passage of the act leaves everything up in the air—that the new law is a kind of loaded gun that could fire in any direction.

"Nobody knows that it's going to do," Johnston said. "The doctrine of unintended consequences will come into action—I know that."

APPENDIX 1: Deficit Reduction on Automatic Pilot

On Jan. 10, a kind of automatic deficit-cutting machine will grind into motion. Then it will idle until Aug. 15, when the machine starts up again, beginning what could be an annual fall cycle of budget projections, congressional action to meet deficit targets and, if the action fails, automatic spending cuts.

Here is how the 1985 Balanced Budget and Emergency Deficit Control Act is to work until the act expires in 1991:

Initial Deficit Estimates   On Aug. 15 of every year, the Office of Management and Budget (OMB) and the Congressional Budget Office (CBO) will estimate the amount, if any, by which the deficit for the coming fiscal year will exceed the maximum that the new law allows. The ceilings are $144 billion in fiscal 1987, $108 billion in 1988, $72 billion in 1989, $36 billion in 1990 and zero in 1991. Both offices will base their projection on the laws then on the books; Congress would not get credit for spending cuts or tax increases still in the works, even though the process of enacting a budget is almost never completed by August. Their report will also make new economic projections and calculate the allocation of any projected automatic cuts to every government program, project and activity.

GAO Arbitration   If the two offices produce differing estimates, they first must try to agree and, failing that, must average their results. They send their report on Aug. 20 to the General Accounting Office (GAO), which makes the final determination of the size of any deficit overage in a report issued on Aug. 25. The GAO is instructed to try to adhere to the OMB-CBO report but is also to ensure a consistent and reasonable final forecast. If the deficit excess is of $10 billion or less, it is ignored. If it is more, the whole amount of the excess must be cut.

Sequestration Order   On Sept. 1, the President issues an order for automatic spending cuts, which the new law calls sequestration, adhering to the requirements set in the GAO's report. The President could also send Congress an alternative plan to eliminate the excess deficit, but that plan would have no special standing with Congress, which could ignore it.

Congressional Response   Congress then has through September to enact additional spending cuts or tax increases to eliminate the deficit overage. In the Senate only, a procedure is established to channel additional budget action through the Budget Committee.

Automatic Spending Cuts   On Oct. 5, OMB and CBO present the GAO with a revised deficit forecast reflecting congressional action as of that date. On Oct. 10, the GAO issues its revised estimates. If the projected deficit is still $10 billion above the target, automatic spending cuts based on the revised estimates become effective on Oct. 15.

Special Provisions for Fiscal 1986   House Democrats, who have a shot at regaining Senate control next year, did not want any pain that the measure causes to be delayed until after the 1986 elections. So they insisted that the measure include automatic spending cuts for fiscal

1986, which began last Oct. 1. For 1986, there is no $10 billion safety margin: Any projected deficit in excess of $171.9 billion must be eliminated. It now seems likely that the projected deficit will be well above the target, and so automatic spending cuts seem almost assured. For 1986 only, the total of automatic spending cuts is limited to about $11.7 billion. As in every year, half of the total will be cut from defense and half from domestic spending.

Special Timetable for Fiscal 1986 The OMB and CBO deficit report will be made on Jan. 10 and reported to the GAO on Jan. 15. On Jan. 20, the GAO issues the final report to the President. On Feb. 1, the President issues his order for automatic spending cuts. On March 1, the automatic cuts take effect. The law contains no provision in fiscal 1986 giving Congress credit for steps taken to reduce the deficit after Feb. 1.

Recession Escape Clause A major fear raised by the measure is that it fails to provide Congress with a way to adjust the deficit goals to the state of the economy. If in any year, OMB or CBO forecasts two or more consecutive quarters of negative economic growth—that is, a recession—the House and Senate Majority Leaders must introduce a joint resolution suspending automatic spending cuts for that year. The same would happen if the economy were in its second consecutive quarter of growth of less than 1 per cent at the time when OMB and CBO issue their deficit forecasts. But the following year's deficit target would not be adjusted, requiring Congress to make up all the lost ground—potentially a mammoth task that could deepen any recession.

Constitutional Fallback Mechanism The act sets up an expedited court review procedure. If the automatic imposition of spending cuts is held to be unconstitutional, Congress would vote each fall on the amount of spending cuts necessary, much as it votes now on an annual budget resolution. Thus spending cuts would no longer kick in automatically.

APPENDIX 2: Trying to Tie the President's Hands

The goal of the 1985 Balanced Budget and Emergency Deficit Control Act is to give the President virtually no discretion in administering any automatic spending cut ordered under the new law. The inevitable result: a detailed, complicated procedure for allocating automatic spending cuts.

Here, step by step, is the way in which the amount and distribution of automatic spending cuts will be determined.

Program Base Most of the budget—more than 70 per cent, according to an informal analysis—is off limits or would be subject to limited cuts. In fiscal 1986, a pot of about $265 billion would bear the brunt of automatic spending cuts. Of that, about two-thirds is defense spending, the rest domestic spending.

Outlay Base In calculating the size of the pot from which cuts are taken, the act includes only those outlays, or actual spending, that are projected to flow from new budget authority and, in defense programs only, from budget authority uncommitted in prior years. (Budget authority is the amount of money that Congress grants programs for current or future fiscal years.) Obligated money from earlier years—money tied up in contracts—is not counted.

For example, suppose some defense program in fiscal 1987 has been granted new budget authority of $100 million and that in that year, it will actually spend $50 million: $10 million of its new budget authority, $10 million in unobligated money left over from prior years' budget authority and $30 million committed in prior-year budgets. For the purposes of automatic spending cuts, this would be a $20 million program, because the $30 million in obligated money would be ignored. If it were a nondefense program, the $10 million in left-over money would also be ignored, leaving only $10 million in outlays that are subject to cuts.

Defense-Domestic Split   Now suppose that the General Accounting Office (GAO) decrees an automatic spending cut (or sequestration, in the act's language) of $20 billion. To calculate the amount of an automatic cut, first split the money evenly between defense and domestic cuts, with $10 billion coming out of each category.

Retirement COLA Cuts   Next, take the total amount of projected cost-of-living adjustments (COLAs) in federal retirement programs (in fiscal 1986, about $1.1 billion) and divide it in two. Half of the COLA cuts must come from canceling or reducing the COLAs of the Pentagon's civilian and military pensioners; the other half, from nondefense federal retirees' COLAs. Those would work out to roughly equal percentage cuts for both groups.

Further Defense Cuts   After cancellation of the defense COLAs, any further cuts that are needed in defense must come by reducing every Pentagon program, project and activity—a very fine level of detail—by an equal percentage. The Pentagon accounts for about 28 per cent of federal spending, but much of that is tied up in contracts, which can be cut only under special procedures. So the defense pool across which automatic cuts must be spread is only about $175 billion in fiscal 1986. A hypothetical sequestration of $20 billion would thus require a $9.5 billion cut from defense (in addition to the COLA cut) or a 5.5 per cent cut in every program and project.

Further Domestic Cuts   After the domestic retirement COLAs are canceled, cuts are applied to several programs—most importantly, guaranteed student loans—that are to be reduced under special rules. Next cuts of at most 2 per cent are made in medicare, community health programs and health programs for veterans and Indians. All of these program cuts would save about $2 billion-$2.5 billion in fiscal 1986. All the rest of the hypothetical $10 billion in domestic cuts must come out of uniform percentage reductions in every domestic program and activity. Out of a domestic pool of about $90 billion, a $10 billion sequestration would require an across-the-board cut of about 9 per cent after cutting COLAs and health programs.

Special Rules for Defense Contracts   Defense money tied up in contracts (about $100 billion in fiscal 1986) from prior years isn't necessarily off limits: The President has discretion to cut contracts, as long as he fulfills the requirement of taking half of the automatic spending cut from defense. It would be up to contract and procurement managers to decide which, if any, contracts to go after. If the President wants to cut a contract, he must give the GAO a detailed statement of how much the cut will save, and the GAO must review and approve the statement before the cut is allowed. Few people think that the President will find much money to cut here. In any event, no contract can be cut by more than the percentage by which other programs are cut, and so weapons systems, for example, could not be killed.

Special Rules for Fiscal 1986   The President can exercise some discretion within accounts—major spending categories—in cutting Pentagon spending this winter only, but he is constrained by a variety of rules in doing so.

Broad Guidelines   The President cannot eliminate any program, project or activity. If he finds a way to cut some programs or projects by different percentages than others, and if the courts uphold him, the whole sequestration process is nullified. This is a fail-safe mechanism in case Reagan finds ways to shift the burden of cuts away from defense and toward domestic spending.

APPENDIX 3: OMB, CBO and GAO on Spot

An acquaintance of Rudolph G. Penner, the director of the Congressional Budget Office (CBO), says that Penner has been asking his friends to pray for him.

The 1985 Balanced Budget and Emergency Deficit Control Act has handed the CBO, the Office of Management and Budget (OMB) and the General Accounting Office (GAO) difficult new responsibilities and has, to varying degrees, cast each of those agencies in an unaccustomed and potentially difficult role.

In particular, CBO and GAO reports have until now had no special standing with Congress. Under the Balanced Budget Act, however, the offices' deficit estimate is itself enough to trigger potentially major policy changes—that is, automatic spending cuts—unless Congress either changes the law or acts to reduce deficits.

"It changes the nature of our operation, in a number of ways," Penner said. "It's a very different world for us."

For one thing, the CBO is in the somewhat awkward position of having to decree policy to its boss, Congress. And giving the CBO and GAO, which are legislative branch agencies, a direct role in administering budget and policy changes may be unconstitutional, a question which is headed for the courts.

Past joint efforts between OMB and CBO, one an executive and the other a legislative agency, have been small in scope and rare. The 1985 act requires them to work jointly on detailed annual reports that, when approved by the the GAO, would serve to trigger automatic cuts. The first is due on Jan. 20.

The workload involved in preparing such a report is enormous. For example, calculating the distribution of automatic spending cuts means collecting and processing information on hundreds, perhaps thousands, of programs and activities, whose spending practices vary over an enormous range.

Moreover, the GAO must examine and either approve or reject every presidential request to cut contracts in order to meet the terms of automatic spending cuts. Harry S. Havens, an assistant comptroller general and former budget official at OMB, is heading the GAO's 15-30 member team that will work on administering the Balanced Budget Act.

Penner, who said that the CBO will get the job done, allowed that "it is a terrible, terrible drain on our resources." As for OMB, which is in the throes of preparing a fiscal 1987 budget request, he said, "They have a bigger problem than we do."

Edwin L. Dale Jr., a spokesman for OMB, said the task of meeting the new law's requirements will go to the budget review division, which is also in charge of putting the budget together. "It's a hell of a big project," Dale said.

APPENDIX 4: Where Ax Would Fall

It may be that Congress will act to avoid the triggering of automatic spending cuts of any great magnitude. If it does not, however, a small portion of the federal budget would be cut to the core.

By the time Congress was through exempting some major programs and writing special rules for others, not much was left. Of almost $1 trillion in federal spending, about 27 per cent—of which two-thirds is defense spending and the rest domestic—would bear almost all of any major automatic cut. After subtraction of some $3 billion in cuts from health programs and from the cancellation of cost-of-living adjustments (COLAs), half of the total amount of any automatic spending cut—which could be tens of billions of dollars— would have to come out of less than $100 billion in domestic spending.

Not by accident, virtually every major domestic program providing direct payments or benefits to individuals is exempt or exposed to only limited automatic cuts. The programs left to be cut heavily are those providing more generalized benefits and services: transportation, aid to state and local governments, housing, education, infrastructure, energy, environmental quality and general government.

According to an unofficial House analysis, here's the breakdown of which programs would be exempt, which would take limited cuts and which would bear the brunt of automatic spending cuts (spending shows outlays in billions of dollars; percentages may not add to totals because of rounding):

	Fiscal 1986 spending	Per cent of budget
Exempt programs		
Social security	$202	21%
Interest on the national debt	142	15
Nondefense spending obligated in prior years	78	8
Major low-income programs*	61	6
Unemployment compensation	20	2
Veterans' pensions and compensation	14	1
Offsetting receipts	−52	−5
Total exempt	$465	48%
Programs taking limited reductions		
Defense spending obligated in prior years (contracts)†	$100	10%
Medicare, veterans' health, other health programs‡	86	9
Retirement programs with COLAs§	48	5
Total taking limited reductions	$234	24%
Programs bearing the brunt		
Domestic: discretionary spending (newly budgeted only)	$74	8%
Domestic: minor entitlements	11	1
Domestic: other	6	1
Defense: new spending	164	17
Defense: unspent from prior years	10	1
Total bearing the brunt	$265	27%

*Medicaid, aid to families with dependent children, special supplemental feeding program for women, infants and children, supplemental security income, food stamps and child nutrition
†Contracts can be cut or modified at President's discretion
‡Cannot be automatically cut more than 1 per cent in fiscal 1986 and 2 per cent thereafter
§Only COLAs can be automatically cut; rest of spending exempt

QUESTIONS FOR DISCUSSION

1 What is *sequestration?* Under the Gramm-Rudman-Hollings (GRH) bill, what conditions trigger sequestration? To what extent is whether sequestration takes place under the law a result of economic *forecasts,* as opposed to "hard numbers"? What potential problems does reliance on forecasts raise?

2 What provisions does GRH make for the occurrence of a recession? Do you think that these provisions adequately deal with the danger that preprogrammed fiscal contraction will exacerbate an economic slowdown? Use the aggregate demand–aggregate supply diagram to illustrate your answer. Be sure to discuss (*a*) the effects of the GRH rule that the deficit target for the year following the recession is not adjusted, and (*b*) the potential role for monetary policy in offsetting the effects of GRH.

3 Under the law, if sequestration occurs, which budget areas would feel the heaviest effects? The least effects? Discuss the political reasons underlying the allocation of cuts. How does the distribution of cuts under sequestration affect the incentives of individual members of Congress to pass deficit-cutting legislation that would keep sequestration from happening?

4 The article above appeared in January 1986. Since then the Supreme Court has ruled some of the "automatic pilot" provisions of the bill unconstitutional. Many legislators argued, however, that Congress should still attempt to meet the Gramm-Rudman targets.

Compare the effects Gramm-Rudman is having on the federal budgetary process with the conjectures made in the article. Does Congress appear to be successful in reaching the deficit targets?

A BALANCED BUDGET CONSTITUTIONAL AMENDMENT: ECONOMIC COMPLEXITIES AND UNCERTAINTIES

Daniel B. Suits
Ronald C. Fisher

Attempts have been and continue to be made to force a balanced budget and restrict the growth of government through a constitutional amendment. Most discussion of these attempts has focused on whether a balanced budget is politically and economically desirable. This article considers this issue at a much more basic level in asking whether, in practice, such an amendment would be enforceable.

Deficits have become the normal form of operation for the federal government. The last federal budget *not* to show a deficit occurred in fiscal year 1969, and since 1980, the total outstanding federal debt has risen from about $900 billion to more than $2.0 trillion and now represents more than $7,000 for every man, woman and child in this nation. The current annual deficit, running in excess of $200 billion, exceeds total state taxes collected by all 50 states combined. Most alarming, however, is not where we are, but where we are potentially heading, for the non-partisan Congressional Budget Office now forecasts deficits in the $200 billion range through the end of this decade.

The manifest inability of President and Congress to dam the flood of federal deficits has led to the proposal of a Constitutional amendment requiring that the federal budget be balanced. To many, such an amendment appears as a simple and direct way to force on politicians what they have not accomplished by themselves, but as with most issues of law and economics, the problem is more complex than appears on the surface.[1] It is the purpose of this analysis to explore some of these complexities.

Daniel B. Suits and Ronald C. Fisher, "A Balanced Budget Constitutional Amendment: Economic Complexities and Uncertainties," *National Tax Journal*, December 1985, pp. 467–477. Reprinted by permission.

[1]For a similar opinion, but from the viewpoint of political science, see Shepsle (1982).

It is unfortunate that virtually all of the public discussion of the proposed amendment has centered on the question of whether the budget ought to be balanced. Surely it can be generally agreed both that, as a general principle, the budget should be balanced, and that there are times when deficits should be permitted.[2] The natural disagreements over how the exceptions are to be identified, and on the procedure by which the exceptions are to be enacted (for example, whether by simply majority vote of Congress, or by some sort of super-majority) are directed to questions or wording, rather than to the merit of the amendment itself. The really basic question is whether it is possible to formulate a workable amendment that will, in fact, force Congress and the President to balance the budget.[3] This is the question we propose to address.

I. THE AMENDMENT

Typical of proposed amendments is Senate Joint Resolution 58, which passed the Senate, 4 August 1982.[4] Nearly identical versions have been subsequently introduced or proposed. The substantive sections are quoted here in full:

> Section 1. Prior to each fiscal year, the Congress shall adopt a statement of receipts and outlays for that year in which the total outlays are no greater than total receipts. The Congress may amend such statement provided revised outlays are no greater than revised receipts. Whenever three-fifths of the whole number of both Houses shall deem it necessary, Congress in that statement may provide for a specific excess of outlays over receipts by a vote directed solely to that subject. The Congress and the President shall, pursuant to legislation or through exercise of their powers under the first and second articles, ensure that actual outlays do not exceed the outlays set forth in such statement.
>
> Section 2. Total receipts for any fiscal year set forth in the statement adopted pursuant to this article shall not increase by a rate greater than the rate of increase in national income in the year or years ending not less than six months nor more than twelve months before such fiscal year, unless a majority of the whole number of both Houses of Congress shall have passed a bill directed solely to approving specific additional receipts and such bill has become law.
>
> Section 3. Congress may waive the provisions of this article for any fiscal year in which a declaration of war is in effect.
>
> Section 4. Total receipts shall include all receipts of the United States except those derived from borrowing and total outlays shall include all outlays of the United States except those for payment of debt principle.
>
> Section 5. Congress shall enforce and implement this article by appropriate legislation.

There is an interesting relationship between the first and second sections of the proposed amendment. Section 1 is intended to compel Congress and the President to agree on and enforce a balanced budget, in keeping with the objective stated earlier. Section 2, however, is addressed to an entirely different objective, that of limiting the

---

[2]For a review of these issues, see Ackley (1982).

[3]Others who have focused on the likely effectiveness of any amendment are Olson (1980), Schultze (1980), and Wildavsky (1980).

[4]S.J. Res. 58 passed the Senate by a vote of 69 to 31 and was defeated in the House by a vote of 236 to 187, short of the 2/3 necessary for Congressional approval of a proposed constitutional amendment. S.J. Res. 5, a nearly identical version, was introduced in the next Congress. To date, 32 state legislatures have passed resolutions calling for a Constitutional Convention to consider a balanced budget amendment.

growth of revenues. The two sections combined would serve to restrict the growth of government to that of national income. Section 1 is necessary for the attainment of the objective of limiting the growth of government, but section 2 is in no way required to mandate a balanced budget. This asymmetry lends itself to the conjecture that the framers of the amendment were less concerned with how government is financed than with limiting the size of government. In any event, the title "Balanced Budget Amendment" is a misnomer. The Senate proposal might better be called the "Balanced Budget and Revenue Limitation Amendment." In what follows, both aspects of the proposed article will be addressed.

Past discussion has made it apparent that there has been some disagreement among those who wish to constitutionally constrain the federal budget, some preferring an attempt to *balance* the budget, others preferring action to *limit* the *growth* of the budget. The factors which contribute to the different focus have been detailed by Stubblebine (1980), who argues first, that expenditure limitation provides more benefits with fewer costs than does budget balancing and second, that revenue limitation may be the only workable method of limiting expenditure growth. As noted above, the amendment now most often discussed includes both features.

II. WHAT IS A "BALANCED BUDGET"?

A governmental budget consists of an array of proposed programs together with the projected outlays needed to carry them out, and an array of receipts projected to result from existing and proposed tax legislation. A "balanced" budget is one in which projected outlays (other than repayment of debt) equal projected receipts (other than receipts from borrowing).

Since budgets must be compiled well in advance, both actual receipts and cash outlays generally differ in the event from what had been set forth in the budget. On the receipts side, tax revenues exceed or fall short of those contemplated in the budget as income, employment and profits exceed or fall short of levels on which budget projections were based. Many budgeted outlays are also projections. For example, benefits paid to unemployed workers are budgeted on the basis of projected future levels of unemployment rates. When unemployment fails to conform to the projection, actual cash layouts for unemployment compensation vary accordingly.

In other words, whether a budget is "balanced" or not depends partly on how the compilers view the unknown future of the economy. In August, 1984 the deficit in the budget for fiscal year 1985 was projected by the administration at $172 billion. Four months later, this estimate was revised to $210 billion, with about half of the revision attributed to "slower than expected economic growth."

The economic outlook, always illusive, is subject to such widely differing interpretations that it is impossible to demonstrate in advance the difference between an accurate forecast and pure wishful thinking. In 1980, supply-siders predicted that their tax reduction program would balance the federal budget by the year 1984. The outcome was a record deficit, but the forecast had been embraced by enough people to enact the proposal, and none of the skeptics could have proven, in any objective sense, that the projection was in error at the time it was made. Given this uncertainty, who is to say that a given budget is not balanced if the President and Congress agree that it is?

Past administrations of all complexions have enlisted the wide margin of uncertainty in economic forecasts to project an economic outlook that would improve the cosmetics of their own budgets. In view of this proclivity, it would appear that one probable result of a balanced budget amendment would be merely an increase in the amount and scope of political game-playing with economic forecasts, rather than any material improvement in the budgetary process.

To be sure, the proposed amendment addresses more than the projected budget. Section 1 concludes with the instruction to the President and Congress to "ensure that actual outlays do not exceed [budgeted] outlays . . ." but there are difficulties here as well. In the first place, the budget is most sensitive to economic fluctuations on the revenue side. Once tax laws are in place, Congress and the President have practically no control over receipts. Once the budget has been declared "balanced," then, a short-fall of receipts can leave it seriously out of balance in the event, despite restriction of actual outlays to those initially voted. It is this problem which led Schultze to conclude that "The federal government would have a major interest [under a balanced budget regime] in finding taxes that do not decline sharply in recession" (Schultze, 1980, p. 123). But that incentive could lead the federal government into the arena of property or wealth taxes, which are more stable than income or consumption taxes.

In addition, however, many outlays are unavoidably linked to economic conditions. Most notably, these include interest on the national debt, roughly a third of which must be refinanced annually at current interest rates. If the total of outlays is to be maintained at the budgeted level, in the face of rising interest rates, other programs must be reduced to compensate.

Once put in place, however, a program is not easily modified in response to unforeseen developments in another part of the budget. Efficiency and economy require that the program be carefully reviewed, rescaled and modified. Due process demands that hearings be held and, essentially, that the entire appropriation process be repeated. There is, of course, an escape clause by which three-fifths of both houses "may provide for a specific excess of outlays over receipts . . ." but this provision would make the functioning of government hostage to a minority when urgent matters demand attention, and could invite the same kind of political posturing and maneuvering that now often accompanies the periodic vote to increase the debt ceiling.

It would, however, be unnecessary to resort frequently to the escape clause, if President and Congress regularly included substantial contingency allowances in the budget to provide for unexpected increases in uncontrollable outlays. Total outlays could then be maintained at budgeted levels without jeopardizing individual programs.

III. WHAT IS INCLUDED IN THE BUDGET?

An additional problem is that "the budget" is not a clearly defined document. There are all manner of budgets for different purposes, and "the Budget of the United States" includes whatever Congress defines it to contain. Supporters of constitutional limitation on the federal budget have, of course, recognized this problem of definition and enforcement, but perhaps none so clearly as Wildavsky, commenting in a series of lectures on ways to limit government spending:

All along I have proceeded on the assumption that the real question about outlays is how large or small should they be, not what they are. I was afraid, to tell the truth, that a trip through these lectures might seem unnecessary if I began by confessing that outlays is a contested concept. (Wildavsky, 1980, p. 93).

The problem is, of course, compounded when both receipts and outlays are to be limited.

To be sure, section 4 of the proposed amendment defines total receipts as "all receipts of the United States except those derived from borrowing" and total outlays as "all outlays of the United States except those for repayment of debt," but this merely rewords the question. What is a receipt or an outlay of "the United States?" There is a recognized distinction between the United States and agencies of the United States. Outlays and receipts of the former are included in the Budget of the United States. Those of the latter are not, and which are which is defined by act of Congress.

From its inception in 1936 until 1968, the entire Social Security program functioned outside the budget of the United States. Social Security taxes were receipts, not of the U.S. Treasury, but of the Social Security Trust Fund, and benefits to retired persons were outlays of the Trust Fund. The excess of receipts over outlays was invested in special Treasury bonds, so during these years, part of the "deficit" in the United States budget was matched by a "surplus" in the Trust Fund. With the introduction of the unified budget in 1969, both Social Security taxes and benefit payments were included in the budget.

From the founding of the Republic until it was turned over to the U.S. Postal Service as an independent agency, the Post Office was part of the U.S. budget. Among the most important off-budget agencies operating today are the Rural Electrification and Telephone Revolving Fund, the Rural Telephone Bank, and the Federal Financing Bank. The activities of these agencies are, by act of Congress, excluded from the unified budget. The most important of these, the Federal Financing Bank, borrows directly (off-budget) from the U.S. Treasury and relends the funds to a variety of other governmental agencies such as the Export-Import Bank, the Farmers Home Administration, the Rural Electrification Administration, and to certain Health Maintenance Organizations.

The Economic Report of the President for 1985 shows the federal budget deficit both under current law and when off-budget outlays are included. That comparison is summarized below:

Year	Deficit (current law)	Federal budget outlays	Total deficit
1980	$ −59.6	$14.2	$ −73.8
1981	−57.9	21.0	−78.9
1982	−110.6	17.3	−127.9
1983	−195.4	12.4	−207.8
1984	−175.4	10.0	−185.3
1985[a]	$−209.8	$12.5	$−222.2
	(billions of dollars)		

[a]Estimate

In a similar vein, Eisner (1984) recently identified nine separate federal government budget accounts which he combined into twelve different deficit measures. For 1982, the alternative deficit measures varied from $20 billion to $301 billion or from less than 1 percent of GNP to nearly 10 percent.

Off-budget outlays have grown substantially from only $0.1 billion in 1973 and $1.4 billion in 1974, the first years for which they were separately reported. While the President has proposed in his budget that these "off-budget" outlays be subsequently included in the budget, that also clearly demonstrates the statutory authority to define "the budget."[5]

There is no economic or functional reason to classify any particular agency as "off-budget." Except for the target groups they benefit, the activities of the (off-budget) Rural Electrification and Telephone Revolving Fund do not differ materially from those of the (on-budget) Small Business Administration. Yet outlays by the latter contribute to total budgeted outlays, whereas those of the former do not. In 1984, total new lending by the Federal Financing Bank constituted an estimated $24 billion that did not appear in the budget and was not counted as part of the deficit.

It is the practice of the present administration to present and analyze the detail of all off-budget items as part of the budget message, and there is considerable sentiment to end the separation as far as these agencies are concerned. The point is that the possibility of defining an activity out of the budget presents an additional complication in the path of an effective constitutional amendment. Since the budget includes only what Congress and the President agree it does, any constitutional requirement that it be "balanced" can be at least partly circumvented by shifting appropriate outlays off the budget.

Another alternative to shifting outlays off the budget is to substitute a subsidized loan program for direct outlays. If the federal government, or its off-budget agency the Federal Financing Bank, issues securities and reloans the resulting funds to private firms at less than market rates paid by private borrowers, no receipts nor outlays appear in the federal budget as long as defaults on those loans are not large enough in aggregate to offset the interest rate differential used to insure against that risk. Similarly, federal guarantees of private market loans, which allow for lower interest charges, will not usually result in budget outlays. But in both cases, the lower borrowing costs are equivalent to government grants to those private borrowers. One limitation on the possible substitution of loans for direct expenditures is the potential for increased rates on all government securities, which would increase the budgeted outlay for service on the federal debt.

According to the Economic Report of the President, about two-thirds of federal government borrowing each year is borrowing to finance the budget deficit. Five percent is borrowing to finance the off-budget deficit and the rest, more than 25 percent, is accounted for by borrowing for federal government loan purposes. In 1985, government sponsored enterprises such as the Farm Credit Administration, the Federal Home Loan Bank Board, the Federal National Mortgage Association and the Student Loan Marketing Association are expected to borrow more than $44 billion. In addition, federal

---

[5]For a detailed review of off-budget activities, see Bennett and Dilorenzo (1983) and Carron (1981).

agencies are expected to guarantee about $20 billion of private borrowing in 1984. These government sponsored enterprises are expected to make more than $185 billion worth of loans in 1984 on top of more than $63 billion of federally guaranteed loans and nearly $55 billion of direct loans by the government. The use of (often off-budget) loans and guarantees is another reason, therefore, why a balanced budget amendment does not necessarily reduce either government involvement in credit markets or government influence over the economy.

To resolve these problems of defining "the budget" by an amendment might require, as Charles Schultze has said, "twenty pages of accounting definitions in the Constitution, and even that would not be enough" (1980, p. 121). If that approach is taken, then surely the courts would be called upon to adjudicate fine variations or cases not covered by the definitions. To leave the definitions to Congress merely continues the current system.

IV. REVENUE LIMITATION

Section 2 of the proposed amendment limits the rate of increase in budgeted "total receipts" to the past rate of increase in national income. It is unclear whether this limit is to apply to budgeted receipts for the coming year as compared to those budgeted initially for the preceding year, or to those actually received. Presumably the first is intended, for—at least under the present budget cycle—the President's proposed budget for the coming fiscal year is presented to Congress early in the second quarter of the current fiscal year. Likewise, it is unclear whether section 2 means that reduction in national income must be matched by a corresponding reduction in receipts, or merely that, when increased, budgeted receipts are to rise by no more than the designated limit.

Whatever the interpretation, it is very important that the amendment avoid too close linkage of the budget with economic activity. That is, the growth of receipts should not be tied to the erratic year-to-year movements of business cycles, since this would tend to intensify rather than iron out economic fluctuations. Section 2 partially avoids this danger by permitting the rate of increase in national income to be measured as a trend over a limited period of time, rather than by movements in individual years.

However, the combined effect of balancing the budget and limiting the growth of receipts when starting from an existing deficit is likely to be a reduction in the amount of federal government outlays. For instance, suppose that outlays equal receipts in the first year the amendment takes effect and that receipts grow at the same rate as national income. Then

$$E^1 = R^1 = R^0(1 + n)$$

where E^1 = outlays in year 1

$\quad R^1$ = receipts in year 1

$\quad R^0$ = receipts in year 0

$\quad n$ = growth rate of national income

If the budget before the amendment takes effect is in deficit, then

$$E^0 = R^0(1 + d)$$

where 1 = ratio of deficit to receipts. It follows that $E^1 < E^0$ if $n < d$. That is, if national income does not increase enough to tax finance expenditures previously financed by the deficit, then outlays must fall. Given the magnitude of current deficits, a relatively long transition period would be required to avoid an expenditure decrease.

Although section 2 appears to present a well-defined limit to the permissible growth in "receipts," it does not provide an effective limit to the growth of government. In the first place, as noted, Congress and the President are free to define which receipts are part of the budget (and hence subject to the limitation) and which are the receipts of off-budget agencies and exempt from the limitations. Since Social Security taxes alone constitute almost a third of all receipts in the unified budget, restoration of Social Security to its former off-budget status would leave plenty of room for government to grow despite the limitation on budgeted receipts. Similarly, government could grow by expansion of its credit programs.

A. Tax Expenditures

Not only can government programs be shifted to off-budget agencies, they can also be replaced by tax expenditures. Tax expenditures occur whenever governmental objectives are accomplished by tax deductions or credits without the outlay of explicitly budgeted funds. For example, under existing tax law, contributions for the support of many activities are deductible from personal income before federal income taxes are calculated. In consequence, the contribution of $1,000 by a taxpayer in the 50 percent bracket provides the agency with $1,000, but costs the taxpayer only $500. The net effect is exactly the same as if the government had allowed no deduction for the contribution, but rather had supplied a dollar-for-dollar matching grant for contributions to the agency. The only difference is that under a matching grant system, both budgeted outlays and budgeted receipts would have been $500 higher than when the support is provided via tax expenditure.

Similarly, a government program to subsidize firms that hire unemployed workers in central cities would, if incorporated in the budget, involve specified outlays and receipts. When the same thing is accomplished by means of a corporate tax credit, neither outlay nor receipt appear. Budgeted programs are clearly and openly part of the government's demand on the resources of the community, and taxpayers are aware that they are footing the bill. When the same programs are financed by means of tax expenditures, the same resources may be diverted for the purpose, but the actual size of government is disguised, nor is it easy for the taxpayer to perceive who bears the cost.

For clarification, support for an agency by a budgeted matching grant is compared in the following table with support by tax expenditure. As shown at the left, when government matches the taxpayer's contribution, both tax receipts and budgeted outlays must be adequate to fund general government and the agency. At the right, however,

Support of an agency by budgeted matching grant		Support of an agency by tax expenditure	
The budget			
Outlay		Outlay	
General government	$10,000	General government	$10,000
Matching grant	500		
Total	$10,500	Total	$10,000
Receipts		Receipts	
Taxes	$10,500	Taxes	$10,000
Taxpayer's position			
Tax liability	$10,500	Tax liability (before contributions)	$10,500
		Deduction	−500
		Net tax liability	10,000
Contribution	500	Contribution	1,000
Total burden	$11,000	Total burden	$11,000

when the taxpayer's contribution to the agency reduces tax liability, the taxpayer is again supporting both general government and the agency, but this time, agency support appears in neither budgeted outlays nor receipts. Yet government is the same size and carries out the same policy in both situations, and the burden on the taxpayer is identical.

Tax expenditures are already employed to finance a broad range of governmental purposes. Federal tax expenditures, as reported in the Special Analyses section of the proposed 1986 budget, are estimated to be equivalent to more than $400 billion of budget outlays. These tax expenditures include programs in nearly every functional area of the government and are expanding. In recent years, even without a balanced budget requirement, tax expenditures have been rising faster than direct federal expenditures, and their use could be expanded indefinitely if government receipts were limited by a balanced budget amendment.[6]

For instance, it would be possible to finance some, or even all, military outlays through tax expenditure. It would only be necessary to establish an independent "Defense Finance Agency," operating under the direction of the Secretary of Defense, to receive voluntary contributions from any interested taxpayers. Taxpayers, in turn, would receive a credit against their tax liability equal to the amount of their contributions. (If a 100 percent tax credit did not, for some reason, elicit enough contributions, nothing would prevent Congress from allowing contributors—up to some limit—to receive tax credit in excess of their contributions.) Of course, as in the table above, legislated tax rates would have to be high enough to leave sufficient revenue

---

[6]Wildavsky (1980) appears to be alone in arguing that use of tax expenditures would not rise if a balanced budget were required. He argues that with revenue limitation lower tax rates will be required, thus reducing the effectiveness of tax deductions and exemptions (although tax credits, the effect of which are not related to rates, could still be used). For a contrary view, see Break (1982).

after tax credits to finance the rest of the government's operation, but the entire military program would be removed from the budget.

B. Efficiency of Government

An additional alternative to direct government spending is provided by government regulation of private economic activity. For example, the government can appropriate funds to the Environmental Protection Agency to clean up toxic waste sites or, alternatively, adopt and enforce a regulation that such sites must be cleaned up by private sector users. The total cost burden is the same, but in one case it appears in the budget and in the other case it does not. Although supportive of a balanced budget amendment, Wagner (1982, p. 48) notes "anything that can be accomplished through the taxing and spending aspects of the budget can be accomplished instead through government regulation." He subsequently concludes "one major impact of a budget limit would be to induce a greater use of the police power to achieve . . . [results] that otherwise would be accomplished through the budget" (Wagner, 1983, p. 138).

The total cost to society of achieving public policy objectives depends partly on the means employed. Taxes, subsidies, and regulation all have costs of their own. (Think of the cost of preparing tax returns under the present complex tax system.) A balanced budget amendment induces the federal government to substitute off-budget activities, loans, tax expenditures or regulations for budgeted expenditures and these may simply be more expensive means of reaching policy objectives. For example, Feldstein (1980) has explicitly compared tax expenditures and direct government expenditures as alternative means and concludes that "in a number of important cases, the tax subsidy may be better [same effect at lower revenue cost] than direct spending" (Feldstein, 1980, p. 122). Of course, the converse also holds and there is no presumption that all current tax expenditures are better than direct spending. In other words, in our view, a balanced budget amendment would not only fail to limit the true size of the federal government, but would raise the total cost of government to taxpayers.[7]

V. EVIDENCE FROM THE STATES

As has often been the case, state governments have preceded the federal government in experimentation, this time with balanced budget requirements. A report by The Council of State Governments shows that 18 states have constitutional or statutory requirements that the budget be balanced, either as proposed or appropriated. Moreover, 20 states have provisions calling for budget action to eliminate deficits that occur as the fiscal year proceeds. By including state constitutional debt limitations, ACIR concluded that "all states (except Vermont) are required to balance their budgets" (ACIR, 1985, p. 6). Their experience is instructive.

---

[7]On this point, we are in agreement with Charles Schultze, who argues that "mandating an annually balanced federal budget in the Constitution would set in motion some major forces . . . virtually all of which would, I think, impose onerous burdens on business firms, state and local governments, and individual citizens" (1980, p. 123).

For instance, Michigan has operated under a balanced budget requirement since its constitution was rewritten in 1963. The operative sections read, in part, as follows:

> Art. 5, Sec. 18. The governor shall submit to the legislature . . . a budget for the ensuing fiscal period setting forth in detail, for all operating funds, the proposed expenditures and estimated revenue of the state. Proposed expenditures from any fund shall not exceed the estimated revenue thereof.
>
> Art. 5, Sec. 20. . . . The governor, with the approval of the appropriating committees of the house and senate, shall reduce expenditures authorized by appropriations whenever it appears that actual revenues for a fiscal period will fall below the revenue estimates on which appropriations for that period were based.

The Michigan Constitution requires, therefore, a balanced state budget both as proposed *and* implemented. In addition, the Michigan Constitution was amended in 1978 by the addition of a revenue limitation. State revenues, excluding federal aid, may be no greater a fraction of state personal income in any fiscal year than they were in 1978. In effect, long-run revenue growth is limited to the growth in personal income.

As would be predicted from the foregoing, however, Michigan has resorted to ways to avoid both the balanced budget and the revenue limitation. The state lottery, which brings in net receipts of more than $250 million annually, is not classified as revenue for purposes of the limitation. In addition, government support for higher education and related activities has been partially shifted to tax expenditure by the provision of a 50 percent income-tax credit for contributions (up to $200 per joint return) to Michigan colleges and universities, public libraries, and broadcasting stations. Moreover, over the period 1975–1982, despite the apparently strict constitutional provision, Michigan accumulated budget debts totaling $850 million, a debt equal to more than 15 percent of the 1982 general-fund, general-purpose budget. This accumulated debt resulted from the practice of using accounting changes and internal borrowing from earmarked funds to meet the letter of the balanced budget requirement, but not the spirit.

As shown in Chart 1, these accumulated budget deficits reached crisis proportions in fiscal year 1983. The accumulated debt plus a projected $900 million current year budget deficit precipitated one of the most serious financial emergencies in the state's history. Indeed, the state's short-term, cash-flow borrowing at the start of that fiscal year had been possible only because of a letter of credit supplied by a consortium of Japanese banks. As the fiscal year's difficulties unfolded, however, Michigan was effectively excluded from the credit markets and faced payless paydays or default without substantial budget adjustments. In short, the constitutional balanced budget requirements had not resulted in truly balanced budgets in Michigan. A fiscal crisis and closure of the financial markets were the factors forcing a fiscal plan to generate balanced budgets and repay the debt.

The experiences of other subnational governments provide similar evidence. The fiscal crisis of New York City in 1975 followed a long period of improper accounting and lackadaisical fiscal oversight. Each year's budget deficit was advanced to the following fiscal year and financed by successively growing borrowing. Each adopted budget appeared to be balanced, and as with Michigan, only a near default and the lack of further borrowing opportunity brought forth fiscal restraint and a move toward truly balanced budgets.

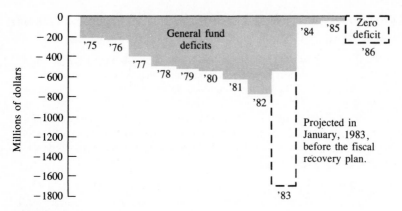

CHART 1
State of Michigan General Fund Balances (computed on the basis of generally accepted accounting principles). *Note:* Fiscal years 1975–1980 are estimates. Fiscal years 1984–1986 are projections. (Source: Budget Message of the Governor, *for fiscal year 1986, State of Michigan, Lansing, 1985, p. 6.*)

This year, the Governor of New York, a state with a Constitutional requirement for balanced budgets, advanced a plan to repay the state's accumulated budget debts, which now total about $4.5 billion, and move the state toward budgeting based upon generally accepted accounting principles. In effect, he is recognizing a past of accounting alterations and borrowing to generate "balanced budgets" on paper, though not in reality. The *Wall Street Journal* (2/27/85) recently noted:

> Every April the state starts its fiscal year with a short-term "spring borrowing" so massive that it crowds out the U.S. Treasury for several weeks. Some of the loan goes for normal cash flow. A great deal more covers state aid to towns and school districts whose fiscal years go on for another quarter . . . Another portion of the hidden deficit, vastly expanded since 1981, is straight deficit juggling, usually through deferred income-tax refunds.

The reaction to the Governor's proposal may be summarized as: why move so fast toward fiscal responsibility? In the same *Wall Street Journal* editorial quoted above, the conclusion is:

> This deficit would have stayed well hidden if New York state in its post-crisis cleanup hadn't committed itself to the world according to GAAP. Under the old accounting, the state budget has been balanced every year but one.
>
> But is it more urgent to pay down the debt or keep cutting taxes? . . . Tax cuts should come first.

The State of New York does not yet face the requisite fiscal crisis.

To be sure, state and local governments operate in a substantially different economic environment than the federal government. Subnational government economies are substantially more open than the national economy which limits the opportunity for effective fiscal policy, and subnational governments do not have, even indirectly, any monetary authority. Yet balanced budget amendments have not controlled the temptation to use deficit finance to separate the benefits of outlays from the costs of financing among subnational governments.[8]

VI. CONCLUSIONS

In principle, there is much to be said in favor of an amendment that would compel the President and Congress to balance the budget, at least if ample provision is made for appropriate exceptions. But it is by no means apparent that the proposed amendment or any other formula can accomplish the desired end. There are so many readily available ways to circumvent the provisions of the proposed amendment that it can neither assure a balanced budget, nor provide an effective limit to the size of government. To block the many escape routes would require, at a minimum, that the entire budget process, including codification of forecasting procedures, be constitutionally specified, and quite probably it would be necessary to embody the structure of the budget itself, together with the tax laws, in the amendment.[9]

Individual states have long written tax laws into their constitutions creating serious problems of inflexibility in times of fiscal crisis, but a balanced budget amendment sufficiently detailed to be effective would go far beyond this. The result, even if it could be written and passed, would be dangerously limiting for the government of a dynamic, continually changing society. In a very real sense, the budget is a detailed expression of what the President and Congress are doing to govern the nation. An effective balanced budget amendment would remove most, if not all, of the political aspect of the government, and replace it by an inflexible formula.

It may be argued that the picture we have drawn of the weaknesses of the proposed amendment is distorted and unrealistic. Even granting that lawmakers have the power to base expected receipts on exaggerated optimism about the economic outlook and to remove activities from the budget in various ways, would they resort to such tactics? Clearly, they might not. But if they didn't, it would be their own political decisions, not because anything about the amendment prevented it. This point, too, seems to be understood by some proponents of Constitutional limitation. Even while arguing for a Constitutional amendment to limit federal outlays and considering what he calls "end runs," Aaron Wildavsky concludes that the operation of "the amendment is totally dependent on some support and on the absence of persistent political opposition. The purpose of the amendment, as bears repeating, is not to replace the political process but to perfect it" (Wildavsky, 1980, p. 101). Here it seems he comes close to agreeing with Mancur Olson, that "just as the demand for alcohol persisted and the profits for supplying alcohol persisted even under prohibition, . . . so the demands of voters and

---

[8]Wildavsky also notes that state balanced budget requirements "do not appear to be entirely effective," although he argues that expenditure limitation at the federal level could be more effective because only expenditures, not revenues, would need to be defined and because the absence of a federal capital budget removes another avenue of fungibility available to many states. (1980, p. 188). For a review of state tax and expenditure limits, see Kenyon and Benker (1984).

[9]Blinder and Holtz-Eakin (1984) recently examined survey results about voter attitudes regarding a balanced budget amendment. A 1980 Gallup Poll asked respondents to rank arguments in favor and arguments against an amendment. The offered arguments against included "Will hurt the economy," "Too restrictive," "Will reduce necessary programs," but, unfortunately, not that it won't work.

pressure groups . . . will not disappear just because a constitutional amendment bans deficit financing" (Olson, 1980, p. 92).

In short, after all the effort expended to compel Congress to act in a specific manner, we would still have to depend on Congress to legislate in accordance with the desired objectives. Since one cannot mandamus a legislature, we would find ourselves essentially back where we are today.

REFERENCES

Ackley, Gardner, "You Can't Balance the Budget By Amendment," *Challenge,* November–December, 1982, pp. 4–13.

Bennett, James T. and Thomas J. DiLorenzo, *Underground Government: The Off-Budget Public Sector,* Cato Institute, Washington, 1983.

Blinder, Alan S., and Douglas Holtz-Eakin, "Public Opinion and the Balanced Budget," *American Economic Review,* May, 1984, pp. 144–149.

Boskin, Michael J., "Federal Government Deficits: Some Myths and Realities," *American Economic Review,* May 1982, pp. 296–323.

Break, George F., "Issues in Measuring the Level of Government Economic Activity," *American Economic Review,* May 1982, pp. 288–295.

Budget Message of the Governor, 1985–86 Fiscal year, State of Michigan, Lansing, January 1985.

Carron, Andrew S., "Fiscal Activities Outside the Budget," in *Setting National Priorities, The 1982 Budget,* J. Pechman, ed., Brookings Institution, Washington, 1981, pp. 261–269.

"Chicken and Egg," *The Wall Street Journal,* (February 27, 1985), editorial.

Economic Report of the President, Annual Report of the Council of Economic Advisers, U.S. Government Printing Office, Washington, February 1985.

Eisner, Robert, "Which Budget Deficit? Some Issues of Measurement and Their Implications," *American Economic Review.* May, 1984, pp. 138–143.

Feldstein, Martin, "A Contribution to the Theory of Tax Expenditures: The Case of Chartable Giving," in H. Aaron and M. Boskins, eds., *The Economics of Taxation,* The Brookings Institution, 1980, pp. 99–122.

Kenyon, Daphne A., and Karen M. Benker, "Fiscal Discipline: Lessons from the State Experience," *National Tax Journal,* Vol. 37, No. 3, September, 1984, pp. 433–446.

Limitations on State Deficits, The Council of State Governments, Lexington, Kentucky, April 1976.

Olson, Mancur, "Is the Balanced Budget Amendment Another Form of Prohibition?" in *The Constitution and the Budget,* W. S. Moore and R. G. Penner, eds., American Enterprise Institute, Washington, 1980, pp. 91–94.

Schultze, Charles L., "Politics and Economics of a Balanced Budget Amendment," in *The Constitution and the Budget,* W. S. Moore and R. G. Penner, eds., American Enterprise Institute, Washington, 1980, pp. 120–124.

Shepsle, Kenneth A., "The Budget: Will a Constitutional Amendment Help?" *Challenge,* July–August, 1982, pp. 53–56.

Significant Features of Fiscal Federalism, 1984 Edition, Report M-141, U.S. Advisory Commission on Intergovernmental Relations, Washington, 1985.

Special Analyses, Budget of the United States Government, Fiscal year 1986, Office of Management and Budget, Washington, February 1985.

Stubblebine, W. Craig, "Balancing the Budget versus Limiting Spending," in *The Constitution and the Budget*, W. S. Moore and R. G. Penner, eds., American Enterprise Institute, Washington, 1980, pp. 50–56.

Wagner, Richard E., *Public Finance, Revenues and Expenditures in a Democratic Society*, Little, Brown and Company, Boston, 1983.

Wagner, Richard E., Robert D. Tollison, Alvin Rabushka, and John T. Noonan, Jr., *Balanced Budgets, Fiscal Responsibility, and the Constitution*, Cato Institute, Washington, 1982.

Wildavsky, Aaron, *The Politics of the Budgetary Process*, Little, Brown and Company, Boston, 1979.

Wildavsky, Aaron, *How to Limit Government Spending*, University of California Press, Berkeley, 1980.

QUESTIONS FOR DISCUSSION

1 Why do the authors believe that "one probable result of a balanced budget amendment would be merely an increase in the amount and scope of political game-playing with economic forecasts . . ."? How would forecasts of each of the following affect the projected budget deficit: (*a*) GNP growth, (*b*) interest rates, (*c*) inflation?

2 Give some examples of "off-budget" federal expenditures. What problem does the existence of off-budget items pose for the enforcement of a balanced budget amendment?

3 A loan guarantee is a federal government promise to a bank that, if the bank makes a loan to a specified borrower (such as a student under the Guaranteed Student Loan program), the government will make good any losses to the bank arising from a default on the loan. Suppose that the government replaces a program of direct (on-budget) federal lending with a program of loan guarantees. What is the economic effect of this switch? The effect on the official government budget?

4 The article states that "the growth of receipts [as mandated by the amendment] should not be tied to the erratic year-to-year movements of business cycles, since it would tend to intensify rather than iron out fluctuations." Explain.

5 Define the concept of a *tax expenditure*, and explain why tax expenditures cause problems for statutory attempts to restrict the size of government.

6 Why do the authors think that a balanced budget amendment would lead to an increase in government regulation?

DOES PRIVATE SAVING ADJUST TO OFFSET INCREASES IN THE GOVERNMENT DEFICIT?

The so-called Ricardian equivalence theorem, first stated by the great nineteenth-century economist David Ricardo and now most closely associated with the name of University of Rochester economist Robert Barro, argues that (to a first approximation) it does not matter for net national savings whether the government finances its spending with taxes or by borrowing. If private individuals can "see through" the veil of government finances to recognize that the government's debts are ultimately their own, then they will increase their own savings to offset any increase in the government deficit. Thus, for example, government borrowing need not "crowd out" private investment.

The first of the two short articles below states the Ricardian proposition in greater detail. The second argues that recent U.S. savings behavior does not appear to conform to the Ricardian theory.

Reading 13 Kevin D. Hoover and Joseph R. Bisignano, "Classical Reflections on the Deficit," *Weekly Letter,* San Francisco Federal Reserve Bank, October 14, 1983.

Joseph Bisignano, "Impervious Savings Behavior," *Weekly Letter,* San Francisco Federal Reserve Bank, September 28, 1984.

CLASSICAL REFLECTIONS ON THE DEFICIT
Kevin D. Hoover and Joseph R. Bisignano

IMPERVIOUS SAVINGS BEHAVIOR
Joseph Bisignano

Classical Reflections on the Deficit

Kevin D. Hoover and Joseph R. Bisignano

The primary long-term effect of deficits is to reduce the rate of capital formation. Government borrowing crowds out private borrowing and causes a lower rate of investment. The lower rate of capital formation hurts productivity, decreases growth, limits the rise in real incomes and weakens our international competitiveness. (Martin Feldstein, Chairman of the President's Council of Economic Advisers in the *Wall Street Journal,* July 15, 1983.)

Everybody's jumping to the conclusion that [crowding out] is going to happen in 30 days . . . it's not going to happen in three months. (Secretary of the Treasury, Donald T. Regan, quoted in the *Washington Post,* August 23, 1983.)

With the prospect of large federal government deficits during this year and perhaps for several years to come, the question as to what their effects will be is in the forefront of discussions of economic policy. Reasonable people evidently differ on the answer. Unfortunately, it is not always clear from their pronouncements what the basis of their judgments is. Close examination shows that what may lie at the heart of their differences are some fundamental conceptual issues in economic theory—in particular, whether taxation and government borrowing are economically equivalent forms of government finance, and whether it makes a difference if government debt takes the form of interest-bearing bonds or non-interest-bearing currency and bank reserves. This *Letter* builds

Kevin D. Hoover and Joseph R. Bisignano, "Classical Reflections on the Deficit," *Weekly Letter,* San Francisco Federal Reserve Bank, October 14, 1983, pp. 1–3.

on a discussion by the nineteenth century English classical economist David Ricardo to help clarify these issues.

GOVERNMENT'S BUDGET CONSTRAINT

All federal expenditures must be paid for, but there is a choice of sources for the needed funds. The Treasury can raise taxes, or it can go into debt. Its debt may either be held by the public at large or by the Federal Reserve System, which although formally independent of the executive branch, can be treated for our purposes as part of the government. When the Federal Reserve buys Treasury debt, it pays with an increase in the monetary base which will be held either as reserves of depository financial institutions or as currency in the hands of the public. This transaction is sometimes called "monetizing the debt," and it leaves the public holding more non-interest bearing government liabilities in the form of money and fewer interest-bearing liabilities in the form of Treasury securities.

Government's expenditure is constrained to equal the sum of taxes plus the sales of debt to the public (including banks) plus the creation of monetary base by the Federal Reserve. Since deficits are the excess of government expenditure over taxes, the budget constraint may also be expressed as: deficits must equal the sales of debt to the public plus the creation of monetary base by the Federal Reserve.

RICARDIAN EQUIVALENCE

The current policy debate centers on whether or not different compositions of government finance result in crowding out. In particular, does issuing more debt and lowering taxes raise real interest rates and *crowd out* private investment? Ricardo gave an early analysis of the problem in his *Principles of Political Economy and Taxation* (1821).

He argued that if taxpayers fully understood that government borrowing only postpones the payment of taxes, it would not matter at all how deficits were financed. If the government chose to finance a given expenditure through taxes, each taxpayer could borrow enough to pay his taxes (i.e., sell a bond) and then would immediately have to pay only the interest and some portion of the principal on the loan. If the government financed the same deficit by selling its own bonds to the public, the taxpayers would be taxed to pay the interest and the currently maturing principal on the government bonds. In either case, the taxpayer might pay the taxes without borrowing the money, but if he treated the amount paid as a loan to himself, he would find that the portion of his income available for consumption would be no less than if he had actually borrowed the money. Ricardo argued, in effect, that the composition of government finance for the same level of expenditure made no difference since taxpayers can make exactly compensating adjustments in their own portfolios.

Ricardo's argument for the equivalence of debt and taxation rests on at least two implicit assumptions. The first is that taxpayers are economically similar. If this assumption were relaxed, then taxpayers' after-tax incomes would be affected by the method of government finance. Suppose, for example, that some people are seen by lenders to be a greater risk than others and are, therefore, charged a higher rate of interest. Lowering taxes and issuing an equal amount of debt means that high-risk borrowers have more cash in hand and pay it back through taxes at a lower rate than they would pay if they had borrowed it privately. Debt finance would thus affect their incomes. In the same way, if the people who buy most of the bonds differed from those who pay most of the taxes, substituting debt for taxes would affect incomes. The second assumption is that taxes are not distorting, that they do not alter the optimal allocation of resources. If this assumption were relaxed, for example, if taxes were levied only on consumption (e.g., sales tax), then lowering taxes and raising debt would favor consumption at the expense of investment.

Ricardo recognized that his argument for the equivalence of debt finance and taxation was a theoretical one that depended crucially on accurate anticipations of future taxes. He believed that, in practice, there would "debt-illusion" in the sense that taxpayers would save enough to pay only the taxes that cover the interest on the debt and forget about the need to repay the principal in the future. Debt finance would then appear to be more stimulative than tax finance when the economy is operating at less than full employment.

If Ricardo's theoretical argument held in practice, different splits between taxes and debt finance would not affect spendable incomes. Private saving would always adjust to the amount needed to service the debt, and interest rates would not be affected. On the other hand, if Ricardo's practical judgment were correct, taxpayers would feel richer when government expenditure is financed by debt rather than by taxes. They would want to spend more, but since they would not actually be richer, they could only spend more by saving less. To induce them to save enough to cover the debt, the interest rate on government bonds would have to rise. Higher interest rates would then discourage private investment. Thus, when there is debt illusion, the more the method of government finance opts for debt over taxes, the lower would be the level of private investment and the higher the level of private consumption.

THE BURDEN OF DEBT

Despite showing that debt and taxes *could* be equivalent, Ricardo believed that government should favor taxes over debt even if there were no debt-illusion. His reason was that present taxes are immediate and hard to escape, but a large debt implying high future taxes would encourage emigration to avoid paying future taxes. Ricardo's argument can be reformulated to show that the present generation can escape taxes by incurring debt that must be paid by generations that live long after the present one is dead and gone. It is said that "the past is another country." The present generation, in effect, would emigrate to the past by shifting the burden of debt onto its descendants. That burden can be measured by the degree to which the capital stock is smaller because previous generations invested less as a response to higher interest rates caused by the choice of debt financing.

This theoretical analysis raises two questions: First, can the burden of debt actually be shifted onto future generations? That is, are taxes and debt finance equivalent across generations? Second, is it desirable to shift the burden of debt? The answer to the second question depends on one's values, but its importance depends on the answer to the first question.

Ricardo believed that the burden of government debt can be shifted to other generations. His implicit assumption is that the debt must eventually be paid off by the taxpayers, but that it can be postponed by issuing more debt. If this were done continuously, no future generation would be taxed to pay off the debt. And each generation would believe falsely that it was richer, and interest rates would remain high to ensure that savings were sufficient to buy newly issued debt.

Critics of this idea argue that there is some debt size, or some ratio of the debt to national income, beyond which no one would want to buy government bonds, that is, at which the government has limited "collateral." At that point, the debt must eventually be paid off. How much collateral the government is supposed to have is not clear. Nevertheless, the critics believe that at the point at which the government could not sell any more debt, it would have to cover its deficits by creating monetary base. And they believe that this monetary expansion could cause inflation.

Can this implicit distinction between the economic effects of an increase of the interest-bearing debt and of the monetary base be sustained? One could argue, in theory, that an expansion of the debt at a rate much faster than the rate of growth of national income would require ever-rising interest rates. And since money yields a zero or fixed rate of return, these high rates would induce people to hold more government bonds and less money. Such a situation is equivalent to a rise in the velocity of circulation of money, which would support a higher rate of inflation.

In practice, we are not facing such a hyperexpansion of government debt. Instead, we are facing a large increase in the ratio of interest-bearing government debt to non-interest-bearing monetary base. In the long-run, since both are nominal liabilities of the government, it may make little difference which is used to finance the deficit. In the short-run, however, the government can sell more debt to the private sector only by offering a higher rate of return to increase its attractiveness. That this rise in interest rates will crowd-out private investment is the principal fear of those who oppose further increases in the interest-bearing government debt.

CONCLUSION

Compared with the recent past, current monetary and fiscal policy in the United States places relatively more weight on deficit finance than on taxation, with the deficit being financed more by government debt than by money creation. What effects this policy stance should be expected to have on the economy in the long-run depends on how one decides the main issues discussed in this *Letter*. In other words, which Ricardo does one believe? The "practical" Ricardo expects present policy to crowd out investment, but the "theoretical" Ricardo expects few ill effects to result from the large government deficits currently facing the U.S.

Impervious Savings Behavior

Joseph Bisignano

One argument made a few years ago by proponents of large federal tax cuts was that the resulting massive federal deficits could automatically be financed by the private sector. In part, the argument relied on the hypothesis that the fall in tax rates would create an incentive for the private sector to increase its saving rate, and that the increase in private saving would finance the federal deficits and obviate any increase in market interest rates.

Such arguments no longer appear in the financial press because the reality is that we live in a country of deficit domestic saving. This deficiency is easily measured. It is simply the difference between gross *private domestic* investment and gross domestic saving in our national income accounts. Gross saving is the sum of gross private saving (personal and business) and the saving of the government sector.

In the second quarter of this year gross *private* saving totalled $663 billion. Added to the $54 billion surplus of state and local governments and the $167 federal deficit— the "dissaving" of the federal government, we find that the gross saving of the entire economy in the second quarter of 1984 amounted to $550 billion, at an annual rate. In contrast, gross private domestic investment totalled $626 billion. Domestic investment therefore exceeded domestic saving. The balance of about $76 billion was made up in essence by borrowing from abroad. Foreigners can be viewed as having provided about 12 percent of the funds needed to finance U.S. private investment in the second quarter, or as having financed about 45 percent of the federal deficit.

HOW THE PRIVATE SECTOR SEES THE GOVERNMENT

Before the proponents of large federal tax cuts made their claims about probable private sector responses to increased federal deficits and higher after-tax rates of return, they should have studied the post-war behavior of gross domestic private saving. Despite recent economic events such as changes in federal income tax rates and high real interest rates, the gross domestic private saving rate whether measured as a percent of GNP or of national income has remained relatively stable.

From 1975 to 1983, gross domestic private saving as a percent of gross national product varied between 16.5 percent and 18.2 percent. In the last three years, its rate has moved narrowly between 17.1 and 17.3 percent. The same stability does not describe the government saving rate. Since 1975, federal, state and local financial positions combined have yielded a government saving rate (as a percent of GNP) that has ranged from about zero in 1979 to negative 4 percent in 1983. Gross domestic private saving, has, then, seemed insensitive to the financial position of the government

Joseph Bisignano, "Impervious Savings Behavior, *Weekly Letter,* San Francisco Federal Reserve Bank, September 28, 1984.

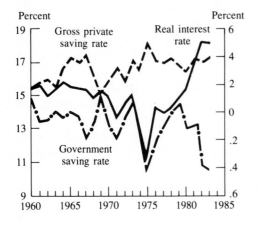

CHART 1

Saving and Real Interest Rates. Real interest rate defined as the 1-year Treasury bill rate less the annual rate of change in the GNP price deflator.

sector as well as to the extraordinarily high level of real interest rates in recent years. (See Chart 1.)

While the gross domestic private saving rate has been relatively stable, its two components—personal saving and business saving have not. As noted by Edward F. Denison three decades ago, personal saving and corporate saving often appear to move in opposite directions. In a sense, the personal sector appears to incorporate the saving behavior of the corporate sector in its own decisions to save and to consume. This is not unreasonable. Since the non-business (personal) sector "owns" the corporate sector, it considers corporate saving, composed of undistributed corporate profits and depreciation of corporate and noncorporate business, a close substitute for personal saving. This implies, as noted by Denison, that personal consumption expenditures are unaffected by corporate dividend behavior.

The offsetting saving behavior of the personal and corporate sectors leads to stability in the gross private domestic saving rate. The relationship is clearly observable in the two saving rates in just the last few years (Chart 2). Business saving as a percent of

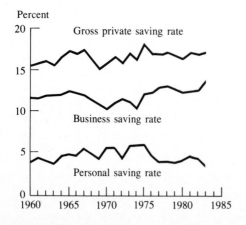

CHART 2

Saving Rates as a Percent of GNP.

GNP grew from 12.6 to 13.7 percent between 1981 and 1983. Personal saving as a percent of GNP, on the other hand, fell from 4.6 to 3.6 percent from 1981 to 1983. The net effect was to produce gross private saving rates (as a percent of GNP) of 17.24, 17.07, and 17.30 percent in 1981, 1982 and 1983, respectively.

Domestic private saving has truly been impervious to the level of real interest rates in recent years and to the financial status of the federal government, whose deficits have nearly tripled during the period from 1981 to 1983. While the personal sector seems to continue to incorporate the saving status of the business sector in its own saving decisions, it appears to have disregarded the financial status of the government sector.

NOT INTERNALIZING GOVERNMENT FINANCIAL BEHAVIOR

The debate over the effect of the federal government deficit on the real economy centers on the degree to which taxpayers recognize any current and future costs associated with paying for government expenditures with the sale of bonds rather than through immediate taxation. At the local community level, one might argue that taxpayers quickly recognize that bond issuance will involve a future financial burden to the local residents. These residents would alter their saving behavior in recognition of the future financing burden. In a sense, bond finance may be viewed as deferred taxation. A similar argument applied to federal deficits has gained popularity recently among some academic economists. However, it is difficult to observe any major change in private domestic saving behavior in response to the outbreak of large federal deficits.

The stability of the gross private saving rate in the face of federal budget deficits amounting to 5-6 percent of GNP, and expected to remain in the 3-4 percent range for the next several years, is inconsistent with recent arguments promoted by some academics that current federal deficits, entailing future principal and interest servicing costs, are equivalent to and interpreted by consumers as future taxes. Their argument presupposes that consumers realize that the only real "tax cut" is a government spending cut. Since they recognize this equivalence, according to the argument, they would not have interpreted recent personal income tax cuts as real tax cuts. Instead, they would have recognized the need to obtain additional interest-earning assets in order to pay for the future costs of servicing the increased federal deficit and saved *all* of the tax cut. The result should be a rise in the gross private saving rate. Chart 1 shows that in 1969 and 1975, for example, the gross private saving rate and the government saving rate moved in opposite directions, as suggested by the theory. Recent facts, however, do not support this argument. Between 1981 and 1983, the gross private saving rate averaged 17.20 percent compared with an average saving rate of 17.18 percent of GNP between 1975 and 1980. The tax cut and resulting federal deficits do not appear to have disturbed the general stability of the gross private saving rate.

THE SAVING GAP

The apparent insensitivity of the gross private saving rate to changes in after-tax rates of return means that gross domestic saving likely will fall short of gross private domestic investment if the federal government goes substantially into deficit. The resulting shortfall may be called the "domestic saving gap." This gap totalled about $34 billion in 1983 and was closed by importing foreign capital, observable in our large and growing current account deficit.

The existence of both large federal deficits and large current account deficits has sometimes led to the claims that the former "causes" the latter. This is not necessarily true. The current account deficit could decline significantly, that is, the saving gap could close, even in the face of large federal deficits if domestic private investment would decline—the textbook case of "crowding out." Eliminating the domestic saving gap therefore requires either a fall in domestic investment or a reduction in the federal deficit.

But is the current saving gap necessarily pernicious, something to be avoided? Not necessarily. What we observe in the United States is that capital investment is more cyclical and more interest-sensitive than private saving. Hence, the saving gap is altered by cyclical swings in investment. For example, between 1978 and 1982, the ratio of gross private domestic investment to GNP fell from almost 18 percent to 13.5 percent, while the gross private saving rate was 17.3 and 17.1 percent.

The cyclical recovery beginning in late 1982 coupled with the reduction in after-tax interest costs of business capital investment and the resulting pick-up in investment led to the emergence of a saving gap and the need for the U.S. to import capital to finance what has turned out to be almost a capital investment boom in 1984. The saving gap currently reflects the very strong cyclical growth in business capital investment as well as the deficit status of the federal government. But unlike earlier recoveries, the saving gap is not expected to decline because the government saving rate is not expected to become less negative as it did between 1975 and 1979.

In part, the present situation is not unlike what occurred after the Civil War, when rapid U.S. economic growth and a declining price level led to massive importation of foreign capital. From 1861 to 1899, the United States was more often than not a financial capital importer. Only in nine years during this period did the United States experience a capital outflow. And not until the end of the 19th century did the United States turn from importing to exporting financial capital. This comparison of saving behavior in the 19th century with that in 1984 is meant simply to emphasize the fact that rapid economic growth and low inflation is often accompanied by capital importation, particularly if rates of return on real and financial investments are higher than they are abroad, which now appears to be the case.

The stability of the gross domestic private saving rate in the United States means that a significant pick-up in capital investment would lead to a cyclical shortfall of private domestic saving available to finance private investment. The private saving gap can be filled either by saving in the government sectors or by importing of foreign capital. In the long-run, it makes a considerable difference how the private saving gap is closed. Interest payments on the federal debt to foreign bond holders represent a real future tax burden to U.S. citizens. One could argue that the heavy importation of foreign capital is financing current government consumption and not private investment and hence the deficit represents the mortgaging of future income to pay for this excess consumption.

TAX POLICY IMPLICATIONS

Changes in neither the personal income tax structure nor real after-tax interest rates have affected the U.S. gross domestic private saving rate. As a result, a large and possibly structural, that is, noncyclical, domestic saving gap has emerged, resulting in U.S. dependence on foreign capital to finance both capital formation and the deficit of the federal government.

Should aggregate tax policy be changed to reduce the saving gap? This is obviously a sensitive and politically charged question, but we can conjecture that as the tax *cut* seems to have had no effect on the gross private saving rate, so a personal tax *increase* would most likely leave it unchanged. If the corporate tax rate is left unchanged, it is possible, although quite conjectural, that a tax increase on consumers *alone* might help close the saving gap without greatly affecting the growth of capital investment. That is, a tax increase on consumers might contribute to lowering the federal deficit without changing the gross private saving rate. Such a change in tax policy would recognize the insensitivity of the gross private saving rate to changes in taxes and real interest rate and the sensitivity of capital investment to both.

QUESTIONS FOR DISCUSSION

1 What are the three ways of financing government spending? What relation among these three means of finance is described by the "government budget constraint"?
2 What is "monetization" of the government debt? Do high government deficits necessarily imply that there will be monetization?
3 "There is no choice between taxes and debt; there is only a choice between taxes now and taxes later." Discuss this statement and relate it to the Ricardian proposition.
4 If most people are concerned about the economic welfare of their children and grandchildren, will this make the Ricardian proposition more or less likely to hold, relative to a world in which people are not concerned about their descendants?
5 What is the relation between personal and corporate savings noted by Denison? What is the analogy between Denison's law (as this relationship is called) and the Ricardian proposition?
6 National savings (gross savings) is the sum of private savings and government savings. Explain how private savings and government savings are defined. What relationship between national savings and government savings is implied by the Ricardian view? Did this relationship appear to hold during the 1980s?
7 Show using national income accounting that national savings (private plus government savings) equals private domestic investment plus net exports. Explain how net exports may be thought of as a "use" of savings. Using this accounting identity, define the term *domestic savings gap*. How is a savings gap financed? What is the implication of a savings gap for the trade balance?

THREE

MONEY AND
MONETARY POLICY

THE CASE FOR OVERHAULING THE FEDERAL RESERVE

Milton Friedman*

Milton Friedman is the originator and leading proponent of the school of economic thought called *monetarism*. Over the years, monetarists have been generally critical of the Federal Reserve's handling of monetary policy and have advocated a number of reforms—the most famous of which is Friedman's suggestion that the money supply not respond to current economic conditions but simply be made to grow at a fixed rate. Below is a recent statement of Friedman's views on the Fed and monetary policy.

Monetary policy can be discussed on two very different levels: the tactics of policy— the specific actions that the monetary authorities should take; and the strategy or framework of policy—the ideal monetary institutions and arrangements for the conduct of monetary policy that should be adopted.

Tactics are more tempting. They are immediately relevant, promise direct results, and are in most respects easier to discuss than the thorny problem of the basic framework appropriate for monetary policy. Yet long experience persuades me that, given our present institutions, a discussion of tactics is unlikely to be rewarding.

Reprinted from "Monetary Policy for the 1980s" in *To Promote Prosperity: U.S. Domestic Policy in the Mid-1980s,* edited by John H. Moore, with permission of Hoover Institution Press. ©1980 by the Board of Trustees of the Leland Stanford Jr. University.

*Milton Friedman, a 1976 Nobel laureate, is a senior research fellow at the Hoover Institution, Stanford University, and Paul Snowden Russell Distinguished Service Professor of Economics at the University of Chicago.

The temptation to concentrate on tactics derives in considerable part from a tendency to personalize policy: to speak of the Eisenhower, Kennedy, or Reagan economic policy and the Martin, Burns, or Volcker monetary policy. Sometimes that approach is correct. The particular person in charge may make a major difference to the course of events. For example, in *Monetary History of the United States, 1867–1960,* Anna Schwartz and I attributed considerable importance to the early death of Benjamin Strong, first governor of the Federal Reserve Bank of New York, in explaining monetary policy from 1929 to 1933. More frequently, perhaps, the personalized approach is misleading. The person ostensibly in charge is like the rooster crowing at dawn. The course of events is decided by deeper and less visible forces that determine both the character of those nominally in charge and the pressures on them.

Monetary developments during the past few decades have, I believe, been determined far more by the institutional structure of the Federal Reserve and by external pressures than by the intentions, knowledge, or personal characteristics of the persons who appeared to be in charge. Knowing the name, the background, and the personal qualities of the chairman of the Fed, for example, is of little use in judging what happened to monetary growth during his term of office.

If the present monetary structure were producing satisfactory results, we would be well advised to leave it alone. Tactics would then be the only topic. However, the present monetary structure is not producing satisfactory results. Indeed, in my opinion, no major institution in the United States has so poor a record of performance over so long a period yet so high a public reputation as the Federal Reserve.

The conduct of monetary policy is of major importance; monetary instability breeds economic instability. A monetary structure that fosters steadiness and predictability in the general price level is an essential precondition for healthy noninflationary growth. That is why it is important to consider fundamental changes in our monetary institutions. Such changes may be neither feasible nor urgent now. But unless we consider them now, we shall not be prepared to adopt them when and if the need is urgent.

THE TACTICS FOR AVOIDING A CRISIS

Three issues are involved in the tactics of monetary policy: adopting a variable or variables as an intermediate target or targets; choosing the desired path of the target variables; and devising procedures for achieving that path as closely as possible.

The Intermediate Targets

The Fed has vacillated between using one or more interest rates or one of more monetary aggregates as its intermediate targets. In the past decade, however, it joined monetary authorities in other countries in stressing monetary growth. Since 1975, it has been required by Congress to specify explicit numerical targets for the growth of monetary aggregates. Although many proposals have recently surfaced for the substitution of other targets—from real interest rates to sensitive commodity prices to the price of gold to nominal GNP—I shall assume that one or more monetary aggregates remains the intermediate target.

In my opinion, the selection of a target or of a target path is not and has not been the problem. If the Fed had consistently achieved the targets it specified to Congress, monetary growth would have been highly stable instead of highly variable, inflation would never have become the menace it did, and the United States would have been spared the worst parts of the punishing recession (or recessions) from 1979 to 1982.

The Fed has specified targets for several aggregates primarily, as I have argued elsewhere, to obfuscate the issue and reduce accountability. In general, the different aggregates move together. The exceptions have essentially all been due to the interest-rate restrictions imposed by the Fed under Regulation Q and the associated development of new forms of deposit liabilities. And they would not have arisen if the Fed had achieved its targets for any one of the aggregates.

The use of multiple intermediate targets is undesirable. The Fed has one major instrument of monetary control: control over the quantity of high-powered money. With one instrument, it cannot independently control several aggregates. Its other instruments—primarily the discount rate and reserve requirements—are highly defective as instruments for monetary control and of questionable effectiveness in enabling it to control separately more than one aggregate.

It makes far less difference which aggregate the Fed selects than that it selects one and only one. For simplicity of exposition, I shall assume that the target aggregate is M1 as currently designed. Selection of another aggregate would alter the desirable numerical targets but not their temporal pattern.

The Target Path

A long-run growth rate of about 1 to 3 percent per year for M1 would be roughly consistent with zero inflation. That should be our objective. Actual growth in M1 was 10.4 percent from fourth quarter 1982 to fourth quarter 1983; 5.2 percent from fourth quarter 1983 to fourth quarter 1984. A crucial question is how rapidly to go from such levels to the 1 to 3 percent range. In my opinion, it is desirable to proceed gradually over something like a three- to five-year period, which means that the rate of growth should be reduced by about 1 to 1.5 percentage points a year—a very different pattern from the erratic ups and downs of recent years.

The Fed has consistently stated its targets in terms of a range of growth rates. For example, its initial target for M1 for 1983 was a growth rate of 4 to 8 percent from the fourth quarter of 1982 to the fourth quarter of 1983. That method of stating targets is seriously defective: it provides a widening cone of limits on the absolute money supply as the year proceeds and fosters a shift in base from year to year, thereby frustrating accountability over long periods. This is indeed what happened. In July 1983, Chairman Volcker announced a new target of 5 to 9 percent for the second quarter of 1983 to the second quarter of 1984 but from the second-quarter 1983 base, which is 3 percent (6 percent at an annual rate) above the top of the earlier range.

A better way to state the targets is in terms of a central target for the absolute money supply plus or minus a band of, say, 1.5 percent on either side—about the range the Fed has specified for annual growth rates. [Since this was written and initially published, the Council of Economic Advisers has made the same suggestion, and Chairman Volcker has expressed support for such a change.]

Procedures for Hitting the Target

There is a widespread agreement both inside and outside the Federal Reserve System that current procedures and reserve regulations make accurate control of monetary growth over short periods difficult or impossible. These procedures and regulations do not explain such long sustained departures from the targets as the monetary explosions from April 1980 to April 1981 or July 1982 to July 1983 or the monetary retardations from April 1981 to October 1981 or January 1982 to July 1982. However, they do explain the wide volatility in monetary growth from week to week and month to month, which introduces undesirable uncertainty into the economy and financial markets and reduces Fed accountability for not hitting its targets.

There is also widespread agreement about the changes in the procedures and regulations that would enable the Fed to come very much closer to hitting its targets over fairly short periods. The most important such change was the replacement of lagged reserve accounting, introduced in 1968, by contemporaneous reserve accounting comparable to that prevailing from 1914 to 1968. The obstacle to controlling monetary growth posed by lagged reserve accounting has been recognized since 1970 at the latest. Unfortunately, the Fed did not act until 1982, when it finally decided to replace lagged contemporary reserve requirements. However, it delayed implementation until February 1984—the longest delay in implementing a changed regulation in the history of the Fed. There was no insuperable technical obstacle to implementing the change more promptly.

The other major procedural changes needed are:

1 Selection by the Fed of a single monetary target to end the Fed's juggling between targets;

2 Imposition of the same percentage reserve requirements on all deposit components of the selected target;

3 The use of total rather than nonborrowed reserves as the short-term operating instrument;

4 Linking of the discount rate to a market rate and making it a penalty rate (neither this change nor the preceding was feasible for technical reasons under lagged reserve accounting; they are now feasible, but neither has been adopted);

5 Reduction of the churning in which the Fed engages in the course of its so-called defensive open-market operations.

Even without most of these changes, it would be possible for the Fed to put into effect almost instantaneously a policy that would provide a far stabler monetary environment that we have at present, even though it would by no means be ideal. The obstacle is not feasibility but bureaucratic inertia and the preservation of bureaucratic power and status.

A simple example will illustrate. Let the Fed continue to state targets for M1 growth. Let is estimate the change in its total holdings of U.S. government securities that would be required in the next six months, say to produce the targeted growth in M1. Divide that amount by 26. Let the Fed purchase the resulting amount every week on the open market, in addition to any amount needed to replace maturing securities, and make no other purchases or sales. Finally, let it announce this schedule of purchases in advance and in full detail and stick to it.

Such a policy would assure control over the monetary aggregates, not from day to day, but over the longer period that the Fed insists is all that matters. It would enable the market to know precisely what the Fed would do and adjust its own actions accordingly. It would end the weekly guessing game that currently follows each Thursday's release of figures on the money supply. The financial markets have certainly demonstrated that they have ample flexibility to handle whatever day-to-day or seasonal adjustments might be needed. It is hard to envisage any significant adverse effects from such a policy.

A few numbers will show how much difference such a policy would make to the Fed's open-market activities. In 1982, it added an average of $176 million a week to its total holdings of government securities—an unusually high amount. In the process of acquiring $176 million, it purchased each week an average of $13 *billion* of securities and sold nearly as much. About half of these transactions were on behalf of foreign central banks. But that still leaves roughly $40 of purchases or $80 of transactions for every one dollar added to its portfolio—a degree of churning of a customer's account that would send a private stockbroker to jail, or at least to limbo.

Increased predictability, reduced churning, the loss of inscrutability—these are at the same time the major reasons for making so drastic a change and the major obstacles to its achievement. It would simply upset too many comfortable dovecotes.

A FRAMEWORK FOR BASIC REFORM

The chief problem in discussing the framework of monetary policy is to set limits. The subject is old, yet immediately pertinent; numerous proposals have been made, and few, however ancient, do not have contemporary proponents. In view of my own belief that the important desiderata of structural reform are to reduce the variability of monetary growth, to limit the discretion of the monetary authorities, and to provide a stable monetary framework, I shall limit myself to proposals directed at those objectives, proceeding from the least to the most radical.

Imposing a Monetary Rule on the Fed

I have long argued that a major improvement in monetary policy could be achieved without any significant change in monetary institutions simply by imposing a monetary rule on the Fed. From an economic point of view, it would be desirable to state the rule in terms of a monetary aggregate such as M1 that has a close and consistent relation to subsequent changes in national income. However, recent years have demonstrated that the Fed has been unable or unwilling to achieve such a target, even when it sets it itself, and that it has been able to plead inability and thereby avoid accountability. Accordingly, I have reluctantly decided that it is preferable to state the rule in terms of a magnitude that has a somewhat less close relation to national income but that unquestionably can be controlled within very narrow limits within very brief time periods, namely, the Fed's own non-interest-bearing obligations, the monetary base.

In *Free to Choose,* my wife, Rose, and I proposed a specific form of rule as a constitutional amendment: *"Congress shall have the power to authorize non-interest-bearing obligations of the government in the form of currency or book entries, provided that the total dollar amount outstanding increases by no more than 5 percent per year and no less than 3 percent.*

"It might be desirable to include a provision that two-thirds of each House of Congress, or some similar qualified majority, can waive the requirement in case of a declaration of war, the suspension to terminate annually unless renewed."

A constitutional amendment would be the most effective way to establish confidence in the stability of the rule. However, it is clearly not the only way to impose the rule. Congress could equally well legislate it, and, indeed, proposals for a legislated monetary rule have been introduced in Congress.

I remain persuaded that a monetary rule that leads to a predictable long-run path of a specified monetary aggregate is a highly desirable goal—superior either to discretionary control of the quantity of money by a set of monetary authorities or to a commodity standard. However, I am no longer so optimistic as I once was that it can be effected by either persuading the monetary authorities to follow it or legislating its adoption. Congressional attempts in the past decade to push the Fed in that direction have repeatedly failed. The Fed has rhetorically accepted monetary targets but never a firm monetary rule. Moreover, the Fed has not been willing even to match its performance to a rhetorical acceptance of monetary targets. All this suggests that a change in our monetary institutions is required in order to make such a rule effective.

Separating Regulatory from Monetary Functions

A modest institutional reform that promises considerable benefits is to separate the regulatory from the monetary functions of the Fed. Currently, regulatory functions absorb most of the Fed's attention. Moreover, they obscure accountability for monetary control by confusing the two very separate and to some extent inconsistent functions.

As has recently been proposed in a study of the Federal Deposit Insurance Corporation, the Fed should be stripped of its regulatory functions, which would be combined with the largely overlapping functions of the FDIC, the Federal Savings and Loan Insurance Corporation, and the comptroller of the currency. Such a combined agency should have no monetary powers. It also might well include the operating functions of the Federal Reserve Banks—the monitoring of reserve requirements, issuance of currency, clearing of checks, reporting of data, and so forth.

A separate monetary-control agency could be a very small body, charged solely with determining the total quantity of high-powered money through open-market operations. Its function would be clear, highly visible, and subject to effective accountability.

Ending the Independence of the Fed

An approach that need involve relatively little institutional change—although it is far more drastic than the preceding—and that could be implemented by legislation would be to end the independence of the Fed by converting it into a bureau of the Treasury Department. That would end the present division of responsibilities for monetary and fiscal policy that leads to the spectacle of chairmen of the Fed blaming all the nation's ills on the defects of fiscal policy and secretaries of the Treasury blaming them on the defects of monetary policy—a phenomenon that has prevailed for decades. There would be a single locus of authority that could be held responsible.

The immediate objection that arises is that it would make monetary policy a plaything of politics. My own examination of monetary history indicates that this judgment is correct, but that it is an argument for, not against, eliminating the central bank's independence.

I examined this issue at length in an article published more than two decades ago entitled "Should There Be an Independent Monetary Authority?" I concluded that it is "highly dubious that the United States, or for that matter any other country, has in practice ever had an independent central bank in [the] fullest sense of the term. . . . To judge by experience, even those central banks that have been nominally independent in the fullest sense of the term have in fact been closely linked to the executive authority.

"But of course this does not dispose of the matter. The ideal is seldom fully realized. Suppose we could have an independent central bank in the sense of a coordinate constitutionally established, separate organization. Would it be desirable to do so? I think not, for both political and economic reasons.

"The political objections are perhaps more obvious than the economic ones. Is it really tolerable in a democracy to have so much power concentrated in a body free from any kind of direct effective political control? . . .

"One [economic] defect of an independent central bank . . . is that it almost inevitably involves dispersal of responsibility. . . .

"Another defect . . . is the extent to which policy is . . . made highly dependent on personalities. . . .

"A third technical defect is that an independent central bank will almost inevitably give undue emphasis to the point of view of bankers.

"The three defects I have outlined constitute a strong technical argument against an independent central bank."

The experience of the past two decades has led me to alter my views in one respect only—about the importance of personalities. They have on occasion made a great deal of difference, but additional experience and study has impressed me with the continuity of Fed policy, despite the wide differences in the personalities and backgrounds of the persons supposedly in charge.

For the rest, experience has reinforced my views. Anna Schwartz and I pointed out in *Monetary History* that subservience to congressional pressure in 1930 and 1931 would have prevented the disastrous monetary policy followed by the Fed. That is equally true for the past fifteen years. The relevant committees of Congress have generally, though by no means invariably, urged policies on the Fed that would have produced a stabler rate of monetary growth and much less inflation. Excessively rapid and volatile monetary growth from, say, 1971 to 1979 was not the result of political pressure—certainly not from Congress, although in some of these years there clearly was pressure for more rapid growth from the Administration. Nonetheless, no political pressures would have prevented the Fed from increasing M1 over this period at, say, an average annual rate of 5 percent—the rate of increase during the prior eight years—instead of 6.7 percent.

Subordinating the Fed to the Treasury is by no means ideal. Yet it would be a great improvement over the existing situation, even with no other changes.

Competitive Issue of Money

Increasing interest has been expressed in recent years in proposals to replace governmental issuance of money and control of its quality by private market arrangements. One set of proposals would end the government monopoly on the issuance of currency and permit its competitive issue. Another would eliminate entirely any issuance of money by a government and, instead, restrict the role of government to defining a monetary unit.

The former set of proposals derives largely from a pamphlet by F. A. Hayek entitled *Choice in Currency: A Way to Stop Inflation*. Hayek proposed that all special privileges (such as "legal tender" quality) attached to government-issued currency be removed, and that financial institutions be permitted to issue currency or deposit obligations on whatever terms were mutually acceptable to the issuer and the holder of the liabilities. He envisaged a system in which institutions would in fact issue obligations expressed in terms of purchasing power either of specific commodities, such as gold or silver, or of commodities in general through linkage to a price index. In his opinion, constant-purchasing-power moneys would come to dominate the market and largely replace obligations denominated in dollars or pounds or other similar units and in specific commodities.

The idea of a currency unit linked to a price index is an ancient one—proposed in the nineteenth century by W. Stanley Jevons and Alfred Marshall, who named it a "tabular" standard—and repeatedly rediscovered. It is part of the theoretically highly attractive idea of widespread indexation. Experience, however, has demonstrated that the theoretical attractiveness of the idea is not matched by practice.

I approve of Professor Hayek's proposal to remove restrictions on the issuance of private moneys to compete with government moneys. But I do not share his belief about the outcome. Private moneys now exist—traveler's checks and cashier's checks, bank deposits, money orders, and various forms of bank drafts and negotiable instruments. But these are almost all claims on a specified number of units of government currency (of dollars or pounds or francs or marks). Currently, they are subject to government regulation and control. But even if such regulations and controls were entirely eliminated, the advantage of a single national currency unit buttressed by long tradition will, I suspect, serve to prevent any other type of private currency unit from seriously challenging the dominant government currency, and this despite the high degree of monetary variability many countries have experienced over recent decades.

The recent explosion in financial futures markets offers a possible new road to the achievement, through private market actions, of the equivalent of a tabular standard.

This possibility is highly speculative—little more than a gleam in one economist's eye. It involves the establishment of futures markets in one or more price indexes—strictly parallel to the markets that have developed in stock-price indexes. (The Commodities Futures Trading Commission has authorized the Coffee, Sugar, and Cocoa Exchange to begin futures trading in the Consumer Price Index as of June 21, 1985.) Such markets, if active and covering a considerable range of future dates, would provide a relatively cost-less means of hedging long-term contracts against risks of changes in the price level. A combination of an orthodox dollar contract plus a properly timed set of futures in a price level would be the precise equivalent of a tabular standard, but would have the advantage that any one party to a contract, with the help of speculators and other hedgers in the futures market, could have the benefit of a tabular standard without the agreement of the other party or parties.

Recent changes in banking regulations have opened another route to a partial tabular standard on a substantial scale. The Federal Home Loan Bank has finally authorized federally charted savings and loan associations to offer price-level-adjusted mortgage (PLAM) loans. Concurrently, the restrictions on the interest rate that can be paid on deposits by a wide range of financial institutions have been eased and removed entirely for deposits of longer maturities.

This would permit financial institutions simultaneously to lend and borrow on a price-level-adjusted basis: to lend on a PLAM and borrow on a price-level adjusted deposit (PLAD), both at an interest rate specified in real rather than nominal terms. By matching PLAM loans against PLAD deposits, a bank would be fully hedged against changes in inflation, covering its costs by the difference between the interest rate it charges and pays. Similarly, both borrowers and lenders would be safeguarded against changes in inflation with respect to a particular liability and asset.

As yet, I know of no financial institutions that have proceeded along these lines. I conjecture that no major development will occur unless and until inflation once again accelerates. When and if that occurs, PLAMs and PLADs may well become household words and not simply mysterious acronyms.

Freezing High-Powered Money

The final proposal combines features from most of the preceding. It is radical and far-reaching, yet simple.

The proposal is that, after a transition period, the quantity of high-powered money—non-interest-bearing obligations of the U.S. government—be frozen at a fixed amount. These non-interest-bearing obligations now take two forms: currency and deposits at the Federal Reserve System. The simplest way to envisage the change is to suppose that Federal Reserve deposit liabilities were replaced dollar for dollar by currency notes, which were turned over to the owners of those deposits. Thereafter, the government's monetary role would be limited to keeping the amount constant by replacing worn-out currency. In effect, a monetary rule of zero growth in high-powered money would be adopted. (In practice, it would not be necessary to replace deposits at the Federal Reserve with currency; they could be retained as book entries, so long as the total of such book entries plus currency notes was kept constant.)

This proposal would be consistent with, indeed require, the continued existence of private institutions issuing claims to government currency. These could be regulated as now, with the whole paraphernalia of required reserves, bank examinations, limitations on lending, and the like. However, they could also be freed from all or most regulations. In particular, the need for reserve requirements to enable the Fed to control the quantity of money would disappear.

Reserve requirements might still be desirable for a different though related reason. The new monetary economists argue that only the existence of such government regulations as reserve requirements and prohibition of the private issuance of currency explains the relatively stable demand for high-powered money. In the absence of such regulations, they contend, non-interest-bearing money would be completely dominated by interest-bearing assets, or, at the very least, the demand for such money would be rendered highly unstable.

I am far from persuaded by this contention. It supposes a closer approach to a frictionless world with minimal transaction costs than seems to me a useful approximation to the actual world. Nonetheless, it is arguable that the elimination of reserve requirements would introduce an unpredictable and erratic element into the demand for high-powered money. For that reason, although personally I would favor the deregulation of financial institutions, thereby incorporating a major element of Hayek's proposed competitive financial system, it would seem prudent to proceed in stages: first, freeze high-powered money; then, after a period, eliminate reserve requirements and other remaining regulations, including the prohibition on the issuance of hand-to-hand currency by private institutions.

Why zero growth? Zero has a special appeal on political grounds that is not shared by any other number. If 3 percent, why not 4 percent? It is hard, as it were, to go to the political barricades to defend 3 rather than 4, or 4 rather than 5. But zero is—as a psychological matter—qualitatively different. It is what has come to be called a Schelling point—a natural point at which people tend to agree, like "splitting the difference" in a dispute over a monetary sum. Moreover, by removing any power to create money it eliminates institutional arrangements lending themselves to discretionary changes in monetary growth.

Would zero growth in high-powered money be consistent with a healthy economy? In the hypothetical long-long-run stationary economy, when the whole economy had become adjusted to the situation, and population, real output, and so on were all stationary, zero growth in high-powered money would imply zero growth in other monetary aggregates and mean stable velocities for the aggregates. In consequence, the price level would be stable. In a somewhat less than stationary state in which output was rising, if financial innovations kept pace, the money multiplier would tend to rise at the same rate as output, and again prices would be stable. If financial innovations ceased but total output continued to rise, prices would decline. If output rose at about 3 percent per year, prices would tend to fall at 3 percent per year. So long as that was known and relatively stable, all contracts could be adjusted to it, and it would cause no problems and indeed would have some advantages.

However, any such outcome is many decades away. The more interesting and important question is not the final stationary-state result but the intermediate dynamic process.

Once the policy was in effect, the actual behavior of nominal income and the price level would depend on what happened to a monetary aggregate like M1 relative to high-powered money and what happened to nominal income relative to M1—that is, on the behavior of the money multiplier (the ratio of M1 to high-powered money) and on the income velocity of M1 (the ratio of nominal income to M1).

Given a loosening of the financial structure through continued deregulation, there would be every reason to expect a continued flow of innovations raising the money multiplier. This process has in fact occurred throughout the past several centuries. For example, in the century from 1870 to 1970, the ratio of the quantity of money, as defined by Anna Schwartz and me in *Monetary History,* to high-powered money rose at the average rate of 1 percent per year. In the post-World War II period, the velocity of M1 has risen at about 3 percent per year, and at relatively steady rate. Above, in specifying a desirable target for the Fed, I estimated that the rise in velocity would slow to about 1 or 2 percent per year. However, a complete end to the rapid trend in velocity is not in sight.

There is no way to make precise numerical estimates, but there is every reason to anticipate that for decades after the introduction of a freeze on high-powered money, both the money multiplier and velocity would tend to rise at rates in the range of historical experience. Under these circumstances, a zero rate of growth of high-powered money would imply roughly stable prices, though ultimately, perhaps, slightly declining prices.

What of the transition? Over the three years from 1979 to 1982, high-powered money grew an average of 7.0 percent a year. It would be desirable to bring that rate to zero gradually. As for M1 growth, about a five-year period seems appropriate—or a transition that reduces the rate of growth of high-powered money by about 1.5 percentage points a year. The only other transitional problem would be to phase out the Fed's powers to create and destroy high-powered money by open-market operations and discounting. Neither transition offers any special problem. The Fed, or its successor agency, could still use part of the existing stock of high-powered money for similar purposes, particularly for lender-of-last resort purposes, if that function were retained.

The great advantage of this proposal is that it would end the arbitrary power of the Federal Reserve System to determine the quantity of money, and would do so without establishing any comparable locus of power and without introducing any major disturbances into other existing economic and financial institutions.

I have found that few things are harder even for knowledgeable nonexperts to accept than the proposition that twelve (or nineteen) people sitting around a table in Washington, subject to neither selection nor dismissal, nor close administrative or political control, have the power to determine the quantity of money—to permit a reduction by one-third during the Great Depression or a near-doubling from 1970 to 1980. That power is too important, too pervasive, to be exercised by a few people, however public-spirited, if there is any feasible alternative.

There is no need for such arbitrary power. In the system I have just described, the total quantity of any monetary aggregate would be determined by the market interactions of many financial institutions and millions of holders of monetary assets. It would be limited by the constant quantity of high-powered money available as ultimate reserves. The ratios of various aggregates to high-powered money would doubtless change from time to time, but in the absence of rigid government controls—such as those exemplified by Regulation Q, fortunately being phased out—the ratios would change gradually and only as financial innovations or changes in business and industry altered the proportions in which the public chose to hold various monetary assets. No small number of individuals would be in a position to introduce major changes in the ratios or in the rates of growth of various monetary aggregates—to move, for example, from a 3 percent per year rate of growth in M1 for one six-month period (January to July 1982) to a 13 percent rate of growth for the next six months (July 1982 to January 1983).

QUESTIONS FOR DISCUSSION

1 Friedman's premise in this article is that the best monetary policy is one that is stable, predictable, and unresponsive to short-run economic conditions. What are the arguments for and against this view? (Refer to your text. Also see Readings 15, 16, and 19.) Why does Friedman believe that the Federal Reserve, as it is currently set up, cannot be relied on to run monetary policy in this way?

2 Why does Friedman oppose the Fed's practice of simultaneously targeting more than one monetary aggregate (M1, M2, etc.)? Consider both (*a*) whether hitting multiple targets is possible in practice, and (*b*) the effect of multiple targets on Fed "accountability."

3 Explain why each of the following institutional changes would, according to Friedman, help improve the Fed's control over the money stock. Which of these changes has already been put into place?

a Contemporaneous rather than lagged reserved accounting

b Uniform percentage reserve requirements for all of the different types of deposits that make up the targeted monetary aggregate

c Specifying an absolute level of the monetary aggregate as the target, rather than a rate of growth

d Reduced "churning" of the Fed's portfolio

4 It has been argued in some quarters that "Paul Volcker's personality is worth two points of inflation reduction." Why might this be so (see Reading 17 on Fed credibility)? Would Friedman agree with this statement?

5 In the article Friedman suggests the possibility of abandoning M1 growth targets in favor of focusing on high-powered money—whose growth would either be "frozen" at zero or limited by a constitutional amendment. Why does he advocate this switch? What effects does he think a freeze of high-powered money would have on inflation and output growth?

6 Friedman supports making the Fed a branch of the U.S. Treasury Department. Evaluate the arguments for and against this proposal.

MONETARISM:
AN EBBING TIDE?

James Tobin

James Tobin, the Nobel Prize–winning economist and leading proponent of
Keynesianism, has often disagreed with Milton Friedman (see Reading 14) about
the conduct of macroeconomic policy. Here is Tobin's critique of monetarism.

Monetarism became influential doctrine in the late 1960s and the 1970s. Economists,
financial pundits, central bankers and legislators flocked to its banner, disillusioned
with the eclectic synthesis of Keynesian and neo-classical economics that had become
mainstream macroeconomics after the second world war. Inflation displaced unemployment as the salient economic evil. Keynesian theories and policies were blamed,
justifiably or not, for the Great Stagflation. Monetarism offered the way out. Thus
were the tables turned. The Keynesian revolution of the 1930s succeeded because the
orthodoxy of the day, including the essentials of monetarism without the label, appeared
to offer neither explanation nor remedy for the mass unemployment of the Great
Depression.

Now that inflation has subsided and unemployment has soared in most economically
advanced democracies, will there be another switch? What are the legacies of monetarism to doctrine and to policy in this decade and the next? It is too soon to know
the answers, but the questions provide a background for a review of the present status
of monetarism.

Monetarism has several meanings, variously emphasized by its adherents.

James Tobin, "Monetarism: An Ebbing Tide?" *The Economist,* April 27, 1985, pp. 23–25. Reprinted
by permission.

THE ALTERNATIVE TO "FISCALISM"

The word "monetarism" was coined as antinomy to "fiscalism" in the 1960s. Professor Milton Friedman had long been fighting endemic scepticism of the efficacy of monetary policies, inherited from the Depression and perpetuated by some Keynesians. Particularly in Britain, the view that money and financial markets are a self-contained sideshow to the main macroeconomic performance held sway for much too long. Mainstream American Keynesians did not dispute Friedman's contention that "money matters". But we also advocated and practised fiscal management of aggregate demand, and resented the popular monetarism/fiscalism dichotomy. We opposed Professor Friedman's stronger contention, that money is all that matters in the sense that fiscal policy has insignificant effects on such macroeconomic outcomes as real gnp, employment and prices.

Like Keynes, himself, we believed that generally both policies work. The mix of monetary and fiscal measures is open to choice, and some mixes are better than others. The non-monetarist theory of policy mix is very relevant today; the United States has stumbled into a bizarre and extreme mix, hazardous to its health and to that of the world economy.

To talk about the efficacies of monetary and fiscal instruments and their proper mixture in demand management presupposes, of course, that they are technically and politically separable. If, for lack of markets for non-monetary government debt or of political will to pursue an independent monetary policy, the central bank automatically finances government deficits, monetary and fiscal policy are essentially one. The debate on the efficacy of fiscal measures concerned pure fiscal policies, with budget deficits not monetised by the central bank.

In theory, this debate turned on the question whether fiscal stimulus can systematically raise the velocity of money. We Keynesians said yes, by raising interest rates and inducing businesses and households to manage their transactions with smaller holdings of cash. Both theory and evidence supported this view, and monetarists shifted ground to the more basic propositions reviewed below.

The patent success of fiscal stimulus in promoting recovery in the United States in 1983-84 reinforces the Keynesian side of this old debate, as does the stagnation of European economies under restrictive fiscal policies reminiscent of the early 1930s. Of course Mr Reagan's deficits, if not corrected, bode serious trouble 10 or 20 years hence. The same logic that says deficits absorb saving and stimulate spending when it is needed to pull the economy out of recession says that they crowd out productive domestic and foreign investment when saving and output are limited by productive capacity. Mainstream Keynesians say that the United States could have had—should have had—the same recovery with a different policy mix, tighter budget and easier money, yielding lower interest rates and a less expensive dollar.

MONETARY TARGETS

During the 1970s monetarists persuaded most major central banks to gear their operations to announced targets for one or more intermediate monetary aggregates. The word "intermediate" denotes a variable which the authorities can control only indirectly and imperfectly, via the effects of their market interventions on the behavior of banks and the general public. At the same time, the economic and social importance of an intermediate target is not intrinsic but is derived entirely from its indicative or causal relation to measures of macroeconomic performance that really matter: production, employment and prices.

Adoption of intermediate monetary targets downgraded central banks' attention to interest rates, "credit conditions", international reserves, exchange rates and the many other kinds of financial and economic information to which central banks formerly responded with discretion and imprecision.

In the United States, congress requires the Federal Reserve to report targets twice a year to committees in both houses. The Fed obliges with three Ms for money, one L for liquidity, and one D for total debt. Its mechanics of monetary control have also changed in response to monetarist pressure. In October, 1979, the Fed stopped targeting interest rates altogether, abandoning the practice of setting a narrow band for the overnight "Federal Funds" rate for the five or six weeks between meetings of its open market committee. Instead, the traders at its New York desk were to be instructed to supply certain quantities of bank reserves, letting interest rates move as they will.

Money targets and quantitative operating procedures prevent the central bank from

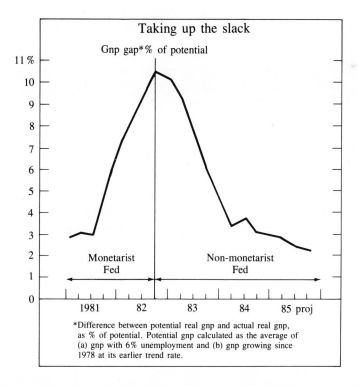

Taking up the slack

Gnp gap*% of potential

Monetarist Fed

Non-monetarist Fed

1981 82 83 84 85 proj

*Difference between potential real gnp and actual real gnp, as % of potential. Potential gnp calculated as the average of (a) gnp with 6% unemployment and (b) gnp growing since 1978 at its earlier trend rate.

accommodating unexpected and unwelcome shocks in demand for goods and services. To this virtue corresponds a vice. When the same targets and rules prevent accommodation of unexpected shocks to monetary velocity, they generate unwelcome booms or recessions.

Generally the central bank cannot discern which kind of shock, demand for goods or demand for money, is the source of upward or downward pressure on interest rates. Then its best bet is a compromise between (a) sticking to a money-stock target and (b) holding to the interest rate that target was expected to imply. In pre-monetarist days, the Fed's vague policy of "leaning against the wind" was a rough compromise.

In principle, the degree of partial accommodation in response to an interest-rate surprise should be smaller the greater the likelihood it came from a shock to goods-demand rather than to money-demand. One article of monetarist faith is that goods-demand shocks are much more likely than money-demand shocks. Non-monetarists do not assert the opposite, but instabilities in monetary velocities (see chart) vindicate their scepticism.

Money-demand shocks have been particularly disturbing recently, as the pace of technological, institutional and regulatory change in financial industries has quickened. The Fed has had to redefine its aggregates repeatedly and re-interpret its targets accordingly. Even so, 1982 was a disastrous year. Velocity not only fell far short of its expected growth trend: it actually declined. The money stock targets supported much less nominal gnp than the Fed had expected. In desperation the Fed suspended its monetary growth targets, allowed a surge of money creation that lowered interest rates three points, turned the American economy around, and saved the world from financial disaster. The strict monetarist regime of October, 1979, had lasted just three years.

The rationale for targeting intermediate monetary aggregates never was convincing. The most popular aggregate, M1, gains semantic appeal as "transactions money", immediately usable to buy goods and services. But that has never meant that fixing its total supply is either necessary or sufficient to control aggregate spending. Its speed of turnover is quite volatile. Near-monies quickly and easily convertible into M1-cash are abundant, and the ingenuity of financial entrepreneurs armed with modern technologies is endless. A different rationale for M1 and the other Ms is that they give advance information on gnp and other truly important variables. Yet any expert forecaster knows better leading indicators.

None the less, recent reforms in the United States have sought to identify M1 more closely with "transactions money", and to enhance the Fed's technical capacity to control M1 so defined (by imposing uniform contemporaneous reserve requirements on all depository institutions and only on those liabilities transferable by cheque or wire on demand). The irony is that these technical changes are occurring just when their purpose, closer control of M1, is losing favour both at the Fed and outside.

There are two ways to go. One is to move closer to instruments under the direct control of a central bank—central bank liabilities, base money, or bank reserves. This direction appears to be the latest preference of Mr Friedman and other monetarists. The other is to target the growth of nominal income, or of output and prices in some other combination, making explicit the objectives that logically guide the settings of intermediate targets anyway. Both approaches could be used: macroeconomic goals

for a year or two ahead and instrument targets consistent with those goals for one to
three months. The intermediate targets, neither fish nor fowl, are at best redundant
and at worst destructive.

PRIORITY FOR ANTI-INFLATION GOALS

Price surges accompanying the second oil shock in 1979-80 provoked major governments and central banks to launch in concert the single-minded anti-inflation crusades
that dominated the world economic scene of the early 1980s. The crusades certainly
succeeded in breaking the back of inflation, but at great costs in production, employment and investment, costs that have scarcely abated in most of the OECD outside
North America. The United States broke ranks from the anti-inflation war in October,
1982, in effect declaring victory even though the inflation rate remained above 4%.
Perhaps the Fed chairman, Mr Paul Volcker, heeded the wise counsel of the late
Senator George Aiken on the war in Vietnam: declare victory and get out.

The recessions of 1980-82 were a blow to the "credible threat" strategies of modern
monetarists. Their idea was that a determined policy of monetary restriction, accompanied by warnings that the authorities would not relent even to save jobs and businesses, would induce faster and less painful wage and price disinflation than previous
bouts of tight money. This time, they alleged, workers and businesses would not wait

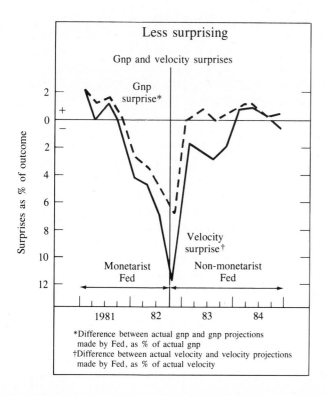

*Difference between actual gnp and gnp projections
  made by Fed, as % of actual gnp
†Difference between actual velocity and velocity projections
  made by Fed, as % of actual velocity

for the government to reflate. Experience under Mrs Thatcher and Mr Volcker did not confirm these hopes.

ENDING COUNTER-CYCLICAL MANAGEMENT

The 1979 commitment to disinflation exemplifies the monetarist approach to policy. Active variation of fiscal and monetary instruments in hope of taming the business cycle is taboo. Derided as "fine-tuning" and blamed for the ills of the 1970s, counter-cyclical demand management is replaced by commitments to hold those instruments steady, in faith that the economy will then be stable too. Rules replace the discretion of policy-makers—and blind rules at that, not to be altered in response to new information or second thoughts every week, every committee meeting or every legislative session.

Professor Friedman always questioned the wisdom, motivation and backbone of central bankers and politicians, and doubted that even the wisest, best-intentioned and firmest of them could outguess and improve nature. Better to rely, he said, on the capacity of the economy to adjust to shocks and to adapt to predictably steady policies. In his famous presidential address to the American Economic Association in 1967, he warned against dedicating monetary policy to any unemployment target. The target might be too low, and then the result would be spiralling inflation. If not—well, the economy will gravitate to its own "natural rate" of unemployment without the help of the central bank or the government budget.

Although Mr Friedman advised against demand management, his theory did not completely shut the door. Stimulative measures when unemployment was surely unnaturally high could hasten the economy's return to the natural rate without adding to inflation.

Newer monetarists, more royalist than the king, did slam the door. In their theories, buttressed by "rational expectations" logic, monetary policies can never alter unemployment—except temporarily when the central bank's moves surprise and confuse the public. Once any monetary policy is generally understood and expected, it will have no real effects at all; it will just be absorbed in prices.

These ideas and prescriptions are now orthodox over most of western Europe. The architects of policy probably do not read Professors Lucas, Sargent, Barro and other apostles of the "new classical macroeconomics"; these new monetarists are not popular evangelists like Mr Friedman. But the spirit of their ideas is in the air. Policies are to be governed by rules: balance the budget, and fix money growth at a non-inflationary number; disregard the state of the economy, especially the unemployment rate.

Prime ministers and central bankers wait and watch for their economics to adjust, recover and prosper. They have been waiting and watching for half a decade already, and their constituents have been remarkably patient. Yet every month of high unemployment sharpens the challenge to the new orthodoxy.

In the United States, in contrast, new monetarist doctrines and policies, fashionable though they are in academic economics, have lost in practical influence. Since October, 1982, the Fed's policy has been oriented to macroeconomic performance, responsive

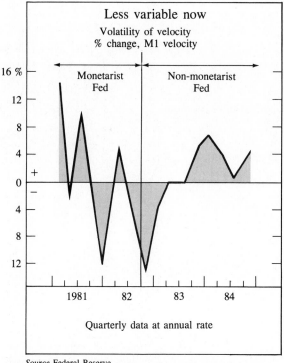

Less variable now

Volatility of velocity
% change, M1 velocity

Monetarist
Fed

Non-monetarist
Fed

Quarterly data at annual rate

Source Federal Reserve

to the actual and projected state of the economy, designed to guide the economy to a "soft landing" at the natural rate of unemployment. The Fed has been willing to encourage and finance unemployment-reducing cyclical growth so long as it is not too exuberant and inflation is not increasing. Yes, they have been "fine-tuning".

The Fed's report to congress of February 20, 1985, confirms this policy. As much attention is paid to velocity as to money supplies. Although the upper limit of the M1 target range for 1985 is one percentage point lower than for 1984, the Fed states clearly its intention to offset velocity surprises by adjustments of money stocks within their target ranges and one may infer, outside them if necessary.

In effect the Fed is targeting "velocity-adjusted" monetary aggregates. That amounts to targeting nominal gnp. Consequently the regular summary of the gnp, price and unemployment "projections" of the seven Federal Reserve governors and the 12 Federal Reserve Bank presidents assume major importance. These projections, for the fourth quarter of 1985, follow the "soft landing" recovery track. Their reported "central tendency" is a 7.5-8% growth in dollar gnp from the final quarter of 1984; a modest 3.5-4% inflation rate; a 3.5-4% growth of real gnp and, consistent with that, an unemployment rate of 7% or just below. These "projections" may well be the true targets of Fed policy. In summary, Mr Volcker has announced that the Fed will continue to support recovery, but more cautiously than in the past two years.

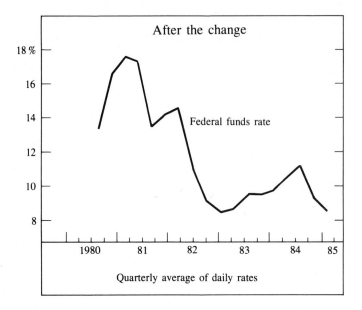

The Fed has pursued this course in an economy receiving massive fiscal stimulus, no less effective in creating demand because it was labelled "supply-side". Consequently the Fed, in order to stay near its desired path, has had to brake the economy much more and keep interest rates and the exchange value of the dollar much higher than if moderate pre-Reagan fiscal policies had remained in effect. On this crucial issue—the fiscal/monetary policy mix and its correction—monetarisms new or old are no help.

Monetarism, in its several meanings and messages, has greatly influenced economic thought and government policy over the past 20 years. Much of its influence is durable. Central banks' duty to hold in check the inflationary institutions and proclivities of their societies is widely understood and accepted. But this duty allows large scope for choice among alternative operating procedures, targets and short-term goals. It definitely does not exclude counter-cyclical demand management.

Mechanical monetarism, stressing targets for intermediate monetary aggregates, is waning in professional opinion and in central-bank practice, especially in the United States. History since 1979 has not been kind to the monetarist prescriptions of stable policies blind to actual events and new information. In the United States the Fed appears to have subordinated monetary targets and rules, and oriented its month-to-month decisions to macroeconomic performance. While the Fed has not become soft on inflation, it seems prepared to engineer further recovery so long as prices do not threaten to accelerate. European governments and central banks remain wedded to noninterventionism. The resulting stagnation must be counted as an unhappy legacy of monetarism.

QUESTIONS FOR DISCUSSION

1 The word *monetarism* was coined as an opposite for *fiscalism*. What were the original meanings of those terms? How do they relate to Tobin's current views?

2 Tobin states that the debate between traditional monetarism and fiscalism turned on whether "fiscal stimulus can systematically raise the velocity of money." (Velocity is the ratio of GNP to the money supply.) Explain this statement. Show, using the *IS-LM* diagram, how fiscal policy can affect velocity. For what slopes of the *IS* and *LM* curves is fiscal policy most effective at changing velocity? Least effective?

3 The economy is hit over time by "goods demand" shocks (that is, random disturbances to the *IS* curve) and "money demand" shocks (disturbances to the *LM* curve.)

  a Suppose the Fed can always observe both interest rates and output. Show that it can then distinguish *IS* shocks from *LM* shocks (assuming they come one at a time). If the goal is to stabilize output, how should the Fed react to each type of shock?

  b Now assume (realistically) that, because of data collection lags, the Fed cannot observe current output (it can still see interest rates). Show that, if most shocks are *IS* shocks, a constant-money-stock rule helps stabilize output; however, if most shocks are *LM* shocks, that the Fed would be better off if it tried to stabilize interest rates rather than money.

4 What is *fine tuning*? Do monetarists support the use of fine tuning? Why or why not? According to Tobin, what is the recent position of U.S. and European policy makers on the fine-tuning issue?

5 Tobin objects to the "policy mix" used by the United States in the early eighties. To what is he alluding? What are the potential problems with the U.S. policy mix? What mix would Tobin prefer?

U.S. MONETARY POLICY IN RECENT YEARS: AN OVERVIEW

Stephen H. Axilrod

This article, written in 1984 by the Staff Director for Monetary and Financial Policy of the Federal Reserve System's Board of Governors, provides a descriptive summary of U.S. monetary policy from the mid-1970s until the end of Reagan's first term. Axilrod first discusses the "need for credibility" that prompted the 1979 change in Fed operating procedures, then turns to the problems with velocity and the measurement of monetary aggregates that resulted in the 1982 deemphasis of money targets.

U.S. monetary policy in recent years, in terms of basic thrust, has aimed at curbing inflation and setting the stage for sustainable economic growth. In the process, the shorter-term policy stance and the day-to-day operating procedures have been complicated by, and have had to be adapted to, a variety of powerful exogenous forces. Among the more important from the mid-1970s through the early 1980s have been large oil price increases, a credit control program, deregulation of and innovations in banking and deposit markets, emergence of a large structural budget deficit, a large current account deficit in the balance of payments accompanied by what many believe to be an overvalued dollar on exchange markets, and strongly embedded inflationary expectations.

Not all exogenous forces are purely exogenous. Rising inflationary expectations in the late 1970s were in part the product of earlier monetary policies (as well as other events) as these policies affected attitudes toward the future, but once embedded

Stephen H. Axilrod, "U.S. Monetary Policy in Recent Years: An Overview," *Federal Reserve Bulletin,* January 1985, pp. 14–24.

the expectations were exogenous to and influenced current policies—as in October 1979. The present deficit in the current account and the high foreign exchange value of the dollar also could be viewed in part as endogenous to policies being pursued, or at least to the mix of fiscal and monetary policies; however, the deficit and the exchange rate have also been exogenous to policy in the degree that they have reflected shifts in preferences toward dollar assets, for any given interest differential, on the part of foreigners and U.S. residents who normally would have invested abroad.

This paper analyzes how monetary policy has evolved over the recent period in response to the exogenous forces facing it—forces that have also shaped the responses of financial and goods markets to the stance of policy. The review starts around the mid-1970s in order to set in relief the more recent period, beginning in late 1979, when there was a significant shift in monetary strategy—a shift that was designed not only to provide greater assurance that actual inflation would be curbed but also to reduce inflationary expectations with less of a lag, given past price behavior, than might otherwise occur. A relatively prompt abatement of expectations might be accomplished if the public's belief in the credibility of monetary's policy's will to achieve price stability over time were greatly enhanced. If that were to lead to quicker wage, price, and interest rate adjustments for any given money supply target, the adjustment process to a noninflationary environment would be eased. In one sense, monetary strategy in recent years can be viewed as a continuing struggle to attain and maintain credibility in the face of continuing shocks and disturbances in money, credit, and goods markets.

THE PERIOD BEFORE OCTOBER 1979

The change in operating procedures announced by Chairman Volcker at an unusual Saturday press conference on October 6, 1979, was, at the time and more so in retrospect, a watershed event. It signaled a shift to greater emphasis on reserve aggregates in carrying out monetary policy, and, by implication, greater concern with achieving goals for monetary aggregates (especially M1) and less concern with interest rates. The shift had its historical basis partly in experience over the several years following the first oil shock in late 1973 and early 1974.

That shock contributed to a sharp rise in the U.S. consumer price index of more than 12 percent from the end of 1973 to the end of 1974, following a rise of almost 9 percent over the preceding year. Annual price increases had generally been in the area of 1 to 2 percent in the last half of the 1950s and first half of the 1960s. Subsequently, there had been a step up to price increases in the range of 3 to 6 percent for the years from 1966 to 1972.

Some part (a third to a half) of the faster price increases of 1973 and 1974 can be attributed to the oil and other commodity price shocks of the time, abstracting from the impact of the phaseout of price controls during the period. Money growth had accelerated earlier in that decade, producing with some lag (of a year or two) upward pressures on the aggregate price level. But with M1 growth averaging around $7^1/_2$ percent annually in 1971 and 1972, the degree of acceleration did not seem sufficient in itself to produce price increases as large as we saw in the aftermath of the first oil shock.[1]

However much one might apportion, on technical econometric grounds, the price increases after the oil shock to the shock itself or to monetary policy, the price increases appear to have led to a rise of inflationary expectations. Despite the ensuing recession, consumer prices rose 7 percent over 1975 (when they probably still reflected some of the direct impact of import price increases) and expanded in a range of 5 to 7 percent during the next two years of recovery. Thus, after the initial response to the oil price shock, inflation did not revert to its earlier range, but was somewhat higher—even during recession and the early stages of recovery—reflecting, as well as providing an impetus to, higher inflationary expectations.

The tendency for inflationary expectations to worsen was buttressed in 1978 when price increases accelerated further and the dollar deteriorated markedly on exchange markets. Efforts by monetary policy to curb these adverse developments involved the conventional approaches of the period. In late 1978, for instance, a package was announced that encompassed an increase of 1 percentage point in the discount rate, a supplementary reserve requirement of 2 percent on large time deposits (the deposit instrument most readily employed by banks at their own initiative to finance growing credit demands), a tightening of conditions in the money market through more re-strained open market operations, and, together with the U.S. Treasury (and with the cooperation of foreign official institutions), mobilization of a large amount of dollars to help support the currency on exchange markets.

In the event, this package had little success in stemming inflationary pressures and attitudes. That outcome can probably be attributed in part to the overhanging effect of the monetary policy pursued over the preceding several years as well as to the behavior of monetary aggregates during much of 1979.

In 1977 and 1978, M1 growth had accelerated to a pace of slightly more than 8 percent per year, after growing by an average of $5^1/_2$ percent per year over the previous two years. Not only did this acceleration itself appear to signal that policy was becoming more expansionary, but also the credibility of policy was being eroded by the consistency with which actual M1 growth came in above adopted target ranges in a strong economy. This psychological effect was made even worse in the circumstances of the time by the fact that new one-year target ranges were adopted quarterly, with the most recent quarter serving as a base (so that for any year there were four one-year target periods ending in successive quarters of a year) and with no apparent effort to make up for the preceding overshoots. This became known as "base drift." The erosion of credibility because the targets were missed and because the process of target setting also led to a perception that the targets were perhaps not serious constraints fueled inflationary expectations.

In addition, it appears with the benefit of hindsight that the actual growth of M1 in 1975 and 1976 was much more expansive than suggested by the relatively low

---

[1]Alan S. Blinder, "The Anatomy of Double-Digit Inflation in the 1970s," in Robert E. Hall, ed., *Inflation: Causes and Effects* (University of Chicago Press for the National Bureau of Economic Research, 1982).

growth rates at the time—rates that were within targets adopted for those years.[2] There were a series of financial market innovations in that period spurred by relatively high market interest rates that greatly increased the opportunity cost of holding non-interest-bearing demand deposits and led cash managers to seek other outlets for highly liquid funds.[3] Depositors shifted funds out of demand deposits to other newly emerging, highly substitutable instruments at banks and other depository institutions—savings accounts that became available mainly to smaller businesses, accounts with telephone and preauthorized transfers, and so forth. Demand deposit holders probably also shifted funds into market instruments in the process of re-evaluating their whole approach to cash management. It is probable that the change in approach to cash management in that period reduced the desire to hold M1, given actual income and interest rates, on the order of 3 to 4 percent in each of the two years.[4] This means that $5^1/_2$ percent a year of M1 growth should, in terms of its economic effect, be construed as more on the order of 8 to 10 percent—quite expansionary and well above target.

Growth of M1 failed to slow over the first three quarters of 1979. At the same time, prices were placed under additional upward pressure by the second oil shock in the early part of the year. Overall price increases moved into the double-digit area. That had also occurred in 1974, but in the earlier period there had been less of a buildup in inflationary expectations and less of an erosion in the credibility of the Federal Reserve's will and capacity to control the situation.

THE PERIOD FROM OCTOBER 1979 TO THE FALL OF 1982

The conditions facing monetary policy in the fall of 1979 were in some respects similar to those in the fall of 1978. Inflation was worsening, as signaled not only in the domestic markets but also by a sharp drop in the dollar's value on exchange markets. However, by the fall of 1979 it had become even clearer that the cumulative lessening of confidence in monetary policy had contributed additionally to a substantial worsening of inflationary expectations.

Thus the policy announced on October 6, 1979, contained a new approach to implementation of open market operations, in addition to the more conventional rise of 1 percentage point in the discount rate and an additional reserve requirement applicable to increases in large time deposits and certain other managed liabilities. An important objective of the new approach was to help convince the public that the Federal Reserve would in practice achieve its monetary targets—was indeed changing its fundamental operating procedures to do so—and thereby increase the credibility of monetary policy and facilitate the transition to a noninflationary environment.

[2]The first "year" for which M1 targets were announced was the period from March 1975 to March 1976. Subsequently, there were one-year targets based on each quarter of the year. Starting with the 1978:4 to 1979:4, monetary targets have pertained only to calendar years.
[3]While demand deposits by law earn no explicit interest, there are implicit positive returns, more sizable for large businesses than for consumers and small businesses.
[4]Richard D. Porter, Thomas D. Simpson, and Eileen Mauskopf, "Financial Innovation and the Monetary Aggregates," *Brookings Papers on Economic Activity, 1:1979,* pp. 213–29.

This new approach has been amply described and evaluated elsewhere.[5] Its essence was to secure direct control of aggregate bank reserves—for operational purposes, nonborrowed reserves—and let interest rates vary as a product of the interaction between the nonborrowed reserve path and the emerging demand for reserves. It was believed that this approach would increase the odds that money growth, particularly M1 (the aggregate most closely related to the reserve base), would in fact be controlled within target ranges, given a relatively predictable relationship between the supply of reserves and the supply of money over a reasonable length of time. Previous efforts to control money growth used money market conditions—typified in much of the 1970s by the federal funds rate (the rate charged on overnight loans of reserve funds among banks)—as the guide for open market operations. Such efforts had foundered partly on policymakers' innate caution in adjusting any policy instrument and partly, and more fundamentally, on the difficulty in predicting the relationship between market interest rates and money growth—a difficulty that was compounded by uncertainties about the interpretation and significance of nominal market rates being introduced by inflationary expectations.

The change in policy procedure, in addition to whatever merits it may have had on its own as a more effective means of controlling money, was an effort to counteract the building of inflationary expectations that was a major obstacle to an orderly reduction of inflation. As noted earlier, those expectations may have been partly the result of earlier monetary policies. Inflationary expectations were also the product of two successive oil price shocks. One impact was to shift the Phillips curve upward, leading to a higher rate of inflation given the natural unemployment rate. The policy adaptation in that context represented an effort to improve the tradeoff between unemployment and the rate of inflation by itself leading to a shift in attitudes in labor and product markets that would bring the curve back down.

In undertaking that change, it was clearly understood that the desirability of M1, or other monetary aggregates, as a policy target depended on its having a reasonably stable or predictable relationship to the ultimate objectives of policy—sustained economic growth with general price stability. Thus M1 would be less desirable as a policy target, or certainly as a relatively rigid one, the more the uncertainty about public preferences for it, given income and interest rates, as had been the case in the mid-1970s. However, evidence from econometric models suggested that the large-scale demand shifts of that period had not been repeated (or reversed) in later years of the decade.

Still, there were in process innovations and regulatory changes affecting the public's disposition to hold M1, as well as other monetary assets, that had to be taken into account in setting target ranges and that also necessitated a redefinition of M1 and

[5]Stephen H. Axilrod and David E. Lindsey, "Federal Reserve System Implementation of Monetary Policy: Analytical Foundations of the New Approach," *American Economic Review,* vol. 71 (May 1981, Papers and Proceedings, 1980) pp. 246–52; Stephen H. Axilrod, "New Monetary Control Procedure: Findings and Evaluation from a Federal Reserve Study," *Federal Reserve Bulletin,* vol. 67 (April 1981), pp. 277–90; Stephen H. Axilrod, "Monetary Policy, Money Supply, and the Federal Reserve's Operating Procedures," *Federal Reserve Bulletin,* vol. 68 (January 1982), pp. 13–24. For a more critical assessment see Karl Brunner and Allan H. Meltzer, "Strategies and Tactics for Monetary Control," with related comments and replies by Axilrod, and Brunner and Meltzer, Carnegie-Rochester Conference Series on Public Policy, vol. 18 (Spring 1983), pp. 59–116.

other aggregates. Interest-bearing accounts against which checks could be written (termed NOW accounts), offered by both banks and thrift institutions, were introduced first in New England and then in a few other states. M1 was redefined in 1980 to include such accounts, and certain other definitional changes affecting it and the broader aggregates were also made at the time.[6] Later, NOW accounts were introduced on a nationwide basis at the beginning of 1981. The annual growth ranges for M1 set from 1979 through 1981 attempted to make allowance for shifts in funds that would take place in the course of the year in response to the introduction of the new accounts. Effects of the shifts were confined almost entirely to M1, since shifts among various deposit instruments were offsetting in the higher-order aggregates.

Tying policy operations more closely to the behavior of M1 to reduce inflationary pressures and inflationary expectations heightened the need to assess on an ongoing basis whether, and to what extent, institutional change was affecting the public's attitudes toward and use of the aggregate in relation to estimates made when the targets were set. This assessment was made more complicated by the increased instability of M1, month by month and quarter by quarter, as compared with earlier periods. A question naturally arises about whether that short-run instability was itself the product of the particular operating procedure used.

That seems doubtful in the conditions of the time. Much of the variation was associated with the credit control program introduced in the spring of 1980 and re-scinded several months later. The program as such was mild, but the psychological impact on the public was strong—leading to a sharp rundown in debt, the money supply, and interest rates after inception and followed by a ballooning of all three after rescission. Beyond that, the financial innovations, variations in credit demands, and general uncertainties about the future, which were engendered as an almost in-evitable by-product of the fight against inflation and questions about its ultimate suc-cess, were associated with large variations in attitudes toward financial assets and, concomitantly, money. Given these conditions, it seems as if money variations had been the product mostly of short-run demand disturbances; thus, if money growth somehow could have been stabilized from month to month, the probable result would have been even greater interest rate volatility.[7]

THE SHIFT IN POLICY APPROACH IN LATE 1982

The policy adopted in October 1979 was successful in reducing the rate of inflation—with the rate of increase in consumer prices dropping rapidly from about $12^1/_2$ percent in 1980 to about 4 percent in 1982. M1 growth fell to $7^1/_2$ percent in 1980, 5 percent in 1981, and about 6 percent (annual rate) over the first three quarters of 1982—after growing at an annual rate of a little more than 8 percent in the two and three-fourths years before October 1979.

The cost of the reduction in inflation was a substantial recession with relatively

---

[6]"The Redefined Monetary Aggregates," *Federal Reserve Bulletin,* vol. 66 (February 1980), pp. 97–114.
[7]Peter A. Tinsley and others, "Money Market Impacts of Alternative Operating Procedures," in Board of Governors of the Federal Reserve System, *New Monetary Control Procedures,* vol. 2 (Board of Governors, 1981).

high levels of unemployment. In that sense, the new operating procedure for monetary policy had not led to a very large, virtually miraculous downward shift of the Phillips curve, lowering the inflation rate sharply for any given unemployment rate. Still, so far as can be judged from qualitative information, the willingness to stick to the new procedure through a very difficult and volatile period greatly increased the Federal Reserve's credibility in fighting inflation. Thus it seems likely that, as time went on, the approach itself did have at least some beneficial impact on attitudes in labor and product markets and on the position of the Phillips curve.

Some "casual" empirical evidence that is at least not inconsistent with this conclusion may be found in recent wage and price data. Through the first year and a half of an exceptionally rapid economic recovery accompanied by a sharp drop in the unemployment rate, consumer prices have increased relatively moderately—remaining around 4 percent at an annual rate. True, prices typically do not tend to accelerate noticeably until later in an expansion. But wage settlements have thus far been unusually modest given the reduction in the unemployment rate.

Moreover, the policy shift in late 1982—when the new operating procedure was abandoned as M1 was de-emphasized, followed by a very rapid surge of M1 growth— did not tend to exacerbate inflationary expectations. Even though M1 expanded at near an $11^1/_2$ percent rate from mid-1982 to mid-1983, long-term interest rates declined sharply over the period, and the dollar actually appreciated somewhat on exchange markets. Thus it may be concluded that the credibility obtained during the period of a rather strict reserve-aggregate-M1-oriented operating procedure was at least in some part responsible for enabling the Federal Reserve to accommodate to a sharp reacceleration of M1 growth without igniting inflationary expectations. Of course, the weakness of the economy at the time was another and very important factor in keeping inflation expectations from reviving.

The De-emphasis of M1

The precipitating event for the de-emphasis of M1 was the maturity of a very large volume ($31 billion) of all savers certificates in October 1982, and uncertainty about how M1 might be affected in the process of the public's reinvesting those funds in other instruments.[8] In addition, movements of funds into and out of M1 were also going to be affected in uncertain amounts by regulatory changes scheduled within a couple of months permitting the introduction of money-market-type accounts at banks and thrift institutions. But the more sustained de-emphasis of M1 as a guide to policy implementation was connected basically with the change that was becoming observable in the public's preference for holding liquid assets in the form of M1. There was evidence of increased demand for M1, given income and interest rates, leading to historically atypical, sharp declines in the velocity of M1, or increases that were smaller than usual at the same time that M1 growth was moving above target ranges in the latter part of 1982 and through much of 1983.

---

[8]The certificates, which bore a very favorable yield and originally a one-year maturity, had been authorized by law a year earlier as part of a special effort to channel funds into agricultural and housing loans. The large volume issued in the first month matured in October 1982, and most holders did not have the option of reinvesting in the certificates.

While it was uncertain how long such a shift in preference would last, it seemed at least in part related to the change in the structure of deposits that had taken place in the previous years and in the role played by the new assets in M1 in the public's portfolio choices. In particular, NOW accounts had grown by that time to nearly $100 billion, or almost 30 percent of the deposits in M1, and these accounts—whose turnover on average was low relative to demand deposits—served both as a repository for longer-term savings and as a means of payment. As interest rates declined in reflection of weakening credit demands and abatement of inflationary expectations, the public increased the amount of funds it was willing to place in NOW accounts, just as it was also increasing the amount of funds flowing into ordinary savings accounts. As market interest rates declined, the opportunity cost of holding money in interest-bearing NOW accounts dropped relatively more rapidly than did that of demand deposits that bore no explicit interest. Thus, incentives for holding M1-type assets had shifted favorably.

Even without the change in the structure of M1 caused by the introduction of NOW accounts, one might well have expected a decrease in M1 velocity as interest rates dropped sharply. And the drop relative to a prior trend might have been expected to be permanent in the degree that it reflected a downward adjustment of inflationary expectations (with increased demand for money relative to goods) and an associated sustained lower level of market interest rates (with increased demand for money relative to other financial assets).

It has been much debated whether the observed reduction in velocity reflected a movement along an existing money demand curve as interest rates dropped; a shift in the existing demand curve; the emergence of a new demand curve with a different interest elasticity and implying a different long-run trend in velocity; or simply aberrant behavior related to special, nonrecurrent circumstances of the time, such as uncertainties affecting financial and other markets, that may have heightened precautionary demands for highly liquid assets.[9] Even now, it is probably too soon to be certain of the explanation, or of the relative importance of various explanations. But in view of all the unusual circumstances and institutional changes through the early 1980s, it seems unlikely that monetary policy was dealing simply with a movement of money in relation to income implied by a preexisting demand curve. Of course, even if it had been, and even if that curve implied a sufficiently large interest elasticity of money demand, it would still be the case that rapid money growth would have needed to be encouraged.

That conclusion would be drawn on the assumption that the demand for goods and services at any given level of interest rates had fallen exogenously (as was quite likely given the reduction of inflationary expectations), so that an especially large actual money growth was required both to encourage economic expansion and to satisfy the demands of money holders. In other words, given a downward shift in the demands for goods and services, the velocity of money would tend to drop for any given money

---

[9]Stephen H. Axilrod, "Issues in Monetary Targeting and Velocity," in Federal Reserve Bank of San Francisco, *Monetary Targeting and Velocity,* Proceedings of a Conference, December 1983 (December 1983), pp. 4–13; Thomas D. Simpson, "Changes in the Financial System: Implications for Monetary Policy," *Brookings Papers in Economic Activity, 1:1984,* pp. 249–72; Flint Brayton, Terry Farr, and Richard Porter, "Alternative Money Demand Specifications and Recent Growth in M1" (Board of Governors of the Federal Reserve System, Division of Research and Statistics, May 1983).

supply; the choice for policy is whether the drop was to be reflected more in rising money or in lower income.

Since the latter part of 1983, the income velocity of M1 has been rising at a pace not far from that of earlier cyclical experience. This has contributed to some restoration of confidence in that aggregate as a guide, though it has not been restored to the role it had before late 1982. It is still too soon to be sure about the underlying trend, not to mention the cyclical behavior, of the velocity of M1, given the changed composition of the aggregate as well as the new deposits and fund outlets (such as money market deposit accounts and money market funds) in other, higher-order aggregates that also serve as both a means of payment and a store of liquidity.

Many take the view that the trend increase of M1 velocity has been lowered on the thought that, with deregulation of deposit rates, the pace of technological innovation may diminish. Also, with deposits in M1 affected more by saving motives, the elasticity of demand with respect to income may be higher than it has been. But the intensifying competition for financial and payments services and the still evolving deposit markets leave considerable room for doubt about any such conclusion with respect to M1 and have also complicated and made more uncertain the interpretation of the other monetary aggregates.

In all of these circumstances, while the aggregates remain as important guides to policy operations and policy objectives are presented in terms of money and credit aggregates, ongoing money supply behavior has needed to be interpreted, more so than usual, in light of surrounding economic and financial conditions. The implementation of policy has thus necessarily become more judgmental than it was in the period from late 1979 to late 1982. The result is that changes in pressures on bank reserve positions do not respond more or less automatically to variations in money demand as they affect the demand for reserves relative to a fixed path for nonborrowed reserves. Rather, the reserve path is adjusted more frequently, on a week-to-week basis, to accommodate to short-run money behavior, with the degree of reserve pressure embodied in the path—indexed by the amount of borrowing allowed for at the discount window—set judgmentally, in light of incoming information, as is thought consistent with desired money and credit growth over a longer period.

Partly in view of the uncertainties that came to affect the monetary aggregates because of institutional change, the Federal Reserve also introduced a broad credit aggregate—the debt (whether incurred in domestic markets or abroad) of domestic nonfinancial sectors—for monitoring purposes, and began stipulating annual growth ranges for that aggregate as well as for measures of the money supply. A debt aggregate is less affected by shifts in preferences for differing financial assets, and provides a basis for assessing the interaction of credit and money demands in relation to the underlying policy objective of sustained economic growth and reasonable price stability.

The Impact of Fiscal Policy

The credit variable and its components have proved to be especially useful in evaluating the impact of fiscal policy on credit markets and in relation to monetary policy. Fiscal policy, as measured by growing high-employment deficits (accompanied by even larger actual deficits), has been a major element in shaping the rapid recovery and expansion following the 1981–82 recession. In 1983, U.S. government debt expanded $21^1/_2$ percent, whereas it had risen less than $8^1/_2$ percent on average in the first year of five previous recoveries. At the same time, private debt rose about 8 percent, close to its pace in the first year of earlier recoveries. Spurred evidently by the rise in federal borrowing, total debt rose almost 11 percent last year, about 3 percentage points more than the average for earlier recoveries, while nominal GNP grew about the same as it did on average in the comparable earlier periods.

By the second year after a cyclical low in economic activity, federal debt expansion normally slows sharply, to about a 4 percent rate. In the first half of 1984, however, federal debt expansion, while slowing somewhat from the year before, still was at a very rapid 15 percent annual rate. At the same time, private debt expansion accelerated to about 11 percent annual rate (abstracting from growth of merger-related debt issues), about the same as in comparable periods of earlier recoveries. The sustained strength of federal debt expansion brought total debt growth in the first half of 1984 to an annual rate of a little less than 12 percent (again abstracting from merger-related debt)— above the range for the year anticipated by the Federal Reserve in setting its money and credit ranges and also nearly 4 percentage points more than in the second year of earlier expansions.

With fiscal policy remaining quite stimulative into the second year of expansion, and with the market concerned that deficits will remain large even as economic growth continues, nominal and presumably real interest rates have remained relatively high. Indeed, market rates rose into the summer of 1984. However, after midyear, and through early fall, first long-term and later short-term interest rates declined somewhat, retracing a part of their rise earlier in the year.

The behavior of interest rates during the current year has been consistent with growth of M1 and M2 within target ranges. The money demand function, which behaved atypically during the recession and very early in the recovery, has seemed in late 1983 and thus far in 1984 to be more consistent with historical expectations. Thus the rise of interest rates in the first part of 1984 can be viewed more as the result of strong credit demands stemming from an upward shift in the demand for goods and services, impelled in part by the continued federal deficit. Subsequent declines of rates probably reflected moderation, or expected moderation, of private credit demands, and demand for money as economic growth slowed over the summer and as indications of upward price pressures remained limited. In addition, there was some lessening of tension in the financial system as Latin American debt negotiations were in process of resolution and problems with certain large depository institutions were contained.

The Balance of Payments and the Dollar Exchange Rate

The strength of demands for goods so far in 1984 has not been reflected in additional upward price pressures, or conventional signs of anticipated upward price pressures such as intentions to accumulate inventories well ahead of sales. While this good price performance partly reflects the still relatively sizable amount of unused labor and plant resources, it may also reflect the strengthened conviction that monetary policy will in fact restrain inflation and work toward price stability. But the ability of U.S. demands for goods and services to increase unusually rapidly in the first 18 months of recovery without signs of further price pressure also needs to be considered in relation to the relatively high value of the dollar on exchange markets and the sharp turn toward deficit in the U.S. current account of the balance of payments—a deficit that reached $42 billion in 1983 and may be estimated at close to $90 billion at an annual rate in the first half of 1984 (with trade deficits that are some $15 billion to $20 billion deeper).

The deficits have permitted expansion of spending by domestic sectors without concomitant pressure on U.S. productive capacity and resources. Over the first six quarters of recovery, real GNP rose $7\frac{1}{4}$ percent (annual rate) while real spending increased $8\frac{3}{4}$ percent (annual rate). As an aspect of those developments, private investment and the federal deficit were financed to a greater extent than normal by net inflows of foreign saving. Such inflows amounted to almost $12\frac{1}{2}$ percent of the sum of net private investment and the federal deficit in 1983 and rose to 20 percent in the first half of 1984.

More remarkable than these arithmetic relationships to GNP and its components is the fact that the current account deficits have not been accompanied by any significant tendency for the dollar to decline in value on exchange markets. Indeed, quite the opposite: from the end of 1982 through September 1984, the dollar rose about 22 percent on a multilateral trade-weighted basis. Foreigners have been quite willing to finance U.S. consumption in excess of output and private investment and a budgetary deficit in excess of domestic saving. The question naturally arises whether this willingness should be construed as an event exogenous to policy or as the product of policies in place.

It is probably some of both. As a response to policies, it would seem to be related less to monetary policy alone than to the mix between fiscal and monetary policies—a mix that has worked, through shifts noted above in the demand for goods and services induced by fiscal policy, to keep interest rates higher than they otherwise would be. As an event exogenous to policy, it reflects the shift of international investment preferences toward the United States, for any given interest differential, caused by political disturbances abroad, reduced confidence in countries burdened with debt crises, and a positive change in attitude toward the United States as confidence in its economy revived (signaled first, perhaps, by the huge stock market rally in the second half of 1982).

Particularly to the extent that dollar exchange rates have remained high for exogenous reasons, one might view the current account deficit as determined by the capital account rather than vice versa. In that sense, the growing demand for goods and services could be accommodated in part by "artificially" low-priced imports, taking pressure off domestic resources and keeping the level of domestic prices lower than it would otherwise be. Once the exogenous shift in investment preferences toward the dollar is completed, and particularly if it begins to be reversed, there is the risk that domestic prices will adjust upward—although any such rise could be moderated to the extent that domestic demands are reduced commensurately (by, for example, more fiscal restraint) or to the extent that foreigners absorb a reduction in home-currency profits more than they usually do. However that eventually works out, the unusually large current account deficit and relatively high exchange rate make it difficult to be certain that progress toward price stability has been as great as the published price series may suggest.

CONCLUDING OBSERVATIONS

This broad review of monetary policy in the United States during recent years suggests a number of general observations, as well as observations more specific to current conditions.

1 Monetary policy has been confronted by shifts both in the demand for goods and services, given interest rates, and in the demand for money, given interest rates and income. Downward shifts in the demand for goods and services seemed evident from the psychological impact associated with initiation of the credit control program in early 1980 and during the recession of 1982 when inflationary expectations began to wane; upward shifts appeared as the credit control program was lifted and more recently in the wake of the turn to a quite expansionary fiscal policy. The shifts related to the psychological impact of the credit control program were very short run in nature, disturbances of no more than a quarter or so. The impacts of other shifts noted were sustained over a longer period. Meanwhile, through much of the period since the mid-1970s there were widespread institutional and regulatory changes introducing new instruments to serve as money or money substitutes, or affecting the implicit or explicit price of old instruments, that also led to shifts in the demand for money relative to historical experience.

2 It is by now very conventional wisdom that a money supply target for monetary policy will produce better policy in the face of shifts in the demand for goods and services than it will in the face of shifts in the demand for money. It does not necessarily follow that a money supply target, or guide, should be abandoned when there are shifts in the demand for money. So long as shifts in demand for goods and services are with us—and I suspect that they are, except on some occasions, the dominant type of shift—there is obvious value to a money supply guide, but one that necessarily entails certain judgmental adjustments to allow for, among other things, shifts in money demand.

3 Shifts in money demand may be most easily and clearly allowed for in advance in monetary targets when a regulatory change is known to be about to take place, such as payment of interest on demand deposits (to which the introduction of NOW accounts was tantamount), with fairly predictable one-time effects. When institutional change is taking place from an internally generated market process, as in 1975–76, it is extremely difficult to know what will happen in advance, requiring adjustments on an ongoing basis as best that may be estimated. Or after the initial adjustment to a regulatory change, like the introduction of NOW accounts nationwide, has been accomplished, it may also be some time before one can be reasonably certain in advance how the public will respond in varying economic circumstances, given the changes in the composition of money assets and presumably also in the motives and sensitivity to changing market conditions of money holders.

4 The advantage of retaining money guides is that they provide protection against the ever-present, unanticipated shocks to demand for goods and services and provide the public with a sense that there is a discipline on the central bank, even though uncertainties about money demand tend to argue for a more judgmental approach to policy implementation, including a willingness to adjust targets in light of evolving circumstances. For instance, one might argue that money growth targets should have been lowered in 1975–76, just as the M1 target was effectively raised in 1982–83. The ability of a central bank to adjust or miss monetary targets without impairing its credibility in fighting inflation depends on the underlying conviction in the marketplace that the central bank has the will to encourage price stability. That obviously depends on surrounding circumstances, actual price behavior, and the whole historical background that goes into determining a central bank's "image." In the late 1970s, money target misses and evidence of accelerating prices eroded the market's confidence in the Federal Reserve's will. That has not happened thus far in the 1980s, reflecting, one might judge, the credibility gained by the policy approach taken from late 1979 to the fall of 1982 and the continuing moderate behavior of prices after that policy approach was dropped and a more judgmental one (but one still based on money targets) adopted. Moreover, money growth in 1984, as measured by M1 and M2, has been well within target ranges.

5 While the credibility of monetary policy has increased in recent years, there is probably some way to go before the public is fully convinced that policy is aimed at and will achieve price stability over some reasonable period of time. Considerable progress has been made in curbing inflation, but there can be doubt about the exact extent of progress to date, in part because of the still relatively strong dollar exchange rate in the face of persistent large current account deficits and in part because the more intense upward price pressures normally come later in an expansion. The prospects for curbing inflation further are also subject to doubt because the lack of progress so far in reducing planned federal deficits raises questions in the minds of market participants about the will of the government generally.

6 Nominal market interest rates that have been high relative to the comparatively low increase observed in the average level of prices as the current economic expansion has continued may be taken as an indication that inflationary expectations, though lower than in the early 1980s, remain well above zero. However, interest rates appear to have been high in real as well as nominal terms, reflecting in part the exogenous upward shift in the demands for goods and services engendered by the continuing stimulative fiscal policy.

7 In contrast to the behavior of interest rates in credit markets, price and wage behavior in labor and product markets does not seem to suggest particularly strong inflationary expectations. Unless one takes the view that the real rate of return on investment goods over time will be exceptionally high, the question arises as to why borrowers have been willing to pay the prevailing high nominal and real market interest rates. Business borrowers would do so to finance longer-term capital outlays either if they expected inflation to accelerate or if they expected market rates to decline. In the latter respect, while the present yield curve does not suggest future rate declines, corporate financing has been concentrated in the short-term market or in floating-rate obligations, an approach consistent with expectations, or hopes, that current capital outlays can be refinanced later at lower market rates. There is an obvious potential for problems if there are expectational differences about inflation between real and financial markets—or between expectations in both markets and intentions on the part of monetary policymakers. A conflict in expectations between financial and real markets cannot be long sustained: it is resolved either as expectations in financial markets improve or as they worsen in real markets. An improvement of inflationary expectations in financial markets could take the form of shifts out of money-type assets into inter-mediate- or longer-term securities, with consequent downward impacts on interest rates on such securities, as well as on short-term interest rates as reserves were provided to maintain money growth. A worsening of expectations in real markets would be manifested in upward price pressures needed, among other reasons, to generate the income for servicing debt bearing high interest rates (as it became more feared that existing debt would not turn out to be refundable at lower rates). Assuming U.S. monetary policy is in fact on a course toward reasonable price stability over time, an early improvement in financial market expectations represents the smoother process of adjustment—an improvement that would be greatly promoted by a turn toward a less expansionary fiscal policy.

QUESTIONS FOR DISCUSSION

1 According to this article, what was the state of inflationary expectations in the United States in 1979? What events of the 1970s caused inflationary expectations to reach the point that they did? What did the change in inflationary expectations over the 1970s do to the Phillips curve tradeoff?

2 What was the change in Federal Reserve operating procedures ordered by Volcker in October 1979? Were the new operating procedures equivalent to "targeting" monetary aggregates, such as M1 and M2? Why or why not?

3 The author argues that a major reason for the Fed's 1979 switch in procedures was its need to increase its credibility. What is meant here by *credibility?* Why is Fed credibility important? *Hint:* What is the relation of Fed credibility to inflationary expectations and the Phillips curve? (See question 1; see also Reading 17.) Why does the author think that the 1979 policy switch was more likely to generate Fed credibility than the package of anti-inflationary policies undertaken in 1978?

4 What happened to real GNP growth and inflation during 1979–1982? Is this more consistent with a characterization of monetary policy as "loose" or "tight"? What do you think happened to the state of Fed credibility over this period?

5 Velocity, the ratio of GNP to the (measured) money stock, fell sharply in 1981–1982. Two explanations for this decline are (*a*) the fall in nominal interest rates during this period and (*b*) shifts in money demand associated with financial deregulation and innovation. Explain how each of these factors could have contributed to the decline in velocity. Given the Fed's operating procedures during this period, why was the fall in velocity a source of concern?

6 (*More difficult*)
   a In an *IS-LM* model with nominal interest rates and real GNP on the axes, show that (*a*) a fall in inflationary expectations moves the *IS* curve to the left, and (*b*) an increase in money demand, given GNP and interest rates, moves the *LM* curve to the left.

b Show, using an *IS-LM* diagram, that if the 1981–1982 velocity decline were due to falling inflation expectations, that a Fed policy of fixing the money supply would have been less contractionary than a policy of manipulating the money supply so as to keep nominal interest rates fixed. Show also that, if the decline in velocity were due to increased money demand, that stabilizing interest rates would have been a better policy than fixing the money supply. (This question is based on a well-known analysis by William Poole; see your text. See also the previous reading by Tobin.)

7 How did Fed policy shift in 1982? Based on U.S. inflation experience since then, would you say that the 1982 shift led to a loss in Fed credibility? Why or why not?

8 Did changes in the value of the dollar make the Fed's fight against inflation harder or easier? Explain.

TIME INCONSISTENCY: A POTENTIAL PROBLEM FOR POLICYMAKERS

Herb Taylor*

In the article on recent monetary policy by Axilrod (Reading 16), it was argued that *credibility* is an important asset of the Federal Reserve. Below, Herb Taylor of the Philadelphia Federal Reserve Bank's research department takes a closer look at the credibility issue. He shows that a problem called *time inconsistency* can cause the Fed to inflate even if it really doesn't want to; but that this problem can be solved if the Fed can develop a credible reputation for noninflationary behavior.

Many industrialized countries, including the United States, experienced high rates of inflation throughout the 1970s. In most of these countries prices have risen at more modest rates over the last several years, but concern over the long-term inflation outlook lingers. The fear usually expressed is that after a few years of low inflation everyone will forget how costly and disruptive high rates of inflation are, and that as industrial economies slow, their central banks will be tempted to pursue inflationary monetary policies to boost real growth. But the difficulty with maintaining a low-inflation monetary policy over the long-term may be more fundamental than that. Using simple examples, economists have demonstrated that even when a central bank recognizes that inflationary monetary policies cannot stimulate real growth and it wants to achieve a low rate of inflation, it may *still* wind up pursuing a high-inflation policy. The

Herb Taylor, "Time Inconsistency: A Potential Problem for Policymakers," *Business Review*, Philadelphia Federal Reserve Bank, March–April 1985, pp. 3–12.

*Herb Taylor is a Senior Economist in the Macroeconomics Section of the Research Department of the Federal Reserve Bank of Philadelphia. The author would like to acknowledge his intellectual debt to Gary Gorton, while absolving him from any responsibility for errors.

problem is that low-inflation policies suffer from what has been called time inconsistency. As a result, even though low-inflation policies always seem best when the central bank lays its plans for the future, they never seem best when the time comes to act on them, and consequently they are not implemented.

Time inconsistency is not unique to monetary policy; the problem often arises in other policymaking situations. But the idea that time inconsistency keeps central banks, such as the Federal Reserve, from sustaining low-inflation monetary policies has generated a great deal of interest among monetary economists recently. This article presents the basic elements of the current debate: What is time inconsistency? How does it arise in the monetary policy context? Does it create a significant problem for monetary policymakers?

TIME INCONSISTENCY: AN UNFAMILIAR NAME FOR A COMMON PROBLEM

The "time inconsistency of optimal plans" is not a concept with which many are familiar, but the problem itself is very common.[1] In fact, time inconsistency problems are, as the game show host used to say, "something often found in the home." Those exasperating situations in which parents find themselves with their children, for instance, frequently arise because parents' policies are time inconsistent and their children know it. An example best illustrates the point.

The Case of George and Martha

George and Martha's daughter, Betsy, is graduating from high school and wants to go to college in the fall. Betsy is willing to work in order to help pay her college expenses, but she cannot earn enough over the summer to pay all of them. So George and Martha discuss the situation and devise a plan.

After the high school graduation ceremony, George and Martha call Betsy into the living room and say to her, "Betsy, we want you to go to college and further your education, but we also want you to get a job and learn some responsibility. So if you get a job for the summer and save your pay, we will make up the difference between your savings and your college expenses in the fall. But if you don't get a job and save this summer, you'll get nothing from us for college in the fall."

George and Martha are happy with the way they have handled the situation. They know that their daughter wants to go to college and is willing to work for it, so they are confident that she will work and save all summer, start college in September, and emerge from the whole experience a more responsible and better educated person. But things do not go according to plan. First, Betsy does not get a job that summer. In fact, she doesn't even try very hard to find one. Second, when the fall comes, Betsy starts college anyway, and George and Martha pick up the tab.

---

[1]Kydland and Prescott (1977) introduced the notion of time inconsistency. The paper provides a mathematical characterization of the problem as it confronts policymakers, and a number of examples, including a version of the monetary policy example discussed later in this article.

What went wrong? Did George and Martha misjudge Betsy's desire to go to college and her willingness to work? Did they then simply lose interest in developing Betsy's sense of responsibility? No, it is not that George and Martha misunderstood Betsy, or that their commitment to certain principles suddenly weakened. George and Martha's plan came apart because it was not time consistent—that is, it was not the plan that would serve their best interest when the time came for them to act—and because Betsy realized this from the beginning.

Dissecting George and Martha's Plan

Right after Betsy's parents explained their policy to her, Betsy went to her room and rationally assessed the situation. As a member of the Pac-Man generation, she recognized that her parents had set up a kind of game. In this game, Betsy would make the first move, choosing either to get a summer job or not to get a summer job. Her parents would get their turn in the fall, when they would choose whether or not to pay her college expenses. The game had four possible outcomes. Betsy knew her parents' goals, so she knew how each outcome would measure up in their eyes. Figure 1 summarizes the situation.

Betsy's parents had just told her how they *planned* to play the game and Betsy could see that the plan was optimal from their perspective. If Betsy chose "Get a Job" on her turn, her parents planned to choose "Pay Betsy's Expenses" on their turn. If Betsy chose "Do Not Get a Job" on her turn, her parents planned to choose "Do Not Pay Betsy's Expenses" on their turn. Thus, the plan, if followed, would force Betsy

FIGURE 1

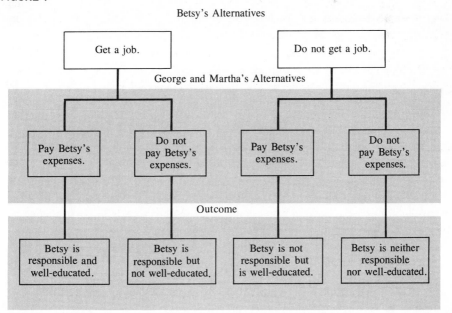

Betsy's Alternatives

to choose between two possible paths: she could either get a job and go to college or not get a job and not go to college. Given that choice, she would take the former, producing what George and Martha saw as the optimal outcome: a responsible, well-educated daughter.

But Betsy realized that it did not matter how her parents *planned* to play the game in June. What mattered is how they would *actually* play the game in September. And since Betsy knew what her parents' goals were, she could figure out how they would actually respond when it came time for them to make their move. She thought:

> Suppose I get a job over the summer. When the fall comes, will George and Martha better serve their goals by paying my college expenses or by not paying them? Well, I will already have worked and learned some responsibility, whether they pay my expenses or not. But by paying my expenses, they will enable me to become well-educated too. So they will choose to pay.
>
> Now suppose I don't get a summer job. When fall comes, will George and Martha better serve their goals by paying my college expenses or by not paying? Well, I will have been without work all summer and I will not have learned any responsibility. But whether they pay my expenses or not will not change that. It will be too late; the summer will be over. And if they do pay my college expenses, then at least I will get an education, which is better than nothing. So they will choose to pay.

Thus Betsy deduced that whether she chose "Get a Job" or "Do Not Get a Job" on her turn, her parents would find it best to choose "Pay Betsy's Expenses" on their turn. So Betsy's choice was really between getting a job before going to college, and taking a vacation before going to college. Given this pair of alternatives, her decision was easy—she took the vacation.

The Perennial Problem of Time Inconsistency

Time inconsistency in George and Martha's optimal plan kept them from achieving their goal of getting Betsy to work for the summer. But the problem can affect anyone trying to influence the behavior of others—and that includes anyone making social or economic policy. For instance, the FDIC wants to maintain a sound financial system, so it tries to discourage people from depositing their funds with banks that undertake risky investments by announcing that it will not insure large deposits (those over $100,000) in the event of a bank failure. But the public realizes that once a bank does fail, the FDIC's desire to maintain confidence in the financial system is likely to dictate that it insure the deposits, so they deposit their funds with risky banks. Similarly, national governments want to protect their citizens from terrorists, so they announce that they will not negotiate with skyjackers. But terrorists realize that once they have seized an airliner, the government's concern for the hostages is likely to dictate that the government negotiate, so the terrorists take the plane. Whatever the particulars of the situation, the problem created by time inconsistency follows the same pattern.[2]

A policymaker sets out to achieve goals which involve getting other individuals to

---

[2]Kydland and Prescott (1977) develop a tax policy example. Newberg (1981) discusses the problem of maintaining the oil cartel in the context of dynamic inconsistency.

behave in certain ways. The policymaker realizes that how these individuals choose to behave depends on how they expect him to react to their choices, and he takes this into account in formulating his optimal plan of action. (George and Martha want Betsy to get a summer job. They realize that how Betsy decides to spend her summer depends on how she expects them to react at tuition time, so they tell her that they plan to link what she does about a summer job with what they will do about her college expenses.)

But there is a difficulty. When it comes time to act, the policymaker will be free to reassess the situation and decide what course of action seems best *at that time*. And generally he will find that following the original plan is no longer in his best interest. Why? Because when the original plan was formulated, it took into account the impact of the policymaker's planned actions on the individuals' behavior. But when it comes time to act, taking the planned actions can no longer influence individuals' behavior. They have already chosen how to behave. Now the policymaker must choose the course of action that brings him closest to achieving his goals *given* the individuals' previous behavior. (So when the fall comes, George and Martha will abandon the plan designed to *influence* Betsy's summer behavior and select the original plan of action which best meets their goals *given* her summer behavior.)

Unfortunately for the policymaker, individuals realize from the beginning that the policymaker will take the time consistent plan of action—the plan which seems best *at the time the action is to be taken*—rather than the one which seemed optimal to the policymaker initially. So from the beginning, individuals' behavior deviates from that called for by the policymaker's optimal plan. (Betsy knows in June that her parents will pay her expenses in September no matter what, so she takes the summer off.)

In sum, time inconsistency is a general problem facing policymakers of all types. And recently economists have been giving serious consideration to the way in which time inconsistency can undermine central banks' abilities to contain inflation. But to appreciate how the problem arises for the makers of monetary policy, it is useful to consider what motivates central banks' choice of monetary policy actions and how the economy responds to them.

HOW TIME INCONSISTENCY CAN FOIL POLICYMAKERS' LOW-INFLATION PLANS

Monetary policy is widely acknowledged to have a direct impact on the rate of inflation, but central banks are also held responsible, to varying degrees, for the level of real economic activity in their countries. Consequently, a central bank's goals generally include not only maintaining a low rate of inflation, but maintaining a low rate of unemployment as well. In the United States, for example, the Full Employment and Balanced Growth Act of 1978 requires that the Fed testify before Congress annually, indicating how its plans fit into Congress' long-term objectives of achieving zero inflation and a 4 percent unemployment rate.

Until about ten years ago, discussions of monetary policy were often predicated on the notion that the central bank faced a fairly stable tradeoff between achieving its inflation and unemployment goals: rapid growth of the money supply would bring low unemployment but high inflation; slow money growth would bring a low rate of inflation but a high rate of unemployment. However, the anomalous behavior of inflation and unemployment in the 1970s—high and even increasing inflation accompanied by high and sometimes increasing unemployment in most industrialized countries—prompted macroeconomists to reformulate their views about the economy's response to monetary policy. Perhaps the two most important ideas to emerge from the recent reformulation are the so-called "natural rate" and "rational expectations" hypotheses. Taken together, these two ideas imply that the growth rate of the money supply directly affects the rate of inflation in the economy, but it has no systematic impact on the unemployment rate. Consequently, to the extent that these two hypotheses are correct, there is no tradeoff between inflation and unemployment for the central bank. Its choice of a monetary policy influences only the inflation rate, not the unemployment rate.[3]

For some time now macroeconomists have been stressing the obvious implication of the natural rate and rational expectations hypotheses: regardless of the central bank's concerns about unemployment, the monetary policies which produce low inflation are generally optimal. It is only recently that economists have paid much attention to a more subtle implication of the two hypotheses: because of the central bank's concerns about unemployment, monetary policies which produce low inflation may also be time inconsistent.

Choosing the Optimal Monetary Policy

According to the natural rate hypothesis, the economy tends toward a natural rate of unemployment which is independent of the stance of monetary policy. It may be possible for monetary policymakers to keep the actual unemployment rate from settling at its natural rate, at least temporarily, but only if they are able to create rates of inflation that the public had not been expecting.

For instance, the monetary authority might consider the natural rate of unemployment too high, and so decide that it will stimulate the economy by increasing the growth rate of the money supply. More rapid money growth increases the growth in private sector demand for goods and services. The increased demand puts upward pressure on prices, and the inflation rate rises. But will the higher inflation rate bring a lower unemployment rate? Not necessarily, according to the natural rate hypothesis. It depends on the public's inflation expectations. If firms and workers had been expecting the central bank to generate a high inflation rate and had figured this into their current wage agreements, then the higher inflation will not induce firms to hire any more workers than they intended to, so unemployment will remain at its natural rate. It is only if firms and workers had been expecting the central bank to generate low inflation and had signed contracts for low wage increases that the high-inflation policy would give firms the incentive to hire additional workers, and thus push unemployment below its natural rate.

---

[3]Criticisms of the standard "Phillips Curve" tradeoff between inflation and unemployment, and development of the alternative notions of the natural rate hypothesis and rational expectations have become nearly standard components of textbooks in macroeconomics and monetary theory. See, for example, Ritter and Silber (1983), Chapter 2, for a good summary.

Conversely, if the monetary authority considered the current inflation rate too high, and so decided to reduce the growth rate of the money supply, the response of unemployment would likewise depend on inflation expectations. As long as firms and workers had expected a slowdown in money growth and inflation when they forged current wage agreements, unemployment will remain at its natural rate. Lower inflation would be accompanied by an increase in the unemployment rate only if labor market participants had signed contracts for high wage increases and the lower inflation took them by surprise.[4]

The natural rate hypothesis leaves the door open for the central bank to affect the unemployment rate, if it can generate an inflation rate which the public does not expect. Proponents of the rational expectations hypothesis slam the door shut by arguing that the central bank cannot systematically engineer any inflation "surprises." According to rational expectations, the public knows as much about the way the central bank conducts monetary policy as the central bank does, so the central bank cannot count on doing anything that participants in the economy did not expect. Consequently, the central bank cannot plan on using monetary policy to drive the unemployment rate away from its natural rate.[5]

If the natural rate and the rational expectations hypotheses were perfectly accurate descriptions of the way the economy worked, then monetary policy would not affect the unemployment rate, and it clearly would be optimal for the central bank to concentrate its efforts on keeping the inflation rate low. Yet even in these circumstances the central bank may wind up pursuing a high-inflation monetary policy. How can this be? Because as long as the central bank would be willing to trade high inflation for low unemployment, the low-money-growth, low-inflation policy is not time consistent. A simple example demonstrates the central bank's predicament.

Dissecting the Optimal Plan For Monetary Policy

Suppose that at the beginning of the year all of the workers and firms in an economy are in the process of negotiating their annual wage agreements. Before the agreements are signed, the central bank announces that it intends to follow a low-money-growth, low-inflation monetary policy during the year. Having received the central bank's statement, the firms and workers in the labor market must decide whether to sign contracts for low wage increases or for high wage increases. What should they do?

Labor market participants realize they are locked into a game with the central bank. In this game, they get the first move, at the beginning of the year, when they choose between signing labor contracts with low wage increases or signing contracts with high wage increases. The central bank takes its turn next, during the year, when it chooses between creating a low rate of money growth or creating a high rate of money

---

[4]Analyses of the impact of surprise inflation on the unemployment rate based on the wage rigidity introduced by labor contracts are presented by Fischer (1977) and J. Taylor (1980). An alternative analysis based on a firm's initial inability to distinguish between general inflation and an increase in the demand for its product is developed by Lucas (1973).

[5]The conclusion that monetary policy systematically affects the inflation rate but has no systematic influence on real output or unemployment was given a clear exposition in Sargent and Wallace (1975).

growth. The game will produce one of four possible outcomes for the economy (see Figure 2).

The firms and workers in the economy understand that the central bank's announced plan seems optimal under the circumstances. The blanket statement that it will pursue a low-money-growth policy seems to leave labor market participants with the choice between signing contracts for low wage increases which will match the rate of inflation and put unemployment at its natural rate, or signing contracts for high wage increases which will outstrip inflation and push unemployment above its natural rate. Since labor market participants will settle on wage increases which just keep pace with expected inflation, the central bank anticipates they will choose low wage increases. So, if all goes according to plan, workers and firms will sign for low wage increases, and the central bank will then follow with the low-money-growth policy which they had expected. As a result, inflation will come in low and unemployment will come in at the natural rate—the optimal outcome.

Of course, the question in the mind of labor market participants is "Will the central bank still see the low-money-growth, low-inflation policy as best after the contracts are signed and it is time for the central bank to carry out its policy?" And in this case, the answer is "No," because the central bank is willing to trade off higher inflation for lower unemployment.

Suppose, for instance, that the firms and workers in the economy were to agree on contracts specifying low wage increases. Now the monetary authority can choose

FIGURE 2

Labor Market Alternatives

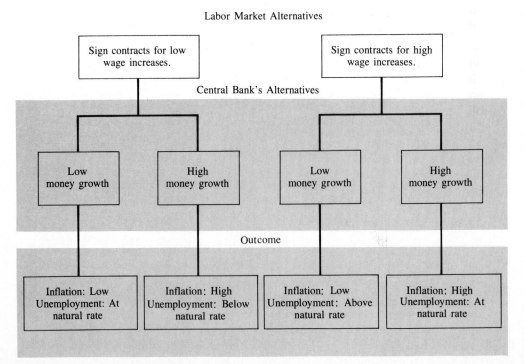

between the low-inflation policy called for by the optimal plan and a high-inflation policy which will drive the unemployment rate below its natural rate. The central bank is presumed to be willing to pursue a high-inflation policy if it would reduce unemployment, and with low wage increases already locked in, the central bank would have its chance. So it would pursue the high-inflation policy.

On the other hand, suppose the labor market participants signed contracts specifying high wage increases for the year. Again, the monetary authority has to choose between the low-inflation policy called for by the optimal plan and a high-inflation policy. But this time the low-inflation policy would drive unemployment above its natural rate. And if the monetary authority is willing to run a high-inflation monetary policy to push unemployment below the natural rate, it is surely willing to do so in order to keep unemployment from rising above it. So the monetary authority would again pursue the high-inflation policy.

In short, the firms and workers of the economy enter into their wage negotiations with the realization that pursuing a high-money-growth, high-inflation policy is the only time consistent plan for the central bank to follow. So their choice is obvious—they sign contracts for high wage increases at the beginning of the year. During the year, the central bank pursues the high-money-growth policy that they expected, so inflation comes in high. And with both wage increases and inflation running high, unemployment settles at its natural rate. So, as a result of the time inconsistency of the optimal low-inflation policy, the central bank winds up creating a high rate of inflation even though it gains nothing on the unemployment front.[6]

A POSSIBLE SOLUTION: CREDIBLE PRECOMMITMENTS TO THE OPTIMAL PLAN

One weakness with the analysis thus far is that it seems to imply that individuals understand the policymaker's situation better than the policymaker does. But surely if Betsy can figure out that her parents' original plan is time inconsistent, so can her parents. Likewise if the workers and firms in the economy recognize that a low inflation policy is not time consistent, so must the central bank. And if policymakers are aware of the time inconsistency in their original optimal plans, isn't there something they can *do* about it? At least in principle, it seems there is—they can take measures to make their original plans time consistent.

In order for the original optimal plan to work it must be time consistent. Everybody must recognize *at the outset* that when the time comes for the policymaker to act, following the original optimal plan will still represent the policymaker's best course of action. The policymaker can ensure this by making some additional arrangements which will make deviating from the optimal plan very costly to him—so costly that he will not choose to deviate from the plan when he acts. Once the policymaker has established this *credible precommitment* to the original optimal plan, so that individuals (rightly) expect him to follow it in the future, they too will behave according to the optimal plan when they make their decisions.

---

[6]A mathematical presentation of the dynamic inconsistency in low-inflation monetary policies along these lines is carefully developed by Barro and Gordon (1983a).

George and Martha might apply this approach to overcoming the time inconsistency in their optimal plan: before talking to Betsy they can have all of their savings put into a trust account with the provision that the trust manager not disburse funds to finance Betsy's education unless she can document that she has worked a summer job. Then when they tell Betsy that they will help her with her college expenses only if she gets a summer job, Betsy will get the job, because she knows that they are committed to the optimal policy and they will not pay her expenses if she does not get a job.

Similarly, one solution to the time inconsistency problem in our simple economic example is for the central bank to begin the year, not simply by announcing that it considers a low-inflation policy optimal, but by establishing a credible commitment to the low-inflation policy. For example, the central bankers themselves may agree to forfeit their position on their personal wealth if money growth or the inflation rate exceeds some announced percent for the year. Once firms and workers realize that it will still be in the central bank's best interest to run a low-inflation monetary policy during the year, they will sign contracts for low wage increases at the beginning of the year, and the economy can achieve the natural rate of unemployment at a low inflation rate.[7]

While arrangements establishing a credible precommitment to low inflation monetary policies can be devised, such arrangements are not likely to be implemented. Governments seem to be unwilling to impose the necessary system of penalties on their central banks, and central bankers are unlikely to do so themselves (see Donald J. Mullineaux's "Monetary Rules and Contracts: Why Theory Loses to Practice" in this issue of the *Business Review*). But all is not lost. Even in the absence of formal arrangements, there are forces at work to push the time consistent policy closer to the original optimal low-inflation rate.

THE ADVANTAGE OF HAVING A GOOD REPUTATION

Both the family example and the monetary policy example consider only a single interaction between the policymakers and the individuals they were trying to influence. But parents try to influence their offsprings' behavior, and central banks try to influence economies' performances, every day. And this repeated interaction itself may help bridge the gap between the optimal plan and the time consistent one.

When the encounter between the policymaker and other individuals is part of a long sequence of encounters, the policymaker becomes concerned about how the present encounter will affect his "reputation"—others' expectations about how he will act in the future. Adhering to the optimal plan in the current encounter presumably will enhance the policymaker's reputation, so that in future encounters, when he announces that he intends to follow the optimal plan, people are more likely to believe him and behave in accordance with that plan. On the other hand, deviating from the optimal

---

[7]The role of the monetary authority's credibility in the disinflation process is discussed in J. Taylor (1982).

plan in the current encounter will impair the policymaker's reputation, so that his announcement of an intent to follow the optimal plan in the future will be less credible, and people will be more likely to act on the assumption that he will deviate from it. In short, adhering to the announced optimal policy today improves the policymaker's prospects for obtaining optimal outcomes tomorrow. Thus, building a reputation functions in the same way as an explicit precommitment to the optimal policy; it raises the relative cost of deviating from the optimal policy, and so keeps the policymaker to the original optimal policy when the time comes to act. Individuals realize this, anticipate the policymaker following the optimal plan, and so behave in accordance with the optimal plan from the beginning.

For example, suppose George and Martha realize that by adhering to their optimal plan and refusing to pay for Betsy's freshman year in college unless she gets a summer job, they will reap the benefit that Betsy will find that policy credible during the summers before her sophomore, junior, and senior years. She may even find similar policies credible on other occasions. And maybe Betsy's younger brothers and sisters will do the same. On the other hand, by abandoning the optimal plan after that first summer and paying Betsy's tuition bill when she does not work, George and Martha forgo all the benefits of having a reputation for adhering to their optimal plans. If the long-run benefits of sticking with the optimal plan and maintaining a reputation outweigh the short-run benefits of sending Betsy to college on schedule, George and Martha will stick to their optimal plan. Betsy will realize this, she will find their optimal policy credible, and she will get a summer job.

Similarly, in the case of monetary policy, suppose that by sticking with the optimal low-inflation policy one year, the central bank reaps the benefit of convincing the public that it will stick with this policy in future years. As long as the central bank weighs this future benefit more heavily than any current benefits from a high-inflation policy, it will stick to its optimal plan. Firms and workers realize this, and, seeing the announced low-inflation policy as credible, sign contracts for low wage increases at the beginning of the year.

There is no guarantee that the central bank's concern about preserving its reputation will work as well as an explicit precommitment to keep the central bank to low-inflation policies. The central bank in our example has a simple choice: high inflation or low inflation. Either the perceived benefits of building its reputation are sufficient to make the low-inflation policy time consistent or they are not. In reality, the central bank chooses from a continuum of possible inflation rates and the greater the benefits of building its reputation the closer the inflation rate associated with the time consistent policy will be to the inflation rate associated with the optimal policy. For instance, if the central bank takes a long-run view of its policies' impacts and sees prospects of high inflation in the future as a serious problem, then it will value its reputation more highly. Similarly, if the central bank knows that the public's confidence is easy to lose and hard to regain, then it will weigh reputation considerations more heavily in its policy decisions. Such considerations will push the time consistent monetary policy closer to the optimal one, and hence push the actual inflation rate closer to the optimal one. A central bank might consider that adherence to the optimal monetary policy today pays a rich enough dividend in terms of lower inflation tomorrow to warrant sticking with that policy, but that would be the extreme case.[8]

CONCLUSION

Decisionmakers charged with setting social policy, from parents to Presidents, often face the problem that their optimal plans are time inconsistent—the plans will no longer seem optimal when the time comes for the policymaker to act. The individuals whose behavior the plans are supposed to affect realize this and, as a result, behave in a way that keeps the policymakers from achieving their original goals.

Some economists are now exploring the notion that the Fed's efforts to reduce inflation are plagued by time inconsistency problems. Simple examples have been developed to show how a central bank that is willing to use inflationary monetary policies to drive unemployment below its natural rate may find itself producing chronic high inflation and never reducing unemployment.

No one is quite ready to argue that time inconsistency spells an inevitable return to double-digit inflation. There are ways around the problem. First of all, time inconsistency can be overcome if the central bank can establish a credible precommitment to follow a low-inflation policy. Admittedly, this solution has yet to be adopted by any country today, but a more practical solution or near-solution may be at work already. A central bank which realizes that its current policy actions influence the public's expectations about the future of monetary policy will find it nearly as much in its self-interest to pursue a low inflation policy as it would if an explicit precommitment had been made. Viewed from this perspective, the recent emphasis that preserving the central bank's reputation has been given in monetary policy discussions, both in the United States and abroad, represents a substantive step forward in containing inflation over the long term.

BIBLIOGRAPHY

Barro, Robert J., and David B. Gordon (1983a), "A Positive Theory of Monetary Policy in a Natural Rate Model," *Journal of Political Economy,* pp. 589–610.

——, and —— (1983b), "Rules, Discretion and Reputation in a Model of Monetary Policy," *Journal of Monetary Economics,* pp. 101–121.

Fischer, Stanley (1977), "Long Term Contracts, Rational Expectations and the Optimal Money Supply Rule," *Journal of Political Economy,* pp. 191–206.

Kydland, Finn E., and Edward C. Prescott (1977), "Rules Rather Than Discretion: The Inconsistency of Optimal Plans," *Journal of Political Economy,* pp. 473–491.

Lucas, Robert E., Jr. (1973), "Some International Evidence on Inflation-Output Tradeoffs," *American Economic Review,* (June), pp. 326–334.

Newberg, D. M. G., (1981), "Oil Prices, Cartels, and the Problem of Dynamic Inconsistency," *Economic Journal* (September), pp. 617–645.

---

[8]Barro and Gordon (1983b) emphasize the role of reputation in helping to reduce the impact of dynamic inconsistency problems on inflation.

Sargent, Thomas J., and Neil Wallace (1975), "Rational Expectations, the Optimal Monetary Instrument, and the Optimal Money Supply Rule," *Journal of Political Economy,* pp. 241–254.
Taylor, John B. (1980), "Aggregate Dynamics and Staggered Contracts," *Journal of Political Economy,* pp. 1–23.
―――― (1982), "Establishing Credibility: A Rational Expectations Viewpoint," *American Economic Review, Papers and Proceedings,* (May), pp. 81–85.

QUESTIONS FOR DISCUSSION

1 In the example given in the article, why is George and Martha's promise not to pay Betsy's college expenses time-inconsistent and therefore not credible? Answer this question by working through the tree diagram of Figure 1 *from the bottom up*. That is, first consider what George and Martha will do in the second stage, given each of the possible actions that Betsy could have taken. Having determined how George and Martha will respond in each case, find Betsy's best action (from her point of view).
2 Suppose that George and Martha can *commit* themselves to carrying out their threat (say by putting Betsy's college money in a trust fund, as described in the article). Use Figure 1 to find out what Betsy's best action is now. How has precommitment changed the outcome? Explain how the development of a reputation for keeping promises by George and Martha can have the same effect as precommitment.
3 A wealthy family, concerned about kidnappers, makes a public statement that they will never pay ransom. Is this likely to help protect them against kidnappers? Would this family support the passage of a law forbidding the payment of ransom to kidnappers? Answer this question by setting up a tree diagram as in Figure 1, in which the decision makers are "Family" and "Potential kidnappers."
4 If workers have rational expectations, why would only *unexpected* inflation tend to drive unemployment below the natural rate?
5 Work through Figure 2 (*from the bottom up*), finding the optimal move by the Fed and by workers at each stage. Why does the time inconsistency problem lead to high inflation? (*More difficult:* Why doesn't time inconsistency lead to *infinite* inflation?)
6 In the situation described in Figure 2, suppose that the Fed initially has no credibility for its promises not to inflate. To develop credibility, it decides to stick to a low-money-growth strategy, come what may. What will happen to the economy during the "transition period," in which the public has not yet learned of the Fed's new approach? Relate this to the effects of monetary policy on the economy after the 1979 switch in Fed operating procedures.
7 "A maximum rate of money growth should be specified by the U.S. Constitution." Discuss.
8 Reread the article on the Gramm-Rudman balanced budget act (Reading 11). How do the concepts of credibility and commitment help explain why Congress passed a law of the form of Gramm-Rudman? Is Congress' strategy working?

MARKET VIEWS OF MONETARY POLICY AND REACTIONS TO M1 ANNOUNCEMENTS

Jan G. Loeys*

Since 1979, the Fed's weekly announcements of the M1 money supply have been carefully watched by financial market participants and have been associated on occasion with sharp changes in bond and stock prices. Jan G. Loeys argues that this is due to the effect of the announcements on investors' beliefs about the course of monetary policy.

The highlight of the week for any true "Fed watcher" is the Thursday afternoon announcement of the Federal Reserve's most recent estimates of the monetary aggregates.[1] In recent years, financial markets throughout the world have reacted strongly to these announcements. The markets' preoccupation with these weekly money numbers has been the subject of a lot of controversy; some have even likened it to a "giant crap game."[2] The markets' response to these money stock announcements may not be irrational, however. Rather, money stock data may contain information that market participants use to revise their expectations about future monetary policy actions and credit market conditions.

These market expectations presumably depend upon the public's perception of the Fed and its policies. If the market changes its view of monetary policymaking, it will

Jan G. Loeys, "Market Views of Monetary Policy and Reactions to M1 Announcements," *Business Review*, Philadelphia Federal Reserve Bank, March–April 1984, pp. 9–16.

*Jan Loeys is Economist at the Federal Reserve Bank of Philadelphia. Excellent research assistance was provided by Sabrina Lee.

[1]Between February 1980 and February 1984, these estimates were released on Friday afternoon.

[2]Marcia Stigum, *The Money Market: Myth, Reality, and Practice*. (New York: Dow Jones-Irwin, 1983), p. 272.

also change the way it interprets monetary data and how it reacts to the money stock announcements. Therefore, observing changes in market reactions to the weekly money stock announcements may provide interesting information on how the public's perception of monetary policymaking has changed in recent years.

M1 ANNOUNCEMENTS AND MARKET REACTIONS

Every Thursday at 4:30 P.M., after the New York Stock Exchange closes, the Fed makes public a series of statistical releases. The release that has drawn the most attention is H.6, which contains detailed statistical information on the various money stock measures and their components. The public tends to focus on the Fed's latest weekly estimate of M1.[3]

The public's preoccupation with this weekly M1 number is evident in the turbulent motion in financial markets whenever the M1 estimate differs from what was expected. If the M1 estimate is higher than expected, interest rates on assets of all maturities tend to rise; if the M1 estimate is unexpectedly low, most interest rates tend to drop.[4] Figure 1 shows how, in recent years, interest rates on different maturities have reacted to the announcement of an unexpected 1 percent increase in M1. The negative slope of the response curve indicates that short-term interest rates have reacted more strongly than interest rates on long-term assets.

At first glance, this phenomenon seems to contradict economic theory, which suggests that an increase in the money supply is associated with a *drop* in short-term interest rates (other things being equal), not a rise. But such a conclusion fails to recognize that money supply data are released with a lag. The M1 number announced on a Thursday afternoon measures the average M1 level in the week that ended *ten days prior*. Therefore, the inverse relation between money and interest rates should be observed two weeks before the announcement. So it would be a mistake to look for rate declines just when the information is made public. Rather, there must be something about the announcement itself that causes interest rates to rise.

Economists have suggested that the explanation lies in what announcements about past money stock levels lead the market to expect about the future. It may be rational for market participants to use money data as a signal of Fed intentions for monetary policy. In particular, markets are likely to be concerned with how the Fed itself will react to the money supply figure.

INTERPRETING THE ANNOUNCEMENT

Since the early 1970s, the Fed has increasingly defined its long-run policy in terms of how fast it wants the money supply to grow. At the beginning of each year, the

---

[3]M1, the narrowest monetary aggregate, consists of currency, nonbank travelers checks, demand deposits, and other checkable deposits.

[4]The impact of money stock announcements can be felt in many markets, such as those for stocks, commodities, and foreign exchange. Economists have shown how, in recent years, the announcement of an unexpected rise in M1 has been followed by lower equity and commodity prices and a stronger value of the dollar vis-à-vis foreign currencies. For a survey of these studies, see Bradford Cornell, "The Money Supply Announcements Puzzle," *American Economic Review* (September 1983), pp. 644–655.

Basis points

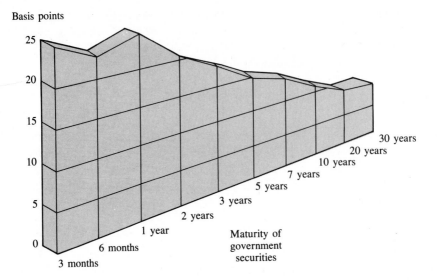

FIGURE 1
The Average Response of Interest Rates to Money Announcements over the Period
November 1977–December 1983. This graph and the graphs that follow illustrate the
rise in interest rates over the whole maturity spectrum one working day following the
announcement of an unanticipated 1 percent rise in M1 (this amounts to $3 to $5
billion during this period). An unanticipated M1 change is measured as the announced
M1 change minus the median change forecasted in a survey of government securities
dealers.

Fed sets targets for growth in several measures of the money supply over a four-quarter
horizon. The targets, expressed as ranges, are announced publicly during Congressional
testimony by the Fed Chairman. The Chairman also will indicate how the monetary
objectives are related to the Fed's ultimate policy goals of price stability and sustainable
economic growth.

Financial market participants are concerned about the money supply for the same
reasons the Fed is. In particular, people recognize that sharp fluctuations in the money
supply can have damaging effects on the economy. If money grows too fast, inflation
will accelerate. If money is in short supply, the pace of economic activity will falter.
To gauge the future behavior of the economy, therefore, people will keep a careful
watch on the behavior of money. And since the Fed plays a key role in influencing
the money supply, people also keep an eye on the Fed.

In the eyes of many, the Fed's role is to keep the money supply "well behaved,"
that is, consistent with its ultimate goals of price stability and economic growth. If a
particular movement in the money supply seems likely to inflict some damage on the
economy, the Fed needs to take some corrective action to get money "back on track."
Unfortunately, however, short-term movements in the money supply are highly volatile, and it is very difficult to know when a given change in money portends future
trouble. Both the Fed and the public must make some judgments, nevertheless, about

whether the behavior of money is getting out of hand. While the Fed makes little public comment on its views about short-run money movements, the market's interest rate response to money supply announcements tells us something about how people *expect the Fed to react* to a money supply fluctuation. If people expect a prompt offsetting response by the Fed to a sharp rise in the money supply, short-term rates should rise, generating what's called a "policy anticipation effect." If market participants believe the Fed is delaying a necessary offsetting response to a bulge in the money supply, then long-term rates should increase with the announcement, producing an "expected inflation effect."

Suppose M1 rises above target and the market believes the Fed will act promptly to bring M1 back to target. How does the Fed do this? It tightens the supply of reserves to financial institutions, which will force short-term interest rates to rise. In fact, the very expectation of this Fed action causes short rates to rise immediately.[5] (The reason involves rational behavior on the part of financial institutions. If banks expect reserves to be more expensive in the future, it pays to acquire them today. But if all banks try to acquire reserves today, they drive up the interest rate on federal funds, the market where banks borrow reserves from one another.) Moreover, the more vigorously and the faster the market expects the Fed to react, the more short-term rates will rise. Thus, the policy anticipation effect explains an increase in short-term interest rates on the heels of the announcement of an unexpected money stock increase.

In reality, people do not always know where exactly the Fed wants M1 to be at each moment in time, in part because the annual targets for the monetary aggregates are expressed as ranges (rather than single points) and because the Fed does not make weekly announcements of its intentions. Moreover, because the monetary control mechanism is far from perfect, the Fed has not always been able to meet the annual target ranges for M1. In the face of this uncertainty about future money growth, the best forecast presumes the Fed will only partially compensate for a sharp rise above the long-run target, tightening up somewhat, but perhaps not enough to bring M1 "back on target."[6] This presumption implies that long-term money growth may be higher than previously expected. Since more rapid money growth leads to higher inflation, but with a lag (averaging 18 months to 2 years in empirical research), long-term interest rates will rise because lenders require a higher "inflation premium" to

---

[5]Short rates may rise even without the Fed tightening the supply of reserves. Between September 1968 and February 1984, during any given Thursday-to-the-following-Wednesday period, banks were required to hold a certain amount of reserves, as a percentage of deposits outstanding two weeks before. At the beginning of the statement week, a bank knows the exact amount of reserves it is required to hold on average during the coming seven days, but it does not know how much other banks must hold. The H.6 release published during any given week, however, contains estimates of the aggregate level of deposits for the week on which current reserve requirements are based. If these deposits, which make up most of M1, were higher than anticipated, banks know that total market demand for reserves during the current week is stronger than expected. As a result banks will raise the level of the federal funds rate they think clears the market, unless they believe the Federal Reserve will take offsetting actions. This 2-week lag in reserve requirement accounting was reduced to 2 days starting in February 1984, so this effect should have disappeared by now.

[6]This point was first developed by Gikas Hardouvelis, "Market Perceptions of Federal Reserve Policy and the Weekly Monetary Announcements," *Mimeo,* U.C. Berkeley (March 1983).

compensate their expected loss of purchasing power.[7] This has been called the "expected inflation effect."

Uncertainty about Fed intentions for long-run money growth, therefore, explains how both short and long rates can rise after the announcement of an unexpected surge in M1: short rates rise in anticipation of some Fed tightening, and long rates rise in anticipation of higher long-term money growth and, hence, inflation. The more uncertain people are about long-run money growth, the more likely they are to raise their long-run money growth expectations after the announcement of an unexpected jump in M1, and the less they will expect the Fed to tighten up in the near future. In other words, the higher this uncertainty, the more responsive long rates will be to money announcements, and the less responsive short rates will be.

HAS THE MARKET'S VIEW OF MONETARY POLICY CHANGED IN RECENT YEARS?

We have examined how the public's perception of monetary policy can affect the way interest rates react to money stock announcements. Observing changes in the response pattern of interest rates may, therefore, reveal something about how the public adjusts its views of monetary policymaking. An econometric analysis of the reaction of interest rates to money announcements over the period November 1977 to December 1983 suggested that there were three distinct shifts in the interest rate response pattern.

The October 1979 Shift

The first shift occurred in October 1979. Figure 2 shows that before this date only short rates reacted in any significant way to money announcements, but in October 1979 interest rates over the whole maturity spectrum began to respond much more strongly. The impact of the announcement of an unanticipated 1 percent rise in M1 on the 3-month rate rose from 7 to 37 basis points, while the response of the 30-year yield rose from essentially zero to 14 basis points.

The most likely cause of this shift is the October 1979 change in Fed operating procedures, which was essentially a change in its instrument to control the money supply. Prior to October 1979 the Fed focused on the federal funds rate as its instrument to control M1. If M1 grew too fast, the federal funds rate would be forced up, while,

---

[7]Another possible explanation for the reaction of long rates is based on the expectations theory of the term structure. According to this theory, yields on assets of different maturities are not independent of each other because they apply to partially overlapping periods. For example, a five-year yield and a two-year yield overlap for the first two years. The three-year yield over the period starting two years hence—implicit in the difference between the five-year and the two-year rate—is called a forward rate. To assure that a movement in the yield on a longer-term maturity is not due merely to its overlap with a shorter-term maturity, the announcement effects also have been estimated using these forward rates (see Jan G. Loeys, "Federal Reserve Operating Procedures, Policy Uncertainty, and the Weekly Money Stock Announcements," Federal Reserve Bank of Philadelphia, *Working Paper* (1983)). The estimated response curves were slightly lower than those for spot rates but were still significantly above zero—at least, up until the seven-year mark— except for the periods before October 1979 and during 1982. This result suggests that the overlap with short-term rates is not enough to explain the response of long-term rates of interest to money announcements.

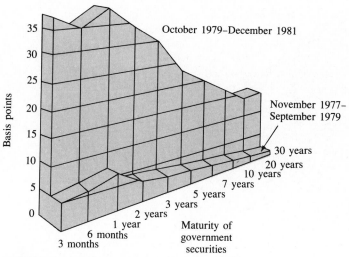

FIGURE 2
The Response Curve Moves Up Sharply in October 1979. . . .

if M1 grew too slowly, this rate would be moved down. This approach did not work particularly well, however, because it did not allow enough flexibility in the federal funds rate to keep M1 on track. Consequently, more often than not the Fed failed to achieve its monetary targets.

Following October 1979 the Fed's operating procedures focused more on bank reserves in controlling money, which allowed more variability in short-term interest rates. It was argued that this approach would give the Fed better and closer control of M1 over shorter time horizons. The increased response of short rates immediately after the new procedures were announced indicates that financial markets expected that the Fed would indeed act faster and more vigorously to keep M1 under control.

The strong response of long-term rates of interest was surprising at first. It suggests that the abrupt change in policy made it difficult initially for market participants to determine exactly what the Fed was up to.[8] In particular, there may have been high uncertainty about what long-run money growth would be. Although the Fed was expected to act faster to keep M1 on target—and would thus control it over shorter time horizons—it was not immediately obvious what that target was.

Another consequence of the new operating procedures also bears considering. The federal funds rate became very volatile after the shift towards a reserves-based operating procedure. Therefore, changes in this rate could not be "read" anymore as signals of the Fed's policy intentions. But reserves were also very volatile following the policy shift, and, therefore, also "unreadable." In consequence, market participants have come to rely more on money movements as signals of sustained deviations from the

---

[8]Recall that there had been no such abrupt change in Fed policy since World War II.

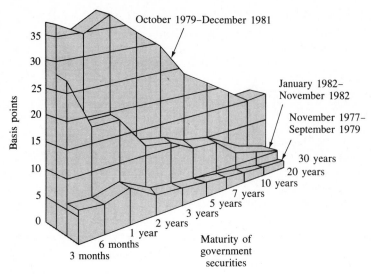

FIGURE 3
. . . But Drops Again in January 1982.

longer-run paths of money growth.[9] These two factors, higher uncertainty about the direction of long-run monetary policy, and the increased importance of M1 fluctuations as potential signals of where the Fed is heading, may explain why long-term bond markets became more sensitive to money stock announcements.

The January 1982 Shift

The second shift in the interest rate response curve took place around January 1982. Figure 3 shows that the curve moved back down, although not to its pre-October 1979 level. One explanation might be that, because of the recession that started in July 1981, financial markets expected the Fed to follow a policy directed more towards smoothing interest rates than towards keeping the monetary aggregates close to target. However, there is no evidence that such a policy change did take place around this time: in fact, during 1982, the federal rate was as volatile as in 1980–81.

A more likely explanation is that after two years under the new operating procedures the public had gained some experience—and confidence—with how the Fed would react to money stock fluctuations. The drop in the response of the 3-month rate, for example, is not very significant, which suggests that the market had only marginally revised its perception of the Fed's tolerance for short-run deviations of money from target. The response of long rates, on the other hand, dropped to a point that was

---

[9]For more details on this argument, see Loeys, "Federal Reserve Operating Procedures, Policy Uncertainty, and the Weekly Money Stock Announcements," Federal Reserve Bank of Philadelphia, *Working Paper* (1983).

statistically not very different from zero during 1982, which indicates uncertainty about long-run monetary policy.

The December 1982 Shift

The third shift took place around the end of 1982, this time taking the form of a significant *rise* in the reaction of long rates together with a *drop* in the reaction of short rates (Figure 4). This flattening of the response curve occurred just two months after the Fed had decided to de-emphasize M1 in favor of the broader aggregates, M2 and M3. This decision was taken because of technical problems that were judged to make M1 unreliable as a guide to policy. The decline in the reaction of short-term rates to M1 announcements suggests that market participants "believed" the Fed's statements concerning the reduced role of that aggregate in the policy process. The fact that the response curve did not drop to its pre-October 1979 level, however, indicates that financial markets did not perceive that the Fed had returned to targeting the federal funds rate directly. M1 still played a significant role, in the market's view, though less so than before.

The increased response of long rates indicates that in 1983, financial markets may have become more uncertain once again about the direction of long-term monetary policy. Articles in the financial press during 1983, for example, showed a lot of confusion about the stance of monetary policy, and the shape of the recovery. Perhaps market participants judged that prospects had increased that the Fed would fail to keep long-term money growth from accelerating. If so, this would account for the increased responsiveness of long rates to money announcements.

FIGURE 4
In December 1982 the Response Curve Turns Flat.

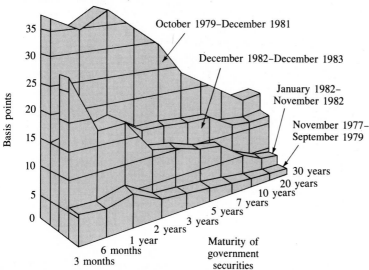

CONCLUSION

The impact of monetary policy actions upon the economy depends crucially upon the behavior of consumers and businesses, which, in turn, is influenced by their expectations of future monetary policy. The way financial markets react to releases of the Fed's money stock estimates can provide valuable information on how markets perceive monetary policy operations. In general, the more short-term interest rates react to money announcements, the faster the Fed is seen to correct deviations of money from target. The more long rates react relative to short rates, on the other hand, the more uncertain the market may be about long-term money growth, or the more the market may be using M1 numbers as signals of where monetary policy is heading.

An analysis of the pattern of interest rate reactions to money announcements during recent years turned up three major shifts. The first shift, just after the October 1979 change in Fed operating procedures, reflects a market perception that the Fed would act faster and more vigorously to control M1 in the short run, although this abrupt policy change did seem to create some confusion about the Fed's long-run monetary policy intentions. A few years under the new operating procedures seems to have made the market more confident about the direction of monetary policy, as suggested by the second shift in the market's response to money announcements, in early 1982. The third shift—around December 1982—is consistent with the October 1982 de-emphasis of M1 as an intermediate target of monetary policy, although the market did not seem to believe that the Fed had returned to a federal funds rate policy such as it followed before October 1979. Like the October 1979 change, however, this policy change did create some uncertainty among market participants about the direction of monetary policy.

QUESTIONS FOR DISCUSSION

1 What has been the effect in recent years of unexpectedly high money supply announcement on short-term interest rates? On long-term interest rates? Is this consistent with the usual view that money supply increases lower interest rates? Explain.

2 Were market reactions to announcements relatively stronger or weaker during the 1979–1982 period? What does this say about market perceptions of monetary policy during this period?

3 Footnote 4 reports the result that unexpected M1 increases also lead to lower stock and commodity prices (commodities are primarily raw materials, like metals and agricultural goods) and to a stronger dollar. Explain why this might be so.

4 (*More difficult.*) It has been argued by some, as an alternative to the view presented in this article, that short-run money surprises are not closely related to monetary policy at all. Instead, they are due to unanticipated shocks to autonomous aggregate demand. How could an anticipated positive shock to, say, autonomous investment demand lead to a higher-than-expected money supply? (*Hint:* A key part of the argument is that the money multiplier increases when interest rates rise; see your text.) In this case, why would positive money surprises affect interest rates? Is this explanation consistent with the greater sensitivity of interest rates to announcements during 1979–1982?

RULES PLUS DISCRETION IN MONETARY POLICY: AN APPRAISAL OF OUR EXPERIENCE SINCE OCTOBER 1979

Frank E. Morris*

Many recent writers on monetary policy have followed the lead of Milton Friedman (Reading 14) in arguing that the Federal Reserve should concentrate only on controlling the growth of a basic monetary aggregate, such as M1 or M2 (that is, use a monetary "rule"). The author of the following article, who is the President of the Federal Reserve Bank of Boston, here argues for an approach that uses rules but adds an element of "discretion" (that is, departure from rules under certain circumstances).

One of the oldest arguments in economic theory is whether monetary policy should be guided by rules or discretion. My object in this paper is to assess what we have learned about this subject since the famous Federal Open Market Committee (FOMC) meeting of October 1979. This is purely a personal assessment, not a Federal Reserve position.

Rules for monetary policy seem to have an intuitive appeal to many people. To some they seem to offer easy answers to complex problems. To others the rules offer a discipline which they think we would not impose upon ourselves.

All rules for monetary policy, whether they be based on the growth of money, the exchange rate, the price of gold or a basket of commodities, must rest on one of two assumptions. One assumption is that the behavior of the object to be controlled is

Frank E. Morris, "Rules Plus Discretion in Monetary Policy—An Appraisal of Our Experience Since 1979," *New England Economic Review,* September–October 1985, pp. 3–8.
*Frank E. Morris is President, Federal Reserve Bank of Boston. Remarks presented to The Money Marketeers, New York, New York, September 11, 1985.

predictably related to the nominal GNP. The only alternative assumption is that monetary policy should be directed solely toward controlling inflation and that the central bank should have no responsibility or concern for the level of employment or output.

I will argue that the events of recent years demonstrate that neither of these assumptions is viable. At the same time, our experience with monetary targeting, for all of its problems, has brought two substantial advantages to the conduct of monetary policy. First, monetary targeting automatically forces the FOMC to consider the longer-run consequences of actions taken to meet short-run objectives. This is an important discipline for the Committee. It reduces the risk of excessive reactions to temporary shortfalls in employment and output. Changes in the guidelines, while they may have to be made from time to time, require an overt decision by the FOMC and cannot be viewed as a casual matter. Second, monetary targeting has made it easier for the Federal Reserve to communicate its policies to the public and the Congress. It automatically injects into the dialogue with the Congress the long-run consequences of alternative policies in a way that no purely discretionary regime could do. These are advantages not to be discarded.

I conclude, therefore, that monetary policy should be one of rules, tempered by discretion. This is not a neat solution but the world is, unfortunately, too complex for neat solutions.

THE PROBLEMS WITH PURE RULES REGIMES

No one, to my knowledge, has demonstrated predictable relationships between the exchange rate, the price of gold, or the price of a basket of commodities and the nominal GNP. Thus any advocate of a pure rules regime in targeting these variables must necessarily assume that the central bank will concern itself solely with the inflation rate, regardless of the short-term impact on employment or output. The revealed unpredictability of the relationship of the monetary aggregates to the nominal GNP is leading some monetarist economists to the same position.[1]

This transition should not be difficult. Implicit in monetarist theory has always been the proposition that the public should accept any short-run consequences of a monetary rule, secure in the knowledge that in the long run, monetary growth rates are neutral with respect to employment and output. However, the monetarist long run is certain to be too long to be relevant for public policy unless some other policy instrument could assure a reasonably acceptable level of employment and output in the shorter run.

The supply-side-monetarist policy mix of 1981 was to have accomplished this. While a policy of gradually reducing monetary growth was to deal with inflation, the tax reduction program was to generate rapid and sustained economic growth. Most economists had difficulty in seeing how a monetary policy tight enough to bring down the inflation rate substantially could coexist with rapid economic growth. The reconciling element was to have been a massive change in inflationary expectations, which would produce declining interest rates despite rapid economic growth.

---

[1]See Milton Friedman's latest views in *Challenge,* July/August 1985 (reading 14).

In the event, we learned that long-term expectations do not change rapidly. It took a number of years of high inflation rates before the bond investor demanded an adequate inflation premium. It will take a number of years of low inflation rates for that premium to be eliminated.

Looking back to 1951 with our inflationary mindset, it seems amazing that the Federal Reserve could still be pegging government bonds at $2^1/_2$ percent despite six years of rather strong economic growth following World War II. It was possible only because the long-term expectations of 1951 were still dominated by the experience of the 1930s. Policymakers should beware of any policy whose success requires a rapid change in the long-term expectations of the buyers of stocks and bonds.

The most critical recent demonstration of the need for discretion in monetary policy occurred in the summer of 1982. In the first half of 1982, M1 grew at a 7 percent rate, substantially above our policy range of 2.5 to 5.5 percent. During the same period, the nominal GNP grew at an annual rate of only 2.2 percent and real GNP declined at a rate of 2.8 percent.

Both Federal Reserve and private forecasters were predicting an upturn in the third quarter. The strong M1 growth in the first half was felt to presage such an upturn. As we moved into the third quarter, however, it became apparent that the widely forecast upturn was not occurring. The economy was still contracting. The FOMC responded by setting aside the M1 target, permitting interest rates to decline despite the M1 overshoot.

Sufficient time has passed to assess the wisdom of this judgment. Suspending the rule did not lead to excessive real growth or to a reacceleration of inflation.

Milton Friedman has argued that monetary policy should ideally be conducted by a few clerks at the New York Fed who should be instructed to provide a constant and low rate of growth of the money supply. He argues that Federal Reserve officials reject this advice only because it would eliminate their power. One can only speculate what would have happened if Milton's clerks were running monetary policy in the last half of 1982. The rate of inflation would probably be even lower than it is today, but the costs in terms of employment and output would have been prohibitive. Furthermore, the impact of a rigid monetary rule on an already shaky financial structure, both domestic and international, might have been catastrophic. It was a classic case of the occasional need for rules to be tempered by discretion.

In the last half of 1982, monetary policy was the only instrument that could have been applied quickly and powerfully in response to the unexpected weakness of the economy in the third quarter. In 1985, with fiscal policy almost completely immobilized, it is even more unrealistic to contemplate focusing monetary policy solely on inflation control.

WHAT TO TARGET

Three years ago, I published an article in which I argued that we could no longer measure the money supply in the United States; that is, we could no longer distinguish balances held for transactions purposes from other balances. I argued that we could not assume that the historical relationship of M1 and M2 to the nominal GNP would prevail in the future.[2]

The reasons were simple. In the case of M1, we could not assume that interest-bearing "money" would behave in the same way as the old non-interest-bearing money. In the case of M2, we could not assume that deposits bearing market-determined rates would behave in the same way as deposits bearing regulated rates. To the extent that bankers kept the rates on money market deposit accounts reasonably in line with market rates, we should expect M2 to be much less interest-elastic than in the past.

In the place of M1 and M2, I argued that we should target on those aggregates that were sufficiently broad so as not to be impacted by financial innovation—specifically, total liquid assets and total, nonfinancial debt (hereafter, debt).

With the passage of three years, it is clear that financial innovation has, indeed, changed the behavior of M1 and M2, but factors other than financial innovation have also been at work which have affected the behavior of all the financial aggregates.

Goodhart's Law* worked with amazing swiftness with respect to debt. No sooner had the FOMC adopted a monitoring range for debt than it became apparent that the very stable relationship which Benjamin Friedman of Harvard had found between debt and the nominal GNP over a number of decades had gone off the track. We can explain a large part of it. In recent years, the debt aggregate has been inflated by massive substitutions of debt for equity, in buy-out situations and in the actions of corporations to protect themselves against buy-outs. It has also been inflated by advance refunding issues of state and local governments. These debt issues do not generate economic activity. However, even after making a rough adjustment for these factors, it appears that more debt is now required to generate a dollar of nominal GNP than was required in the 1970s.

In addition to financial innovation, M1 behavior has been impacted by large changes in interest rates which have dramatically changed the opportunity costs of holding M1-type assets. The introduction of the Super NOW account, which can pay a market rate, was expected to have reduced the interest-elasticity of M1. In fact, because of the way these accounts have been priced, the introduction of the Super NOW has increased the interest-elasticity of M1.

Bankers have been quick to reduce the rate paid on Super NOWs when interest rates declined, but loath to raise the rate when market rates rose. In contrast, when pricing money market deposit accounts, bankers promptly adjusted MMDA rates in both directions. (See Charts 1 and 2.) As a result of this pricing practice, the opportunity cost of holding Super NOWs can vary substantially. In early 1984 the opportunity cost of holding Super NOWs instead of money market mutual funds was about 1.5 percent and Super NOWs were growing at about a 30 percent rate. By the third quarter of 1984, the opportunity cost of holding Super NOWs had risen to 3 percent and the

---

[2]Frank E. Morris, "Do the Monetary Aggregates Have a Future as Targets of Federal Reserve Policy?" Federal Reserve Bank of Boston, *New England Economic Review* (March/April 1982). See also Frank E. Morris, "Monetarism without Money," Federal Reserve Bank of Boston, *New England Economic Review* (March/April 1983.)

Editor's note: Goodhart's Law states that any financial aggregate targeted by the central bank will immediately lose the stable relationship it had previously had with GNP.

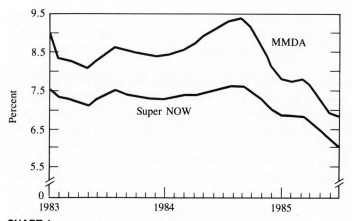

CHART 1
Yields of Super NOW and Money Market Deposit Accounts.
(Source: *Board of Governors of the Federal Reserve System.*)

CHART 2
Super NOW Accounts. (Source: *Board of Governors of
the Federal Reserve System.*)

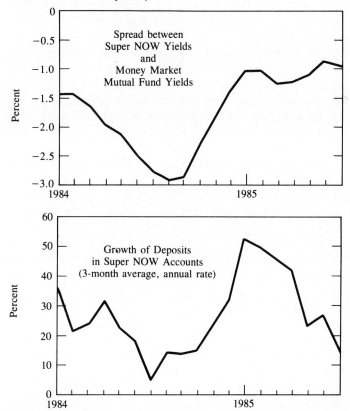

growth rate of Super NOWs fell below 10 percent. By early 1985, the opportunity cost had dropped to 1 percent and the growth rate surged to 40 percent. This interest sensitivity accounted for a significant part of the changes in M1 growth rates in 1984–85.

The M1/nominal GNP relationship has become even more predictable than I anticipated three years ago. In the autumn of 1983, prominent monetarist economists forecast that the economy would move into recession in the first half of 1984 and that the inflation rate would accelerate sharply in the second half.[3] The combination of two such seemingly contradictory events would have been most unusual in business cycle history. The forecasts were based on rules of thumb with respect to the lagged relationships of M1 growth, nominal GNP and the inflation rate, rules of thumb that had often been reliable in the past. In the annals of economic forecasting there can be few forecasts with such large misses. Instead of moving into recession, the first half of 1984 showed a real growth rate of 8.4 percent and, instead of a sharp escalation in the inflation rate in the last half, the inflation rate actually declined. Forecasting the nominal GNP and the inflation rate on the basis of past M1 growth has become a chancy enterprise, indeed.

In three out of the past four years, the FOMC has either set aside the M1 target (1982) or rebased the target on the second quarter level (1983 and 1985). Only in 1984 did the original target set for M1 prove to be compatible with a reasonably acceptable outcome for the nominal GNP. This fact speaks volumes about the suitability of M1 as a target for monetary policy.

We have been pointing to financial innovation and large interest rate changes as the source of aberrant behavior by the aggregates. The information presented in the table and Chart 3 suggests a third factor. Shown on the table and chart are the cumulative deviation of velocity from the 1970–80 trend for M1, M2, M3, total liquid assets (L) and debt (D).[4] Although the amplitudes of the deviations differ widely, all of the

---

[3]See Edward Mervosh, *Business Week,* December 12, 1983, "Milton Friedman's Recession Forecast Sparks a Controversy":

Milton Friedman, the Nobel laureate economist, is playing Scrooge this holiday season. While most economists and Administration officials are enjoying the steady diet of cheerful economic news coming from Washington, Friedman, the guiding light of monetarism, is gloomily predicting that the Federal Reserve is setting the U.S. up for a return to stagflation next year, possibly as early as the first half.

Friedman's scenario is based on straightforward monetarist analysis: By letting the money supply grow too fast from mid-1982 to mid-1983, the Fed has insured a sharp reacceleration of inflation at least by the second half of 1984. Beginning this summer, the Fed reined in the growth of the money supply, and Friedman argues that if the money growth continues its limp performance for another couple of months, the economy will be heading into a sharp slowdown or even a recession early next year. 'If money growth continues at its present rate for another two months, we are almost sure to have a recession in the first half of 1984,' he predicts.

Friedman holds out little hope that money growth will accelerate soon enough to head off the impending disaster.

See also: Walter Guzzardi, *Fortune,* March 19, 1984, "The Dire Warnings of Milton Friedman":

Still, when Friedman takes his eye off the [tennis] ball to regard the economy, he is depressed. He forecasts a slow current quarter, with real growth of the gross national product running at an annual rate of only 1%; he also sees a strong possibility that by the end of this year inflation could reach an annual rate of 9%.

[4]I am indebted to my colleague, Richard W. Kopcke, for this analysis.

RECENT BEHAVIOR OF VELOCITIES: DEVIATION FROM 1970–1980 TRENDS
(Percent)

	M1	M2	M3	L	D
1981:I	1.9	6.3	5.0	3.7	2.1
1981:II	0.3	5.1	4.8	2.9	1.3
1981:III	1.7	6.0	4.2	3.2	2.1
1981:IV	0.2	4.1	2.1	1.0	0.6
1982:I	−3.9	1.6	−0.2	−1.5	−1.6
1982:II	−3.4	1.0	−1.1	−2.6	−2.3
1982:III	−5.1	−0.8	−2.8	−4.4	−3.8
1982:IV	−9.1	−2.3	−3.9	−5.5	−5.2
1983:I	−10.7	−5.4	−4.3	−6.0	−5.4
1983:II	−11.7	−5.1	−3.4	−5.4	−4.9
1983:III	−12.7	−4.7	−3.0	−5.5	−5.2
1983:IV	−12.6	−4.3	−2.7	−5.1	−5.3
1984:I	−11.5	−2.7	−1.3	−4.3	−5.0
1984:II	−11.5	−1.9	−1.1	−4.6	−5.5
1984:III	−12.2	−2.3	−1.9	−6.1	−7.2
1985:IV	−12.1	−2.9	−2.7	−6.5	−8.7
1985:I	−14.3	−4.6	−3.8	−7.5	−10.6
1985:II	−16.5	−4.8	−3.7	−7.5	−12.1
		Mean absolute error			
1970:I–1980:IV	1.0	2.2	2.2	1.6	0.7

CHART 3
Velocity of Financial Aggregates: Deviations from 1970–1980 Trends.

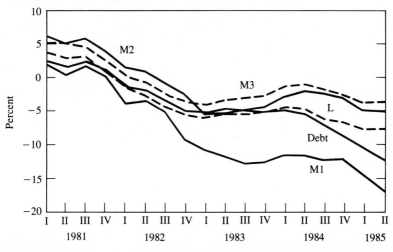

aggregates showed larger than expected velocity gains in 1981 and much larger than expected velocity declines in 1982–85.

This suggests a third factor at work which has affected all of the aggregates in different degree but in a similar fashion. Perhaps the third factor is the sharp decline in the rate of inflation, which since 1981 has led people to be willing to hold more financial assets relative to real assets and relative to income.[5]

If we are to target financial aggregates, which should we use? My answer is that the only ones we should use are those with a long track record and those whose character has not changed in recent years. This leaves out M1 and M2, since they are new aggregates, even though they bear old designations. The behavior of M3 since 1980 has been fairly good, but it has to be a very suspect aggregate in an era when the regulatory authorities are pressing banks and thrifts to improve their capital ratios. It is quite possible, in fact, that the fairly decent behavior of M3 has been a consequence of banks moving substantial assets off their books to improve their capital ratios. M3 may also not mean what it used to mean.

What about my two candidates of three years ago? I will confess that when I recommended total nonfinancial debt as a target three years ago, it never occurred to me that American corporations would be issuing vast quantities of debt for the sole purpose of retiring equity. I will not comment on the sanity of this in an already over-leveraged economy, but it is clear that if we are to utilize a debt target, we will have to differentiate debt that will generate economic activity from debt that will not.

This leaves me with total liquid assets. It seems to me that if we can no longer measure transaction balances, the next logical step would be to concentrate on controlling liquidity. I can emphasize how very personal a view this is by telling you that I doubt I could get two votes for this proposition on the FOMC, even if one of the votes were mine.

How has total liquid assets performed as a target during the last four years? Better than the rest. It had a disastrous year in 1982, when its velocity was 6.5 percent below trend. But 1982 was a disastrous year for all of the financial aggregates, with deviations from trend velocity ranging from -5.8 percent for debt to -9.3 percent for M1. In the other three years, the velocity for total liquid assets fell 0.7 percent faster than its trend, with the largest deviation being -1.4 percent in 1984.[6]

Since 1981 we have seen an increased willingness to hold liquid assets relative to income. This has impacted all of the aggregates. When the adjustment to a lower inflation rate has been completed, there is every reason to believe that the relationship of total liquid assets to the nominal GNP will be similar to that of earlier years. This, however, is not the case with the new interest-bearing M1. There is no basis for thinking that its future velocity will be similar to that of the old non-interest-bearing M1. We will need at least another decade of data before we can be confident in forecasting the velocity of the new M1.

[5]This was suggested to me by Donald L. Kohn of the staff of the Federal Reserve Board of Governors among others.
[6]The velocity deviations from trend are measured fourth quarter to fourth quarter.

TO SUM UP

Asked the question "What have we learned since October 1979?" I would list the following:

1 A targeting procedure for monetary policy has great disciplining values which we should not discard.

2 There is no variable that the Federal Reserve can target which has a highly predictable relationship to the nominal GNP.

3 It is not feasible for monetary policy to focus solely on the price level, since there is no other policy tool available with which to deal with an unexpected weakness in the economy—à la 1982—or unexpected strength.

4 If one accepts the first three propositions, then it follows that the optimum monetary policy regime is one of rules tempered by discretion.

5 I would choose a total liquid assets rule for two reasons: (1) unlike all of the other aggregates its meaning has not been changed by the events of the past 10 years; and (2) if we can no longer measure transaction balances, controlling liquidity is the next best choice.

QUESTIONS FOR DISCUSSION

1 What does the author consider to be the two principal advantages of monetary rules? Do these arguments for rules differ from the ones put forward by monetarists?

2 The author states that the relationships between nominal GNP and variables such as the exchange rate, the price of gold, or the monetary aggregates (M1, M2) tend to be unpredictable. If this is true, why is this bad news for supporters of "rules"?

3 The super NOW account, a kind of checking account that pays interest, is one of the recently introduced financial assets included in M1. How has the rate of growth of super NOW accounts varied over time? How does this complicate the operation of monetary policy?

4 Why does the author feel that the Federal Reserve was right to abandon its monetary rule in 1982?

5 Legislative disagreements and lags have probably reduced the flexibility of fiscal policy as a tool for stabilizing the macroeconomy. What implication (according to this author) does this fact have for the conduct of monetary policy?

6 A monetarist would argue that the policy recommended here of rules plus discretion is effectively a policy of no rules at all—a return, perhaps, to the pre-1979 approach when the Fed tried actively to fine tune the economy. What do you think? Relative to a no-rules regimen, would a rules-plus-discretion regimen (*a*) constrain Fed overactivism or (*b*) improve the Fed's inflation-fighting credibility (see Readings 16 and 17)?

THE FUTURE OF MONETARY POLICY: THE RATIONAL EXPECTATIONS PERSPECTIVE

Mark H. Willes*

The theory of rational expectations holds that people will make efficient use of all available information in forming their expectations about the future. In this article (written just after the 1979 change in Fed operating procedures), the President of the Minneapolis Fed discusses some implications of rational expectations for monetary policy and for the idea of an inflation-unemployment tradeoff.

Nobody is very happy with the conduct of monetary policy. The economy has performed badly, particularly in terms of inflation and the large costs that go with it. And the near-term outlook for the performance of the economy is grim. Many critics accuse the monetary authorities of failing to deal effectively with the problems we have faced, and virtually every policymaker admits that, in hindsight, we have made some mistakes that have added to our economic woes.

The critical questions now are, Can and will the Federal Reserve do better in the future? My own assessment is that we clearly can do better than we have, but it is too soon to tell whether we really will. Not that we don't all want to do better. I am absolutely convinced that all of my colleagues strive diligently to recommend and pursue those policies that are best designed to improve economic conditions. But we

Mark H. Willes, "The Future of Monetary Policy: The Rational Expectations Perspective," *Quarterly Review,* Minneapolis Federal Reserve Bank, Spring 1980, pp. 1–7. This reading first appeared as a paper presented at the Allied Social Science Association Annual Meeting in Atlanta, Georgia, December 29, 1979, and previously published by the Center for Research in Government Policy and Business (Reprint CS-7). The author gratefully acknowledges the assistance of his staff, and Arthur Rolnick in particular, in preparing these remarks.

*Mark H. Willes is President, Federal Reserve Bank of Minneapolis.

don't all agree on what *best* policies are. It is these intellectual and analytical differences that raise questions about the future directions of monetary policy.

TWO BASIC QUESTIONS

Recent experience has raised two fundamental questions about the ability of the monetary authorities to manage the economy. One is how the Federal Reserve can best control the monetary aggregates. The other, more important question is whether policymakers can trade off lower rates of real growth and employment (or higher rates of unemployment) for lower rates of inflation.

The question of how to control the monetary aggregates has created considerable controversy. Recognizing the need to improve its operating procedures, the Fed recently announced a new procedure that is designed to control the aggregates by manipulating bank reserves. Many people have doubts, however, about the effectiveness of this new procedure, for in some ways it appears to be just the old one in disguise. It may take a while before this controversy is resolved. Within a year or so, we will have enough experience with the new procedure to decide whether the Fed has controlled the aggregates better than it did under the old procedure and whether the new approach has made the difference. I have some serious misgivings about how we are conducting this new experiment, but I am willing to wait and hope we refine the process so that it becomes a real success.

The question of the existence of a trade-off between inflation and unemployment (the Phillips curve relationship) has also stirred a major controversy, and this is the most basic disagreement facing economic policymakers, since it goes to the heart of what we can and cannot do. The controversy actually started several years ago, sparked by a new theory of expectations that has radical implications for policy analysis. Advocates of this theory, *rational expectations,* contend that there is no simple trade-off between inflation and unemployment and that analyzing economic policy is much more subtle and complex than standard macroeconomic models lead us to believe. If the rational expectations theory is correct, some of the main problems of the last several years are really only outgrowths of the problems of the last ten years, problems caused in part by inadequate theory which led to counterproductive policy. The implication is that we could have done more good by doing less—that is, by making fewer attempts to offset economic fluctuations. The corollary implication is that future monetary policy will be more effective if it is less active. In my judgement, it is the resolution, or lack thereof, of the controversy surrounding this point that will determine both the direction and the success of monetary policy. Consequently, what I would like to do is discuss why I think rational expectations should be taken seriously and why it has such fundamental implications for the conduct of monetary policy.

Economic Analysis Needs a Theory of Expectations

In the last few years, policymakers as well as academicians have been recognizing the importance of expectations in economic decision making. They have found that expectations can be a key factor in a wide range of consumption, investment, and policymaking problems. In fact, it is hard to imagine an economic problem which does not include expectations. Most economic problems are inherently dynamic; in some way, time is involved. Time can be a cost of production, an element in the planning horizon, or an influence on preferences. Whatever the problem, though, once time becomes a factor, expectations must also, for what we think is going to happen tomorrow will affect the choices we make today.

The consumption-saving problems faced by economic agents illustrates the key role of expectations in the decision process. One of the most successful theories for explaining consumption and saving has been the *permanent-income hypothesis*. Roughly speaking, it says that today's consumption and saving depend not only on today's spendable income, but on expected future income as well. Expected life-span, expected future tax liability, and expected earning potential can all affect economic agents' decisions on how much income to consume now and how much to save for the next period. People who expected a shorter life-span, a new tax on consumption, or a higher salary might greatly increase their current consumption or saving.

Investment decisions are another kind of problem in which expectations play an obviously important role. What individuals invest today clearly depends on what returns and what risks they expect over the life of the investment. One major influence on their expected returns and risks is their expected future tax liabilities. For example, congressional consideration of a windfall profits tax has undoubtedly increased the risks and reduced the investment individuals are willing to make in the oil industry.

It would be easy to enumerate many other economic problems that are inherently dynamic and require a theory of expectations, but perhaps it is unnecessary. At least to some extent, economists have always agreed that expectations are critical at this level of analysis. Only recently, though, have they become aware that expectations are also important for analyzing economic stabilization policies.

Like most other economic problems, stabilization policies must be analyzed in a dynamic framework. What government does today—how it raises taxes, spends its revenues, and finances its deficits—affects the economic environment of the future. (And the government presumably cares about the future economy as well as the present.) Once again, where time is a factor, expectations are critical. People's decisions today depend on expectations of the future. Because government policies affect future outcomes, they affect people's expectations and thus affect people's current decisions. If today's policy actions do not take expectations into account, they may not have their intended effects.

A theory of expectations, therefore, is a major ingredient for almost any analysis of economic behavior. In particular, it's a prerequisite for any model that is going to explain how economic decisions are made and how optimal government policies are formulated.

THE ADAPTIVE EXPECTATIONS THEORY

Recognizing the importance of developing a theory of expectations has proved much less controversial than agreeing on the best theory. Many have believed that the *adaptive expectations theory*, which assumes that expectations are simply an extrapolation of past trends, is the best we could do. But recent theoretical challenges, as well as recent experience, have raised serious doubts about the validity of modeling expectations this way.

Model builders' initial attempts at constructing a theory of expectations were based on relatively simplistic assumptions. These attempts assumed either that agents expected no change or that they expected the change tomorrow to be the same as it was today. After some experimenting, econometricians found that they could get better fitting equations if they assumed that expected changes would be equal to a weighted average of past changes. This adaptive expectations model went virtually unchallenged until the 1970s.

The substantive issues economists first discussed about this theory were not those dealing with the validity of adaptive expectations but rather those questioning the size of the weights and the length of the lag distribution. If the weights were small and the lags were long, models that used the adaptive expectations scheme predicted that the trade-off between inflation and unemployment was quite favorable. Stimulative policy only had to increase inflation a little in order to lower real wages and boost employment and production for a relatively long time. If the weights were large and the lags were short, however, the inflation-unemployment trade-off was much less favorable. Then reducing real wages required significantly more inflation, and the employment and production benefits didn't last nearly as long.

The discussion of weights and lags was not trivial as long as the adaptive expectations

Inflation and Unemployment, 1960–79
(Sources: *U.S. Departments of Commerce and Labor.*)

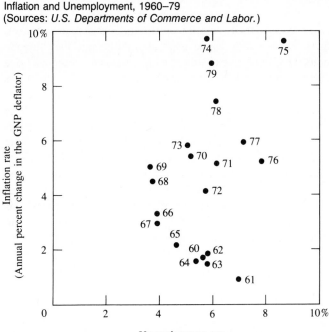

Unemployment rate
(Unemployment as a percent of the labor force)

scheme remained unchallenged. The debate about the characteristics of the large distribution continues even today as we hear both policymakers and economists argue about the costs and benefits of stimulating a recessionary economy that is suffering from double-digit inflation. Such debates, though, ignore more fundamental issues.

While some economists are still trying to estimate the trade-off between inflation and unemployment, others are questioning the validity of the underlying theory. Models based on adaptive expectations, which worked well in the 1960s, failed dramatically in the 1970s. In the early 1970s such models predicted, with a high degree of confidence, that the United States could drive its unemployment rate down to 4 percent if it were only willing to live with a 4 to 5 percent rate of inflation; with a 5 to 6 percent rate of inflation, it could virtually eliminate unemployment. There was some debate about whether this trade-off could be repeatedly exploited, but most economists agreed that at least in the short run such a trade-off existed. The actual 1970s inflation and unemployment statistics were a serious rejection of these models. Whether by design or not, we got much more inflation than most expected, yet unemployment climbed above 9 percent instead of falling to zero as predicted.

To some, this empirical rejection of standard macroeconometric models came as no surprise because the theory of adaptive expectations is inconsistent with the rest of economic theory. The fundamental principle underlying virtually all economic theory has been that agents always do the best they can for themselves, given their income, wealth and technological constraints. With the resources and tools available, firms produce until any extra output brings less revenue than the extra cost of production—that is, until maximum profits are collected. Likewise, individuals consume until any extra current consumption is worth less than than tomorrow's consumption—that is, until consumption is maximized over time. And likewise, workers continue working until any extra income they earn is worth less to them than the leisure they forego. The theory of adaptive expectations is not consistent with this principle of optimization. The adaptive expectations equations used for forecasting generally imply that agents don't optimize. They imply, instead, that agents can be systematically fooled so that obvious profits can go uncollected.

Adaptive Expectations Are Irrational

A few examples will illustrate how agents fail to optimize when they base their expectations just on historical relationships, as the adaptive expectations.

Suppose the government announced a new higher rate of price supports for wheat. And suppose this policy change was advertised well in advance and had complete congressional approval. The wheat farmers who based their production and storage decisions only on past price behavior would make some very big mistakes—just as they would if they ignored the price implications of a new report on the Russian wheat harvest or a recent change in weather. The wheat farmers who based their decisions on such readily available information, as well as on the historical behavior of past prices, would obviously do much better.

In adaptive forecasting schemes, agents also fail to optimize in the wage bargaining process. If workers or their unions use only historical data to forecast future inflation, they can easily be misled into working for wages with lower purchasing power than desired. Suppose the government announced that the accumulated federal deficit in the 1980s was going to grow twice as fast as it did in the 1970s and that the Federal Reserve was going to buy most of this new debt. Those unions that assumed prices were going to behave just as they did in the 1970s would agree to contracts that allowed their members' real wages to decline. Those unions that paid attention to the correlation between government financing and inflation would make much better deals for their members.

Under adaptive expectations, agents also fail to optimize when OPEC announces a change in its pricing policy. Suppose OPEC planned to double its price tomorrow. Firms that used a lot of energy would seriously understate their expenses if they only looked at the historical prices of oil—not at probable future prices. The efficient firm would take this new information into account and make a much better decision.

By not using available information about current and future events, agents who form expectations adaptively can make some very obvious mistakes, leaving very obvious profits uncollected. The criticism of the adaptive expectations theory, though, goes much deeper. It is not only that mistakes are obvious, but also that they persist. Thomas Sargent (1976a, pp. 316–18) has shown that when agents form expectations adaptively, one can easily devise a future path for any policy variable that can systematically and forever fool them. Adaptive expectations, therefore, are generally irrational expectations.

THE RATIONAL EXPECTATIONS THEORY

Recognizing the nonoptimality of the adaptive expectations approach, several researchers began to take a new theory pioneered by John Muth (1961) more seriously. Muth's idea was to model expectations the same way economists model other economic behavior: by assuming agents maximize their objective functions, subject to the constraints they face. With this in mind, Muth assumed that agents' subjective probability distributions are equal to the objective or actual probability distributions plus a random term, the variance of which depends on the information available to agents. He defined such expectations as *rational*. Rationality, therefore, is not perfect foresight; people can make mistakes. In fact, people can make lots of mistakes, but they will not be systematically wrong.

By assuming that agents use information efficiently, Muth was able to construct a theory of expectations that was consistent with the rest of economic theory. Like other economic theories, Muth's implies that obvious uncollected profits do not persist. Constructing such a theory, however, was not the breakthrough that led a significant number of economists to abandon standard models.

The major breakthrough came when Robert Lucas showed that rational expectations models can explain a correlation between inflation and unemployment, a correlation similar to that represented by the Phillips curve. Standard macroeconomics began with the notion that we could not explain unemployment with classical equilibrium models. In a nonstochastic, frictionless classical model, in which agents optimize and markets clear, monetary policy is neutral. There is no correlation between inflation and unemployment, for there is no unemployment; in equilibrium, all who want to work can work. As the money supply increases and prices rise, real wages remain unchanged. Workers concerned about the purchasing power of wages raise their money wage demands, but firms are willing to pay the higher wages because their prices have increased. In the new equilibrium, nominal wages rise by the same amount as prices, leaving employment and production unchanged.

To explain the inflation-unemployment correlation represented by the Phillips curve, macroeconomists have argued that we had to abandon the assumptions of clearing markets and optimizing agents. James Tobin (1947), for example, assumed that agents were *irrational* in the labor markets. He recognized that such agents were incompatible with optimizing agents, but he contended that the only way to construct a model consistent with the correlation between inflation and unemployment was to drop the optimizing assumption. The nonoptimality assumption also implied that the correlation represented a trade-off that could be exploited by expansionary fiscal and monetary policies. We could reduce unemployment if we were willing to pay the price of a higher inflation rate.

Lucas' contribution was to show that the classical model was abandoned prematurely (Lucas 1972, 1975). He proved that an essentially classical model—one based on the classical principle of optimizing agents and clearing markets—could generate a correlation between inflation and unemployment. He did this by extending classical theory to include uncertainty and information costs. In Lucas' *new classical* approach, agents face an information problem. In general, they do not know whether a change in the price of their labor is a real change (due, say, to an increase in demand for their services) or simply a reflection of a general rise in all prices. If an increase in the price of their labor occurred because of a real change in supply or demand, then agents would want to respond somehow. For instance, they might adjust the number of hours they were willing to work. If the increase in the price of their labor was merely the result of inflation, however, then they wouldn't want to respond. The problem they face is that they don't know whether any specific change in their own price is real or not, so they don't know how to respond. When agents face this kind of uncertainty, some of them respond as if the price changes were real and not just the result of a general change in the price level. Under these conditions, *unexpected* movements in prices can generate real effects, such as the correlation between inflation and unemployment.

CHALLENGES TO MACRO MODELS AND POLICIES

The policy implications of this new micro theory are obviously much different from those of standard macroeconomics. The theory suggests that there is no simple way to stimulate demand and move the economy along the Phillips curve toward higher output. In fact, Sargent and Neil Wallace (1975) have shown that even within a standard macro framework, the inflation-unemployment trade-off doesn't exist when rational expectations are imposed. While policies can have real effects, the effects are much more subtle and complex than standard models have led us to believe.

Sargent and Wallace first showed that in ad hoc macroeconomic models, under certain conditions, rational expectations imply that policy is neutral. [They define an *ad hoc model* as one that is not derived from a consistent set of assumptions about individuals' and firms' objective functions and available information (Sargent and Wallace 1975, p. 241).] If the public and monetary authority have access to the same information and if agents have identical preferences, then "the probability distribution of output is independent of the deterministic money supply rule in effect" (p. 242). In an ad hoc model, one nonrandom money supply rule is as good as another.

They went on to show that, when these assumptions are relaxed, monetary policy can affect the distribution of output, but constructing the right policy nevertheless becomes very hard. When the monetary authority has more information than the public, for example, policy can affect the variance of output (though not the mean). To choose the right policy, however, the monetary authority must know precisely how the public's information differs from its own. When the public is slow to learn about a policy change, for another example, the monetary authority can affect real output. But here again, the monetary authority must know precisely what the public knows, plus how it learns, before it can devise the right policy. Policy analysis no longer rests on estimating a simple relationship between inflation and unemployment. It now requires the policymaker to know precisely how information sets differ and how people learn. As Sargent and Wallace point out, this is such a subtle task it is likely to be an intractable econometric problem.

These results of the rational expectations research are often misinterpreted. Many think the theory of rational expectations says that monetary policy does not matter, that whatever the monetary authority tries to do, rational agents will undo. This, however, is the wrong implication. More accurately, the Sargent-Wallace results are a strong indictment of ad hoc macro models because they point out how little these models tell us about the impact of inflation. We know that inflationary policies matter. We know, for example, that inflation makes the real return on money negative; therefore, inflation must generally cause a decline in all other real rates. We also know that inflation affects the value of agents' endowments and that not all agents are identical; therefore, inflation must affect real consumption and saving decisions. Further, we know that agents' information sets differ among themselves and differ from the information sets of the monetary authorities; therefore, inflation must have an effect on the distribution of output. Yet, ad hoc macro models tell us nothing about these effects; they are not explicit enough to capture the impact of monetary policy. Without more explicit theories, we cannot even begin to understand how inflation affects the economy and how to construct appropriate policies.

THE DOMINATING THEORY

Some have alleged that the assumptions behind rational expectations are too unrealistic, that people just are not smart enough to be rational. They argue that people don't have enough information to make rational forecasts or that they don't know how to use the information efficiently. Both allegations are misleading. Most useful theories, after all, make some superficially unrealistic assumptions. Furthermore, rationality does not depend on how they use their information. No matter how little information they have, therefore, agents have enough to satisfy the premises of rational expectations. The substantive issue is thus whether they use their information efficiently. *Using information efficiently* means only that agents cannot be systematically wrong forever. This is a realistic enough assumption. Although absolutely efficient use of information may not be descriptively realistic, would it be more realistic to assume people use information inefficiently? That is, would it be more realistic to assume people are 95 percent, 50 percent, or 25 percent efficient? I doubt it. Any number would be difficult to defend strictly on realistic grounds. Furthermore, anything less than 100 percent efficiency implies obvious uncollected profits, since people can be consistently fooled. Surely this implication cannot be justified on grounds of realism.

Most economists would agree that only empirical results can provide tests for choosing among competing theories. In economics, however, testing alternative theories is usually not very easy. Choosing between rational and adaptive expectations is a classic example. On the one hand, advocates of rationality contend that their theory can explain the shifting Phillips curve observed in the 1970s. The curve shifted, they believe, because inflation did not continue to surprise people. On the other hand, proponents of adaptive expectations claim that the Phillips curve shifted for reasons that had little to do with inflationary expectations. They argue that changes in the composition of the work force and the pricing policies of OPEC were the major causes of the instability in the Phillips curve. Once these extraneous factors are taken into account, their autoregressive equations fit the 1970s very well.

Based on goodness of fit, then, neither theory of expectations is clearly superior. But Sargent (1976b) has shown that in a period when only one policy rule is in effect, this criterion can never be used to determine which theory is better. An adaptive expectations model can be constructed to fit the data just as well as a rational expectations model when there has not been a change in the policy rule.

Sargent's findings, however, do not rule out all tests; they only make the task more difficult. A way to test the validity of these theories is to test their stability under alternative policy rules. The only study I know of that has performed such a test found the rational expectations model superior. Salih Neftci and Sargent (1978) identified a break in monetary policy rule in 1968. After estimating a standard version of a macroeconometric model for the years before 1968, they applied the model to the years after 1968 and found that it failed dramatically. It was not stable. The rational expectations results, while not spectacular, were considerably better. The model marginally passed a test of stability. This is an important test because an economic model must remain invariant when policy changes if it is to be useful for evaluating policies. With the empirical evidence available, then, the rational expectations theory cannot be dismissed, nor should its policy implications be ignored.

CONCLUSION

The rational theory gives us a new perspective on policy analysis. For the first time, it gives us a coherent approach to modeling expectations that may be applied to many aspects of economic analysis. Equally important, the rational expectations theory has some very negative implications. It says that we currently know very little about the appropriate use of economic policies. It says that macroeconomists have to develop more explicit models of economic behavior. It says that the answers we seek are much more subtle and complex than we once believed.

Because we know so little, economists and policymakers should be considerably humbler in their policy prescriptions. Simple correlations between inflation and un-employment, for instance, cannot be reliable guides to policy. At most, we can say that since policy actions can easily add to the economic uncertainty, whatever rules we happen to choose should be well defined and well understood. For policymakers to advocate much more than this will require significant theoretical and empirical breakthroughs in research. In the meantime, it seems to me the best we can do is to follow policy rules which are stable and long-run. Who knows; we might even like the results we get.

REFERENCES

Lucas, Robert E., Jr. 1972. Expectations and the neutrality of money. *Journal of Economic Theory* 4 (April): 103–24.

———.1975. An equilibrium model of the business cycle. *Journal of Political Economy* 83 (December): 1113–44.

Muth, John F. 1961. Rational expectations and the theory of price movements. *Econometrica* 29 (July): 315–35.

Neftci, Salih, and Sargent, Thomas J. 1978. A little bit of evidence on the natural rate hypothesis from the U.S. *Journal of Monetary Economics* 4 (April): 315–19.

Sargent, Thomas J. 1976a. Interest rates and expected inflation: a selective summary of recent research. *Explorations in Economic Research: Occasional Papers of the National Bureau of Economic Research* 3 (Summer): 303–25.

———.1976b. The observational equivalence of natural and unnatural rate theories of mac-roeconomics. *Journal of Political Economy* 84 (June): 631–40.

Sargent, Thomas J., and Wallace, Neil. 1975. "Rational" expectations, the optimal monetary instrument, and the optimal money supply rule. *Journal of Political Economy* 83 (April): 241–54.

Tobin, James. 1947. Money wage rates and employment. In *The new economics: Keynes' influence on theory and public policy,* ed. Seymour Harris, pp. 572–87. New York: Knopf.

QUESTIONS FOR DISCUSSION

1 *Adaptive expectations* is an approach to modeling the public's expectations which assumes that expectations about any variable in the future are a simple extrapolation of the past behavior of that variable. When might this be a reasonable assumption? Would adaptive expectations be useful:

   a If we are trying to predict consumption in a poor country in which major oil reserves have just been discovered?

   b If we are trying to forecast investment demand during a normal recovery from a recession?

   c If we are trying to predict the effects of extensive wage-price controls in an economy which has not previously experienced controls?

2 Give a government policy action (other than in the monetary area) whose impact on the economy depends in an important way on the public's expectations about this policy. Describe how modeling expectations as adaptive or rational might affect predictions about how the policy will work.

3 What conclusion does the author draw from the fact that the stable unemployment-inflation relationship of the 1960s appeared to break down in the 1970s? How would Keynesians explain this apparent breakdown? (Refer to your text.) Do events since 1979 (see Reading 16 on recent monetary policy) support one or the other of these views?

4 According to Lucas's new classical theory, why do increases in the average price level tend to be associated with higher output? Why is Lucas's theory sometimes called the *misperceptions hypothesis?* If Lucas's theory is right, would a fully anticipated, announced-in-advance increase in money and the price level have any effect on output? Why or why not?

5 *The expectations-argumented Phillips curve* states that unemployment differs from its natural level only when expected inflation differs from actual inflation. (Refer to your text.) What then does the rational expectations view imply about the unemployment costs of a sustained anti-inflationary monetary policy, relative to the cost implied by adaptive expectations?

6 "The rational expectations approach implies that monetary policy has no role in stabilizing the economy." Discuss.

7 Wages are often set by labor contracts, which are negotiated once every few years. Assume that firms and workers set contract wages based on rational expectations of what economic conditions will be over the life of the contract. What are the implications of this for the ability of monetary policy to systematically affect output in the short run? In the long run?

NEW VIEWS OF THE BUSINESS CYCLE: HAS THE PAST EMPHASIS ON MONEY BEEN MISPLACED?

Carl E. Walsh*

Economists have long recognized that "real" factors (such as technological or productivity shocks, weather, or wars) are important in the explanation of macroeconomic fluctuations, and have treated these factors as complementary to money in the theory of the business cycle. However, recently some new classical macroeconomists (using models which assume continuous market clearing and rational expectations) have claimed that real factors *alone* are sufficient to explain the historical pattern of cycles; no active role for monetary shocks is necessary. In the following article, Carl Walsh compares and assesses the real and the monetary theories of cycles.

Monetary policy has been a central element in virtually all analyses of business cycles during the past twenty years. Many analysts claim that fluctuations in the growth rates of monetary aggregates are the dominant factor causing cycles in real economic activity and in the rate of inflation. Recently, however, economists have seen a revival of interest in the role played by nonmonetary events in causing business cycles. This revival has led to the development of *real business cycle theories*. Real business cycle theories take the view that historical cycles in the U.S. have been caused largely by "real"—rather than monetary—shocks, such as sharp changes in supplies of raw ma-

Carl E. Walsh, "New Views of the Business Cycle: Has the Past Emphasis on Money Been Misplaced?" *Business Review,* Philadelphia Federal Reserve Bank, January–February 1986, pp. 3–13.

*Carl E. Walsh, Senior Economist at the Federal Reserve Bank of San Francisco, prepared this article while he was a Visiting Scholar at the Federal Reserve Bank of Philadelphia and Assistant Professor of Economics at Princeton University. The author gratefully acknowledges helpful comments from Robert DeFina, Steve Meyer, Aris Protopapadakis, and Jeremy Siegel.

terials, shifts in productivity, or technological changes. These theories show how such "real" shocks, whether striking the economy as a whole or confined initially to one sector, can cause a business cycle.

A major impetus to the development of real business cycle theories was the general agreement that oil and food supply shocks, rather than monetary shocks, were the primary causes of the 1974–75 recession. Another is that monetary theories' predictions about some key economic quantities—like real wages—do not mesh with empirical observations. Real business cycle theories, unlike their monetary counterparts, offer a simple explanation of the observed behavior of real wages over the cycle. At the same time they offer a consistent explanation of the cyclical behavior of monetary aggregates and many other key economic quantities. In their current form, real business cycle theories suggest that most of the cyclical movement of U.S. real output can be explained by nonmonetary factors, and that money has played predominantly a passive role in past business cycles.

The investigation of modern real business cycle theories is in its infancy. At this stage the formal models that are being developed do not allow any role for monetary shocks. There are, however, good reasons to believe that *both* "real" shocks and monetary shocks have a role in business cycles (see appendix). The hope is that the continuing investigation and the development of these theories will sharpen our understanding of U.S. business cycles, and that this understanding will lead to better economic policies.

WHAT IS A BUSINESS CYCLE?

A simple definition of a business cycle is that it consists of parallel and persistent expansions and contractions in output across most sectors of the economy. The National Bureau of Economic Research, for example, identifies a recession in a business cycle as a *widespread* contraction in the output of goods and services (real GNP) that *persists* for two or more consecutive quarters. Fluctuations in the level of output that occur only in a single sector of the economy do not constitute a business cycle. Figure 1 illustrates this feature of business cycles in the U.S.; it shows fluctuations of real output in agriculture, manufacturing, and wholesale and retail trade from 1948 to 1983. While the movements are similar, different sectors do not move in exactly the same way. For example, wholesale and retail trade conforms much more closely to the movement in real GNP than does agricultural output.

In addition to being widespread, the rise and the fall of both aggregate and sectoral output persists over time in a business cycle. During an upturn, real output typically expands for several quarters before reaching a peak and reversing direction. For example, the average expansion (trough to peak) during the period from October 1949 to November 1984 was 15 quarters. Similarly, contractions are characterized by several consecutive quarters of very slow or negative growth. Contractions historically tend to be shorter than expansions; contractions averaged 3.6 quarters over this same period. Of course, these averages can hide much of the variation that distinguishes one cycle from another. For example, the shortest complete cycle during this period lasted only

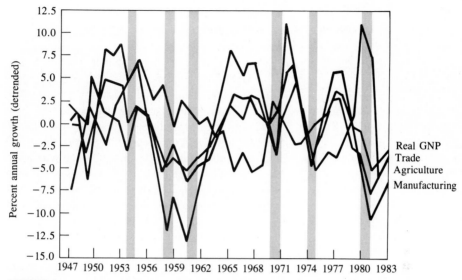

FIGURE 1
Output in Major Sectors Moves with Real GNP. *Note:* Shaded regions denote business cycle
contractions as dated by the National Bureau of Economic Research. In order to bring out
clearly the cyclical behavior of each series, an estimate of trend growth rate has been subtracted
from each series. The trend growth is estimated by regressing the log of real GNP on time and
time squared.

18 months (January 1980–July 1981), while the longest lasted 116 months (April
1960–December 1969).

The behavior of real GNP is the criterion by which business cycles are measured,
but many other important economic quantities move with the business cycle. For
example, the money stock (as measured either by M1 or M2) tends to grow faster
than average during expansions and slower than average during recessions—that is,
it behaves *procyclically*. Also, employment, inflation, investment, and capacity utilization behave procyclically. Real wages (wages expressed in terms of their purchasing
power) and the size of the labor force are generally procyclical, but their relation to
real GNP is not as obvious. Unemployment, on the other hand, rises above its average
value during recessions and falls below it during expansions—it behaves *counter-
cyclically*.

Any theory of business cycles is an attempt to explain the essence of how some
economic events—often referred to as shocks—can initiate cycles, and how such shocks
can lead to the parallel and persistent movements in real GNP that characterize business
cycles. Monetary theories of business cycles, and the more recent real business cycle
theories, describe this cyclical behavior according to two different perspectives on
how the economy works. These perspectives have different implications not only for
the causes of cyclical behavior of real GNP, but also for other important economic
quantities, such as the monetary aggregates, real wages, and the labor force.

A MONETARY PERSPECTIVE ON BUSINESS CYCLES

The standard monetary theories of business cycles argue that changes in the money stock are a major cause of fluctuations in real economic activity. A recession, for example, would be explained by a decline in money growth—a monetary shock. Such a fall in money growth could be policy-induced, or it could result from events affecting the banking industry, such as major regulatory changes. The slowdown in money growth results in a temporary shortage of money and credit, which causes interest rates to rise. The rise in interest rates slows real spending, particularly investment spending and purchases of durable goods. Initially firms respond to the slowdown in spending on their products by cutting back production and laying off some workers. The laid-off workers also reduce their spending, which causes further drops in the demand for goods and services and spreads the decline throughout the economy. As demand drops, firms slow the rise in their prices, and they accept lower profit margins in an attempt to maintain their sales; in some sectors prices may even fall.

According to these monetary theories, wage rates do not decline immediately along with prices, however. Rather, wages adjust slowly because of the existence of multiyear contracts which often have built-in raises, and because of the general practice of adjusting noncontract wages infrequently, usually once a year. Therefore, as inflation slows, real wages rise, and with them the real labor costs to firms. Employment falls further and the recession worsens. Unemployment rises because the laid-off workers cannot find work elsewhere at the going wages, since wages fall only slowly in response to the decline in the demand for labor. This is a key feature of these monetary theories, because it is the sluggish wage adjustment that is responsible for the rise in unemployment. If nominal wages and other prices adjusted readily, then monetary shocks would not cause business cycles in these theories.[1]

If no other shocks occur, the higher unemployment and lower inflation associated with the recession eventually will lead to smaller wage increases, or to wage concessions, as new labor contracts are negotiated and noncontract wages and salaries gradually adjust. Firms start hiring more labor as real wage costs moderate. Output, employment, real wages, and the labor force return gradually to their trend growth rates. These trend growth rates are determined by such fundamental factors as the population growth rate, the rate of technological change, and people's attitudes towards work, leisure, and saving.

Different economists have emphasized different aspects of this general story, and they often differ over how long a monetary expansion or contraction affects real activity. However, most economists share this general view of how monetary fluctuations would

---

[1]The widely accepted version of the "monetary theory" discussed here requires that goods prices and/or wages adjust slowly to economic events. In this sense the monetary theory of business cycles depends on temporary disequilibria in some markets. More recent monetary theories of business cycles do away with the assumption of slow price and wage adjustment, and instead attribute cyclical behavior to incomplete information. In these theories, only unanticipated changes in the money supply matter. The empirical evidence on the success of these new monetary theories is mixed, at best. See R. Barro, "Unanticipated Money, Output and the Price Level in the United States," *Journal of Political Economy*, (August 1978), pp. 549–580; F. Mishkin, *A Rational Expectations Approach to Macroeconomics*, (Chicago: University of Chicago Press, 1983); R. McGee and R. Stasiak, "Does Anticipated Monetary Policy Matter?" *Journal of Money, Credit and Banking*, (February 1985), pp. 16–27.

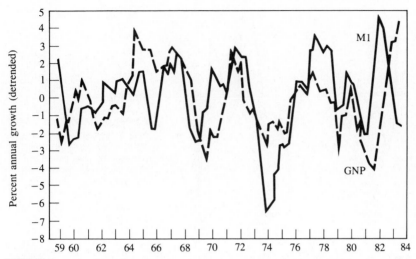

FIGURE 2
The Growth Rates of M1 and of Real GNP Follow Each Other Closely. *Note:* In order
to bring out clearly the cyclical behavior of each series, an estimate of its trend
growth rate has been subtracted from each series. The trend growth is estimated by
regressing the log of each variable on time and time squared.

cause business cycles. Most economists also would agree that such money-induced
business cycles have been common in the U.S. To assess how well monetary theories
account for business cycles it is useful to see how they stand up to the evidence from
U.S. business cycles. If they describe business cycles accurately, then two of the
fundamental features of their mechanism should be apparent in economic data. First,
fluctuations in the rate of growth of the money supply should be related closely to
cyclical fluctuations in real GNP. Second, real wages should tend to be countercyclical,
rising after the onset of the recession—which worsens the recession—and falling during
the early part of expansions—which allows the return to trend growth.[2]

Money and Real GNP Behave As Predicted . . .

Over the period from 1960 to 1984 there is, on the whole, a close relation between
the growth rate in real GNP and the growth rate of M1 (see Figure 2). Thus, M1's
cyclical pattern is roughly consistent with monetary theories of the business cycle.[3]
While the relation between money and real output is prominent, it is not characterized

[2]Naturally, monetary theories predict the behavior of most other important economic variables as well,
such as real interest rates, investment, and so forth. The discussion here focuses on real wages because
real wage behavior is a crucial aspect of the workings of both monetary and real business cycle theories,
and because the two theories differ in their predictions of real wage behavior.
[3]Taking an even longer perspective, Milton Friedman and Anna Schwartz, in *A Monetary History of
the U.S. 1867–1960* (Princeton University Press, 1963), document a similar relation between money growth
and real GNP for over a century.

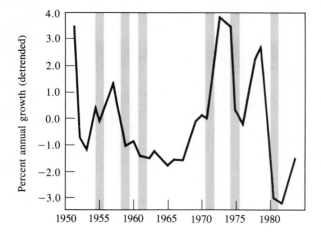

FIGURE 3
The Index of Real Monthly Earnings Is Procyclical. *Note:* In order to bring out clearly its cyclical behavior, this series is adjusted by subtracting the estimated trend growth from the growth rate. The trend growth is estimated by regressing the log of the index on time and time squared.

by any rigid link; rather, as Milton Friedman has claimed frequently, the relation is characterized by "long and variable lags."

... But Real Wages Do Not

Over the period from 1950 to 1982 real wages do not show the countercyclical movement that monetary theories predict. For instance, the real hourly earnings index of the Bureau of Labor Statistics is procyclical (see Figure 3). During each recession since 1950 (except the 1981–82 recession), this index fell relative to its trend. Also, many studies find procyclical behavior in sector-by-sector real wage data.[4] This discrepancy between the monetary theories' predictions and the actual behavior of real wages over cycles represents a serious weak point in monetary models.

Some attempts have been made to modify monetary theories to account for the procyclical behavior of real wages. These attempts show that the cost to employers of laying off and rehiring workers, and the ability of employers to offer overtime, may make measured real wages procyclical, while the underlying straight-time hourly rate may be countercyclical. For instance, if a temporary rise in the real hourly wage reduces the firm's demand for labor, it may respond by cutting back overtime em-

[4]R. Bodkin, "Real Wages and Cyclical Variations in Employment: A Re-examination of the Evidence," *Canadian Journal of Economics,* (August 1964), pp. 353–374, finds real wages to by procyclical. J. Altonji and O. Ashenfelter, "Wage Movements and the Labor Market Equilibrium Hypothesis," *Economica,* (August 1980), pp. 217–245, argue that changes in the average manufacturing real wage are not cyclical in nature at all. However, J. Heckman, in "Comment on Ashenfelter and Kydland," in *Essays on Macroeconomic Implications of Financial and Labor Markets and Political Processes,* (Carnegie-Rochester Conference Series on Public Policy, Volume 21, Autumn 1984) pp. 209–224, points out that industry-by-industry data do reveal procyclical behavior of real wages. Also see M. Mitchell, M. Wallace, and J. Warner, "Real Wages Over the Business Cycle: Some Further Evidence," *Southern Economic Journal* 51,4 (April 1985), pp. 1162–1173. S. Neftci, in "A Time-Series Analysis of the Real Wages-Employment Relationship," *Journal of Political Economy* (April 1978), pp. 281–291, suggests that real wages and employment are negatively related if account is taken of the dynamic aspects of their relationship.

ployment first. Since firms have to pay a premium for overtime, this reduction in overtime may cause the *average* wage paid by the firm to fall, while the underlying straight-time hourly rate is rising.[5] However, real wage measures—such as the earnings index in Figure 3—which correct for this shift between overtime and straight-time pay, still reveal a procyclical pattern.

A more conspicuous weakness of monetary theories has been their inability to account for the 1974–1975 recession, the most severe since World War II. This shortcoming helped encourage the formulation of real business cycle theories which look for "real" shocks as the source of protracted upturns or downturns in real GNP from trend. Real business cycle theories suggest that business cycles are caused primarily by the ripple effect of "real" shocks as they work their way through the economy. Indeed, the procyclical behavior of real wages is an integral part of real business cycle theories; and, at the same time, these theories offer a possible explanation for the close relation between money growth and real GNP.

THE REAL BUSINESS CYCLE PERSPECTIVE

Real business cycle theories, like monetary theories, emphasize that the economy's trend real growth rate is determined by nonmonetary factors (population growth, technological innovation, consumer preferences, and so forth). Prices and wages constantly adjust if shortages or surpluses occur in any of the markets. These adjustments serve to keep the economy close to its trend growth. In the view of real business cycle theorists, any apparent sluggishness of some prices and wages is not of sufficient importance to prevent the economy from remaining close to its trend growth. From this perspective, then, fluctuations in real economic activity are attributed to changes in the real, nonmonetary factors, which determine this trend growth.[6]

Business cycles arise in these theories when "real" shocks change the economy's real productivity or wealth, and upset the economy's equilibrium. "Real" shocks can take a variety of forms, such as the disruption in oil supplies in the 1970s, shifts in demand from one sector of the economy to another, or a technological change like the development of computer microchips. Strikes and productivity shifts in specific industries are further examples, as are shifts in household attitudes towards saving or working.[7] These changes then set in motion economy-wide adjustments in consumption, production, labor supply, and saving that ultimately re-establish a new equilib-

---

[5]See R. E. Lucas, Jr. "Capacity, Overtime, and Empirical Production Functions," *American Economic Review* (May 1970), pp. 23–27, T. J. Sargent and N. Wallace, "The Elasticity of Substitution and Cyclical Behavior of Productivity, Wages and Labor's Share," *American Economic Review,* (May 1974), pp. 257–263, and T. J. Sargent, "Estimation of Dynamic Labor Demand Schedules under Rational Expectations," *Journal of Political Economy,* (December 1978), pp. 1009–1055.

[6]The recent work on real business cycles has its roots in earlier nonmonetary theories of the cycle. For a survey of the older theories, see Gottfried Haberler, *Prosperity and Depression* (Harvard University Press, 1960). Recent contributions include J. Long and C. Plosser, "Real Business Cycles," *Journal of Political Economy* (February 1983), pp. 39–69, and R. King and C. Plosser, "Money, Credit, and Prices in a Real Business Cycle," *American Economic Review,* (June 1984), pp. 363–380.

[7]Recent empirical studies of the role of real shocks include D. Lilien, "Sectoral Shifts and Cyclical Unemployment," *Journal of Political Economy* (August 1982), pp. 777–793, and J. Hamilton, "Oil and the Macroeconomy since World War II," *Journal of Political Economy* (April 1983), pp. 228–248.

rium. The important contribution of real business cycle theories has been to explain how these adjustments to "real" shocks can generate business cycles.

To understand better how "real" shocks can cause business cycles, suppose there is a temporary decline in one sector's productivity that reduces real income in that sector. Initially, this reduction in real income leads individuals who earn their living in that sector to decrease their consumption of goods and services from their own and all the other sectors. However, people generally do not reduce immediately their current consumption by the full amount of the temporary decline in their real income. Instead, they want to spread over time the effect of the real income reduction by decreasing both their planned consumption and their planned saving. This response of consumer demand not only causes the initial real income shock to spread to other sectors of the economy, but it also means that it takes time before the economy can work its way out of the repercussions of the initial shock. Thus, real business cycle theories can explain both the parallel and the persistent movement in economic activity that marks a business cycle.

The decline in output induced by the initial "real" productivity shock leads firms to want fewer workers at the going wage. The developing slackness in the labor market causes workers to lower their wage demands promptly in an effort to get the relatively scarce jobs. Since, according to real business cycle models, wages adjust readily in response to market pressures, real wages fall temporarily. Thus real business cycle theories predict that real wages move in the same direction as real GNP—that is, procyclically—which accords well with observed behavior.[8]

A key mechanism that causes cyclical variations in employment in these models is the response of individuals to temporary fluctuations in real wages. The real wage earned by an individual represents the return to working. So, if the real wage is perceived to be low relative to its average level, the return to working is low temporarily, and workers will work fewer hours and have more leisure and lower incomes. This type of substitution between work and leisure can take a variety of forms. Employed workers might reduce their hours of work by limiting overtime hours or quitting second jobs. Individuals who had been unemployed and are looking for work may, in response to lower real wages, spend more time searching before taking a job, or they may stop searching altogether and drop out of the labor force. Such individuals perceive the benefits from more extensive job search, or from leisure, to outweigh the net gain from working at the temporarily lower real wage.[9] Thus, according to these real business cycle models, the supply of labor falls in response to temporary real wage declines. One interesting aspect of the existing real business cycle models is that

---

[8]Strictly speaking, this prediction is true because real business cycle models emphasize supply shocks. However, certain "real" disturbances could lead to countercyclical real wage movements. Shifts in workers' tastes for leisure would cause real wages to fall (rise) as output rose (fell). Such disturbances, however, have not been emphasized in the literature on real business cycles.

[9]Households may also respond to *permanent* changes in real wages. However, since business cycle theories attempt to explain the factors leading to *temporary* deviations of output from its trend growth path, the focus has been on the role of temporary movements in real wages. Factors that might produce a permanent change in real wages would influence the economy's trend growth path. For a discussion of the responses of primary and secondary workers to real wage changes, see B. Horrigan, "The Flat-Tax Rate Controversy: A Guide for the Perplexed," this *Business Review*, (May/June 1985), pp. 3–15.

they do not allow for *involuntary* unemployment, because wages are assumed to respond readily to changes in labor supply and demand. Each individual is either working, does not wish to work, or else is in the process of searching for the best possible job, that is, voluntarily unemployed.[10] Real business cycle theories then predict that, just like real GNP and real wages, labor supply will fall (or rise) in response to an adverse (or favorable) "real" shock.

Labor Supply is Procyclical . . .

Current empirical research finds that generally labor supply varies procyclically, in accordance with real business cycle theories.[11] However, the response of labor supply to real wages varies greatly across different demographic groups in the population. For example, working, married males respond only slightly to real wage changes. In contrast, the supply of labor by married females varies a great deal more with real wages. Much of this greater responsiveness is due to the effect real wages have on the decisions to enter or leave the labor force.[12]

. . . But It Is Not the Whole Story

Real business cycle theories hold that the cyclical variation in employment comes from cyclical variation in labor supply. Unfortunately, it is not clear whether this last prediction is consistent with observation. U.S. experience shows that most of the cyclical variation in employment is accounted for by changes in the employment rate, rather than by changes in the supply of labor—the number of individuals seeking work or the number of hours each of these individuals wants to work. For example, only a relatively small fraction of the variation in total hours of employment in the U.S. private business sector is due to changes in hours per worker. Most is due to variation in the number of employed workers.[13] Also, most of the variation in the number of

---

[10]See R. E. Lucas and L. E. Rapping, "Real Wages, Employment, and Inflation," in E. Phelps, et al., *Microeconomic Foundations of Employment and Inflation Theory,* (NY: W. W. Norton 1970), pp. 257–305. However, economists have developed models of labor markets that generate *involuntary* unemployment in equilibrium, even though prices and wages are fully flexible. Involuntary unemployment in these models is generated because firms use high wages to induce workers to perform well on the job. This type of behavior has not been incorporated into real business cycle models as yet. For a survey of this literature, see Janet Yellen, "Efficiency Wage Models of Unemployment," *American Economic Review* (May 1984), pp. 200–205.

[11]The supply of labor, or the labor force, conventionally is defined as those individuals currently employed plus those who have actively sought work during the previous four weeks. That is, labor supply, or the labor force, consists of those employed plus those who declare themselves unemployed regardless of the reason.

[12]Orley Ashenfelter summarizes recent evidence in "Macroeconomic Analysis and Microeconomic Analysis of Labor Supply," in *Essays on Macroeconomic Implications of Financial and Labor Markets and Political Processes* (Carnegie-Rochester Conference Series on Public Policy, Volume 21, Autumn 1984) pp. 117–156. See also Joseph Altonji, "The Intertemporal Substitution Model of Labour Market Fluctuations: An Empirical Analysis," *The Review of Economic Studies,* Special Issue, (1982), pp. 783–824, and J. Heckman and T. McCurdy, "A Life-Cycle Model of Female Labor Supply," *Review of Economic Studies,* (January 1980), pp. 47–74.

[13]BLS *Handbook of Labor Statistics,* Table 96. See also Heckman's comment on Ashenfelter and Kydland, footnote 4, above.

employed workers is due not to variations in the number of individuals in the labor force, but to variations in the fraction of the labor force which is employed. Particularly during recession years, very little of the decline in total employment is explained by declines in the measured labor force. For example, in the recent recession year of 1982, only about 3 percent of the decline in employment was attributable to reductions in the labor force.[14] While real wage movements may affect some individuals' decisions about whether to work at all and, if so, how many hours, variation from this source seems to account for little of the fluctuation in total employment that characterizes a business cycle.

Real business cycle theorists do have an explanation for this observation that changes in unemployment (rather than changes in the labor force) account for changes in employment. They claim that the collected unemployment statistics do not correspond correctly to the economic concept of unemployment—involuntary unemployment. They claim that many workers now counted as unemployed should not be counted in the labor force at all. These are workers who are not willing to work at the *going* wages and in *available* jobs, though they may want to work at their previous (higher) wages in their former jobs. Also, there are some workers counted as unemployed who are spending their time searching the job market. These workers are employed in job search, which is a useful activity, and they are not unemployed in an economic sense. According to real business cycle theorists, if the unemployment and labor force statistics are adjusted to measure only involuntary unemployment, it would become clear that the bulk of changes in employment come from changes in the labor force, in accordance with the predictions of real business cycle models. Unfortunately, sufficient data are not available to make such adjustments to the statistics on unemployment and the labor force. Thus, the extent to which real business cycle theories fully account for movements in employment remains an open issue.[15]

An important challenge for real business cycle theorists is to give a consistent explanation of the cyclical behavior of money. Money's close relation to GNP during a cycle is the cornerstone of monetary theories, which view changes in the stock of money as the *cause* of cycles. Real business cycle theories, which posit nonmonetary shocks as the causes of cycles, have to show that the close relation between money and GNP is, instead, an *effect*.

REAL BUSINESS CYCLES: WHY IS MONEY PROCYCLICAL?

Real business cycle models explain the close relation between monetary aggregates and real output by focusing on the connection between the level of output and the demand for the transaction services money provides. Money is demanded because of its usefulness in lowering the transaction costs involved in transferring goods from their producers to their consumers. As output expands or contracts during a business

---

[14]BLS *Handbook,* Table 1.

[15]Most economists, however, would attribute this apparent inability to explain the magnitude of observed employment fluctuations to the real business cycle models' assumption that wages are flexible and can adjust quickly to equilibrate labor supply and demand.

cycle, so does the volume of transactions. Thus, the demand for money will tend to expand and contract along with real output.

Furthermore, according to real business cycle theories, an increase (or decrease) in the *demand* for money elicits an increase (or decrease) in the *supply* of money. A rise in output causes both the demand for money and interest rates to rise. As rates rise, banks attempt to reduce their holdings of excess reserves, which earn no interest, by purchasing interest-earning assets, such as government securities, or by making new private loans. Since all such new loans end up as demand deposits (or their close substitutes) at some bank, the money supply expands in response to a rise in market interest rates. This expansion occurs even if monetary authorities keep the total reserves supplied to the banking system unchanged.[16] Consequently, broadly similar movements in the monetary aggregates and real GNP can result even if reserves supplied by the monetary authority to the banking system do not vary over the business cycle.

Real business cycle theorists also cite the Federal Reserve's operating procedures to help explain the close relation between money growth and real GNP after World War II. In most of this period, the Federal Reserve set short-term interest rate targets as a means of managing money growth. Under such a policy, if the demand for money increases, then the monetary authority attempts to counter the resulting higher interest rates by increasing reserves to the banking system, thus increasing the money supply. Given such an operating procedure, any disturbance that causes real output to vary would also cause the money stock to change in the same direction.

The parallel movement of money and output, then, is consistent with both monetary theories and real business cycle theories, even though in real business cycle theories, fluctuations in money growth do not cause business cycles.

CONCLUSION

Real business cycle theories explain how "real" shocks in one or more sectors of the economy can generate output and employment movements across all sectors and through time—the hallmarks of business cycles. Thus real business cycle theories can account for recessions not obviously generated by monetary shocks. Real business cycle theorists, however, go further and argue that most observed business cycles in the U.S. have been caused by nonmonetary factors. Real business cycle theories also can account for the observed close correlation between monetary aggregates and real GNP—the observation that traditionally has provided the key support for monetary business cycle theories. In contrast to monetary theories, real business cycle theories also imply that real wages are procyclial, which seems consistent with the U.S. experience.

An apparent weakness of real business cycle theories, however, is that they rely on labor supply movements to explain the fluctuations in employment over a business cycle. It is not clear whether movements in the labor force can explain the actual fluctuations in employment that occur during a business cycle.

---

[16]For extensive discussions of the money supply process, see S. Goldfeld and L. Chandler, *The Economics of Money and Banking,* 8th ed. (New York: Harper & Row, 1981) Chapter 6, or C. Henning, W. Pigott, and R. Scott, *Financial Markets and the Economy,* 3rd ed. (NY: Prentice-Hall, 1981), Chapter 4.

Perhaps the most important contribution of real business cycle models at this stage of their development lies in the reminder they provide that monetary shocks are not the only cause of business cycles. A more complete understanding of business cycles almost surely will require a broader theory that incorporates the key elements of both monetary and real business cycle theories.

APPENDIX: The Case History of a Real Business Cycle? November 1973–March 1975

The recession that began in November 1973 and ended in March 1975 was the most severe since the end of World War II. From the fourth quarter of 1973 to the first quarter of 1975, real GNP fell by 4.8 percent, and the unemployment rate averaged 8.5 percent in 1975—up from 4.9 percent in 1973. Is it possible to identify "real" shocks to the economy that might account for this recession?

Two such shocks were much in the news at the time. First, 1972 marked the beginning of a series of bad harvests worldwide which continued into 1973. As a result, food prices rose dramatically. From December 1972 to December 1973, the food component of the Consumer Price Index (CPI) rose 20.1 percent. The second real shock was associated with the OPEC oil embargo and the energy price increases resulting from the Arab-Israeli War that started in October 1973. The energy component of the CPI rose 16.8 percent from December 1972 to December 1973, and another 21.6 percent from December 1973 to December 1974. In contrast, the CPI for all items other than food and energy rose only 4.7 percent from December 1972 to December 1973, and 11.3 percent from December 1973 to December 1974.[1] The energy price increases and the resulting supply distribution difficulties reduced consumer real income and, since energy is a factor of production, reduced aggregate supply.

Real business cycle models predict that both current consumption and saving would fall as consumers attempted to spread the impact of such an income reduction over time. Consumption of food and autos did fall in the fourth quarter of 1973. Total consumption then rose slightly over the first three quarters of 1974 before collapsing in the last quarter. This large decline in the last quarter of 1974 is what made the recession so severe. But it is difficult to explain the timing of this decline as a response to any perceived new "real" shock to the economy.

As real business cycle models would predict, average real wages and the labor force both fell relative to trend during the recession. The average real wage in the private nonagricultural sector declined by 0.1 percent in 1973, by 2.8 percent in 1974, and by 0.7 percent in 1975. The labor force, as a fraction of the civilian population, fell by 0.2 percent in 1975. However, employment relative to the population fell by 3.1 percent.[2] Hence, almost all of the fall in employment was due to a rise in the fraction of the labor force that was unemployed, and not to worker withdrawal from the labor force in response to the decline in real wages. Total labor hours in the private business sector did fall about 4 percent in 1975. However, only about one-eighth of this decline can be attributed to a fall in hours per worker. Almost all the reduction took the form of a decline in the number of employed workers.

---

[1]Data on the CPI are from the *Economic Report of the President,* (February 1985), Tables B55 and B56.

[2]The average growth rates for these series for 1962–1982 are .5 percent for real wages, .4 percent for the ratio of the labor force to civilian population, and .2 percent for the ratio of employment to civilian population.

While bad harvests and oil supply disruptions were shocks of the type emphasized in real business cycle models, there is evidence to suggest that monetary factors contributed to the onset of the recession in late 1973. M1 grew at an average rate of 8.3 percent during 1972, and it declined slightly in the first quarter of 1973 to 8.2 percent. It then decelerated, and averaged only a 4.7 percent annual growth rate during the last three quarters of 1973. Given the pattern of real GNP, the mechanism postulated by real business cycle models cannot explain fully these large changes in the growth rate of M1. Coinciding with this monetary deceleration was the removal of the remaining price controls during late 1973 and early 1974. The removal of price controls produced a rapid rise in all prices, and the real quantity of money fell 8 percent from the first quarter of 1973 to the first quarter of 1975. This analysis suggests that, while real disturbances played an important role in the recession, so did monetary factors.[3]

QUESTIONS FOR DISCUSSION

1 Define *business cycle*. What distinguishes a "real" from a "monetary" business cycle?
2 Show how the author's description of a money-induced business cycle (both the decline and the recovery) can be represented in the *IS-LM* and aggregate demand–aggregate supply diagrams. What implication of this story does the author pick out as not being consistent with the data?
3 According to the real business cycle approach, what effects should an adverse oil supply shock have on output, employment, real wages, and the labor force? How do these predictions differ from those of the traditional analysis of an oil supply shock (as represented by the *IS-LM* and aggregate demand–aggregate supply diagrams)? What actually happened during the 1973–1975 oil shock recession?
4 Empirical studies have tended to find that (*a*) the real wage, although slightly procyclical, does not vary much over the business cycle; (*b*) employment varies quite a bit over the business cycle; and (*c*) the elasticity of labor supply with respect to the real wage appears to be fairly small, at least for most workers. If these three findings are all true, are they good news or bad news for the real business cycle approach?
5 Suppose that the demand for money depends positively on expected future output as well as positively on current output. Show in an *IS-LM* graph that, if the Fed is targeting interest rates, an increase in expected future output will raise today's money supply. Why is the existence of such an "anticipations effect" on money important for the real business cycle story?
6 What is the real business cycle explanation of the existence of unemployment? How do real business cycle theorists respond to critics who argue that the relatively small variation of labor supply over the cycle (as compared to the variation in employment) is evidence against their approach?

---

[3]A detailed discussion of this recession can be found in Alan S. Blinder, *Economic Policy and the Great Stagflation*, (NY: Academic Press, 1981).

PART FOUR

FOUR

INFLATION, UNEMPLOYMENT, AND GROWTH

WHAT CAUSED INFLATION TO DECLINE SO SHARPLY IN THE EARLY EIGHTIES?

Between 1980 and 1985, inflation in the United States fell from double-digit levels down to the 3 to 4 percent range, a rather remarkable decline. We reprint below three articles from *Challenge*'s September-October 1985 symposium, "What Caused Inflation to Collapse?" Each article focuses on a different set of factors that contributed to the subsidence of inflation.

Reading 22   Allen Sinai, "The Soaring Dollar Did It," *Challenge,* September-October 1985, pp. 18–22.

Reading 23   David McClain, "Stabilizing Oil and Farm Prices Holds the Key," *Challenge,* September-October 1985, pp. 23–26.

Reading 24   Roger E. Brinner and Kenneth S. Kline, "A New Market Realism: Wage Moderation," *Challenge,* September-October 1986, pp. 27–29.

THE SOARING DOLLAR DID IT

Allen Sinai*

Since 1980, inflation rates have dropped no less than 11 to 13 percentage points. In March 1980 inflation, measured on a year-over-year basis, was ranging from 13.9 percent to 14.7 percent, depending on the index used. By mid-1985, the Producers' Price Index (PPI) was rising at only a 1 percent rate and the Consumer Price Index (CPI-U) was at 3.7 percent, year over year. This decline of inflation has been greater than for any other five-year period since the early 1950s. Indeed, the unexpected shift from a highly inflationary environment to one of disinflation challenges explanation.

Whatever happened to inflation? How did so pronounced a disinflation occur? Were the recessions of 1980 and 1981–1982 the major cause? Or was it disinflationary oil- and food-price shocks? Were there new special factors that came into play, such as shifting patterns of wage-setting, deregulation, or productivity growth? Did the exceptional rises in the value of the dollar have a substantial effect on U.S. inflation?

Five extraordinary developments mark the recent disinflation experience. First, the downturns of 1980 and 1981–1982—the only time in the past forty years when recessions occurred in three consecutive years—created record slack in product and labor markets and pushed price and wage inflation downward: manufacturing-capacity utilization fell to 68.2 percent in November 1982, a postwar low. And the unemployment rate reached 10.7 percent, a postwar high.

Second, disinflationary oil price shocks in March 1983 and February 1985 helped

Allen Sinai, "The Soaring Dollar Did It," *Challenge,* September–October 1985, pp. 18–22. Reprinted with the permission of the publisher, M. E. Sharpe, Inc., 80 Business Park Drive, Armonk, NY 10504, USA.

*Allen Sinai is Chief Economist at Shearson Lehman Brothers, Inc., and Adjunct Professor of Economics at New York University. This article is based on a paper presented by the author and Russell Robins, formerly an economist at Shearson Lehman Brothers, at the Eastern Economic Association Annual Meeting, in March 1985.

lower inflation. Declines in OPEC oil prices from $34 to $29 a barrel in 1983—$28 more recently, and still lower since early 1985—reversed the upward spiral in oil and energy prices of the 1970s.

Third, the pattern of wage-setting changed, with employers tending to pass downward pressure on prices into wages as a means of preserving growth in profits. In more and more wage agreements, lower inflation is now accepted as an assumption.

Fourth, deregulation of the transportation, banking, and financial industries increased competition and helped lower inflation, particularly through diminished monopsony power of unions.

Finally, the dollar, as measured against the Morgan Guaranty trade-weighted average of fifteen OECD currencies, appreciated by 47.6 percent in nominal terms from July 1980 to the end of February 1985, both directly and indirectly lowering inflation. Over the previous five years the dollar had depreciated by 12.1 percent, adding to inflationary pressures.

While all of these considerations have been key to the disinflation of the 1980s, the role of the dollar is probably the most significant. Many of the factors in the 1980s disinflation process stem, at least in part, from dollar appreciation.

The effects of dollar appreciation on inflation were both direct and indirect. The prices of goods and services purchased abroad declined, directly reducing the inflation rates of prices in various stages of processing. The indirect effects operated mainly through a new dimension of competition for U.S. producers—imports that are both low in cost and high in quality. The soaring dollar increased, albeit with lags, the relative prices of U.S. exports and lowered the purchasing power of foreigners for U.S. goods and services. Import prices, on the other hand, dropped sharply on an absolute and relative basis, making foreign goods irresistible to American consumers and businesses.

The weakening of exports and surge of imported goods imposed a pricing discipline on U.S. business never experienced in the postwar era. Competitive pressures on prices have been felt keenly in product markets ranging from autos to semiconductors, and they have been transmitted to wages and costs. The deep slack in the domestic economy from the early 1980s recessions has helped make the competitive pressures stick. Another effect has been on oil prices, with the strengthening dollar raising the oil bills of most nations and thereby dampening their demands for oil and energy. This has produced extra pressure on OPEC to hold oil prices down.

Why did the dollar rise so much and how did that lower inflation? Just how much disinflation has arisen from the dollar? And can the disinflationary effects of the strong dollar linger?

WHY THE DOLLAR SOARED

A key factor was the loose-fiscal, tight-money policy mix in the U.S. economy since 1980. Large federal budget deficits (Table 1) contributed to strong growth and made substantially higher nominal and real interest rates inevitable, given the Federal Reserve's strategy of targeting monetary growth. The dollar's rising value reflected promising growth prospects and high real returns on U.S. investments; its extraordinary

TABLE 1
FEDERAL BUDGET DEFICITS, THE DOLLAR, AND TRADE DEFICITS*

Year	Unified budget deficit (billion dollars, fiscal years)	Dollar (percent change, calendar years)	Merchandise trade deficit (billion dollars, NIA calendar years)
1975	−43.6	0.1	8.7
1976	−60.6	3.6	−9.0
1977	−45.0	−0.4	−30.5
1978	−40.9	−8.2	−33.6
1979	−27.7	−1.5	−30.6
1980	−59.6	−0.1	−24.2
1981	−57.4	9.9	−28.4
1982	−110.7	10.3	−35.4
1983	−195.4	4.0	−60.4
1984	−175.4	7.2	−104.2
1985-to-date	−156.2	8.8	−111.0

*Percent appreciation or depreciation vs. the Morgan Guaranty trade-weighted average exchange rate of 15 foreign currencies from OECD countries.

appreciation was more the result of international capital than tradeable goods flows. A stronger dollar, in turn, contributed to a lower inflation rate. The lower inflation rate—given the policy mix—raised real interest rates, coming round full circle to strengthen the dollar. This "virtuous" cycle, a kind of positive feedback loop, then worked to raise the U.S. trade deficit and foreign debt. U.S. interest rates and the dollar had to stay high enough to attract foreign capital and to curb domestic capital outflows so that the budget and trade deficits could be financed. Competitive pressures in the form of falling market shares for the goods side of the economy, both from rising imports and declining growth in exports, intensified the disinflation in the manufacturing sector. Weakness in the tradeable goods and manufacturing sectors maintained the slack in product and labor markets, increased price competition, and helped establish new patterns in wage settlements. Downward pressure on oil prices, wages, and speculative elements of inflation can all be related to the strength of the dollar. As a result, we have experienced the biggest disinflation in thirty years.

As the dollar soared, the impact of foreign competition grew. Not only have U.S. consumers and businesses expanded travel and purchases abroad, but more and more U.S. manufacturers are using foreign components and materials as inputs into production. American companies are increasingly locating factories and establishments abroad. And exports of what were once highly exportable goods, such as agricultural products, are growing only slowly, if at all. Thus, by the end of this year, the merchandise trade deficit will have more than doubled since 1983. With intense foreign competition across a wide range of goods and the diversion of so many purchases overseas, U.S. prices have remained under intense downward pressure.

THE DOLLAR AND DISINFLATION—THE PROCESS

In the contemporary U.S. economy, now more open to trade and capital flows than ever before, the dollar affects inflation in numerous ways. Most obvious are the effects on the prices of goods and services bought directly from abroad. Basic commodities such as food, metals, raw materials, and oil become cheaper to U.S. consumers and producers. At the same time, however, since foreigners have to make payments for oil and other commodities in more expensive dollars, the costs to foreigners rise and the quantities demanded fall. Lower costs of materials to U.S. producers work through various stages of processing to reduce intermediate- and finished-goods prices and thereby help lower retail prices to consumers. The impact has been especially great on oil prices, since payments are settled in dollars.

A second effect of the dollar's appreciation on inflation is through real costs of financing. A stronger dollar lowers inflation and raises the real cost of financing purchases of goods for sale or for inventories. Speculative purchases and the hoarding of inventories can be a major source of inflationary pressure and has been absent in recent years.

A third effect is the slack in the economy that is created by declining net exports. Since the fourth quarter of 1982, real net exports in the United States have dropped $57.5 billion. In five other postwar expansions that have lasted this long, the average change in real net exports was a plus $1.5 billion. Recent declines in trade have cost the United States two to three percentage points of real economic growth each quarter. The gap between actual demand and potential output has remained wider as a consequence, considerable losses of jobs have occurred, and there has been a related rise in the failure rate of business and financial institutions.

A fourth effect is indirect: the combination of increased foreign competition, the loss of market shares in the tradeable goods industries, outsourcing, and the erosion of goods-producing activities, makes price and cost reductions necessary as a response.

Fifth, there are direct and indirect effects on wages. Labor costs abroad become cheaper, encouraging the construction of capacity overseas. Unit labor costs are held down as U.S. workers lose jobs to employees of foreign goods producers.

Because of interactions among materials costs, labor costs, and other prices in the stages-of-processing pricing mechanism, the net result is a much larger effect on inflation from shifts in the dollar than might be expected. This is especially so now, as compared with periods when the U.S. economy was less open and exchange rates were not fully flexible.

THE DOLLAR AND DISINFLATION—ESTIMATES

Using a newly developed 25-equation model of the inflation process, we attempted to assess quantitatively the role of the dollar in the recent U.S. disinflation experience. In this model, inflation rates reflect the behavior of 1) the exchange rate; 2) oil and energy price shocks; 3) agricultural prices; 4) wage costs; 5) productivity growth; and 6) aggregate demand in relation to potential output. This model allows for interactions

TABLE 2
INFLATION WITH NO APPRECIATION OF THE DOLLAR: 1980:3 TO 1984:4*
(Cumulative Changes, Percentage Points)

Year	PPI-finished goods	CPI-U	Implicit GNP deflator
1980	0.2	0.1	0.1
1981	2.1	1.3	1.0
1982	4.0	3.1	2.3
1983	5.0	4.2	3.5
1984	6.8	5.0	4.4

*This computer simulation of the 25-equation inflation model used the dollar exchange rate set at its value of 1980:3. Interactions between the various price and wage equations were permitted, but no other feedback was allowed. The "gap," unit-labor costs, crude oil prices, the exchange rate itself, interest rates, and other variables were not permitted to vary in response to the changes in inflation.

among prices in a stages-of-processing chain of costs and prices. In this framework based on stages of processing, the commodity-based PPI quickly reflects fluctuations in the dollar. Changes in the value of the dollar affect prices of crude materials, intermediate goods and supplies, and finished goods. These goods comprise the PPI, which therefore responds more sensitively to the dollar fluctuation than the CPI-U, since the latter includes a mixture of goods and services prices. More general measures of inflation in the U.S. economy, such as the implicit GNP deflator, are more likely to be affected slowly and by smaller amounts.

To assess how much the dollar's appreciation affected the disinflation of the early 1980s, we used the model to remove the 45.3 percent appreciation of the dollar, as measured against the Morgan Guaranty trade-weighted average exchange rate, between the third quarter of 1980 and the fourth quarter of 1984 (see Table 2).

According to the results of these computer simulations, inflation rates would have been $4^1/_2$ to about 7 percentage points higher by 1984 than if the dollar had remained unchanged, taking into account both the direct and indirect effects of the dollar's appreciation. The effect of the dollar's appreciation on inflation was greatest for the PPI with different responses for Crude Materials (7 percentage points); Intermediate Goods and Supplies ($4^1/_2$ percentage points); and Finished Goods (6.8 percentage points). Without the dollar appreciation, the rate of inflation for the CPI-U would have been 5 percentage points higher by 1984. For the implicit GNP deflator, the estimate is 4.4 percentage points.

The effects cumulate over time, with the greatest impacts in 1983 and 1984, when the dollar surged the most. Wage costs were estimated to be one percentage point higher in the first year without any dollar rise. The effect was 3.9 percentage points by 1984.

It should be noted that if the simulations had been performed with a large-scale model of the U.S. economy, the feedback effects from higher interest rates and lower economic growth would have reduced the indicated disinflation. Therefore, the reported estimates must be regarded as upper bounds of the possible disinflationary effects stemming from the dollar's appreciation. Nevertheless, these impacts are considerably higher than those which other economists typically have estimated. This is perhaps not too surprising given the unusual configuration of factors affecting trade, growth, and inflation since 1980.

WHAT NEXT?

After nearly five years of appreciation, the dollar finally began to decline in March 1985. Between late February and midyear, the dollar had dropped 11 percent against the Morgan Guaranty trade-weighted average of fifteen OECD currencies; 25.1 percent against the British pound; 16.6 percent against the German deutschemark; 15.7 percent against the French franc; 15.2 percent against the Italian lira; and 8.5 percent against the Japanese yen. Has the string run out on the disinflationary effects of a rising dollar?

We used another computer simulation to demonstrate how much a hypothetical, sustained 10 percent depreciation of the dollar would worsen inflation between the fourth quarter of 1979 and the fourth quarter of 1984 (see Table 3). The sensitivity test shows sizeable rises in all price indices, although there are differences in magnitude and timing, depending on the specific index used to measure inflation.

A falling dollar has the quickest impact on the PPI-Finished Goods; inflation accelerated by 2.0 percentage points in the initial six months following the dollar's decline, by 2.2 percentage points after one year, and by 2.4 points after two years. The prices of Intermediate Goods and Supplies respond less sensitively, as the more sensitive basic commodities prices appear mostly in the Crude Materials stages-of-processing price index. The CPI-U is 1.4 percentage points higher in the first year and 2.1 percentage points greater after three years. Some 53 percent of the CPI-U measures goods prices and 47 percent is for services. Finally, the implicit GNP deflator is only 1.1 percentage points higher in the first year of impact, 1.9 percentage points greater after three years, and two percentage points higher five years later.

The sensitivity of inflation to changes in the value of the dollar is sizeable, therefore, and relatively immediate, assuming a fixed path for other determinants of prices. This implies that a sustained, permanent reduction in the value of the dollar could be a

TABLE 3
SENSITIVITY OF INFLATION TO DOLLAR WEAKNESS*
(Changes from History, in Percentage Points)

Year	PPI-finished goods	CPI-U	Implicit GNP deflator
1980	1.9	1.0	0.8
1981	2.2	1.9	1.4
1982	2.3	2.0	1.5
1983	2.5	2.1	1.8
1984	2.8	2.0	1.8

*10 percent drop in the Morgan Guaranty trade-weighted average exchange rate of 15 OECD countries.
Note: The simulations were performed over the period 1980:3 to 1984:4. Simulations with econometric models should be regarded as only approximations, since the results are one set in a potential distribution of many, and the shocks analyzed can alter the equation coefficients themselves.

threat to U.S. inflation, and that concern over accelerating inflation caused by a falling dollar is justified.

But although the effects of the dollar's fluctuations on inflation are considerable, other factors may prevent the price responses to the dollar's recent decline from being quick and large. The disinflationary effects of a still relatively strong dollar outweigh the inflationary effects of the dollar's recent decline. While the results reported in Table 3 hold constant the other factors that affect inflation, slack in the U.S. economy has been growing—especially in the manufacturing, mining, and agricultural sectors—that tends to moderate price increases. At the same time, labor-market slack also persists, with the unemployment rate still over 7 percent. Oil prices are declining, as are most food prices, and unit labor costs are rising slowly. Consequently, a lower dollar suggests inflation rates higher than might otherwise be the case, but not necessarily much higher than currently and perhaps even lower, depending on the other determinants of inflation.

Another relevant factor that moderates price increases are the decisions by foreign producers to hold on to the market shares they gained in the last few years. As dollar prices decline relative to prices in the rest of the world, foreign producers are likely to take lower profit margins in efforts to retain market shares in the face of lower prices.

Eventually, however, the upside potential on inflation from a sustained dollar depreciation will be realized, especially as the trade balance improves enough to push the U.S. economy closer to full capacity. The dollar as one of the two or three major determinants of U.S. inflation is here to stay, especially so for an economy that is increasingly integrated into the rest of the world and one that must function in a regime of flexible exchange rates.

QUESTIONS FOR DISCUSSION

1 Taking as given that the major cause of dollar appreciation is high U.S. real interest rates, explain how the U.S. monetary-fiscal mix helped strengthen the dollar. To the extent that the strong dollar was primarily itself a result of U.S. macroeconomic policy, in what sense if any was the dollar's value a *cause* rather than an *effect* of disinflation?

2 Name at least three ways in which the strong dollar acted to moderate wage demands in the United States.

3 How did the strong dollar affect the price of oil? Of food?

4 As of this writing, the dollar has fallen sharply from its recent heights, but no strong inflationary effect has been seen. Why does the author argue that, in the short run, a decline in the dollar would not create significant inflationary pressure? What does he predict for the long run? What in fact has happened to the inflation rate since the end of 1985? (You may wish to consult the *Economic Report of the President*.)

STABILIZING OIL AND FARM PRICES HOLDS THE KEY

David McClain*

Conventional wisdom about the disinflation experience of the first half of the 1980s has it that the back-to-back recessions of 1980 and 1981–1982 were the unpalatable medicine the economy had to take to purge itself of the disease of double-digit inflation. Analyzing the behavior of inflation through 1982 or 1983, many mainstream economists have concluded that the cure worked just about the way the textbooks would have suggested, when allowance is made for the size of the dose. Some have noted that the drug seems to have been a bit more effective on wage inflation. But all credit the recessions, and the policies that produced them, with bringing down the economy's inflationary fever.

By examining a full cycle of recession and recovery, however, I find that while the 1980s disinflation does appear to have been a textbook case, the doctors may have been looking at the wrong page. The curative powers of cyclical downturns appear to have been overrated, and several other factors—particularly the *mere stabilization* of oil and farm prices at historically high levels—seem to have been responsible for a larger-than-realized share of the disinflation. Such a conclusion suggests that the social costs of containing inflation with a policy of restrained aggregate demand may have been too high for the patient's own good.

David McClain, "Stabilizing Oil and Farm Prices Holds the Key," *Challenge,* September–October 1985, pp. 23–26. Reprinted with the permission of the publisher, M. E. Sharpe, Inc., 80 Business Park Drive, Armonk, NY 10504, USA.

*David McClain is Associate Professor and Chair of the Department of Finance and Economics at the School of Management, Boston University. This article is adapted from papers delivered at the December 1984 and March 1985 meetings, respectively, of the American Economic Association and the Eastern Economic Association.

A TEXTBOOK CASE?

According to the mainstream view of the inflation process, the early 1980s experience should reflect the historical inflation-unemployment trade-off embodied in the "old-fashioned" Phillips curve, as well as the impact of changes in farm and oil prices, and in the dollar. In this scenario, high unemployment and favorable price shocks reduce the actual rate of inflation, which in turn leads to further slowdowns in wage and price increases by lowering expectations of inflation, as they are embodied in explicit and implicit contracts that come up for renegotiation. Thus, a restrictive monetary policy reduces inflation slowly and indirectly via unemployment, general excess capacity, and a rising dollar.

In contrast, the "credibility" school argues that the disinflation experienced in this decade cannot be explained by reference to historical relationships alone. They stress that the commitments to reducing inflation embodied in the Reagan administration's "Program for Economic Recovery," and in the October 1979 reorientation of Federal Reserve operating procedures, were without precedent in the postwar period. As such, the credibility school believes, these commitments have contributed independently to the inflation reduction by *directly* affecting expectations of inflation, and by encouraging workers and firms to renegotiate *sooner than normal* the terms of the implicit and explicit contracts that are responsible for the inflation inertia characteristic of the mainstream perspective.

In order to evaluate both points of view, I have conducted a simulation of the early 1980s experience using a traditional Phillips curve. It is one I formulated while on the staff of the Council for Economic Advisers, with Steve Cecchetti, Michael McKee, and Dan Saks. (We originally calibrated the model with data from 1964–1978, and used it to analyze the impact of the second oil-price shock in 1979 and the Carter administration pay and price standards.) This model's structure is quite stable when 1979–1984 are added to the sample, and consequently it tracks the recent wage and price disinflation quite well, as the first two rows of Table 1 indicate. For price inflation, in particular, the model suggests essentially no role for credibility effects in the 1980s disinflation.

On the wage side, the credibility factor also appears to be of limited significance. However, the dollar's real trade-weighted exchange rate seems to have been statistically significant in the 1964–1984 sample (but not 1964–1978). There are several possible explanations. Perhaps fluctuations in the real exchange rate serve as a bellwether of future profitability, conditioning firms' wage negotiations with workers. Its increased significance over the 1979–1984 period may reflect the rather recent growth in the exposure of domestic producers to international competition. On the other hand, possibly such considerations always have been important, but the real exchange rate has varied enough only in the last six years to allow them to be discovered statistically.

A plausible case also can be made that during this period the exchange rate was the most visible evidence of the credibility of the Federal Reserve's new emphasis on controlling the rate of growth of the monetary aggregates, since dramatic innovation in the financial industry had made it difficult to interpret measures of the money supply.

One caveat: it is only during the 1981 period that the real exchange rate contributes significantly to explaining the variance of wage inflation. That coincides with the air

TABLE 1
ACCOUNTING FOR DISINFLATION
(Deceleration of Inflation* from 1980:4 to Date Indicated)

	Adjusted hourly compensation (% deceleration)		Private nonfarm (ex housing) output prices (% deceleration)	
	1982:4	1984:3	1982:4	1984:3
Actual percent deceleration	2.8	5.6	7.4	7.5
Simulated: base	3.9	6.1	7.7	8.8
Simulated: no recession	1.6	4.1	6.8	7.2
Impact of recession	2.3	2.1	0.9	1.6
% of base deceleration	59%	34%	12%	18%
% of actual deceleration	82%	37%	12%	21%
Simulated: no favorable shocks	3.2	5.2	6.5	7.8
Impact of favorable shocks	0.7	1.0	1.2	1.0
% of base deceleration	18%	15%	15%	12%
% of actual deceleration	24%	17%	16%	14%
Simulated: no recession and no favorable shocks	0.9	3.1	5.6	6.2
Impact of recession and favorable shocks together	3.0	3.0	2.1	2.6
% of base deceleration	76%	49%	28%	30%
% of actual deceleration	106%	54%	29%	35%

*These figures show the reduction of inflation (measured by 4-quarter percent changes) from 1980:4 to the quarter indicated.

traffic controllers' strike. Consequently the performance of the real exchange rate may reflect the improved credibility, not of the monetary authorities, but of the executive branch at that time.

In summary, then, with regard to the effect of credibility on wages one must render the Scottish verdict "not proved." The data are insufficient to confirm or deny conclusively the existence of such effects. On balance, one might attribute some transitory importance to them at the beginning of the Reagan administration, but not thereafter.

ACCOUNTING FOR DISINFLATION: WHICH PAGE OF THE TEXTBOOK?

If the slowdown in inflation the United States has experienced since 1981 can be explained largely by traditional descriptions of the inflation process, the question remains: which factors in particular are responsible, and to what degree? Did high unemployment do most of the work in braking the momentum of inflation, or do favorable oil, food, and exchange-rate shocks—actual reductions in oil and farm prices, and increases in the dollar's real value—deserve most of the credit?

Admittedly, any separation of these exogenous forces is artificial, since the weaker U.S. economy, and the policies that produced it, contributed to the rise in the dollar and promoted the reduction in prices of agricultural output and the break in oil prices. Nonetheless, this approach is consistent with the late Otto Eckstein's decomposition of inflation into demand, shock, and core components, and it does effectively account for the two principal aggregations of temporary forces affecting measured inflation.

In apportioning credit for curing our inflation ills, one must also ask whether, and how much, inflation would have come down anyway had we not experienced the deep 1981–1982 recession and the favorable shocks noted above. After all, the stabilization of oil prices after the 1973 shock at the historically high level of $12 a barrel contributed to the reduction of inflation experienced in 1975–1976. Since high prices are not rising prices, they provide no continuing momentum to inflation.

To determine the sources of the disinflation we have experienced, I have conducted three alternative simulations based on my "old-fashioned" Phillips curve for the 1981–1984 period. The first assumes the 1981–1982 recession and 1982–1984 recovery never occurred. The second holds oil and farm prices at their late 1980/early 1981 peak levels, while the dollar is not permitted to increase in real terms above 1980 levels. The third simulation combines the effects of the first and second.

The table displays the results for adjusted hourly compensation and the private nonfarm (ex housing) output price deflator. Recession and favorable shock effects together are responsible for about three-quarters of the *simulated* deceleration in the inflation of compensation from 1980:4 to 1982:4, and those effects equal approximately all of the *actual* deceleration. Extending the simulation interval seven quarters, to 1984:3, lowers substantially (to about 50 percent) the combined contribution of these two factors. Cyclical effects account for only about one-third of the deceleration of the simulated wage inflation. As the dollar continued to appreciate and oil prices dropped in the spring of 1983, favorable shock factors maintained their roughly 15 percent contribution to the increased deceleration.

The results for output-price inflation and consumer-price inflation (not shown) are a variation on the same theme. By the third quarter of 1984, the share of disinflation attributable to cyclical forces is about 20 percent, while that attributable to favorable shock factors is slightly less.

Why did recession and favorable shock forces contribute so little (about 50 percent for wages and 30 percent for prices) to the deceleration of inflation during 1981–1984? Given the self-limiting character of the wage-price spiral, the *stabilization* of external cost impulses from oil and farm prices and from the real exchange rate is enough *in and of itself* to bring inflation down substantially. In this setting, to maintain the 1979–1980 momentum of inflation (and increase the contribution of shock factors to the disinflation), oil and farm prices would have had to *continue* to increase, and the real exchange rate would have had to depreciate.

It is possible that these simulations underestimate the effects of cyclical forces taken alone because, as I have noted, this Phillips curve contains no causal relation between the unemployment rate or GNP gap on the one hand and oil and farm prices and the dollar on the other. But the maximum impact of demand and favorable shock forces taken *together* must be gauged properly, assuming that the rest of the model is accurate, unless one believes that in a nearly fully employed economy (a) OPEC could have continued to boost its price above the $38.72 peak value reached in late 1980, (b) farm prices would have continued to rise, and (c) the real exchange rate would have depreciated further from 1980 levels. The real price of oil had risen by 250 percent in 1979–1980, nominal oil prices had stabilized and real oil prices were eroded after the 1973–1974 shock, farm prices in 1980 were at historic highs, and the market forces moving assets—not goods—were dominating the dollar's course. Consequently—even though some of these developments in the assets markets can be attributed to the policies which contributed to the recession—I find it implausible to argue that a recession was necessary to halt the rise in nominal oil and farm prices and to stabilize the dollar. Indeed, it seems to be that some of the actual decline in nominal commodity prices, as well as the rise in the dollar's real value, would have occurred without a recession.

WAS IT WORTH IT?

In order to arrive at some measure of costs and benefits that result from restrictive demand policies, let's make the perhaps generous assumption that the recession did in fact lead to the fall in nominal oil and farm prices and to the real rise in the dollar. Accordingly, the above exercises suggest that the "output-sacrifice ratio"—measured as the percent of potential output lost as a result of restrictive aggregate demand policies per each percentage point reduction in the inflation rate—amounts to about 6 in the early 1980s. That result is consistent with that found by other researchers. Given the output price inflation deceleration (see Table 1), and estimates of the efficiency costs of inflation-induced distortions in the economy (in terms of lost real GNP) available in the literature at the end of the 1970s, one can calculate (assuming a social discount rate of 3 percent) that the benefits of pursuing recessionary policies outweighed the costs by about 30 percent.

However, financial deregulation and tax-law modifications have reduced the distortions caused by inflation as measured at the end of the last decade. If, as is quite likely these changes have shrunk the distortions by more than 25 percent, then the resulting revised calculation suggests that the benefits of restrictive aggregate-demand policies fall short of the costs. If, for example, the inflation distortions have been reduced by 33 percent, then the cost-benefit ratio of fighting inflation with higher unemployment—even allowing for favorable feedback effects via international commodity and foreign exchange markets—is 1.16. If the distortions have been halved, costs exceed benefits by over 50 percent.

Not embodied in these estimates is the benefit of reducing the risk of hyperinflation, in which inflation begins to feed on itself with such force that no amount of institutional adaptation can contain the efficiency costs. Clearly, the statements of some policy authorities during 1981–1982 indicate that they felt the 1979–1981 average rise in the GNP deflator of over 9 percent was too close to this range. (It is difficult to assess whether this zone begins in the United States at a 10 percent inflation rate, 15 percent, or higher.)

In summary, then, with financial deregulation and some tax reform in train, with oil and farm prices likely to stabilize at current high levels, and with further dollar depreciation unlikely, the case in the late 1980 for engineering a recession in the ensuing months in order to lower inflation was not overwhelming. If the benefits did exceed the costs, they did so only marginally—unless the United States was on the precipice of hyperinflation.

WHAT'S NEXT?

What does a mainstream model of the inflation process have to say about the outlook for prices in 1985–1986? In the current year, soft oil and farm prices and a dollar that has yet to slip below second-half 1984 levels should prevent any acceleration in inflation. Indeed, if productivity growth had held up, a further decline in inflation would have been possible this year. For 1986, inflation could increase by no more than 0.5 to 1.0 percentage points if real output growth reaccelerates modestly, farm and oil prices firm, and the dollar loses roughly 10 percent of its trade-weighted value.

Thus it seems likely that, barring a new dose of monetary restraint, the disinflation of the 1980s is at an end. It has been a time of structural upheaval and bizarre and contrasting combinations of national economic policies and of regional and individual economic well-being. Most probably, at least half the disinflation would have occurred without a recession or favorable price shocks. There must have been a better way to go from 1981 to 1986.

QUESTIONS FOR DISCUSSION

1 The author contrasts the "old-fashioned Phillips curve" and "credibility" models of the fall in wage and price inflation. Explain this distinction, using the aggregate supply–aggregate demand framework and the expectations-argumented Phillips curve. What evidence does the author give to support his conclusion that the old-fashioned view is the right one for this case?

2 The author points out that, while oil and food prices were *high* in the early eighties they were no longer *rising*. Why is this distinction important?

3 See if you can understand the results reported in Table 1. According to the author's simulation, how much did the 1981–1982 recession contribute to the actual deceleration of inflation between 1980/IV (the fourth quarter of 1980) and 1982/IV? Between 1980/IV and 1984/III? What were the contributions of "favorable shocks" (by which he means falling oil and food prices, and the strengthening dollar) over these two periods?

4 On what basis does the author make the inference that the leveling out of oil and food prices was in itself important in the deceleration of inflation? Does this seem reasonable to you? What alternative inference(s) might one draw from his simulation results?

A NEW MARKET REALISM: WAGE MODERATION

Roger E. Brinner
Kenneth J. Kline*

Over the past three decades American wage bargaining appears to have changed substantially as the economy has moved through different phases. These changes were not simply matters of price inflation or unemployment cycling up and down to produce variations in wage increases through time. They were structural shifts. New factors have entered into the process and old ones have dropped out or lost importance. Recently there has been a visible trend toward greater market realism, with wages coming to reflect the commercial value of labor in competitive international markets.

During the 1950s and early 1960s, the dominant factor driving each change in pay appears to have been the balance between labor supply and demand during the prior twelve quarters: a percentage point change in the unemployment rate implied a three-quarter percentage point change in wage inflation. Consumer-price inflation was also part of the bargaining climate, although only approximately one-half of a price change would pass through to wages, with a similar lag. Wages were essentially reactive, set in a backward-looking mode: when "the business cycle" produced more unemployment, wage increases were subsequently moderated. If consumer prices rose sharply after a prior settlement, then new contracts reflected this in higher earnings.

During the late 1960s and early 1970s, the strength of the economy and the emergence of rapid inflation appear to have diverted bargaining attention from unemployment conditions to consumer price inflation. Each percentage point of price inflation brought a full point of wage inflation, while the influence of unemployment explicitly

Roger E. Brinner and Kenneth J. Kline, "A New Market Realism: Wage Moderation," *Challenge,* September–October 1985, pp. 27–29. Reprinted with the permission of the publisher, M. E. Sharpe, Inc., 80 Business Park Drive, Armonk, NY 10504, USA.

*Roger E. Brinner is chief Economist and Group Vice President in the U.S. Economic Service at Data Resources, Inc., and Kenneth J. Kline is an economist with DRI.

contradicted the "Phillips curve" hypothesis of a nonlinear relationship which would produce higher inflation increments at lower unemployment rates. Although the shifts in coefficients pointing to these conclusions are not always statistically significant, the changing qualitative conclusions of researchers over the past two decades and changing quantitative results across a wide range of equation specifications are very clear. Most students of the Phillips curve literature will recall that the first half of the 1970s brought with it the first empirical "proof" that price increases were fully passed through into wages. This led to the "accelerationist" denial of a stable tradeoff between nominal changes in wages and unemployment: if wages fully reflect price changes and prices fully reflect nominal labor-cost movements, then there exists only a short-run tradeoff between inflation and unemployment. In such circumstances, the available short-run choices will always be dependent on the initial conditions, such as the recent history of demand shocks, raw material crises, or policy changes (e.g., minimum-wage or payroll-tax legislation).

This second regime, however, is still essentially reactive, the only differences being the greater extent of the price pass-through and the lesser sensitivity to unemployment. Institutional evidence of these phenomena also exists in the spread of cost-of-living adjustment (COLA) clauses in union contracts: in 1968, only 22 percent of collectively bargained contracts covering over 1,000 workers included such clauses, but by 1975 the share had increased to 49 percent. Moreover, anecdotal evidence suggests that informal cost-of-living adjustments came to be a standard part of nonunion and even managerial pay discussions: "real" wages were negotiated and consumer, not producer, prices were the basis of the inflation adjustment from nominal to real. As a result, the employer bore the immediate risk of paying too much, and the employees bore a later risk of losing their jobs by pricing themselves and the goods they produced beyond customer willingness to pay.

That's exactly what happened during the decade beginning in 1974. First, the OPEC oil price shocks raised consumer prices without correspondingly raising the prices for domestically produced goods. Following old procedures, wages would have increased more rapidly than the value of the corresponding output. Second, productivity growth slowed due to decelerating investment in R&D and fixed capital. The "normal" positive margin of 2.5–3.0 percent between growth rates of wages and prices could no longer be justified in the marketplace. Finally, international competition became an increasingly important factor. As the dollar appreciated 45 percent in real terms from 1980 to 1984 and the United States lost market share at home and abroad, it became clear to workers and managers that U.S. wages and profit margins could not be maintained at previous levels. (Indeed, COLA adjustments were present in only 35 percent of pay adjustments in 1983.) An econometric analysis of recent behavior indicates that each of these factors can now be identified as playing a visible role in wage determination.

TODAY'S REALISTIC WAGE CLIMATE

The third regime of today's economy is thus one of greater market realism: wages are based on output prices, not consumer prices, and influenced by changes in productivity growth; wages are reduced by an appreciating dollar and a declining market share for

TABLE 1
EQUATIONS ESTIMATED WITH 1955–65 AND 1955–74 DATA

	1955–65	1966–70	1980–84
	Equation estimated with 1955–65 data		
Actual wage inflation	3.6	7.0	6.0
Predicted value	3.6	5.2	3.3
	Equation estimated with 1955–74 data		
Actual wage inflation	3.6	7.0	6.0
Predicted value	4.9	5.7	8.0

U.S. producers. Each of these market factors is significant *in addition* to the traditional unemployment rate effect. Now wage levels are not merely passive, adjusting after unemployment develops, but proactive, reading market signals.

That structural changes have occurred in wage determination is supported by empirical evidence (Table 1). It shows actual wage inflation for various subintervals and values which an "old fashioned" Phillips curve model would have predicted. When data from 1955–1965 are used to estimate the regression coefficient, subsequent wage growth is underestimated, since this equation does not capture the importance of consumer-price increases fueled by the Vietnam war and commodity- and oil-price shocks in the early 1970s. Including the 1966–1974 data in the equation's estimation helps to explain the inflation experienced in 1975–1979, but still fails to reflect structural changes that occurred since 1980.

This most recent shift to a more realistic wage climate was necessary, because the extreme sensitivity of wages to prices that had developed during the 1965–1974 period

TABLE 2
WAGE INFLATION AND ITS DETERMINANTS

	Split interval				Full interval 55–84
	55–65	66–74	75–79	80–84	
Wage inflation	3.6	6.5	7.7	6.0	5.7
Consumer price inflation	1.6	5.4	7.8	5.6	4.7
Civilian unemployment rate	5.3	4.6	7.0	8.3	5.9
At full employment	4.1	4.6	5.1	5.1	4.6
Difference	1.2	0.0	1.9	3.2	1.3
Output price inflation	2.1	5.1	7.0	6.0	4.7
Productivity growth	2.5	1.5	1.1	1.9	1.8
Import share (average)	7.1	10.0	11.1	13.3	9.6
Real exchange rate growth (*1)	−0.1	−2.2	0.5	6.4	0.5

Due to data availability, the '55 to '65 and '55 to '84 growth rates use 1958 for their starting point.

would have priced American labor far too high relative to the value of the output being produced. The evidence shows (Table 2) that price increases for output fell short of consumer-price inflation in the 1966–1974 and 1975–1979 periods, and productivity growth was rather weak.

Rather than strictly emphasizing consumer prices and unemployment as in "traditional" explanations of inflation, output prices, productivity growth, and variables reflecting trade pressures are used as explanatory variables in addition to consumer-price inflation. This analysis reflects the influence of COLA clauses and the difference between the actual civilian unemployment rate and its full employment norm. (See the box and Table 3 for some of the technical details.)

WAGE INFLATION AND ITS DETERMINANTS

A one percent change in the following explanatory variables produces the indicated change in wage inflation.

TABLE 3

	Alternative specifications			
	1	**2**	**3**	**4**
Unemployment rate*	− 0.68	− 0.69	− 0.66	− 0.70
Output price inflation	0.63	0.48	0.62	0.62
Consumer price inflation	0.20	0.31	0.20	0.22
Productivity growth	0.28	0.30	0.21	0.28
Nominal exchange rate (% change)			− 0.23	
Change in import share†				− 0.16
"Goodness of fit"				
R-bar squared	0.875	0.864	0.882	0.876
Standard regression error	0.747	0.781	0.730	0.746

*In this regression, the personal-consumption price deflator is used rather than the GNP deflator. Difference between the civilian unemployment rate and its full employment norm.

†Import share is defined as total real imports (1972 prices, NIA basis) divided by real consumption less housing plus producer spending on durable equipment plus the change in nonfarm inventories: the change is this share lagged one-quarter less the value lagged five-quarters.

Output prices do outperform consumer prices as explanatory variables (Column 1). When the personal-consumption price deflator is used rather than the output-price deflator (Column 2), regression error rises and the R-bar squared declines, indicating that "goodness of fit" has been sacrificed. In both cases, approximately 30 percent of the variation of productivity growth from trend is passed through to wages. The final two regressions include measures which reflect foreign trade pressures. Either term—the exchange rate or the change in import share—reduces equation error relative to the base case (Column 1).

FUTURE IMPLICATIONS

Considering the variables in this alternative specification, wage growth is likely to be moderate in the near term. Even though the dollar began a decline in the second quarter of this year, the share of domestic markets captured by imports will not be easily or quickly eroded. Continuing trade pressures mean further restraint on producers' ability to command higher prices for their output and therefore on their ability to grant extensive wage increases. With unemployment remaining well above its historical average and both full employment norm and productivity growth reflecting recent history, the new "market realism" leaves neither producers nor their workers in a position to renew a wage-inflation spiral.

QUESTIONS FOR DISCUSSION

1 What were the three regimes of wage-setting practices in the postwar United States, as described by the authors? According to the authors, why did modes of wage-setting change over time? What institutional changes accompanied these regime changes? (For more on recent wage-setting practices, see Reading 25.)
2 The oil shock of 1974 led to significant increases in unemployment. Assuming that this article's thesis is correct, what would be the effect of an oil shock of similar size today?
3 Is the change in wage-setting behavior since 1980 an exogenous (that is, unexplained) change, or is it related to more fundamental macro variables? Discuss. What do you think would happen to wage-setting practices if the United States were now to go through ten years of low and stable inflation?
4 In Table 3, what are the effects of (*a*) a change in the exchange rate and (*b*) a change in the U.S. import share on wage inflation? Are these two results consistent with each other?

ADJUSTMENT TO MACROECONOMIC SHOCKS IN EUROPEAN AND AMERICAN LABOR MARKETS

Until the mid-1970s, the major western European economies averaged much lower rates of unemployment than did the United States. But the difference in unemployment rates began to fall sharply in 1976–1980 (see the table below); and, in the worldwide recession of the early 1980s, Europe suffered unemployment rates comparable to those in the United States. The period since 1983 has shown a remarkable divergence in U.S. and European unemployment rates, and in an unaccustomed direction. While output and employment have recovered strongly in the United States, unemployment in Europe has remained at high levels.

EUROPEAN AND U.S. UNEMPLOYMENT, 1961–1986

	United States	United Kingdom	France	West Germany
1961–1970	4.7	1.9	.9	.8
1971–1975	6.1	2.8	2.6	1.8
1976–1980	6.7	5.2	5.3	3.7
1980	7.1	6.0	6.4	3.4
1981	7.6	9.2	7.7	4.8
1982	9.7	10.6	8.7	6.9
1983	9.6	11.6	8.8	8.4
1984	7.5	11.8	9.9	8.4
1985	7.3	12.0	10.7	8.4
1986*	7.2	11.7	10.9	8.0

Source: Annual Economic Review, Commission of the European Communities, 1986; cited by Olivier Blanchard and Lawrence Summers, "Hysteresis and the European Unemployment Problem," in S. Fischer (ed.), NBER Macroeconomics Annual 1986 (MIT Press, Cambridge, Mass.).
*Forecast.

Why has European recovery from the recession been so slow? The next two readings provide background material for an analysis of this question. Of special interest is the possibility, which has been suggested by some economists (notably Jeffrey Sachs of Harvard), that differences in labor market structure in the United States and Europe have allowed the U.S. to adjust more quickly to macroeconomic shocks.

Robert S. Gay, in Reading 25, describes the adjustment of wages and employment in the United States in the early 1980s. While this adjustment was painful, it appears that in the United States high unemployment led to more moderate real wage demands. This in turn promoted the recovery of output and employment.

In Reading 26, Swedish economist Assar Lindbeck addresses the causes of high European unemployment. Although he points to a number of explanations, he particularly mentions "rigidities" in European labor markets (such as created by unions and restrictive labor laws) as a factor inhibiting macroeconomic recovery. He goes on to suggest a number of labor market reforms.

Reading 25   Robert S. Gay, "Union Settlements and Aggregate Wage Behavior in the 1980s," *Federal Reserve Bulletin,* December 1984, pp. 843–856.

Reading 26   Assar Lindbeck, "What Is Wrong with the West European Economies?" *The World Economy,* June 1985, pp. 153–170.

UNION SETTLEMENTS AND AGGREGATE WAGE BEHAVIOR IN THE 1980S

Robert S. Gay*

Since 1979, at least 3 million union members in the United States, one out of every six, have accepted labor contracts that freeze or reduce wages and fringe benefits or alter work rules. Initially, such deviations from traditional union wage practices were confined to a few financially troubled firms. But as the economy went through back-to-back recessions during the early 1980s and unemployment climbed to postwar record levels, deviations from customary practices appeared with increasing frequency in union contracts and often were negotiated on an industry-wide basis. By 1982, wage freezes and pay cuts had become as commonplace as wage increases in major collective bargaining settlements. Moreover, despite the rebound in economic activity and in profits since late 1982, managements have continued to press for cost-reduction measures, and wage cuts and freezes remained prominent features of union negotiations in 1984.

These developments coincided with an unusually large reduction in aggregate wage inflation. As recently as mid-1981, the rate of wage increase averaged close to double digits, whereas just three years later, wage adjustments had dropped on balance to less than 4 percent—the smallest rate of increase since the mid-1960s. The change in the size of union settlements has been even more dramatic. Average wage adjustments exclusive of cost-of-living payments during the first year of new union contracts dropped from about 10 percent in 1981 to $2^{1}/_{2}$ percent during 1983 and the first nine months of 1984 (chart 1).

*This article was prepared by Robert S. Gay of the Federal Reserve Board's Division of Research and Statistics. Anne Peters and Maura Shaughnessy helped prepare the data.

Robert S. Gay, "Union Settlements and Aggregate Wage Behavior in the 1980s," *Federal Reserve Bulletin*, December 1984, pp. 843–856.

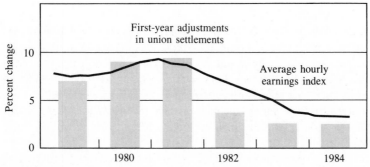

CHART 1
Union Settlements and Aggregate Wage Change. Hourly earnings index is the change from four quarters earlier; first-year adjustments are annual data, except 1984, which represents the first nine months. (Source: *Bureau of Labor Statistics.*)

In summarizing recent union wage developments, the discussion will focus on three issues. First, what were the nature and extent of nontraditional bargaining and how much did it contribute to the unusually sharp reduction in wage inflation during the past several years? Similar contract modifications have occurred with some regularity in the past, but the recent episode clearly involved unprecedented numbers of workers and industries. Under some conservative assumptions, aggregate wage inflation would have been at least $1/2$ percentage point higher in 1983 and 1984 in the absence of pay cuts and freezes. This estimate could be substantially larger if nontraditional bargaining had a major influence on other wage decisions. For the most part, however, the evidence suggests that spillovers outside of traditional channels have not been widespread. In industries that were less severely affected by the recession, both unionized and non-unionized, wage changes generally have shown fairly typical cyclical responses to rising unemployment and lower inflation.

Second, what factors contributed to the recent changes in union wage practices? Exceptionally large and prolonged declines in output and employment in many un-ionized industries often precipitated unscheduled reopenings of contracts and modi-fications to traditional wage formulas. That adversity was not solely cyclical. It stemmed also from longer-term influences, such as the secular rise in the relative wage of union workers and intensified competition from domestic nonunion or foreign firms, and from the relaxation of barriers to entry under deregulation of the transportation and communications industries.

Third, what aspects of recent settlements may reflect permanent changes in union wage determination and what aspects may prove transitory? Unions have shown no tendency to abandon certain key features of traditional contracts—multiyear settlements and escalator clauses. However, many union workers appear to have scaled back their expectations for annual improvements in real wages and have shown a willing-ness to experiment with profit-sharing and various cooperative labor-management programs to enhance productivity. These innovations may endure if competitive pressures persist.

UNION WAGE PRACTICES AND DISINFLATION

By the 1970s, the basic institutional features of union wage determination were well established. Multiyear contracts had become the predominant format for labor negotiations, and formal cost-of-living adjustment (COLA) provisions had spread to cover a majority of union workers. Prospective wage settlements were fairly predictable as many large unions adhered to a policy of negotiating identical fixed increases in each contract year—often referred to as the annual improvement factor—plus COLAs. When annual improvement factors were established during the 1950s and 1960s, they were perceived as paralleling productivity trends, but by the 1970s they had become more a matter of custom than a projection of current or future productivity performance. To the extent that COLA formulas did not pass the full increase in prices through to wage increases, first-year wage increases in succeeding contracts were adjusted to make up the difference—a so-called catch-up adjustment. In contracts without escalator provisions, negotiators had to build into future adjustments their expectations for inflation over the course of the contract or include contingency clauses for reopening the agreement.

These wage-setting practices often were cited as a major factor underlying the persistence of wage inflation in the United States. In particular, three-year contracts with staggered expiration dates, often buttressed by escalator clauses, were viewed as building inertia into the wage-determination process, thereby limiting the response of inflation to aggregate demand policies designed to reduce it. Some observers extended the inertia argument beyond union agreements by noting contract-like regularities in nonunion wage practices.

One rationale for attributing a central role in the inflation adjustment process to overlapping, multiyear contracts rests on the presumed importance of wage comparisons. In this view, workers' notions of an equitable wage have a major influence on wage-setting practices. Such notions may be based on wages paid to other, similar workers or on expectations of real wage gains that have been ingrained by experience. Given workers' perceptions of equity, union leaders feel pressure to emulate other settlements or to retain traditional guaranteed wage increases in escalated contracts; otherwise, they risk a rejection of the contract by their memberships. Thus key contracts reached in a bargaining round often appeared to set the tone for subsequent settlements, especially in related industries, even if economic conditions had changed in the interim.

Factors other than wage comparisons also influence union settlements. Negotiators ultimately must take into account current and prospective macroeconomic conditions as well as longer-run trends in their own industries. Evidence from the postwar period up to the 1980s indicated an asymmetric sensitivity to macroeconomic conditions: union wages were highly responsive to inflation but relatively insensitive to slack demand.

A closer look at the traditional features of multiyear contracts discussed above reveals why union wages were not very responsive to cyclical fluctuations in demand. First-year negotiated wage changes under new settlements, which dictate only a portion of all union wage adjustments in any given year, are fairly sensitive to unemployment. But that cyclical responsiveness is overwhelmed by the rigidities introduced by fixed wage increases that were scheduled under contracts negotiated in previous years, when

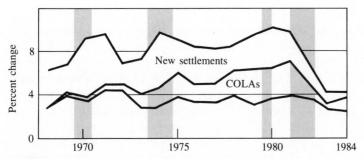

CHART 2
Effective Union Wage Change and Its Components. Annual data;
1984 represents first nine months at annual rates. Shaded areas denote
recessions. (Source: *Bureau of Labor Statistics.*)

economic conditions may have been decidedly different. In contrast, COLA clauses generate far less wage inertia than deferred adjustments. Many COLA formulas call for frequent reviews, making union wages highly responsive to price changes. Thus to the extent that macroeconomic policies designed to curb inflation in fact do so, COLAs help to moderate wage adjustments with only a brief delay.

Important aspects of the cyclical response of union wages have changed in the 1980s. To illustrate the changes that have occurred, chart 2 displays data on the components of union wage changes—first-year adjustments, deferred adjustments, and COLAs. For most of the period since 1968, the data relate the traditional story told above. First-year adjustments under new settlements show the greatest cyclical variance, albeit with some delay, while the deferred component displays relatively little variance. The inertia generated by deferred increases under earlier settlements can be seen most vividly in the years when total effective wage change decelerated sharply, as it did in 1972 and 1982; in those years, deferred increases accounted for an unusually large proportion of the average change in union wages. The contribution of COLAs rose dramatically during the 1970s—from only 5 percent of wage changes received by union workers in the late 1960s to about one-third in 1977–78. Part of that secular trend was attributable to a higher average inflation rate during the 1970s; but, more important, COLA provisions were added to many contracts early in the decade so that the proportion of union workers covered by such provisions rose from about 25 percent to around 60 percent.

EMERGENCE OF NONTRADITIONAL BARGAINING

The deceleration in union wage changes since 1980 has differed from past patterns in two key respects. First, the reduction in the size of first-year adjustments was exceptionally large after 1981, primarily because an unprecedented number of union workers accepted freezes on base wage rates or pay cuts. Second, the COLA component also declined sharply. Most of the reduction in COLAs can be traced to the general deceleration in price increases rather than to deferred or forgone payments under some union contracts.

Even though a contraction in activity in some unionized industries began as early as mid-1979, relatively few workers agreed to contract reopenings or deviations from traditional patterns until late 1981. According to data from the Bureau of Labor Statistics on major settlements that cover only bargaining units of 1,000 or more workers, about 35,000 workers took wage cuts or freezes in 1980. A separate tally from press reports and other published sources that was made by the Federal Reserve Board staff put the figure at 67,000 workers; this estimate includes salaried employees who agreed to terms similar to those granted by their union coworkers and other workers at nonunion firms. Often these early contract modifications took the form of a temporary deferral of scheduled wage adjustments or COLAs, and they generally were confined to financially troubled firms with recent records of poorer profitability than other companies in their industries. As the period of slack demand lengthened, however, wage cuts and freezes not only became pervasive but also were frequently negotiated on an industry-wide basis and extended over the life of multiyear contracts.

In 1981, roughly 190,000 union workers, or 8 percent of those reaching new settlements in the private sector, accepted first-year wage cuts or freezes, according to the data from the Bureau of Labor Statistics shown in table 1. By 1982, that figure had climbed to almost 1.5 million. The corresponding figures from the tally by the Federal Reserve Board staff were 365,000 workers in 1981 and 2.3 million workers in 1982. Many of the larger agreements broke with traditional wage-setting practices by eliminating guaranteed annual increases over the life of the contracts. This new format became the standard for union workers in the automobile, trucking, and rubber industries in 1982, and was adopted in 1983 by the aluminum, metal container, shipbuilding, copper mining, and farm machinery industries. Significant deviations from the industry standard were negotiated at companies with particularly acute financial problems. All told, more than two-fifths of workers covered by large new settlements accepted first-year wage freezes in 1982, and in manufacturing the proportion was one-half.

TABLE 1
DISTRIBUTION OF WORKERS BY FIRST-YEAR WAGE ADJUSTMENT
IN MAJOR COLLECTIVE BARGAINING SETTLEMENTS, 1980–84
(Percent Except as Noted)

Wage adjustment	1980	1981	1982	1983	1984 (first nine months)
Decrease	0	5	2	15	6
No change	0	3	42	22	21
Increase					
0–4 percent	4	3	9	14	33
4–8 percent	25	9	23	39	37
8 percent and over	71	81	24	10	3
Memo					
Mean adjustment (percentage change)	9.5	9.8	3.8	2.6	2.5
Number of workers (thousands)	3,790	2,382	3,257	3,089	1,447

Source: Bureau of Labor Statistics, *Current Wage Developments,* various issues.

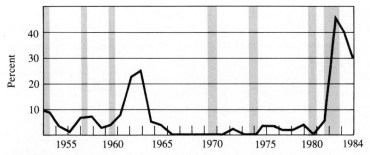

CHART 3
Union Workers Receiving No Wage Increase or a Wage Cut. Annual data
for collective bargaining agreements covering 1,000 or more workers;
1984 represents first nine months. Shaded areas denote recessions.
(Source: *Bureau of Labor Statistics,* Current Wage Developments,
various issues.)

In 1983, the distribution of first-year union settlements shifted even more dramatically toward wage cuts. Settlements in the steel, airline, and meatpacking industries
called for initial wage reductions ranging from 10 to 20 percent. In addition, half of
unionized construction workers signed new agreements calling for pay reductions or
freezes. Altogether, about 1.1 million workers under large union contracts in the private
sector accepted wage cuts or freezes in 1983. The tally by the Board staff found that
at least 1.3 million employees were subject to new wage cuts or freezes in 1983.
Modifications to past wage practices continued to be a prominent feature of union
negotiations during the first nine months of 1984, despite the strong rebound in overall
economic activity and profits over the preceding year. About one-fourth of the 1.5
million workers negotiating new contracts accepted initial wage cuts or freezes. In the
construction industry, the average wage adjustment was about 1 percent, the lowest
figure recorded for the industry since the Bureau of Labor Statistics began publishing
these data in 1968.

Chart 3 puts the recent period in historical perspective. Although wage cuts were
common during the Great Depression, the experience with distressed bargaining after
World War II is more instructive because by that time modern institutions of collective
bargaining were well established. Two other episodes of distressed bargaining occurred
during the postwar era: one during the 1953–54 recession and another in the late 1950s
and early 1960s. Both episodes were highlighted by the spread of wage cuts or freezes
to a substantial portion of the unionized workforce in a few select industries. Usually,
these industries were undergoing extensive structural change at the same time.

In the early 1950s, the textile industry faced considerable excess capacity, largely
as a result of foreign competition, technological advances, and the introduction of
synthetic fibers. To forestall plant closings, union workers accepted pay cuts. Despite
these revisions to pay scales, industry employment continued to decline over the next
two decades. During the late 1950s and early 1960s, the meatpacking industry also
experienced structural upheaval. Nonunion firms paying wages below the union scale
had entered the market by building highly efficient production facilities. Unionized

companies, which had once dominated the market, generally failed to keep abreast of technological and marketing advances, and cost disadvantages threatened their long-term viability. Contracts eventually were reopened in 1962 and 1963, and pay and work rules were changed.

Wage cuts were rare outside the meatpacking industry in the early 1960s, but decisions not to increase negotiated rates for base wages were fairly common. Some observers viewed the prevalence of moderate settlements at that time as evidence of success of the wage-price guideposts program or attributed it to a tougher stance taken by management after a period when unions had extracted fairly generous wage increases. Concern arose among union workers about the impact of automation and the employment problems caused by closures of outmoded plants. Despite all the factors restraining wage adjustments, the extent of pay cuts and freezes in union settlements did not approach that recorded during the past three years.

Apart from a few instances, most situations of distressed bargaining during the postwar period before 1982 were specific to individual firms or plants. Almost invariably, these situations involved financially weak firms, and managements were able to convince workers that changes in labor contracts were necessary to assure the firm's survival or to avoid plant closure. Cyclical layoffs even on a large scale generally did not provoke extensive modifications to traditional wage formulas. A prime example is the experience during the 1974–75 recession. Negotiations for most major multiyear settlements were completed before the severity of the recession was evident. Yet, although employment and output fell sharply in many industries, existing contracts were not reopened, as they have been recently. The reason for the sharp contrast between the experiences of 1974–75 and 1980–84 apparently was that in the earlier period, union workers did not perceive job losses to be permanent.

As discussed earlier, the COLA component of effective union wage changes also has declined precipitously since 1981 after a decade of increase. The observed contributions of COLAs to total effective union wage changes are the product of three factors: (1) the proportion of union workers covered by COLAs; (2) the recovery rate— the extent to which COLA formulas pass the change in consumer prices through into wage increases; and (3) the rate of change in consumer prices. Historical data on these factors affecting the COLA contribution are presented in table 2. Note that the diminished role of COLAs in total union wage adjustments recently cannot be attributed to union workers giving up COLA provisions in their collective bargaining agreements. COLA coverage has remained fairly stable at just under 60 percent since 1976. Even in distressed situations, union workers showed little willingness to eliminate entirely contractual provisions indexing wages to movements in the general price level. The only major exceptions to this generalization have appeared in contracts negotiated for airline and food store workers, in which abandonment of escalator clauses has reduced COLA coverage from around 70 percent of the union workforce in these industries to less than 20 percent over the past four years.

Instead of abandoning COLA provisions altogether, some unions agreed to defer or forgo some payments (as in the auto and steel contracts), or to divert payments to help defray the rising costs of fringe benefits (as in the Master Freight Agreement), or to lengthen the period between reviews, which in effect reduces employers' total

TABLE 2
FACTORS AFFECTING COLA COMPONENTS OF EFFECTIVE UNION WAGE CHANGES, 1968–84
(Percent, Except as Noted)

Year	Portion of total due to COLAs (percentage points)	Proportion of union workers covered by COLAs	Recovery rate[1]	Price change[2]
1968	.3	23.6	34	4.7
1969	.3	25.0	26	6.1
1970	.6	25.9	67	5.5
1971	.7	27.8	92	3.4
1972	.7	40.6	59	3.4
1973	1.3	39.4	47	8.8
1974	1.9	39.2	48	12.2
1975	2.2	51.5	68	7.0
1976	1.6	59.4	73	4.8
1977	1.7	61.2	58	6.8
1978	2.4	60.4	55	9.0
1979	3.1	58.9	51	13.4
1980	2.8	58.1	58	12.5
1981	3.2	58.2	67	8.7
1982	1.4	56.7	70	3.9
1983	.6	57.6	53	3.3
1984: first nine months[3]	1.1	57.3	53	4.1

[1]The data for 1968–80 are Federal Reserve Board staff estimates of the passthrough of price changes into wage adjustments under COLA clauses based on data on the average size of cost-of-living adjustments for workers who actually received payments during the calendar year as a percent of the December-to-December change in the consumer price for urban wage earners and clerical workers (CPI-W). After 1980, the data are estimates by the Bureau of Labor Statistics, which are based on the change in consumer prices over the actual period of the COLA review.
[2]December-to-December change in the CPI-W.
[3]Nine-month change at a compound annual rate.
Sources: COLA contribution and recovery rates after 1980 are from *Current Wage Developments,* various issues; COLA coverage is from *Monthly Labor Review,* vol. 107 (January 1984), p. 31, and previous January issues; price change data are from the Department of Labor.

costs. In addition, some settlements, notably in the steel industry, set limitations on COLAs so that payments are based only on increases in consumer prices in excess of a threshold inflation rate. Most of the alterations to COLAs appear to be temporary and are often scheduled to terminate before the expiration of the contracts.

All of these modifications to COLA provisions should affect the recovery rate. Estimates of the recovery rate are shown in column 4 of table 2. In the early 1980s, COLA formulas on average compensated workers for roughly two-thirds of the rise in consumer prices. Modifications to COLA formulas lowered the recovery rate to around one-half in 1983. These data suggest that modifications to COLAs accounted for perhaps $1/2$ percentage point, or one-fifth of the deceleration in the COLA component of total effective union wage changes. The remainder was attributable to the general slowdown in price increases.

IMPACT OF CONTRACT MODIFICATIONS
ON AGGREGATE WAGE INFLATION

The unprecedented number of wage cuts and freezes after 1981 coincided with a halving of the average rate of wage inflation from 9 percent in that year to around 4 percent recently (table 3). At least two aspects of this wage deceleration contrast with the experience in previous postwar downturns. First, union wage change actually began to decelerate long before there was any sign of a slowdown in nonunion wages. Second, wage inflation fell more rapidly in the union sector than elsewhere—from 11 percent in 1980 to about $3^1/_4$ percent thus far in 1984.

As indicated by the data from the employment cost index, the slowdown in union wage inflation began in 1981. Even so, wage adjustments for union workers on balance exceeded those received by nonunion workers, as they had throughout most of the

TABLE 3
THE DECELERATION OF WAGES, 1979–84
(Percentage Change)

Measure	1979	1980	1981	1982	1983	1984 (first nine months)
Employment cost index, wages and salaries[1]						
Private nonfarm	8.7	9.0	8.8	6.3	5.0	3.9
Union	9.0	10.9	9.6	6.5	4.6	3.3
Nonunion	8.5	8.0	8.5	6.1	5.2	4.2
Manufacturing	8.6	9.4	8.7	5.6	4.3	4.1
Union	9.4	11.0	8.9	5.8	3.6	3.9
Nonunion	7.9	7.9	8.3	5.6	4.7	4.3
Nonmanufacturing	8.8	8.8	9.0	6.5	5.5	3.9
Union	8.5	10.8	10.2	7.1	5.5	2.7
Nonunion	8.8	8.1	8.6	6.2	5.5	4.2
Hourly earnings index[2]						
Private nonfarm	8.0	9.6	8.3	6.1	3.9	3.1
Manufacturing	8.7	10.9	8.8	6.0	2.7	3.3
Construction	6.9	7.7	8.3	5.4	1.5	1.2
Transportation and public utilities	9.0	9.3	8.5	6.1	4.3	3.1
Trade	7.5	8.7	6.9	5.4	4.7	2.4
Services	7.6	9.3	9.1	7.0	4.9	4.1
Finance, insurance, and real estate	7.7	10.1	8.0	7.7	6.0	3.9
Major collective bargaining agreements[3]						
Total effective wage change, private sector	9.1	9.9	9.5	6.8	4.0	4.0
First-year adjustments under new settlements, private sector	7.4	9.5	9.8	3.8	2.6	2.5

[1]December to December; data for 1984 are from December 1983 to September 1984 at a compound annual rate, not seasonally adjusted.
[2]Fourth quarter to fourth quarter; data for 1984 are from 1983:4 to 1984:3 at a compound annual rate.
[3]Wage adjustments put in place during the calendar year, except for 1984, which covers only the first nine months.

past decade. By 1982, however, union wages on average were rising at about the same rate as nonunion wages. Much of this early deceleration probably was attributable to smaller COLAs in contracts with escalator clauses, as consumer price increases slowed from $12\frac{1}{2}$ percent in 1980 to just 4 percent in 1982. Not until mid-1982 did a substantial number of union workers actually forgo scheduled wage adjustments or COLAs. As the cumulative total of workers negotiating wage cuts and freezes rose, the average change in union wages fell below that for nonunion workers and has remained below it over the first three quarters of 1984. During the past two years, changes in union wages have averaged about $\frac{1}{2}$ to 1 percentage point less than those in nonunion wages.

The direct influence of distressed bargaining also can be seen in wage data by industry. Wage cuts and freezes were particularly prevalent in manufacturing, construction, and transportation; and these industries also showed the greatest deceleration in average wage changes, especially after 1981. According to the hourly earnings index, wage adjustments in manufacturing fell from 11 percent in 1980 to around 3 percent during the past two years. In construction, where wage cuts and freezes in union contracts were widespread in 1983 and 1984, wage changes have averaged only 1 percent lately, compared with about 8 percent in 1981. The direct influence of distressed bargaining is less noticeable in the aggregate wage index for transportation, communications, and public utilities—probably because wage settlements at public utilities were well above average in recent years while wage cuts and freezes were confined largely to trucking firms and airlines.

Distressed bargaining also appeared to have some limited influence on other wage decisions. For example, many union contracts contained provisions requiring "equality of sacrifice" from nonunion counterparts at the same firm. Also, once wage cuts or freezes were negotiated in certain key contracts, other, similar settlements soon spread to industries in the same "sphere" of union wage setting, in a pattern that has been evident for many years. The automobile settlement set precedents for revised agreements in automotive parts, truck manufacturing, and farm and construction equipment; the master steel settlement influenced negotiations in nonferrous metals and metal containers; and intercity trucking settlements were imitated in local trucking agreements, by truckers at retail food stores, and at bus companies.

Even in these examples, it is difficult to distinguish whether the behavior followed a pattern set by one industry or was the independent responses of the individual industries to acute financial problems all of them faced. The contracts negotiated within traditional spheres of influence clearly were tailored to fit the economic conditions of each industry. The steel contracts, for example, cut pay substantially (although the reductions are to be restored over the contract term) and limited COLAs for two and a half years, whereas related settlements merely froze base wage rates. Settlements for truck and bus drivers also have varied widely according to market conditions and companies' fortunes. In short, even within traditional spheres of imitation, there has been considerably greater diversity of wage settlements than in the past.

Outside distressed industries, union settlements also moderated after 1981, but the deceleration appeared to be no greater than might be expected during a period when inflation dropped sharply and unemployment rose. For those workers who received wage increases, first-year adjustments under new settlements exclusive of COLAs dropped from 11 percent in 1981 to 4.2 percent in the first nine months of 1984. This slowdown can be explained largely by reduced inflationary pressures, which mitigated demands for catch-up increases and moderated expectations of future inflation. With consumer prices rising less than 4 percent annually during the past two and a half years, union workers who received wage increases enjoyed, on balance, fairly substantial gains in real wages. Indeed, the rise in real wages over the life of contracts expiring recently is a key factor in the virtual disappearance of initial wage increases in excess of 8 percent in 1984. Thus the unionized workforce divided into two camps during the early 1980s: in industries afflicted by sweeping changes in product market conditions, heightened competition spurred employers and unions to reduce labor costs; in industries facing less stringent product market pressures, negotiators stuck with traditional wage-setting practices.

Wage decisions in unrelated, nonunionized industries also did not appear to be influenced greatly by the extraordinary developments in the union sector. Nonunion wages rose less rapidly than union wages in 1980 and 1981, as was the case throughout most of the 1970s. If strong spillovers from union to nonunion wages existed, the persistent widening of union-nonunion wage differentials over more than a decade could not have occurred. After 1981, when pay cuts and freezes became widespread for union workers, increases in nonunion wages declined, but the reduction was far less than that for union workers. Apparently, nonunionized employers did not feel that product market conditions warranted drastic measures to cut costs; indeed, employment in many nonunionized industries in the service-producing sector continued to rise during the back-to-back recessions of the early 1980s.

A crude calculation may be made of the impact of distressed bargaining on aggregate wage inflation. Roughly 3 million union workers were directly covered by wage cuts or freezes. Spillovers to nonunion workers might double the number of workers affected to 6 million, or about 8 percent of private nonfarm payroll employment in 1983. A realistic assumption is that these workers received no increase in wages on balance. (Small wage adjustments generated by COLAs in many contracts that froze base wage rates probably were counterbalanced by steep wage cuts in some other contracts.) If, instead of having their wages frozen, these workers had received wage increases of $5^1/_4$ percent, commensurate with traditional formulas (a 3 percent annual improvement factor plus COLAs), the average wage change for all workers reported in the employment cost index would have been $5^1/_2$ percent rather than 5 percent in 1983. In other words, recent modifications to traditional wage formulas may have held down overall wage inflation since 1982 at least $1/_2$ percentage point per year. This estimate understates the impact on aggregate wage inflation because the definition of contract modifications used here is confined to freezes on base wage rates and pay cuts.

FACTORS INFLUENCING RECENT SETTLEMENTS

Developments leading up to the recent wave of wage cuts and freezes were complex in their origins and varied across industries, but many of these situations had common characteristics. Frequently, the affected industries were among those hardest hit, in terms of sales and profits, by the prolonged slump in economic activity. Yet the problems facing financially troubled firms were not solely cyclical in nature. At least three developments that evolved during the 1970s probably would have forced unions to modify their traditional wage formulas even in the absence of the back-to-back recessions during the early 1980s.

First, wage dispersion across industries widened dramatically over the past decade as average union wage increases consistently exceeded average nonunion wage increases. By the early 1980s, the union-nonunion wage differential had reached a historic high. Second, productivity trends deteriorated markedly across a wide range of industries, particularly after 1973. As a result, real wage increases for many union workers tended to outstrip productivity gains, exacerbating cost pressures on prices. Third, new competition emerged. For heavily unionized "smokestack" industries, the challenge came from foreign suppliers that made dramatic inroads into U.S. markets. In several highly unionized industries less subject to import competition, domestic nonunion firms paying lower wages captured an increasing share of the market. For the airline and trucking industries, the new competition has been the result of deregulation, which effectively removed barriers to entry into basically competitive markets. The twin recessions of the early 1980s and the strengthening value of the dollar relative to foreign currencies clearly added to these burgeoning market pressures on unions and hastened modifications to traditional wage practices.

Layoffs and Plant Closings

Almost invariably, unions have accepted major contract modifications only when bankruptcy, extensive plant closings, or massive layoffs were an immediate threat. Job losses were particularly widespread among union workers during the early 1980s. Table 4 shows cumulative declines in employment from peak levels (usually in 1979) to the recession lows for numerous heavily unionized industries in which wage cuts and freezes became widespread. In many cases, including automobiles and steel, more than one-third of the prerecession workforce was laid off. In the meatpacking, trucking, and airline industries, the overall declines in employment undoubtedly understate the adversity faced by union workers, because the number of nonunion jobs expanded or at least contracted less than the number of union jobs. By 1982, many union workers had been separated from their former jobs for nearly three years, and prospects for regaining them were highly unfavorable. Indeed, by mid-1984, after one and one-half years of economic recovery, employment in these industries generally was still well below prerecession levels.

A puzzling question is why crisis situations must develop before unions are willing to modify traditional wage practices. One possible explanation is that unions do not perceive the wage–employment tradeoff, especially in the short run. Under some circumstances, this lack of perception is understandable. If the short-run elasticity of demand for union labor is low, as some evidence suggests, employed workers must sacrifice a lot in wages to generate a small gain in employment for their unemployed counterparts. Elasticities of labor demand tend to be low when unions effectively control their jurisdictions and when the ratio of labor costs to total costs is low. For

TABLE 4
JOB LOSSES IN SELECTED INDUSTRIES RECEIVING WAGE CONCESSIONS
(Percent)

	Cumulative change in employment	
Industry	Prerecession peak to recession trough[1]	Prerecession peak to July 1984
Copper ores	−50.4	−51.3
Construction	−29.8	−4.6
Metal cans	−28.8	−27.1
Primary aluminum	−37.7	−24.1
Fabricated structural metal	−29.5	−23.5
Farm machinery	−48.4	−43.2
Construction machinery	−59.6	−44.0
Metalworking machinery	−28.6	−19.0
Motor vehicles and equipment	−35.7	−17.4
Blast furnace and basic steel products	−43.7	−41.2
Meat packing plants	−17.2	−12.0
Tires and inner tubes	−27.9	−20.7
Trucking and trucking terminals	−17.3	−4.8
Air transportation	−5.4	4.7
Food stores	...[2]	13.5
Ship and boatbuilding	−20.7	−10.9
Total private nonfarm	−4.4	4.9

[1]Peaks and troughs are specific to the individual industries. The absolute decline in employment totaled about 4 million in the industries listed; private nonfarm employment fell 1.9 million between February 1980 and December 1982.

[2]There was no trough for this industry.

Source: U.S. Department of Labor, *Supplement to Employment and Earnings* (July 1984), and recent monthly issues of *Employment and Earnings.*

many of the industries in which wage formulas ultimately were altered, including steel, autos, meatpacking, and tires, the ratio of labor costs to total costs is one-third or less. A sizable wage cut, even if fully passed through into prices, would translate into only a moderate reduction in product prices, which in turn would stimulate output and employment only a little in the near term. Thus low short-run elasticities of labor demand may account in part for the reluctance of unions to accept cost-reduction measures until they saw clear signs of a long-term crisis.

Institutional considerations also can forestall or even preclude contract modifications during recessions. Workers often distrust their companies' claims of financial distress. Lacking membership support, union leaders are reluctant to recommend pay cuts that would alienate their members and threaten their leadership within the union. Moreover, revisions to customary wage formulas in even one firm often are viewed by union leaders as undermining union strength because they can subject the union to demands for equal treatment by other organized firms.

A key role in union decisionmaking is played by senior workers, who generally constitute a majority and whom seniority systems insulate to some extent from layoffs. Unless the job security of senior workers is threatened, a consensus in favor of contract reopenings and revised settlements is unlikely to emerge. The jobs of senior workers rarely were threatened during the postwar period before the 1980s, and the responsiveness of wages under multiyear contracts to cyclical changes in economic conditions was sharply limited. By contrast, crisis situations that threatened senior workers— imminent threats of bankruptcy or permanent plant closings—extended far beyond marginal firms during the early 1980s and afflicted a much greater number of industries.

Long-Run Influences

Although massive layoffs were the catalyst for recent changes in collective bargaining, a confluence of developments during the 1970s had added to market pressures on unions and probably would have forced modifications to traditional wage formulas in any event. These difficulties included high domestic labor costs, a narrowing or even the elimination of the U.S. productivity advantage, and the failure of some unionized industries to adapt quickly to changes in technology and in consumer preferences. As these problems evolved, numerous unionized industries became increasingly vulnerable to import and nonunion competition, which in turn eroded union bargaining power.

In key manufacturing industries, the new competition came from imports. During the 1970s, foreign suppliers made steady inroads into U.S. markets formerly dominated by domestic firms. For example, by 1982, foreign cars accounted for 28 percent of total U.S. auto sales, compared with only 9 percent in 1968. The import share for steel almost doubled over the same period to 22 percent (table 5). Likewise, imports of apparel, tires, leather goods, and machine tools rose sharply as a share of domestic sales. The sharp increase in the foreign exchange value of the dollar beginning in late 1980 put added pressure on domestic producers by reducing the relative price of imported goods. Since late 1982, the strong recovery of aggregate demand has bolstered sales of domestic producers but has not stemmed the tide of imports. Indeed, the U.S. merchandise trade deficit reached record levels during the first three quarters of 1984.

In a number of industries in which imports are not a factor, the emergence of nonunion competition eroded union bargaining power. Unionization in construction, meatpacking, and retail food stores shrunk during the 1970s, and the deterioration appeared to accelerate during the early 1980s. For the highly unionized airline and trucking industries, deregulation effectively removed barriers to entry into basically competitive markets, and new low-cost nonunion firms offering discount rates have thrived. Whatever its source, the heightened competition exacerbated the cyclical decline in union employment and undoubtedly was a major influence on workers' perceptions of their firm's long-term prospects. More important, greater competition in product markets made it more difficult for businesses to pass on higher costs into prices.

Underlying these fundamental changes in product markets were marked cost differences between union firms and their competitors. During the 1970s, wage increases varied considerably across industries, and the dispersion of wage rates widened dra-

TABLE 5
IMPORT PENETRATION RATIOS[1]
(Percent)

Industry	1968	1981
Food and kindred products	1.0	4.2
Tobacco manufacturers	.3	2.0
Textile mill products	5.2	5.9
Apparel and related products	4.2	13.7
Lumber and wood products, except furniture	8.3	8.7
Furniture and fixtures	1.6	4.8
Paper and allied products	5.8	6.4
Printing, publishing, and allied products	.6	1.0
Chemicals and allied products	2.3	4.4
Petroleum and coal products	3.9	6.8
Rubber and miscellaneous plastic products	3.0	7.7
Tires and inner tubes[2]	2.3	11.7
Leather and leather products	8.9	24.7
Stone, clay, and glass products	3.0	5.1
Primary metal products	8.8	14.5
Steel[3]	12.2	21.8
Fabricated metal products, except machinery and transportation equipment	1.7	3.9
Machinery, except electrical	4.0	3.9
Metalworking machinery[2]	4.8	16.3
Machine tools[2]	14.6	29.4
Electrical machinery, equipment, and supplies	4.0	8.0
Transportation equipment	5.7	14.8
Motor vehicles and parts[2]	5.7	21.7
Measuring, analyzing, and controlling instruments; photographic and optical goods; watches and clocks	4.9	11.3
Miscellaneous manufactured commodities	10.6	23.6
All manufacturing industries	4.3	8.4

[1]Import penetration ratios are defined as imports divided by total industry shipments plus imports. Changes in industry classifications as of 1972 affected import penetration ratios in a few industries, notably petroleum; basic trends for most two-digit industries, however, are not distorted by comparing figures for 1968 and 1981.
[2]Data are from the Census of Manufactures, 1967 and 1982.
[3]Data are from the American Iron and Steel Institute, 1967 and 1982. Exports are netted out in this volume-based data.
Source: Bureau of Labor Statistics, except as noted.

matically after a decade of relative stability (chart 4). The causes of the increased dispersion in wages are open to debate, but it is clear that many of the union workers granting wage cuts or freezes in the early 1980s were among those who had received the largest wage increases during the 1970s. For example, union wage scales in autos, steel, rubber, and trucking—industries recently marked by wage cuts and freezes—

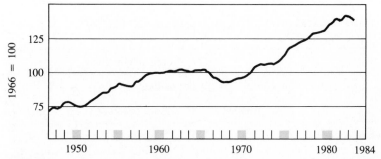

CHART 4
Dispersion of Average Hourly Earnings across Industries. The summary statistic plotted is the coefficient of variation for average hourly earnings in 44 three-digit industries for which data are available since 1947; data are indexed to equal 100 in 1966. A similar widening in interindustry wage differentials during the 1970s was evident for a larger sample of 120 three-digit industries for which data are available since 1958. Weighting the earnings data by industry employment also did not change the basic pattern of dispersion. (Source: *U.S. Department of Labor.*)

climbed from a level 30 to 40 percent higher than the average wage for all private nonfarm production workers in the late 1960s to a level 50 to 80 percent higher in 1981 (table 6). In the meatpacking industry, older unionized plants paid substantially higher wages than the new nonunion plants with advanced technology, and large settlements in the construction industry during the early 1980s undoubtedly widened the wage gap between union and nonunion workers.

Many industries in which labor contracts were modified recently also experienced a slowdown in productivity growth after 1973 (table 7). One consequence of that slowdown was a compounding of cost disadvantages for unionized firms in these industries relative to foreign or domestic nonunion competitors. Before the 1970s, strong productivity gains appeared to warrant annual increases in real wages of 2 to 3 percent that were embedded in union wage formulas. For nearly a decade after 1973, however, few heavily unionized industries experienced productivity gains of that mag-

TABLE 6
RATIO OF HOURLY EARNINGS IN SELECTED INDUSTRIES TO AVERAGE FOR
PRIVATE NONFARM PRODUCTION WORKERS

Industry	1969	1973	1977	1981	1983
Trucking[1] (Master freight agreement)	1.31	1.59	1.63	1.73	1.63
Autos[2]	1.39	1.45	1.57	1.70	1.67
Steel[3]	1.34	1.42	1.64	1.81	1.67
Rubber[4]	1.38	1.33	1.38	1.53	1.54

[1]Straight-time hourly wage rates are specified in Master Freight Agreements.
[2]SIC 3711, motor vehicles and car bodies.
[3]SIC 3312, blast farmers and steel mills.
[4]SIC 301, tires and inner tubes.
Source: U. S. Department of Labor and Master Freight Agreements for various years.

TABLE 7
PRODUCTIVITY GROWTH IN SELECTED INDUSTRIES, SELECTED PERIODS
(Average Annual Percentage Change)

	Productivity growth[1]		
	Earlier period		
Industry	Change	Years covered[2]	1973–81
Motor vehicles and equipment	3.7	1957–73	1.9
Steel	1.8	1947–73	.8
Tires and inner tubes	4.0	1947–73	2.9
Primary aluminum	4.4	1947–73	− .3
Farm and garden machinery	2.5	1958–73	.5
Intercity trucking	2.7	1954–73	.3
Air transportation	7.5	1947–73	2.6
Metal cans	2.3	1947–73	3.8
Copper mining, crude ore	3.7	1955–73	2.2
Retail food stores	2.8	1958–73	− .6
Construction machinery	2.1	1958–73	.1
Machine tools	1.5	1958–73	− .7
Meatpacking	3.2	1967–73	3.2
Fabricated structural metal	2.3	1958–73	− .4
Total private nonfarm	2.5	1947–73	.6

[1]Output per employee hour.
[2]The period covered was determined by the availability of data.
Source: Productivity Measures for Selected Industries, 1954–81, Bureau of Labor Statistics Bulletin 2155 (December 1982).

nitude, yet traditional annual improvement factors remained largely intact. At the same time, foreign producers, particularly in Japan, were able to raise productivity substantially, thereby narrowing or even eliminating the U.S. advantage in production efficiency.

LONG-RUN PROSPECTS FOR COLLECTIVE BARGAINING

Traditional union practices governing wage determination and other key outcomes of collective bargaining underwent sweeping changes during the early 1980s in response to heightened competition in many unionized markets. This response was the inevitable result of the significant widening of union-nonunion wage differentials or, in the case of import-sensitive industries, the worsening of labor cost disadvantages vis-à-vis foreign producers during the 1970s. Union wage-setting practices remained stable as long as trend productivity growth matched the annual improvement factor built into traditional wage formulas. But when productivity gains slowed, the use of mechanistic formulas resulted in settlements that were at odds with the market conditions facing individual firms or industries. After the longer-term consequences became evident in the form of declining market shares, affected unions began to modify traditional wage formulas and to experiment with alternate approaches to wage administration in an effort to lower costs. Which modifications in recently negotiated contracts are likely to be enduring features of union settlements during the remainder of the 1980s? What are the implications for union wage behavior?

If the only change in union wage determination were that workers did not recoup traditional wage adjustments that were forgone, then the moderation in wage inflation would be transitory. Wage *levels* would be indefinitely lower than they would have been without the recent wage cuts and freezes, but future wage *changes* would be indistinguishable from those in the past; that is, the past relationship between union wage behavior and its basic determinants—inflation and unemployment—would re-emerge as modified contracts expire. There are some indications, however, that the structural upheaval in many unionized markets has redirected the attention of union workers to the long-run adverse consequences that higher labor costs have for employment—a development that could presage longlasting changes in traditional union wage practices.

One fundamental change could be the scaling back of annual improvement factors. The absence of this factor from so many contracts during the past several years suggests that workers no longer automatically expect real wage improvements of 3 percent annually and will accept more modest goals in order to preserve jobs. Other joint efforts by labor and management to curb costs can be seen in recent contract provisions that diminish the economic impact of published wage scales. Such cost-saving provisions include two-tier wage systems under which new hires are paid less than incumbent employees for doing the same job, measures to hold down the rapid rise in benefit costs, and the elimination of costly work rules.

A survey by the Bureau of National Affairs found that nearly 6 percent of the 1,800 nonconstruction agreements reached between January and July 1984 specified some sort of dual pay plan. The potential savings from lower pay for new hires will vary depending on the size of the wage differential, on labor turnover rates, and on the extent to which new hires remain at the lower pay scales. Some observers of industrial relations fear that two-tier schemes could affect morale and productivity adversely if they create animosity between new hires and incumbents. Perhaps for that reason, many of these plans are temporary or graduated systems that allow new employees to progress to top-tier or regular wage scales over a specified period of time.

Negotiators also have sought to curtail the rapid rise in benefit costs, particularly the costs of medical plans. Union contract provisions covering medical plans often are specified in terms of benefit coverage rather than benefit costs. As medical costs rose, they were absorbed automatically by employers in addition to any negotiated improvements in benefit coverage. To curb rising costs, negotiators have turned to such measures as employee-paid deductibles and so-called cafeteria plans, under which employees are offered a choice of medical plans varying in cost and coverage while employers pay for a fixed dollar amount of their cost. These provisions are meant to encourage workers to avoid unnecessary medical expenditures and excessive insurance coverage. Improvements in benefits also have been scaled back or eliminated, and in some contracts a portion of COLAs has been diverted to help cover benefit costs.

A potentially more far-reaching change may be found in union agreements to lift work rules that have evolved over the past five decades. There is a growing consensus that many contractural rules governing the performance of work are no longer appropriate, particularly for industries faced with rapid technological change or increased competition.

Two major types of work-rule changes are being negotiated. One type leaves the existing organization of work intact but makes it more efficient. Examples include allowing management greater flexibility in scheduling work, relaxing the use of seniority in job assignments, and reducing the number of separate job classifications by combining duties and eliminating superfluous jobs. Generally, work-rule changes of this type give only a one-time boost to the level of productivity, unless they signal an ongoing effort to increase flexibility in the workplace. More fundamental changes involve revamping the organization of work entirely. An example is the introduction of team work, whereby workers learn all of the jobs in their work areas rather than perform narrow job functions, the usual practice. These developments may mark an emerging trend away from the traditionally adversarial atmosphere of U.S. labor-management relations toward a more cooperative framework with a long-term commitment to enhancing productivity.

Other innovations negotiated recently include profit-sharing arrangements and new job security provisions. Both of these innovations may be viewed as evidence of the new emphasis that unions are placing on preserving jobs. Because profits are heavily influenced by cyclical fluctuations in demand, profit-sharing plans tend to make labor compensation more sensitive to the ups and downs of the business cycle. Greater flexibility in compensation and prices could tend to smooth out cyclical fluctuations in sales, production, and employment. More stable employment in turn could reduce the costs of job security provisions such as lifetime employment guarantees or income maintenance plans for workers who are laid off because of plant closings. Over the longer term, preserving jobs will depend on remaining competitive; so managements often have offered new job security provisions in return for union commitments to negotiate improvements in productivity.

Whether profit-sharing plans will have a major influence on the cyclical behavior of union wages depends on (1) the proportion of the union workforce covered by profit sharing; (2) the size of bonuses as a share of total compensation; and (3) the extent to which bonuses replace other features of union settlements such as guaranteed wage increases and COLAs, which contributed to wage inertia in the past. Although the number of plans indexing compensation for union workers to company performance has increased sharply since 1980, overall coverage under these plans is still fairly low. Only about 10 percent of the workers in large bargaining units were covered by profit-sharing plans as of late 1983. Moreover, the size of bonuses under existing plans has yet to become a substantial proportion of total compensation. Thus, unless more unionized industries adopt profit-sharing plans and unions continue to accept bonuses in lieu of guaranteed wage increases, the impact of such plans on the cyclical behavior of aggregate union wages will be limited.

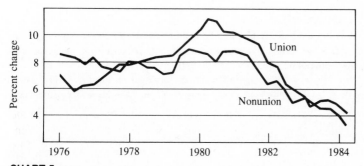

CHART 5
Wage Changes. Change from four quarters earlier. (Source: *Employment Cost Index, Bureau of Labor Statistics.*)

Although unions and management may continue to experiment with alternative forms of wage administration, there is no evidence of either a permanent move toward shorter contracts or a willingness to abandon COLA clauses. A recent survey found that management would strongly oppose any legal restrictions on the duration of collective bargaining agreements. The disadvantages of short-term contracts cited by management include an increase in the time and money spent on negotiations, an increase in the incidence of strikes, and adverse consequences on employee morale and productivity. Some of these objections may not be warranted, but it is clear that U.S. employers still feel that multiyear contracts are extremely important to maintaining stability in labor-management relations. At the same time, unions have been very reluctant to eliminate COLA provisions, even during a period of duress. Thus wage changes under multiyear agreements probably will remain highly sensitive to inflation.

Nevertheless, the secular developments that led to the unprecedented wave of wage cuts and freezes recently may keep downward pressure on union wage changes. Apart from a few cases of steep wage cuts, recent modifications to traditional wage formulas have not yet substantially narrowed labor cost disadvantages. During the past two years, the rise in union wages on balance has averaged only $1/2$ to 1 percentage point less than the rise in nonunion wages. That compares with a widening of the overall union–nonunion wage differential of perhaps 10 percentage points during the 1970s (chart 5). Given remaining cost disadvantages, the highly competitive conditions in many product markets are likely to persist. In unionized markets subject to foreign competition, domestic firms still have incentives to shift production abroad. In other unionized industries, recent inroads by nonunion firms have reduced the ability of unions to maintain wage premiums for their members. Barring any concerted actions to raise protectionist barriers or toward the reimposition of regulation, which merely would postpone market adjustments, these factors imply a sustained moderation in the rise of union labor costs in the years ahead and perhaps some reversal of the widening in union–nonunion wage differentials that took place during the 1970s.

QUESTIONS FOR DISCUSSION

1 What is a COLA? Why did the percentage of union contracts with COLA provisions increase dramatically during the 1970s? How did the existence of COLA provisions increase wage responsiveness to macroeconomic conditions in the early 1980s?

2 In what ways were "traditional" wage-setting practices modified during the 1980s? Under what conditions were firms or industries most likely to experience large departures from traditional wage-setting? Were wage agreements in the 1980s sensitive to unemployment or the threat of unemployment?

3 Unionized workers experienced more severe wage cuts than nonunionized workers during the recent period. What explanations does the author advance for this? What effect did the fact that unions are more prevalent in manufacturing, as opposed to service, industries have on the relative performance of union wages?

4 Union decisions are typically controlled by the more senior workers, who are the last to be laid off during bad times. According to the author, what possible implications does this fact have for the responsiveness of union wages to unemployment in severe recessions versus the responsiveness of wages to unemployment in milder recessions?

5 What roles have foreign competition, the presence of a large nonunion sector, and deregulation played in the recent evolution of union wages?

6 The article reports that some unions, in order to avoid layoffs, are including profit sharing plans (in which workers take part of their pay in the form of a fixed share of company profits) in their contracts. Why does profit sharing tend to stabilize employment over the cycle? (*Hint:* What happens to labor costs during a recession under profit sharing?) [For more on profit sharing, see Martin Weitzman, *The Share Economy* (Cambridge: Harvard, 1984).]

WHAT IS WRONG WITH THE WEST EUROPEAN ECONOMIES?

Assar Lindbeck*

It is well known that the drastic deterioration in the performance of the Western economies since the mid-1970s has been more pronounced in Western Europe than in the United States.[1] Growth in both output and labour productivity has dropped more in Western Europe than in the United States.[2] Moreover, contrary to previous experience, unemployment since about 1983 has been higher in Western Europe than in the United States.

When trying to assess the long-term outlook for the countries of Western Europe, it is important to understand the factors behind this deterioration in economic performance. For that purpose it is useful to make a distinction between three different,

Assar Lindbeck, "What Is Wrong with the West European Economies?" *The World Economy,* June 1985, pp. 153–170. Reprinted by permission.

*Professor of International Economics, and Director of the Institute for International Economic Studies, University of Stockholm, Sweden; author of *A Study in Monetary Analysis* (1963), *Swedish Economic Policy* (1975) and *Inflation: Global, International and National Aspects* (1980). This article is a revised version of the Finlay Lecture which Professor Lindbeck delivered at University College, Dublin, on 9 November 1984.

[1]In preparing this article, the author is grateful to Karl-Gustav Hansson for research assistance.

[2]For instance, while the rates of GDP growth in Western Europe (weighted average) dropped from 4.7 per cent in the period 1960–73 to 1.8 per cent in 1973–84, the corresponding drop in the United States was from 4.0 to 2.4 per cent. Moreover, while the rate of GDP growth *per employed person* dropped from 4.3 to 1.9 per cent in Western Europe between the periods 1960–73 and 1973–84, the corresponding fall in the United States was from 2.0 to 1.4 per cent. (These figures are from sources of the Organisation for Economic Cooperation and Development, as are other figures in the article, unless otherwise stated.) The conclusion of a larger drop in growth in labour productivity in Western Europe than in the United States seems to hold (in absolute terms) also if the figures are adjusted for differences in capacity utilisation. See Robert J. Gordon, 'Wage-price Dynamics and the Natural Rate of Unemployment in Europe, Japan and North America', mimeograph, Centre for Economic Policy Research, London, March 1985.

although complementary, explanations of what has gone wrong with the West European economies.

1 The most obvious factor is perhaps the *specific economic shocks* of the early 1970s—not only the dramatic oil-price hikes but also the large increases in nominal wage costs in Western Europe around 1970 and 1975. On both occasions, these increases in wage costs were accompanied by increases in the *real* wage costs—that is, the so-called 'product wage rates'—relative to labour productivity, creating the notorious 'real wage gap' in Western Europe. The increases in product wages around 1975 occurred in a situation when in fact a reduction was required to protect the profitability of production, employment and investment, *inter alia* because of the oil-price increases and the slowdown of productivity growth.

To these disturbances were then added various *stabilisation-policy shocks,* in particular when governments finally refused to accommodate fully the cost shocks, in the sense that governments started to fight the inflationary consequences of these shocks by way of restrictive—that is, demand-reducing—economic policy, the inevitable consequence being a fall in capacity utilisation and hence a further rise in unemployment. This meant that so-called 'Keynesian' unemployment, due to deficient aggregate demand, was added to the 'classical' unemployment which had arisen in the 1970s as a result of the combination of drastic increases in real energy prices and drastic increases in product wage rates. In some countries, there was a reduction of foreign demand for domestic output, for prices increased more than in competing nations. (Whether this should be called 'classical' or 'Keynesian' unemployment is a moot question.)

The prolonged fall in profitability and capacity utilisation had long-lasting effects on growth in both output and productivity, due to the negative effects on capital formation. For instance, in Western Europe the share of investment in gross national product (GNP) has fallen from 24.7 per cent of GNP in the period 1965–74 to 19.7 per cent in 1981–84. These consequences for investment suggest that the negative 'scale effect' on capital accumulation of higher product wage rates (via a reduction in the rate of return on capital) and of lower capacity utilisation, *in the aggregate,* have dominated the positive substitution effect on capital of the higher price of labour relative to capital.

If these shocks had been the only reasons for the deterioration in the economic performance of the Western economies, one could perhaps be confident that a recovery would take place when the shocks had worked themselves out of the economic system, even though the policy failures of the last decade have left a legacy for the near future in terms of high unemployment and a smaller capital stock than otherwise.

2 But there are other, and more profound, reasons for the deterioration in economic performance. One such reason is the *gradual and inevitable subsidence of a number of exceptional circumstances for economic growth* in the 1950s and 1960s: (i) the large gains from reallocation associated with the rapid outflow of labour from agriculture, where a large reservoir of labour was available after World War II; (ii) the once-and-for-all increase in output due to the reconstruction after the war as well as the gains from reallocation arising from the lifting of war regulations and the liberalisation of international trade in the 1950s and 1960s; and (iii) the terms-of-trade improvements due to a downward trend of real prices of imported energy until 1973.

These favourable factors were particularly important for Western Europe, where the reserves of labour in agriculture were especially large, where the potential gains from increased trade were substantial—because of the small size of the domestic markets—and where large amounts of energy were imported. Like Japan, the countries of Western Europe could also exploit the possibility of 'catching up' with American technological levels, which was facilitated by heavy investment in physical and human capital. Indeed, while the share of investment in GNP in Western Europe was about 25 per cent in 1965–74, it was only about 19 per cent in the United States.

Together with the previously mentioned shocks, the subsidence of these exceptional factors takes us a long way in explaining the fall in growth of both output and productivity since the mid-1970s.[3]

3 It will also be argued, however, that there is another important set of factors behind the recent unsatisfactory performance of the West European economies, namely a long-term *gradual deterioration in the functioning of some basic mechanisms of these economies*. The two most obvious factors are perhaps (i) increased costs and inflexibilities in labour markets due to higher and, highly-distorting, taxes as well as more detailed regulations of employment and activities with environmental consequences *and* (ii) the increased inability of both real and relative wage rates to equilibrate various parts of the labour market and to adjust to new circumstances.

Behind the high, and often highly-distorting, taxes in Western Europe lies a rapid increase in public spending relative to GNP, as well as attempted redistributions of incomes; that is, policies which voters and members of labour unions have strongly endorsed. For instance, in Western Europe the ratio of public expenditures (including transfers) to GNP increased from about 30 per cent in 1973 to about 51 per cent in 1984. The corresponding increase in the United States was from 31 per cent to 36 per cent. (In the most 'advanced' welfare states in Western Europe, such as Sweden, Norway, Denmark and the Netherlands, the figure was over 60 per cent in 1984.)

I would argue, however, that the gradual deterioration in economic performance was also a consequence of a more 'subtle' process: (iii) The previous success of the full-employment policy to some extent carried the seeds of its own destruction. What I mean is that wage and price formation gradually became more inflationary, for labour unions and firms started to believe that they could not—at least not collectively—price themselves out of the market since it was the government, rather than the parties in wage negotiations, which had the responsibility for full employment. Previously perceived limits to wage and price increases were exceeded more and more. As a result, governments were later forced to 'clamp down' on an ever-faster rate of inflation—a policy shift which was greatly speeded up by the inflationary effects of the earlier-mentioned cost shocks. The consequence was that governments, in order to squeeze out inflation, destroyed the guarantees of full employment which they had earlier given electorates.

In other words, at first, the guarantee of full employment contributed to growth in investment and output by creating confidence in high capacity utilisation. But when,

---

[3]For an attempt to quantify the importance of these factors behind the slowdown in productivity growth, see Assar Lindbeck, 'The Recent Slowdown of Productivity Growth', *Economic Journal*, March 1983.

later on, people adjusted not only spending behaviour but also price and wage behaviour to these expectations, governments eventually felt forced to crack down on high and rising inflation and hence to break the confidence which they had created in the first place by the full-employment 'guarantees'.

A problem with the hypothesis of a *gradual* deterioration in the basic mechanisms of the West European economies is that the increase in unemployment, and the slow-down of output and productivity growth, occurred quite *abruptly* during the 1970s. But the point is that, as long as the requirements for rapid adjustments in the allocation of resources were not large (perhaps apart from the contraction of agriculture), existing rigidities did not pose severe problems. And, as long as the economy was not exposed to drastic supply shocks, downward rigidities in real wage rates did not create severe unemployment problems, for firms could afford to 'hoard' labour during short recessions. But when abrupt changes in relative costs and international competition required a large and rapid reallocation of resources, the rigidities started to become a severe disadvantage to the West European economies. And when a drastic drop occurred in productivity growth, and strong inflationary cost impulses emerged, the demand for compensation from employees not only accentuated inflation; it also created a severe threat to the opportunities for employment.

FUTURE ECONOMIC POSSIBILITIES FOR WESTERN EUROPE

What, then, are the future possibilities and problems for the West European economies? And how do they compare with those for the American economy? Only two main aspects of these questions will be discussed: (i) unemployment and (ii) productivity growth. As shall be seen, the explanations for both problems partly coincide, although an economy which is able to absorb a rapidly expanding labour force, without a large increase in the rate of capital accumulation, has to accept a more modest growth in labour productivity than has an economy with a stagnant labour force.

Unemployment

The first prerequisite to achieve low levels of unemployment is a mitigation of the inflationary bias in the West European economies, in particular of *wage formation*. Otherwise restrictive unemployment-creating policies will be regarded as necessary from time to time. At least four types of reform relating to the system of wage formation may therefore be worth considering.

1 One possibility is to introduce new types of wage contracts, for instance with bonus systems. The purpose would be to stop the present practice of trying 'to share the pie before it is baked'—a practice which, in a world of uncertainty about the future path of real value added, often has the effect of making the 'pie' shrink due to reduced profitability. In more concrete terms, low wage contracts at the beginning of a year could be combined with variable bonus payments at the end of the year. In other words, the size of the wage increases would be contingent on the *actual* increase in value added during the year rather than the increase that was *expected* at the beginning of the year. Such bonus systems may also be a way of making the marginal cost of labour lower than the average remuneration (including bonus), so bringing about a reduction in the average remuneration of labour when the labour force of a firm expands.[4] Thus bonus systems would be expected both to prevent 'accidental' over-shootings of real wage rates and to make it possible to operate the economy systematically at lower levels of unemployment than today.

2 A further step in the direction of *ex post* profit sharing would be to launch systems of individual employee ownership which may also increase the tolerance of profits among individual employees.

3 But labour unions and firms, in particular, have to understand that in the long run a strong inflationary bias in wage formation is a threat to high capacity utilisation and full employment. Thus the idea would be to make the agents of wage bargaining take a greater responsibility for the level of employment. A way of helping to bring about such understanding and responsibility might be declarations by the government that it is not willing to accommodate large increases in wages by means of an expansion of nominal aggregate demand and the money stock—or by means of exchange-rate depreciations in countries with fixed rates of exchange. The purpose of such declarations would *not* be to create more unemployment, but to prevent rates of inflation becoming so high that, in the end, governments are forced to pursue a policy which does, indeed, generate heavy unemployment.

Clearly there are severe 'credibility problems' associated with such announcements, for it is tempting for a government, in spite of earlier announcements about a non-accommodating strategy, nevertheless to accommodate *after* sizeable increases in wages have actually occurred, not only to mitigate social problems but also to avoid being blamed for the increase in unemployment. This credibility problem is accentuated by the tendencies of opposition parties to blame governments merely for not providing enough of such accommodation. The credibility of non-accommodating strategies could perhaps be enhanced for small countries if formal agreements were made between leading political parties to tie the rate of exchange to a large 'non-inflationary' country or to a basket of currencies. Indeed, that was a usual defence of the old Bretton Woods system.

Another obvious problem with announced non-accommodating strategies is that, while aggressive policies by labour unions may be pursued by employees with relatively safe jobs, for instance due to seniority or jobs in the public sector, the consequences of a non-accommodating policy could hit, in particular, private employees without much seniority. Such a policy could also be especially damaging to 'outsiders' like people already unemployed and new entrants into the labour force. This consequence is, indeed, difficult to avoid, although greater flexibility in relative wage rates would mitigate the problem. Government policies designed to give the 'outsider' better training, as well as to remove various privileges for labour unions, may also reduce the problem. Moreover, to the extent that firms close down entire plants rather than reduce the labour force in existing plants, the seniority status often does not make much difference.

[4] See Martin Weitzman, *The Share Economy* (Cambridge, Massachusetts: Harvard University Press, 1984).

4 A further method of creating incentives among labour unions to show wage constraint may be to allow members of specific unions to finance the system of unemployment insurance to a larger extent than at present. In principle, this would make it more costly for them to raise wage rates excessively relative to growth in labour productivity. There are many difficulties connected with a reform like this, perhaps the most severe one being strong opposition among unions. There would also be consequences for income distribution, to the disadvantage of employees in industries with large cyclical instability as well as in declining ones, although such consequences may vary well be rational from the point of view of efficiency in the allocation of resources.

A second prerequisite for a return to low levels of unemployment in Western Europe is more *flexibility of real and relative wages*—in the sense that the product wage rate adjusts more smoothly in accordance with market-clearing requirements in various parts of the labour market. The problem is not that real and relative wages are 'fixed' in Western Europe, but rather that they sometimes change in the 'wrong' directions (as in several countries in 1974–76), while at other times they adjust too slowly in the 'right' direction. It would seem that, in this respect, the economic system functions much better in the United States than in Western Europe. In particular, it is striking to note that since 1973 more than 20 million new jobs have been created in the United States, while there has been a virtual stagnation in Western Europe. It is also interesting to note that the average period of unemployment is much longer in Western Europe than in the United States where unemployment probably 'rotates' among a somewhat larger fraction of the labour force than in Western Europe.[5] The better performance of the American economy than the West European ones is reflected in this ability not only to absorb an increasing labour force but also to recover from recessions and to shift resources—labour as well as capital—to expanding industries.

It may be argued that, for given employees, 'rotating unemployment' is associated with smaller social problems than is 'permanent unemployment'. It is also tempting to suggest that rotating unemployment implies that more people are likely to be aware of the risks of unemployment than in a system with permanent unemployment among largely the same group of people. It may therefore be hypothesised that rotating unemployment keeps down the rate of increase in nominal wages more than does permanent unemployment.

It has proved difficult to establish conclusively, by econometric methods, that there is a 'causal' relationship between the product wage rate and the level of unemployment. In my opinion, however, this difficulty reflects the limitations of 'mechanical' statistical techniques in economic analysis rather than the absence of such a relationship in the real world. Theoretical considerations, common sense and careful observations of

[5]According to Michel Albert and R. J. Ball, *Towards European Recovery in the 1980s*, Working Document No. 31 (Strasbourg: European Parliament, 1983), the periods of unemployment are six times as long in the countries of the European Community than in the United States. Moreover, while people who have been unemployed for over a year accounted for 40 per cent of total unemployment in Western Europe in 1983 (as compared with 27 per cent in 1979), the corresponding figure for North America was 13 per cent (4 per cent in 1979). See *OECD Employment Outlook* (Paris: OECD Secretariat, 1984) p. 9.

events in individual countries all suggest that such a relationship does exist in the real world.

For instance, during the period 1961–81 growth in output was almost the same in the United States and the European Community, namely about 3.5 per cent a year. But, while employment grew by about 2 per cent a year in the United States, it was basically constant in the Community. At the same time, the capital stock seems to have been increasing much faster in the Community than in the United States: 4.5 per cent a year in the Community as compared with 1 per cent in the United States. It is natural to hypothesise that this difference between the United States and the Community in the development of employment and the capital stock was largely a result of the different paths of the costs of labour relative to capital. While real labour costs per man-year increased by 3.5 per cent a year in the Community, they did not rise by more than 1.5 per cent in the United States. While labour costs relative to the return on capital increased by 1.8 per cent a year in the Community, the comparable statistic was zero in the United States.[6]

Thus substitution between capital and labour was stimulated less in the United States than in Western Europe. While this factor has certainly implied a drag on growth in labour productivity in the United States, it helped the American economy to absorb the increased supply of labour.

Less is known about what has happened to the structure of *relative* wage rates in Western Europe as compared with the United States. There is evidence, however, that the overall dispersion in wages is much greater in the United States and that it widened during the 1970s in the United States (as well as in Japan), while it contracted in Western Europe.[7] It is conceivable, perhaps even likely, that the low and falling frequency of unionisation in the United States, relative to Western Europe, is a partial explanation for this difference in wage formation between the two areas.

The disadvantages for Western Europe of not adjusting real and relative wage rates to demand and supply for labour is accentuated today by the more rapid rate of growth of the potential labour force during the 1980s than in the 1960s and 1970s. The reason is to be found not only in demographic factors; the desired participation in the labour force of married women is also likely to have increased recently in a number of West European countries.

In popular discussions, an additional reason for unemployment is often singled out, namely technological advances. The phantom of technological unemployment, how-

---

[6]The figures are from Michael Emerson, *Thema,* Economic and Financial Papers (Turin: Sanpaolo Bank di Torino, 1985). Moreover, while the product wage rate during the period 1971–79 rose by some ten percentage points more than growth in labour productivity in Western Europe, it fell by about two percentage points relative to growth in labour productivity in the United States (the entire economy). See Gordon, *op. cit.;* Jeffrey Sachs, 'Real Wages and Unemployment in the OECD Countries', *Brookings Papers on Economic Activity,* Vol 14, No. 1, 1983; and Albert and Ball, *op. cit.* Also see Manfred Wegner, *The Employment Miracle in the United States and Stagnating Employment in the European Community: a Tentative Explanation,* Economic Paper No. 17 (Brussels: Commission of the European Community, 1983).

[7]*Labour Market Flexibility,* Report prepared by Working Party No. 1 of the Economic Policy Committee (Paris: OECD Secretariat, 1985). Also see *Employment and Earnings,* Bureau of Labor Statistics, United States Department of Labor, Washington, December 1984; and *Wages and Total Labour Costs for Workers: International Survey, 1972–1982* (Stockholm: Swedish Employers Association, 1984).

ever, is not convincing if it is interpreted as something more long-term, and 'inevitable', than distortions of relative factor prices, as discussed above. There are really no 'technological' limits to increased employment. Historically, productivity growth through technological advances has expanded output rather than reduced employment. On the other hand, to experience such a favourable outcome in the future as well certainly depends on a number of conditions relating to the functions of both economic policies and the market system. In particular, expansion of real demand in line with productivity growth has to be 'allowed' by the economic policy authorities; and (approximately) equilibrating real and relative wage rates have to be accepted by employers, labour unions and governments. Although there has recently been considerable moderation in real wages in several countries of Western Europe (at least in the manufacturing sector),[8] some of these countries certainly have a long way to go to achieve real wage rates that are consistent with 'reasonable' profit levels. It is my belief that several West European countries have an even longer way to go to achieve *relative* wage rates which reflect the distribution of demand and supply for labour in various sub-markets.

But even if real and relative wage rates in Western Europe were to adjust better to market conditions in the future than in the past, it might be difficult to return to the levels of profitability that were usual in the 1950s and 1960s. One reason is that the capital-intensive economies of today would be expected to generate lower rates of return on capital (along equilibrium paths) than did the less capital-intensive economies of the 1950s and 1960s.[9] Another reason is that the increased inter-dependence of national economies has resulted in stiffer competition and hence flatter demand curves for firms which, as a consequence, would be expected to result in lower profit margins.

Flexibility of relative wage rates is probably of particular importance for the services sector where, as a rule, relative wage rates are higher and less flexible in Western Europe than in the United States, especially for labour with modest skills.[10] Against this background, it is interesting to note that about 70 per cent of the huge increase in employment in the United States during the last decade has taken place in 'private services', as compared with 15 per cent each in manufacturing industry and government. In addition, the higher marginal rates of tax in many countries of Western Europe than in the United States are unfavourable for an expansion of private services (outside the 'underground' economy), for the taxes stimulate households to undertake 'do-it-yourself' work rather than to purchase services in the open market. Moreover, in some West European countries, in particular in north-western Europe, the public sector has

[8]Gordon, *op. cit.*

[9]Profit shares (of value added) will fall during a process of substitution between labour and capital if the elasticity of substitution is smaller than unity without this development reflecting disequilibria of relative factor prices.

[10]See Wegner, *op. cit.* According to this paper, relative wage rates in the United States are particularly low in industries like hotels, retail trade, personal services, amusement and recreation, educational services and some 'social' services. Moreover, while real labour costs outside manufacturing seem to have increased by about 19 per cent in the four major West European countries in the period 1973–81, they seem to have *declined* by 3 per cent in the United States (wage cost deflated by output prices). The difference in change of real wage costs between Western Europe and the United States seems to have been smaller in manufacturing. See *OECD Economic Outlook,* OECD Secretariat, Paris, July 1984, p. 45.

monopolised service production to a large extent, which makes it difficult for private services to flourish.

A third prerequisite for a return to full employment in Western Europe is less regulation of *the hiring and firing of labour*. Hiring currently represents a heavy investment in several countries of Western Europe due to the expense and difficulties of laying off redundant or inappropriate labour. Obviously this reduces the willingness of firms to employ workers, although the quantitative importance of this factor is difficult to determine. Moreover, the firing of labour, like the closing down of plants, is important for the creation of new and highly-paid jobs in the long run. The reason is that the old production structures often stand in the way of new ones. In addition, reallocations of the factors of production are particularly important today in order for economies to adjust to the build-up of production and export capacity in certain manufacturing industries in the so-called newly industrialising countries.

Besides the unemployment-creating effects of inappropriate real and relative wage rates, and of high costs of hiring and firing, it is also obvious that the restrictive fiscal policies during the first half of the 1980s have been a major reason for the drastic increase in unemployment in Western Europe. By contrast to the United States there are no asserted 'supply-siders' that pursue expansionary Keynesian demand-management policies in Western Europe. The rather restrictive fiscal policies in Western Europe presumably reflect a fear of inflation and a belief that budget deficits should be kept down. Indeed, the more flexible supply side in the United States than in Western Europe makes Keynesian demand-management policies more effective in the United States than in Western Europe. Probably many governments also believe that the individual countries in Western Europe are too small to reflate alone. It is therefore difficult to escape the conclusion that a major reduction of unemployment in Western Europe today could be brought about by means of a joint fiscal stimulus of the West European governments, although not without risks of higher inflation again.

Productivity Growth

If the explanations for the slowdown of productivity growth mentioned at the beginning of the article make sense, it is not likely that the rate of productivity growth in Western Europe will be as high in the future as it was during the 1950s and 1960s. But it could certainly be greater than in the 1980s, for new 'specific shocks' of the same magnitude as in the 1970s are probably not likely to occur.

The United States even has a chance of increasing its productivity growth relative to that of the 1950s and 1960s. The reason is that (total) productivity growth in the country during the 1950s and 1960s was restrained by the expansion of *the technological frontier,* while Western Europe could rely more on technological 'catching up'. Now, when the technology gap is smaller, and when the technological frontier is being pushed out by research and development in many countries, the frontier will probably move faster than before.

Some of the main obstacles to productivity growth in Western Europe have already been specified: (i) low factor mobility and rigidity of real and relative factor prices; (ii) government regulation of production, investment and employment; and (iii) distortions of markets and disincentives for work, saving, investment and entrepreneurship—including, occasionally, low profitability, high and highly-distorting marginal rates of tax and strongly-selective subsidies (these last euphemistically called 'industrial policy'). In addition, several countries in Western Europe suffer from highly *unstable* rules concerning the tax systems and regulations which makes the 'pay-off functions' for individuals and firms very uncertain. If individuals wake up every morning to find that what they did yesterday was wrong because the 'rules of the game' were changed during the night, individual agents are certainly not encouraged to make long-term commitments in the official production system.

It is clearly important that these problems should be removed if the Europeans want to return to a considerably more successful economic performance than during the 1970s. Another, probably important, handicap for Western Europe is that, unlike the United States, it does not have a large and integrated capital market.

In order to avoid painting too idyllic a picture of the United States, it should be mentioned that the American economy is also plagued by severe problems, such as low aggregate saving, a problem which has been aggravated recently by the large budget deficit. It is also a commonplace that the high real rates of interest in the United States, and the high rate of exchange of the dollar since 1982–1983, seriously threaten the country's economic growth, in particular in the tradeable sector, where in the mid-1980s a large 'wage gap' has emerged which certainly threatens production, investment and employment in that sector. It would seem that the wage gap in manufacturing in the United States became even *larger* than in Western Europe from about 1983, partly due to the slowdown of nominal-wage increases in Western Europe, associated with heavy unemployment, and partly due to the appreciation of the dollar. On the other hand, this means that it is not obvious that the *mechanisms* which in the 1970s generated huge wage gaps in Western Europe, relative to the United States, have disappeared permanently; the gap may re-emerge and widen again if unemployment falls in Western Europe and the dollar's rate of exchange goes down.

Thus an appreciation of the dollar seems to pose a threat to the tradeable sector in the United States similar to that posed by the nominal-wage explosions to the production activities in several countries of Western Europe. Moreover, if the huge current-account deficit, partly caused by the high rate of exchange of the dollar, continues during the next few decades in the United States, the widening gap between gross domestic product (GDP) and gross national income will certainly damage the standards of living of future generations.

Moreover, the United States has a number of 'ailing' industries with highly distorted relative wages, the automobile and steel industries being perhaps the best-known examples. Casual observation also suggests that there are problems with product quality in these industries, as well as in industries like textiles.

A difference between the United States and Western Europe, though, is that in the former there are more expanding industries around the ailing ones—not just high-tech manufacturing but also low-tech services. Moreover, the expected slower growth of the number of new entrants in the American labour market in the coming decade, than in the past, is favourable for productivity growth—through substitution between capital and labour as well as through a more experienced labour force.

INFLUENCE OF THE UNITED STATES ON WESTERN EUROPE

It has been argued above that the economic problems of Western Europe are firmly embedded in its economic and political structure. This point is in some conflict with prevalent complaints in Western Europe to the effect that its economic problems are to a considerable extent caused by the economic policy of the United States—in particular the high real rates of interest, which are often claimed to be a consequence mainly of the Federal budget deficit. It is reasonable, however, to consider the high real rates of interest in the world economy in the mid-1980s to be a result not only of the large structural budget deficit in the United States but also of the disappearance of the huge savings of the members of the Organisation of Petroleum Exporting Countries (OPEC). Likewise, the low real rates of interest in the world economy in the 1970s may be viewed as a consequence of a high propensity to save in the world economy after the international redistributions of income to the high-saving OPEC countries associated with the oil-price hikes.

Certainly this is not the *only* reason for high real rates of interest now. Recorded real rates of interest (as measured by current rather than expected inflation) always tend to be high immediately after periods of rapid inflation, due partly to long-term loan contracts, partly to great uncertainty about the expected rate of inflation and partly to expectations which lag the actual rate of inflation. Thus, in a short-term perspective, real rates of interest would be expected to come down somewhat when the memory of the high and wildly fluctuating rates of inflation in the late 1970s and early 1980s recedes. In a more long-run perspective, however, the remedy for high real rates of interest could only be lower (structural) budget deficits or higher household and business propensities to save in the world economy relative to real propensities to invest. The theory behind these assertions is that real rates of interest are determined by real propensities to save and real propensities to invest in the world economy and not by the monetary policy of national central banks, which then, in a medium-term and long-term perspective, mainly influences the rate of inflation and nominal rates of interest.

There is a tendency among economists today to adjust the *statistics* of the budget deficits by both 'inflation accounting' and cyclical adjustments, which often means that the measured deficits tend to disappear, at least in Western Europe. It is certainly useful to make such adjustments when one is interested in the development of the wealth position of a government. But it is important to point out that the deficits which are thus 'removed' from the public sector 'pop up', instead, in the statistics for the private sector. The *aggregate* saving ratio is not influenced by such recalculations (to the extent that the debt is domestically held).

The main point to be stressed in this context, however, is that West European governments, and economic commentators, strongly exaggerate the negative effects on their economies of the budget deficit in the United States. First of all, high real rates of interest did not stop the cyclical business upswing in the United States in the 1983–84 period, even though the United States, too, is hurt by high rates of interest. Although one reason may be that the deductibility of rates of interest is more liberal in the United States than in most countries of Western Europe, I would suggest that the main reason is that in a situation of low capacity utilisation it is not the capital cost but rather the existence of large excess capacity which is the most significant constraint on investment. More importantly, it is not reasonable to analyse the effects of high rates of interest in the United States, or other parts of the world economy, on business conditions *without also analysing other effects of the policies which have resulted in the high rates of interest*. And these policies, more specifically the expansionary fiscal policies in the United States, have certainly increased the demand for products not only in the United States but also in the rest of the world—an effect that has been accentuated by the high rate of exchange of the dollar, which is another obvious outcome of, among other factors, the large budget deficit in the United States.

Thus, in summary, the expansionary fiscal policy in the United States has created two expansionary effects and one contractive effect on Western Europe (and elsewhere). The high level of demand in the United States and the high rate of exchange of the dollar, by themselves, have stimulated economic recovery in Western Europe, while the high rates of interest, by themselves, have had the opposite effects. It is an empirical question whether it is the positive or the negative effects which dominate. It has been argued above that in deep recessions, where capacity utilisation rather than capital costs is probably the main obstacle to investment, the two *positive* effects are likely to dominate.

Thus it would seem that the attempts by politicians and economic commentators in Western Europe to blame the United States for its problems are not well founded. A cynic might say that Western Europe's only remaining superiority today is its ability to blame the rest of the world for its problems.

WHICH COUNTRIES CAN REFORM THEMSELVES?

It is difficult to predict which countries in Western Europe have the best chances of (i) removing the obstacles to cyclical recovery, (ii) achieving a drastic reduction in unemployment and (iii) restoring a rapid rate of productivity growth. Indeed, views on this important issue have to be mere speculations, which nevertheless might be worth making.

1 For instance, which countries are likely to be the most successful in reducing marginal rates of tax, in removing distortions in the tax structure and in deregulating? This is not only an issue of bourgeois *versus* social democratic governments, for many bourgeois governments have been highly interventionist and have also contributed to a rapid expansion of public spending (such as in Italy, Ireland, Belgium and Sweden) while some social democratic governments, in particular in the 1950s and 1960s, pursued very liberal economic policies and in some cases have also been careful with public spending (for instance, in Austria and Finland).

2 Another important issue in this context is whether it will be an advantage or a disadvantage in the long run to have private and public sectors that are *well organised*— as, for instance, in the Federal Republic of Germany, Sweden, Norway and Austria. A provocative speculation might be that a good organisation in the long run may be a cause of 'arteriosclerosis', for example rigidities. It is well known that innovations usually come from *outsiders*. In the long run, therefore, efficient routine administration may be an obstacle to innovation and renewal. Could it even be the case that the most successful countries in the long run will be those which are characterised by what may be called a 'functioning chaos', as in Italy, with poor administration in the public sector and, perhaps, rather chaotic conditions in some of the large firms in the private sector. The reason for the possibility of long-term success of countries like these could then be that rigid structures and policies, which might block new initiatives, would not exist. Of course, certain parts of the public sector *have* to function reasonably well—for example, the infrastructure in transport and energy and the education system. In this respect Italy certainly has problems.

A brave speculation might be that the best type of public administration is a small and efficient one, the second best a large and inefficient one which is unable to thwart individual initiatives, while the worst public administration, from the point of view of long-run economic vitality, is a large and efficient one which succeeds in its attempt to regulate private activities and initiatives. From that point of view countries like France and Sweden, with large and rather efficiently functioning public administrations, might have long-term problems concerning vitality and flexibility.

3 It might also be asked if it is advantageous for a country to have weak labour unions which do not cooperate much with firms and the government, as in the United States, or strong unions which are willing to cooperate with the government, as in Austria and, occasionally, the Federal Republic of Germany and some of the Scandinavian countries. Again, we do not really know. But loyal firm-specific labour unions, as in Japan, seem to be particularly favourable for productivity growth. Most likely, the worst alternative is strong and non-cooperative unions, as in the United Kingdom.

4 Another speculative question is whether a deteriorating economic system in terms of efficiency, like the United Kingdom, Benelux and Sweden, can be revitalised. For instance, while the deterioration in the functioning of the Swedish economy since the late 1960s has probably been accentuated by government interventions, in particular perhaps the high and strongly distorting marginal rate of tax, it is important to realise that the decline in productivity growth in the United Kingdom cannot be regarded as a consequence only, or perhaps even mainly, of government interventions and the build-up of a welfare state. The decline in the United Kingdom started much earlier, at the turn of the nineteenth century. It was really the private sector itself which lost its vitality at that time. Technological 'catching up' by other countries to British levels of technology could be an important factor behind the decline in productivity growth in Britain *relative* to other countries at the turn of the century—in the same way as productivity growth was slow in the United States, relative to Western Europe, in the 1950s and 1960s. Cultural factors, however, can hardly be excluded. It may be speculated that the decline of vitality in the British economy started when the new business class acquired the habits of the old class of rich landowners—and, indeed, married into their families!

Again, it has to be said, however, that not much is really known about the mechanisms by which a civilisation loses its previous vitality, for instance via changes in values, habits and institutions. The most pessimistic outlook is perhaps provided by Mancur Olson, of the University of Maryland.[11] His theory is that rigidities necessarily accumulate over time if there are no drastic overhauls of the institutional structures, such as by way of wars, revolutions and similar drastic events. The idea is that it takes time and stability to build up interest groups which are more interested in the zero-sum games of redistributing income to themselves than in increasing productivity; in other words, groups which believe that more is to be gained from obtaining large slices of a fixed, or even shrinking, cake than by contributing to making the cake larger.

Although, for the above reasons, it would probably be wrong to put *all* the blame for 'Euro-sclerosis' on government policies, including the welfare state, it is certainly true that government regulations, and disincentives associated with public-sector growth and the tax structure, are important reasons for the rigidities and distortions in Western Europe. Indeed, the private interest groups have been able to play their zero-sum games just by using an expanding public sector and the tax system as their basic means.

It is also true that we do not know for sure at what levels of public spending and taxes (relative to GNP) serious economic problems start to emerge. In practice, there are really no non-distorting taxes, which means that expansion of 'the tax bite' necessarily means increased distortions. My casual observation is that the problems were probably not *severe* as long as public spending was less than 40–50 per cent of GNP and inflation was low (2–4 per cent). Total public spending is now some 45–65 per cent of GNP in most countries of Western Europe, at the same time as high inflation in the late 1970s and early 1980s accentuated the distortions of the tax system, which is mainly nominalistic—that is, constructed for a non-inflationary world. But it is not the size of public spending by itself relative to GNP that creates distortions and efficiency losses; it is high, and highly-differentiated, *marginal tax wedges* between productive contributions and individual rewards. There is a rapidly expanding body of empirical research which indicates that the efficiency losses (so-called 'excess burden') of the increases in marginal rates of tax during the 1970s were quite large.[12]

CONCLUDING REMARKS

The main message of this article is that the problems of heavy unemployment and slow growth in productivity cannot be solved just by a more 'clever' use of discretionary policies of various types. Improvements in some *basic mechanisms* of the West European economies are necessary. It is not too difficult to say what types of reforms are potentially useful (i) to restore mobility in factor markets and flexibility of real and relative wage rates, (ii) to remove, or at least reduce, the inflationary bias in wage

[11]Mancur Olson, *The Rise and Fall of Nations* (New Haven: Yale University Press, 1982).

[12]See K. E. Browning, 'The Marginal Costs of Income Redistribution', *Southern Economic Journal,* July 1978, pp. 1–17; Ingemar Hansson, 'Marginal Costs of Public Funds for Different Tax Instruments and Government Expenditures', *Scandinavian Journal of Economics,* Vol. 86, No. 1, 1984, pp. 113–30; Dale Jorgenson and Kon Young Yun, 'Tax Policy and Capital Allocation', *Scandinavian Journal of Economics,* 1986 forthcoming; and J. B. Shoven, 'Applied General Equilibrium Tax Modelling', *IMF Staff Papers,* June 1983, pp. 394–420.

formation, (iii) to bring about less distortions and non-symmetries in the taxation of work, saving and asset holding, which certainly requires a reduction of marginal rates of tax, and (iv) to bring about more stable rules so that the 'pay-off functions' for individuals become more predictable than at present.

A factor underlying many of the problems is the rapid expansion of public spending and the associated increases in marginal rates of tax. It is clearly necessary to do something about this expansion. One possibility is to shift to more reliance on actu-arially fair social-insurance systems, whereby the fees become prices rather than taxes. In principle, the tax burden can also be kept down by fees on public services, which would turn some taxes into prices. Lesser ambitions to redistribute income within the middle of the distribution of income, as well as from top-income brackets, would also help to reduce marginal rates of tax. Finally, there is the possibility of allowing more private services in competition with public services, for this would not only reduce the rates of tax but also contribute to more efficiency in the production of services, which today are largely monopolised by public agencies.

By now, however, it should be realised that it is not enough to recommend policy actions to politicians. It is even more important *to suggest reforms of the mechanisms by which political decisions are undertaken.* My favoured explanation for the rapid expansion of public spending is that, while publicly-provided benefits are usually *specific,* the taxes to finance them are usually *general.* This creates a strong incentive for individual voters, and groups of voters, to accept offers from politicians of higher benefits on the assumption that the costs in terms of higher taxes are mainly paid by others. This is probably one of the principal reasons why the welfare state tends to turn into a 'free-for-all' competition for public benefits with an apparently 'limitless' expansion of public spending as a result—possibly also a shift of the burden of part of this spending to future generations via budget deficits.[13]

Against this background, let me conclude with a few examples of how political institutions and mechanisms may be modified in order to reduce the political pro-pensities for the expansion of public spending. Conceivable examples are constitutional reforms for the purpose of (i) making expenditure and tax decisions simultaneously, so that parliament is not allowed to raise public spending without, at the same time, raising taxes to finance the higher spending, (ii) requiring a qualified majority for spending and/or tax decisions, (iii) using frequent referenda, (iv) having permanently broad coalition governments and (v) introducing a more decentralised structure into the political system ('federalism').

For instance, it is likely that the requirement of a two-thirds majority for tax increases in Finland is one important reason why her public spending is a smaller percentage of GNP than in the other Nordic countries. There would still be a risk, however, that the expansion of public spending could continue, financed by increased public deficits rather than taxes. If so, some constitutional ties on borrowing or spending are perhaps also necessary; at least, some removal of public privileges in borrowing, as compared with private agents, could be considered.

[13]See Lindbeck, 'Redistribution Policy and the Expansion of the Public Sector', *Journal of Public Economics,* 1986 forthcoming.

It might also be asked why public spending is 68 per cent of GNP in Sweden but only 30 per cent in Switzerland. Do the preferences differ that much between the voters in the two countries? Or is the reason that these two democracies have different political constitutions—Switzerland being characterised by a federal structure, permanent coalition governments and frequent referenda, while Sweden is characterised by a centralised public sector, partisan governments in hard competition with an equally strong opposition and hardly any referenda?

If the answer, as I personally believe, is that differences in the political constitution play an important part here, the possibility of reducing the rate of expansion of public spending has partly to be found in reforms of the *decision rules* and hence *the constitution* in the Western democracies. Indeed, this position has been held for a long time by at least one outstanding American economist, James Buchanan, who has emphasised the importance for political decision making of 'constitutional rules'.

QUESTIONS FOR DISCUSSION

1 What shocks and long-run forces does Lindbeck blame for the increase in European unemployment during the 1970s? Which of these, if any, hit Europe harder than the United States?

2 The author alludes to the "gradual deterioration in the functioning of some basic mechanisms of [the west European] economies." What does he have in mind? According to the author, what role do European governments have in this process of deterioration?

3 The author argues that the practice of governments "guaranteeing" full employment tended to generate more and more inflation in Europe.

   a Use an aggregate demand–aggregate supply diagram to show that, if the government always uses monetary and fiscal policies to maintain full employment, there is nothing "tying down" the rate of wage and price inflation. What happens if the government then "cracks down" on high and rising inflation?

   b The author suggests that governments announce in advance that they will not "accommodate" large wage increases; but he then admits such announcements might not be "credible." Why would these announcements not be credible? If they are not credible, is any purpose served by making these announcements? (If you have read Reading 17, on policy credibility, make a tree diagram of the "game" between the policy makers and the wage-setters; show why incredible announcements won't achieve their desired goal.)

   c What actions could a government take to increase the credibility of its announcements? Do you think that European governments are currently increasing their credibility?

4 What were the average rates of growth of output, employment, and the capital stock in the United States and Europe during 1961–1981? What explanation does Lindbeck give for the United States–European difference?

5 In many European countries, government regulations make it difficult for firms to fire workers. How could such regulations be responsible for increased, rather than decreased, unemployment?

6 Lindbeck argues that recent U.S. fiscal policy has had two positive effects and one negative effect on European economic growth. List and explain these effects.

7 The article cites a hypothesis due to Mancur Olson as a possible explanation of "Eurosclerosis." What is this hypothesis? Do you think it is a plausible explanation of national or regional differences in economic vitality? (For further discussion, see the cited book by Olson, as well as R. D. Norton, "Industrial Policy and American Renewal," *Journal of Economic Literature*, March 1986, pp. 1–40.)

THE LIFE CYCLE OF WAGE AND PRICE CONTROLS

George P. Shultz
Kenneth W. Dam

One device for fighting inflation, used relatively infrequently in the United States, is the imposition of wage and price controls. Our most significant postwar experience with controls occurred when President Nixon used them from 1971 to 1974. These controls were not successful in restraining inflation, which actually *rose* significantly over the period! In this article, Shultz and Dam give an insiders' view of the political and administrative difficulties, as well as the economic problems, associated with controls.

President Nixon stated before his election and on a number of occasions thereafter his opposition to government intervention in wage and price decisions. But by late 1970 conflicting views on this subject emerged within the administration, and by August 1971 a freeze was imposed on wage and price movements, to be followed by an elaborate system of controls. Both of us were at Camp David with the President and others during that fateful weekend when his decision was made final to impose a freeze, along with other actions of great and lasting significance. And we both participated in the continuing struggle to administer the controls, once instituted. The controls experience reveals much about all dimensions of economic policy; the subject—unfortunately, in our view—is destined to have continuing practical importance.

Important segments of our society may at any time be found at almost any point on the spectrum of views about wage and price controls. Some people oppose their

George P. Shultz and Kenneth W. Dam, "The Life Cycle of Wage and Price Controls," in George P. Shultz and Kenneth W. Dam (eds.), *Economic Policy beyond the Headlines* (Stanford Alumni Association, Stanford, Calif., 1977), chap. 4, pp. 65–85. Reprinted by permission.

use in any form, whether as a formal system, a set of guidelines used informally, or any variation in between. Others think that some formal or informal incomes policy should be a permanent instrument of economic policy. Still others believe such intervention in individual wage and price decisions can occasionally be useful, even though it may not be desirable as a permanent fixture. Whatever the state of advocacy at a particular time, it will almost surely change. Even if incomes policies are not used, intense debate about their desirability will periodically become prominent in public discussion of economic policy, and the discussion itself may have an impact on the decisions of both private and public economic institutions.

In reflecting on the 1971–74 experience with wage and price controls, we shall not attempt a comprehensive discussion, either chronological or analytical. Nor shall we attempt to evaluate the costs and benefits of controls. There have already been a plethora of such efforts. Rather we shall concentrate on the dynamics of an incomes policy, a central problem in any future attempt to institute a formal or informal controls program. The problem may take the form of a question: Why is it not possible through careful advance planning to design a simple controls program that can be put in place, once and for all, to control wages and prices for the indefinite future?

Whatever one thinks of direct regulation of particular industries by the independent regulatory agencies or of indirect regulation, say, through the tax system, these kinds of regulatory programs have been much less volatile and sporadic than controls programs have been in this and other countries. Adjustments have necessarily been made in these other regulatory programs from time to time because of changes in technology and other underlying conditions, but the adjustments have usually been infrequent and have seldom altered the programs' basic operation. In contrast, a short life and frequent changes in method (called phases in the 1971–74 experience) have been a peculiar, and we believe inherent, characteristic of controls programs.

In puzzling over this central question, we have come to the conclusion that wage and price controls programs have a "life cycle" of their own. This phenomenon occurs to some extent in other regulatory areas, but controls programs appear unique in both the inevitability and the remarkable shortness of their life cycles. The controls life cycle is quite unlike cycles in the physical universe where, for example, one spring is much like another and leads inexorably through high summer to autumn and winter and then back to spring again. A controls program does not leave the economy where it was at the outset, much less at the point intended when the program was instituted. Rather, the loop itself spirals and winds to a new level, so that the cycle of controls produces a new and usually unforeseen situation. One important residue of a controls cycle, for example, is a set of fears, expectations, and conjectures about the possibility of a new cycle.

Before turning to a study of the controls life cycle, it is useful to consider four themes that come through "loud and clear" in wage and price controls. These themes help to explain the existence of the life-cycle phenomenon.

SOME PROMINENT THEMES

The first is the problem of dealing with anticipations and expectations. Although this problem is most visible prior to the start of any formal controls program, it remains a concern throughout. People always speculate about whether and when changes will be made in the rules and regulations—let alone the coverage—of the controls, and anticipations themselves have an effect on private-sector behavior in a way not always consonant with the goals of the program.

Second, it is a gross oversimplification to believe that the private sector of the economy can be subjected to a new government action or regulation and remain reasonably passive. The administration of controls must take into account at all times that the tableau to which the controls are applied is itself changed by them. Controls illustrate the continually interactive relationship between public and private actions.

Third, any new and important program, especially one so pervasive as wage and price controls, brings a new element into the advocacy system in which government policy is made. Issues formerly submerged in a specialized bureaucracy dedicated to a particular interest are thrown into a more general governmental policymaking framework and into public discussion. Interconnections that were once obscured thus emerge into public view. New considerations are brought to bear, and old ones are reweighted, often with severe policy repercussions which may even bring down the whole program. In any event, the advocacy element in the making of public policy is brought into sharp relief during the administration of wage and price controls.

Fourth, the controls life cycle demonstrates the dynamic nature of most public programs. One step leads to the next—often a misstep—until those in charge eventually find themselves nowhere near the intended destination. Thus, a sense of strategy is imperative if the momentum of tactical evolution is to be turned in a desired direction.

THE 1971 FREEZE

The life cycle of the 1971–74 controls program had its beginning in earlier actions and discussions. The jawboning and arm-twisting of the Johnson administration had been consciously put aside in the early days of the Nixon administration. The game plan was for a continuation of the bipartisan effort to cool the economy, an effort begun in mid-1968 with a tax increase and attempts to hold down spending, thereby reducing the large full-employment deficits of the fiscal 1967 and 1968 budgets. This fiscal effort to stabilize the economy—initially opposed by the expansionary policies of the Federal Reserve in the latter half of 1968 but then buttressed by the extraordinarily tight money policy throughout almost all of 1969—brought on the mild recession of 1970. The general price level was slow to respond, perhaps because of that mildness; real GNP declined only in the quarter of 1970 in which there was a protracted General Motors-United Automobile Workers strike. But the rate of increase in consumer prices did fall from a little over 6 percent in 1969 to about 5.5 percent in 1970 to 3.7 percent in the eight months of 1971 preceding wage and price controls.

That rate of inflation and the progress in bringing it down were not, however, satisfactory to the American public. The unease and impatience of the public and the increasing insistence that the government step in and "do something" were reflected in the attitudes and demands of labor and management. To be sure, the business community wanted some government leverage on the rate of increase in wages, whereas labor was concerned primarily with prices. Nevertheless, both labor and management were at least talking about—and in a great many instances clearly pushing for—some form of intervention in wage and price decisions.

Congress had earlier, as a political dare, granted the President sweeping authority to impose controls on the American economy. But as 1971 wore on, the drumbeat in Congress for a formal incomes policy became more insistent, and many within the administration privately joined Federal Reserve Board Chairman Arthur Burns, who called publicly for the President to change his course. An anticipatory response was clearly gaining momentum, with many industrial prices raised in order to beat any possible change in policy.

To grasp the political dimension of such an important economic policy decision, the reader might ask himself what he would have done if he had been the President, facing this insistent demand for direct action and possessing a broad grant of authority, especially if he had decided that politically he had no choice but to respond in some way. Widespread public discussion and congressional hearings about the form, structure, and timing of formal restraints would only add to the momentum of price increases instituted in anticipation of possible controls.

Under these circumstances, any President would be sorely tempted to impose a freeze on wages and prices. However arbitrary a freeze might be, it would readily gain public support and it would provide him with an essential breathing space—a respite from anticipatory behavior—during which a more elaborate incomes policy or controls mechanism could be designed.

A freeze would also command attention. As it happened, the debate over an incomes policy coincided with a growing realization among U.S. trading partners that the dollar was overvalued and a growing unease about the large and persistent negative balance in our international payments. By mid-July 1971, the President and his economic advisers knew that the dollar could not continue to be tied to gold at the fixed price of $35 per ounce and would have to be, in effect, devalued. However much sense this might make from the standpoint of healthy trading relationships, we also knew that it was bound to have an inflationary impact. Furthermore, the idea of "devaluation" would probably have adverse political overtones unless surrounded by other major decisions. And so, on August 15, 1971, the "New Economic Policy" was born: stimulate the economy toward faster growth, close the "gold window," impose a surcharge on imports to force a fairer deal for American products on world markets, and impose a freeze on wages and prices to deal with potential inflationary consequences.

Any such freeze, it is clear at the outset, cannot last very long. It is inherently arbitrary. In view of the complexities and the dynamism of the American economy, wages and prices cannot be frozen for any length of time without creating serious distortions. At the same time, a freeze presents an administrative nightmare. A freeze is beautifully simple, or perhaps a better word is simplistic, but it does tend to have an immediate and clear effect. People love it. As soon as discussion turns to the possible alternatives to follow the freeze, the general reaction may very well be, and certainly was in 1971, why change it?

Early in the game, therefore, it is necessary to take one's heart in one's hands and state unequivocally that the freeze will end within a very short, prescribed period of time. Ninety days was the period selected. That was the minimum time judged necessary to develop a wage and price control structure with some staffing, at least at the top. After 90 days the freeze, known as Phase I, would end and Phase II, a system of bureaucratically administered controls, would begin.

THE EFFORT TO GAIN AND MAINTAIN SUPPORT

For the subsequent controls program—let alone the original freeze—to be at all effective, it must have wide support, not only from the public generally but also more specifically from the principal parties immediately involved, especially labor, management, and farmers. A broad acceptance of the rules and a willingness to live by them, at least for the time being, must be developed. Apart from the need to design a program that is inherently fair, understandable, and workable, this point suggests the importance of certain procedural considerations.

Wide and visible consultation before the controls program itself is decided upon is essential. Once the regulation-writing process is rolling, the publication of draft regulations with opportunity for comment, coupled with a genuine willingness to change in the face of justified criticism, will help. The composition of administering boards must be arranged so that the parties can feel that their arguments will be heard attentively and, at the same time, the public will retain confidence in the integrity of the process.

The wage side of such institutional arrangements has always received special treatment. The historic pattern of developing a tripartite wage board reflects the importance of involving both labor and management in the program; such involvement is needed to obtain their input into the wage control policies and their administration and to generate acceptance of the program. Under a tripartite board, though all members are presumably acting in the public interest, the labor and management members are also expected to bring, and do bring, the point of view of their respective constituencies.

The proper and expected role of the public members on a tripartite wage board is not so clear. To some degree, they must mediate between opposing views of labor and management, which has been their typical role in the past. However, in a period of buoyant labor markets it is not at all clear that labor and management interests will diverge. It is all too typical that labor and management make joint applications in particular cases for settlements that exceed whatever standards have been set out. A strong case can therefore be made that the public members should be thought of as a genuine "third force" in the situation, not oblivious to their role of mediator, but certainly not limited to that conception of their duties. We had this "third force" idea very much in mind as appointments were made to the Pay Board in 1971. Some of the abrasiveness in the early days of the Pay Board may well have stemmed from that decision.

The activities of those to whom controls will be applied—labor and management— will also be affected by their perception of how long their freedoms will be curtailed. If they think that the controls are to last indefinitely, their natural reaction will be to dig in administratively and learn how to live within the rules while still attaining as many of their private objectives as possible. Labor will seek the maximum wage package possible under the rules. Management will seek the maximum immediate profit under the rules or at least a use of permissible costs that will buttress a firm's long-range position.

On the other hand, if a program is viewed as temporary, designed to solve an immediate and short-term problem, then the reaction may be more one of living within the spirit of the program and refraining from extensive sharpshooting at the rules. With this point in mind, we placed considerable emphasis on the transitory nature of the controls program, partly because that was what the President and his close advisers felt was proper, but also because a permanent system seemed likely to call forth a pattern of behavior sharply and undesirably different from what a temporary effort would evoke. In short, anticipations about the system have important consequences for behavior under the system, illustrating the interactive process of public policy and private reactions.

In any case, the life cycle of controls will be heavily influenced by a set of early decisions not only about what is to be done but also about how it is to be done. A primary objective in these decisions will be to develop support for the program. Without at least tacit support from the principal parties involved, controls will certainly not last long.

REACTIONS TO CONTROLS

However the post-freeze controls mechanism may be designed, experience with it over a period of time, say, six to eight months, leads to several developments. Distortions of various kinds emerge. With all of the goodwill and intelligence and hard work in the world, the controllers cannot possibly master the vast and complicated economy with which they must deal. The application of a set of rules to a dynamic economy and a changing business environment renders some necessary goods relatively un-profitable. People stop making them. This process leads to artificial scarcities, artificial in the sense that they represent a misallocation of resources induced by the controls themselves. But since these artificial scarcities are nonetheless real, they tend to slow production and projects and can gradually have a debilitating impact on economic growth.

Distortions arise not only in product markets but also in the collective bargaining process itself. Although the wage board may have a role to play in settling a dispute between a particular union and management, the more likely event, as labor markets tighten, will be that the board's wage-increase guidelines will be below what both labor and management would prefer. Sometimes management may find the path of least resistance to be no resistance, and will join the union in an application to the board, fully expecting that the board will do management's job for it by cutting the union's demands down to size. Wage controls may thus generate a decline in the vigor of collective bargaining.

At the same time, it is almost inevitable that people soon start questioning whether this so-called transitory program is not taking on a rather permanent appearance. Once the suspicion of permanence sets in, gamesmanship develops between the private and the public sectors. It becomes apparent that the controls process is not a one-way street in which the government does something to the private sector; rather, it is a two-way street, with the government taking an action, the private sector reacting to it, the government reacting in turn, and so forth. It is a continual process of interplay and interrelation through which those "controlled" develop ways of doing whatever they really want to do, but within the rules of the controls system. It is an impressive tribute to the ingenuity of private enterprise and collective bargaining how quickly and skillfully people find loopholes in any set of rules.

For a while the controllers engage in a process of plugging loopholes, changing a regulation here and there, and trying to keep things more or less in balance, but eventually these emerging problems in product markets and in collective bargaining will lead those in charge of the controls program to conclude that it is time to change the model. They say to themselves, "We have set out some rules and developed governmental bodies to administer them and these have all worked reasonably well for a while, but now the sharpshooters are getting to them, distortions of various kinds are arising, and so we had best do something different." In the meanwhile, one important result (perhaps achievement) of the program has been delay of the inevitable price increases. A delay of a few months in the rise of any particular price means that the average rate of increase in the price indices is reduced, at least for a time.

CHANGING THE MODEL

By the time the controls program has progressed to this point, it has undoubtedly developed a strong and loyal bureaucracy. When the controls agency is new, many employees find the work exciting and interesting, they find satisfaction in working long hours, and their work is heavily covered by the press. Such a bureaucracy can quickly develop aspirations for permanence. As it acquires a life of its own, the bureaucracy seeks to perpetuate that life. Those in charge of the program may thus conclude that if a new model is to be brought out, it should encompass a change in the institutions running the controls program, as well as a change in the substance of the program itself.

This analysis contains some of the rationale for the shift in January 1973 from Phase II to Phase III in the recent controls experience. Institutional rearrangements were made: The new system of administration was designed to emphasize the continued concept that controls were a transitory matter, and a renewed effort was made to enlist the support of labor, management, and other groups for the new version of the system.

DISENGAGEMENT

As the controls system proceeds in its life cycle, the realization grows that the system is a wasting asset—if it can be called an asset at all. The system may work for a while, or at least appear to. Presidents have certainly found it good politics, again for a while. But it grows more and more apparent that the system's useful life is limited. Having grabbed this tiger by the tail, those in charge must inevitably start thinking about how they are going to let go. This need to disengage has engulfed every controls program, even when those in charge were not so set on limiting the period of controls as they were in the most recent experience.

The classic means of disengagement for a controls program has been a blowup. The system puts out an edict of some kind, the private sector defies it, and the whole thing just blows up. In the past, labor has usually said, in effect, "We believe in free collective bargaining, we don't accept the decision of the wage board, we withdraw from the board, and we will strike against any effort to impose its will on us." As a matter of strategy, those in charge might view a labor boycott of the program as a tenable way out and decide to let it happen. On the other hand, the effort to administer the program in a responsible and orderly manner leads to a desire for more orderly disengagement.

The process of orderly disengagement can propel a controls program in a number of directions. One such direction is to cut down on the scope of the controls system itself by eliminating small firms from coverage and by exempting sectors of the economy where the burden of controls could lead to disaster. Letting go of rent control at the start of Phase III, for example, was both extraordinarily difficult and critically important to the health of the housing industry.

During Phase III, self-administration accompanied reduced coverage. The central idea behind this approach was to relieve companies and unions of the bureaucratic entanglements of the controls system. The rules, the duties, and the possibility of fines and rollbacks in the event of violation would all remain the same as in Phase II. But instead of administering the rules by the Phase II process of application and administrative review, followed by disapproval or approval in whole or in part, companies and unions would self-administer.

The guiding principle was that once the rules were published, it was up to those to whom they applied to self-administer them properly. It was, as was said at the time, "as voluntary as your income tax." The taxpayer fills out his own form and sends it in to the IRS at his peril. The IRS judges whether or not he has complied with the rules and, if not, the taxpayer is punishable, subject to the possibility of judicial review. For the most part, taxpayers self-administer honestly and the system works.

One important effect of the self-administration strategy of disengagement is that the tactic of delaying wage and price increases drops out of the system: The parties decide for themselves whether to raise a wage or a price, and if the increase is permissible under the rules, they simply act. Consequently, when the gears are shifted from bureaucratic review to self-administration, a bulge in wage and price increases is almost inevitable—simply because all of the increases in the bureaucratic pipeline are released at the moment of the shift.

OTHER TACTICS OF DISENGAGEMENT

The Phase III effort to disengage through self-administration was abandoned because it was blamed for a development with which it actually had little connection. The composition of the price increases during the first half of 1973 shows clearly that price increases outside the scope of the program led to an escalating rate of overall price increases, which in turn undermined confidence in the program. During Phase III, food and energy prices—essentially internationally traded commodities not subject to controls—increased by 20 percent and 19 percent, respectively. In contrast, nonfood commodities and services, which were largely subject to self-administered controls, increased by 4.8 percent and 4.3 percent, respectively. If the country again has the misfortune to be saddled with controls, the facts concerning self-administration should not be overlooked.

The experience with disengagement under Phase III strongly suggests that, regardless of the reasons for a bulge in prices, political tolerance limits the size of an "acceptable" price bulge. The 1973 bulge was politically unacceptable, and the reaction was apparent in press and congressional criticism and in a move toward a congressionally imposed freeze. In response, the President imposed his own freeze in June 1973, followed by a severe form of bureaucratically administered wage and price controls, known as Phase IV. The President's economic advisers vigorously opposed this second freeze and, in fact, this Labor-Management Advisory Committee met in special session and expressed its opposition to even a tightening of controls, let alone a freeze. Perhaps we should have seen the handwriting on the wall when, in response to Chairman of the Council of Economic Advisers Herb Stein's remark, "You know, Mr. President, you can't walk on water twice," the President replied, "Maybe you can if it's frozen."

The second freeze came at a bad time in the economic cycle, compared with the timing of the first one. In 1971, seasonal factors worked in its favor in the food area, international prices were relatively stable, and the general tide of inflation was already receding. In 1973, by contrast, all these forces were working strongly in the reverse direction, and U.S. price levels were also feeling the full effects of two devaluations. Whatever political justifications may be offered for this decision to impose a second freeze, only one thing can be said for it on the substantive side: The results were so bad that everyone could see the inherent limitations of controls.

After reimposing a mandatory set of controls, complete with notification periods and other means of reinstituting delay in wage and price changes, a different disengagement strategy was necessary. A sector-by-sector approach evolved. Decontrol by sectors is at best a very tricky process. Because the American economy is such a closely interrelated and interdependent system, if something is done to one part of it, other parts will be affected, often quite rapidly. The interrelationships that exist between products are often surprising. Fertilizer and explosives, for example, both use the same raw material, ammonium nitrate. If fertilizer is decontrolled, allowing that use of the raw material to become relatively profitable, the raw material will be drained away from explosives. If keeping coal mines going is a good thing, then decontrol of fertilizer without decontrol of explosives (of vital use in mining) is not a wise idea.

The director and staff of the Cost of Living Council closely monitored such interconnections, and on the whole the sector-by-sector approach succeeded moderately well. The controllers bargained with the private sector, price by price and, to a degree, wage by wage, since wages and prices in an industry were almost always decontrolled at the same time. Those who wanted to be decontrolled were asked for a variety of guarantees: about average price behavior over some period into the future, investment plans and commitments, limitations of export of critical materials, and the development of improved structures of collective bargaining.

Whenever any price was decontrolled, a slight bulge in overall price indices resulted. The sector-by-sector strategy of decontrol is based on the premise that only so much of a bulge is politically tolerable; any greater bulge will lead the political process to throw the program back into a tight bureaucratic system. The goal is to disengage as rapidly as possible without incurring a politically intolerable bulge at any one time.

In the end, Congress provided the final act of disengagement by refusing to extend the life of the Economic Stabilization Act beyond April 30, 1974. By that time, labor and management were thoroughly fed up with the whole thing, and the President's Labor-Management Advisory Committee had some time earlier publicly recorded its view that controls should end.

Unfortunately, however, total disengagement is not the end of the life cycle of controls. The fact that controls were used remains very much in the public mind and has created a set of attitudes that complicates the problem of dealing with inflation. Although the 1971–74 episode provided some public education about the limitations of controls, there nevertheless seems to be an undying willingness to believe that, somehow or other, with enthusiastic administration, controls will work.

Controls have the political appeal of action: A legislator who wants to "do something" about inflation can always espouse controls, and a President who wants to be seen as a man of action can impose them. Public discussion by highly placed people can in turn easily lead to the kind of anticipatory price increases that tend to force a government to reinstitute controls. In a sense the problem then becomes, assuming one wants to stay out of the wage and price control business, how to keep the barn door open long enough to allow the stolen horses to be returned.

LIMITATIONS OF THE "LARGE-UNIT" APPROACH

Controls or almost any other type of incomes policy will almost inevitably be directed primarily at the large units—unions as well as companies—of the economy. They are the ones that can be dealt with directly, that have public visibility, and that, particularly on the company side, fear public criticism.

This large-unit approach conforms to one popular and continuously propagated theory of how the economy operates. According to this "administered-price" school of thought, the big units in our economy administer prices and wages to a considerable degree at their own discretion, and their decisions in turn tend to dominate the economy. From this point of departure, those favoring controls but desiring (for whatever reason) to exempt small firms from the controls argue that if the big units decide to follow a moderate course, then smaller firms will follow suit. They will follow, so the argument goes, in part because as competitors they must do so in order to sell their products, in part because as suppliers they feel pressure from the buying power of large units, and in part because a tone is set creating an environment to which everyone must conform.

The administered-price view—the intellectual foundation for the large-unit approach to controls—is widely held among politicians and is supported by a substantial number of economists. The popularity of this view is attributable primarily to the brilliant polemics of a few members of the economics profession. But the weight of the evidence is against the idea that firms in relatively concentrated industries (e.g., steel, autos, rubber) have higher-than-average price increases during a period of inflation and are, therefore, in part "responsible" for the inflation. Consequently, there is little analytical support for the proposition that if their prices were moderated somewhat, a broad beneficial impact would be enjoyed. As Albert Rees, at the time executive director of the President's Council on Wage and Price Stability, commented in testimony before the House Committee on Banking, Currency, and Housing (June 17, 1975):

Although it is probably true that concentrated industries charge higher prices than they would charge if they were more competitive, it does not appear to be true that prices in these industries rise more rapidly than other prices. This last hypothesis would require not only that concentration confer a price advantage, but also that this advantage be continuously increasing.

Any attempt to use controlled prices of large firms to discipline prices charged by smaller ones breaks down in a period when the commodity is in short supply. Then, control of large firms' prices would simply result in a flow of the commodity to smaller firms that could buy it and subsequently sell it at the higher price. Over a long enough period, we would have large firms with low prices and nothing to sell.

Whatever the merits of the arguments for and against the administered-price view, the facts of life during most of the recent controls period differed from assumptions of the large-unit theory. Prices and wages rose most rapidly in the sectors of the economy that were (1) competitive (composed of small units), (2) characterized by special problems on the wage side, (3) dominated by government, or (4) heavily involved in international markets, either on the importing or exporting side. It was the increase in these prices that caused the overall price indices to rise so rapidly and that generated the political demands for further government action.

In the health sector, for example, there was a rapid escalation of prices to the consumer in an industry populated by local hospitals and many individual entrepreneurs, most importantly doctors, who are organized into what may be viewed as a union, the American Medical Association. The steady escalation of costs was largely a direct result of the vast and increasing flow of federal funds to this area. A tremendous effort was made to adapt the idea of controls to this situation, and some success was achieved in concept, if not indeed in actual effect on health service prices: A labor-management panel and health advisory committee were formed to generate ideas from knowledgeable people and transmit information and decisions to those affected, and direct limits were placed on increases in the prices of many health services. The rate of increase in these costs did slow for a time (and for the first time in a long while). The basic problem, however, was one of grappling with government-induced cost increases, a far cry from the stereotyped problem of dealing with price increases imposed by large companies.

Food was another sector of the economy that plagued the controls program. The rapid increases in consumer food prices were basically caused by price increases in highly competitive markets for raw food materials. These markets were in turn strongly affected by worldwide crop failures and resulting scarcities in international markets, on the one hand, and by government policies tending to restrict supply in domestic markets, on the other. The fruitful ways of dealing with scarcity-induced price increases surely do not include lowering price below cost in the markets where the problem originates.

An example is useful. Although raw agricultural products were exempt from controls on the solid justification that to cover them would discourage supply and therefore be self-defeating in the long run, broilers were covered. The problem was that, whether one starts with the chicken or the egg, by the time the product emerges at its first point of sale, it is no longer "raw." It has been plucked and prepared for use. At the same time, the underlying raw material—feed grain—was, as a raw agricultural product, free of all controls. The resulting interaction between rising prices for feed grains and controlled prices for broilers was disastrous for profit margins in the broiler industry. Yet the Price Commission was loath to permit much of an increase in broiler prices because of consumer sensitivity. The predictable consequence of holding price below cost was a drying up of supply as broiler producers literally could no longer afford to stay in business. In the end broilers were declared a raw agricultural product, and their price, automatically released from controls, shot up by over 50 percent. Supply responded rapidly, however, in this short-production-cycle industry and within a matter of months the price had fallen to near its original level.

The theory that controlling prices charged by large units in the economy would strike at the essence of the inflation problem thus simply had no application to the sectors of the economy where prices were rising most rapidly. The relevance of the large-unit theory to the inflation problem is paralleled by the old story of the drunk who was looking for a key under a lamp post. When asked by a passerby what he was doing, he replied that he was looking for a lost key. When the passerby asked where he lost the key, the drunk replied that he had lost it down the street. "Well, then," he was asked, "why are you looking here?"—"Because the light is so much better."

To continue the analogy, the drunk is like the politician who knows the political mileage to be gained by pushing around the big boys in the economy, whether or not it makes any economic sense. Attention in any controls program will thus inevitably be directed at the large units because they are what the controllers can most readily get their hands on, and the administered-price school of thought provides a ready justification. But as we have seen, concentrated industries often are not where the problem lies. The focusing of controls on large units is thus a distinct and inherent limitation on their potential usefulness and may contribute in turn to public dissatisfaction with their performance and to their eventual collapse.

INTERACTIONS WITH OTHER POLICIES

A wage and price controls system interacts not only with the private sector which it seeks to regulate but also with a host of government policies that bear directly or indirectly on the general price level and on particular prices. One of the most powerful and important of these interactions is the potential impact of controls on fiscal and monetary policy. The proclaimed existence of controls almost inevitably creates the feeling that the controls policy is contending, at least in some fashion, with the problems of inflation. It follows from this feeling that the government can be more aggressive in stimulating the economy. Those who find tough monetary or fiscal policies inconvenient or contrary to their interest conclude that easier monetary and fiscal policies have become feasible.

This line of thinking was at least implicit in the August 1971 package, which included some fiscal stimulants to the economy. The same view can be discerned in the plea from the Federal Reserve for an incomes policy, a plea frequently heard when the rate of inflation calls for a tight monetary policy. The argument is that monetary policy has carried too much of the burden of controlling inflation and cannot do the job alone, and therefore some help from an incomes policy is needed. Certainly the implication is that if an incomes policy is adopted, then monetary policy can be easier. This tendency toward self-deception is a central problem with controls. It is the explanation for the otherwise puzzling fact that countries using controls the least tend to have the best record in fighting inflation. The outstanding example, of course, is West Germany, which has enjoyed a consistently superior performance in fighting inflation.

This point deserves particular emphasis for those inclined toward econometric studies of the effects of controls. The studies typically start with a given fiscal and monetary policy and then compare price and wage performance under controls with what might have been expected without controls. Such studies have the fatal weakness that they leave out of account what is perhaps the most important variable—the impact of the existence of controls on changes in fiscal and monetary policy.

A second important interaction is the interplay between controls and international economic policy. In the case of the United States, the 1971 and 1973 devaluations and the institution of a flexible system of exchange rates undoubtedly aggravated the inflation problem. A correction in the exchange value of the dollar was long overdue. Moreover, the more flexible system now in place enables individual countries to maintain a more independent fiscal and monetary policy, if they choose to do so. Be that as it may, these results were achieved only with considerable pain. The first effect of a devaluation is to raise the price of imports and, by adding to the capacity of the international community to buy domestic products, to bid up domestic prices. An upward movement of the price indices inevitably results. In addition, in 1971 the refusal of some major countries to accept what the United States regarded as an adequate devaluation resulted—through their purchase of dollars in foreign exchange markets in order to maintain exchange rates favorable to their export industries—in a great increase in their foreign exchange reserves. This increase in the world money supply was a major contributor to the worldwide inflation in the 1972–75 period.

A third interaction is between a domestic price controls policy and developments in international markets for particular commodities. In any discussion of the design of a controls program it is almost instantly and universally agreed that costs of internationally traded goods must be passed through in the product price if the country is not to be cut off from access to those supplies. Articles produced and used in the United States but also exported present a more difficult and potentially more dangerous dilemma. Agricultural commodities are leading examples. If the controlled price of a domestically produced good is below the world market price, exports will surely rise. The obvious alternatives must be to put up with the scarcity, to allow the price of food to rise to the world price, or to impose controls on exports.

The attempt in 1973 to deal with this latter problem through export controls demonstrates how a controls program tends to spread from one area to others. Fortunately, the United States was not drawn very far into export controls. Although the pressure for widespread export controls on food was great, they were imposed—and then but briefly—only on soybeans. The experience with soybean export controls, though short and perhaps justifiable as a short-term measure, provides a lesson in what *not* to do. These controls tended to undermine the confidence of other countries in the United States as a secure source of supply. Soybean export controls were also a blow to farmers who depend on exports of that crop for their livelihood. In addition, some of the demand for soybeans spilled over into markets for other feed grains, illustrating the inherent indivisibility of the economy.

Here, also, the existence of authority to impose controls on exports and the fact that this authority was used on at least one occasion produced a problem in anticipations that aggravated an already difficult situation. Intentions to export were artificially pumped up as exporters guarded against a possible program of export controls that would allow them to export some fixed percentage of their "intended" amount. Since this possibility created an incentive to inflate intentions, it became more difficult to judge true export demand—a difficulty that occurred not only in soybeans but in many other agricultural commodities as well.

Any comprehensive controls system must eventually face up to the dilemma produced by attempts to control the domestic price of an internationally traded commodity. It is worth noting also that commodity agreements worked out internationally can very well spread into the domestic area, a point U.S. negotiators must keep in mind as they deal with insistent demands to stabilize prices through international agreements. Foreign and domestic markets are intimately intertwined; over any period of time it is impossible to control one market without affecting the other.

GOVERNMENT POLICIES TOWARD SUPPLY

If one area of genuinely constructive experience were to be singled out from the 1971–74 controls period, it would be the impact of the controls system on government actions affecting supply. In the economic package announced in August 1971, President Nixon coupled the imposition of wage and price controls with a request to Congress for reinstitution of the investment tax credit. Congress approved both the credit and a previously announced administrative liberalization of the depreciation provisions of the federal income tax code. Both were actions taken to increase supply. Another was the sustained and partially successful effort to limit price increases of certain commodities by selling out of government stockpiles articles no longer considered "strategic." Similarly, in the process of disengagement from controls, strenuous efforts were made to obtain a commitment to greater capacity in bottlenecked industries of the economy, such as fertilizer.

Perhaps the most interesting development was the emergence of a new center of advocacy within the government. With economic policies for the most part in the hands of departmental bureaus and congressional committees representing special interests, governmentally imposed restrictions on supply, designed to gain a higher price for those interests, are commonplace. In an advocacy system of government, there has been little organized resistance to these raids by special interests.

The controls system created a new group within the executive branch devoted to keeping prices down and, therefore, to expanding rather than restricting supplies of almost everything. The Cost of Living Council and its staff and the more recent Council on Wage and Price Stability were the institutional base for this new advocacy group to represent the general public interest. With a staff large enough and expert enough to develop independent information and analysis, this group was able to challenge departmental views and, with presidential backing, to change many decisions. Excessive set-asides in planting, compulsory empty backhauls by trucks, restricted car-loading of certain commodities, size standards for produce, and a myriad of other such restrictions were brought into question. In many cases important changes were made that relaxed government restrictions on supply. For example, marketing orders (under which restrictions were placed on the permissible volume of shipments of certain commodities) were discovered by people outside the Department of Agriculture, and a system was set up to review them.

It would, of course, be naive to believe that all or even most of these battles could be won, because the political forces that produced the restrictive measures in the first place are usually alert and powerful. Nevertheless, some battles were won, and the fact that a confrontation might develop undoubtedly has a healthy restraining influence on new measures to restrict supply. This function, which yielded important results during the 1971–74 controls period, holds the prospect for positive contributions to public policy with or without an economic stabilization program. It would be highly worthwhile for this effort, now the responsibility of the Council on Wage and Price Stability, to be made a permanent feature of the government.

SOME ADMINISTRATIVE INSIGHTS

Any formal system of controls will require an administrative apparatus to interpret the rules and regulations, to police compliance with them, and to provide service throughout the country. Particularly when the program is conceived of as temporary, it will be advantageous from the standpoint of the program to use an existing bureaucracy. Immediately, then, the Internal Revenue Service springs to mind. The IRS is large, has offices all over the country, and is a respected and to a certain extent feared organization (nobody likes to have a visit from the IRS). The Service's employees are also competent in the process of writing and interpreting regulations. The temptation is thus strong to give the IRS the duty of day-to-day administration, knowing that other tasks will easily absorb its manpower when this temporary program disappears.

Despite its appeal, such a choice presents an interesting dilemma for government organization. The IRS has an important job to do—collecting taxes. Manpower and budget support for that job are scarce and should not be unnecessarily diluted. Furthermore, one of the attractions of using the IRS is that its tax-enforcement role gives it special clout. But that fact itself raises serious questions about the propriety of attempting to harness the taxpayer's fear of tax enforcement for the achievement of an unrelated end, such as controlling prices.

Over the decades the practice has grown up of using IRS records and personnel in the effort to control organized crime, to deal with the problem of drug abuse, and so on. To its everlasting credit, the IRS is one bureaucracy that is not disposed to seek an enlargement of its jurisdiction. The attitude within the IRS is that the job of collecting taxes is important and should not be diluted by sharing the IRS stage with other responsibilities. There is much to be said for this view. In the event of another outbreak of the wage and price control disease, some other means of administration should be found.

As in other experiments with controls in the United States, in the most recent episode a tripartite wage agency (the Pay Board) was adopted. The Pay Board hammered out the broad policies pursued throughout the entire 1971–74 stabilization period. Nevertheless, the Pay Board's discussions of administrative as well as policy matters were marked by considerable acrimony, and the situation gradually deteriorated. Most of the labor members eventually decided to walk off the board near the end of Phase II, an action that under some circumstances would have brought the whole program to an end. In this case, however, one labor member stayed and he was paired, so to speak, with one management member. The other management members chose to resign in order to maintain labor-management parity and to give a majority to the public members. All five public members stayed on the board, and it thereby became an essentially public body.

This structural change made the administrative processes of the board, which were then the predominant activity, much more efficient and workmanlike. The labor staff members continued to work with the Pay Board and the board's activities were more or less accepted, no doubt in large part because labor had participated in the formulation of the policies being pursued. The design of the wage side of the Phase III program took a lesson from this experience. A Labor-Management Advisory Board was formed, and it operated quite successfully on the policy level. Its views on the desirability of ending the controls were instrumental in creating a climate in which that could be done. At the same time, the administrative effort during Phase III and Phase IV was lodged with the Cost of Living Council, whose director, John Dunlop, was responsible for the administration of both wage and price controls.

This experience underscores an important distinction between policy formulation and administrative action, particularly where wages are concerned. The participation of labor in the formulation of policy during the early months of controls was not only more important than its participation in administration but was a vital condition of labor's willingness to cooperate with those administering wage controls.

THE POLITICS OF CONTROLS

One of the most difficult problems in the administration of controls is how to insulate the process from political pressures exerted by special interests. Although the advocacy process is present in both the executive and legislative branches, it is more pronounced in the latter. One can predict, for example, that a running battle will ensue with certain congressmen and senators whenever a marketing order emanating from the Department of Agriculture is challenged by executive branch officials concerned with expanding supply. The politics of special interests in controls is dramatized by the experience of President Truman, who advocated a wage and price controls system after World War II but had to veto the bill that Congress ultimately passed. His grounds for the veto were that the bill was so loaded with debilitating amendments that it could not possibly work. The executive branch officials in charge of controls must somehow contend with a kind of political guerrilla warfare, in which particular members of Congress strongly advocate controls, on the one hand, and, on the other, continually slip into bills riders that would exempt from controls an industry or group very important to their own constituency.

A controls program must have administrative integrity if it is to survive. The administrators of the controls program must be in contact with Congress if the program is to be understood at all sympathetically. They must reconcile themselves to being denounced for the record and on the record and be satisfied with a wink and a nod that is supposed to tell them not to take the denunciation either personally or too seriously. It is up to the President, his cabinet officers, and the President's political assistants to provide a buffer shielding the administrators of the program from the most intense political heat. If ground must be given to special interests, those providing this political buffer must be prepared to take the responsibility for making that decision.

In short, the 1971–74 experience with wage and price controls shows how tempting it is to adopt controls and how difficult it is to get rid of them. They virtually assure easier and more inflationary fiscal and monetary policies. To yield to these temptations is to give bad medicine at a bad time. Once having put the economy on a regime of controls, policymakers will find that they have to change the dosage and the method of administration constantly. Even as the life cycle of controls seems to have run its course, its legacy remains: fear that another dose may will be in the offing.

QUESTIONS FOR DISCUSSION

1 According to the authors, why was President Nixon "forced" to impose wage-price controls in 1971? What other policies to fight inflation had he already tried?

2 The authors argue that any wage-price freeze would have to be temporary. What problems would arise if wage-price controls were instituted permanently?

3 What are some of the major groups in the economy that must support a controls program if it is to have any chance of success? How did the Nixon administration attempt to win the support of these groups?

4 Why was the second freeze imposed in June 1973? Why did it fail?

5 What is the *large-unit theory* of inflation? What does this theory suggest about the effectiveness of controls? Did the large-unit theory work well for 1971–1974? Why or why not?

6 "Wage-price controls can be successful only insofar as they reduce inflationary expectations." Discuss, using the aggregate supply–aggregate demand curve for framework. (*Hint:* Show that the inflationary expectations of workers govern how fast the aggregate supply curve moves northward over time.) What does this suggest about the sort of monetary and fiscal policies that should accompany a freeze, if inflation is to be reduced?

THE DUAL PROBLEMS OF STRUCTURAL AND CYCLICAL UNEMPLOYMENT

Council of Economic Advisers

Written at a time when the unemployment rate was at its postwar high, the following excerpt from the *Economic Report of the President* provides an overview discussion of the phenomena of cyclical and structural unemployment, their causes, and possible policy responses.

Unemployment is the most serious problem now facing the United States. By December 1982 the number of unemployed had risen by more than 4 million since the beginning of the recession in July 1981. The unemployment rate was higher in December 1982 than at any point since the Depression, with over 12 million persons counted as unemployed. Even after the economy recovers from the recent recession, it is likely that the unemployment rate will reach a plateau between 6 and 7 percent.

This chapter analyzes the two major types of unemployment: cyclical and structural. The high level of cyclical unemployment now prevailing in the United States is a major problem, but it should prove transitory. Only a healthy and sustained recovery from the recent recession can effectively diminish cyclical unemployment. Even after full recovery, however, a serious structural unemployment problem will remain unless measures are taken to improve the functioning of labor markets. Reducing structural unemployment will require attacking the special problems of young people and the long-term adult unemployed.

This chapter begins by describing the dimensions of the cyclical and structural unemployment problems. It then examines the potential of public employment pro-

U.S. Council of Economic Advisers, *Economic Report of the President: 1983,* chap. 2 (excerpt), "The Dual Problems of Structural and Cyclical Unemployment," pp. 29–43.

grams and macroeconomic policies to lower cyclical unemployment. Finally, policies for reducing structural unemployment are considered.

THE RECENT RECESSION

The unemployment rate in December 1982 stood at 10.8 percent of the civilian labor force. Since the recent period of economic slack that began in January 1980, the unemployment rate has risen by 4.5 percentage points. During the recent recession, which began in July 1981, the unemployment rate rose by 3.6 percentage points. Historical experience suggests that the unemployment rate tends to increase for several months after the level of production bottoms out and it is possible that the unemployment rate will reach 11 percent at some point during 1983.

Beyond those officially counted as unemployed, the recent recession has prevented many Americans from working as much as they would like. In December 1982 there were over two million persons involuntarily working part time. The Bureau of Labor Statistics also reported that there were over 1.8 million discouraged workers in December. These are individuals who have given up looking for work because they believe they cannot find jobs.

Unemployment is often linked to economic hardship. While many of the unemployed receive unemployment insurance and live in families that have other members who work, many unemployed individuals and their families suffer economic distress. Table 1 presents information of the incomes of families in which the husband, wife, or head of household experienced unemployment during 1981. (Data for 1982 are not yet available.) Three types of families are distinguished: (1) families in which both husband and wife worked, (2) families in which only the husband or male head worked, and (3) families in which only the wife or female head worked. For all of the family types, unemployment experienced by husband, wife, or head of household significantly lowered median family income. For example, single-earner families in which the husband (or male head) was never unemployed had a median income in 1981 of $25,000. In contrast, the median income of similar families in which the male head experienced

TABLE 1
MEDIAN FAMILY INCOME BY UNEMPLOYMENT AND FAMILY STATUS, 1981
(Current Dollars)

	Unemployment status of husband, wife, or head of household		
Family status	Person never unemployed	Person unemployed less than 26 weeks	Person unemployed more than 26 weeks
Husband and wife both work	$31,600	$23,000	$17,900
Only husband or male head works	25,000	16,500	10,200
Only wife or female head works	18,900	15,200	11,200

Source: Department of Labor, Bureau of Statistics.

1 to 26 weeks of unemployment was $16,500. Families in which the male head was unemployed for more than 26 weeks had a median family income of $10,200.

The financial losses of the unemployed are not the only costs of a prolonged economic decline. Considerable anxiety and emotional distress is experienced by those who have lost their jobs or who fear that they might lose their jobs in an economy with a declining number of employment opportunities. Protracted unemployment is frequently associated with poor health, psychological problems, and gradual erosion of job-related skills.

THE COMPOSITION OF CYCLICAL AND STRUCTURAL UNEMPLOYMENT

The unemployment problem can be divided into two components, cyclical and structural unemployment. The term *cyclical unemployment* is used to refer to the unemployment associated with cyclical downturns in aggregate economic activity. The incremental unemployment associated with the recent recession would fall into this category. The term *structural unemployment* is used to refer to the unemployment that remains even after cyclical recoveries in aggregate economic activity.

In large part, structural unemployment is a natural concomitant of a dynamic economy with constantly changing patterns of demand. Labor markets are in constant flux, with people entering and leaving the labor force, losing or quitting old jobs, and looking for and acquiring new jobs. Some amount of structural unemployment is an inevitable aspect of a large modern industrial economy such as ours. It is important to realize that although expansionary macroeconomic policies cannot reduce structural unemployment permanently, certain microeconomic policy interventions can affect the ease and speed of the process that matches workers with jobs.

Some insight into the differences between cyclical and structural unemployment can be obtained by comparing the characteristics of the unemployed in 1982 and in a period of low cyclical unemployment. Since the unemployment rate in 1978 was 6.1 percent, close to most observers' estimates of full employment, data from that year will be used to illustrate the characteristics of structural unemployment. The next two sections examine the composition of the unemployed population in 1978 and 1982 in terms of demographic composition and reasons for unemployment. A third section analyzes the dynamics of unemployment.

Demographic Composition

Chart 1 provides information on the demographic composition of the unemployed population in 1978 and in 1982. The chart shows that young people under age 24 account for a substantial fraction of unemployment both when the economy is weak and when it is strong. Persons under 24 accounted for 49 percent of total unemployment during 1978 and 41 percent of unemployment in 1982. The decline in the share of youth unemployment reflected the large increase in unemployment among adult males in cyclically sensitive sectors of the economy, such as manufacturing.

A pattern that appears in Chart 2 is the cyclical sensitivity of unemployment among

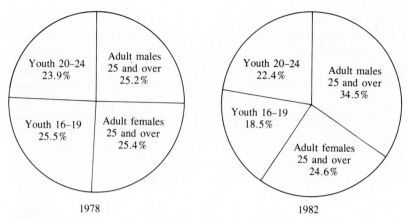

CHART 1
Distribution of Unemployment by Age and Sex. *Note:* Data relate to
persons 16 years and over. (Source: *Department of Labor.*)

those who provide the primary financial support for a family. The share of unemployment among husbands, wives, and family heads in families without a working spouse rose from 20 percent in 1978 to 24 percent in 1982. Because unemployment undoubtedly imposes its greatest hardship when it hits a worker upon whom others depend for their sole support, this increase is particularly distressing.

A continuing tragedy in both good and bad times is the very high rates of unem-

CHART 2
Distribution of Unemployment by Family Status. *Note:* Data relate to
persons 16 years and over. (Source: *Department of Labor.*)

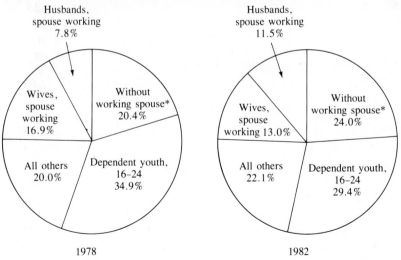

*Husbands and wives whose spouse does not work and persons who maintain families.

ployment of blacks and other minorities. This group accounts for a share of unemployment that is greatly disproportionate of its share of the labor force. While blacks and other minorities comprised 13 percent of the labor force in 1982, they comprised approximately 23 percent of the unemployed. Chart 3 shows that the recent recession raised the unemployment rate of blacks and other minorities proportionally less than that of the rest of the population.

However, black and other minority unemployment rates increased sharply during the recession and continue to greatly exceed those of the entire population. The unemployment rate for black and other minority adult males was 16.2 percent in 1982, compared to 7.8 percent for white males. For black and other minority teenagers the unemployment rate was 43.9 percent, compared to 20.4 percent for white teenagers.

Reasons for Unemployment

Analyzing the problem of unemployment requires understanding the process by which people become unemployed. The unemployed are often described in stereotyped terms as the victims of permanent layoffs by firms that are either partially or fully shutting down. Even during the recent recession, however, this characterization applied to less than half of the unemployed.

As part of the monthly Current Population Survey, the unemployed are asked a number of questions designed to elicit the reasons for their unemployment. The answers to these questions permit a breakdown of the unemployed into five groups: (1) persons laid off who can expect to return to the same job; (2) persons who have lost jobs to which they cannot expect to return; (3) persons who have quit their jobs; (4) reentrants who are returning to the labor force after a spell of neither working nor looking for work; and (5) new entrants who have never worked at a full-time job before but are now seeking employment.

CHART 3
Distribution of Unemployment by Race. *Note:* Data relate to persons 16 years and over. (Source: *Department of Labor.*)

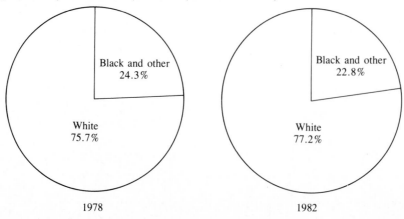

Black and other
24.3%

White
75.7%

1978

Black and other
22.8%

White
77.2%

1982

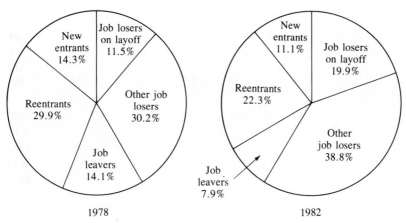

CHART 4
Distribution of Unemployment by Reason. *Note:* Data relate to
persons 16 years and over. (Source: *Department of Labor.*)

Chart 4 shows that the distribution of the unemployed among these categories is
very sensitive to cyclical conditions. The share of persons who have lost their jobs,
either temporarily or permanently, is particularly sensitive, rising from 42 percent in
1978 to 59 percent in 1982. Over this period the number of job losers on temporary
layoff tripled and the number of permanent job losers more than doubled. The decline
in alternative employment opportunities resulted in a decline in the share of unemployment traceable to workers leaving their jobs voluntarily during the recession—
from 14 percent in 1978 to 8 percent in 1982. Finally, because the number of labor
force entrants and reentrants is relatively constant, their share in total unemployment
declined somewhat during the recession.

The data on reasons for unemployment indicate a major difference between cyclical
and structural unemployment. Almost 90 percent of the increase in unemployment
during cyclical downturns involves increases in job losses and layoffs, as firms respond
to declines in demand for their products. On the other hand, almost 60 percent of
structural unemployment is comprised of voluntary job leavers, labor force entrants,
and reentrants. The remainder are job losers. As described below, the very different
causes of cyclical and structural unemployment suggest that different policy responses
are appropriate.

The Dynamics of Unemployment

An essential feature of the unemployment problem is its dynamic character. The
appropriate design of policies to reduce unemployment depends on whether most of
the unemployed are out of work for a long time and must wait for an economic upturn
to find jobs or whether they are a group whose membership changes rapidly, even
during recessions.

The principal source of information on the duration of unemployment is the monthly

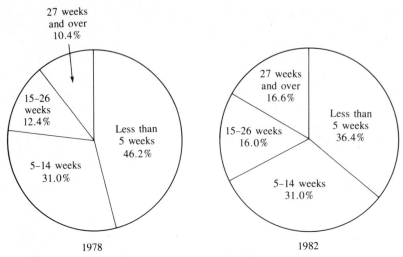

CHART 5
Distribution of Unemployment by Duration. *Note:* Data relate to
persons 16 years and over. (Source: *Department of Labor.*)

Current Population Survey, which asks persons who report themselves as unemployed
to report how long they have been unemployed. Chart 5 presents information on the
duration of unemployment in 1978 and 1982. The clearest difference between cyclical
and structural unemployment emerges in the incidence of long-term unemployment.
In 1982 the number of unemployed individuals who reported that they had been out
of work for 6 or more months was almost three times the corresponding number in
1978, when the economy was operating without significant cyclical unemployment.

While the incidence of long-term unemployment increases sharply during recessions, it is important to recognize that many of the unemployed find jobs or withdraw
from the labor force relatively quickly. Of all the persons who became unemployed
in September 1982, over 45 percent were not longer unemployed by October, and
over 65 percent were no longer unemployed by November. However, evidence on the
duration of employment is not purely indicative of the ease or difficulty with which
persons find jobs since almost half the unemployed leave the labor force without
finding jobs.

While most persons who become unemployed look for work only briefly, this group
does not comprise a large part of the unemployment problem. It is long-term unemployment that is of special concern. A recent study found that in 1978, more than 40
percent of total unemployment was due to the 15 percent of the unemployed population
who were out of work a total of 6 months or longer during the year. This concentration
of long-term unemployment among a relatively small group of the unemployed is
particularly pronounced during cyclical downturns. Data on this subject are not yet
available for 1982. During 1975, however, when the unemployment rate was 8.5
percent, an estimated 52 percent of the unemployment was due to the 22 percent of
the unemployed population who were out of work more than 6 months.

These findings suggest several conclusions. First, even during recessions, most persons who become unemployed either find jobs or leave the labor force relatively quickly. Second, the unemployment problem is most serious for those who are unemployed for prolonged stretches. Third, the incidence of long-term unemployment is very sensitive to cyclical conditions, which suggests that it will diminish as the economy recovers. Even after a recovery is well underway, however, a sizable fraction of total unemployment will involve protracted joblessness. The needs of the long-term unemployed deserve special recognition in the designing of policies to attack structural unemployment.

COMBATING CYCLICAL UNEMPLOYMENT

High rates of cyclical unemployment, which the American economy is now experiencing, are largely a consequence of fluctuations in aggregate demand caused by macroeconomic policies and shocks to the economy. The historical experience of the United States and other countries suggests that disinflation is generally associated with lost output and increased unemployment. During periods of disinflation and recession, the measures available to reduce the pain of the transition from accelerating inflation to price stability are limited. Greater fiscal or monetary stimulus might increase employment, but only at the risk of igniting inflation.

The Limits of Macroeconomic Policy

The only way to reduce current high levels of cyclical unemployment is for the United States to achieve a sound recovery from the recent recession. Avoiding future recurrences of high cyclical unemployment requires avoiding an expansion so rapid as to lead to rapidly increasing inflation. Historical experience suggests that the change in the rate of inflation depends both on the rate at which economic activity is expanding and on the level of economic slack. If the slack in the economy declines too rapidly, or capacity utilization is held at too high a level, inflation will tend to increase. The lower limit on unemployment below which inflation will tend to increase is referred to as the *inflation threshold* unemployment rate.

While it is not easy to pinpoint the inflation threshold unemployment rate precisely, it probably lies between 6 and 7 percent. Econometric studies of historical data suggest that when unemployment is close to 6 percent, the rate of inflation tends to accelerate. For example, during 1978 when the unemployment rate was 6.1 percent, inflation as measured by percentage changes in the gross national product (GNP) deflator rose to 7.4 percent from 5.8 percent in 1977. An even larger increase occurred in 1979 when the unemployment rate averaged 5.8 percent.

The Effect of Demographic Factors There are a number of reasons to believe that the inflation threshold unemployment rate increased during the 1960s and 1970s. Many economists believe that demographic factors may have contributed to the increase. Persons with little labor market experience tend to have high rates of unemployment as they move from job to job in an effort to obtain a desirable career position.

In the last 15 years, the children of the baby boom have reached maturity thus raising substantially the share of inexperienced workers in the labor force. In addition, women with little recent labor market experience have entered the labor force at an unprecedented rate during the last 15 years. It has been estimated that if the labor force had the same demographic composition today as it had in 1958, the unemployment rate would have been about three-quarters of a percentage point lower in 1982. The share of young people in the labor force will decline sharply over the next decade due to a dramatic reduction in the birth rate throughout the late 1960s and the 1970s. This provides grounds for cautious optimism that the inflation threshold unemployment rate will decline.

Social Insurance Programs Other factors which have increased the inflation threshold unemployment rate in recent years are less likely to be reversed in the next decade. These include the effects of social programs. While providing important financial support to their recipients, these programs also have both behavioral and reporting effects on the measured unemployment rate.

Behavioral effects of social insurance programs such as unemployment insurance include the encouragement of firms to lay off workers and the inducement of persons to prolong their spells of unemployment. These effects are discussed in more detail below. Reporting effects occur when programs induce persons to change reporting of their labor force status, without changing their behavior. For example, some experts believe that the Federal Supplemental Benefits program instituted during the 1975 recession caused persons who otherwise would have withdrawn from the labor force to report that they were unemployed because of job search requirements. There is some evidence to suggest that the work registration requirements in the food stamp and AFDC programs have had a similar effect.

Wage Rigidity A number of studies show that wages and prices are much more rigid now than prior to World War II, and that rigidity has increased within the post-War period. Increased wage rigidity is likely to raise the economy's inflation threshold level of unemployment, since less flexible wages increase the inevitable unemployment associated with the sectoral shocks which buffet the economy.

The reasons for this change are not well understood. A side effect of the provision of a "safety net" program is that employees may become more resistant to wage reductions, leading to increases in wage and price rigidity. To the extent that the two-earner family is a form of private "safety net" against the financial losses of unemployment, the recent growth in the number of two-earner families may also have contributed to increasing wage rigidity in the United States over time.

Increasing Structural Change A final factor that may have contributed to a rising inflation threshold unemployment rate is the increasing rapidity of structural change in the economy. This acceleration, which is in part caused by the economy's increasing sensitivity to events in the world economy, is evidenced by increasing dispersion across industries and localities in rates of unemployment. Because transfers of human and physical resources are costly and take time, increased unemployment is a concomitant of structural change.

While the separate impacts of these factors—changing demographic composition, larger social insurance programs, increased rigidity, and increased structural change—are difficult to quantify, it is reasonable to conclude that together they may have significantly increased the inflation threshold unemployment rate. Expansionary macroeconomic policies are unlikely to reserve the effects of these changes.

Public Works Employment Programs

Direct provision of public works jobs by the government is a politically popular response to cyclical unemployment during recessions. Available evidence suggests, however, that public works programs adopted in past recessions proved counterproductive, and that the inherent capability of public works programs to combat cyclical unemployment is limited.

The Timing of Public Works Expenditures   Public employment programs that produce useful goods or services generally take time to plan and implement. Therefore, such programs often have their greatest effects on public employment long after an economic recovery has begun. For this reason, public employment programs have sometimes exacerbated rather than mitigated cyclical fluctuations in aggregate demand. A study of the Accelerated Public Works program enacted in September 1962 by the Congress to combat the high unemployment rate of the early 1960s found that the number of jobs created by the program peaked in June 1964, 37 months after the bottom of the recession. More recent experience also confirms that lags in implementation are long. A recent study by the Office of Management and Budget found that 90 percent of the outlays for local public works projects designed to stimulate recovery from the 1974–75 recession occurred more than $2^1/_2$ years after the trough of the recession. The lags in implementing public works programs result in their having destabilizing effects, since a large share of the resulting spending occurs during periods of economic expansion.

The Effect of Federal Funding of Public Works on State Expenditures   Even when spending for these programs begins immediately after they are enacted, many public works projects do not yield a net increase in employment. Because of the long planning and implementation lags, most of the projects available for immediate funding are those that were planned before the recession began. Thus, Federal expenditures on these projects often substitute for outlays that would have taken place anyway.

A major effect of Federal public works expenditures may be to alter the timing of public works projects. The expectation of new public works programs may induce State and local governments to delay making outlays during the early stages of economic downturns in the hope that they will receive Federal funds for projects they have "on the shelf." The importance of this possibility is suggested by experiences with the Local Public Works Capital Development and Investment Act of 1976 and the Public Works Employment Act of 1977, programs intended to spur recovery from the 1975 recession. Three characteristics of these programs may have created incentives for local governments to delay their own discretionary spending until they could see whether the Federal Government would pay their entire bill: (1) projects were financed fully by the Federal Government; (2) grants were limited to quick-starting projects; and (3) there was considerable uncertainty and lengthy delays in the process of awarding money to State and local governments. One study found that State and local public works expenditures fell substantially in mid-1976 and decreased further between 1976 and 1977. It suggested that this may have occurred because States and local governments delayed projects in anticipation of funds becoming available under the 1976 and 1977 public works programs. The study also suggested that these measures may have caused the postponement of as much as $22 billion in total government spending.

Crowding Out of Private Sector Employment   Another reason for discounting the efficacy of public works measures is their adverse side effects on private employment. If public works outlays are financed by additional taxes, the income and spending of consumers are reduced, decreasing the number of jobs in the private economy. Alternatively, insofar as public works outlays are financed by borrowing from the public, interest rates are raised, crowding out some forms of private spending and reducing private employment. The higher interest rates resulting from increased Federal borrowing also discourage capital investments that help create future employment.

Benefits to Workers   An additional reason to discount the efficacy of accelerated public works projects is their limited value to participants. Most jobs in countercyclical public works projects are of extremely short duration and are unlikely to provide participants with lasting job skills. Under the Public Works Impact Program, initiated in fiscal year 1972, the average duration of employment amounted to only 4.1 weeks. Almost 60 percent of all employees worked 2 weeks or less. Data for the local public works programs initiated in 1976 and 1977 and described above, indicate that the average job lasted only 3.5 weeks.

Although public works programs are motivated by a desire to provide jobs for the unemployed, very few jobs are actually filled by unemployed workers. Under the Public Works Impact Program, only 27 percent of all jobs were filled by the previously unemployed. Under the more recent public works programs of 1976 and 1977, it has been estimated that only 12 percent of all jobs were filled by previously unemployed workers.

COMBATING STRUCTURAL UNEMPLOYMENT

The preceding analysis suggests that it would be imprudent to use macroeconomic policies to reduce the unemployment rate below its inflation threshold level of 6 to 7 percent. Such an effort would increase inflation, and ultimately prove counterproductive as increased inflation was followed by recession. This does not mean that unemployment rates in the 6 to 7 percent range are either inevitable or desirable. The inflation threshold level of unemployment can be reduced by policies that consider the special problems of two groups of workers: (1) young people, and (2) adults experiencing long-term unemployment. It can also be reduced by reforms of the unemployment insurance system, which, while providing valuable insurance, may increase the incidence of unemployment.

The Problem of Youth Unemployment

At times of low cyclical unemployment, about half the unemployed are young people between the ages of 16 and 24. Close to one-fourth of all the unemployed are teenagers aged 16 to 19. While unemployment clearly imposes hardships on youths, it has very different economic impacts than it does for adults. Many unemployed youths are in school and looking for part-time work. Most of this group, and many other young people who have left school, are not economically independent, but rather live at home and rely on their parents for financial support. Many other young people experience only brief periods of unemployment as they move from one job to the next.

Table 2 provides information on the labor market activities of young men and women aged 16 to 19 in October 1981, when the teenage unemployment rate was 24.1 percent. Data for 1982 are not yet available. As the table reveals, only 5 percent of all teenagers were out of school and measured as unemployed (because they were looking for work). A striking feature of the youth labor market is the large fraction of young people who are out of school but are neither working nor looking for work. Over 30 percent of female and 14 percent of male out-of-school teenagers were not in the labor force. The factors underlying this labor force withdrawal by young people are not well understood. In some cases, young people may withdraw from the labor force because they are discouraged about their prospects for finding suitable employment. In other cases, labor force withdrawal may reflect a desire for leisure.

The observations about the dynamic character of unemployment made elsewhere in this chapter are especially true of young people. Most young people find jobs or

TABLE 2
EDUCATIONAL AND LABOR MARKET ACTIVITIES OF YOUTH AGED 16 TO 19, BY SEX, OCTOBER 1981

Item	Males			Females		
	Number (thousands)	Percent of subgroup	Percent of population	Number (thousands)	Percent of subgroup	Percent of population
Total population	8,036		100.0	8,059		100.0
Enrolled in school	5,683	100.0	70.7	5,526	100.0	68.6
Employed	2,024	35.6	25.2	1,829	33.1	22.7
Unemployed	424	7.5	5.3	429	7.8	5.3
Not in labor force	3,235	56.9	40.3	3,268	59.1	40.6
Unemployment rate (percent)	17.3			19.0		
Not enrolled in school	2,353	100.0	29.3	2,533	100.0	31.4
Employed	1,585	67.4	19.7	1,340	52.9	16.6
Unemployed	434	18.4	5.4	417	16.5	5.2
Not in labor force	334	14.2	4.2	776	30.6	9.6
Unemployment rate (percent)	21.5			23.7		

Source: Department of Labor, Bureau of Labor Statistics.

leave the labor force fairly quickly. It was recently estimated that of those male teenagers who become unemployed in a given month only 42 percent remain unemployed in the next month.

Youth unemployment is nevertheless a critical economic problem. A large part of the youth unemployment is traceable to the small group of teenagers who experience extensive unemployment. More than 52 percent of all unemployment experienced by teenage males aged 16 to 19 in 1981 was due to the 4.4. percent of the male teenage population of this group who were out of work for more than 6 months during that year.

Evidence also suggests that certain teenagers who suffer extensive unemployment earn lower wages later in life. The direction of causation is very difficult to establish since persons with low skills may simply fare poorly both early and late in life. However, the best evidence available suggests that poor labor market experiences early in life caused reduced wages during adulthood. This suggests the importance of developing policies to improve employment opportunities for the long-term unemployed and to reduce job turnover.

Training, Unemployment, and the Minimum Wage A major problem in the youth labor market is the dearth of "career-oriented" employment opportunities. While people who participate in post-secondary schooling are generally subsidized by the public sector, public support of equivalent magnitude has not been available for the post-high school training of youth who choose to enter the labor force after high school.

Employers may find it very difficult to offer such training because of the constraints imposed by minimum wage legislation. These laws discourage employers from hiring unskilled workers at very low wages and compensating them further by providing training. This may help explain very high job turnover among youths as they move rapidly in and out of "dead-end" jobs. Another consequence of minimum wage laws is that they prevent some young people from acquiring the training that would permit them to find steady, well-paying employment as adults. Statistical studies provide evidence that minimum wages significantly depress the accumulation of valuable skills and resulting growth in earnings among youths who are paid the minimum wage. There is also evidence that the negative effects of the minimum wage on employment and training are concentrated disproportionately among youths with the fewest labor market skills. Thus, although the stated purpose of the minimum wage is to reduce poverty, experience suggests that it may actually decrease the lifetime earnings of some of the poor and thereby increase income inequality.

QUESTIONS FOR DISCUSSION

1 Define *cyclical unemployment* and *structural unemployment*. At the worst point of the recession in 1982, about what fraction of the total unemployment rate could have been attributed to each of these two categories? What would be the approximate breakdown as of today?
2 Of a working teenager, still living at home, and an adult breadwinner, who is *relatively* more likely to be "structurally unemployed"? Who is relatively more likely to be "cyclically unemployed"? What does this suggest about the costs (to both individuals and society) of structural versus cyclical unemployment?

3 Although the long-term unemployed are a relatively small fraction of the total unemployed population at any given time, they make a large contribution to the overall unemployment rate. Explain how this seemingly paradoxical result can be true (a numerical example would be helpful). What happens to the number of long-term unemployed and their contribution to the unemployment rate during recessions?

4 Explain how the government's provision of unemployment insurance (UI) can raise the measured unemployment rate; distinguish between "behavioral" and "reporting" effects. Can you think of a way in which the existence of UI today might act to lower the unemployment rate in the future? (*Hint:* What is the effect of longer periods of search on the quality of job that a worker eventually finds?) Does the tendency of UI to raise unemployment provide grounds for eliminating this program?

5 Why does the *Report* argue against the use of public works programs to combat cyclical unemployment? Would these arguments have applied during the great depression, when extensive use was made of public employment?

6 ". . . Although the stated purpose of the minimum wage is to reduce poverty, experience suggests that it may actually decrease the lifetime earnings of some of the poor and thereby increase income inequality." Discuss.

7 Much unemployment seems to be associated with "declining industries," such as steel. Compare and evaluate the following two alternative policy responses to this problem: (*a*) subsidies and tax breaks to the declining industry to try to induce it to expand production and employment; (*b*) retraining and migration assistance to the workers, to help them find jobs in other sectors.

ON THEORIES OF UNEMPLOYMENT

Robert M. Solow*

Economists usually argue that market forces will act to bring supply and demand into balance. Does this maxim apply in the labor market? Some economists, the so-called new classical macroeconomists (see Readings 20 and 21) argue that it does. In the following article (which was an American Economic Association Presidential Address), the prominent Keynesian economist Robert M. Solow explains why he feels that the supply-equals-demand rule may not be very helpful when we are studying certain labor market phenomena, particularly unemployment.

This reading is difficult in places. It will be understood more easily by those who have had an intermediate course in microeconomics.

There is a long-standing tension in economics between belief in the advantages of the market mechanism and awareness of its imperfections. Ever since Adam Smith, economists have been distinguished from lesser mortals by their understanding of and—I think one has to say—their admiration for the efficiency, anonymity, and subtlety of decentralized competitive markets as an instrument for the allocation of resources and the imputation of incomes. I think we all know this; for confirmation one can look at the results of a paper (James Kearl et al.) presented at the last annual meeting, reporting the responses of professional economists to a sort of survey of technical opinion. The propositions which generated the greatest degree of consensus were those asserting the advantages of free trade and flexible exchange rates, favoring cash trans-

Robert M. Solow, "On Theories of Unemployment," *American Economic Review,* March 1980, pp. 1–11. Reprinted by permission.

*Presidential address delivered at the ninety-second meeting of the American Economic Association, December 29, 1979, Atlanta, Georgia. Like most people, I get by with a little help from my friends, in this case especially Paul Samuelson, George Akerlof, Arnold Kling, and James Tobin.

fers over those in kind, and noting the disadvantages of rent controls, interest rate ceilings, and minimum wage laws.

Views on these policy issues did not seem to represent mere conservative ideology: half of the respondents agreed and another 30 percent agreed "with provisions" that redistribution of income (presumably toward the poorest) is a legitimate function of government policy. The profession's reservations about rent control, interest rate ceilings, and minimum wage laws do not appear to reflect a rejection of the goals of those measures, but rather a feeling that nonprofessionals simply do not understand fully the consequences, often unexpected and undesired, of messing around with the market mechanism. Most of us are conscious of a conflict that arises in our minds and consciences because, while we think it is usually a mistake to fiddle the price system to achieve distributional goals, we realize that the public and the political process are perversely more willing to do that than to make the direct transfers we would prefer. If we oppose all distorting transfers, we end up opposing transfers altogether. Some of us seem to welcome the excuse, but most of us feel uncomfortable. I don't think there is any good way to resolve that conflict in practice.

Simultaneously, however, there is an important current in economics that focuses on the flaws in the price system, the ways that real markets fail because they lack some of the characteristics that make idealized markets so attractive. I think that outsiders, who tend to see economists as simple-minded marketeers, would be astonished to learn how much of the history of modern economic analysis can be written in terms of the study of the sources of market failure. The catalog runs from natural and artificial monopoly, to monopolistic competition, to the importance of public goods and externalities of many other kinds, to—most recently—a variety of problems connected with the inadequate, imperfect, or asymmetric transmission of information and with the likelihood that there will simply be no markets for some of the relevant goods and services.

Even the vocabulary can be revealing. Market "imperfection" suggests a minor blemish of the sort that can make the purchase of "irregular" socks a bargain. Market "failure" sounds like something more serious. To take a more subtle example, I mentioned that one kind of flaw in the system can be the absence of certain markets. The common generic term for the reason why markets are missing is "transaction costs." That sounds rather minor, the sort of thing that might go away in due course as accounting and information processing get cheaper. But some of the cases of missing markets really go much deeper. The fact that distant future generations can not participate directly in the markets for nonrenewable resources will not be remedied by improvements in communication. Nor are the residents of densely populated areas ever likely to be able to dicker effectively with the dozens or hundreds of sources of barely traceable pollutants whose health effects, if any, cumulate over many years.

There is a large element of Rohrschach test in the way each of us responds to this tension. Some of us see the Smithian virtues as a needle in a haystack, as an island of measure zero in a sea of imperfections. Others see all the potential sources of market failure as so many fleas on the thick hide of an ox, requiring only an occasional flick of the tail to be brushed away. A hopeless eclectic without any strength of character, like me, has a terrible time of it. If I may invoke the names of two of my most awesome predecessors as President of this Association, I need only listen to Milton Friedman talk for a minute and my mind floods with thoughts of increasing returns to scale, oligopolistic interdependence, consumer ignorance, environmental pollution, intergenerational inequity, and on and on. There is almost no cure for it, except to listen for a minute to John Kenneth Galbraith, in which case all I can think of are the discipline of competition, the large number of substitutes for any commodity, the stupidities of regulation, the Pareto optimality of Walrasian equilibrium, the importance of decentralizing decision making to where the knowledge is, and on and on. Sometimes I think it is only my weakness of character that keeps me from making obvious errors.

The critics of the mainstream tradition are mistaken when they attribute to it a built-in Panglossian attitude toward the capitalist economy. The tradition has provided both the foundations for a belief in the efficiency of market allocations and the tools for a powerful critique. Economic analysis by itself has no way of choosing between them; and the immediate prospects for an empirically based model of a whole economy, capable of measuring our actual "distance" from the contract curve, are mighty slim. The missing link has to be a matter of judgment—the Rohrschach test I spoke of a minute ago. For every Dr. Pangloss who makes the ink blot out to be of surpassing beauty, give or take a few minor deviations—the second-best of all possible worlds, you might say—there is a Candide to whom it looks a lot like an ink blot. Maybe there are more Panglosses than Candides. But that was true in Voltaire's time too—just before the French Revolution, by the way—and has more to do with the state of society than with the nature of economics.

The tension between market efficiency and market failure is especially pointed in discussions of the working of the labor market, for obvious reasons. The labor market connects quickly with everything else in the economy and its performance matters more directly for most people than that of any other market. Moreover, the labor market's own special pathology, unemployment, is particularly visible, particularly unsettling, and particularly frustrating. The fuse leading from theory to policy in this field is short, and has been known to produce both heat and light throughout much of the history of economics.

Contemporary macro-economic theory, though apparently full of technical novelties, has revived many of the old questions in only slightly different form. One of the points I want to make is that underneath the theoretical innovations—some of which are interesting and important—the basic controversial issues that come to the surface are the same ones that occupied earlier literature. The most important among them is really the old tension between market efficiency and market failure. Should one think of the labor market as mostly clearing, or at worst in the process of quick return to market-clearing equilibrium? Or should one think of it as mostly in disequilibrium, with transactions habitually taking place at non-market-clearing wages? In that case presumably the wage structure is either not receiving any strong signals to make it change in the right direction or is not responding to the signals it receives. My own belief in this case lies with the market-failure side. That is to say, I believe that what looks like involuntary unemployment is involuntary unemployment.

Of course that conclusion only leads to another question. If the labor market often fails to clear, we had better figure out why. There is no shortage of candidate hypotheses. Here I think it is worthwhile to insist on a commonplace: although it is natural for academic people to seek a single weighty Answer to a weighty Question, if only because it is so satisfying to find one, it is quite likely that many of the candidate hypotheses are true, each contributing a little to the explanation of labor-market failure. Now the second general point I want to make is one that I am surprised to hear myself making. While I find several of the candidate hypotheses entirely believable, I am inclined to emphasize some that might be described as noneconomic. More precisely, I suspect that the labor market is a little different from other markets, in the sense that the objectives of the participants are not always the ones we normally impute to economic agents, and some of the constraints by which they feel themselves bound are not always the conventional constraints. In other words, I think that among the reasons why market-clearing wage rates do not establish themselves easily and adjust quickly to changing conditions are some that could be described as social conventions, or principles of appropriate behavior, whose source is not entirely individualistic.

I said that I am a little surprised at myself. That is because I am generally stodgy about assumptions, and like to stay as close to the mainstream framework as the problem at hand will allow. In any case, I think that the unconventional elements in what I have to say are only part of the story. And I assure you that I am not about to peddle amateur sociology to a captive audience. All I do mean to suggest is that we may predispose ourselves to misunderstand important aspects of unemployment if we insist on modelling the buying and selling of labor within a set of background assumptions whose main merit is that they are very well adapted to models of the buying and selling of cloth. Far from advocating that we all practice sociology, I am pleasantly impressed at how much mileage you can get from the methods of conventional economic analysis, if only you are willing to broaden the assumptions a little.

I

It might be interesting to have a history of the evolution of economic ideas about unemployment, and their relation both to the internal logic of the subject and to the parallel evolution of the institutions of the labor market. I am not sufficiently well read to provide that kind of survey. To make my point about the persistence of the market-efficiency market-failure tension, I took a short cut. I went back to reread Pigou's *Lapses from Full Employment,* a little book I remember having been assigned to read as a student just after the war. And that in turn sent me back to its parent book, Pigou's *Theory of Unemployment.* The Preface to *The Theory of Unemployment* is dated April 1933, after a decade of poor performance and relatively high unemployment in Great Britain, well into the Great Depression, and before the publication of the *General Theory.* The Preface to *Lapses from Full Employment* (another example of a revealing vocabulary) is dated November 1944, after five years of the war that put an end to the depression, and well after the appearance of the *General Theory.* That seemed like an interesting approach to the historical question, because current controversies in macro-economic theory are often described as a debate between "Keynesians" and others—"monetarists," "Classicals," or "equilibrium theorists"— and because Pigou, besides being a great economist, was in particular the embodiment of the Marshallian tradition, the leading figure in the "classical economics" that the Keynesian revolution was explicitly intended to overthrow.

Lapses makes interesting rereading. It emphasizes the money wage, whereas its predecessor was written almost entirely in terms of the real wage. The general macro-theoretic framework, in which the discussion of the labor market is embedded, clearly has an eye on Keynes. The underlying model could be *IS-LM* without doing much violence to the argument. There are little anachronisms: Pigou tends to think of the interest rate as being determined in the goods market (by Savings = Investment) and nominal income as being determined by the demand for money. Today we take simultaneity seriously, but the *General Theory* more or less speaks as if real output is determined in the goods market and the interest rate by liquidity preference. After what is to me a confusing description of a Keynesian low-level liquidity-trap equilibrium, Pigou invokes the Pigou effect to explain why the low level might not be as low as all that and then, characteristically, remarks that none of it is very important in practice anyway. All this is relevant here only as background for the treatment of the labor market.

Pigou says the obvious thing first, and I agree that it is the first thing to say: if there is "thorough-going competition" among workers, then the only possible equilibrium position is at full employment. That is little more than a definition of equilibrium. He is aware that he is taking a lot of dynamics for granted. Expectations of falling wages could perversely reduce the demand for labor; and he discusses the possibility that under some conditions, with the interest rate at its practical floor, nominal wage rates and prices may chase each other down and thus prevent the real-wage adjustment needed for an increase in employment. (This is where the Pigou effect makes its appearance, of course.)

It is what comes next that interests me. It is obvious to Pigou, writing in 1944, that the labor market does not behave as if workers were engaged in thorough-going competition for jobs. With the common sense that seems somehow to have escaped his modern day successors, he wonders why it does not. And he discusses three or four of the institutional factors that a reasonable person would mention even now as obstacles to the classical functioning of the labor market.

First of all, he realizes that the labor market is segmented. Not everyone in it is in competition with everyone else. I am not referring here to the obvious fact that abilities, experience, and skills differ, so that unemployed laborers can not compete for the jobs held by craftsmen. That fact of life merely reminds us that "labor" is not a well-defined homogeneous factor of production. Even within skill categories or occupational groups, however, workers have ties to localities, to industries, to special job classifications, even to individual employers. These ties can be broken, but not easily. It is interesting to me that even the *Theory of Unemployment* of 1933 devotes a lot of space to the analysis of a labor market in which there are many "centers of employment"—to use the neutral term chosen by Pigou to describe segmentation of the labor market—between which mobility is absent or slow. Of course he observes that even in a completely segmented labor market, if there is thorough-going competition within segments, full employment will be the rule, although there may be wage differentials between centers of employment for otherwise identical workers. I think that the fact of segmentation is very important, not only because it limits the scope of competition but because its pervasiveness suggests—though it can not prove—that habit and custom play a large role in labor market behavior. From the prominence that he gives it, I gather that Pigou might have agreed.

A second factor, which has been more often discussed, is trade unionism. Pigou does not have very much to say about collective bargaining, but what he says makes sense.

> Of course, these agencies in their decisions have regard to the general state of the demand for labour; they will have no wish to set wage rates so high that half the people of the country are thrown out of work. Nevertheless, there is reason to believe that they do not have regard to demand conditions in such degree as would be necessary to secure, as thorough-going competition would do, the establishment of full employment. [1945, p. 26]

Later on in the book, Pigou makes an observation that is not explicitly connected with collective bargaining. He does connect it with "actual life" however, and it fits organized workers very well, and perhaps others besides:

> In periods of expansion employers might be willing to agree to substantial advances in wage rates if they were confident that, when prosperity ended, they would be able to cancel them. They know, however, that in fact this will not be easy, that elaborate processes will have to be gone through, and that their work-people will put up a strong rear-guard action. . . . In periods of depression wage-earners, for precisely similar reasons, hold out against wage reductions, which they might be ready to concede if it were not for the difficulty that they foresee in getting them cancelled when times improve. . . . A widespread desire for 'safety first' helps to make wage rates sticky. [1945, p. 48]

These casual remarks raise more questions than they answer about the determination of nominal wages by collective bargaining. The first excerpt can be taken as a redefinition of full employment when the labor market is not competitive; the second, however, advances an account of wage stickiness and is therefore on a different footing. It would help to explain the failure of the labor market to clear on any reasonable definition, and thus provide a connection between nominal demand and real output.

The third institutional factor mentioned by Pigou has also been the subject of much analysis, past and present: the provision of unemployment insurance. There are several channels by which the availability of unemployment compensation can add to the recorded amount of unemployment. The prolongation of search is only the most obvious. My own impression is that this is currently a significant factor. As an indication of the complexity of the issues, let me just mention here that some recent research by my colleagues Peter Diamond and Eric Maskin suggests the possibility that in some environments search activity conveys a positive externality. So the optimal search strategy for the individual might provide less than the socially optimal amount of search, and unemployment compensation could be regarded as a corrective subsidy. This is a neat twist on the theme of the counterpoint between market efficiency and market failure. In any case, it can hardly be doubted that the unemployment compensation system is an important determinant of behavior on both sides of the labor market, and complicates even the definition of full employment.

The last comment of Pigou's that I want to cite is especially intriguing because it is so unlike the sort of thing that his present day successors keep saying. Already in the 1933 *Theory of Unemployment* he wrote: ". . . public opinion in a modern civilized State builds up for itself a rough estimate of what constitutes a reasonable living wage. This is derived half-consciously from a knowledge of the actual standards enjoyed by more or less 'average' workers. . . . Public opinion then enforces its view, failing success through social pressure, by the machinery of . . . legislation" (p. 255). A similar remark appears in *Lapses*. Such feelings about equity and fairness are obviously relevant to the setting of statutory minimum wages, and Pigou uses them that way. I think they also come into play as a deterrent to wage cutting in a slack labor market. Unemployed workers rarely try to displace their employed counterparts by offering to work for less; and it is even more surprising, as I have had occasion to point out in the past, that employers so rarely try to elicit wage cutting on the part of their laid-off employees, even in a buyer's market for labor. Several forces can be at work, but I think Occam's razor and common observation both suggest that a code of good behavior enforced by social pressure is one of them. Wouldn't you be surprised if you learned that someone of roughly your status in the profession, but teaching in a less desirable department, had written to your department chairman offering to teach your courses for less money? The fact that nominal wage rates did fall sharply during the early stages of the depression of the 1930's, and the fact that the Chrysler Corporation has been able to negotiate concessions from the UAW certainly show that wage rates are not completely rigid. But those very instances seem to me only to confirm the importance of social convention in less extreme circumstances. After all, people have been known to try to claw their way into a lifeboat who would never dream of cheating on a lift-line.

I think I have made the case that the most eminent representative of orthodox economics in the 1940's was fully aware of the many obstacles to "thorough-going competition" among workers, that is, of the many ways in which the labor market may "fail." In particular, one cannot under those circumstances expect the labor market always to clear. Pigou certainly drew that conclusion. He says, in the Preface to *Lapses:* "Professor Dennis Robertson . . . has warned me that the form of the book may suggest that I am in favour of attacking the problem of unemployment by manipulating wages rather than by manipulating demand. I wish, therefore, to say clearly that this is not so" (p. v).

Pigou clearly felt the tension between market efficiency and market failure. Nevertheless, he did not come down on the side of market failure, even after the 1930's. The very title of *Lapses from Full Employment* tells us that much. Evidently he concluded that the tendency of the capitalist economy to seek (and find) its full-employment equilibrium was strong enough so that departures from full employment could be regarded as mere episodes. Is that surprising? Well, to begin with, there is no accounting for Rohrschach tests. One person's ink blot is another person's work of art. But I think there is also something more systematic to be said.

In the *Theory of Unemployment*, Pigou gives an elaborate analysis of the short-run elasticity of demand for labor. He is very careful: he allows for the elasticity of supply of complementary raw materials; he allows for the (presumably very high) price elasticity of demand for exports; he discusses the effects of discounting future returns

to labor. It is a masterly attempt to get a grip on orders of magnitude. It is all based
on the presumption that the only possible starting point is the elasticity of the marginal-
product-of-labor curve. Let me remind you that in the old standby, two-factor Cobb-
Douglas case, the elasticity of demand for labor with respect to the real wage is the
reciprocal of the share of capital. Everybody's back-of-the-envelope puts the capital
share at $1/4$ and the elasticity of demand for labor at 4. This is not exactly the way
Pigou proceeds, but he reaches the same conclusion: the initial estimate of the elasticity
is "certain to be (numerically) much larger than -1 and may well amount to -5 or
more." There follow some modifications, but the conclusion remains that in times of
depression, the aggregate elasticity of demand for labor with respect to the real wage
"cannot, on the least favourable assumption here suggested, be numerically less than
-3 and may well be larger than -4" except perhaps in the very shortest run.

For practical purposes, one would want to know the elasticity of demand with
respect to the nominal wage, taking account of the likelihood that prices will follow
wages down, at least partially. (Obviously if product prices fall equiproportionally
with wage rates, as Keynes thought might happen in unlucky circumstances, the real
wage doesn't move at all and employment will not improve.)[1] The details of Pigou's
calculations do not concern us, but his conclusion does: ". . . we may . . . not un-
reasonably put the elasticity of the money demand for labour in times of deep depression
at not less numerically than -1.5."

If I could believe that, I too could believe that the labor market generally clears.
To reduce the unemployment rate by 6 percentage points is to increase employment
by about 6 percent, if we ignore for this purpose the side effects that go to make up
Okun's Law. If that could be accomplished by a real-wage reduction of 2 percent, or
even less, that is, by foregoing one year's normal productivity increase, then I could
imagine that the labor market might easily learn to adjust smoothly to fluctuations in
aggregate demand. I could even imagine that workers might accept the necessary 4
percent reduction in nominal wages, in the expectation that half of it would be offset
by lower prices. The trouble is that Pigou's demand elasticities are way too high. A
recent econometric study by Kim Clark and Richard Freeman, based on quarterly data
for U.S. manufacturing, 1950–76, puts the real-wage elasticity of demand for labor
at about one-half, a whole order of magnitude smaller than Pigou's guess.[2] And the
Clark-Freeman work is presented as revisionist, a counterweight to other estimates
that are typically *lower,* averaging out at about 0.15 according to a survey by Daniel
Hamermesh. To my mind, smooth wage adjustment seems intrinsically unlikely in a
world with such a small demand elasticity and institutions like those sketched earlier.
Nothing I read in the newspapers suggests to me that 6 percent of nonfrictional

[1]Neither Pigou nor Keynes invoked Kaldor's notion that prices can be expected to fall faster than wages
in a recession with the resulting rise in real wages providing the force for recovery from the demand side,
through a distributional shift toward wage incomes which generate more spending per dollar than other
incomes do.
[2]The Clark-Freeman estimates are based on quarterly data for aggregate U.S. manufacturing. Their
difference from other work appears to rest on allowing wage changes to operate with a lag different from
other factor prices. According to their results the lag of employment behind wage changes is quite short;
it is complete in about two quarters.

unemployment produces a threat adequate to set off a quick 12–15 percent fall in the real wage, or a drop in nominal wage rates twice as large. Sellers facing inelastic demands usually try to discourage price cutting; why should workers be different?

The modern classical school seems curiously remote from all this. When they try to explain how the equilibrium volume of employment can fluctuate as widely as actual employment does in business cycles, their only substitute for Pigou's high elasticity of demand is a high elasticity of supply (of labor) in the face of a perceived temporary opportunity for unusual gains, which in this case reflects wages that differ from average expected (discounted) future wages. In other words, people who give the vague impression of being unemployed are actually engaged in voluntary leisure. They are taking it now, planning to substitute extra work later, because they think, rightly or wrongly, that current real wages are unusually low compared with the present value of what the labor market will offer in the future. They may be responding to changes in real wages or to changes in the real interest rate.

It is astonishing that believers have made essentially no effort to verify this central hypothesis. I know of no convincing evidence in its favor,[3] and I am not sure why it has any claim to be taken seriously. It is hardly plausible on its face. Even if the workers in question have misread the future, they are merely mistaken, not confused or mystified about their own motives. It is thus legitimate to wonder why the unemployed do not feel themselves to be engaged in voluntary intertemporal substitution, and why they queue up in such numbers when legitimate jobs of their usual kind are offered during a recession.[4]

When they face the market-clearing issue at all, Pigou's successors take a rather abstract line. They regard it as inherently incredible that unexploited opportunities for beneficial trade should be anything but ephemeral—which means merely that they ignore all those human and institutional facts of which Pigou was aware. Or else they argue that one cannot believe in the failure of markets to clear without having an acceptable theory to explain why that happens. That is a remarkable precept when you think about it. I remember reading once that it is still not understood how the giraffe manages to pump an adequate blood supply all the way up to its head; but it is hard to imagine that anyone would therefore conclude that giraffes do not have long necks. At least not anyone who had ever been to a zoo. Besides, I think perfectly acceptable theories can indeed be constructed, as soon as one gets away from foolishly restrictive and inappropriate assumptions.

II

That brings me to the second and last general point I had hoped to make. Suppose one chooses to accept the apparent evidence of one's senses and takes it for granted

---

[3]Just after writing those words, I received a working paper by Robert Hall which (a) concludes that the elasticity of supply of labor required to make the inter-temporal-substitution hypothesis work is actually in the ballpark suggested by other facts, but (b) rejects the whole theory of other empirical grounds. I have done some further experimentation on Hall's data (with the help of Mr. Sunil Sanghvi) with results that cast doubt on the reliability of even the first conclusion. On reflection, I stand by the words in the text.

[4]I have tried to phrase that carefully. For some direct evidence, see "Jobs and Want Ads: A Look Behind the Evidence," *Fortune*, Nov. 20, 1978.

that the wage does not move flexibly to clear the labor market. By the way, my own inclination is to go further and claim that commodity prices are sticky too, at least downward. But it is the persistence of disequilibrium in the labor market that I want to emphasize. How can we account for it?

There is, as I mentioned at the beginning, a whole catalog of possible models of the labor market that will produce the right qualitative properties. Since I have surveyed this literature elsewhere, I will just list a half-dozen possibilities now, with the reminder that they are not mutually exclusive alternatives.

1 There is Keynes's idea that case-by-case resistance to wage reductions is the only way that workers can defend traditional wage differentials in a decentralized labor market. The net result is to preserve the general wage level or its trend, but that is an unintended artifact.

2 There is a complementary hypothesis about the behavior of employers that I have proposed myself: if employers know that aggressive wage cutting in a buyer's market may antagonize the remaining work force, hurt current productivity, and make it harder to recruit high-quality workers when the labor market tightens, they will be less inclined to push their short-run advantage.

3 Pigou realized that widely held notions of fairness, enforced by social pressure or by legislation, might have to be part of any serious account of wage determination. George Akerlof has pursued this trail further, documented the prescription of codes of good behavior in manuals of personnel practice, and showed formally that such codes of behavior can be self-enforcing if people value their reputations in the community. Obviously there are no Emily Post manuals to consult as regards the behavior of laid-off workers, but you would certainly not be astonished to learn that self-esteem and the folkways discourage laid-off workers from undercutting the wages of their still-employed colleagues in an effort to displace them from jobs. Reservation wages presumably fall as the duration of unemployment lengthens; but my casual reading suggests that this pattern shows up more in a willingness to accept lower-paid sorts of jobs than in "thorough-going competition" for the standard job. The cost to the worker of this sort of behavior is diminished by the availability of unemployment insurance. It is worth remembering that the acceptance of lower-grade jobs is itself a form of unemployment.

4 I need only touch on the Azariadis-Baily-Gordon implicit-contract theory, because it has been much discussed in the literature. Here wage stability is a vehicle by which less-risk-averse firms provide income insurance for more-risk-averse workers, presumably in exchange for a lower average wage.[5] It is now understood that the theory works well only when workers have some source of income other than wages, unemployment compensation for instance. This is not really a disadvantage in a world with well-developed unemployment insurance systems. In any case such implicit contracts do

---

[5]Unemployment generated by this mechanism is, in a sense, voluntary. Workers reveal a preference for steady wages over steady employment. But the aggregate welfare cost of the system can still be reduced by stabilization policies. This comment applies equally to the social customs described in the preceding paragraph of the text. One can ask why workers cling to such costly conventions. It is the job of sociology to answer that question. But it is the job of economics to point out that, whatever the reason, the narrowly economic cost of such conventions can be reduced by the stabilization of aggregate demand.

not themselves account for unemployment. Their effect is to reduce the average amount of unemployment below the level that would occur in a simple spot market. The theory belongs in my list because I suspect it does help to account for the habit of wage inertia and therefore the vulnerability of employment to unexpected fluctuations in aggregate demand.

5 Wherever there is collective bargaining in our economy, the standard pattern, with few exceptions, is that wage rates are specified in the contract, and the employer chooses the amount of employment. This is not exactly simple monopoly, because the union cannot set the wage schedule unilaterally. To the extent that it can, another source of wage stickiness can be identified. Under a reasonable assumption about what the union maximizes, it turns out that the only aspect of the demand for labor that has any effect on the monopoly wage is its elasticity. So if the demand curve for labor shifts down nearly isoelastically in a recession, the contractual wage will change little or not at all, and the full effect of the fall in demand will bear on employment. The amount of unemployment compensation available plays a role here too. (There is much more to be said along these lines, and Ian McDonald of the University of Melbourne and I hope to say it on another occasion.)

6 As a last example, I recall Pigou's observation that wage changes may be seen by the parties as hard to reverse without a struggle whose duration and outcome cannot be foreseen. The resulting uncertainty causes employers to drag their feet when demand increases temporarily and workers to reciprocate when demand falls. The result is wage stickiness in the face of fluctuating employment.

Only what Veblen called trained incapacity could prevent anyone from seeing that some or all of these mechanisms do indeed capture real aspects of the modern capitalist economy. Assessing their combined significance quantitatively would be a very difficult task, and I do not pretend to be able to do that. We are all interpreting this ink blot together. Obviously I would not be giving this particular talk if I did not think that wage stickiness is a first-order factor in a reasonable theory of unemployment.

To make my position plausible, I want to try to summarize the sort of general characteristics that the labor market should have if the particular mechanisms that I have enumerated are to be important. By the way, I have no reason to believe that my list is anything like exhaustive; you may think of others. Simply to narrow the field, I have deliberately left out of account factors relating specifically to age, sex, race, and other characteristics that normally form the basis for discussions of structural unemployment as distinct from cyclical unemployment.

The sort of labor market I have in mind is segmented. It often makes sense to think of an employer or definable group of employers as facing its own labor pool. Some members of the labor pool may be unemployed, but still belong to it. Although transportation, information, and transaction costs are possible sources of segmentation, they need not be among the most important. The buildup of firm-specific or industry-specific human capital may be more fundamental, and equally a kind of mutual knowing-what-to-expect that gives both parties in the labor market a stake, a rent, in the durability of the relationship. This point is close to the distinction between auction markets and customer markets made by Arthur Okun in a different context. The labor market, at least the "primary" labor market, is a customer market; this may be one of the important facts that differentiates the primary from the secondary labor market.

A second general characteristic is the availability of some nontrivial source of nonemployment income. The obvious one is unemployment compensation, but I imagine that fringe activity ranging from hustling to home maintenance can function in much the same way. I suppose in some societies the possibility of returning temporarily to farming is now as important as it once was here. The presence of a second earner in the family can make an obvious difference. One consequence is that it becomes easier to maintain a labor pool in the presence of fluctuating employment. In addition, as I mentioned a few moments ago, several of the specific sticky-wage mechanisms in my catalog depend for their operation on this characteristic.

Third, the stability of the labor pool makes it possible for social conventions to assume some importance. There is a difference between a long-term relationship and a one-night stand, and acceptable behavior in one context may be unacceptable in the other. Presumably most conventions are adaptive, not arbitrary, but adaptiveness may have to be interpreted broadly, so as to include pecuniary advantage but not be limited by it. Critics who deride the notion of "economic man" have a point, but usually the wrong point. Economic man is a social, not a psychological, category. There are activities in our culture in which it is socially acceptable and expected that individual pecuniary self-interest will be the overriding decision criterion: choosing a portfolio of securities, for example.[6] There are others in which it is not: choosing a mate, for example. The labor market is more complicated than either, of course, and contains elements of both. Perhaps in nineteenth-century Manchester labor was bought and sold by "thorough-going competition" but I think that is unlikely to be a good approximation to contemporary wage setting. In particular, as I have emphasized, there is nothing in the data or in common observation to make you believe that moderate excess supply will evoke aggressive wage cutting on either side of the labor market.

III

I draw two conclusions from this whole train of thought, one about economics and the other about the economy.

About economics: it need not follow that we old dogs have to learn a lot of new tricks. It still seems reasonable to presume that agents do the best they can, subject to whatever constraints they perceive. But in some contexts the traditional formulations of the objective function and constraints may be inappropriate. In the labor market, the participants are firms and groups of firms on one side, and individual workers, organized trade unions, and informally organized labor pools on the other. Grant me that all feel constrained, to some nontrivial degree, by social customs that have to do with the wage and wage-setting procedures. The result is that factor prices turn up in our equations in unfamiliar ways. Let me just mention a few examples from my earlier list of hypotheses. If Keynes was right about the conventional significance of relative

---

[6]The emotion aroused by the case of South Africa strikes me as one of those extreme exceptions that proves the rule.

wages, then ratios of wage rates appear in the objective functions on the labor side. If the current or future performance of workers depends on their feelings that wage levels are fair, then wage rates appear in the production functions constraining firms. If the individual worker's utility function depends quite conventionally on current income, then the collective objective function of a labor pool of identical workers might reasonably be a weighted average of the utility of the wage and the utility achievable when unemployed, with weights equal to the employment and unemployment fractions. This objective function contains both wage and volume of employment as arguments; and it has the interesting property that the marginal rate of substitution between wage rate and employment can depend very sensitively on the size of the unemployment insurance benefit. Constrained maximization and partial or complete reconciliation in the market can still be the bread and butter of the macro theorist. Spread with more palatable behavior assumptions, they make make a tastier sandwich, and stick to the ribs.

About the economy: if the labor market is often not in equilibrium, if wages are often sticky, if they respond to nontraditional signals, then there is a role for macro policy and a good chance that it will be effective. Equilibrium theories that conclude the opposite may conceivably turn out to have the right answer, but they simply assume what they purport to prove. It is not my argument that standard textbook policy prescriptions are bound to be right. That has to be worked out case by case. All I do claim is that a reasonable theory of economic policy ought to be based on a reasonable theory of economic life.

REFERENCES

G. Akeriof, "The Case Against Conservative Macroeconomics: An Inaugural Lecture," *Economica*, Aug. 1979, *46*, 219–37.

C. Azariadis, "Implicit Contracts and Unemployment Equilibria," *J. Polit. Econ.*, Dec. 1975, *83*, 1183–202.

M. N. Bally, "Wages and Employment under Uncertain Demand," *Rev. Econ. Stud.*, Jan. 1974, *41*, 37–50.

K. Clark and R. Freeman, "How Elastic Is the Demand for Labor?" Nat. Bur. Econ. Res. work. Paper no. 309, Cambridge, Mass., Jan. 1979.

P. Diamond and E. Maskin, "Externalities and Efficiency in a Model of Stochastic Job Matching," working paper, Mass. Inst. Technology, forthcoming.

D. F. Gordon, "A Neo-Classical Theory of Keynesian Unemployment," *Econ. Inquiry*, Dec. 1974, *12*, 431–59.

R. Hal, "Labor Supply and Aggregate Fluctuations," Nat. Bur. Econ. Res. work. paper no. 385, Stanford, Aug. 1979.

D. Hamermesh, "Econometric Studies of Labor Demand and their Applications to Policy Analysis," *J. Hum. Resources*, Fall 1976, *11*, 507–25.

J. Kearl, C. Pope, G. Whiting and L. Wimmer, "A Confusion of Economists?," *Amer. Econ. Rev. Proc.*, May 1979, *69*, 28–37.

A. Okun, "Inflation: Its Mechanics and Welfare Costs," *Brookings Papers*, Washington 1975, *2*, 351–90.

A. C. Pigou, *The Theory of Unemployment,* London 1933.

——, *Lapses from Full Employment,* London 1945.

R. Solow, "Alternative Approaches to Macroeconomic Theory: A Partial View," *Can. J. Econ.,* Aug. 1979, *12,* 339–54.

QUESTIONS FOR DISCUSSION

1 Solow argues that much unemployment is involuntary; by this he means that, at going wages, there is frequently more labor supplied than demanded. Depict a situation of involuntary unemployment on a conventional microeconomic supply-demand diagram. Why is it puzzling to economists that unemployment can persist? Why does Solow call unemployment a "market failure"?

2 (*Continuation of question 1*) Depict a situation of Keynesian involuntary unemployment in a (macroeconomic) *aggregate* supply and demand diagram. Using the same diagram, show how fiscal or monetary policy can eliminate involuntary unemployment. In terms of the microeconomic supply-demand diagram of question 1 above, what does the fiscal or monetary policy do that allows a restoration of full employment?

3 What three institutional factors were cited by Pigou as reasons that labor markets might clear slowly? Critically analyze these factors using the microeconomic supply-demand diagram. Do they provide a rationale for *involuntary* unemployment?

4 Solow stresses the importance of equity, fairness, and social conventions in the labor market. Explain why such factors might impede wage-cutting in the labor market. Do these factors provide a rationale for involuntary unemployment?

5 Solow also makes an argument, elsewhere called the *efficiency wage hypothesis,* that firms might avoid wage cuts for fear that such cuts would act to lower the productivity of their workers. How might wage reductions lower workers' productivity? If the efficiency wage hypothesis is true, could it be a source of involuntary unemployment?

SUPPLY-SIDE ECONOMICS: OLD TRUTHS AND NEW CLAIMS

Martin Feldstein*

The announced goal of President Reagan's fiscal policies (see Reading 5), as well as many of his other economic policies, was to increase productivity and growth by stimulating aggregate supply. In this article, Martin Feldstein of Harvard, a former chairman of Reagan's Council of Economic Advisers, gives his assessment of supply-side economics.

Experience has shown that the notion "supply-side economics" is a malleable one, easily misused by its supporters, maligned by its opponents, and misinterpreted by the public at large. Perhaps now, five years after supply-side economics became a slogan for a changing economic policy, it is possible to assess what supply-side policy really means and how the policies adopted under that banner have fared.

The term supply-side economics originated as a way of describing an alternative to the demand side emphasis of Keynesian economics. The essence of Keynesian analysis is its conclusion that the level of national income and employment depend on the level of aggregate demand, and that easy money and expanded budget deficits, by stimulating demand, can increase output and employment. Although this may have been an appropriate emphasis during the depression years of the 1930's when Keynes developed his theory, by the 1960's and 1970's it was clear to most economists that

Martin Feldstein, "Supply-Side Economics: Old Truths and New Claims," *American Economic Review,* May 1986, pp. 26–30. Reprinted by permission.

*Professor of Economics, Harvard University, Cambridge, MA 02138, and President, National Bureau of Economic Research.

it was wrong to focus exclusively on demand and to ignore the factors that increase the potential supply of output—capital accumulation, technical progress, improvements in the quality of the labor force, freedom from regulatory interference, and increases in personal incentives. Many of us also concluded that the persistently high level of measured unemployment did not reflect inadequate demand but was due to government policies like unemployment insurance, welfare restrictions, and the minimum wage that reduced the effective supply of labor.

In all of these ways, many of us were supply siders before we ever heard the term supply-side economics. Indeed, much of our supply-side economics was a return to basic ideas about creating capacity and removing government impediments to individual initiative that were central in Adam Smith's *Wealth of Nations* and in the writings of the classical economists of the nineteenth century. The experience of the 1930's had temporarily made it easy to forget the importance of the supply factors, but by the 1970's they were returning to the mainstream of economics. (See my 1981, 1982 papers.)

It is important in any discussion of supply-side economics to distinguish the traditional supply-side emphasis that characterized most economic policy analysis during the past 200 years from the new supply-side rhetoric that came to the fore as the decade began.

I. THE SHIFT IN POLICY

Economic policy took a few hesitating steps in the traditional supply-side direction in the late 1970's with deregulation in the transportation industry, a significant reduction in the tax on capital gains, and the partial taxation of unemployment compensation. But it was only in 1981 that Congress enacted the major tax bill that has become the centerpiece of supply-side economics.

The emphasis throughout the tax legislation was on changing marginal tax rates to strengthen incentives for work, saving, investment and risk taking. For individual taxpayers, the basic features of the Economic Recovery Tax Act of 1981 were a 25 percent across-the-board reduction in personal tax rates, an extra tax reduction for two-earner families, an increased exemption for long-term capital gains, and the creation of universal Individual Retirement Accounts that effectively permit the majority of American employees to save as much as they want out of pretax income and pay tax on those savings on a consumption tax basis. Personal tax brackets were also indexed to prevent inflation from raising real tax burdens (although this indexing was only scheduled to begin in 1985). For businesses, the 1981 legislation contained accelerated depreciation schedules that significantly reduced the cost of investment in plant and equipment, and an increased tax credit for research and development.

The Reagan Administration also began an unprecedented reversal of the share of *GNP* absorbed by government nondefense spending. Those outlays declined from 15.1 percent of *GNP* in fiscal year 1980 to 14.1 percent of *GNP* in FY 1984. When the Social Security and Medicare outlays are excluded, this spending declined from 9.3 percent of *GNP* in 1980 to 7.4 percent in 1984. These spending reductions were significant not only because they released resources that could be used to finance tax rate reductions, but also because they were often achieved by shrinking programs that in themselves had adverse incentive effects.

President Reagan also provided strong support for the anti-inflationary Federal Reserve policies. The sharp fall in inflation between 1980 and 1982 significantly reduced the effective tax rates on the return to corporate capital, increasing the real after-tax return to savers as well as reducing the uncertainty of saving and investment.[1]

II. EXCESSIVE CLAIMS

These policies were a major step in the direction recommended by supply-side economists of both the new and old varieties. What distinguished the new supply siders from the traditional supply siders as the 1980's began was not the policies they advocated, but the claims that they made for those policies.

The traditional supply siders (although I dislike labels, I consider myself one of that group) were content to claim that the pursuit of such tax, spending, and monetary policies would, over the long run, lead to increased real incomes and a higher standard of living. We recognized that the key to this process was increased saving and investment and knew that that would take a long time to have a noticeable effect.[2]

The "new" supply siders were much more extravagant in their claims. They projected rapid growth, dramatic increases in tax revenue, a sharp rise in saving, and a relatively painless reduction in inflation. The height of supply-side hyperbole was the "Laffer curve" proposition that the tax cut would actually increase tax revenue because it would unleash an enormously depressed supply of effort. Another remarkable proposition was the claim that even if the tax cuts did lead to an increased budget deficit, that would not reduce the funds available for investment in plant and equipment because tax changes would raise the saving rate by enough to finance the increased deficit. It was also claimed that the rapid rise in real output that would result from the increased incentive to work would slow the rate of inflation without the need for a rise in unemployment because the increased supply of goods and services could absorb the rising nominal demand.

Probably no single individual made all of those claims—at least not at the same time. And anyone who feels the need to defend his name can argue that the administration's 1981 economic program was not enacted exactly as proposed. Nevertheless, I have no doubt that the loose talk of the supply-side extremists gave fundamentally good policies a bad name and led to quantitative mistakes that not only contributed to subsequent budget deficits, but also made it more difficult to modify policy when those deficits became apparent.

---

[1]The effects of inflation on effective tax rates on investment in plant and equipment are analyzed in the papers collected in my book (1983a).

[2]Some of us were also nervous about the magnitude of the enlarged tax cut that emerged from the bargaining between the congressional Democrats and Republicans. I advocated making a large part of the personal tax cut an immediate indexing of the tax brackets (to eliminate the risk of a real tax cut that was either bigger or smaller than needed to offset bracket creep during the years 1981–85) and phasing in much of the remaining tax cut only as spending cuts were achieved.

III. GROWTH AND RECOVERY

To assess the claims of the new supply siders, it is useful to compare the actual growth of real *GNP* between 1981 and 1985 with the growth that the supply siders initially projected. The record shows that real *GNP* increased 10.9 percent between 1981 and 1985, only slightly more than half of the 19.1 percent predicted in the Reagan Administration's original economic plan.[3]

This 45 percent shortfall in economic growth cannot be blamed, as some of the new supply siders would now do, on a failure of the Federal Reserve to supply as much money and credit as the plan originally envisioned. The 1981 *Program for Economic Recovery* assumed that "the growth rates of money and credit are gradually reduced from the 1980 levels to one-half those levels by 1986" (p. 23) while the actual money growth rates have hardly declined at all since 1981.

Although the original forecast of nearly 5 percent a year real growth from 1981 to 1985 was improbable on the basis of both historic experience and economic theory, the short-fall was clearly exacerbated by the recession that depressed *GNP* from the third quarter of 1981 until the final quarter of 1982. The new supply siders were naively optimistic when they claimed that the double digit inflation of 1980 and 1981 could be halved in a few years without any increase in unemployment simply by increasing output enough through improved incentives to absorb the excess demand.

Most of the new supply siders have now conveniently forgotten the substantial discrepancy between their growth forecast and the subsequent experience. But some of the supply-side extremists even claim that the recovery was delayed because individuals preferred to "consume leisure" and were waiting to return to work until the final stage of the tax rate reduction had occurred. Anyone who believes that that explains the 10.7 percent unemployment in December 1982 has not studied that data on the composition and timing of unemployment or on the relation between the spending upturn and subsequent reductions in unemployment. And those who wish to believe that the cut in the tax rate stimulated a major increase in the number of people wanting to work will be disappointed by the data on labor force participation rates.

During the first four quarters of the recovery, real *GNP* increased at about the average pace of the previous recoveries. In the second year of the recovery, the rise in *GNP* exceeded the past norm. But now, eleven quarters after the recovery began, the cumulative rise in *GNP* has settled back to the middle of the range of past recoveries.

How much of the recovery has been due to the stimulus to increased supply that was provided by the new policies?[4] I have already commented on the lack of evidence of an induced increase in the number of people wanting to work. But it would be equally wrong to view the recovery as the result of the fiscal stimulus to demand as some traditional Keynesians have done (for example, James Tobin, 1984).

In fact, the rise in nominal *GNP* since 1982 can be more than fully explained by the traditional relationship to the lagged increase in money (*M*1). The division of the

---

[3]See The White House, page S-1. This official forecast predicted less growth than some of the more ardent new supply siders anticipated.

[4]The remainder of this section is based on my 1986 article.

nominal *GNP* increase between *GNP* and inflation was, however, more favorable than would have been expected on the basis of past experience; somewhere around 2 percent of the 15 percent rise in real *GNP*, since the recovery began cannot be explained by the increase of nominal *GNP* and the past pattern of inflation and might therefore be attributed to supply side factors. However, the rise in the exchange rate fully explains the relatively favorable inflation experience and leaves no unexplained rise in real *GNP*. Of course, it might be argued that supply-side factors contributed to the dollar's rise. Only further research will resolve whether supply-side influences have contributed to the rise in real *GNP* since 1981.

Let me emphasize that, to a traditional supply sider like me, the positive but apparently modest supply-side effect is neither surprising nor disappointing. Although we would expect some increase in work effort from the reduction in the highest marginal tax rates, past evidence all points to relatively small changes. The favorable effects of improved incentives for saving and investment can only be expected after a much longer period of time.

IV. TAX REVENUE

Perhaps the most dramatic claim of some of the new supply siders was that an across-the-board reduction in tax rates would be self-financing within a few years because of the increased output that results from the enhanced after-tax pay.[5] It is, of course, very difficult to disentangle the effects of the tax legislation from other things that influenced tax revenue. But a very careful study by Lawrence Lindsey (1985a,b) indicates that in 1982 the response of taxpayers did offset about one-third of the effect of the tax cut on federal receipts.

Lindsey reports that about 65 percent of the induced offsetting rise in tax revenue reflects higher pretax wages, salaries, and business profits than would have been anticipated without the change in tax rates and tax rules, 25 percent reflects an increase in realized capital gains, and the remaining 10 percent is due to reductions in various itemized deductions. These induced offsetting effects are very small among taxpayers with incomes below $20,000. Only among taxpayers whose initial marginal tax rates exceeded 50 percent was there evidence that the rate reduction did not reduce federal revenue at all.

Only time will tell whether this first-year tax response overstates the long-term effect (because it reflects a shift in the timing of income receipts and deductions rather than a more fundamental change in behavior) or understates the long-term effect (because it takes time for taxpayers to adjust their behavior to new tax rules). But the effect for 1982 is clearly an economically significant one. Although the increase in taxable income fell far short of the claims made by the overoptimistic new supply siders and may have been due in large part to a restructuring of income (for example,

---

[5]The administration never made such a claim although the unusually strong real growth that it predicted for the first five years would have been sufficient to recoup between one-half and three-quarters of the proposed 30 percent tax cut.

from fringe benefits to cash) rather than an increase in work effort, the rise in taxable income is a reminder that the traditional revenue estimation method that ignores the behavioral response to tax changes can be very misleading (see my 1983b report).

V. CONCLUSION

The experience since 1981 has not been kind to the claims of the new supply-side extremists that an across-the-board reduction in tax rates would spur unprecedented growth, reduce inflation painlessly, increase tax revenue, and stimulate a spectacular rise in personal saving. Each of those predictions has proven to be wrong.

But it would be unfortunate if this gave a bad reputation to the traditional supply-side verities that the evolution of a nation's real income depends on its accumulation of physical and intellectual capital and on the quality and efforts of its workforce. Moreover, nothing about the experience since 1981 would cause us to doubt the time-honored conclusion of economists that tax rules influence economic behavior and that high marginal tax rates reduce incentives.

Indeed, the evidence suggests that the reduction in tax rates did have a favorable effect on work incentives and on real *GNP,* and that the resulting loss of tax revenue was significantly less than the traditional revenue estimates would imply. Traditional supply-side considerations are undoubtedly important in the design of economic policies in general and of tax policies in particular. But the miraculous effects anticipated by some of the new supply-side enthusiasts were, alas, without substance.

REFERENCES

Feldstein, Martin, "The Retreat from Keynesian Economics," *The Public Interest,* Summer 1981, *64,* 92–105.

———, "The Conceptual Foundations of Supply Side Economics," in *Supply Side Economics in the 1980's,* proceedings of a conference sponsored by the Federal Reserve Bank in Atlanta and the Emory University Law & Economics Center, May 1982.

———, (1983a) *Inflation, Tax Rules and Capital Formation,* Chicago: University of Chicago Press, 1983.

———, (1983b) *Behavior Simulation Methods in Tax Policy Analysis,* NBER Project Report, Chicago: University of Chicago Press, 1983.

———, "The 1983 Economic Recovery: Lessons for Monetary and Fiscal Policy," forthcoming, 1986.

Lindsey, Lawrence, (1985a) "Taxpayer Behavior and the Distribution of the 1982 Tax Cut," NBER Working Paper No. 1760, 1985.

———, (1985b) "Estimating the Revenue-maximizing Top Personal Tax Rate," NBER Working Paper No. 1761, 1985.

Tobin, James, "Unemployment in the 1980s: Macroeconomic Diagnosis and Prescription," in Andrew Pierre, ed., *Unemployment and Growth in the Western Economies,* New York: Council on Foreign Relations, 1984.

The White House, *America's New Beginning: A Program for Economic Recovery,* Washington: USGPO, February 18, 1981.

QUESTIONS FOR DISCUSSION

1 According to Feldstein, to what weaknesses in the standard Keynesian approach was supply-side economics reacting?

2 Explain Feldstein's distinction between "traditional" and "new" supply-side approaches. What problem does he have with the new approach?

3 What were the major components of Reagan's shift in policy, starting in 1981? How were these policies supposed to affect (*a*) the labor force participation rate, (*b*) the unemployment rate, (*c*) output per worker (productivity), (*d*) the national savings rate, (*e*) the fraction of GNP devoted to business fixed investment, (*f*) the inflation rate, (*g*) the ratio of government spending to GNP, (*h*) the ratio of taxes to GNP? Using the *Economic Report of the President*, find data on each of these variables for 1981 and for the current year, and compare. What is your assessment of supply-side economics?

4 Both supply-side and Keynesian approaches predict that a (say) 20 percent cut in tax rates will reduce actual government revenue by less than 20 percent; however, the reasons given by the two schools of thought for this effect differ. Explain, from each of the two points of view, why revenue should fall less than tax rates. What evidence is given by Feldstein that the supply-side explanation may have at least some relevance?

INDUSTRIAL POLICY:
A DISSENT

Charles L. Schultze*

Concern over the slowdown in the growth of productivity and output in the United States has given rise to a number of proposals to combat the problem. Some of these proposals (e.g., from supply-siders; see Reading 30) have advocated greater reliance on market forces; others have supported a larger government role in the allocation of resources. A number of policy suggestions of the latter sort have been grouped under the general name of *industrial policies*. In the following article, written just after the 1981–1982 recession (which slowed growth even further), Brookings Institution economist Charles Schultze presents a critique of the industrial policy approach.

The last ten years have been a time of troubles for most of the world's industrial economies. The growth of output and productivity has slowed. Both inflation and unemployment have averaged substantially higher than in earlier postwar years. And the decade has produced the two worst recessions of the postwar period.

In the United States, this experience has spawned two new economic doctrines, each purporting to explain the source of at least some of our economic ills and offering a plan of action to deal with them. These economic theories originated outside of the mainstream of professional economic thought. The first of them is supply-side economics, which is based on a vast exaggeration of the incentive effects of lower taxes.

From *The Brookings Review*, Fall 1983. Copyright © 1983 by The Brookings Institution, Washington, D.C.

*Charles L. Schultze is a senior fellow in the Economic Studies program at Brookings. He was chairman of the Council of Economic Advisers from 1977 to 1980 and director of the U.S. Bureau of the Budget from 1965 to 1967. His books include *The Public Use of Private Interest*.

It has had a spectacular political success, and was installed in early 1981 as official U.S. government policy.

The second of these new theories—and the latest entry in the competition for the hearts and minds of political candidates—is a set of economic ideas and policy recommendations that goes by the name "industrial policy." It has been the subject of a growing stream of books and articles; it has been endorsed as a concept by the AFL-CIO; its precepts have been incorporated in a number of bills now before the Congress; and it is receiving a sympathetic hearing from many of the candidates for the 1984 Democratic presidential nomination.

The phrase "industrial policy" means somewhat different things to different people; it refers not so much to a single theory as to a loose collection of similar diagnoses and proposals. The diagnoses generally cluster around two basic propositions:

First, the United States has been "de-industrializing." The share of national output generated by manufacturing has been falling in recent years while the share attributable to services has been growing. Within manufacturing a number of essential heavy industries are in absolute decline, and the United States is no longer at the cutting edge of technological advance in the newer, high-tech industries. We are becoming increasingly uncompetitive in world markets. These are the symptoms of deep-seated structural problems; they will not be cured by macroeconomic measures aimed at overall economic growth. The private market is not directing investment to the right places; older manufacturing industries cannot find the funds they need to rehabilitate themselves, and promising new firms in the advancing sectors are often unable to secure as much venture capital as they need for growth. American labor finds it difficult to make the necessary transition from older, declining industries to newer ones with good growth potential and high value-added per worker; this is partly because investment is being directed to the wrong industries and partly because laid-off workers do not have the skills needed or are not in the right locations. And when these dislocated workers eventually do get reemployed it is too often in low-skill jobs paying low wages. We are in danger of becoming a nation of hamburger joints and boutique shops.

Second, some other countries—Japan being the preeminent example—have developed governmental policies that successfully promote vigorous industrial growth. The Japanese government identifies potential winners in the competition for world markets and encourages their growth, while simultaneously protecting and easing the burden of adjustment for older but essential heavy industries. Farsighted officials in the Japanese Ministry of International Trade and Industry (MITI), working closely with cooperative Japanese business leaders and bankers, plan and organize, years in advance, such industrial achievements as the penetration of world automobile markets, the development of automated steel mills producing at water's edge for exports, the 256K memory chip, and now the ultimate supercomputer.

The various proponents of industrial policy offer a wide range of suggestions to deal with the structural problems they identify. Many of their proposals involve new or modified federal initiatives in traditional areas: expanded support for technical education; research and development; and programs to retrain workers. Whatever the merits of these ideas, they do not constitute a major new thrust in economic policy.

What is new, however, is the proposal that government deliberately set out to plan and create an industrial structure, and a pattern of output and investment, significantly different from what the market would have produced. Two leading advocates of industrial policy, Ira Magaziner and Robert Reich, put the matter this way: "We suggest that U.S. companies and the government develop a coherent and coordinated industrial policy whose aim is to raise the real income of our citizens by improving the patterns of our investments rather than by focusing only on aggregate investment levels."[1]

Industrial policy thus aims to channel the flow of private investment towards some firms and industries—and necessarily, therefore, away from others. The government develops, at least in broad outline, an explicit conception of the direction in which industrial structure ought to be evolving, and then adopts a set of tax, loan, trade, regulatory, and other policies to lead economic activity along the desired path.

Industrial policy typically has two aspects—"picking the winners" and "protecting the losers"—and proponents sometimes disagree as to the relative emphasis to be placed on each. "Picking the winners" involves identifying industries that are at the cutting edge of economic progress, with such characteristics as high growth potential and high value-added per worker, and then providing investment subsidies, research support, and other assistance to existing firms and new entrants in those industries. "Protecting the losers," on the other hand, involves supporting and presumably helping to rehabilitate major declining industries. The government measures that would be deployed for this purpose include creation of barriers against competition from imports, special tax breaks, subsidized loans, and selectively favorable regulatory treatment. In most versions of industrial policy, the government, in a switch from current practice, would require that labor and management in these declining industries accept major reforms—wage restraint, reduction of featherbedding rules, and improved managerial practices—as preconditions for assistance.

In addition to the two explicit propositions noted above—that America has been de-industrializing and that the government of Japan has successfully managed industrial adjustment—there are two *implicit* premises on which the case for a U.S. industrial policy rests. The first of these is that the government has the analytical capability to determine with greater success than market forces what industrial structure is appropriate, who the potential winners are, which of the losers should be saved, and how they should be restructured. The second is that the American political system would (or could) make such critical choices among firms, individuals, and regions on the basis of economic criteria rather than political pressures.

In fact, as we shall see, reality does not square with any of the four premises on which the advocates of industrial policy rest their case. America is *not* de-industrializing. Japan does *not* owe its industrial success to its industrial policy. Government is *not* able to devise a "winning" industrial structure. Finally, it is *not* possible in the American political system to pick and choose among individual firms and regions in the substantive, efficiency-driven way envisaged by advocates of industrial policy.

---

[1] Ira Magaziner and Robert Reich, *Minding America's Business,* Harcourt Brace Jovanovich, New York, 1982, p. 4.

DE-INDUSTRIALIZATION: A NONEXISTENT TREND

America has not been de-industrializing. Throughout the industrial world, economic performance in the 1970s did fall behind the record of the 1960s. But relative to the industries of other countries, American industry performed quite well by almost all standards.[2]

During the decade of the 1970s, before the current recession began, the United States was vastly superior to the major European countries and to Japan in the generation of new jobs. Total employment grew by 24 percent in the United States during that decade. The next best performer was Japan, with a 9 percent increase. Other countries were far behind; in Germany, for example, employment actually fell. Moreover, the United States was one of only three major industrial countries—Italy and Canada having been the others—with any increase in *manufacturing* employment. According to OECD data, manufacturing production in the United States, while rising less rapidly than production in Japan, grew faster than the European average and outstripped the gains made in Germany, a country that is usually mentioned, along with Japan, as a leading example of industrial strength.[3]

Manufacturing production in the United States typically rises more in business cycle expansions, and falls further in contractions, than does total GNP. After adjustment for this regular cyclical pattern—and contrary to popular impression—the share of private domestic GNP produced by manufacturing industries did not decline significantly in the 1970s.[4] The proportion of total U.S. employment accounted for by manufacturing has been falling throughout the postwar period, but this principally reflects the fact that productivity growth (output per person) has continued to grow faster in manufacturing than in most other parts of the economy.

The relatively good performance of the industrial sector in the 1970s was partly due to a very large increase during the decade—in fact, a doubling—in exports of American manufactured goods. This was a good bit less than the rise in Japanese exports, but substantially higher than the increase experienced by Europe. America's export strength was aided by a decline in the real exchange value of the dollar, from

---

[2]In a forthcoming Brookings book, Robert Z. Lawrence documents in substantial detail the absence of any trend toward de-industrialization in the United States during the 1970s and, in particular, the fallacy of the proposition that international trade has contributed to depressing output and employment in American manufacturing. This section of the paper owes much to his work.

[3]To reduce distortions caused by cyclical influences (U.S. recessions in 1970 and 1980), average output in 1969–70 and 1979–80 was used to make the decade output comparisons. The European average was held down by the very poor performance of the United Kingdom, but even if the United Kingdom is excluded from these calculations, the growth of manufacturing output in the United States still exceeded that of the rest of Europe as reported by the OECD data. The U.S. Bureau of Labor Statistics produces an alternative set of manufacturing output measures for selected countries; according to these data, the United States outperformed Germany and the average of eight European countries, but grew less than the European average (33.5 versus 36 percent) if the United Kingdom is excluded.

[4]During the cyclical peak of the Vietnam war boom, 1965–69, the constant-dollar manufacturing share averaged slightly higher (30 percent) than it did in both the early years of that decade (28.2 percent) and the last years of the 1970s (28.6 percent), but by no more than can be explained by the strength of the boom. In a regression equation fit to data from 1955–80 that linked the manufacturing share to a cyclical variable and a time trend, the time trend did have a very small negative coefficient of marginal statistical significance. The trend was so slight that it would require some thirty years to reduce the share by one percentage point. There was no evidence that the trend became larger in the 1970s.

an overvalued level at the beginning of the decade to what many people believed was a somewhat undervalued level at the end. Since it is unlikely that the value of the dollar will fall steadily over the long run, the share of U.S. economic activity accounted for by the manufacturing sector could conceivably decline very slowly. That would be a natural development, however, in no way reflecting a structural malaise requiring new governmental policies.

The United States does have some old-line heavy industries with deep-seated structural problems—especially the steel and automobile industries. But they are not typical of American industry generally. There is no evidence that in periods of reasonably normal prosperity American labor and capital are incapable of making the gradual transitions that are always required in a dynamic economy, as demand and output shift from older industries to newer ones at the forefront of technological advances.

Indeed, American industry successfully made some important and desirable structural adjustments in the 1970s, even though that was a decade of economic difficulties throughout the world. Thus, Robert Lawrence of Brookings reports that the U.S. international trade *surplus* in the products of high-tech industries grew from $12 billion in 1972 to $40 billion in 1979, while the trade *deficit* in other manufactured products rose from $15 billion to $35 billion over the same period. Yet, according to a study done for the National Commission for Employment Policy, dislocated workers— defined as unemployed people whose last jobs were in declining industries and who had been out of work for more than eight weeks—amounted to only 0.4 percent of the labor force in March, 1980.[5] In addition, although the total unemployment rate was higher in the United States than in most large European countries as the 1970s drew to a close, long-term unemployment was substantially lower.[6]

But even if it is true that the United States was not de-industrializing in the 1970s, has not the industrial sector performed very much worse than the economy in general during the past several years? Yet, it has. From 1981 through the fourth quarter of 1982—the trough of the recession—GNP declined by 2.2 percent while manufacturing production fell by 10.6 percent. But the outsized drop in manufacturing production occurred for two reasons having nothing to do with de-industrialization. First, as noted above, manufacturing production *always* falls faster than GNP during recessions, and rises faster during booms. In the first half of 1983, for example, as GNP began to recover at a 5.9 percent annual rate, manufacturing production jumped up at a 16.2 percent rate. Second, the huge rise in the real exchange value of the dollar over the last two years discouraged U.S. exports and encouraged foreign imports—a development that had an especially depressing effect on American manufacturing industries. But the overvaluation of the dollar was obviously not caused by structural deficiencies

[5]Marc Bendick, Jr., and Judith Radlinski, "Workers Dislocated by Economic Change: Do They Need Federal Employment and Training Assistance?" National Commission for Employment Policy, *Seventh Annual Report*, Appendix B.

[6]Long-term unemployment rates (percent of the labor force) in 1979 were: United States (1.14), United Kingdom (1.92), France (4.41), Germany (3.35). The long-term unemployment definition—fifteen weeks or longer for the U.S., fourteen weeks for the U.K., and three months for France and Germany—does bias the U.S. rate down relative to the others, but not by enough to account for those differences. *Economic Report of the President*, January, 1981, p. 127. These findings were confirmed by a later OECD analysis reported in *Economic Outlook*, July, 1983, p. 46 (Table 15).

in American industry; it was principally the result of the combination of tight money and loose budgetary policy that gave us unprecedentedly high interest rates. What is needed is a better mix of macroeconomic policies, not a new government agency to influence the pattern of industrial investment.

What about the dramatic fall in the rate of productivity growth in the United States during the 1970s? Does that not reflect, at least in part, a major structural problem in U.S. manufacturing sector? The pace of productivity growth did, indeed, decrease. While the reasons for this decline are still something of a mystery, a few things are known. First, the decline was worldwide—and its magnitude in the United States was about midway down the list of industrial countries. Second, the decline was not concentrated in manufacturing industries; in fact, by most estimates it was somewhat smaller there than in the other sectors of the economy, and productivity growth has continued to be higher in manufacturing than in most sectors. Third, the decline was not caused by a shift in production away from high-productivity manufacturing industries to low-productivity service industries.[7]

Productivity growth is the source of rising living standards. The sharp decline in that growth, in manufacturing and elsewhere, is the most serious long-run problem facing the U.S. economy. But there is no evidence that this decline stems from a tendency for the private market system to allocate investment to the "wrong" places—away from the manufacturing sector or, within manufacturing, to the wrong firms or industries. The decrease in productivity growth in no way bolsters the case for an industrial policy.

A CLOSER LOOK AT THE JAPANESE SUCCESS

The postwar flourishing of Japan's economy is frequently cited as the premier example of how successful an industrial policy can be. The Japanese do have a way of working cooperatively towards national economic objectives without getting strangled in bureaucratic red tape or dulling competition among business firms. But the contributions of MITI and of industrial policy to Japan's postwar success have been far overstated. Other factors were primarily responsible for the phenomenal growth that the Japanese economy enjoyed until very recently.

First, over the past two decades, the Japanese saved and invested some 30 to 35 percent of their GNP, compared to 17 to 20 percent in the United States.[8] Second, with an industrial plant technologically far behind those of the United States and Western Europe, Japanese business firms were able to put the huge savings to work at moderate risk and with good returns by upgrading their capital stock with known technologies. Countries that were much nearer to the technological frontier, like the

---

[7]Martin Neil Baily estimated, more generally, that none of the slowdown in American productivity growth since 1973 can be explained by a shifting composition of output among major American industries. Baily, "The Productivity Growth Slowdown by Industry," *Brookings Papers on Economic Activity*, 2:1982, pp. 445–51.

[8]Based on OECD estimates of gross fixed capital formation as a percent of gross domestic product (GDP). *Economic Outlook 1960–1980*, Table R-3. The difference between GDP and GNP is small and does not affect the basic comparison between the United States and Japan.

United States, had to depend more heavily for their economic growth on the gradual advance of technical knowledge. Third, the Japanese appear to have developed a unique set of cooperative labor-management relationships that promote high quality work and rapid productivity growth.

Throughout the postwar period, the Japanese government in general, and MITI in specific, did act on a broad view of what was required for rapid economic growth in the particular circumstances facing Japan. For example, private savings and investment were encouraged by tax laws and other measures. Up through the early 1970s, macroeconomic policies were highly expansive, but with a combination of very stimulative monetary policies and large budget surpluses. Thus, the government endeavored to encourage the rapid expansion of both demand and supply. Since it needed to import virtually all of its fuel and raw materials, Japan discouraged the import of manufactured goods. Especially in the earlier part of postwar history, when it was still lagging behind other major countries in industrial technology, Japan protected large segments of its home market against import competition.

But while a broad strategy along these lines did guide Japanese economic policy during the postwar period, that strategy did not dictate the detailed structure of Japanese industry. The major decisions about where funds would be invested were made by Japanese business leaders, not by MITI. Hugh Patrick, professor of Far Eastern economics at Yale, has put forward this assessment:

> Indeed, looking at Japanese industrial development as a whole in the postwar period, I think the predominant source of its success was the entrepreneural vigor of private enterprises that invested a good deal and took a lot of risks. The main role of the government was to provide an accommodating and supportive environment for the market, rather than providing leadership or direction. Unquestionably government planning bodies were important in a few industrial sectors, but not in many others, which flourished on their own.[9]

The Japanese government, through its Fiscal Investment and Loan Program (FILP), does control substantial investment sums, amounting in 1980 to some $80 billion in direct investments, subsidized loans, and loan guarantees. Such a large investment budget does seem to offer potential leverage for carrying out an industrial policy. In fact, however, as Brookings' Philip Trezise carefully documented in the Spring, 1983, issue of the *Review,* the government's investment portfolio is spread across a wide range of enterprises in response to regional, political, and special interest pressures. In 1979, the FILP budget was allocated among some fifty separate agencies, plus a number of local governments. The local governments, together with four agencies (a housing loan corporation, two small business financing entities, and the Japanese National Railways), got a total of 60 percent of the funds. Another 27 percent went to such entities as the Ex-Im Bank; the Japan Highway Corporation; the Japan Housing Corporation; the Agriculture, Forestry, and Fisheries Corporation; and the Japan Development Bank.

---

[9]Interview in *Manhattan Report on Economic Policy,* Manhattan Institute for Policy Research, Vol. II, NO. 7, October, 1982.

The Japan Development Bank (JDB), in turn, seems a likely candidate for the role of financing an industrial policy aimed at building up major growth industries. The facts belie this conjecture, too. In the first twenty years of the JDB's life, according to Trezise, three-quarters of its funds went to merchant shipping, electric utilities, and regional and urban development. The burgeoning steel industry, on the other hand, received during these two decades less than one percent ($110 million) of the JDB's financing. Since 1972, in Japan as in the United States, public investment has emphasized energy and pollution control—and the JDB budget reflects this trend. But JDB investment in the development of new technologies outside of the energy industry has averaged only $313 million a year over the past decade.

Thus, in Japan as in any other democratic country, the public investment budget has been divvied up in response to diverse political pressures. It has not been a major instrument for concentrating investment resources in carefully selected growth industries. Indeed, if one changed the institutional labels, the Japanese government's investment budget looks remarkably like what might have emerged from a House and Senate conference committee on public works in the United States Congress.

All of this is not to suggest that MITI had no influence on the direction of Japanese industrial investment. For example, MITI is widely, and probably quite correctly, cited as having played a major role in organizing the very successful Japanese penetration of the memory chip segment of the world semiconductor markets. As Paul Krugman has pointed out, however, the relevant question is whether this particular use of Japanese savings generated a higher return for the nation than would have been earned had the market allocated the funds.[10] It may have done so, but we do not yet know the answer.

MITI has also had some major failures. For instance, MITI tried very hard—and, as is evident, to no avail—to keep Honda out of the automobile business and to consolidate Japanese auto production into a few giant companies. MITI also attempted to get a major commercial aircraft industry going in Japan, but the banks failed to follow MITI's lead and would not provide the necessary capital. Those who attribute Japan's economic success principally to MITI's industrial policy seem to be suggesting that without MITI the huge 30 to 35 percent of GNP that the Japanese invested in the past several decades would have gone mainly into such industries as textiles, shoes, plastic souvenirs, and fisheries. This is sheer nonsense. Given the quality of Japanese business executives, those massive investment funds probably would have wound up roughly where they actually did. And to the extent that there would have been differences, there is no reason to believe that MITI's influence, on balance, improved the choices in any major way.

The combination that worked so well for Japan—a huge saving rate, aggressive business leaders, and a backlog of modern technology waiting to be exploited—may now be faltering. In particular, as Japan has caught up to the technological frontier of other Western countries, the potential for large returns from investment in known

---

[10]Paul Krugman, "Targeted Industrial Policies: Theory and Evidence," a paper prepared for the Conference on Industrial Change and Public Policy, sponsored by the Federal Reserve Bank of Kansas City, August 25–26, 1983, pp. 46–49.

technologies has been reduced. The propensity to save remains high, but investment opportunities appear to have dwindled. Partly for this reason, Japanese economic growth, while still above that in other advanced countries, fell from an average of 9.9 percent a year between 1960 and 1973 to 3.5 percent a year between 1973 and 1983.[11]

IDENTIFYING THE "RIGHT" INDUSTRIAL STRUCTURE

Despite the lack of evidence that the United States has been de-industrializing or that the key to Japan's economic success has been its industrial policy, advocates of an industrial policy for the United States nevertheless propose that the federal government play a much enlarged role in determining the structure of American industry. The centerpiece of an industrial policy is some kind of a development bank—a new Reconstruction Finance Corporation—with authority to do some or all of the following: provide loans, loan guarantees, and subsidies to business firms and regional development bodies; certify firms as being eligible for special tax breaks; recommend measures to protect domestic industries against competition from imports; and negotiate restructuring agreements with labor and management in firms and industries that are in trouble and are candidates for assistance. In many versions of industrial policy, the new RFC would be governed, or at least be advised, by a tripartite body made up of representatives from business, labor, and government. The powers of the Corporation would be exercised in pursuit of explicit industrial objectives designed to achieve some combination of the two broad goals—stimulating the emergence and growth of new high-tech industries and protecting and rehabilitating older industries.

The first problem for the government in carrying out an industrial policy is that we actually know precious little about identifying, before the fact, a "winning" industrial structure. There does not exist a set of economic criteria that determine what gives different countries preeminence in particular lines of business. Nor is it at all clear what the substantive criteria would be for deciding which older industries to protect or restructure.

Originally, comparative advantage and international specialization among countries were thought to derive principally from the relative abundance or scarcity of the factors of production—labor, capital, and various natural resources. The United States and other advanced industrial countries do in fact have a broad advantage in the production of those goods that are research-based and technologically sophisticated, and that require for their production an educated labor force. It is also demonstrably the case that the availability of certain kinds of natural resources can play an important role in determining comparative advantage. But beyond these very broad principles, there are no general criteria that allow one to predict the industries in which a country will be particularly successful.

Advanced industrial countries both export and import a wide range of goods that covers almost the entire spectrum of their manufacturing industries. Exports are not concentrated in one set of selected industries and imports in another. One study has

[11]1983 growth as forecast by the OECD, *Economic Outlook*, July, 1983.

shown, for example, that in major countries very few industries, classified at a medium (three digit) level of detail, had less than 30 percent of their international trade as *intra*-industry trade—i.e., in most categories of industrial goods, international trade involved significant volumes of *both* exports and imports, rather than exclusively one or the other. The distribution among advanced nations of the production of various manufactured products is not principally a function of some broad set of national characteristics, but arises in large part from quite different causes.

In an insightful article on industrial policy, Assar Lindbeck of the University of Stockholm has analyzed the origins of industrial specialization among advanced countries.[12] He argues that what a country will specialize in is determined by a combination of historical coincidence and momentum. Individual entrepreneurs search for a niche in the market. Once one or more firms in a country successfully establish a foothold in the market for some special product, forces come into play that can heighten, at least for a while, that country's comparative advantage in the manufacture of that product. A growing market leads to economies of scale for the original producers. Ancillary firms spring up to supply the new industry's special needs. Workers and managers acquire skills and know-how. Success tends to breed success.

In short, the winners emerge from a very individualistic search process, only loosely governed by broad national advantages in relative labor, capital, or natural resource costs. The competence, knowledge, and specific attributes that go with successful entrepreneurship and export capability are so narrowly defined and so fine-grained that they cannot be assigned to any particular nation. The "winners" come from a highly decentralized search process, the results of which cannot be identified on the basis of abstract criteria. As Lindbeck points out, there is nothing in Swedish natural resources or national character that would have foreordained that Sweden would be preeminent in the production of ball bearings, safety matches, cream separators, and automatic lighthouses. Nor, it might be added, is there a basis in observable national characteristics to have predicted Japanese dominance in the motorcycle industry or the American success in pharmaceuticals and the export of construction management and design.

There are, of course, overall policies that government can pursue to create the kind of environment in which a decentralized search process is most likely to be fruitful. What government cannot do—except perhaps in a country that is far behind the leaders and simply trying to catch up by imitating them—is to identify in advance the particular lines and products in which its country will be successful.

Some have argued that a new industrial policy should particularly seek to reallocate investment towards industries with high value-added per worker and away from those with low value-added. The argument for such a reallocation implicitly assumes (1) that there are large numbers of skilled American workers trapped in low-paying jobs in industries with low value-added per worker; (2) that there are large untapped markets for the products of high value-added industries employing skilled workers; and (3) that this situation exists because of a propensity on the part of American business to invest too much in the low value-added, and too little in the high value-added, in-

---

[12]Assar Lindbeck, "Industrial Policy as an Issue in the Economic Environment," *The World Economy*, December, 1981, pp. 391–405.

dustries. Government policies designed to improve the skills of the labor force make good sense. But given the current mix of skills in the labor pool, there is no evidence that market forces in the United States have tended to ignore potentially large returns in industries with high value-added per worker and to channel excessive investment to those with low value-added. Indeed, as Krugman points out, government redistribution of a fixed aggregate investment from low value-added to high value-added industries would tend to lower employment and output, since capital-labor and capital-output ratios are higher in the latter industries.[13]

There are equally formidable barriers to designing substantively defensible criteria to govern a systematic government policy of trade protection and investment assistance for declining older industries. No one seriously suggests a policy of indiscriminate aid to *all* such industries, so some criteria for choice are necessary. One litmus test that is proposed is the importance of an industry to the national defense; that, however, is almost always a red herring. The national defense essential industry argument is usually presented in an all-or-nothing mode, as though, in the absence of import protection, the affected industry would disappear. In fact, what is almost always at stake is a much less dramatic change in the industry's fortunes, of a magnitude that is irrelevant to national defense. Whether, for example, the domestic steel industry meets 80 percent of the nation's peacetime needs, as it does now, or only 60 percent is of no significance to the nation's security.

It has also been suggested that we assist those particular older and troubled industries that other governments are heavily subsidizing. The industries we would end up supporting under this decision rule would most likely be those with worldwide excess capacity, in which the returns to investment are unusually low, since those are the ones most apt to be getting help from other governments. A systematic reallocation of investment away from other American industries towards these would lower the growth of national output and real wages.

Ironically, the systematic provision of import protection to various industries, in an effort to "restructure" them, would indirectly weaken the most dynamic and progressive sector of American industry. Import protection would initially worsen the trade balances of the countries against whom it was directed. As a result, their currencies would tend to depreciate against the dollar. In turn, this would impair the competitive position of American export industries, which, by their very nature, are likely to be at the leading edge of economic progress. We would trade jobs and output in the leading sectors for jobs and output in the losing sectors.

In practice, the motivation behind most existing efforts to protect the losers is not so much to improve economic performance as to lessen the pains of economic change. Almost by definition, a dynamic economy is one in which change is continually at work—change in technology, in tastes, and in world markets. And while change creates new opportunities, it also forces some firms, workers, and communities to make painful adjustments.

A decent concern for the human costs imposed by economic change is one hallmark of a compassionate society. But society can act to reduce those costs in two quite

---

[13]Krugman, op. cit., pp. 6–8.

different ways. First, it can short-circuit market forces and try to slow the pace of change through subsidies, trade protection, and regulations designed to prop up declining firms. Second, it can attempt to accommodate and ease the transitions dictated by changing economic conditions through the provision of reasonable unemployment compensation, relocation assistance, and generous training opportunities to those facing major adjustment problems. Neither approach will fully insulate workers and communities from the pains of economic change. But systematic application of the first approach, while preventing some pain for some people, will over time sap the economy of dynamism and hold down growth in living standards. The second option is far from perfect, but it offers the potential of reducing transition costs with much less impairment of the dynamism that generates economic growth.

INDUSTRIAL POLICY AND THE AMERICAN POLITICAL SYSTEM

Not only would it be impossible for the government to pick a winning industrial combination in advance, but its attempt to do so would almost surely inflict much harm.

There are many important tasks that only governments can do—and, with constant effort and watchfulness, they can do those tasks passably well. But the one thing that most democratic political systems—and especially the American one—cannot do well at all is to make critical choices among particular firms, municipalities, or regions, determining cold-bloodedly which shall prosper and which shall not. Yet such choices are precisely the kind that would have to be made—and made explicitly—for an industrial policy to become more than a political pork barrel.

The government can, and continually does, adopt policies that have the indirect consequence of harming particular individuals or groups. But a cardinal principle of American government is "never be seen to do direct harm." The formal and informal institutions of the political system are designed to hinder government from making hard choices among specific individuals, rewarding some and penalizing others. So it is, for example, that we have an Economic Development Administration, created to help "depressed areas," that has eligibility criteria so broad that they encompass over 80 percent of the counties in the United States. The same pattern—that of obviating the necessity of choice—is evident in the evolution of the Model Cities Program. Two decades ago, planners in the Johnson administration set out to test the proposition that a very comprehensive assistance program—directed at physical capital, education, retraining, social services, and so on—that concentrated large investment in a few areas could overcome the inertial force and vicious cycle of inner city poverty and decay. A demonstration of this approach was initially designed to be carried out in a very limited number of cities; hence the name "Model Cities Program." By the time the concept had made its way through the political thickets of the administration and the Congress, the Model Cities Program encompassed one hundred and fifty cities, each receiving only a fraction of the funding needed.

It is not surprising that the American political system is seldom capable of making express choices among individuals, firms, or regions. The American government, after all, was not established to bring order and authority out of social chaos. Quite to the contrary, it originated in an effort to reduce what was seen as too much authority on the part of the British king and parliament. Its founders were principally concerned to constrain legislative and executive authorities so that they could not make arbitrary and invidious choices among individuals. In the American system, most decisions that discriminate among specific citizens and firms are reached through litigation in the courts, where "fairness," rather than "efficiency," is the major criterion for setting disputes. When it is necessary to permit executive officials to make such decisions, their exercise of discretion is hedged about by complex procedural safeguards, including the right of appeal to the courts. The Administrative Procedures Act, which governs the exercise of regulatory authority, is a prime example of this approach.

The governmental choices that an industrial policy contemplates have little to do with fairness and much to do, at least ostensibly, with exacting economic criteria. As we have seen, these are precisely the sorts of decisions that the American political system makes very poorly. A new RFC would do not better. For every twenty new entrants into the high-tech race, nineteen will probably perish and only one succeed. But the federal government's portfolio would likely carry all twenty forever.

To be anything more than a universal protector of inefficiency, a systematic program of assistance to declining industries would have to call for some very hard-headed decisions among particular firms, cities, and groups of workers—that the Youngstown plant can live but the Weirton one must close, for example, or that the cotton textile industry has a reasonable chance to rehabilitate itself but the wool textile industry is a hopeless case and must die. Or that in order for the steel industry to compete successfully in world markets, the large increases over the last fifteen years in its wages and fringe benefits relative to those of the rest of industry must be eliminated. Quite apart from the inability of any staff to make such substantive calls correctly, can anyone seriously imagine an American RFC being left alone to make such decisions, with its authorizations and appropriations controlled by the Congress and its policies supervised by a president interested in his own and his party's political success? Rather, we can expect a combination of patterns to emerge: Some assistance would be made available, on a formula basis, to all industries that were in trouble; the wheels with the loudest squeaks might get a bit of extra financial grease; and protectionist interests would have a new and highly vulnerable pressure point to exploit. In the process, resources would be misallocated, incentives for industrial efficiency reduced, and competitive forces blunted.

THE FALSE ALLURE OF "COORDINATION"

One of the most frequently heard arguments for industrial policy is that it would bring a much-needed coordination to government policy-making. Those who make this argument begin by pointing out that the government already has in place many individual policies that affect the industrial structure, often in illogical, contradictory, or harmful ways. They go on to ask why we do not, therefore, adopt a positive and coherent industrial policy in place of the current ad hoc array. These advocates often cite examples of the foolishness that ad hoc assistance decisions lead to:

- The U.S. government now spends five times more on research and development for commercial fishing than for steel.
- The U.S. tax code provides almost $750 million a year in tax breaks for the timber industry, but only a small fraction of that amount for semiconductors.
- We now provide substantial import protection for the carbon and specialty steel industries (an illustration presumably adduced on the grounds that with an industrial policy we would be able to extract more competition-oriented reforms from labor and management in the favored industries).

In fact, this argument makes little sense—even if the examples cited are indeed blunders. It might very well be bad policy to spend five times more on R&D for commercial fishing than for steel (although what is relevant is total R&D, private as well as government, and even then it is not self-evident that the payoff from R&D in commercial fishing is less than from R&D in steel). Tax experts long ago concluded that the special treatment of the timber industry was excessively generous. And virtually all economists would argue that the steel protectionist measures are bad for the country. But these conclusions would all be true even if the term "industrial policy" had never been invented, and regardless of whether industrial production was an increasing or a decreasing share of GNP. Indeed, it is curious logic to cite examples of how the American industrial structure has been distorted by political pressures—in support of an argument for entrusting even more economic decisions to the same political system. One does not have to be a cynic to forecast that the surest way to multiply unwarranted subsidies and protectionist measures is to legitimize their existence under the rubric of industrial policy. The likely outcome of an industrial policy that encompassed some elements of both "protecting the losers" and "picking the winners" is that the losers would back subsidies for the winners in return for the latter's support on issues of trade protection.[14]

The argument is also made that we do provide assistance to individual firms, on occasion and in a very ad hoc way; the Chrysler and Lockheed bailouts are usually cited as examples. Should we not, therefore, regularize and rationalize this procedure, rather than making these assistance decisions on a case-by-case basis? In fact, the ad hoc approach is precisely the right approach. To every rule there are exceptions. It may very occasionally be in the public interest to supersede the market's judgment and to prevent the bankruptcy of some major firm. But it is a virtue that a special law is now needed for each case. It is a virtue that each case is, in fact, treated as an exception. Only very exceptional cases are likely to muster the support needed to enact a special law, and the government's bargaining power, to impose needed and painful reforms on management and labor, is consequently enhanced. Should this process of decision by exception be supplanted by an ongoing authority to initiate bailouts, the result would almost surely be a politically vulnerable fund, available to help avoid or delay politically sensitive plant closings.

[14]The chief executive of a firm producing semiconductors has recently argued that his industry does not need special government help—only a "Buy America" provision for its products.

SOME REAL PROBLEMS

To say that industrial policy is a dangerous solution for an imaginary problem is not to say that the United States has no serious economic difficulties. It has a number of them.

Our most immediate set of problems is macroeconomic in nature. Recovery from the deepest recession of the postwar period has just begun. Having paid a very high price for partially wringing out a stubborn inflation fifteen years in the making, we—along with every other industrial country—will have to walk a very fine line to sustain an economic recovery vigorous enough to make substantial inroads on unemployment, but not so buoyant as to risk a resurgence of inflationary pressures or inflationary expectations.

In addition, we in the United States face the special problem of a political impasse that threatens to perpetuate very sizeable federal budget deficits even as the economy recovers towards full utilization of its resources. Since the Federal Reserve is most unlikely to accommodate these high employment deficits with large and inflationary increases in the money supply, failure to break the impasse with tax increases and spending cuts would extend today's high real interest rates—or, more likely, even higher ones—into the indefinite future. This outcome would have particularly serious consequences for the health of America's industrial structure. High interest rates would tend to perpetuate overvaluation of the U.S. dollar, and would continue to penalize American exports and encourage imports. At home, the high interest rates would especially depress purchases of durable manufactured goods. Finally, the ability of new and young enterprises, at the frontiers of technological advance, to raise new capital could be seriously impaired to the extent that the actuality and the expectation of continued high interest rates depressed stock market values.

Getting America's monetary and fiscal policies in order is far more important for the health of the nation's industrial structure than any conceivable set of new industrial policies. What now seem to be serious problems of industrial structure would quickly shrink and become far more manageable with a few years of balanced economic recovery at lower real interest rates.

After the achievement of a sustained and balanced recovery, the prospects for which depend heavily on how the government uses its macroeconomic tools, the next most important factors influencing industrial performance are mainly beyond the government's control—such things as the pace of technological progress, the course of labor-management relationships, and the stability of world markets. There is, however, a variety of governmental microeconomic policies that can affect, favorably or unfavorably, the vigor and adaptability of American industry. Choices among alternatives in this area sometimes pose very difficult tradeoffs between economic efficiency and other social goals. For example, environmental considerations compete with the objective of keeping industrial costs low. The provision of generous tax incentives for risk bearing has to be balanced with the objective of a more equal distribution of income. Additional federal support for scientific and technical education would conflict with the goal of budget expenditure control. In other cases, what is at issue is not a tradeoff among competing national objectives, but the reform or elimination of provisions in tax or regulatory codes that distort the pattern of investment among different industries. The 1981 liberalization of depreciation allowances, for example, was desirable in the aggregate but very arbitrary as among investments of different types. It sharply skewed rates of return and distorted investment incentives among industries. Determining the federal government's stance on these and other thorny issues will continue to provide grist for the legislative and political mills in the years ahead. How they are settled will have an important, even if not overwhelming, influence on the behavior of American industries.

The most critical and vexing structural problems that American society will have to face in the coming decade have little to do with the issues raised by industrial policy. Even with a return to prosperity, unemployment among America's black youth will remain scandalously high. Large parts of American central cities will continue to be afflicted by serious financial constraints, social problems, and physical decay. And, if recent studies are to be believed, the quality of American education has been deteriorating for a number of years. Unfortunately, no one yet seems to have a very clear idea of exactly how the federal government can best play a constructive role in fundamentally reversing these very troubling structural trends. But we must keep searching for solutions—and where federal outlays are required to experiment with promising approaches, these are the areas, unlike most others, where the benefit of the doubt ought to be given a little more rather than a little less funding.

In sum, there are changes in federal fiscal and monetary policies that could help the economy generally, and industry in particular, attain a more satisfactory level of economic prosperity. There are microeconomic policies that we know could contribute to an environment that is favorable to the creation of new and rapidly expanding lines of business and to the adaptability of American industry. In many cases, formulating these policies requires making some very difficult choices among competing national objectives.

In addition, there are a few very important structural problems for which, at the moment, no convincing solutions are in sight. Yet it is absolutely essential that we keep searching and experimenting to try to solve them.

One structural problem, however, that does *not* exist is the de-industrialization of American industry. And one set of government measures that we do *not* need is an industrial policy under which the federal government tries to play an important role in determining the allocation of resources to individual firms and industries.

We have enough real problems without creating new ones.

QUESTIONS FOR DISCUSSION

1 What is meant by *industrial policy*? What is the fundamental philosophical difference between industry policy advocates and supporters of supply-side economics?
2 What is MITI? Why are the activities of this organization often cited by proponents of industrial policy? How does author Schultze's view of MITI differ from that of industrial policy supporters?
3 Explain the distinction between the "picking the winners" and the "protecting the losers" variants of industrial policy. Which approach would you prefer, and why? What factors might

induce a given politician to support one or the other of these strategies? Does the author of this article favor one or the other?

4 Schultze cites two macroeconomic factors to explain the weak performance of manufacturing in the early 1980s. What were those factors? Are they relevant today? Find data on manufacturing employment (you might try the *Economic Report of the President*) to see if it has grown since the early 1980s.

5 What are the "human costs imposed by economic change"? According to Schultze, what is the industrial policy approach to reducing these costs? What is Schultze's alternative and why does he prefer it? Do you think Schultze's alternative is (or can be made) consistent with the generally pro-market tone of his article?

6 What political problems does Schultze see in actually implementing industrial policies? Do you think such problems could be overcome? How does the U.S. experience with government administration of wage-price controls (Reading 27) bear on this issue?

PART FIVE

INTERNATIONAL MACROECONOMICS, TRADE, AND DEVELOPMENT

IS THE UNITED STATES TOO DEPENDENT ON FOREIGN CAPITAL?

Craig S. Hakkio
Bryon Higgins*

In recent years a series of large trade deficits has transformed the United States from a creditor to a debtor nation. In this article, Craig Hakkio and Bryon Higgins of the Kansas City Fed argue that the trade deficits, and the associated capital inflows, are the result primarily of U.S. fiscal deficits.

The growing U.S. foreign trade deficit in recent years has been accompanied by an increasing net inflow of foreign capital. As a result of these net capital inflows, the United States has become—or soon will become—a net debtor to the rest of the world. Indeed, unless the trends are reversed, this country will soon become the largest debtor nation in the world.

The growing net capital inflows have caused many to be concerned that the United States is increasingly dependent on foreign capital. They argue that increased borrowing from foreigners is both unsustainable and dangerous.[1] One danger is that at some point foreigners will be reluctant to provide additional capital to the United States, creating the potential for a precipitous decline in the exchange value of the dollar and an attendant rise in interest rates to ration the limited domestic supply of credit. Another concern is that the large net capital inflows threaten to drain capital from Europe and

Craig S. Hakkio and Bryon Higgins, "Is the United States Too Dependent on Foreign Capital?" *Economic Review,* Kansas City Federal Reserve Bank, June 1985, pp. 23–36.

*Craig S. Hakkio is a senior economist at the Federal Reserve Bank of Kansas City. Bryon Higgins is a vice president and economist at the bank.

[1]See, for example, the statement by Henry Wallich, member, Board of Governors of the Federal Reserve System, before the House Subcommittee on International Economic Policy and Trade, March 22, 1985, or the statement by C. Fred Bergsten, director, Institute for International Economics, before the Senate Subcommittee on International Finance and Monetary Policy, June 6, 1984.

elsewhere that will be needed to finance real investment abroad. Many of those who consider the net capital inflow dangerous think it results from high federal government budget deficits in the United States. They argue that high budget deficits have forced up U.S. interest rates, thereby attracting foreign capital. Their recommendation, therefore, is to reduce the budget deficit to bring down interest rates, the exchange rate, the trade deficit, and capital inflows.

An alternative point of view is that the net capital inflows are not dangerous because they merely reflect the U.S. economy's vitality, which is attributed to the 1981 tax cuts and the improved inflation outlook in the United States.[2] Those who hold this point of view deny that budget deficits cause high interest rates and conclude that reducing budget deficits would not deter continued net capital inflows. In addition, they do not agree that the United States is increasingly dependent on foreign capital or that the reluctance of foreigners to acquire additional U.S. assets threatens to disrupt exchange or domestic credit markets. Part of this sanguine attitude results from a certain interpretation of the balance of payments statistics. This interpretation holds that the increase in net capital inflows has resulted from a reduction in gross capital outflows rather than from an increase in gross capital inflows. They conclude from this interpretation that the United States has not become increasingly dependent on foreign capital.

This article argues that the United States has become increasingly dependent on foreign capital and that this dependence poses risks for the balance and stability of the domestic and world economies. The first section discusses the causes of the rise in net capital inflows, concluding that the large government budget deficit has been a major factor. The second section discusses the two points of view regarding the consequences of the net capital inflow and argues that continued large net capital inflows are likely to pose problems for both the U.S. economy and the world economy. The conclusion from this analysis is that reducing the budget deficit would help reduce dangerous U.S. dependence on foreign capital.

CAUSES OF THE NET CAPITAL INFLOW

Several explanations have been offered for the large U.S. net capital inflows. Some of these explanations mistake symptoms for causes, however. The ultimate determinants of capital inflows are domestic spending and saving. To see why this is so, it is useful to see how capital flows fit into the overall balance of payments and to develop a framework for analyzing net capital inflows.

Capital Flows in the Balance of Payments

A country's balance of international payments is a summary statement of all transactions between residents of that country and the rest of the world. The balance of payments has three basic components.

---

[2] This point of view has been expressed by supply-side economists and members of the Reagan administration. See, for example, Paul Craig Roberts, "The Strong Dollar: A Sheep in Wolf's Clothing," *Business Week*, March 11, 1985, and the comments by Treasury Secretary James Baker reported in *Daily Report for Executives*, April 15, 1985.

The most familiar component is the merchandise balance of trade. A surplus in the merchandise balance of trade occurs when more goods are exported than are imported, and a deficit occurs when more goods are imported than are exported.

The second component is the service account balance, which includes net interest income and other services. Net interest payments are equal to interest payments to foreign investors minus interest receipts of domestic residents on foreign investments. Interest payments are included in the services account since they are viewed as current payment for capital services. The balance on other services is the net sale of insurance, real estate, shipping, and similar tradeable services to the rest of the world. The sum of the services balance and the merchandise trade balance is the current account balance.[3]

Capital flows are the final component of the balance of payments. International capital flows pertain to exchanges of assets—mostly financial assets—between countries. There are several categories of international capital flows. One category is official capital flows, which consist of changes in the asset holdings of an official agency in at least one country. This type of capital flow often arises as a result of exchange market intervention or accumulation of reserve assets by central banks. All other capital flows involve the exchange of assets by private citizens or firms. These private capital flows include direct investment, securities purchases, and bank flows.

Since all of a country's international transactions must sum to zero, a net capital inflow must offset a deficit or surplus on the current account. A country with a deficit in its current account must finance that deficit by borrowing abroad—that is, by a net capital inflow.[4] Similarly, a change in the current account balance must be accompanied by an equal but opposite change in the net capital flow.

Most short-run changes in the current account balance result from changes in the merchandise trade balance. Net interest payments change little over short periods, being determined primarily by the size of past capital flows; and flows of other services are smaller and less volatile than merchandise trade flows. Therefore, a change from net capital outflow to large net capital inflow is almost inevitably associated with a surge in merchandise imports or a sharp cutback in merchandise exports.

The United States has experienced such a turnaround in net capital flows in recent years. As shown in Chart 1, the United States had a net capital outflow most of the

---

[3]There is one additional, but small, component to the current account—"remittances, pensions, and other unilateral transfers."

[4]The actual balance of payments accounts are much more complex than suggested by this discussion. However, all of the important conceptual points can be made using the tripartite division of merchandise trade flows, service flows, and capital flows. In the actual balance of payments statistics, measured capital flows need not entirely offset the current account surplus or deficit. Because of measurement problems, there is a large residual category for statistical discrepancy, which amounted to $24.7 billion in 1984. Although large, the statistical discrepancy does not pose insurmountable problems for analyzing balance of payments changes over time, especially those as large as have occurred in the U.S. balance of payments in recent years. However, all empirical estimates using balance of payments figures are subject to unusually large errors because of the large statistical discrepancy.

The discussion in the text should not be interpreted as implying that current account deficits *cause* net capital inflows. The current account and capital account are jointly determined because both are endogenous variables. According to the portfolio balance approach to international economics, changes in capital flows are if anything causally prior to changes in the current account. Statements in the text that could be interpreted otherwise are used only for expositional ease.

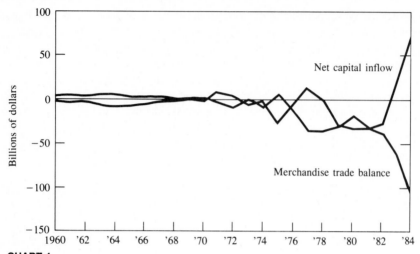

CHART 1
Net Capital Inflow and Merchandise Trade Balance. (Source: *Board of Governors of the Federal Reserve System.*)

net capital inflow, which totaled over $70 billion in 1984. As the chart also shows, the turnaround in net capital flows has been associated with a deterioration in the merchandise trade balance, which has posted large and growing deficits in recent years.

The sources and uses of funds framework shows why the net capital inflow is equal to the difference between domestic uses of funds and domestic sources of funds. Investment spending and the budget deficit are the two domestic uses of funds. Domestic savings and the net capital inflow are the two sources of funds. Therefore, funds to finance investment spending and the budget deficit must come either from domestic savings or from the net capital inflow from abroad. If the domestic uses of funds exceed the domestic sources of funds, the excess must be borrowed from abroad, resulting in a net capital inflow. This relationship can be seen in Equation 1.

$$NKIN = (G - T) + I - S \tag{1}$$

where NKIN = net capital inflow to the United States,
        G = government spending,
        T = government tax revenues,
         I = domestic private investment spending, and
        S = domestic private saving.

The equation shows that a country with a large government budget deficit, good investment prospects, or a low propensity to save will tend to have a net capital inflow. The equation also shows that factors which do not affect budget deficits, investment, or domestic saving do not affect the capital inflow.

Factors Leading to a Net Capital Inflow

The sources and uses of funds framework can be used to analyze the factors contributing to the increased net capital inflow to the United States. In an integrated world economy, almost everything that happens in the United States and other countries affects U.S. capital flows to some extent. However, three factors have been cited as the principal causes of the increased U.S. net capital inflow. These factors are U.S. government budget deficits, the robust economic expansion of the U.S. economy and associated rapid growth in investment spending by U.S. businesses, and the LDC debt crisis and accompanying desire of investors for a "safe haven" for their funds.

Many analysts think the large U.S. government budget deficits are the most important cause of the net capital inflow. This view is based in part on the approximate coincidence of increased budget deficits and increased capital inflows. Capital inflows began rising soon after federal government deficits burgeoned.[5] More importantly, though, is the close economic relationship between budget deficits and capital inflows. As shown by Equation 1, if commensurate reductions in investment spending or increases in domestic saving do not accompany higher budget deficits, the deficits will necessarily lead to higher net capital inflow.

The logic behind this relationship is straightforward. Higher budget deficits lead to increased government demand for credit. Unless this increase in borrowing is offset by a reduction in private demand for credit or an increase in private saving, the net capital inflow from abroad must rise. Such a rise in the net capital inflow could be due to increased borrowing from foreigners, reduced foreign lending by domestic investors, or some combination of the two. Regardless of how it is achieved, though, the increased net inflow of capital to the United States in recent years is thought by many to have been due primarily to the unprecedented size of federal budget deficits.

Similarly, these analysts point to budget deficits as the ultimate reason for the sharp deterioration of the U.S. foreign trade balance in recent years. They argue that increased budget deficits led to increased interest rates to ration the limited credit supply.[6] And higher interest rates in the United States than abroad caused foreign investors to shift funds into U.S. assets, a move that contributed to the sustained rise in the exchange value of the dollar. The strength of the dollar, in turn, was a major factor in the deterioration of the merchandise trade balance. In this way, it is argued, the budget deficit led to massive trade deficits that have accompanied the large net capital inflow.

The robust recovery of the U.S. economy and rapid growth of investment spending

---

[5]The precise timing of increased capital inflow depends on whether published data or data adjusted for introduction of international banking facilities are used. If official data are used, the net capital inflow did not increase appreciably until 1983. If adjusted data are used, the net capital inflow increased steadily beginning in 1981. A fuller explanation of this point is given below.

[6]This argument assumes that an increase in the budget deficit leads to an increase in the real interest rate. There are some who do not believe that such a link exists. For support, they refer to a study published by the U.S. Treasury Department, "The Effects of Deficits on Prices of Financial Assets," January 1984. The argument is that an increase in the budget deficit implies an increase in future taxes, so that savings rise by an equal amount, with no change in interest rates. However, there are also many economists who believe that an increase in the budget deficit does lead to a higher interest rate. For evidence in support of this proposition, see Michael Hutchison and David Pyle, "The Real Interest Rate/Budget Deficit Link: International Evidence, 1973–82," *Economic Review,* Federal Reserve Bank of San Francisco, Fall 1984, pp. 26–35.

in 1983 and 1984 may also have contributed to increased net capital inflows. Economic growth and investment spending in the United States have been very strong, especially when compared with European economies. As a result, private credit demands have increased more in the United States than in most other countries, contributing to higher U.S. interest rates that have encouraged the inflow of foreign capital and discouraged the outflow of domestic capital. Moreover, some argue that the relative strength of the U.S. economic expansion has improved the long-run prospects for a healthy U.S. economy, especially because robust economic growth has been achieved without a reacceleration of inflation. If so, both foreign and domestic investors may have become more inclined to buy U.S. assets, thereby contributing to the increased net capital inflow.

There is no consensus on why the economy and investment spending have grown so rapidly. Supply-side economists and some members of the Reagan administration attribute most of the improved economic performance to the favorable supply-side effects of the 1981 tax cuts. By providing incentives for investment, saving, and work, they argue, the tax cuts led to a boom in investment, productivity, and economic activity. In contrast, other analysts say the primary effects of the 1981 tax cuts were through traditional demand stimulus channels. While admitting that the large business tax cuts increased the profitability of real investment, these analysts attribute most of the rapid economic growth in 1983 and 1984 to the large fiscal stimulus resulting from the reduction in taxes that was not offset by a commensurate reduction in government spending. To the extent that this explanation is correct, part of the contribution of rapid economic and investment growth to the net capital inflow is an indirect effect of increased budget deficits.

Some think the LDC debt crisis contributed to the net capital inflow to the United States. As investors became concerned about the ability of LDC debtors to service their foreign debt, they shifted funds to the United States to guard against capital controls and other financial disruptions. Together with increased political instability in Europe, the financial difficulties of LDC debtors made the United States' reputation as a safe haven for investments more important in investors' portfolio decisions.

Banks in the United States substantially reduced their lending to LDC's after the Mexican debt crisis in 1982. Some analysts claim that the cutback in U.S. bank lending to LDC's has been a major factor in reducing capital outflows from the United States and that the capital flight from Latin America and other areas in search of a safe haven for investments has been a major factor increasing capital inflows to the United States.

The importance of the LDC debt crisis as a cause of the U.S. net capital inflow is questionable, however. Although the financial difficulties of LDC's caused an increase in the net capital inflow to the United States from those countries, the increased flow of funds from LDC's could have been lent to other countries were it not for the deficiency of domestic sources of funds in the United States in the face of rapidly growing credit demands. Since net capital inflows are determined by domestic spending and saving decisions, the LDC debt crisis is a cause of U.S. net capital inflows only to the extent that it lowered U.S. saving or increased U.S. investment and budget deficits. For example, the LDC debt crisis may have stimulated investment or lowered saving in the United States by keeping U.S. interest rates lower than they might otherwise have been. But the size of this effect may well have been small. Therefore, the most significant effect of the LDC debt crisis on U.S. capital inflows has probably been on the channels through which that inflow occurred and the accompanying interest rates rather than on the size of the inflow itself. In short, given the deficiency of domestic saving compared with investment and budget deficits, the United States would have had to attract capital from other countries if not from LDC's. For that reason, neither the LDC debt crisis nor the view of the United States as a safe haven for investment has likely been a major cause of the increase in U.S. net capital inflows.

Empirical Evidence on Causes of Net Capital Inflows

Several types of empirical evidence can be brought to bear in judging what factors have been most important in causing U.S. net capital inflows. One possible source of evidence is the composition of net capital inflows. Some analysts argue that the causes of the net capital inflow can be inferred from the types of assets foreigners have acquired and the channels through which the funds have flowed. According to this reasoning, for example, the large $59.3 billion increase between 1980 and 1984 in net flows of funds through banks could be considered evidence that the LDC debt crisis was responsible for much of the increased net capital inflow. Much of the capital transferred from LDC's into U.S. assets may have been deposited in U.S. banks. In addition, U.S. banks reduced their lending to LDC's. Both of these actions contributed to an increase in the net bank flows from LDC's to the United States.

But this kind of evidence is unreliable. Banks, especially those with foreign branches, obtain funds wherever deposits can be found and lend funds wherever creditworthy borrowers can be found. Moreover, banks are financial intermediaries that arbitrage any interest rate differentials. For these reasons, a significant part of any change in capital flows might occur through banks regardless of the ultimate cause of the change. For example, a capital inflow caused by government budget deficits that caused an increase in U.S. interest rates would lead banks to borrow more abroad, where funds are cheaper, and lend more domestically, where loan rates are higher. Therefore, a rise in net capital inflows might be manifested as increased inflows through banks even if the cause of the net capital inflow were higher budget deficits. Similarly, the relatively small $20.3 billion increase in direct investment between 1980 and 1984 in the United States is not decisive evidence against the claim that the net capital inflow is due to business tax cuts having improved the profitability of real investment in U.S. businesses. Because credit is fungible, the sources of credit and the channels through which it flows are not reliable evidence regarding the causes of the increased demand for credit.

Another type of evidence is the size of changes in the components of domestic saving and spending. These changes can be analyzed in the framework provided by Equation 1. According to that equation, changes in the net capital inflow from 1980 to 1984 must be equal to the change in government budget deficits and investment spending minus the changes in domestic saving. As shown in Table 1, the U.S. net capital inflow increased $104.9 billion from 1980 to 1984. Over the same period, the combined budget deficits of all levels of government rose $92.1 billion, net investment spending rose $125.8 billion, and net private saving rose $129.3 billion. The

TABLE 1
CHANGES IN SOURCES AND USES OF FUNDS, 1980 TO 1984
(Billions of Dollars)

	Net capital inflow	Budget deficit	Net investment	Net private saving
Change from 1980 to 1984	104.9	92.1	125.8	129.3

Notes: The net capital inflow does not equal the budget deficit plus investment minus savings due to several minor factors. These factors reflect statistical discrepancies and differences between the National Income and Product accounts and the Balance of Payments accounts. The budget deficit is the combined federal, state, and local budget deficits; investment is net private domestic investment; savings is net private domestic saving.

larger rise in investment spending than in budget deficits since 1980 might seem to imply that business tax cuts or the robustness of the U.S. economic expansion have been the most important factors causing the net capital inflow. But this conclusion could be affected by the short-run nature of the comparison. In particular, both investment spending and budget deficits were affected in 1980 by the credit control program and the recession. As a result, comparison of changes in sources and uses of funds from 1980 to 1984 is not a reliable way of evaluating the causes of increased net capital inflows.

A more reliable source of evidence is the deviations of sources and uses of funds from their long-run trends. Comparing the ratios of budget deficits, investment, and saving to GNP in recent years with the average ratios in the 1970s sheds light on the factors responsible for the recent scarcity of domestic sources of funds relative to domestic uses of funds. This comparison indicates that the biggest change in recent years has been in the size of budget deficits. Budget deficits averaged only 1.2 percent of GNP in the 1970s. But by 1984, budget deficits had risen to 3.4 percent of GNP. In contrast, the ratios of net investment and net saving to GNP in 1984 were 6.4 percent and 7.4 percent, very close to their average values in the 1970s. Although investment grew rapidly in 1983 and 1984, it started from a very low base. As a result, net investment had only returned to a normal level by 1984. Moreover, the rapid investment growth may have come to an end. Projections based on recent data suggest that business spending on plant and equipment as well as spending on housing will increase only modestly in 1985. This projected dissipation of growth in investment spending conforms with analysis indicating that the effects of the 1981 business tax cuts would have only a temporary stimulative impact on investment spending.[7] Overall, then, comparison of sources and uses of funds in recent years with historical values suggests that increased budget deficits have been an important—perhaps even the predominant—cause of net capital inflows in recent years.

The conclusion that budget deficits are an important cause of the net capital inflow is confirmed by evidence from an econometric model. The staff at the Federal Reserve's Board of Governors has developed a model of international economic relationships.

---

[7]See, for example, John Makin and Raymond Sauer, "Effects of Debt Accumulation on Capital Formation," American Enterprise Institute, 1984.

The model is called the multicountry model (MCM) because it includes models of both the U.S. economy and other major economies. Simulations of the model have been conducted to determine the effect of U.S. budget deficits on the U.S. current account balance.[8] Since changes in the current account balance must be reflected in changes in net capital inflows, these simulations can be used to estimate how much increased budget deficits have contributed to the rise in the net capital inflow in recent years. According to the simulations, the increase in federal budget deficits from $61.2 billion in 1980 to $175.8 billion in 1984 would lead to an increase of more than $50 billion in net capital inflows. Since the actual increase in net capital inflows from 1980 to 1984 was $104.9 billion, the estimates from the MCM suggest that about half of the total increase in net capital inflows has been due to higher federal budget deficits. According to the MCM, therefore, large and growing budget deficits have been an important cause of the U.S. net capital inflow.

CONSEQUENCES OF CONTINUED NET CAPITAL INFLOWS

Net capital inflows to the United States are widely expected to continue for some time. For example, Data Resources Incorporated predictions through 2010 project a current account deficit and associated capital inflow throughout the period. Some have argued that this net capital inflow does not pose any serious problems since it has been and will continue to be due to a decrease in gross outflows rather than an increase in gross inflows. Others, however, believe that a continued net capital inflow poses serious problems. This section investigates both of these arguments.

Does the Composition of the Net Capital Inflow Matter?

According to economic theory, the composition of a net capital inflow is largely unimportant. The theory of international portfolio balance holds that interest rates, exchange rates, and other important economic variables depend on net asset demands— that is, on the difference between the demands for assets denominated in a particular currency and liabilities denominated in that currency.[9] Accordingly, an increase in gross capital inflows to the United States, which results in an increase in foreign

---

[8]Gilles Oudiz and Jeffrey Sachs, "Macroeconomic Policy Coordination Among the Industrial Economies," *Brookings Papers on Economic Activity*, 1984:1, pp. 1–64. Sachs and Oudiz simulate the effect of a fiscal expansion on the current account, using the MCM model. They find, for example, that a $100 billion fiscal expansion leads to a $47 billion worsening of the current account. Peter Hooper, "International Repercussions of the U.S. Budget Deficit," Board of Governors International Finance Discussion Paper No. 246, September 1984, estimates the effect of recent fiscal policy actions on the budget deficit and the current account, also using the MCM model. He finds that such actions worsened the budget deficit by $65 billion and the current account by $30 billion. These estimates imply that 46 percent of the higher budget deficit is reflected in an increase in current account deficits.

[9]See, for example, William Branson and Dale Henderson, "The Specification and Influence of Asset Prices," in Ronald Jones and Peter Kenen, editors, *Handbook of International Economics, Volume 2*, North Holland, New York, 1985.

Strictly speaking, the balance of payments accounts record the increase in foreign claims against the United States (the gross inflow) and the increase in U.S. claims against foreigners (the gross outflow), which is not quite the same as an increase in dollar-denominated assets or liabilities. For simplicity, though, this distinction is not made in the remainder of this article.

holdings of dollar assets, has the same aggregate effects as a reduction in gross capital outflows from the United States, which results in a reduction in dollar liabilities by foreigners. Since both increase the net dollar assets of foreigners, it is not necessary to know the composition of an increase in net capital inflows to the United States to predict their overall impact.

Based on this economic theory, the composition of net capital inflows has little if any effect on the price and quantity of credit to foreigners. If the net capital inflow is due to increased lending by foreigners to U.S. residents, the net capital inflow literally drains capital from abroad. If the net capital inflow is due to a reduction in U.S. lending abroad, the supplement to foreign domestic savings available to foreign borrowers is being reduced. Whether this is characterized as a drain on foreign capital or not, the important point is that reduction of U.S. lending abroad reduces the amount of credit available to foreign borrowers by the same amount as an increase in U.S. borrowing abroad.[10]

Because increased net capital inflows to the United States imply less capital available for foreign borrowers, regardless of the composition of the increased net capital inflow, foreign interest rates must be higher than otherwise to ration the reduced supply of loanable funds. Therefore, an increase in net capital inflows to the United States inevitably reduces the availability of credit to foreign borrowers and increases the interest rate they pay, regardless of the composition of the net capital inflow.

Nor does the composition of a net capital inflow substantially alter the possibility of portfolio saturation, which might cause a precipitous decline in the value of the dollar. If the net capital inflow is due primarily to an increase in gross inflows, foreign investors could decide at some point to stop acquiring dollar assets or even to liquidate their current holdings. Such a decision would presumably be based on a judgment that their portfolios were becoming too risky because they were too heavily tilted toward dollar assets. Diversifying portfolios by including assets denominated in different currencies reduces risk from exchange rate changes and other economic developments that have differential effects on the value of the assets. If there is diminishing marginal risk reduction from continuing to build up dollar assets in a portfolio, investors would become increasingly reluctant to acquire dollar assets as their percentage of the total portfolio increases. In this situation, relatively small changes in expected yields on dollar assets—brought about, for example, by changes in exchange rate expectations—could lead to very large reductions in desired dollar holdings. The resulting liquidation of dollar assets by foreign investors could cause a sharp decline in the exchange value of the dollar. Therefore, an increase in capital inflows can result in portfolio saturation that could increase the risk of a precipitous decline in the dollar.

---

[10]A physical analogy helps demonstrate this equivalence. Imagine a situation in which the amount of water in a bathtub is in "equilibrium" at 100 gallons, with 2 gallons being added and 2 gallons being drained each hour. The amount of water in the bathtub can be reduced 1 gallon an hour either by increasing the outflow of water by 1 gallon an hour or by reducing the inflow of water by the same rate. If the amount of water in the bathtub is considered to be the funds available to foreign borrowers, an increase in the capital outflow from abroad—that is, increased gross capital inflows to the United States—has the same effect as a reduction in the capital inflow from the United States—that is, lower gross capital outflows from the United States. For the same reason that only the difference between inflows and outflows matters in determining the change in the water level in the tub, only the difference between gross capital inflows and gross capital outflows matters in determining the amount of credit available to foreign borrowers.

Analogous reasoning suggests that a reduction in gross capital outflows may pose similar risks. A reduction in gross outflows increases the proportion of dollar assets in the portfolios of U.S. residents. Like foreigners, domestic residents can reduce risk by holding a diversified portfolio containing both dollar and nondollar assets. Although U.S. residents may be less sensitive to expected exchange rate movements, if they too become increasingly reluctant to continue acquiring dollar assets, liquidation of those assets could also disrupt foreign exchange markets and domestic credit markets.

The real world is far more complicated than economic theory suggests. Capital markets are not frictionless; some investors are liquidity-constrained; and domestic investors may evaluate risks differently or have different information available than do foreign investors. For these reasons, the composition of a net capital inflow may have some aggregate effects. But these effects are presumably minor, especially if the net capital inflow results from important changes in both gross outflows and gross inflows.

This leads to the second question regarding the sanguine attitude about increased net capital inflow—the extent to which it has been due to reduced gross outflows rather than increased gross inflows of private capital.

Composition of the Net Capital Inflow

Those who deny the United States has become more dependent on foreign capital have focused primarily on the published balance of payments statistics from 1981 to 1984. According to those statistics, private capital inflows increased only $18 billion from 1981 to 1984, while private capital outflows declined $89 billion. It appears from these figures that the increased net capital inflow was due almost entirely to a cutback in foreign lending rather than to an increase in borrowing from abroad.

A very different picture emerges, however, when 1980 is used as the first year in the comparison. Private capital outflows declined $60 billion from 1980 to 1984, only slightly larger than the increased private inflows of $51 billion. This comparison suggests that the increased net capital inflow has been due in almost equal measure to reductions in foreign lending and increases in foreign borrowing. A similar conclusion is suggested by other comparisons that do not use 1981 as the base year.[11] Thus, the claim that the growing trade deficit has been financed without significantly greater dependence on foreign capital appears to be very sensitive to the choice of the period used.

Closer examination of the data suggests that capital flows in 1981 and 1982 were aberrations from the underlying trends. Private capital outflows jumped $28 billion in 1981 and increased another $7 billion in 1982 before declining sharply in the last two years. Similarly private capital inflows jumped $34 billion in 1981, increased an additional $16 billion in 1982, and then leveled off on balance in the last two years.

The seemingly incongruous capital flow statistics in 1981 and 1982 may well result from aberrations caused by the introduction of international banking facilities (IBF's)

---

[11]For example, comparison of the averages for 1977–80 to the averages for 1981–84 also indicates that the increased net capital inflow in recent years has been about equally divided between a reduction in gross outflows and an increase in gross inflows.

in late 1981. Until then, U.S. banks had conducted much of their international business from offshore branches to avoid the competitive disadvantage of regulations that applied to domestic branches. In response, Congress authorized banks to establish IBF's in the United States to conduct international business on the same basis as U.S. branches of foreign banks. As a consequence, U.S. banks shifted both assets and liabilities from banking offices abroad to domestic offices. This had the effect of raising both reported capital outflows and reported capital inflows substantially in 1981 and 1982. It has been estimated that the introduction of IBF's inflated capital outflows and capital inflows by an average of $58 billion in 1981 and 1982.[12] Although admittedly imprecise, these estimates suggest that the official statistics on capital flows in 1981 and 1982 are so contaminated that use of either year as the base for evaluating the extent of increased dependence on foreign capital can be very misleading. For this reason, the comparisons that do not use 1981 or 1982 as the base—such as those comparing 1984 with 1980—are much more indicative of the trends regarding dependence on capital flows.[13] These comparisons indicate that the United States has indeed become increasingly dependent on foreign capital in recent years.

Consequences of Continued Net Capital Inflows

If continued, large net capital inflows could have several adverse consequences. Among the most important are a reduction in future living standards, a drain of capital needed abroad, and the increased likelihood of disruptions to foreign exchange and domestic credit markets.

Large and sustained net capital inflows threaten to lower future living standards in the United States. A large buildup of foreign net dollar claims implies large future net interest payments to foreigners. To meet these interest obligations, the United States will have to export more goods and services than it imports. As a result, less will be available for domestic consumption, and the average living standard of U.S. residents will be lower than it otherwise would be.

This would not be the case, though, if the capital inflows were being used primarily to finance productive investment in the United States, as was true during much of the 19th century, when the United States borrowed from abroad to finance the building of railroads and other productive capacity. In this case, the increased future production would more than offset the higher future interest obligations, allowing increased living standards. As discussed in the preceding section, though, the predominant reason for the large capital inflows in recent years has been the increase in the federal budget deficit.

Because the high budget deficits have not been associated with investment spending that is high by historical standards, the accompanying net capital inflows represent borrowing from future consumption possibilities to finance current consumption. Ex-

---

[12]Lois Stekler and Peter Isard, "U.S. International Capital Flows and the Dollar: Recent Developments and Concerns," *Brookings Papers on Economic Activity*, forthcoming.

[13]Moreover, using a 1980 base for computing the growing dependence on foreign capital allows an evaluation of the effects of the 1981 tax cuts, which are commonly thought to have been a major factor contributing to net capital inflows.

cept for the possibility that the budget deficit has resulted from increased defense spending essential to the survival of future productive capacity, it seems most likely that recent capital inflows have been due to consumption exceeding current productive capacity. Under these circumstances, the United States cannot continue consuming more than it produces. To offset this current imbalance, U.S. residents will have to produce more in the future than they consume, and "pay" the remainder of the nation's domestic output to foreigners as interest on their holdings of dollar assets. In this sense, large net capital inflows are mortgaging the country's economic future, just as previous capital inflows to LDC's from the United States and elsewhere mortgaged their economic futures by leading eventually to a need to curtail consumption to pay the interest on their foreign debt. Mexico's mortgage has come due; the United States' has not. But the ultimate effect of sustained net capital inflows to finance consumption is unavoidable.

Capital inflows also threaten to drain capital from abroad that is needed for productive investment. As pointed out above, a net capital inflow to the United States reduces the quantity of credit available to foreign borrowers, regardless of the composition of that inflow. Currently, such a drain may be relatively innocuous. Because of the slow recovery of European economies from the worldwide recession of 1981–82 and the LDC debt problems that have effectively precluded their borrowing in the last few years, foreign demand for credit to finance productive investment is comparatively low. But as European economies move toward full employment and LDC debtor countries work their way out of their difficulties, foreign demand for credit could rise substantially. If so, world interest rates would rise, increasingly crowding out domestic and foreign investment. Whereas it used to be thought that budget deficits crowded out only domestic investment, in the current world economy with flexible exchange rates and integrated world capital markets, the crowding out effect of budget deficits is allocated among domestic investment, tradeable goods sectors, and foreign investment.

Continued large net capital inflows also pose the increasing danger of disruptions to exchange and domestic credit markets. Net capital inflows lead to commensurate increases in the net dollar asset holdings of foreigners. Since portfolio decisions depend on net asset positions, continued large net capital inflows could at some point lead to saturation of foreign portfolios with dollar assets.[14] For the same reason, portfolios of U.S. investors could also become saturated with dollar assets because U.S. investors, like foreign investors, prefer to hold portfolios that are diversified between dollar assets and other assets. The desired ratio of dollar assets to nondollar assets is, of course, higher for U.S. residents than for foreigners, and changes in desired holdings may respond somewhat differently to interest rate or exchange rate expectations. But the growing proportion of net dollar claims in both foreign and domestic portfolios could lead to portfolio saturation that poses risk for the smooth functioning of exchange

[14]At the end of 1983, U.S. claims on foreigners were $887 billion and foreign claims on the United States were $781 billion, for a net asset position of $106 billion. The net capital inflow in 1984 was $77 billion, which reduced the net asset position to $29 billion at the end of 1984. This means that the United States will almost surely become a net debtor in 1985.

markets and domestic credit markets. Resistance to acquiring more dollar claims could lead to a sharp fall in the exchange value of the dollar and a sharp rise in U.S. interest rates.

Portfolio saturation is, to be sure, a relative rather than an absolute concept. There is no unique amount of dollar claims beyond which investors refuse to acquire more assets. But, as the relative proportion of dollar assets increases, investors become more reluctant to acquire additional dollar assets. They can be induced to buy more only by increasingly higher expected returns, due either to expected capital gains because of expected exchange rate changes or to higher expected real yields on the assets themselves.

However, portfolio saturation would not necessarily lead to gradual and nondisruptive changes in exchange rates and interest rates. Because asset markets are heavily influenced by expectations, asset prices are highly volatile, even without such extraordinary circumstances as rapid growth in net dollar asset positions resulting from large net capital inflows. With such circumstances, the effects of changes in expectations could be magnified. Moreover, increasing portfolio saturation could itself lead to changes in expectations about exchange rates and interest rates that would, in effect, become a self-fulfilling prophecy. To the extent that either of these developments occur, continued large net capital inflows increase the risk of a precipitous decline in the dollar, accompanied by a sharp increase in U.S. interest rates, that would disrupt both the domestic and world economies.

In contrast, progress in reducing the federal budget deficit could lead to a gradual decline in interest rates and the exchange rate. Reduction in the budget deficit would alleviate the deficiency of domestic credit supplies relative to domestic credit demands. The consequent relief in pressure on interest rates would reduce the attractiveness of U.S. assets to both foreign and domestic investors, thereby reducing the net capital inflow and the exchange value of the dollar. The decline in the exchange value of the dollar to a more sustainable level would improve the competitiveness of U.S. goods in domestic and international markets. And this improved competitive position would lower the trade deficit. Therefore, cutting the budget deficit could set in motion forces that would reduce dependence on foreign capital and improve the prospects for sustainable and balanced real growth of the U.S. economy.

CONCLUSION

The increased net capital inflow and associated growing dependence on foreign capital could pose serious risks for the U.S. and world economies. But policy actions to reduce the dependence on foreign capital are not likely to be successful unless they treat the root causes of the problem. The fundamental problem stems from the United States consuming more than it produces. Attempting to solve the problem through exchange controls, exchange market intervention, expansionary monetary policy, or increased trade barriers would at most only temporarily obscure the fundamental source of the problem. Empirical evidence implies that high government budget deficits have been a major factor contributing to large U.S. net capital inflows. As a consequence, reducing budget deficits would reduce the troublesome U.S. dependence on foreign capital.

QUESTIONS FOR DISCUSSION

1 From an accounting perspective, what does the existence of large capital inflows to the United States imply about the U.S. trade balance? About the relationship between domestic investment and domestic saving?

2 According to the standard theory, how does an increase in the government budget deficit affect the capital account? The trade balance? The difference between domestic saving and investment? What are the mechanisms by which these effects are supposed to occur?

3 Besides the federal deficit, what other explanations have been suggested for the increase in capital flows to the United States? Work through the steps by which these different factors are supposed to have their effects.

4 What evidence do these authors give for their view that budget deficits are a primary cause of the capital inflows?

5 At the level of an individual business, it is considered "sound" to borrow in order to finance expansion of productive capacity, but "unsound" to borrow so as to finance increased dividends for stockholders or larger salaries for managers. Relate this observation to the debate about capital inflows to the United States.

6 What is *portfolio saturation* and why do the authors consider it a source of potential problems for the U.S. economy?

7 Why do the authors feel that increased trade barriers or restrictions on capital flows would not help solve the U.S. current account problem?

8 During the 1980s, U.S. industry has been criticized for losing its competitiveness on world markets. Assuming that the argument of this article is right, explain why the principal blame for lost competitiveness should not be placed on U.S. workers and managers.

THE UNITED STATES IN THE WORLD ECONOMY: STRAINS ON THE SYSTEM

U.S. Council of Economic Advisers

This reading gives a long-term perspective on U.S. trade problems, covering such issues as the trend in U.S. competitiveness, the changing composition of the U.S. balance of payments, the bilateral trade deficit with Japan, and the changing value of the dollar. Written in late 1982 or early 1983, this article also forecasts the large increase in the trade deficit that was to come, and evaluates potential policy responses.

During the 1970s the world's market economies became more integrated with each other than ever before. Exports and imports as a share of gross national product (GNP) reached record levels for most industrial countries, while international lending and direct foreign investment grew even faster than world trade. This closer linkage of economies was mutually beneficial. It allowed producers in each country to take greater advantage of their country's special resources and knowledge, and to take advantage of economies of scale. At the same time, it allowed each country to consume a wider variety of products, at lower costs, than it could produce itself.

Underlying the growth in world trade and investment was a progressive reduction of barriers to trade. The postwar period was marked by a series of agreements to liberalize trade: both multilateral, like the Kennedy Round, and bilateral, like the Canada-U.S. auto pact.

In spite of its huge benefits, however, this liberalized trading system is now in serious danger. Within the United States, demands for protection against imports and

U.S. Council of Economic Advisers, *Economic Report of the President: 1983,* chapter 3, "The United States in the World Economy: Strains on the System," pp. 51–70.

for export subsidies have grown as a combination of structural changes, sectoral problems, and short-run macroeconomic developments has led to a perception that we are becoming uncompetitive in world markets. In Europe, a growing structural un-employment problem, aggravated by the recession, has increased protectionist pressures. In the developing countries a financial crisis threatens the integration of capital markets and is pushing many countries back toward the exchange controls and import restrictions they had begun to dismantle.

These problems must not be allowed to disrupt world trade. If the system comes apart—if the world's nations allow themselves to be caught up in a spiral of retaliatory trade restrictions—a long time may pass before the pieces are put back together.

This reading reviews the strains on the international economic system and the policies by which the United States is attempting to overcome them. The first section discusses long-term changes in U.S. competitiveness. The correction of widespread misconceptions about the competitive position of the United States is essential if we are to get through the difficult period ahead without making major policy mistakes. The second section of this reading is devoted to financial developments and their effects on trade, especially the appreciation of the dollar and its likely effects on the U.S. trade balance.

LONG-RUN TRENDS IN U.S. COMPETITIVENESS: PERCEPTIONS AND REALITIES

Concern over the international competitiveness of the United States is as high as it has ever been. It is argued with increasing frequency that U.S. business has steadily lost ground in the international marketplace. This alleged poor performance is often attributed both to failures of management in the United States and to the support given to foreign businesses by their home governments. Feeding the perception of declining competitiveness is the persistent U.S. deficit in merchandise trade, especially the imbalance in trade with Japan.

Changes in U.S. trade performance must, however, be put into the context of changes in the U.S. role in the world economy. This wider approach reveals that much of the concern about long-run competitiveness is based on misperceptions. Although the recent appreciation of the dollar has created a temporary loss of competitiveness, the United States has not experienced a persistent loss of ability to sell its products on international markets; in fact, in the 1970s the United States held its own in terms of output, exports, and employment. Changes in the relationship of the United States to the world economy, however, have made the United States look less competitive by some traditional measures.

Aggregate Performance of the United States and Other Developed Countries

Discussion of U.S. competitiveness often gives the misleading impression that the United States has consistently performed poorly relative to other industrial countries. The U.S. share of world trade and world GNP did in fact decline throughout the 1950s and 1960s, reflecting the recovery of the rest of the world from World War II, together with the narrowing of the huge and unsustainable U.S. technological lead. In the 1970s, however, this long decline leveled off.

• From 1973 to 1980, real gross domestic product (GDP) in the United States grew at an annual rate of 2.3 percent, compared with 2.6 percent in the other Organization for Economic Cooperation and Development (OECD) countries.
• From 1973 to 1980 the U.S. share of OECD exports remained nearly constant, declining from 17.6 to 17.2 percent.
• Over the same period, employment in the United States grew at 2.1 percent a year, compared with only 0.5 percent in the rest of the OECD countries.

The United States, in part as a side effect of its relatively rapid growth in employment, did do poorly by comparison in one respect, productivity growth. Output per worker grew at only 0.2 percent in the United States, compared with 2.2 percent a year in the rest of the OECD countries. Productivity is, of course, crucial to living standards; ultimately, the level of consumption per capita depends on the level of output per worker. But there is no necessary relation between productivity and competition in international markets. Slow growth in productivity only hampers a country's international competitiveness if it is not offset by correspondingly slow growth in real wages. If U.S. workers, for example, were to receive real wage increases equal to those granted in other countries while their productivity failed to increase at a comparable rate, U.S. industry would find itself increasingly uncompetitive. The fact is, however, that this did not occur, as the comparative experience of the United States and the European Economic Community illustrates. From 1973 to 1980 output per manufacturing worker in the European Economic Community rose at an annual rate of 2.7 percent, but real compensation rose at an annual rate of 4.1 percent. By contrast, output per worker in the United States rose 1.1 percent annually, while real compensation rose only 1.8 percent annually. In fact, until the recent rise in the dollar's exchange rate, it was workers in the European Economic Community, rather than those in the United States, who were probably pricing themselves out of the world market in spite of their relatively good productivity performance.

The overall performance of the United States, then, does not suggest a long-term problem of competitiveness. The shift from persistent trade surplus to persistent deficit which occurred over the last decade is, however, often misinterpreted as a sign of an inability to compete. In fact, changes in the structure of the U.S. balance of payments are more the result of changes in the U.S. saving and investment position than of slow productivity growth.

The Changing Structure of the U.S. Balance of Payments

In the 1950s and early 1960s the United States normally had a trade surplus and invested heavily in other countries. In the years after 1973, however, the United States normally had a trade deficit, and annual investment by foreigners in the United States began to approach annual U.S. investment abroad. The shift in the U.S. trade balance was closely connected with the shift in investment flows.

Taken as a whole, U.S. international transactions always balance. Any force tending to increase or decrease the balance in one category of transactions sets in motion a process leading to exactly offsetting changes in balances in other categories. For example, an increase in foreign demand for U.S. exports tends directly to improve the trade balance, but this improvement leads to a rise in the dollar's exchange rate against foreign currencies. The exchange-rate appreciation in turn leads to increases in imports, a worsened balance on services, and so on. Similarly, an increased desire by foreign residents to invest in the United States is reflected in an increase in the capital account but leads to an appreciation of the dollar and an offsetting decline in other parts of the balance of payments.

The shift in the U.S. trade balance from persistent surplus to persistent deficit was largely an offset to changes in the U.S. capital account. In the 1950s and the first half of the 1060s, rates of return on capital were lower and wage rates were higher in the United States than in other industrial countries. Since the United States suffered no war damage, its capital stock was intact, and the diffusion of U.S. technology abroad created a demand for new capital investment in the recipient countries. The result was that returns to investment were higher abroad than in the United States, and the United States was a heavy net foreign investor. The counterpart to this foreign investment was a persistent surplus on current transactions, including merchandise trade.

By the 1970s the other industrial countries had narrowed or eliminated these differences in capital and labor costs. The result was that the demand for new capital abroad was no longer a great deal larger than it was in the United States. At the same time, the supply of savings in the United States was restricted by a low national saving rate (the lowest among the major industrial countries). Thus the United States ceased to be a major net exporter of capital, and the current account of the balance of payments moved from surplus to rough balance. Meanwhile, the U.S. balance on items other than merchandise trade improved: the deficit in military transactions fell, the surplus in services rose, and , in particular, the accumulation of past foreign investments began to yield increasing income. This meant that a balanced current account was associated with a deficit in merchandise trade.

Table 1 and Chart 1 show how the structure of the U.S. current account has changed, measuring its components as percentages of GNP.

TABLE 1
STRUCTURE OF THE U.S. BALANCE OF PAYMENTS, AS PERCENT OF GNP, 1960–80

Type of balance	Percent of GNP		Change, percentage points
	1960–66	1974–80	
Merchandise trade	0.86	−0.80	−1.66
Investment income	.74	1.06	.32
Military transactions	−.41	−.03	.38
Travel and services	−.04	.12	.16
Remittances	−.44	−.30	.15
Current account	.70	.06	−.64

Source: Department of Commerce, Bureau of Economic Analysis.

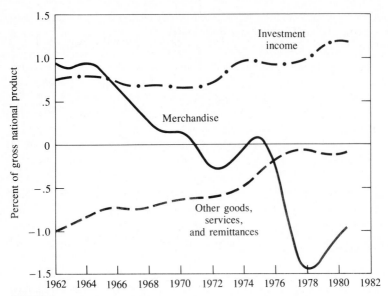

CHART 1
Structural Changes in the Current Account Balance. *Note:* Data are 16-quarter
weighted centered moving averages. (Source: *Department of Commerce.*)

The Issue of U.S. Trade with Japan

The perception of diminished U.S. competitiveness stems not only from the U.S. trade
deficit but from an impression that U.S. trade performance compares poorly with that
of other countries, especially that of Japan. Japan runs a huge surplus in its manufactures trade, while the United States runs only a small one, and Japan also has a
large surplus in its bilateral trade with the United States. These facts are often attributed
to Japanese trade restrictions. Japan does maintain restrictions which seriously hurt
U.S. businesses. Trade restrictions, however, do not in the long run improve the
Japanese trade balance; as discussed more fully below, they lead to offsetting increases
in other imports or declines in exports. The main explanation of Japan's surplus in
manufactures trade and in trade with the United States is that Japan, with few natural
resources, incurs huge deficits in its trade in primary products, especially oil, and with
primary producers, especially the Organization of Petroleum Exporting Countries (OPEC).
The surpluses in the rest of Japan's trade offset these deficits.

Table 2 and Chart 2 show the differences in the structure of the Japanese, European,
and U.S. trade accounts. They show clearly how the huge Japanese surplus in manufactures offsets large deficits in primary products.

Corresponding to the Japanese sectoral deficit in primary products, especially oil,
is a regional deficit with OPEC. Japan makes up for its deficit with OPEC by running
surpluses in its trade with other regions. The extent of this regional imbalance—and
its contrast with the U.S. position—is shown in Table 3. The point here is similar to
that already made with respect to the overall U.S. trade balance: looking at Japanese-

TABLE 2
TRADE BALANCES BY COMMODITY GROUP AS PERCENT OF GDP,
UNITED STATES, JAPAN, AND THE EUROPEAN ECONOMIC COMMUNITY, 1980
(Percent of GDP)

Commodity group	United States	Japan	European Economic Community
Total	−1.45	−0.99	−2.23
Primary products	−1.93	−10.11	−5.41
Food, beverages, and tobacco	.54	−2.15	−1.23
Crude materials excluding petroleum	.40	−1.26	−.41
Mineral funds	−2.87	−6.71	−3.77
Manufactures	.48	9.12	3.18
Machinery and transport equipment	−.42	3.09	.88
Other manufactured goods	.90	6.02	2.30

Source: Organization for Economic Cooperation and Development.

U.S. trade in isolation is misleading. The Japanese surplus in trade with the United States is largely a response to the rise of OPEC.

Although Japanese trade policy does not play a central role in causing the bilateral trade imbalance with the United States, Japanese import restrictions remain a major source of friction. Japan maintains a variety of nontariff barriers against imports. These include import quotas for a number of agricultural products and "red tape" barriers against manufactured goods, such as stringent inspection requirements applied against

CHART 2
Composition of Trade, 1980. (Source: *Organization for Economic Cooperation and Development.*)

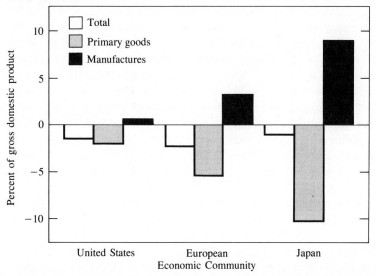

TABLE 3
TRADE BALANCES BY REGION AS PERCENT OF GDP, UNITED STATES AND JAPAN, 1980
(Percent of GDP)

Region	United States	Japan
Industrial countries	0.23	1.92
Oil-exporting countries	− 1.45	− 3.20
Non-oil developing countries	.52	1.46

Source: International Monetary Fund.

imported goods but not against Japanese products. These trade restrictions probably do not lead to a larger overall Japanese trade surplus. If they were removed, the yen would depreciate and increased Japanese imports in the currently protected sectors would be offset by reduced deficits or increased surpluses elsewhere. Japanese trade restrictions do, however, distort the composition of U.S. trade with Japan, imposing serious costs on some U.S. producers. As the fastest growing and second largest market economy, Japan has a responsibility to help sustain the open trading system. A major trade liberalization by Japan would do much to relieve the political strains on that system, while the failure of Japan to make more than token concessions would intensify them.

The Problem of Uncompetitive Sectors

Analysis of the overall U.S. trade deficit and the bilateral deficit with Japan suggests that worries about U.S. competitiveness are based in part on a misunderstanding of the situation. There is no question, however, that increased foreign competition has forced some sectors of the U.S. economy to contract.

This is partly a consequence of the fact that trade has become more important to the U.S. economy. Specialization by nations is the reason for international trade. If the United States is to expand its trade, the U.S. economy must become more specialized. This means that some sectors will grow and others will shrink. During the 1970s the United States developed increasing surpluses in areas in which it already enjoyed a comparative advantage and developed increasing deficits in sectors in which it was at a disadvantage. Some illustrative numbers are given in Table 4.

Specialization of this kind is desirable both for the United States and for its trading partners. Specialization and trade raise the efficiency of the world economy as a whole by allowing each country to concentrate on doing what it does relatively well, and by allowing increased economies of scale. But greater specialization can leave those involved in the contracting sectors worse off, at least temporarily. Attempts to prevent adjustment through trade barriers or subsidies, however, impose severe costs on unprotected sectors.

Some sectoral reallocation of resources, then, is a normal consequence of the increasing U.S. integration into the world economy. This is not the whole story, however. Some sectors of the U.S. economy are confronted by a problem that is not simply the result of market forces. Broadly speaking, these sectors fall into two groups. In one group are sectors where firms or their workers, accustomed to having substantial market power, now find that they have priced themselves out of the world market. In the other group are sectors which are hurt by foreign protectionism or export subsidies.

Market Power and Competitiveness   The "problem" of diminished market power in some sectors actually derives from a desirable aspect of trade: the fact that trade increases competition. One of the major benefits of an increasingly open U.S. economy is that it reduces the problems of monopoly and market power, thus increasing efficiency and helping consumers. But the transition to more competitive markets can prove painful. When an industry accustomed to having domestic market power encounters international competition, it must accept a reduction in the premium in prices and wages it previously commanded over other sectors of the economy. Both firms and workers may be reluctant to accept this implication of increased competition, and idle capacity and unemployment may result. Prices and wages in some U.S. heavy industries are probably too high to be sustainable in an integrated world economy.

Policies of Foreign Governments   A different problem is posed when foreign governments engage in protective or export promotion measures that harm U.S. producers. U.S. trade negotiators have emphasized four particular areas of concern:

1 *Agriculture*. Japan and the European Economic Community have high protective barriers against U.S. agricultural products. Further, the European Economic Community now engages in massive subsidized export of agricultural products to dispose of the surpluses created by its price-support program. These measures depress world prices of agricultural products, imposing substantial costs on U.S. producers in a sector where the United States holds a clear comparative advantage.

2 *High technology*. In recent years, many countries have come to view the high-technology industries as vehicles for economic growth and have sought to promote

TABLE 4
U.S. TRADE BALANCES BY SECTOR AS PERCENT OF GDP, 1972–79
(Percent of GDP)

Item	1972	1979
U.S. comparative advantage		
Research-intensive manufactures	0.93	1.63
Resource-intensive products, other than fuels	.06	.67
Invisibles (services and investment income)	.40	1.44
U.S. comparative disadvantage		
Nonresearch-intensive manufactures	−1.27	−1.44
Fuels	−.27	−2.41

Sources: International Monetary Fund, National Science Board, and Organization for Economic Cooperation and Development.

them through a complex mix of policies—outright subsidies, export credit subsidies, research subsidies, preferential procurement by State-owned enterprises, and so on. The United States holds a comparative advantage in high-technology products, and the U.S. export market share has remained roughly constant since 1973. Nevertheless, there is concern that in some specific areas, especially aircraft, foreign subsidies are threatening the position of U.S. producers.

3 *Services.* The United States has developed an increasingly strong net export position in services. Services, however, have never been recognized as being under the rules of the international trading system, and trade in services is limited by a maze of foreign government regulations.

4 *Investment.* Many countries impose "investment performance requirements" on foreign investors in exchange for the right to invest or to receive investment incentives. Many of those performance requirements are trade-related, requiring foreign companies to export more, reach a specified level of local content, or reduce imports.

Challenges to U.S. Trade Policy

The next few years are critical for the international trading system. Accumulating structural problems have combined with short-run macroeconomic stresses to produce a resurgence of protectionist pressures. The Administration's aim, nonetheless, is to preserve and extend the benefits of freer trade. To do this will require resisting protectionist pressures at home while continuing to urge foreign governments to eliminate their more objectionable trade-distorting policies.

Responding to Foreign Actions   The practices of foreign governments pose extremely difficult issues for U.S. trade policy. The United States customarily seeks to induce other nations to move in the direction of freer trade. The dilemma is how to do this without imposing costs on ourselves that exceed the benefits from changes in other countries' policies.

Trade-distorting measures, whether they take the form of protection against imports or the promotion of exports, hurt the country which adopts them as well as other countries, even when they are a response to foreign trade-distorting practices. If foreign governments limit imports from the United States and we respond in kind, the initial results will be further reductions in economic efficiency at home and higher domestic prices. If foreign governments subsidize exports, depressing world prices for U.S. products, a countersubsidy by the United States will depress prices still further. The belief that departures from free trade are automatically called for if other countries do not play by the rules is a fallacy.

Intervention in international trade by the U.S. Government, even though costly to the U.S. economy in the short run, may, however, be justified if it serves the *strategic* purpose of increasing the cost of interventionist policies by foreign governments. Thus, there is a potential role for carefully targeted measures, explicitly temporary, aimed at convincing other countries to reduce their trade distortions.

There are obvious risks in such a course of action. Instead of inducing other countries to move toward freer trade, U.S. pressure might set off a cycle of retaliation which would leave everyone worse off. There are also domestic political risks. Trade measures intended to be temporary may end up permanent and institutionalized. The need to balance the strategic objective of reducing foreign trade barriers against the harm which might be caused by U.S. retaliatory measures explains the U.S. policy of negotiating for freer trade while holding open the possibility of more direct action as a last resort.

Responding to Problem Industries   The problems of industries which have recently lost their traditional market power also pose a serious policy dilemma. There is strong pressure to give these industries at least temporary relief from imports, in the hope that lower wage and price increases and improved productivity will eventually make them competitive again. On the other hand, protection reduces the incentives for both firms and workers to make these changes. Furthermore, protectionist measures, however temporary they are supposed to be, tend to become permanent. The limitation of protection for these problem industries is a central goal of U.S. economic policy.

EXCHANGE RATES AND THE BALANCE OF PAYMENTS

During 1982 the dollar rose against other major currencies to its highest level since the beginning of floating exchange rates in 1973. The strength of the dollar provided some benefits to the U.S. economy by reducing import prices and thus accelerating progress against inflation. On the other hand, the strong dollar caused severe problems by decreasing the cost competitiveness of exported U.S. goods.

Causes of the Dollar's Strength

Exchange-rate movements are not well understood. Econometric models of exchange-rate determination proposed in the past decade have not shown any consistent ability to track past exchange-rate movements, let alone predict future changes. Nevertheless, careful analysis can narrow the range of plausible explanations of the dollar's rise.

The recent appreciation of the dollar, unlike many earlier exchange-rate movements, did not simply reflect contemporaneous changes in relative price levels. The well-known theory of purchasing power parity suggests that the rate of change in the exchange rate should equal the difference between the foreign and domestic inflation rates. Over the very long run, or in situations of very large differences in inflation rates, the purchasing power parity theory has proved to be a useful guide. But the theory has little or no power to explain the recent rise of the dollar. Price increases over the past 2 years in Germany and Japan, for instance, were lower than in the United States. Yet the dollar appreciated dramatically during that period against both the mark and the yen. Stated differently, the rise of the dollar was not simply a nominal but also a real appreciation, as illustrated in Chart 3.

Large exchange-rate movements may also occur because of shifts in world demand for a country's exports or changes in a country's demand for imports. An example of such an event was Great Britain's discovery of oil in the North Sea, which has played at least some role in the high level of Great Britain's real exchange rate relative to other European currencies.

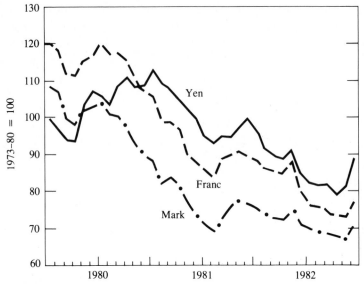

CHART 3
Real Exchange Rates of Major Currencies against the Dollar. *Note:* Consumer prices used as deflator. (Source: *International Monetary Fund.*)

No comparable event accounts for the appreciation of the dollar, although U.S. oil imports have declined sharply. The rise of the dollar was not initially accompanied by a deterioration of the trade balance, a fact which might seem to suggest that there was an increase in demand for U.S. goods. The initial lack of deterioration, however, stemmed from lags in the effect of the exchange rate on the trade balance rather than from a shift in either export or import demand, and the U.S. trade deficit grew rapidly in the second half of 1982.

What the rise of the dollar seems clearly to reflect is a rise not in the demand for U.S. goods, but in the demand for U.S. assets. The reasons for the increased attractiveness of investment in the United States are somewhat controversial, but the effects are not. In order to buy U.S. assets, foreigners must first acquire dollars. The increased demand for dollars drives up the exchange rate.

One important factor in the increased demand for U.S. assets was that real interest rates in the United States were high relative to real interest rates elsewhere. Real interest rates are not directly measurable, since they equal the nominal rate minus *expected* inflation. But some rough measure is attainable by computing the nominal rate minus *actual* inflation. Chart 4 shows the differential in real interest rates computed in this way between the United States and other industrial countries. The chart suggests that the real interest rate in the United States was substantially higher than foreign rates in recent years.

But events in the fall of 1982 cast some doubt on whether real interest rates alone can explain the dollar's strength. As U.S. short-term interest rates fell sharply, the differential between short-term interest rates in the United States and other countries was greatly reduced. Yet the dollar continued to rise. The explanation for this may lie in the difference between short- and long-term rates. Most exchange-rate models suggest that long-term real rates, and not short-term ones, are what affect the real exchange rate. A notable feature of the U.S. financial scene in the fall of 1982 was that long-term rates did not fall nearly as much as short-term rates. At the same time, long-run inflation expectations may have declined, so that it is unclear how much long-term real interest rates actually fell.

Many observers believe that other factors besides real interest rates help explain the dollar's strength. In particular, the unsettled state of the world economy—particularly the problems in Europe and Latin America—may have created a desire on the part of investors for a safe haven for their funds. The United States, according to this argument, is still regarded as the most politically and economically stable of the market economies and has become a financial refuge in troubled times. While the importance of this factor is hard to assess, the worldwide search for financial security may partially explain this country's rising capital account surplus and its growing current account deficit.

Effects of a Strong Dollar on U.S. Trade

The rise of the dollar was associated with a large rise in the production costs of U.S. firms relative to those of foreign competitors. To take one measure, unit labor costs in U.S. manufacturing rose 32 percent relative to those of a weighted average of other industrial countries from their low point in the third quarter of 1980 to the second quarter of 1982. This rise in relative costs has at least temporarily reduced the inter-

CHART 4
International Real Short-Term Interest Rate Differentials. *Note:* Data are U.S. rate minus average of rates for major industrial countries weighted by GNP. Adjusted for differences in consumer price inflation. (Source: *International Monetary Fund.*)

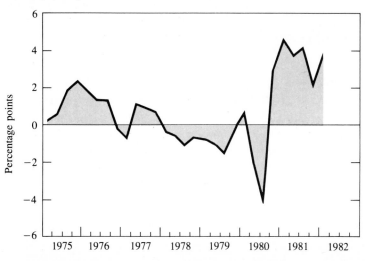

national competitiveness of U.S. industry dramatically. Other U.S. exporting and import-competing sectors, especially agriculture, have also been squeezed.

Despite this deterioration in competitive position, it was only in the third quarter of 1982 that the U.S. trade deficit began to show a significant increase. This delay was in line with previous experience of the effect of exchange rates on trade. The full effect of changes in exchange rates on the volume of exports and imports is felt only after some time has passed, because some trade takes place under contracts signed in advance and because customers do not always change suppliers immediately when relative prices change. The short-term effect of a rise in the dollar is to reduce import prices, which actually tends to *improve* the trade balance. Although the negative effects eventually dominate, some econometric estimates suggest that the full negative effect is not felt for more than 2 years.

As the effects of the strong dollar are increasingly reflected in U.S. trade, the trade deficit will widen. Economic developments elsewhere in the world will also contribute to a widening trade deficit. The recession in other industrial countries will depress the demand for U.S. exports, and financial constraints in developing countries will lead them to import less. Both developments will have negative consequences for U.S. exports. Record trade and current account deficits in 1983 will almost surely result.

Whether the trade and current account deficits persist will largely depend on U.S. macroeconomic policies, particularly on the fiscal side. If large budget deficits are allowed to continue to depress the U.S. national saving rate, real interest rates may rise again, sustaining or even increasing the high real exchange rate of the dollar. In this case the trade deficit could remain high for several years.

A large and sustained trade deficit would result in an economic recovery which would be "lopsided" in the sense that exporting and import-competing sectors would not share in the gains. Should this occur, government, business, and labor officials must bear in mind that even though protectionist foreign trade practices distort the composition of world trade and reduce economic efficiency both in the United States and abroad, large trade deficits are not the result of unfair foreign competition. Large projected U.S. trade deficits are a result of macroeconomic forces, particularly large budget deficits. The main sources of the U.S. trade deficit are to be found not in Paris or in Tokyo, but in Washington.

Responses to the Strong Dollar

The temporary adverse effects of a strong dollar create pressure to do something for the exporting and import-competing sectors. Three kinds of policies might be used: microeconomic intervention in the form of protection or export subsidies, direct intervention in the foreign exchange market, and changes in monetary and fiscal policy.

Protection and Export Promotion   The negative effect of the strong dollar on the competitiveness of many U.S. firms has fueled pressures for an interventionist trade policy. These pressures must be resisted. Protecting import-competing industries or subsidizing exports is not just a harmful long-run policy. With a floating exchange rate, such policies would fail to improve the trade balance or create employment even in the short run.

The exchange rate always moves to clear the market. An increase in exports or a reduction in imports would lead to an increased demand for or reduced supply of dollars on the world market, raising the exchange rate. This would lead to a further loss of competitiveness in the sectors not protected or promoted. An export subsidy for agricultural products would worsen the situation of the auto industry, an import quota on steel would hurt the competitiveness of the aircraft industry, and so on. Although these indirect effects may seem of doubtful importance in the real world, they are not. That governments cannot simultaneously protect everyone is a basic principle of international trade.

Instead of creating additional employment and output, the distortion of trade through protectionist policies or export promotion would probably reduce them. Market-distorting policies reduce the efficiency of the economy. Thus, a turn to protectionism could create a "supply-side" shock that might have the same kind of stagflationary effects as an oil price increase. The effects would prove still worse if, as is likely, U.S. actions were to provoke foreign retaliation.

Although protectionism and export subsidies provide no answer to the problems caused by a strong dollar, the pressure to use them is increasing. Many of the exporting sectors, which make up the traditional constituency for freer trade, appear to have become convinced by the strength of the dollar and the resulting loss of U.S. competitiveness that a more interventionist policy is needed.

Exchange-Market Intervention Since March 1981 the United States has abstained as much as possible from direct intervention in the foreign exchange market. This unwillingness to intervene is based on doubts about whether exchange-market intervention is effective or desirable. As long as the Federal Reserve continues to pursue a policy of targeting monetary aggregates, any U.S. intervention on the foreign exchange market must be *sterilized*—that is, offset by other transactions on domestic financial markets. These transactions are likely to wipe out most of the effect of the initial exchange-market intervention.

The process of sterilization is straightforward. If the U.S. Government attempted to drive up the price of foreign exchange and weaken the dollar by buying foreign securities, the Federal Reserve would issue dollars to pay for the foreign assets. In order to prevent these dollars from increasing the U.S. money stock, however, the Federal Reserve would then have to withdraw an equal number of dollars from the market by selling Treasury bills. The only net result would be that the world's supply of dollar-denominated assets would increase, while its supply of assets denominated in other currencies would fall.

The increase in the level of dollar-denominated assets would probably have little effect on the exchange rate because of the sheer size of world financial markets. The world market in dollar-denominated securities includes not only the dollar assets actually owned abroad—foreign deposits in U.S. banks, foreign holdings of Treasury bills, Eurodollar deposits, and the like—but also all those dollar assets which are potentially tradeable. Thus, the total pool of internationally mobile dollar assets is probably in the trillions of dollars. This makes it questionable whether even very large interventions in the exchange market can have much effect on the exchange rate.

Macroeconomic Policies   Although the government cannot significantly affect exchange rates through direct intervention, monetary and fiscal policies do indirectly affect the exchange rate. A feasible strategy for bringing the dollar down would involve looser monetary policies and tighter fiscal policies. Both of these changes would tend to lower real interest rates (at least in the short run), making capital movement into the United States less attractive and thus driving down the value of the dollar.

Despite its unfortunate effects on the U.S. balance of trade, however, monetary restraint is the prime weapon in the fight against inflation. Disinflation, as we have learned, unfortunately involves substantial costs. Under fixed exchange rates the heaviest costs of monetary contraction and disinflation fell on the interest-sensitive sectors of the economy, such as construction and consumer durables. With floating exchange rates, however, much of the burden also falls on exporting and import-competing sectors, which are injured by the rise in the value of the dollar.

A tighter fiscal policy would also lower real interest rates and lead to a lower dollar. Under fixed exchange rates, budget deficits crowded out domestic investment. With a floating exchange rate they crowd out exporting and import-competing products as well. A reduction in deficits would lead—with some lag—to an improvement in the trade balance as well as higher investment.

The strength of the dollar has put considerable strain on the resolve of the United States to remain committed to free trade. This strain is not unique to the international sector. The recession and high interest rates have also put a strain on the resolve to let other types of markets, from housing to labor markets, operate freely. If there is special reason for concern about the international side, it is because of the danger that mistakes in U.S. policy could set off a spiral of retaliation among all the major trading nations.

The competitiveness of U.S. business as a whole—as opposed to that of particular sectors—and the balance of payments are macroeconomic phenomena. Microeconomic interventions cannot cure macroeconomic problems; they can only make one sector better off by hurting other sectors even more. The most effective strategy the United States can pursue for its exporting and import-competing sectors is to get its overall economic house in order—above all, by bringing budget deficits and real interest rates under control.

QUESTIONS FOR DISCUSSION

1 For what reasons did the authors of this article, which was first published in 1983, believe that the "liberalized [world] trading system is now in danger"? As you read this piece, have the sources of this danger receded?

2 What is *competitiveness?* What factors contribute to U.S. competitiveness (or lack of it)? Why does the *Report* argue that the United States does not have a "long-term problem of competitiveness"? How do changes in the value of the dollar affect their argument?

3 The reading states, "The shift in the U.S. trade balance form persistent surplus to persistent deficit was largely an offset to changes in the U.S. capital account." Explain. Did this continue to be true through the 1982–1986 period? (See the previous reading.) How about as of today?

4 What is the basic "structural" explanation for the large bilateral trade deficit that the United States has with Japan? How was this problem aggravated in the early 1980s by the relative

valuations of the dollar and the yen? Find the current yen/dollar exchange rate. (Try looking in *The Wall Street Journal*.) How does it compare with 1980? With 1984? (Consult the *Economic Report of the President*.)

5 How does increased and freer world trade help the United States overall? What groups may be injured by increased trade, and why? What policy solutions are there to the problems of these groups?

6 The rise in the dollar through 1984 was a real rather than purely nominal appreciation. Explain this distinction. What effect does a real appreciation have on the trade balance? What effect would a purely nominal appreciation have?

7 This reading foresaw the serious deterioration of the U.S. trade balance that occurred after 1982. It stated that the main sources of the U.S. trade deficit "are to be found . . . in Washington." Explain this statement. What policy responses to trade deficits did this reading support? Oppose?

THATCHER AND THE U.K. ECONOMY, 1979–1983

In 1979, Margaret Thatcher became the Prime Minister of Britain, inheriting from her predecessors an economy whose problems included relatively slow output growth, high inflation, and a weak currency. To address these problems, Thatcher undertook a number of significant policy actions, including tighter monetary policy, fiscal reform, and increased privatization of the economy.

The results of these initiatives appear to have been mixed, at best. After a temporary surge, inflation came down quite a bit. The pound became quite strong for a while, then weakened. Probably most significantly, however, the British economy underwent a very severe recession; and, although output has by now recovered somewhat, as of 1986 unemployment remains extremely high.

The following two readings give alternative views of the sources of the British recession. The first, an excerpt from an article by Stephen A. Meyer, attributes the slowdown to excessively tight monetary and fiscal policies. The second, by K. Alec Chrystal, points the finger at the negative effect of North Sea oil on British manufacturing competitiveness—the so-called Dutch disease.

Reading 34 Stephen A. Meyer, "Margaret Thatcher's Economic Experiment," *Business Review,* Philadelphia Federal Reserve Bank, May-June 1982, pp. 3–13.

Reading 35 K. Alec Chrystal, "Dutch Disease or Monetarist Medicine?: The British Economy under Mrs. Thatcher," *Review,* St. Louis Federal Reserve Bank, May 1984, pp. 27–37.

MARGARET THATCHER'S ECONOMIC EXPERIMENT

Stephen A. Meyer*

When Margaret Thatcher became Prime Minister of Great Britain in May 1979, she pledged a new direction for economic policy. Her goal was to reverse Britain's long-term difficulties of slow economic growth, low productivity, and high inflation. She called for lower taxes and for less government intervention in the economy to encourage more output and investment, and for slower growth of the money supply to reduce inflation. Her supporters expected these policies to lead to rapid real growth and less inflation. Instead, the unemployment rate in the United Kingdom more than doubled, real output of the British economy fell sharply, and inflation soared after Mrs. Thatcher took office.

Why did these unexpected problems occur? To answer this question we must look carefully at the actual economic policies put in place in Britain, not at the promised policies.

BRITISH FISCAL POLICIES WERE NOT AS PROMISED

Mrs. Thatcher had promised an economic program intended to deal with Britain's problems of high unemployment and economic stagnation, but the policies adopted were not the promised ones. She had pledged to cut taxes to provide improved in-

Excerpted from Stephen A. Meyer, "Margaret Thatcher's Economic Experiment: Are There Lessons for the Reagan Administration?" *Business Review,* Federal Reserve Bank of Philadelphia, May-June 1982, pp. 3–13.

*Stephen A. Meyer is Senior Economist in the Money and Macroeconomics section of the Philadelphia Fed's Research Department. He also teaches macroeconomics and international finance at the Wharton School, University of Pennsylvania.

centives for individuals to work and to invest, but actually she raised taxes substantially. She also had promised to reduce the size and economic role of the government in order to return economic resources to the private sector, but government spending rose. British fiscal policies pushed the economy into recession rather than promoting growth.

British Taxes Rose Despite Income Tax Cuts

To carry out its campaign promise, the new British government enacted an across-the-board cut in personal income tax rates. As a result, total government revenue was reduced by roughly 5 percent from what it would have been otherwise. Mrs. Thatcher also had pledged to reduce the government's budget deficit. Because cutting income tax rates would have resulted in a larger budget deficit, other taxes were raised to make up the revenue loss. In particular, the value-added tax (VAT), which is similar to a national sales tax, was raised from 8 percent to 15 percent of value-added on most goods.[1] Excise taxes on petroleum products, liquor, cigarettes, and other products were raised also. In addition, taxes on North Sea oil production were increased. These tax hikes were expected to increase total tax revenue by 4 percent above what they would have been otherwise during the 1979 tax year.[2]

Increases in VAT and in excise taxes were large enough to generate an overall tax hike, because they were combined with hidden tax increases caused by bracket creep. Britain's high inflation during 1979 pushed people into higher tax brackets at the same time that tax rates for those higher brackets were cut. Bracket creep largely undid the cuts in personal tax rates; so income tax revenues in Britain stayed roughly constant, in real terms, from the 1978 to the 1979 tax year. During the same period the real value of taxes on consumers' expenditures rose 21 percent. As a result the real value of taxes levied on Britons actually rose by 7.5 percent from the preceding year, which helped to start a recession.

Taxes were raised further in 1980 and 1981 even though the British economy was already in a recession. In its 1980 budget the Thatcher government adjusted income tax schedules to offset most of the bracket creep caused by inflation, but it raised taxes on consumers' expenditures even more. In 1981, income tax schedules were left unchanged, so that real income taxes were effectively raised again as inflation pushed people into higher tax brackets; in addition, excise and other taxes on expenditure were raised yet another time.[3]

---

[1] A value-added tax is levied at each stage of production or distribution on the difference between the price at which a product is sold and the cost of raw materials and parts which are used to make that product (thus 'value-added'). The value added by a retailer is (roughly speaking) the difference between the retail price and the wholesale price he paid for the item. The value added by a manufacturer is the difference between the wholesale price he charges for the item and the cost of parts which go into the item. The value added by the maker of parts is the difference between the price at which he sells the parts and his cost for raw materials. Adding up the value added at each stage, we clearly get the retail price of the item before tax. Thus a 15-percent tax on value added at each stage is like a 15 percent tax on total value, that is, like a 15-percent sales tax.

[2] The British tax year, or fiscal year, begins in April and runs through March of the following year.

[3] A detailed presentation of the first budget adopted by the Thatcher government can be found in *The Economist* for June 16, 1979, pp. 63 ff. The British government's budget for the 1980 tax year is discussed in *The Economist* for March 29, 1980, on pp. 25–36. A similar treatment of the 1981 budget appears in *The Economist* of March 14, 1981, on pp. 51–65.

The British government raised taxes when Britain was in a recession because it focused on the size of the government's budget deficit. Policymakers appear to have ignored the fact that much of the government's budget deficit was caused by Britain's worsening recession. As the British economy turned down, tax revenues collected by the government fell below projected levels because personal income and spending fell (in real terms) as workers were laid off or put on short time. Lower-than-expected tax revenues meant a higher-than-expected budget deficit. The British government apparently interpreted the larger budget deficit as indicating that fiscal policy was too expansionary, and so it raised taxes in an attempt to reduce that deficit. These tax increases made the recession more severe. Mrs. Thatcher was elected on a pledge to cut taxes. Instead her government raised the real tax burden substantially.

Government Spending Was Not Cut

Cutting taxes is not the only pledge that Mrs. Thatcher was unable to carry out. The Thatcher government believed that private individuals and firms would use resources more efficiently than the public sector. If so, giving the private sector command over more resources would increase the efficiency of the British economy, thus raising productivity and the standard of living.

Mrs. Thatcher's program contained two elements designed to reduce the size and economic role of the British government. The first was a pledge to reduce the real value of government spending (after adjusting for inflation) by one percent per year from 1979 to 1984. The second element was to sell some of Britain's nationalized firms to private investors. So far the government has had little success in returning resources to the private sector because it has been unable to implement either element of its program.

Although Mrs. Thatcher pledged to reduce the real value of government spending (after adjusting for inflation) in the 1979 and 1980 tax years, the real value of central government spending rose by 3.4 percent in the first year and by approximately 1.3 percent more in the second year. For the 1981 tax year real government spending remained at roughly the previous year's level. Much of the increase in real government spending since the new government took office was caused by large salary increases for government employees and by growth of transfer payments (such as unemployment compensation) resulting from Britain's recession.

The Thatcher government was only a little more successful in carrying out the second element of its program to reduce the economic role of the government. The British government did manage to sell part of its interest in several high-technology and service companies, and it also sold part of its share of British Petroleum. But the remainder of the nationalized firms, including those in the steel, coal, shipbuilding, and automobile industries, remain under government control. All of these nationalized firms run large losses and require growing subsidies from the central government.

Although the government has not succeeded in reducing its size, neither has it allowed its spending to grow as fast as it did in earlier years. As a result, total tax revenues have risen relative to government spending in Britain since Thatcher's election, making fiscal policy restrictive. The tighter fiscal policy could have been offset, at least in part, by new supply-side incentives. But none were provided.

Tax Changes Did Not Improve Incentives to Work

The Thatcher government did enact an across-the-board cut in marginal tax rates on personal income.[4] Cuts in marginal tax rates on wages and salaries were intended to provide greater incentives for those already working to work longer hours, and for those not working to take jobs. Cuts in marginal tax rates on interest and dividend income were intended to provide greater incentives for people to save and invest.[5]

The highest tax rates were cut drastically. The top tax rates during the 1978 tax year were 83 percent of wages and salaries and 98 percent of interest and dividends for that part of total income above £30,075 (equivalent to approximately $51,000). For the 1979 tax year, Mrs. Thatcher slashed these rates to 60 percent of wages and salaries and 75 percent of interest and dividends. Similar but smaller cuts in tax rates were enacted for people at lower income levels. Most families in Britain found themselves in one large tax bracket which stretched from £3,700 to £12,000 (or $6,300 to $20,400); for these families the marginal tax rate was cut from 33 percent in 1978 to 30 percent in 1979.[6]

Incentives to work, save, and invest may have been increased by cuts in income tax rates, but they were reduced by other policies. While personal income tax rates were cut substantially, at least at higher income levels, much of those cuts was eroded by bracket creep caused by high inflation. The value-added tax was raised at the same time. Most workers discovered that if they worked an extra hour they could take home a slightly bigger fraction of their extra pay (because income taxes were cut), but they also discovered that their extra take-home pay would buy less than before (because consumption taxes went up). The real purchasing power of an additional hour of work was lower after the tax changes, except for families with high incomes.

Fiscal Policy Was Restrictive Overall

The upshot of the tax and spending policies adopted by the government was a contractionary fiscal policy with no offsetting supply-side stimuli. During the first two years of Mrs. Thatcher's tenure, the real value of taxes levied by the central government in Britain rose more than twice as much as government spending. In the 1981 tax year, real government expenditures were held approximately constant while real taxes again rose substantially. These tax increases were not offset by providing greater supply-side incentives; in particular, the total marginal tax bite on extra earnings was not lowered. Thus fiscal policy in Britain has been contractionary, overall.

---

[4]The marginal tax rate is the percentage of any additional income that one must pay to the taxman. When we speak of someone as being in the 50-percent tax bracket, we are referring to that person's marginal tax rate.

[5]All of these are supply-side policies. For a discussion of how these incentives work, and how large they might be, see Aris Protopapadakis, "Supply-Side Economics: What Chance for Success?" *Business Review*, Federal Reserve Bank of Philadelphia, May-June 1981.

[6]The income levels cited here are for the example of a married couple, both working. Incomes are given in 1979 £ throughout, with the U.S. equivalent required to achieve the same purchasing power in the U.S. if the tax systems in the two countries were identical. The tax rates cited are for income tax only; they abstract from Social Security taxes, sales taxes, and other taxes.

The restrictive fiscal policy is one reason why the British economy is undergoing a severe recession. Another reason is that monetary policy was also restrictive—much more restrictive than the government had planned.

MONETARY POLICY WAS TIGHTER THAN INTENDED

The Thatcher government pledged to reduce the rate of growth of the money supply in Britain gradually, in order to bring down the inflation rate while avoiding a credit crunch. The government chose to target a broad measure of money known as sterling M3.[7] For the 1979 fiscal year the target rate of growth of sterling M3 was 10 percent, with an allowable range of 8 percent to 12 percent. The target and its associated range were to be lowered by one percentage point each year, so that by fiscal 1983 the target would be 6 percent money growth with an allowable range of 4 percent to 8 percent. Inasmuch as sterling M3 had grown by almost 12 percent during the 1978 fiscal year, the announced targets represented moderately tighter monetary policy.[8]

By making its tight monetary policy known in advance, the government was trying to lower inflationary expectations. The government hoped that unions would accept lower wage increases and firms would post smaller price hikes if they believed that inflation would decline. British policymakers hoped to reduce inflation without causing rising unemployment and falling sales.

Sterling M3 actually grew by 15 percent in the year after Mrs. Thatcher took office, so it might seem that monetary policy did not become tighter. However, sterling M3 gives a misleading impression of monetary policy; other measures suggest monetary policy was quite restrictive.

Sterling M3 Is a Poor Indicator

By choosing to focus attention on sterling M3, the Thatcher government created confusion about its monetary policy, because sterling M3 is not a very good measure of money. Sterling M3 includes various bank deposits, such as certificates of deposit, which are not transactions balances (cannot be spent directly), but it does not include similar money-market instruments issued by other financial intermediaries. Thus the figures for sterling M3 will rise or fall when individuals shift from certificates of deposit issued by banks to similar instruments from other issuers, or vice versa. But such shifts leave liquidity unchanged. People chose to shift funds into bank certificates of deposit and other bank time deposits and out of other money-market instruments

---

[7]Sterling M3 is defined as currency in circulation *plus* sterling denominated checkable deposits owned by the U.K. private sector *plus* sterling denominated time deposits owned by the U.K. private sector. Thus sterling M3 is a broad monetary aggregate which includes the equivalents of large certificates of deposit and other savings certificates.

[8]In Britain it is the Prime Minister and her cabinet who make decisions about monetary policy targets. The central bank (the Bank of England) exercises considerable discretion in carrying out monetary policy, and also helps the administration in choosing targets. But it is the Prime Minister who has the final authority to set monetary policy. In the United States, by contrast, the central bank (the Federal Reserve System) is an independent agency responsible to the Congress. The President of the United States does not exercise control over monetary policy.

during the second half of 1979 and during 1980, because the British government changed regulations governing banks. The resulting high growth rate of sterling M3 did not represent a high growth rate of liquidity in the economy. By contrast, the growth rate of a broader measure of liquidity which includes both bank deposits and comparable money-market instruments actually fell in the year after Mrs. Thatcher became Prime Minister. Growth of this broader aggregate—PSL2—slowed from 15 percent per year over mid-1977 through mid-1979 to 12.2 percent during mid-1979 to mid-1980.

A monetary aggregate constructed for purposes of monitoring the tightness or ease of monetary policy can quickly become obsolete when government regulation of financial institutions changes. Just such a regulatory change was introduced in Britain in 1979 and 1980 by the Thatcher government: the government removed restrictions on banks' offering certificates of deposit. This change contributed to the shift of funds out of money-market instruments into interest-bearing bank deposits. Thus the regulatory changes in Britain contributed to making sterling M3 a misleading indicator of monetary policy.

A similar difficulty arose in the United States early in 1981 when NOW accounts became available nationwide. As individuals moved billions of dollars from checking accounts and savings accounts into NOW accounts, the money supply figures for the United States were distorted. When someone took funds out of a savings account and put them into a NOW account, the M1B measure of the U.S. money supply went up even though that person's bank balance was unchanged overall. U.S. policymakers adjusted the measured money supply (M1B) to correct for this distortion. But in Britain no such correction was made to sterling M3; the British government continued to set its monetary targets in terms of a misleading indicator of monetary policy.

Monetary Policy Was Extremely Tight

Other, better measures of British monetary policy than sterling M3 indicate that monetary policy became much tighter after Mrs. Thatcher took office. The monetary base (currency in circulation plus bank reserves), which is directly under the control of the central bank, grew by more than 15 percent in each of the two years before the election. In the year after, from May 1979 to May 1980, the monetary base grew much less, by 8.4 percent. Growth of the monetary base slowed further during the following year. From May 1980 to May 1981, the monetary base grew by only 5.3 percent. This sharp decline in the rate of growth of the monetary base is a signal of tighter monetary policy.[9]

The growth rate of M1, a measure of transactions deposits, confirms the monetary base signal that monetary policy was tight.[10] The rate of growth of sterling M1 in Britain slowed from an average rate of almost 19 percent in each of the two years

---

[9]In British terminology, the monetary base is defined as "Notes and coin in circulation with the public *plus* Notes and coin held by banks *plus* Banker's deposits held at the Bank of England." Data can be found in the Bank of England *Quarterly Bulletin*, March 1981, pp. 59–65.

[10]British M1 is defined as "Notes and coin in circulation with the public *plus* U.K. private sector interest bearing and non-interest bearing sight deposits." Thus British M1 corresponds to U.S. M1.

before the election to 6.5 percent in the following year. During the second year of Mrs. Thatcher's tenure, the rate of growth of sterling M1 slowed further, to 1.6 percent.

Tight monetary policy not only helped to push the British economy into its current recession by driving up the real cost of borrowing funds; it also caused the British pound to appreciate on international currency markets, which worsened the recession. Tight monetary policy drove up interest rates in Britain and also reduced the expected future inflation rate, which made British pounds more attractive. As foreigners rushed to buy British pounds, they pushed up the price of pounds in terms of foreign currencies.[11] The appreciation of the pound made British goods more expensive abroad and made foreign goods cheaper in Britain. Both Britons and foreigners bought fewer British goods as a result. This decline in demand for British goods made the recession in Britain more severe.

Although very tight monetary policy helped to cause the British recession, it did not immediately reduce inflation. In fact, the inflation rate doubled in the year following Mrs. Thatcher's inauguration, but not because of the new, tighter monetary policy (see WHY INFLATION SOARED). Slow money growth will take longer than a year to bring down inflation.

RESTRICTIVE ECONOMIC POLICIES
CAUSED THE BRITISH RECESSION

The government's restrictive monetary and fiscal policies caused a sharp reduction in aggregate demand for British goods and services. Taxes were raised substantially, as consumption taxes were raised and real income taxes were not cut. Taxes were raised much more than government spending. Monetary policy was tightened as well, as indicated by sharp reductions in the rates of growth of the monetary base and M1. The effects of tight money were reinforced by the resulting appreciation of the exchange rate.

These restrictive demand-management policies were not offset by new supply-side incentives. British firms found that declining demand for their output was not offset by policies which reduced their costs or improved their profitability.

Given the economic policies actually adopted by the Thatcher government, it is not surprising that the British economy was hit by a recession. With contractionary fiscal and monetary policies and no offsetting supply-side policy, a recession is the most likely outcome. British economic policies were strongly contractionary, so they caused a severe recession. After Mrs. Thatcher took office the unemployment rate more than doubled in the United Kingdom, rising from 5.4 percent in May 1979 to 11.7 percent in January 1982. Real output of the British economy fell sharply; from the second quarter of 1979 to the second quarter of 1981 real output (Gross Domestic Product) fell 7.4 percent, and manufacturing output (other than oil extraction) fell 16 percent (see Figure 1).[12]

---

[11]The British pound increased in value from $2.06 per pound when Mrs. Thatcher took office to $2.40 per pound at the end of 1980.

[12]Economic data for Britain are provided in *Economic Trends*, published monthly by the U.K. Central Statistical Office.

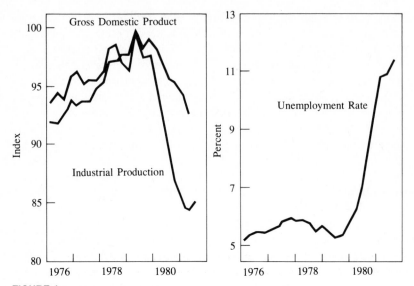

FIGURE 1
U.K. Output and Unemployment. (Source: *U.K. Central Statistical Office,* *Economic Trends.*)

Economic events in Great Britain since Mrs. Thatcher took office lose their mystery in light of the economic policies that she actually adopted. The mystery is why a government that was elected on promises to cut taxes and promote private business did the opposite.[13]

[13]The reader who wishes a more detailed description and analysis of British economic policies and the resulting recession should turn to Willem H. Buiter and Marcus Miller, "The Thatcher Experiment: The First Two Years," *Brookings Papers on Economic Activity* 1981, No. 2, pp. 315–380.

WHY INFLATION SOARED

Monetary policy became much tighter after Margaret Thatcher became Prime Minister. Policymakers expected that tight monetary policy would reduce the inflation rate. But inflation in Britain nearly doubled in the year after Mrs. Thatcher took office. The consumer price index in Britain rose by 11.3 percent in the year ending in June 1979 but jumped by 21 percent in the following year, the first year of Mrs. Thatcher's tenure. In her second year in office prices rose by another 11.3 percent, despite the restrictive monetary policy she adopted. Does this mean that tight monetary policy no longer works to reduce inflation in Britain?

Raising the value-added tax and excise taxes was one cause of higher inflation in the year following the election. A more important cause is that the rate of growth of the money supply

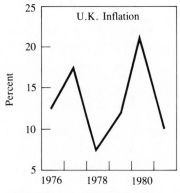 

U.K. Inflation and Money Growth.

had accelerated greatly two years before the Thatcher government took office. Speeding up or slowing down the money supply growth rate usually causes the inflation rate to speed up or slow down one to two years later. The sterling M1 measure of the money supply in Britain (transactions balances) grew by 10.8 percent in the year ending June 1977, but then it accelerated to a growth rate of 22.2 percent from June 1977 to June 1978.* From June to December 1978 the growth rate of M1 was 16 percent per year. Economists would expect the year of more rapid money growth to be followed by more rapid inflation about two years later, in 1979. This is precisely what occurred, as the accompanying Figure reveals. To a large extent, the rise in inflation which occurred in the year after Mrs. Thatcher took office was inherited from the previous government.

Not all of the rise in inflation was inherited, however. In June 1979 Mrs. Thatcher announced an increase in the value-added tax on most commodities from 8 percent to 15 percent. This tax hike was equivalent to an increase in sales taxes in that it raised selling prices directly. From June to July 1979 the consumer price index in Britain rose by 4.4 percent, equivalent to a 67.7-percent annual rate of inflation. In March of 1980 the value-added tax and other expenditure taxes were raised again. From March to April 1980 the British consumer price index rose by 3.4 percent, which is equivalent to an annual inflation rate of 49.4 percent. During the entire year from June 1979 to June 1980 the consumer price index in Britain rose by 21 percent. Somewhat less than one-third of this increase may have been due to the two increases in VAT and expenditure taxes.†

Given the actual monetary policies adopted by Mrs. Thatcher's predecessor and the new consumption taxes imposed by Mrs. Thatcher herself, the acceleration of inflation that occurred during the second half of 1979 and first half of 1980 is not surprising. Nor is it surprising that inflation in Britain slowed in the next year, given the substantial drop in the rate of growth of the money supply which was engineered by Mrs. Thatcher.

*The acceleration of money growth in the U.K. from June 1977 to June 1978 is shown by other measures of money as well as by M1.

†From June 1979 to June 1980 the price index rose by 21 percent. Excluding July 1980 and April 1981, prices rose at an annual rate of 15 percent over that period. I attribute the difference to increases in VAT.

QUESTIONS FOR DISCUSSION

1 Why did Prime Minister Thatcher not cut the overall tax burden and reduce the size of government, as promised? How did her fiscal policy differ from that used starting in 1981 in the United States?

2 Why was the growth of sterling M3 a bad indicator of the tightness of monetary policy during this period, according to the author? What similar problems were encountered by U.S. monetary authorities at about the same time? What indicators of British monetary policy does the author prefer to rely on?

3 Tight monetary policy increased the value of the pound, according to author Meyer. Using the *IS-LM* diagram, augmented by a balance of payments line, show how this effect would work. What effects of the stronger pound on British net exports, output, and employment would be predicted by this analysis?

4 What reasons are given for the sharp increase in inflation during the first year of Thatcher's administration? Using the aggregate demand–aggregate supply framework, show how the large increase in the value-added tax can be interpreted as an adverse supply shock.

DUTCH DISEASE OR MONETARIST MEDICINE?: THE BRITISH ECONOMY UNDER MRS. THATCHER

K. Alec Chrystal*

The performance of the British economy over the past five years has been the object of worldwide curiosity. Much publicity has been focused on the government of Margaret Thatcher and her apparently radical departure from the policies pursued by her predecessors.[1] This alleged policy departure is sometimes considered a "monetarist experiment."[2] Chart 1 illustrates some of the major macroeconomic changes in Britain since Mrs. Thatcher's election to Prime Minister. Inflation first rose through 1980, then fell by 1983 to its lowest level since the mid-1960s. In contrast, unemployment rose after 1979 to its highest level since the 1930s. By the end of 1983, unemployment was more than double that following the previous worst recession (1973–75) in the postwar period.

Critics of Mrs. Thatcher claim that these events are primarily the result of the tight aggregate demand (monetarist) policies of her government and, further, that the price paid for reducing inflation has been too high. The purpose of this paper is to point out that this interpretation of events is misleading.

An important feature of the changing employment levels in Britain has been that job losses occurred almost entirely in the manufacturing sector. In 1979, this sector provided about 28 percent of total employment. Between the end of 1978 and the end of 1982, there was a 1.4 million rise in the number of unemployed. Over the same

K. Alec Chrystal, "Dutch Disease or Monetarist Medicine?: The British Economy under Mrs. Thatcher," *Review*, St. Louis Federal Reserve Bank, May 1984, pp. 27–37.

*K. Alec Chrystal, professor of economics-elect, University of Sheffield, England, is a visiting scholar at the Federal Reserve Bank of St. Louis. Leslie Bailis Koppel provided research assistance.

[1]Mrs. Thatcher came to power five years ago on May 3, 1979. She was reelected for a second term in June 1983 and may stay in office until June 1988 without recourse to a further general election.

[2]See, for example, Gould, Mills and Steward (1981), Kaldor (1982), and Buiter and Miller (1981).

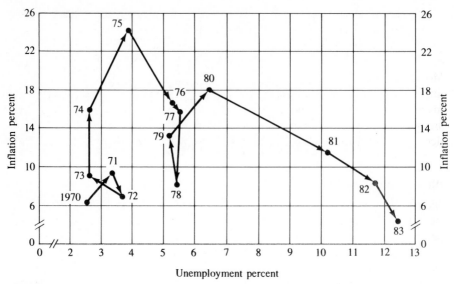

CHART 1
Inflation and Unemployment. Quarterly inflation calculated as $[(CPI_t/CPI_{t-4}) - 1] \cdot 100$.
Annual averages are taken from quarterly figures for inflation and from monthly figures for
unemployment.

period, the number employed in manufacturing industries fell by 1.5 million. This job
loss can be traced to a substantial and sustained collapse of manufacturing production
(chart 2) between late 1979 and the end of 1980.

Thus, any explanation of unemployment's steep rise in Britain must be able to
explain the collapse in the manufacturing sector, a collapse that was essentially completed within 18 months of Mrs. Thatcher taking office. Neither monetary nor fiscal
policy, alone or taken together, has been so tight as to explain sufficiently what has
happened in Britain. Rather, a more likely contributor to unemployment comes from
the structural changes in the British economy caused by North Sea oil production. The
scenario is now widely termed the "Dutch Disease," so-called because of the negative
impact that Dutch oil and gas production had on employment and output in the non-
oil traded goods sector of the Netherlands' economy.

Before discussing the impact of North Sea oil production on the British economy,
however, it is necessary to show why two other widely claimed causes—British policies
and the worldwide recession—are inadequate explanations.

BRITAIN BEFORE THATCHER

Macroeconomic policy in the 1950s and 1960s was dominated by the commitment to
maintain a fixed exchange rate. Fiscal policy was used to stimulate the economy
whenever there appeared to be slack; expansion, on the other hand, was constrained
by the balance of payments. Periodic runs on Britain's foreign exchange reserves led
to policy reversals, causing a budgetary cycle of expansion and contraction that earned
the nickname of "stop-go." A stable exchange rate was maintained, however, for

nearly two decades (1949–67). Indeed, in retrospect, this period seems like a golden age. Inflation averaged 3 percent, unemployment averaged less than 2 percent and was sometimes below 1 percent, and average real incomes grew about 3 percent per year.

Monetary policy in this period was subordinated to the twin requirements of maintaining the exchange rate and funding public sector borrowing. The main policy instrument was the Bank of England's discount rate (Bank Rate), though this was augmented periodically by quantitative ceilings on bank lending. These ceilings were particularly important following the November 1967 devaluation of sterling until 1971.[3]

Heath's "Dash for Growth"

In mid-1970, when the Labour government of Harold Wilson lost a general election to the Conservative party led by Edward Heath, the British economy was in good shape. Both the balance of payments and the government budget were in surplus. Inflation (6 percent) and unemployment (2.2 percent), although high by 1960s standards, were by no means at crisis levels—or so it seems in retrospect.

As unemployment drifted upward through 1971, however, the Heath government embarked upon a stimulative macroeconomic policy known alternatively as the "dash for growth" or the "Barber boom."[4] The stimulation took two forms. First, monetary policy became expansionary in September 1971 following the introduction of a reform

[3]In both the 1960s and 1970s, monetary and fiscal policies were augmented from time to time by incomes policies which attempted to regulate the growth rate of wages. There is some evidence that these policies temporarily restrained wage increases, but had no long-run impact on wage and price inflation. See Henry and Ormerod (1978).

[4]The Chancellor of the Exchequer, chief minister in the Treasury, during the Heath government (June 1970-February 1974) was Anthony (later Lord) Barber, appointed July 26, 1970.

CHART 2
Manufacturing Production Index.

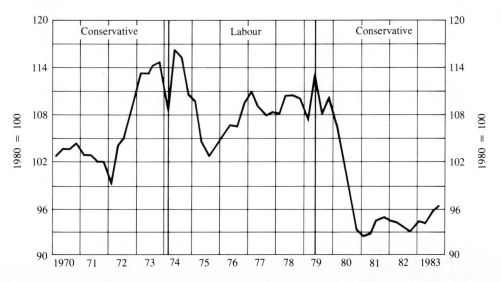

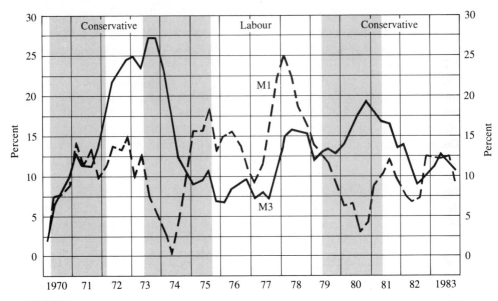

CHART 3
Annual Growth Rates of M1 and Sterling M3. Shaded areas represent recessions, defined as the contraction phase of coincident economic indicators.

package known as Competition and Credit Control. This program removed ceilings on bank lending without replacing them with an effective alternative control mechanism.[5] As a result, money and credit expanded rapidly. Through 1972 and 1973, the annual growth rate of sterling M3 reached levels well in excess of 20 percent (see chart 3).[6]

Second, an expansionary budget was introduced in March 1972. This largely involved cuts in personal taxation, but was later augmented by a substantial expansion in public sector investment programs.

Underlying this dash for growth was the belief that the growth of the British economy had been artificially constrained by the fixed exchange rate (or, equivalently, the balance of payments). In the past, restrictive fiscal policy had to be introduced every time there was a significant run on foreign exchange reserves.

Floating the exchange rate became acceptable, however, following the measures introduced by President Nixon on August 15, 1971, which among other things led to the floating of the U.S. dollar in foreign exchange markets. The pound floated from August 23, 1971, was repegged following the Smithsonian Agreement of December,

[5]See Hall (1983) for a detailed discussion of the scheme. The authorities presumably thought the monetary expansion would be temporary following the removal of ceilings. It proved, however, to be both substantial and sustained.

[6]The monetary aggregates referred to are defined as follows: M1 = notes and coins in circulation with the public + U.K. private sector sterling sight deposits; sterling M3 = M1 + private sector sterling time deposits + public sector deposits. Sterling M3 was the aggregate targeted after 1976, though after 1980 the authorities claimed to be monitoring both narrower and broader aggregates as well as sterling M3.

but floated again on June 23, 1972, after a run on reserves. The float, which was introduced as a temporary measure, has continued ever since.

The expansionary policies were successful for a short time. Industrial production rose 7 percent in 1973 and unemployment fell from 3.7 percent in 1972 to 2.6 percent in 1973 and 1974 (chart 1). Investment, however, did not rise significantly and the boom was short-lived. The oil crisis combined with a sharp reversal in monetary policy to bring the expansion to an end. By 1975, industrial production was back to its 1970 level.

During this time, however, inflation accelerated, reaching 25 percent per year in 1975. Some blamed the inflation on the oil price rise; the major cause, however, was the money stock increases of 1972–73 (see chart 3). As a result of this extremely fast money growth, inflation in Britain went much higher than in other industrial countries. In the United States, for example, it was about 11 percent in 1974 and about 9 percent in 1975.

A Tightening of the "Corset"

The reversal of monetary policy in December 1973 took the form of a return to quantitative ceilings on deposits. This scheme, which became known as the "corset," restricted banks' ability to compete for interest-bearing time deposits.[7] A maximum percentage growth rate was specified for banks' interest-bearing eligible liabilities. If a bank exceeded this growth rate, it was required to place non-interest-bearing "Supplementary Deposits" with the Bank of England (much like the Fed's required reserves). The corset remained in force until June 1980 (apart from two breaks: February 28, 1975, to November 18, 1976, and August 11, 1977, to June 8, 1978).

The upsurge of inflation became a major political concern. A voluntary wage restraint policy was introduced in mid-1975, and a commitment was made that money supply growth would cease to be a source of inflationary pressure in the economy. A target range for the growth rate of sterling M3 was introduced in 1976 by the Labour Chancellor Dennis Healey.[8] The practice of announcing targets has continued to date. The targets have generally been achieved except in periods following relaxation of the corset.

While the inflationary monetary expansion of 1971–73 was moderated after the end of 1973, the fiscal deficit got bigger. From a financial surplus in 1970, public sector finances deteriorated to a position where in 1975 public sector borrowing exceeded 10 percent of GNP. This was partly due to the policies introduced by the Heath government, but also to the efforts of the subsequent Labour government, elected in February 1974, to hold down nationalized industry prices as well as those of some foods. This involved increased subsidies.[9] The argument, initially accepted in official

---

[7]For a retrospective assessment of the corset, see *Bank of England Quarterly Bulletin* (March 1982), pp. 74–85.

[8]It was first announced that money growth would henceforth be noninflationary. A forecast for sterling M3 was then released. Only later did the forecast form the basis of a target range.

[9]A further problem was created by the fact that up to 1975 government expenditures were planned in real terms. When prices rose, nominal expenditure was increased to compensate. Subsequently, cash limits were introduced for public spending.

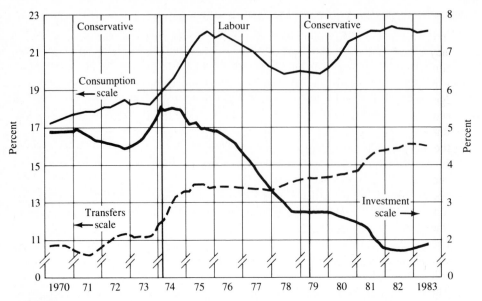

CHART 4
Government Transfers, Consumption, and Investment as a Percent of GDP. *Note:* Figures are four-quarter moving averages of the ratio of expenditures, N.S.A., to GDP, N.S.A.

circles, was that an increased budget deficit represented an appropriate offset to the impact of the oil price rise.

By 1976, the size of the budget deficit had become a major public issue. A crisis was triggered by a substantial fall in the value of the pound. An application was made to the International Monetary Fund (IMF) for a loan to increase foreign exchange reserves. Why this was necessary is not clear, since the pound was floating, but the government introduced a major package of public spending cuts in order to meet IMF conditions for the loan. While current government expenditures on goods and services were held back to a noticeable degree, the major impact of the cuts was in public sector investment programs (see chart 4).

Despite the tightening of fiscal policy after 1976, the economy exhibited moderately strong real growth through 1979. Growth rates of real GDP (gross domestic product, which is gross national product less net income from abroad) were in the 2 percent to 3 percent range. The expansion was aided somewhat by a temporary relaxation of monetary policy in the second half of 1977 and first half of 1978. Partly this expansion resulted from the removal of the corset; it also was induced, however, by substantial foreign exchange intervention *to stop the pound from appreciating*. U.K. foreign exchange reserves rose from $3.4 billion at the end of 1976 to $30.1 billion by the end of 1977. This intervention was clearly reflected in the rapid growth of M1 (see chart 3).[10]

---

[10]This experience with intervention did much to convince the authorities that holding down the value of the pound without generating a rapid rise in the money supply was impossible.

POLICY CHANGES OF THE THATCHER GOVERNMENT

Whereas the 1970–74 Conservative government of Edward Heath had embarked on a money growth and public spending-led boom, Mrs. Thatcher came to power in 1979 committed to a very different strategy. The Thatcher government had two major goals. One goal was to reduce the level of public spending, in order to both eliminate the budget deficit and facilitate lower levels of taxation. This would reverse the alleged crowding out of private sector activity by the public sector and would restore the incentives necessary for industrial growth. Second, inflation was to be squeezed out of the economy by a gradual reduction of the rate of growth of the money stock.[11]

In June 1979, Sir Geoffrey Howe, Mrs. Thatcher's Chancellor of the Exchequer for her first government (May 1979–June 1983), introduced a budget that lowered personal direct taxes and raised indirect taxes. The budget also included a rise in the tax on North Sea oil producers. Planned public expenditures were cut. The target range for the growth rate of sterling M3 was set at 7–11 percent, only 1 percent lower than that set by the previous Labour government. A the same time, however, the Bank of England's Minimum Lending Rate (MLR) was raised from 12 percent to 14 percent (and later raised to 17 percent in November).[12]

The June 1979 policy changes were intended to reduce inflation, which had begun to rise again in 1979. This macroeconomic policy strategy was formalized in the March 1980 budget into a so-called Medium Term Financial Strategy (MTFS), which involved planned reductions in public spending over a four- or five-year horizon to reduce the budget deficit as a proportion of GDP. Reductions in tax rates also were considered. Monetary growth targets were to be reduced gradually over the same period, though there was no change in the range for 1980–81.[13]

The MTFS was effectively abandoned almost immediately. The Public Sector Borrowing Requirement target for 1980/81, set in the March budget, was £8^1/$_2$ billion. By November 1980, the forecast was revised upward to £11^1/$_2$ billion. The expansion of public spending was due partly to high wage settlements in the public sector and partly to an unexpected rise in unemployment.[14] The abandonment of the corset in June 1980 led to growth rates of sterling M3 well in excess of the upper target level.[15]

---

[11]The intention of eliminating inflation solely by monetary policy rather than incomes policies was one reason why Mrs. Thatcher earned the monetarist label. The nature of monetarism is outlined in Batten and Stone (1983). For a discussion of how views about macroeconomic policy had changed over time both in Britain and the United States, see Alt and Chrystal (1983).

[12]Bank Rate was renamed Minimum Lending Rate in 1971. It was intended to be related to market rates, though from time to time it was still used as a policy instrument. See Hall.

[13]Budgets are normally submitted in March. They apply for the following financial year which runs April to April. The convention used here is that 1980/81 refers to the financial year April 1980 to April 1981.

[14]The previous Labour government had set up a Pay Comparability Commission to inquire into public sector pay. This commission recommended substantial pay raises for many groups. Mrs. Thatcher honored these recommendations before winding up the commission and substituting a public sector "pay norm."

[15]Buiter and Miller (1981) argued that monetary policy in Britain was too tight and resulted in an excessive appreciation of sterling. In Buiter and Miller (1983), however, they admit that the evidence is not consistent with a monetary overshooting hypothesis. Indeed, they express concern for the credibility of a monetary policy that frequently exceeded targets. Since 1979, sterling M3 growth has consistently exceeded the inflation rate. M1 growth looks more restrictive, though this also is distorted by the ending of the corset. The freeing of banks to compete for time deposits led to a switch from checking accounts to time deposits. This substitution is voluntary and would not normally be considered to represent policy tightening.

While Mrs. Thatcher intended to cut both taxes and public spending, the opposite generally has occurred. Tax revenue, for example, grew as a proportion of GDP until late 1982 (chart 5).[16] Similarly, both real government consumption (current spending on goods and services) and real transfer payments have risen as a proportion of GDP since 1979 (chart 4). The major exception on the expenditure side is government investment (chart 4), which was cut until mid-1982. The cuts achieved in this category by the Thatcher government, however, were much smaller than those introduced by the previous Labour government.

ARE POLICY CHANGES PRIMARILY RESPONSIBLE?

It is hard to look at what happened in Britain after 1979 and be comfortable with the story that policy changes made by the Thatcher government are entirely responsible. We already have seen that unemployment in 1983 reached a level well over double that associated with the 1973–75 recession. Yet monetary policy was probably no tighter in the Thatcher years than in the previous recession.

Fiscal policy, if anything, was tighter in the 1975–78 period than in the first three years of the Thatcher government. Table 1 presents the change in budget deficit as a proportion of GDP. The first column is based on unadjusted figures. The second column attempts to identify changes due to discretionary policy rather than cyclical factors. It also weights the tax and expenditure changes according to their impact on demand.

---

[16]Revenue from taxes on North Sea oil producers has contributed significantly to this. In 1978, the yield on Petroleum Revenue Tax was close to zero. In 1983, the taxes on North Sea oil yielded £6.1 billion which was 13.5 percent of total tax revenue.

CHART 5

Government Tax Revenues as a Percent of GDP. *Note:* Figures are four-quarter moving averages of the ratio of tax revenues, N.S.A., to GDP, N.S.A.

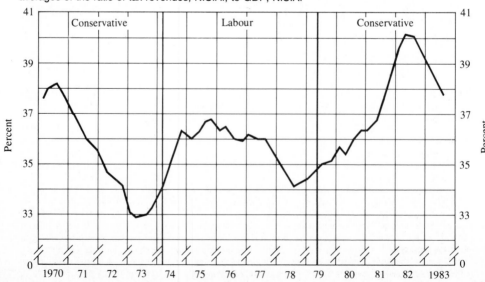

TABLE 1
CHANGE IN THE BRITISH BUDGET DEFICIT AS PERCENT OF GDP

	Unadjusted	Weighted cyclically adjusted
1974/75	2.57%	1.57%
1975/76	0.26	−1.16
1976/77	−1.79	−1.32
1977/78	−1.84	−2.20
1978/79	0.81	0.58
1979/80	−0.97	−0.56
1980/81	0.87	−0.51
1981/82	−2.60	−2.10
1982/83	0.80	0.30
1983/84	−0.10	−0.30

Note: Figures for 1983/84 are partly forecast.
Source: National Institute Economic Review (February 1982), p. 96 and (February 1984), p. 8.

An allowance for the fact that some taxes came from oil, which would have a different impact on demand from, say, personal income taxes, is therefore included in this measure; thus, it provides a better indicator of fiscal policy stance. Negative figures reflect a reduction of the deficit and, therefore, a tightening of policy.

What emerges from these figures is that fiscal policy was mildly restraining in 1979/ 80 and 1980/81. It was tighter in 1981/82, but has been more or less neutral since then. It is noticeable, however, that the fiscal policy of the Thatcher government has been *less restrictive* than that of the previous Labour government in the three financial years 1975/76 to 1977/78, when the cumulative fall in the deficit as a percent of GDP (weighted and cyclically adjusted) amounted to 4.7 percentage points. The fall under Mrs. Thatcher in the three years 1979/80 through 1981/82 totaled only 3.2 percentage points.

WAS THE WORLD RECESSION PRIMARILY RESPONSIBLE?

Britain's economy exports about 25 percent of its GDP. It is conceivable that a decline in world demand could reduce the demand for British exports enough to cause a contraction of manufacturing production. No doubt the worldwide recession of the early 1980s is partly to blame; however, it does not seem to be the main event: the decline in manufacturing in Britain preceded the world recession by several months.

Table 2 shows that world trade in manufactured goods grew strongly through 1980, slowed in 1981, then declined marginally in 1982. The decline in sales of British manufactured goods, however, dates from 1979 at the latest, and the adjustment of production was largely complete by the end of 1980.[17] In both 1979 and 1980, world trade in manufactured goods rose strongly.

---

[17]Manufacturers' stocks of unsold output rose sharply in 1979 indicating a slump in sales. See *National Institute Economic Review* (February 1984), p. 11, chart 5. Production was subsequently cut back and stocks run down through 1980.

TABLE 2
WORLD TRADE, PRODUCTION AND UNEMPLOYMENT

	Volume world trade in manufactured goods, 1975 = 100	Industrial production		Unemployment rate	
		OECD	U.K.	OECD	U.K.
1975	100	100	100	5.2%	4.7%
1976	112	109	103	5.3	6.0
1977	117	113	108	5.3	6.3
1978	123	117	112	5.2	6.3
1979	130	123	116	5.1	5.6
1980	137	123	108	5.8	7.0
1981	139	123	104	6.7	10.7
1982	136	118	106	8.2	12.4
1983	n.a.	122	109	8.7	12.9

Note: Industrial production figures for the United Kingdom include oil and gas.
Source: National Institute Economic Review (February 1984) pp. 93–94.

The figures for industrial production tell a similar story: Organization for Economic Coooperation and Development (OECD) industrial production rose strongly in 1979, leveled off in 1980 and 1981 and declined in 1982. British industrial production fell about two years before the fall in the OECD figure, and by a considerably larger amount.[18]

Before 1976, unemployment in Britain had typically been below the OECD average. From 1976 through 1979, Britain's unemployment rate was a little higher, but followed a similar pattern to the OECD average. Since 1979, Britain's unemployment has risen much further than the OECD average.

Thus, there is no strong case for believing that the world recession provides an adequate explanation of the contraction in Britain in 1980, even when combined with the Thatcher government's monetary and fiscal policies. Indeed, the world recession was most severe in 1982, a year in which Britain's manufacturing production actually recovered somewhat.

THE NORTH SEA OIL EXPLANATION

The emergence of Britain as a major oil producer provides an explanation of some of the changes that occurred in the British economy over the past five years.[19] Up to mid-1976, Britain was entirely dependent upon imported oil; in 1980, Britain became a net exporter of oil. Following such a structural change in the supply side of the

---

[18]Industrial production is a broader aggregate than manufacturing. It includes oil production among other things.

[19]Some commentators such as Buiter and Miller (1981, 1983), Niehans (1981) and Darby and Lothian (1983) have dismissed the effects of North Sea oil. However, Forsyth and Kay (1980) argued that oil production would lead to a sizable contraction in manufacturing. Bond and Knöbl (1982), Laney (1982) and McGuirk (1983) all provide evidence that oil has substantially worsened the competitiveness of U.K. manufacturing. See *Bank of England Quarterly Bulletin* (1982), pp. 56–73, for a description of North Sea oil resources.

economy, the trade balance in manufactured goods, according to theory, would move in the opposite direction of the oil balance.[20] The force that brings this about is an appreciation of the exchange rate, which raises the price of domestic manufactured goods relative to overseas competitors' prices. Consequently, domestic consumers buy a higher proportion of foreign-produced goods, and foreigners buy relatively fewer domestic-manufactured exports. Thus, the manufacturing sector contracts.[21]

Chart 6 shows the oil trade balance and the manufacturing trade balance. Chart 7 shows the dollar-pound exchange rate and the relative wholesale price of British manufactured goods compared with other industrial countries.[22] Until 1973, there was

[20]See, for example, Corden and Neary (1982).

[21]Strictly speaking, this contraction need only be relative to the rest of the economy. What has to be explained is the *switching* of spending from home-produced to foreign-produced manufactured goods. Our claim is that this was largely a relative price effect resulting from the oil-related decline of competitiveness of British manufacturing.

There are relative price effects among inputs as well as outputs. A rise in real wages has caused manufacturers to economize on labor for given output levels. Output per person employed in U.K. manufacturing rose 15 percent between the end of 1980 and mid-1983. Thus, the decline in employment in manufacturing has been greater than the output loss alone would have led to.

[22]Niehans, and Darby and Lothian argue that the appreciation of sterling was due to slow base money growth in the early years of the Thatcher government. This is implausible. Why, for example, was sterling appreciating for two years before Mrs. Thatcher came to power, and why did it depreciate in 1981 when base growth continued to slow? None of the monetary explanations of the exchange rate can explain a sustained rise in relative goods prices over a long period of time, such as that evident in chart 7. Such changes require structural explanation such as is offered by North Sea oil. Many commentators presumed that monetary policy was tight simply because sterling was appreciating. Laney offers evidence that monetary explanations of the U.K. exchange rate broke down after 1977. The price of oil is an important explanatory variable after that date. He also shows that other new oil producers have had comparable experiences. Thus, the event of significance in 1979 may not be the election of Mrs. Thatcher but rather the rise in the price of oil.

CHART 6
Oil and Manufacturing Trade Balance.

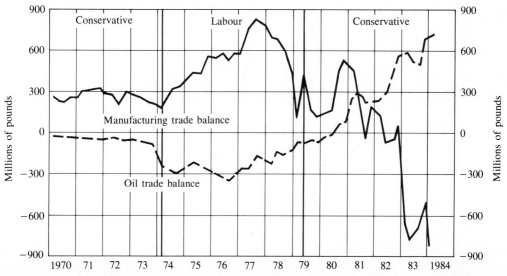

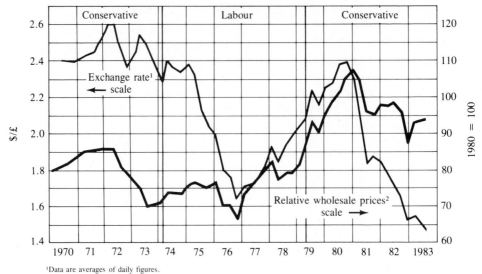

¹Data are averages of daily figures.
²Wholesale prices are for manufacturing relative to 13 other industrial countries.

CHART 7
Dollar/Pound Exchange Rate and Relative Wholesale Prices. (Source: International Financial Statistics, *International Monetary Fund.*)

a small surplus in manufactured trade and a small deficit in oil trade. As the oil deficit grew, so did the manufactured goods export surplus. From III/1976 on, the oil deficit shrank, and was eliminated in 1980. By I/1984, there was a substantial oil surplus.

The manufacturing surplus initially continued to increase as the pound appreciated after 1976.[23] As sterling appreciated further, however, relative demand for British and foreign goods shifted far enough to compensate for the relative rise in price of British goods. After mid-1977, the surplus in manufactured goods fell sharply, until by I/1984 there was a substantial deficit in manufactured goods trade, roughly equal to the oil surplus.

[23]As the currency appreciates, the sterling price of imports falls. In the short run, this improves the manufacturers' trade balance because the same volume of imports costs less. However, as spending patterns adjust to the new relative prices, the volume of exports starts to fall relative to the volume of imports. Once the volumes adjust more than the prices, the balance in manufactured goods starts to decline. This is just the reverse of the "J curve" effect of a devaluation. It arises because demand elasticities are smaller in the short run than in the long run. Because of this, the exchange rate may appreciate "too far" in the process of adjusting to the oil surplus. That is to say that the rise in the relative price of manufactured goods required in equilibrium is less than that actually experienced during transition. This is consistent with events in Britain where relative wholesale prices (chart 7) overshot their ultimate level. This is a different kind of overshooting from that associated with an unexpected tightening of monetary policy analyzed by Dornbusch (1976). The appreciation of the exchange rate is brought about not just by the impact of the changing oil balance on the current account but also by capital inflows which reinforce the process. The 1979 oil price rise boosted a process already under way. McGuirk estimates that a 23 percent fall in competitiveness was required *in equilibrium* to adjust the U.K. trade balance to the effects of oil at the 1980 oil prices. At the 1978 price of oil, this was only 12 percent. A fall in competitiveness is a rise in the relative price of British goods. This is sometimes referred to as a rise in the "real" exchange rate.

In short, we have an explanation of events in Britain that requires neither a major contraction in domestic aggregate expenditure nor a major slump in total world demand to explain the collapse of manufacturing industry in Britain. The dominant factor was a major switch in spending patterns resulting from the rise in relative price of British manufactured goods. The proportion of domestic demand for these goods satisfied by imports rose sharply, while exports of manufactured goods stagnated. The volume of manufactured exports was about the same in 1983 as it was in 1976. Over the same period, the volume of manufactured goods imported *rose 63 percent.*

CONCLUSION

The government of Margaret Thatcher has been blamed by its critics for causing a major contraction of activity in Britain by applying monetarist policies. Without quibbling over whether those policies were indeed monetarist, this article argues that the case for blaming the rise in unemployment and the contraction of manufacturing on deflationary aggregate demand policies is not a strong one, even if one allows for the impact of the world recession. Rather, the production and sale of North Sea oil have had a big negative impact on the British manufacturing sector. The production of oil and the subsequent rise in its price caused an appreciation of sterling and a rise in the relative price of British manufactured goods. As a result, British manufactured goods became uncompetitive and production contracted sharply. Thus, it is impossible to write a balanced history of the British economy over the last few years without reference to North Sea oil production.

REFERENCES

Alt, J. E., and K. Alec Chrystal. *Political Economics* (University of California Press and Wheatsheaf, 1983).

Bank of England Quarterly Bulletin, vol. 22, no. 1 (March 1982).

Batten, Dallas S., and Courtney C. Stone. "Are Monetarists an Endangered Species?" this *Review* (May 1983), pp. 5–16.

Bond, Marian E., and Adalbert Knöbl. "Some Implications of North Sea Oil for the U.K. Economy," *International Monetary Fund Staff Papers,* vol. 29, no. 3 (September 1982), pp. 363–97.

Buiter, Willem, and Marcus Miller. "The Thatcher Experiment: The First Two Years," *Brookings Papers* (2:1981), pp. 315–79.

————. "Changing the Rules: Economic Consequences of the Thatcher Regime," *Brookings Papers* (2:1983), pp. 305–65.

Corden, W. Max, and J. Peter Neary. "Booming Sector and Deindustrialization in a Small Open Economy," *Economic Journal* (December 1982), pp. 825–48.

Darby, Michael R., and James R. Lothian. "British Economic Policy Under Margaret Thatcher: A Midterm Examination," *Carnegie-Rochester Conference Series on Public Policy* (North-Holland, 1983), pp. 157–207.

Dornbusch, Rudiger. "Expectations and Exchange Rate Dynamics," *Journal of Political Economy,* vol. 84, no. 6 (December 1976), pp. 1161–76.

Forsyth, P. J., and J. A. Kay. "The Economic Implication of North Sea Oil Revenues," *Fiscal Studies,* vol. 1 (July 1980), pp. 1–28.

Gould, Bryan, John Mills, and Shaun Steward. *Monetarism or Prosperity* (Macmillan Press Ltd., 1981).

Hall, Maxmillian. *Monetary Policy Since 1971: Conduct and Performance* (Macmillan Press Ltd., 1983).

Henry, S. G. B., and P. A. Ormerod. "Incomes Policy and Wage Inflation: Empirical Evidence for the U.K. 1961–1977," *National Institute Economic Review*, no. 85 (August 1978), pp. 31–39.

Kaldor, Nicholas. *The Scourge of Monetarism* (Oxford University Press, 1982).

Laney, Leroy O. "How Contagious Is 'Dutch Disease'?" Federal Reserve Bank of Dallas *Economic Review* (March 1982), pp. 3–12.

McGuirk, Anne K. "Oil Price Changes and Real Exchange Rate Movements Among Industrial Countries," *International Monetary Fund Staff Papers*, vol. 30, no. 4 (December 1983), pp. 843–84.

National Institute Economic Review, no. 107 (February 1984).

Niehans, Jürg. "The Appreciation of Sterling—Causes, Effects and Policies," Money Study Group Discussion Paper (Social Science Research Council, 1981).

QUESTIONS FOR DISCUSSION

1 To what does Chrystal attribute the sharp decline in British manufacturing output under Thatcher? Using the *IS-LM* diagram, augmented with a balance of payments line, show how this effect is supposed to work. Can this effect explain an overall recession, as well as a recession specific to manufacturing?

2 What factors contributed to the sharp increase in British inflation that started in 1975?

3 What was the "corset"? What problems did its elimination in July 1980 cause for the conduct of monetary policy?

4 Do you agree with the statement that "monetary policy was probably no tighter in the Thatcher years than in the previous recession"? Compare to the discussion of monetary policy in the previous reading. What problem arises in attempting to distinguish the effects of tight money from the Dutch disease effect?

THE UNITED STATES AND ECONOMIC DEVELOPMENT

U.S. Council of Economic Advisers

For many reasons—economic, political, and humanitarian—the United States has a strong interest in the economic progress of the so-called developing countries (DCs). This excerpt from the 1986 *Economic Report of the President* discusses the growth record of the DCs; analyzes the recent problems of the developing world, especially the burden of external debt; and makes a series of recommendations for promoting economic development.

After World War II, the United States in cooperation with other countries established the basic policies and institutions of the open system of world trade and investment that has since guided economic relations among nations. On the whole, the world has enjoyed an extraordinary record of economic progress under this system. Between 1950 and 1984, U.S. real per capita gross national product (GNP) rose at a 1.8 percent average annual rate, allowing nearly a doubling of average real living standards in 34 years. In the other nine largest Western industrial countries, real per capita income rose at a spectacular 3.7 percent average annual rate, implying that real living standards in these countries (as measured by real per capita GNP) rose by more than twice as much as they had in all of previous history. Despite disappointing economic performance of some developing countries, the average annual rate of growth of real per capita income for all developing countries was 2.8 percent between 1955 and 1984, implying more than a doubling of average real living standards in these countries in just 29 years.

U.S. Council of Economic Advisers, *Economic Report of the President: 1984,* chap. 2 (excerpt), "The United States and Economic Development," pp. 71–96.

The progress of developing countries over the past three decades is manifested in other important indicators of human welfare. Between 1955 and 1984, their population nearly doubled. Despite the problems of some developing countries, this increase in population was not accompanied by increasing human misery, as some feared, but rather by generally rising real living standards that were reflected in longer life expectancies, lower infant and child mortality rates, better nutrition and health care, and higher educational attainment. For example, between 1965 and 1983, average life expectancy rose by 9 years in lower income developing countries and by 8 years in middle-income developing countries.

This overall record of economic and social progress provides the context for this chapter's discussion of important economic problems that have recently afflicted a number of developing countries and of the policies that are needed to deal with these problems. The record of long-term economic success of many countries suggests that these problems can be successfully resolved. It also suggests that retention and refinement of the policies and institutions that helped to generate this success, together with reform of practices that have contributed to recent difficulties, is the appropriate prescription for restoring prosperity and reviving growth in countries that have suffered economic slowdown or stagnation.

To develop this main theme, it is appropriate first to discuss the substantial and growing importance of developing countries in the world economy. This is followed by a description of the general economic performance and recent economic problems of developing countries, including the problems associated with the international debt crisis. The reading next examines economic policies that experience suggests are conducive to rapid and sustainable economic growth. The reading concludes with a discussion of contributions that the developed countries can make to the economic performance of the developing countries and of improvements of the international economic system that can benefit all nations.

Before embarking on this discussion, it is important to stress the interest of the United States in seeking more vigorous economic growth in both developed and developing countries. Beyond wishing its friends well, the United States has a strong national interest in the economic prosperity of its allies, and has an important national interest in economic prosperity of developing countries, including especially countries striving to strengthen their democratic institutions. The United States also has an economic interest in the prosperity of other countries. Economic growth appears to be a mutually reinforcing process. For example, the rapid recovery in the United States during the first six quarters of the current expansion contributed significantly to recovery and expansion in other countries and particularly to easing of some of the economic problems of developing countries. Conversely, relatively sluggish recovery of other industrial countries and recent economic problems in many developing countries are seen as factors contributing to the deterioration of the U.S. trade balance during the current recovery and thus perhaps also to the slowdown of that recovery since mid-1984. Thus, for economic as well as broader national purposes, the United States has an important interest in rapid and sustainable growth in other countries.

ECONOMIC PERFORMANCE AND PROBLEMS
OF DEVELOPING COUNTRIES

Developing countries are the home of three-quarters of the world's population. Their aggregate national products in 1983 were more than half of that of the United States and nearly double that of Japan. Merchandise trade (exports plus imports) of the developing countries (including high-income oil exporters) in 1983 accounted for more than a quarter of total world merchandise trade and was more than twice the size of that of the United States, the world's largest trading country. The substantial and growing economic importance of developing countries is reflected specifically in the extent of trade between these countries and the United States and, especially during the past decade, in the flow of credit from the United States and other industrial countries to the developing countries.

Trade between Developing Countries
and the United States

The importance of trade with developing countries has been growing along with the general importance of international trade for the U.S. economy in the postwar period, especially during the past 20 years. In 1965 exports to and imports from developing countries were, respectively, 1.2 and 1.0 percent of U.S. GNP. They rose to 3.0 and 4.4 percent of U.S. GNP, respectively, in 1980. By 1984 the share of exports to developing countries in GNP fell to 2.0 percent, and the share of imports from such countries fell to 3.3 percent. The relatively small shares of exports and imports in U.S. GNP are somewhat deceiving because industries that account for about 70 percent of U.S. GNP produce either services that do not enter into international merchandise trade, or produce products that are largely nontradeable. For the industries that account for the remaining 30 percent of U.S. GNP, international merchandise trade is of considerable importance. On average for these industries in 1984, exports to developing countries accounted for about 7 percent of annual product, and imports from developing countries accounted for about 11 percent of annual product.

Increased imports of some categories of manufactured goods from developing countries have been a particular cause of concern for and complaint by U.S. competitors. Without attempting to judge the merits of individual complaints, it should be noted that the United States has until recently had a trade surplus in manufactured goods with developing countries and still exports large amounts of such goods to these countries. In 1980 the United States exported $60 billion of manufactured goods to and imported $32 billion of such goods from developing countries, for a net export surplus of $28 billion. Although the magnitude of this surplus may have reflected temporary factors such as the weak dollar and the large borrowing of developing countries in 1980, the existence of such a surplus is consistent with past trends. By 1984 exports of manufactures to developing countries fell to $52 billion, while imports of manufactures from these countries rose to $64 billion, yielding a net export deficit of $12 billion. The deterioration in the net trade position in manufactured products with developing countries, however, is proportionately smaller than the deterioration of the overall U.S. net trade position between 1980 and 1984.

The explanation of the behavior of the overall U.S. trade balance or current account balance, of course, cannot be found in analyses of changes in the bilateral trade imbalances between the United States and individual countries or groups of countries. The overall trade balance or current account balance is a macroeconomic phenomenon whose behavior is primarily to be explained by the behavior of other macroeconomic variables, in particular economic growth of the United States in comparison with other countries, levels of saving and investment in the United States and in other countries, expenditure and tax policies of the U.S. Government and the governments of other countries, anticipated real rates of return on investments in different countries, and the real foreign exchange value of the U.S. dollar.

Credit Flows to Developing Countries

The growing importance of financial relationships between developed and developing countries is apparent in the rapid growth of the real flow of financial resources to developing countries, as reported in Table 1. The net flow of funds to developing countries (in 1983 dollars), as estimated by the Organization for Economic Cooperation and Development (OECD), nearly doubled in real terms between 1970 and 1980, from $53.1 billion to $93.9 billion. After peaking in 1983 at $118.3 billion, this flow declined to $92.3 billion in 1984. The sources of these funds have shifted substantially over the past 15 years. In 1970 official development assistance accounted for 42 percent of the net flow of funds to developing countries, while lending by commercial banks accounted for only 15 percent of the total. By 1983 the share of official development assistance declined to 29 percent, while the share of bank lending (including rescheduling) rose to 46 percent. This trend was reversed in 1984, when the share of official development assistance rose to 39 percent of net lending and the share of commercial

TABLE 1
REAL NET FLOW OF FUNDS TO DEVELOPING COUNTRIES, SELECTED YEARS, 1970–84
(Billions of 1983 Dollars)

Type of receipt	1970	1975	1980	1981	1982	1983	1984
Official development assistance	22.2	31.6	36.1	36.2	33.7	33.8	35.8
Grants by private voluntary agencies	2.3	2.0	2.2	2.0	2.3	2.3	2.5
Nonconcessional flows	28.7	51.0	55.7	68.6	60.1	82.1	54.0
Official or officially supported flows	10.4	15.7	22.9	21.6	21.9	19.8	20.0
Private flows	18.3	35.4	32.8	47.0	38.2	62.3	34.0
Direct investment	9.7	16.9	9.9	16.8	11.8	7.8	9.5
Bank lending[1]	7.9	17.8	21.6	29.2	25.9	54.0	24.0
Bond lending	.8	.6	1.3	1.1	.5	.5	.5
Total	53.1	84.6	93.9	106.8	96.1	118.3	92.3

[1]Includes for 1983 and 1984 significant amounts of rescheduled short-term debt.
Note: Detail may not add to totals due to rounding.
Source: Organization for Economic Cooperation and Development.

TABLE 2
INDICATORS OF ECONOMIC GROWTH, 1955–84
(Annual Growth Rate; Percent)

Period	Population	Real GNP	Real GNP per capita
Developing countries[1]			
1955–70	2.2	5.4	3.1
1970–80	2.2	5.3	3.1
1980–84	2.0	3.1	1.1
Low-income countries:			
1955–70	2.1	3.7	1.6
1970–80	2.1	4.5	2.4
1980–84	1.8	6.7	4.9
Middle-income countries:			
1955–70	2.4	6.0	3.5
1970–80	2.4	5.6	3.1
1980–84	2.4	1.8	−.6
Industrial market countries			
1955–70	1.1	4.7	3.6
1970–80	.8	3.2	2.4
1980–84	.5	1.8	1.3

[1]Excludes the high-income oil exporters.
Source: International Bank for Reconstruction and Development.

banks fell to 26 percent. More recent information indicates a further substantial decline in commercial bank net lending to developing countries in 1985.

By 1983 total external liabilities of developing countries reached an estimated $843 billion, equal to about one-third of the annual GNP of these countries and about 10 percent of the annual GNP of the developed countries. More than half of these liabilities were loans from commercial banks, and nearly a third of these bank loans were owed to U.S. financial institutions. The problems recently experienced by several of the high-debt countries in meeting their debt-service obligations, and the consequences of these problems for the financial institutions that hold their obligations, have dramatized the deepening financial relationships between developing countries and the United States and other developed countries.

Economic Problems of Developing Countries

Economic growth in developing countries has been rapid over the past 30 years, on average, as indicated in Table 2. Some countries, however, have not shared in this progress over the long run, and, in the past few years, a number of countries with relatively good long-run performance have experienced economic difficulties. The chronic economic problems of many quite poor countries in Sub-Saharan Africa, South Asia, and Latin America deserve treatment separate from the acute difficulties recently experienced by middle-income countries with large debt burdens.

The low-income developing countries (those with per capita incomes of less than $400 in 1983) had an average growth rate of real per capita GNP of 2.3 percent between 1955 and 1984. This result is dominated by the performance of China and India, which together account for three-quarters of the population of low-income developing countries and which had a combined average annual growth rate of real per capita GNP of 2.4 percent over this period. Interestingly, the combined growth performance of these two large countries has been improving recently as they have adopted more market-oriented, pro-growth economic policies. Some other low-income developing countries have also enjoyed vigorous growth, including some spectacularly successful countries that earlier adopted market-oriented, pro-growth economic policies and have now graduated to the class of middle-income developing countries. In many other low-income countries growth performance has not been very strong. Between 1965 and 1984, real per capita income in the low-income countries of Sub-Saharan Africa rose at only a 0.5 percent average annual rate.

The road to economic prosperity for many of the poorest countries will be a long and difficult one. In some extreme situations, such as the recent and continuing famine in Ethiopia, extraordinary external assistance has been essential to provide the bare requirements of human survival. The success of some formerly quite poor countries, however, gives hope that some of today's poorer countries will be able to graduate to the ranks of the middle-income developing countries by early in the next century.

The middle-income developing countries (those with per capita incomes between $400 and $7,000 in 1983) had good growth performance on average between 1955 and 1984. As a group, they recorded an average annual growth rate of real per capita income of 2.8 percent per year, enabling the real income of the average resident of these countries to rise by 123 percent in just 29 years. Some countries, of course, performed less well than the average, and a few even registered substantial declines in real per capita incomes over periods of two decades or longer. On the other hand, nine countries had growth rates of real per capita income of 5 percent per year or better between 1965 and 1983, implying an increase in real per capita income of more than 140 percent in just 18 years.

The early 1980s have been a period of sharp contrasts in the economic performances of developing countries. For all developing countries, excluding the high-income oil exporters, the average growth rate of real per capita income was only 1.1 percent per year between 1980 and 1984. Thanks primarily to the good performance and large weight of China and India, low-income developing countries registered a 4.9 percent average annual growth rate of real per capita income over these 4 years. Other low-income countries in Asia did about as well as China and India, on average, but low-income countries in Africa suffered a cumulative 8.7 percent decline in average real per capita income over these 4 years. For the middle-income developing countries, average real per capita incomes declined at a 0.6 percent annual rate between 1980 and 1984. Despite the recession in the industrial countries, some of these countries, especially in Asia, continued to enjoy strong real growth. Other middle-income developing countries, especially in Latin America, had enjoyed generally good growth during the 1960s and 1970s, but experienced economic stagnation or decline in the early 1980s.

Effects of External Shocks

For developing countries that experienced poor economic performance in the early 1980s, adverse external economic developments explain part, but only part, of this poor performance. Some countries whose national incomes depend heavily on revenues from oil exports saw their real national incomes decline because of the fall in world oil prices and in the volume of oil exports. However, some oil-exporting countries that saved some of their oil-export revenues in the 1970s have been able to draw on those savings to support domestic consumption and investment during a period of lower oil prices and export volumes. Other oil exporters that spent all of their export revenues and even borrowed from world capital markets to spend on consumption and domestic investment have faced a more difficult task in adjusting to lower oil exports and oil prices. The same is true for developing countries that experienced export booms for other commodities during the 1970s and failed to foresee that these booms might not last forever.

Moreover, evidence suggests that adverse external events are not primarily responsible for the recent poor economic performance of some developing countries. As previously mentioned, other developing countries that faced similar external circumstances continued to perform well in the early 1980s. Table 3 summarizes results from a World Bank study that compared the magnitude of external shocks to developing countries that needed to reschedule their external debts by the end of 1984 with countries that did not need to reschedule. The index of external shocks was calculated as the combined effects on a country's balance of payments of deteriorations in its terms of trade (the ratio of export prices to import prices), declines in world demand for its exports, and increases in interest rates on its outstanding external debt. In 1979–80 and 1981–82, the average adverse external shock was about the same for reschedulers and nonreschedulers. The average of annual growth rates of real gross domestic product (GDP) in 1979–83 for reschedulers, however, was only 0.9 percent, versus 4.3 percent for nonreschedulers.

TABLE 3

EXTERNAL SHOCKS AND REAL GDP GROWTH IN SELECTED DEVELOPING COUNTRIES, 1979–83

Country category	Net external shocks as percent of GNP[1]		Growth of real GDP (percent)[2]
	1979–80	1981–82	1979–83
Reschedulers[3]	−2.6	−9.3	0.9
Nonreschedulers	−2.6	−8.4	4.3

[1]External shocks are defined as the impact on the balance of payments as a percentage of GNP of: (a) changes in the terms of trade; (b) a decline in the growth rate of world demand for a country's exports; and (c) increases in interest rates, averaged across countries.

[2]Averaged across countries and years.

[3]Countries that had rescheduled debt as of the end of 1984.

Sources: International Bank for Reconstruction and Development, *World Development Report, 1985,* and International Monetary Fund, *International Financial Statistic Yearbook, 1985.*

External shocks did, of course, affect developing countries in the early 1980s. The disinflation of the early 1980s was associated with an unwinding of the effects of the inflation of the 1970s on relative commodity prices, including prices of some products exported by developing countries. The recession in the industrial countries in the early 1980s reduced demand for the exports of developing countries. The real burden of the external, dollar-denominated debt of many developing countries rose as the dollar appreciated in foreign exchange markets. Increased nominal and real interest rates, especially in 1981, increased the debt-service requirements of heavily indebted countries with large amounts of floating-rate loans. Countering these adverse developments have been the recovery in the industrial countries, especially the United States, and the decline in interest rates since 1982, plus the recent moderate decline of the dollar.

The effects of movements in interest rates and in the foreign exchange value of the dollar on debt-service burdens were important for developing countries that chose, as a consequence of the policies they pursued, to borrow large sums from international capital markets. The problems of these countries are best understood in the context of a general discussion of the role of international credit flows and the current international debt situation.

The Role of International Credit

The international flow of capital performs at least two important economic functions. It allows countries with more attractive investment opportunities than can be financed out of domestic saving to obtain resources from countries with excess savings. It also allows countries suffering temporary economic difficulties to borrow from world capital markets rather than institute sharp temporary reductions in consumption or costly cutbacks in investment.

International capital flows have performed these functions for many countries over a long span of time. In the 50 years prior to World War I, the United States, Canada, Australia, Argentina, and the Scandinavian countries financed domestic investments with substantial loans from Great Britain and other European countries. The evidence indicates that despite occasional defaults and other difficulties, the providers of this credit earned higher returns than those typically available on investments in their own countries. In most of the period since World War II, the United States has been a net supplier of capital to the rest of the world, especially through the mechanism of direct investment by U.S. firms in foreign countries. The generally higher real growth rates of other industrial countries up to 1975 and of developing countries up to 1980 suggest that this flow of capital out of the United States was generally in the direction of higher returns. During the current expansion, the United States has become a net borrower in world credit markets. This is consistent with the high rate of return on and rapid growth of investment in the United States, in comparison with other countries, and with the need to finance the Federal deficit. The suppliers of credit to the United States are primarily other industrial countries where desired saving rates exceed desired rates of domestic investment.

With the exception of some oil-exporting countries, developing countries have generally been recipients of net capital inflows in the postwar period. Evidence indicates that from the mid-1960s to the late 1970s, there was a generally positive relationship between the growth of external indebtedness of particular developing countries and the growth of investment in these countries. Evidence suggests a similarly positive relationship between the growth of external indebtedness and the growth rate of real gross domestic product. This is consistent with the notion that international capital flows were, on the whole, performing the desirable function of financing investment in countries with good growth opportunities. From 1979 to 1983, however, there is no significant relationship between growth of external indebtedness and growth of investment for developing countries, and there is a negative relationship between growth of external debt and growth of real domestic product.

In the 1960s and 1970s, a few developing countries experienced difficulties in meeting their debt-service obligations and had to reschedule their external debts. At least up to 1979, however, these problems affected no more than two or three countries in any year, and the total amount of debt rescheduled in any year did not exceed $2 billion. In 1979, 7 countries rescheduled $6.2 billion of external debts; in 1980, 6 countries rescheduled $3.7 billion; and in 1981, 13 countries rescheduled $5.8 billion. In 1982 reschedulings fell when 9 countries rescheduled $2.4 billion; but in 1983, 21 countries rescheduled $51 billion; and in 1984, 24 countries (many of them the same as in the preceding year) rescheduled $116 billion. Because rescheduling agreements are typically reached some time after a country begins to experience debt-servicing difficulties, it is reasonable to conclude that by 1982 many of the developing countries with large external debts were already in trouble.

The International Debt Situation

A stylized description of events leading up to the recent international debt crisis is the following. Starting in 1973, growth of balance of payments surpluses of some high-income oil-exporting countries stimulated expansion of the international banking system that recycled these surpluses. Increased availability of credit on attractive terms through the international banking system increased opportunities for many developing countries to become borrowers from that system in the mid-1970s. Initially, debt-service requirements did not rise relative to the export earnings of many of these countries because they enjoyed rapid economic growth and because the inflationary expansion of the 1970s contributed to a boom in demand for their exports. Moreover, nominal interest rates on dollar-denominated loans declined from 1974 to 1976 and rose modestly between 1976 and 1978. Real interest rates became increasingly negative during the late 1970s as inflation accelerated. In addition, depreciation of the dollar relative to the currencies of other industrial countries after 1976 reduced the value of the dollar-denominated debt of many countries, thereby making further borrowing seem even more attractive.

In 1981–83 difficulties arose for many developing countries that had borrowed extensively from the international banking system in the late 1970s and 1980. The recession in the industrial countries, the high level of nominal and real interest rates (especially from late 1980 through mid-1982), the strengthening of the U.S. dollar, and the declines in the dollar prices of many commodities exported by heavily indebted developing countries (associated with the undoing of the inflationary excesses of the 1970s) contributed to an increase in the debt-service requirements of these countries relative to their export earnings, especially for countries with large volumes of dollar-denominated, floating-rate loans. To meet rising debt-service requirements, many debtor nations increased external borrowing. These high levels of borrowing, together with deteriorating export earnings and slackening economic growth, caused concern among lenders about the longer run capacity of these countries to meet their external debt-service obligations.

Table 4 presents data for two groups of debtor countries that are useful in understanding the debt crisis. Group A consists of indebted developing countries that incurred external payments arrears between 1981 and 1983 or rescheduled their external debts between 1981 and mid-1984. The 57 countries in group A accounted for 42.8 percent of GDP and 59.5 percent of the external debt of all developing countries in 1980. Group B consists of those indebted developing countries that did not experience recent debt-servicing difficulties. The 66 countries in group B accounted for 43.2 percent of GDP and 40.5 percent of the external debt of all developing countries in 1980. These two groups had the same average annual growth rate of real GDP, 5.5 percent per year, from 1967 to 1976. Both groups enjoyed substantial growth between 1976 and 1980, although even by this stage, countries in group B (with generally lower external debt burdens) were growing somewhat more rapidly. The growth rate of real GDP for group A fell to 1.1 percent in 1981, to -0.1 percent in 1982, and to -1.9 percent in 1983, and was estimated to be only 2.0 percent in 1984. In contrast, group B continued to enjoy impressive growth rates of real GDP, with annual growth rates of 5.1 percent in 1981, 4.0 percent in 1982, 5.4 percent in 1983, and an estimated 5.7 percent in 1984.

Another important difference between these two groups is the behavior of their respective current account balances. On average, from 1967 to 1976, group A had a slightly larger current account deficit as a percentage of exports of goods and services than group B. By 1977 the current account deficit as a percentage of exports had risen to 25.5 percent for group A, while it was only 6.1 percent of exports for group B. In the late 1970s and early 1980s the current account deficit of group B remained modest, peaking at 14 percent of exports in 1981. For group A the current account deficit remained much larger, peaking in absolute size in 1981, and relative to exports at 33.3 percent in 1982. An important factor contributing to the larger current account deficit of group A was the interest they had to pay on their larger external debt.

A current account deficit implies an excess of national spending over national income that must somehow be financed. The primary means of finance for developing countries is usually external net borrowing. This is shown in Table 4 in the close relationship between net external borrowing as a percentage of exports for both groups of countries. Not surprisingly, debt-servicing difficulties are associated with countries that run large and persistent current account deficits that need to be financed by large and persistent net external borrowing.

Loss of confidence in a country's creditworthiness might be expected to affect internal as well as external creditors, leading to a flight of domestic capital. This is

TABLE 4
DEBT INDICATORS FOR DEVELOPING COUNTRIES, 1967–84

Indicator by country group[1]	1967–76 average	1977	1978	1979	1980	1981	1982	1983	1984[2]
Percent									
Growth of real GDP									
Group A	5.5	5.4	3.7	5.3	3.9	1.1	−0.1	−1.9	2.0
Group B	5.5	6.3	8.2	4.7	4.9	5.1	4.0	5.4	5.7
Billions of U.S. dollars									
Exports of goods and services									
Group A		107.8	117.3	154.5	201.3	207.4	185.4	178.2	192.1
Group B		154.5	183.5	240.1	310.5	328.2	319.1	322.5	354.9
Percent of exports of goods and services									
Current account balance									
Group A	−18.5	−25.5	−31.9	−25.3	−23.7	−32.2	−33.3	−14.4	−7.6
Group B	−13.3	−6.1	−10.6	−9.4	−9.4	−14.0	−12.9	−10.5	−6.5
Net external borrowing									
Group A		29.5	36.1	28.8	32.3	37.5	32.2	18.3	11.0
Group B		8.9	10.9	10.5	10.6	12.9	11.9	10.2	7.2
Net asset transactions plus errors and omissions									
Group A		−7.4	−5.9	−3.4	−10.0	−14.5	−16.7	−6.2	
Group B		−3.1	−1.6	−2.5	−2.2	−2.1	−2.2	−2.7	−2.2
External debt									
Group A		171.7	195.8	178.1	167.1	194.5	246.0	268.1	256.8
Group B		95.3	91.9	81.6	73.6	78.3	91.1	97.0	94.2
Debt-service payments									
Group A		22.3	29.6	30.2	26.9	33.8	41.6	36.2	36.6
Group B		10.0	11.8	11.7	11.0	12.7	14.6	14.4	14.9

[1]Group A: countries with recent debt-servicing problems. Group B: countries without debt-servicing problems.
[2]Estimates.
Source: International Monetary Fund, *World Economic Outlook, 1985.*

reflected in Table 4 in the behavior of net asset transactions plus errors and omissions in the balance of payments. As a percentage of exports, these items remain quite small for group B, which did not experience debt-servicing problems. For group A, however, these items grow quite large in 1980–82.

Adverse external developments can contribute to a loss of confidence in creditworthiness. A decline in export earnings due to a decline in world market demand for a country's exports may cause creditors to worry about the security for their loans. For a country with a large amount of floating-rate debt, an increase in interest rates increases debt-service requirements. This tends to worsen the current account balance, thereby contributing to creditor worries. Such events did adversely affect many heavily indebted developing countries in the early 1980s. However, the extent of these effects depended on the size of a country's external debt. In Table 4, group A has a higher ratio of debt service to exports in both 1977 and 1982 and a larger increase in this ratio between 1977 and 1982 than group B. This is not because group A faced higher interest rates or a larger increase in interest rates. It is because they had a higher ratio of external debt to exports in 1977 and a larger increase in this debt ratio between 1977 and 1982. Especially in developing countries where most external debt is government debt, the effects of changing interest rates on debt-service problems are a mixture of the effects of external events and of past government policies.

When a country experiences debt-servicing difficulties, its creditors tend to want to reduce their exposure by collecting all interest and principal payments as they come due, while extending no new credit. This may be neither desirable nor feasible. For the countries that experienced debt-servicing difficulties to pay all of the interest and principal on their external debts in 1982, without any new gross external borrowing, they would have had to move from net external borrowing equal to 37.5 percent of exports in 1981 to net external lending equal to principal payments on outstanding external loans (probably about 20 percent of exports). This would have required these countries to improve their trade balances in 1982 by more than $100 billion, relative to actual performance. Engineering such a massive change in the trade position of these countries was probably not feasible in so short a time, and it certainly would have been very costly. Moreover, it is questionable whether the major creditor countries, including the United States, would have wished to see a deterioration of more than $100 billion in their own trade balances, which would have been the necessary counterpart of an improvement of similar magnitude in the trade balances of debtor countries. To deal with this problem, debtor countries and their creditors normally attempt to negotiate rescheduling arrangements under which the creditors agree to extend the time period for repayment of the principal and sometimes part of the interest on existing loans.

The Role of the International Monetary Fund

In most cases, debt rescheduling involves formal standby lending arrangements with the International Monetary Fund (IMF). The IMF establishes such arrangements as part of its general function to provide financial support to countries experiencing balance of payments difficulties, provided that they adopt policies holding promise of correcting these difficulties. Typically, under these agreements, the IMF provides only part of the new credit extended to a debtor country, but the agreement is frequently an effective precondition for a rescheduling arrangement with other creditors. As a condition for IMF support, countries agree to pursue policies directed at improving their capacity to meet their external obligations. Usually, the agreed policies seek reductions or limitations of government spending, government borrowing, and credit and money creation. The policies are intended to reduce domestic spending relative to domestic income and thereby improve the current account balance. In many cases, a devaluation of the exchange rate is also adopted as a means of improving the current account balance by increasing the price of internationally traded goods relative to home goods. Such a relative price change tends to reduce imports, increase exports, and shift resources toward the tradeable goods sector of the economy.

The IMF has been criticized, in some quarters, especially in developing countries, on the grounds that it recommends policies that focus too strongly on achieving short-term improvements in the balance of payments, rather than promoting longer term growth, and that contribute downward pressure on economic activity in countries already subject to strong recessionary forces. It is certainly true that several countries that adopted economic policies recommended by the IMF suffered severe recessions in the early 1980s. It is far less clear that these policies were primarily responsible for the severity of these recessions or that, under the circumstances, there was any real alternative to adopting some of these policies. These circumstances included the cumulative effects of past government policies and of adverse external events that contributed to the loss of confidence in the creditworthiness of a number of heavily indebted developing countries. A country that cannot borrow because of lost confidence in its creditworthiness must adopt policies that keep the excess of spending over income within the range of permitted borrowing. Because its own resources are limited, the IMF's capacity to expand the supply of credit (including borrowing to make debt-service payments) depends partly on its capacity to persuade other creditors that policies undertaken by debtor countries offer reasonable hope of restoring creditworthiness. Moreover, some of the countries that have established standby agreements with the IMF have improved their current account balances. This task might well have proved more difficult and more painful without the assistance of the IMF.

The critical issue for the future is how to resolve the economic problems of debtor countries in the manner most advantageous to them, to their creditors, and to the world as a whole. The mutually advantageous resolution is clearly one that restores these countries to paths of rapid, sustainable, noninflationary economic growth, thereby assuring creditors of repayment and benefiting the world economy through a general expansion of trade and economic activity. This most desirable outcome requires that developing countries pursue policies that support their own economic growth and structural adjustment, that the United States and other industrial countries maintain high and stable rates of economic growth, and that the nations of the world cooperate in sustaining an open system of international trade and investment that enables each of them to realize its full economic potential.

POLICIES FOR ECONOMIC GROWTH AND DEVELOPMENT

Achievement of a rapid rate of economic growth has been a key objective of economic policy in many older and newly emergent developing countries for the past three decades. Different countries at different times have pursued a wide array of different policies in their efforts to stimulate and sustain rapid rates of growth, and have enjoyed varying degrees of success in these efforts. From this wealth of experience, it is possible to learn a good deal about economic policies likely to support successful development and about policies likely to inhibit economic growth.

Establishing Appropriate Incentives through Relative Prices

One basic lesson is that the rules governing economic behavior in developing countries do not fundamentally differ from the rules governing such behavior in more economically advanced countries. Allowed the opportunity to pursue their own interests, individuals respond to the incentives implicit in the relative prices of products they consume and produce and of factor services they sell or employ. Hence, it is crucial that economic policies operate to confront individuals with relative prices of products and factors that accurately reflect their true values and allow them to respond appropriately to the incentives embodied in these prices.

The importance of this point has not always been recognized in either developing or developed countries. For example, policies that depress prices of agricultural commodities in many developing countries are often seen as benefiting low-income consumers, without much reducing agricultural production. Experience demonstrates the error of this supposition. When prices of cash crops are depressed by export taxes, overvalued exchange rates, or price controls, production declines as farmers shift to crops with higher market prices or shift back to subsistence agriculture, sometimes with disastrous consequences for the national food supply. The opposite side of this coin has been observed in many developed countries where programs to support prices of agricultural products have generated mountains of surplus grain, oceans of surplus dairy products, and enough sugar production to please even Mary Poppins.

Another recent example of this fallacy is the supposed lack of responsiveness of producers and consumers to changes in the price of energy. After 1973 the U.S. Government imposed controls on the prices paid to domestic producers of oil and natural gas and on standards for energy consumption, including fuel economy standards for automobiles. Part of the rationale for these controls was the supposition that allowing domestic energy prices to rise would redistribute income from energy consumers to domestic energy producers, but would have little effect on the quantities of energy produced and consumed. However, energy production in the United States responded strongly to the incentives provided by higher prices. Similarly, when consumers faced higher energy prices, they demanded higher gas mileage vehicles, better insulated homes and factories, and more energy-efficient equipment and appliances.

The relevance of this point is not limited to the United States. In some oil-exporting countries, domestic fuel prices were kept well below world market levels throughout the 1970s. When the economic situation of many of these countries deteriorated in the early 1980s, there was resistance to raising domestic fuel prices as a means of conserving a valuable resource because it was believed that price increases would reduce real incomes of fuel consumers without stimulating much conservation. Countries that raised domestic fuel prices, however, found that fuel consumption responded to the incentives created by higher prices.

Maintaining Reasonable Fiscal Discipline

A second basic lesson from experiences with economic growth is the virtue of main-taining reasonable fiscal discipline. This requires that governments not run large and persistent fiscal deficits, especially deficits financed by inflationary money creation or by heavy foreign borrowing, and that the size of the public sector be limited.

The "reasonable" size of the fiscal deficit depends on the situation and circumstances of particular countries. A country that enjoys rapid economic growth can usually expand its money supply more rapidly without generating inflation than a country that suffers slower economic growth. A country with good credit standing can finance a temporary fiscal deficit by foreign borrowing, while a country with a poorer credit rating may not have this option. A country that devotes a large fraction of its income to productive and profitable investments can sustain a higher rate of foreign borrowing than a country that does not invest as much in its future growth. However, the experience of many developing countries in the international debt crisis of the early 1980s demonstrates the dangers and disadvantages of policies that lead to persistent, large-scale foreign borrowing.

More generally, experience indicates that countries whose governments run large and persistent fiscal deficits (sometimes exceeding 8 or 10 percent of national income) may enjoy rapid economic growth for a while, but sooner or later they suffer severe economic difficulties. These difficulties may become acute during periods when deficits are being curtailed, thereby complicating observed relationships between fiscal deficits and economic performance. The painful effects of reducing government deficits, how-ever, should be attributed to their basic cause. We suffer hangovers not because we stop drinking, but because we drank too much in the first place.

The appropriate size of the public sector is a critical issue to be resolved by any society. Experience does not provide unambiguous evidence that the size of the public sector, within a certain range, is strongly and negatively correlated with the rate of economic growth, but it does suggest that large public sectors are not associated with superior growth performance. For the industrial countries, the share of government spending in GNP has generally risen over the postwar period, and the rate of economic growth has generally declined. Japan has enjoyed the highest rate of economic growth among the major industrial countries and has also had the lowest share of government spending in GNP. In the 1950s and 1960s, Western European countries generally had higher rates of economic growth than the United States, even though they generally had somewhat larger public sectors. More recently, however, as many Western European countries have increased their share of public spending, their growth perfor-mance has fallen off, both absolutely and relative to the United States. Among de-veloping countries, the evidence is mixed concerning the cross-sectional relationship between the size of the public sector and the rate of economic growth. There are, however, a number of examples where rapid growth of the public sector has been associated with a deterioration of growth performance. Moreover, large public sectors generally need to be supported (sooner or later) by high taxes. High tax rates create disincentives for working, saving, and investing, and, as some evidence shows, tend to be associated with lower rates of economic growth.

For a country with a large public sector, it is especially important that the public sector be run efficiently. Public sector enterprises that provide services similar to those that might be provided by private firms (such as electricity or transportation) should meet the standards of efficiency and profitability normally expected of private sector enterprises. Some public sector enterprises may meet this performance criterion; many do not. Often, employment in public sector enterprises is artificially high and wage and benefit levels for workers and managers of such enterprises exceed levels generally prevailing in the private sector. Public sector enterprises in the United States are less efficient than their private sector counterparts. Evidence suggests that public sector enterprises in developing countries also suffer from serious inefficiencies, implying that substantial gains can be made by making public sector enterprises behave more like private firms or, better still, by shifting their activities to private firms.

Restoring fiscal discipline is a politically painful exercise. The short-run effect of either a reduction in government spending or an increase in taxes may be a decline in economic activity. The longer run effect of higher taxes, which distort economic incentives, is likely to be a lower level of real income. Moreover, the beneficiaries of deficit spending see themselves harmed by spending cuts, by tax-rate increases, or by efforts to expand the tax base. There is an important asymmetry here. Recipients of subsidized public services, transfer payments, or special tax breaks frequently blame governments for reducing these benefits. They do not protest with similar intensity the failure to provide such benefits in the first place. Hence, to maintain reasonable fiscal discipline, it is important not to initiate programs that may become expensive and are likely to generate interest groups supporting their continuation.

Restraining General Price Inflation

A third basic lesson is that a rapid rate of price inflation is generally associated with relatively poor growth performance. For the industrial countries, the higher inflation period of the 1970s and early 1980s generally brought poorer economic performance than the lower inflation period of the 1950s and 1960s. Some developing countries with inflation rates in the range of 20 to 40 percent per year have enjoyed reasonably good real growth. When inflation rates have accelerated to 50 percent per year or higher, however, growth performance has generally been poor relative to lower inflation periods. Inflation rates of 100 percent per year or higher have frequently been associated with economic stagnation or decline. Successful efforts to reduce high inflation rates have usually been associated with higher real economic growth. Countries enjoying the highest real growth rates have generally had low or moderate inflation rates.

The causal linkage between high inflation and poor growth is complex. Because governments often resort to inflationary policies when their economies are not performing well, inflation can be a symptom as well as a cause of poor economic performance. In theory, a country could have a high and predictable rate of inflation, and could adjust its economic institutions (including its tax system) to such inflation. In practice, high inflation rates are usually variable and unpredictable. High and variable inflation rates tend to induce wide variations in relative prices that interfere with the signals concerning the appropriate allocation of resources. With high and variable inflation rates, economic agents divert time, effort, and resources from productive activities into socially unproductive efforts to profit or to avoid losses from inflation and its attendant effects. Inflation frequently interacts with other distortions of the economic system to impair economic performance. For example, taxation of interest and other returns from capital on a nominal rate of return basis produces high real effective rates of taxation in the presence of high inflation. Schemes for indexing wage rates and other economic variables to deal with the problems of inflation can reduce the flexibility of the economy to deal with other types of disturbances. Under general price inflation, controlled nominal prices of basic commodities and public services frequently result in low relative prices of these goods and services. Governments are often reluctant to raise these controlled prices for fear that it will contribute to inflation or stimulate political protests. Enlarged fiscal deficits necessary to finance high real subsidies on basic commodities and to pay for the deficits of public sector enterprises, however, can stimulate increased money creation that in turn accelerates inflation.

Maintaining an Open Policy toward International Trade

A fourth basic lesson is that an outward looking, open policy toward international trade tends to be conducive to rapid economic growth. The essence of such a policy is that internal relative prices of internationally traded goods are not forced to diverge too far from world market prices because of import tariffs or quotas, exports taxes or subsidies, multiple or misvalued exchange rates, or other government policies. An open policy toward international trade allows for relatively unrestricted importation of products cheaply available in world markets and for exportation of products in which a country has or can develop a comparative advantage.

This contrasts with the inward looking, import-substitution policies adopted by many developing countries, early in the postwar period. The objective of these import-substitution policies was to stimulate economic growth by encouraging development of domestic industries to produce products (especially manufactured products) previously imported. The tools were high-import tariffs, restrictive import quotas, foreign exchange licensing schemes, and other protective devices. In a few extreme cases, domestic producers could even obtain absolute prohibitions of imports on the promise that they would supply domestic substitutes.

Many studies have shown that relatively open policies toward international trade provide a better environment for economic growth in developing countries than policies of import-substitution. The most rapidly growing countries generally have relatively open trade policies. Countries that have shifted from import substitution to more open policies have generally improved economic performance. In contrast, import-substitution policies have produced large distortions between the domestic relative prices of tradeable goods and the true costs of these goods, as reflected in world market relative prices. As a result, resources were diverted from potential export activities into production of high-cost domestic substitutes for products that could be purchased more cheaply in world markets. In addition, smaller countries that adopted import-substitution policies lost economies of scale by attempting to produce a diversified range of products for a small domestic market, rather than concentrating on a more limited range of products to be produced for export as well as domestic consumption. In some cases, loss of productive efficiency was exacerbated by a decline in market discipline on domestic firms and their workers because these firms faced little internal competition and were shielded from foreign competition.

Some countries with relatively open policies toward international trade have provided temporary protection for some import-competing industries or have given direct or indirect export subsidies to some industries (including preferential tax treatment and favorable tariff rates on imported inputs used in these industries). In some cases, special privileges accorded to particular industries may merely offset other distortions that impair the exploitation of natural comparative advantage. Although there are a few examples of successful industrial targeting, there are also many examples of industries that have become successful exporters without benefit of specific targeting by government authorities. There are also examples of industries targeted for development that never proved especially successful. Worst of all are the examples of targeted industries that continue to require subsidies or protection long after they were initially selected for special assistance. The general lesson appears to be that industrial targeting may occasionally succeed when a government has the luck to select the right industries for development. But there is a danger that special government privileges will be supplied for long periods to industries with little development potential. Moreover, if private sector investors err in selecting an industry for development, they bear an important part of the cost of that mistake, rather than passing it on to the rest of society. For this reason, there is less danger that the private sector will prolong activities that prove unsuccessful.

Given that most countries will not pursue policies of complete free trade, it is important to recognize that some impediments to trade are worse than others. A uniform ad valorem import tariff applied to all imports is generally less distortionary than a tariff structure with the same average tariff rate but with wide variations in the tariffs applied to individual commodities. This is especially so when imported goods are used as inputs in producing other goods. In this situation, relatively small variations in nominal tariff rates can generate large differences in effective rates of protection for value added in different domestic production activities. Large differences in effective protection rates, in turn, imply large distortions of the incentives to devote domestic resources to different production activities.

In general, import tariffs are less harmful than import quotas that provide the same initial level of protection. Tariffs raise revenue for the government. The implicit revenue associated with an import quota is usually distributed to the private parties who receive quota allocations and who hence have an interest in preserving and enhancing the scarcity value of the right they have received. A tariff generally allows less latitude for the exercise of market power by domestic producers of import substitutes (or by suppliers of factors to such producers) than does an import quota. With an import tariff, the degree of protection for domestic producers relative to foreign competitors is fixed; domestic producers are therefore under pressure to match the efficiency gains of their foreign competitors. With an import quota, the discipline on domestic producers to remain efficient is often diminished because the level of protection rises to offset any deterioration in the efficiency of domestic producers relative to their foreign competitors. Systems of foreign exchange licenses, with different exchange rates for different classes of imports and exports and with complicated mechanisms for the allocation of licenses, share the disadvantages of import and export quotas and frequently offer even greater latitude for harmful manipulation.

Maintaining an Appropriately Valued Exchange Rate

A fifth basic lesson from the growth experiences of developing countries is the importance of maintaining an appropriately valued exchange rate. The exchange rate is the price of domestic money in terms of foreign monies. The economically appropriate exchange rate establishes the correct relationship between internal nominal prices of goods and services in terms of domestic money and the nominal prices of goods and services in terms of foreign monies. For most developing countries that maintain some form of pegged exchange rate, the economically appropriate exchange rate is difficult to identify with great precision. However, there is little doubt that some developing countries have injured their export industries and their overall growth performances by maintaining substantially overvalued exchange rates. Frequently, this has happened because rapid domestic inflation has transformed an initially appropriate nominal exchange rate into a substantially overvalued exchange rate.

The initial effect of an overvalued exchange rate is often to enlarge a country's trade deficit beyond the level that can be financed by the normal equilibrium level of capital inflow. In the short run, to sustain the foreign exchange value of its currency, the government may intervene in the foreign exchange market by using its official reserves or reserves borrowed on the world capital market. Alternatively, a large-scale capital inflow resulting from either official foreign borrowing or from private capital inflows can contribute to overvaluation of the exchange rate by financing an excess of domestic spending over domestic income. To sustain an overvalued exchange rate and stem reserve losses, governments frequently resort to trade restrictions and foreign exchange controls. Although the reason for imposing these restrictions may not be a desire to engage in import substitution, the effect is the same—a distortion of the economically appropriate relationship between internal and external prices and a corresponding distortion of incentives for the efficient allocation of resources.

Limiting Distortions of
Domestic Product and Factor Markets

A sixth basic lesson from the experiences of developed and developing countries is the importance of limiting distortions of domestic product and factor markets. Such distortions can arise from the activities of private economic agents, in particular through the exercise of market power. The appropriate role of government policy in this regard is not to facilitate the exercise of market power by supporting cartels or other anti-competitive practices but to promote competition. Even more important, the government should not allow its own policies to distort excessively the markets for domestic products and factors.

Some distortion of domestic product and factor markets is the inevitable consequence of taxes used to raise revenue to finance essential government operations. The harmful distortionary effects of taxation generally rise more than proportionately with the rate of taxation. They become especially acute when rates of taxation are highly variable across similar products or across different uses of the same factor of production. Hence, it is important to keep overall tax rates as low as possible and to keep tax rates relatively even across similar products and different uses of the same factor of production. Increasingly, experience suggests that low and even tax rates contribute to economic growth, presumably by maintaining incentives to work, save, and invest.

To keep overall tax rates low, it is vital to limit public spending financed by tax revenues. The appropriate rule with respect to public spending is that the marginal social value of such spending should exceed its direct cost by enough to compensate for the distortionary and collection costs of the taxes necessary to finance it. For the United States, the true social cost of Federal Government spending has been estimated at one and one-half times the direct budget cost. For many developing countries that may have higher tax collection costs and more distortionary tax systems than the United States, the marginal social cost of additional government spending is even higher relative to direct budget cost.

Further, public sector enterprises that supply goods and services in competition with private sector enterprises or that might plausibly function as private sector enterprises (such as electric utilities and suppliers of transport services) should charge prices that reflect the true costs of the goods and services they supply (adjusted for externalities associated with consumption or production of these goods and services). Such user charges do not have the distortionary effects of taxation because they make the users recognize the cost of the particular good or service they are using. Normally, public sector enterprises should generate profits that reflect a fair rate of return on the capital that the public has invested in these enterprises. The profits should be returned to the public treasury, not squandered on employment of unnecessary personnel, on excessively high wage rates for workers, or on benefits and perquisites for their managers.

Special tax exemptions, rebates, and privileges frequently cause economic distortions. They increase, sometimes to a great extent, the disparity between tax rates on activities benefiting from them and on similar activities. There also is the need to replace by raising other taxes the revenue lost because of exemptions, rebates, and privileges. Moreover, once granted, special benefits often prove to be politically difficult to remove and may stimulate others to seek similar benefits.

In addition to taxes, many other government policies can harm economic performance by distorting economic incentives. Such policies include regulations of prices, wages, and interest rates. Policies that have maintained low prices of agricultural commodities in a number of developing countries have often discouraged agricultural production, thereby exacerbating problems of hunger and starvation while reducing the real income of rural families who are usually the poorest families in developing countries. Rent controls in both developing and developed countries generate housing shortages. Regulations that hold real wage rates above economic equilibrium levels contribute to unemployment among affected groups of workers. Restrictions on plant closings and work force reductions, such as have been used recently in some Western

European countries, protect specific jobs for specific workers in the short run. However, they discourage workers who have protected jobs from seeking new jobs in which their social product (if not immediately their own income) would be higher. They also discourage creation of new jobs by making prospective employers fear that workers hired to expand output today will be a liability if demand contracts tomorrow.

Distortions also arise from controls on interest rates and credit allocations, especially in inflationary economies. Several developing countries have controlled nominal interest rates on deposits at financial institutions in the face of inflation rates that made real returns of such deposits substantially negative. This discouraged saving and investment and impaired the functioning of financial institutions as intermediaries of credit transactions. When real rates of return on savings were well below those on investment, financial institutions typically employed nonprice mechanisms for allocating the scarce supply of credit. Many factors other than the likely economic productivity of alternative investments can influence the allocation of credit in such an environment.

In its continuing studies of the effects of economic policies on economic growth, the World Bank has estimated for a number of developing countries the extent of economic distortions resulting from inappropriate exchange rates, protection of domestic manufacturing industries from import competition, protection or taxation of domestic agriculture, distortions of domestic capital markets, distortions of domestic labor markets, and distortion generated by inflation. The measures of these classes of distortions have been combined in a general distortion index, which has been related to measures of economic performance of developing countries in the 1970s. The results are summarized in Table 5. Countries with a low distortion index show a higher growth rate of real gross domestic product, a higher domestic savings ratio, a higher growth rate of industrial output, a higher growth rate of agricultural output, and a higher growth rate of exports than countries with a medium distortion index. Medium-distortion countries, in turn, show better economic performance in all of these categories than countries with a high distortion index.

TABLE 5
PRICE DISTORTIONS AND ECONOMIC GROWTH IN THE 1970s
(Percent)[1]

Country category	Annual growth rate of GDP	Domestic saving/ GDP ratio	Return on invest- ment	Annual growth rate of agriculture	Annual growth rate of industry	Annual growth rate of export volume
Low-distortion countries	6.8	21.4	27.6	4.4	9.1	6.7
Medium-distortion countries	5.7	17.8	26.9	2.9	6.8	3.9
High-distortion countries	3.1	13.8	16.8	1.8	3.2	.7

[1]Averaged across countries.
Source: International Bank for Reconstruction and Development, *World Development Report, 1983.*

Maintaining Political Stability

A final general lesson from the growth experiences of many countries over a long span of time is the importance of maintaining reasonable political and economic stability. Economic growth requires current sacrifice to obtain future reward. A political and economic system that does not provide reasonable assurance that those who make the sacrifices will enjoy a fair share of the reward will almost inevitably fail to generate much growth. This is apparent in countries where the insecurity created by war or political turmoil has caused economic stagnation or decline.

Even in less extreme circumstances, it is important that the political and economic system provide reasonable assurance that those who make the greatest contributions to economic progress enjoy a fair share of the fruits of that progress. This means that there is unlikely to be an absolutely even distribution of the benefits of economic growth. Those who work the hardest, save the most, exhibit the greatest skill and inventiveness, and provide the critical entrepreneurial efforts should be able to expect a greater share in the benefits of growth than those who make smaller contributions. On the other hand, economic "progress" that benefits only a very few, perhaps at the expense of a great many, is likely to prove unstable and ephemeral. Sustained economic growth requires the contributions of all elements of society and should be expected to benefit all elements of society.

The broad experience with economic growth and development over the past three decades demonstrates that rapid economic growth does benefit all of society, even if all do not benefit in the same proportion. A developing country that has enjoyed the average growth of real per capita income over the past three decades has more than doubled its real living standard. In some countries with average or better than average growth rates, real per capita incomes of the poorest 20 percent of the population may have risen relatively less than real per capita incomes of the richest 20 percent of the population. But even the poorest 20 percent have benefited substantially from general economic growth. Along the coastline of economic progress the tide may rise more rapidly in some places than in others, but, as President Kennedy observed, "A rising tide lifts all boats."

There is, of course, no absolute guarantee that countries will always achieve rapid rates of economic growth even if their governments recognize the importance of economic incentives, maintain reasonable fiscal discipline, sustain moderate inflation rates, pursue open policies with respect to international trade, keep exchange rates near economically appropriate levels, avoid excessive distortions of their domestic economies, and provide reasonable assurance that those who make the sacrifices necessary for economic progress enjoy a fair share of the benefits of such progress. At times adverse external economic conditions will make growth difficult even for countries with growth-oriented economic policies. Moreover, in the final analysis, successful growth and development do not depend only or primarily on government policies. They depend on the effort, investment, ingenuity, and enterpreneurship of the citizens of a country. The fundamental task for economic policy is to provide the essential environment of economic stability and the right framework of economic incentives so that these basic forces can have their full effect in generating economic progress. The experience of many developed and developing countries indicates that in the longer run societies where economic policies perform these essential tasks do enjoy the fruits of economic progress and the improvements in human welfare that flow from such progress.

QUESTIONS FOR DISCUSSION

1 How has the balance of trade between the United States and developing countries changed recently? What are the reasons for this change? How does this change affect the ability of the developing countries to repay their international debts?

2 How did rates of growth in the low-income and middle-income developing countries compare during 1955–1984? During 1980–1984? Would it be more accurate to characterize the postwar growth experiences of developing countries as being roughly similar from country to country, or as varying widely?

3 What role does international borrowing play in the development process? Under what circumstances does increasing external indebtedness tend to be associated with healthy growth? With stagnation or decline?

4 What is *rescheduling?* Why was a great deal of rescheduling necessary in the early 1980s? Why were the industrialized nations and their banks willing to accept this rescheduling?

5 What role has the IMF played in the international debt crisis? What policies has the IMF tried to impose on debtor countries as a condition for assistance? What effect were these policies designed to have on debtor country current accounts and, hence, on their ability to repay debts? What effects have these policies typically had on the domestic economies of the debtor countries?

6 What policies for development are recommended by the *Report?* What is the relation between these policies and the supply-side economics advocated by the Reagan administration? To what extent has the United States itself tended to follow these recommended policies?

7 Developing countries frequently have very large public sectors. Why do you think this is the case? What problems with a large public sector are pointed out by the *Report?*

8 What is *import-substitution* and what is its goal? This approach is perceived to have worked in some cases; overall, however, the authors of the *Report* disapprove of this strategy. Give their reasons and discuss.

9 A key recommendation of the *Report* is that developing countries avoid distortions in domestic markets. What is meant by *distortion* here? Why do developing countries frequently have this problem? What benefit is seen from eliminating distortions?

THREE COUNTRY STUDIES

For most nations in the world, international considerations (as well as problems of economic development) play a much larger role in macroeconomic policy making than in the United States. The following articles are a set of short, previously unpublished studies of recent macroeconomic policy and performance in three very disparate countries: Canada, Ireland, and Mexico.

Reading 37 M. L. Wernecke, "Canadian Macroeconomic Policy in the 1980s"

Reading 38 Paul Gottlieb, "Macroeconomic Problems and Policies in Ireland"

Reading 39 Gregory T. Everts, "The Mexican Debt Crisis"

CANADIAN MACROECONOMIC POLICY IN THE 1980S

M. L. Wernecke

OVERVIEW OF THE ECONOMY

Canada suffered from slow growth and high inflation in the early eighties, in large part due to the negative effects of the 1979 oil price shock on aggregate supply (see Table 1). The Bank of Canada, operating within a monetarist framework, responded by sharply restricting the money supply in order to restore price stability. The rate of M-1 growth declined from 6.4% in 1980 to 3.6% and 0.7% in 1981 and 1982 respectively. Meanwhile, officials in Ottawa concerned with the high degree of U.S. ownership of Canadian companies, took steps to restrict foreign investment and "Canadianized" the energy industry via the National Energy Plan.

This vigorous application of anti-inflationary monetary policy and anti-foreign investment industrial policy led Canada into its deepest recession since the depression. GNP plummeted 4.4% in 1982, devastating manufacturing and construction sectors. Total employment contracted by 3.3% while an expanding labor force pushed the unemployment rate to 12.8% in the final quarter of the year. Finally, the National Energy Plan prompted considerable capital outflow, undermining a traditional source of support for the Canadian dollar.

An export-led recovery began to take hold in 1983 owing largely to improving conditions in the United States, Canada's major trading partner. Eighty percent of Canadian exports are U.S.-bound, and the leading U.S. expansion provided the growth engine for Canada. Indeed, Canada recorded an unprecedented string of current account surpluses in 1982–84 stemming from the relative cyclical positions of the two North

M. L. Wernecke completed this study while a student in the Woodrow Wilson School of Public and International Affairs at Princeton University.

TABLE 1
CANADIAN MAJOR ECONOMIC INDICATORS

	1980	1981	1982	1983	1984	1985
Real GNP, percent	1.1	3.3	−4.4	3.3	5.0	4.5
CPI, percent	10.2	12.5	10.8	5.8	4.4	4.0
Unemployment	7.5	7.5	11.0	11.9	11.3	10.6
US$/C$	0.837	0.843	0.8098	0.8038	0.7569	0.7114
M1, percent	6.4	3.6	0.7	10.2	3.2	NA
Current account (bn US$)	−0.953	−5.055	2.110	1.365	1.893	−1.900

Sources: Bank of Canada Review [Wharton for 1985 data]; Wharton Econometric Forecasting Associates.

American economies. By 1985, the cyclical positions were again reversed: growth in Canada outstripped that in the U.S. and the Canadian current account reverted to a deficit position as Canadian demand for imports recovered while U.S. demand languished.

In 1986, Canada benefits from broad-based growth and low inflation. However, a weak currency continues to constrain monetary policy as the Canadian dollar hit an all time low in February. Moreover, despite three years of economic expansion, the unemployment rate remains stuck at about 10%. Policymakers face a difficult dilemma as efforts to support the currency hinder Canada's ability to solve its unemployment problem.

THE BANK OF CANADA'S APPROACH TO CURRENCY MANAGEMENT

The Bank of Canada fears a weaker dollar largely because of the inflationary consequences. Historically, the central bank has intervened—both with large direct purchases on foreign exchange markets and by raising domestic interest rates—whenever the Canadian dollar has come under pressure. The "bank rate," which is set 25 basis points above the yield on three month Treasury bills at a weekly auction, is the primary policy lever used by the Bank to signal its intentions. In recent years, a 50 to 100 basis point positive differential between Canadian and U.S. rates has been required to maintain exchange rate stability, although much larger differentials are required at times.

The Bank of Canada must balance a pair of competing economic objectives: it must preserve exchange rate stability while at the same time promoting growth through low and stable interest rates. Additionally, given the interdependence of North American capital markets, the Bank of Canada's options are also constrained by U.S. monetary policy. For example, if the Federal Reserve Board opts to tighten monetary policy (leading to higher U.S. interest rates), the Bank of Canada must follow suit or accept the consequences of a weaker exchange rate.

The Canadian dollar has depreciated about 17% vis-a-vis its U.S. counterpart since 1981. Rather than a gradual decline, the Canadian dollar typically maintains a fairly stable trading range for a number of quarters, then suddenly comes under severe pressure resulting in discrete jumps in the exchange rate. Central bank response during these periods of pressure reveal much about monetary policy priorities at a given point in time.

For example, largely due to capital outflows associated with the "Canadianization" of energy resources, the Canadian dollar came under severe pressure in the first quarter and again in the summer of 1982. The Bank of Canada spent about 40% of its international reserves in the first five months of 1982 in defense of the currency, and pushed Canadian interest rates 400 basis points above comparable U.S. rates. Stagflation characterized the economy, but fighting inflation (rather than combating the rising unemployment rate through easy money) received priority. From 85 U.S. cents* at the end of 1981, the Canadian dollar stabilized at about 81 cents, maintaining an 81–82 cents range until the first quarter of 1984.

In February 1984, the Canadian dollar was pushed below 80 cents, which was considered an important benchmark. At this time, inflation was down to about 5% and the export-driven recovery was struggling to expand to other sectors. In contrast to the 400-basis point differential established in the 1982 crisis, the Bank of Canada responded moderately. Canadian rates stayed within 50 basis points of their U.S. counterparts for the first half of the year, and the currency stabilized at 75–77 cents. Similarly, facing pressure in the first quarter of 1985, the central bank seemed content to accept a permanently weaker currency (72–73 cents) in exchange for lower domestic interest rates.

However, the Bank has drawn the line in 1986. The Canadian dollar came under severe pressure in February, trading at an all time low of 69 cents. The Bank countered with direct purchases reported in excess of $2 billion, and temporarily established a 400 basis point interest rate differential. These measures helped the currency recover to a 72–73 cent range, which appears to be the targeted level. Although the interest rate gap has narrowed, Canadian rates remain considerably above their U.S. counterparts. The prime rate in Canada currently stands at 10.75%, versus 8.5% in the U.S. With about 4% inflation in both countries, real interest rates in Canada are over 200 basis points higher than real U.S. rates. In short, currency management considerations have forced the Bank of Canada to maintain high real interest rates in 1986.

UNEMPLOYMENT: EUROSCLEROSIS VISITS NORTH AMERICA

As in many industrialized countries, the cure for inflation came at the cost of significantly higher unemployment. According to the Conference Board of Canada, 600,000 jobs were lost during the 1979–1982 recession and the average duration of unemployment rose significantly. At the same time, Canada's labor force grew faster than most other OECD nations owing to underlying demographic trends. As a result, the unemployment rate peaked at 12.8% in the last quarter of 1982.

Despite three years of positive real growth, the Canadian unemployment rate has remained stubbornly above 10%. Indeed, job creation has only recently picked up,

*All exchange rates are expressed in US$/C$ terms.

and total employment is just now reaching pre-recession levels. The seriousness of the unemployment situation stems at least in part to the fiscal policy priorities of Prime Minister Brian Mulroney. Mulroney's Conservative government, elected in the fall of 1984, quickly embraced austerity and deficit reduction as key fiscal priorities. This approach was not without cause as Canada's public sector deficit exceeded 6% of GNP in 1984, an imbalance which prompted an IMF reprimand and contributes to the high real interest rates characterizing Canada in recent years.

The current budget, released February 26, seeks to trim the deficit by nearly C$2 trillion in the current calendar year, two-thirds of which will come from higher taxes. The new revenue will come from a 3% surcharge on personal and corporate income taxes and a one percentage point increase in the federal sales tax. Last year's budget also featured a personal income tax surcharge, but only for high income individuals. Government expenditures have been reduced in real terms in both budgets.

Clearly, the new budget does not provide new fiscal stimulus. Instead, the government hopes that measures taken will bolster support for the Canadian dollar, allowing the Bank of Canada to relax monetary policy and thereby stimulate domestic demand. However, the budget was not well received on foreign exchange markets, and relatively high real interest rates have been required to protect the apparently important 72–73 trading range. As a result, the current monetary and fiscal policy mix does little to address Canada's unemployment problem.

ASSESSMENT

Overall, the Bank of Canada deserves good marks for its efforts to manage the currency. The Bank accepted a lower dollar in the 1984–85 period, and took decisive steps to arrest the currency's freefall in the first quarter of 1986. However, the Bank should not become permanently wedded to the 72–73 cent trading range, particularly since lower oil prices will provide some relief on the inflation front in the current year.

In contrast, Prime Minister Mulroney's hopes that austerity will prompt monetary stimulus is an inadequate response to the unemployment situation. In terms of fiscal policy, simple *IS-LM* analysis shows that deficit reduction (which shifts the *IS* curve in through lower government spending and higher taxes) is counter-productive. Moreover, monetary policy is currently constrained by exchange rate considerations. Finally, even if the Bank of Canada did not face a vulnerable Canadian dollar, it is far from certain that central bank Governor Bouey would agree to stimulate the economy given his demonstrated concern with re-inflation.

Instead, Canada could have attacked joblessness from the "supply side." For example, while U.S. tax reform has focused on creating appropriate incentives, Canadian tax reform has been primarily concerned with raising revenue. Specifically, in contrast to the FY1985-86 budget which imposed a surcharge on high income individuals, a supply side approach would have attempted to reduce the marginal tax rates faced by these very same individuals. Finally, at the same time supply siders in the United States were deregulating the airlines, policy makers in Canada were "Canadianizing" the energy industry. In fairness, Prime Minister Mulroney has reversed the Trudeau energy and foreign investment initiatives, but in general, Canada's industries are still far more regulated than their U.S. counterparts.

BIBLIOGRAPHY

Bank of Canada, *Bank of Canada Review,* December 1985.

Green, John. "Canada," *Wharton World Economic Outlook,* Wharton Econometrics Forecasting Associates, May 1986.

Maxwell, T. "The Canadian Economy in 1983 and 1984," presented at the Spring Meeting of Project LINK, 1983.

Organization for Economic Cooperation and Development, *Canada,* July 1984.

Wernecke, M. L. "Canada," *Foreign Exchange Rate Outlook,* Wharton Econometrics Forecasting Associates, various issues.

QUESTIONS FOR DISCUSSION

1 What conflict of policy goals did the Bank of Canada face during the 1981–1986 period? How did the Bank respond?

2 According to the author, what factor led to improvement in the Canadian current account in 1982–1984 and to its worsening in 1985? Did changes in the value of the Canadian dollar tend to strengthen or offset these trends?

3 What was the stance of fiscal policy in Canada in 1985–1986? If carried out, what effects should the proposed fiscal policies have on employment? Real interest rates? The value of the Canadian dollar? The current account?

4 How would you advise the Canadian government to deal with its unemployment problem?

MACROECONOMIC PROBLEMS AND POLICIES IN IRELAND

Paul Gottlieb

What western OECD country

• has large budget and current account deficits that are financed largely through capital inflows?

• has embarked on a program to sharply reduce government deficits by the end of this decade without raising taxes?

• has introduced plans for tax simplification and reduction?

• is a major exporter of high-technology electronic products and chemicals?

• has many citizens who are concerned about the rights of Irish Catholics in Northern Ireland?

If you said the United States, you would be correct. Special congratulations, however, to anyone who guessed "Republic of Ireland" without reading the fifth clue.

The resemblance between the two countries is more than coincidence. Much of Ireland's manufacturing capacity is now American-owned. A program of tax incentives over the past twenty years, combined with ease of trade between Ireland and the continent, has brought a number of subsidiaries of US high-tech companies to Irish soil. About 95% of this output is exported, so that the composition of Irish exports reflects American technical strengths.[1] Returns to American investors have historically been high. Indeed, repatriation of profits (some 5.6% of Irish GDP) explains a large portion of Ireland's current account deficit.[2]

Paul Gottlieb completed this study while a student in the Woodrow Wilson School of Public and International Affairs at Princeton University. This study is copyright 1986 Paul Gottlieb.

[1]Organization of Economic Development and Cooperation, *Economic Surveys: Ireland,* April 1985, p. 55.

[2]Ibid., p. 39.

The use of Ireland as an export platform to the EEC, however, highlights some of the major differences between it and the United States. Ireland has a small, export-oriented economy ($18 billion GDP, $5,120 per capita)[3] with close ties to one trading partner, the UK. Domestic demand and investment are relatively weak, but the public sector is large, employing in typical European fashion almost 28% of the workforce.[4]

But it is another European phenomenon that most sharply distinguishes Ireland from the US. Ireland's 17% unemployment rate is the highest in the OECD—and rising.[5] Much of Irish unemployment can be explained by demographic factors. Ireland has Europe's youngest and fastest-growing workforce, relatively recent urbanization, and a 28% female participation rate which has yet to climb to the EEC average of 46%.[6] So far, manufacturing employment has not grown fast enough to absorb the new workers.

After unemployment, Ireland's problems differ from America's only in magnitude. Inflation has abated, but the balance-of-payments deficit as a percentage of GDP is the second worst in the OECD (after Greece);[7] current budget deficits as a percentage of GDP have been exceeded only by Belgium;[8] while outstanding government debt is the OECD's highest at 128% of GNP.[9] Since much of the budget deficit is financed by public borrowing overseas, interest payments make up an increasingly large part of both the budget and current account deficits.[10]

In short, Ireland has internal and external balance problems similar to those of the US. A high unemployment rate, however, puts Ireland into a classic policy dilemma. Either she expands the economy, worsening trade and budget deficits as she increases employment—or she embarks on an austerity program and risks putting even more people out of work.

The question is whether Ireland's selection of the "American Plan" is an appropriate answer to this dilemma.

POLICY HISTORY

Ireland has been governed in recent years by a series of centrist coalitions. Although particular budgets have caused governments to fall, economic policy has not been fiercely partisan.

1 *Industrial policy.* Ireland's encouragement of export industries, along with the country's general underdevelopment, contributed to an average annual growth rate of

---

[3]Ibid., p. 93.

[4]Ibid., p. 10.

[5]Central Bank of Ireland, *Annual Report for the Year Ended 31 December 1984* (Dublin: Central Bank of Ireland, 1985), p. 43.

[6]Organization of Economic Development and Cooperation, *Economic Surveys: Ireland,* December 1983, p. 36.

[7]Ibid.

[8]Organization of Economic Development and Cooperation, *Economic Surveys: Ireland,* April 1985, p. 29.

[9]Ibid., p. 30.

[10]Ibid, p. 32.

4% from 1973 to 1982, far above the OECD average.[11] But the effect on domestic employment has been disappointing. Many of the new manufacturing firms are capital-intensive and "linkages" to the domestic economy have been few. The Industrial Development Authority is now considering new criteria for investment subsidies that will employ more indigenous labor.

2 *Fiscal policy.* Ireland's boom coincided with expansionary fiscal policy. The oil price shock arrived and the government was still spending: inflation reached a high of 20% in 1981.[12] This was followed quickly by a period of retrenchment. Government spending was reduced and taxes raised slightly in the 1982 and 1983 budgets. Inflation fell, deficits improved, but GNP growth fell below earlier levels and unemployment rose. Ireland was already in the thick of its policy dilemma. In 1984 and 1985, the government began to streamline income tax brackets, increase personal tax allowances, and reduce the VAT for certain goods. Consumption spending rose slightly in these years. In addition, the government embarked in 1984 on a three-year "National Plan" to reduce budget deficits to 5% of GNP without raising taxes.[13] Exports continued to lead the economy, and in 1985 Ireland experienced its first trade surplus in 40 years.[14]

3 *Currency and monetary policies.* In 1979, Ireland linked its currency to the currencies of the European Monetary System ("the snake") while decoupling from the British Pound. Since that time, monetary policy has been used mainly to support the Irish Pound by insuring adequate foreign reserves. To the extent that Irish monetary authorities control the domestic economy, they target interest rates rather than monetary aggregates. Central bankers have nevertheless been too busy with international considerations to consider expanding domestic output.

ANALYSIS

I believe that current Irish macroeconomic policy is sound, given the institutional and economic constraints under which it operates. It has two main components: a contractionary fiscal policy whose goal is the reduction of high budget deficits (the Irish Gramm-Rudman); and tax policies aimed at improving domestic incentives to work, spend, and invest. These policies are appropriate because they help to redress the nation's worst domestic imbalance—the ratio of public to private spending—while reducing the need for overseas borrowing.

But these policies will not work without reliance on an old friend, exports. It is likely that a major currency devaluation will be needed to expand the economy and prevent budget cuts from decimating employment. The IDA should cooperate by targeting subsidies at more labor-intensive industries.

Why this particular policy mix? Why not expand the economy more directly with fiscal or monetary policy?

There is a method of expansion using fiscal policy which is compatible with balance-

---

[11]Organization of Economic Development and Cooperation, *Economic Surveys: Ireland,* December 1983, p. 37.

[12]Ibid., p. 37.

[13]"Republic of Ireland," *ABECOR Country Report,* November 1985, p. 2.

[14]Central Bank of Ireland, *Annual Report for the Year Ended 31 December 1984* (Dublin: Central Bank of Ireland, 1985), p. 16.

of-payment deficits. That method is to expand fiscal policy enough to increase employment, but contract monetary policy in such a way that interest rates are increased and capital inflows help to offset the inevitable deterioration in the current account.

There are several reasons why this would not be a good policy mix for Ireland. It would (1) worsen the government deficit, (2) increase interest payments to foreigners, (3) improve the capital account at the expense of the current account, (4) hurt domestic sectors sensitive to the interest rate (like the moribund construction industry), and (5) be resisted by the monetary authorities.

Currency devaluation, on the other hand, is perfectly compatible with fiscal contraction, allowing internal and external imbalances to be reduced simultaneously. Its major cost is a decline in the standard of living through inflation and a worsening of the terms of trade.

Irish authorities are expected to announce a devaluation within the EMS sometime this year.[15]

Although the Americanization of Irish macroeconomic policy makes sense from an economic point of view, one wonders why there has been so little political fuss over jobs. One possible reason is that the Irish regard their population problem as a fact of life and are secretly relying on a more traditional method of reducing unemployment—emigration.

BIBLIOGRAPHY

Central Bank of Ireland, *Annual Report for the Year Ended 31 December 1984* (Dublin: Central Bank of Ireland, 1985).

Alan Day (ed.), *Government Economic Agencies of the World* (Detroit: Gale Research Company, 1985).

Rudiger Dornbusch and Stanley Fisher, *Macroeconomics* (New York: McGraw-Hill, 1978).

Organization of Economic Cooperation and Development, *Economic Outlook,* December 1985.

———, *Economic Surveys: Ireland,* December 1983 and April 1985.

———, *Main Economic Indicators,* January 1986.

———, *National Accounts, 1960–1983.*

"Republic of Ireland," *ABECOR Country Report,* November 1985.

QUESTIONS FOR DISCUSSION

1 Ireland's exchange rate is fixed. If Irish policy makers wish to avoid devaluation, what constraints does this place on domestic macroeconomic policy? (*Hint:* Focus on the effects of domestic policies on the balance of payments, at the given exchange rate.)

2 What is Ireland's policy dilemma? Suppose that, like some other countries in a similar situation, Ireland opts for austerity (tight monetary and fiscal policies). What does theory say will be the effects in the short run? In the long run? Based on recent experience in Europe (see Reading 26), does the long run seem more likely to be just a few years or many?

3 The author supports a mix of contractionary fiscal policy and currency devaluation. What are the advantages and disadvantages of this approach? Do you agree with the author's recommendation?

[15]"Republic of Ireland," *ABECOR Country Report,* November 1985, p. 2.

THE MEXICAN DEBT CRISIS

Gregory T. Everts

In 1982 Mexico's economy was in a state of crisis. Under the management of President Jose Lopez Portillo, inflation rampaged at 100 percent annually. The government deficit consumed 18 percent of Gross Domestic Product. Real GDP was down .5 percent from the previous year.

Mexico's position vis-a-vis the world was equally dismal. Its trade balance suffered from the declining price of oil, a commodity accounting for 70 percent of export earnings. Foreign debt, public and private, had grown to $88 billion. Mexico was struggling to keep up with scheduled interest payments.

By August 1982, the debt situation was out of control. Faced with interest obligations it could not pay, the Mexican government sought help from the United States and the international financial community. In exchange for new credit and a rescheduling of its debt payments, Mexico agreed to an austerity plan aimed at reducing domestic inflation and restoring a current-account surplus.

BACKGROUND

Mexico has a market economy, with a very large public sector. The government controls more than two-thirds of output. The seeds of Mexico's economic crisis were sown during the 1970s and early 1980s when the government pursued a policy of economic and industrial expansion—an expansion financed by borrowing (Chart 1). U.S. and European banks, flush with petrodollars, were eager to lend—and Mexico, a country

Gregory T. Everts completed this study while a student in the Woodrow Wilson School of Public and International Affairs at Princeton University.

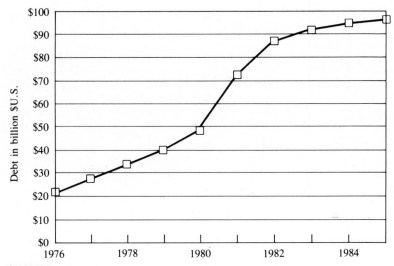

CHART 1
Mexico's Foreign Debt. (Source: The Wall Street Journal.)

with large oil reserves at a time when oil prices were rising, was viewed as a good risk.

The 1979–1982 world recession depressed oil prices and reduced demand for Mexico's non-oil exports. Mexico's controlled peso was over-valued. The U.S. Administration's tight money policy, a weapon aimed at inflation, raised interest rates and made the U.S. dollar—hence, international borrowing—more costly.

AUSTERITY

President Portillo was replaced by Miguel de la Madrid Hurtado, who was sworn in to a six-year term as president in December 1982. Since then, Mexico has pursued an austerity policy of budget cuts, higher food and energy prices, relaxed controls on foreign exchange, controls on imports, and higher taxes.

Budget cuts. As a result of spending cuts, Mexico's government deficit (Chart 2) fell from a high of 18 percent of GDP in 1982 to 9 percent in 1983 and 8 percent in 1984 and 1985 (est.).

Wage controls. Bucking political pressure from Mexico's powerful trade unions, the de la Madrid government slowed the growth of wages. Real wages in 1985 were 30 percent below the 1982 level.

Price controls. In 1982, the Portillo government cut subsidies for bread, gasoline, and electricity, causing prices to rise by 50, 66 and 30 percent respectively. Since then, de la Madrid has further reduced subsidies for bread, gasoline, and electricity, as well as for tortillas, eggs, sugar, and other staples, causing prices to rise sharply.

Currency devaluation. Mexico resumed limited free market trading in the peso in December 1982, ending a policy of strong control. The peso/dollar exchange rate fell

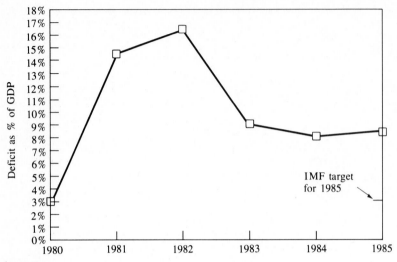

CHART 2
Deficit as % of GDP. (The Economist; *Ministry of Economy data.*)

sharply, immediately raising Mexico's export competitiveness. In December 1984, the government accelerated the official rate at which the peso fell against the U.S. dollar.

Tight money. Currency devaluation and control of the money supply has reduced Mexico's real money supply (Chart 3).

Import controls. Since 1982, the Mexican government has controlled imports through a system of permits and quotas.

CHART 3
Real Money Supply (M2). (Source: Statistical Abstracts of Latin America.)

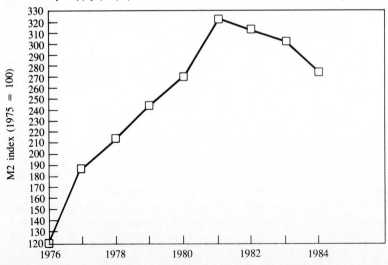

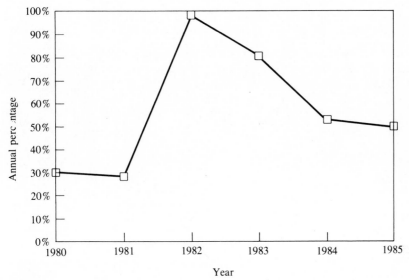

CHART 4
Mexico's Inflation Rate. (Source: *Bank of Mexico.*)

The Effects of Austerity

The austerity measures cut inflation and restored a surplus in the current account but immediately deepened Mexico's recession. Inflation fell from 100 percent in 1982 to 80 percent in 1983, and to roughly 50 percent in 1984 and 1985 (Chart 4). Real GDP, which fell .5 percent in 1982, fell 5.2 percent in 1983. In 1983, it rebounded some-what—growing at 3.5 percent.

By restricting imports and by improving the competitiveness of its exports through peso devaluation, Mexico boosted its trade surplus substantially, from $7.5 billion in 1982 to nearly $13 billion in 1983 and $12.2 billion in 1984 (Chart 5). The increased trade surplus, together with a fortuitous drop in world interest rates, helped ease the interest burden on Mexico's foreign debt.

Both factors—the larger trade surplus and lower interest rates—created for Mexico the first positive current account balance in more than a decade. From a $5.7 billion deficit in 1982, the current account rebounded to a $5.2 billion surplus in 1983 (Chart 6).

A NEW CRISIS?

These improvements were to be short-lived. By mid-1985, Mexico again was in serious trouble. After remaining at 50 percent for two years, inflation began to inch upward. By July, the deficit surpassed the figure projected for all of 1985. Imports increased and export earnings fell. After a healthy showing in 1983 and 1984, Mexico's current account dropped near zero.

Several factors relevant to Mexico's continuing crisis are:

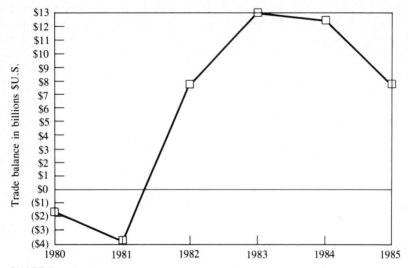

CHART 5
Trade Surplus (Deficit). (Source: *International Monetary Fund.*)

• *The earthquake.* In September 1985, a series of earthquakes devasted Mexico City. Repairing the damage will cost an estimated $4 to $6 billion and require greater government spending and increased imports—both of which counter the goal of austerity.

• *IMF lending policy.* The day the first earthquake struck, it was reported that Mexico had failed to meet the austerity targets set in a $3.4 billion emergency financing

CHART 6
Current Account Balance. (Source: *International Monetary Fund,* International Financial Statistics.)

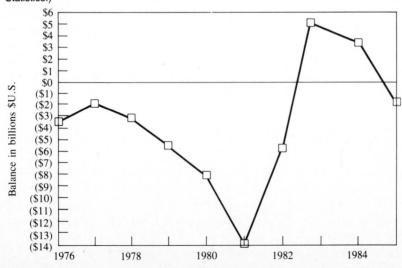

agreement negotiated with the IMF early in 1983. In response, the IMF suspended $900 million in remaining credit. In the aftermath of the earthquake, however, Mexico received new, emergency assistance.

• *Falling oil prices.* In 1985, 70 percent of Mexico's export earnings came from oil sales. For every $1 drop in the price of oil, Mexico loses $500 to $800 million in annual export earnings. Since December 1985, the price of oil has fallen by roughly $15 per barrel, from about $28 to $12–$14. That translates into a loss this year of $7.5 to $12 billion—a loss that is likely to wipe out any trade surplus and throw the current account into a deficit situation.

• *Capital flight.* In 1982 alone, it is estimated that wealthy Mexicans sent more than $14 billion abroad. The Mexican government harshly denounced those who sent money into foreign investments, yet could do little to control it. One result of this capital outflow is that business investment fell sharply in 1982 and 1983 (Chart 7).

CONCLUSION

Mexico's ability to impose austerity measures is not unlimited. The belt-tightening policy has created unrest, and there is growing talk in the Mexican press of a Third World debtors cartel. Efforts to raise prices and dampen domestic demand threaten to undermine the ruling party's political base. Budget cuts alienate the bureaucracy, cuts in food and energy subsidies alienate the poor and middle-class, and lower real wages and higher unemployment antagonize labor.

President de la Madrid and Finance Minister Jesus Silva Herzog argue that economic growth is the only way out of Mexico's crisis. Yet growth will require long-term restructuring of Mexico's debt and new development loans—loans that private lenders are unwilling to supply and that public lenders will supply only if Mexico agrees to conditions involving further austerity. So what next for the Mexican economy?

CHART 7
Change in Private Investment. (Source: *Bank of Mexico, cited in* Curr. Hist.)

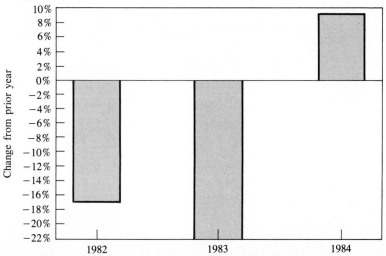

In the short-term, further international aid, on concessionary terms, is essential. Debt restructuring will occur with the approval of international lenders because, without it, Mexico and other debtors will be forced to default.

In the long-run, the crisis may force major structural changes in the Mexican economy and political system. The government has taken some tentative steps to reform existing policies, all of which are likely to be expanded upon in the coming years.

These developments include:

• *Privatization*. The government has experimented with "privatization" by selling off several state-owned businesses.

• *Export diversification*. Mexico is attempting to improve its trade and political relations with Europe and the United States. These efforts have met with some limited success. In 1984, for example, non-oil export earnings rose 18 percent.

• *Reduced protectionism*. Mexico's markets are heavily protected, but Mexico has taken some steps to open them up to foreign competition. President de la Madrid announced last year that Mexico would join GATT, although skeptics believe that domestic political pressure will make it tough for him to implement that decision.

• *Foreign ownership*. Mexican law, which forbids majority foreign ownership in any Mexican enterprise, has inhibited investment. The Mexican government bent this law last year by allowing IBM to come in with majority U.S. ownership, but there is strong resistance to further change due to a long-standing fear of U.S. dominance of Mexico and the Mexican economy.

QUESTIONS FOR DISCUSSION

1 When did Mexico's external debt problem begin? Why did the problem reach a stage of crisis in 1982?

2 What were the elements of Mexico's austerity program? What effects did this policy have on Mexico's internal and external balance? Explain why these effects occurred.

3 What factors led to renewed crisis in 1985? What are the "major structural changes" that the author predicts will be forced on Mexico in the long run? Compare these with the recommendations to developing countries made by the 1986 *Economic Report of the President* (Reading 36). Do you think these changes would increase Mexico's rate of economic growth?

APPENDIX

Tables matching appropriate readings to chapters in *Macroeconomics,* fourth edition, by Robert J. Gordon (Little, Brown); and *Macroeconomics* by Robert Hall and John Taylor (Norton).

Gordon chapter	Suggested readings	Gordon chapter	Suggested readings
1	—	11	—
2	1, 2, 32	12	3, 15, 19–21
3	4, 5	13	—
4	8, 15, 16	14	14–18
5	5, 6, 9, 32	15	5–13
6	—	16	4–6, 13
7	20, 21, 25, 26, 29	17	5, 7, 8
8	22–26	18	33–35, 37–39
9	22, 27	19	5, 30, 31, 36
10	28		

Hall and Taylor	Suggested readings	Hall and Taylor	Suggested readings
1	—	10	6, 9–13, 32
2	1, 2	11	14–16, 18
3	2(*b*)	12	5, 28, 30, 31
4	4, 8, 9, 16	13	20, 21
5	—	14	25, 26, 29
6	15, 19, 20	15	22–24
7	4, 5	16	3, 17, 19, 20
8	5, 7, 8	17	38, 39
9	32–35, 37		